LIST OF CONTRIBUTORS

Yeşim M. Atamer
Istanbul Bilgi University, Turkey

Christina Beardsley
Chelsea & Westminster Hospital, London and St Mary's University, Twickenham, London, England

Jack Byrne
Consultant, TransAction, Auckland, New Zealand

Richard Chisholm
ANU College of Law, Australia; formerly a Judge of the Family Court of Australia

Maria Giovanna Cubeddu Wiedemann
University of Trieste, Italy

Duncan Dormor
University of Cambridge, England

Peter Dunne
Trinity College Dublin, Ireland

Anatol Dutta
University of Regensburg, Germany

Josep Ferrer Riba
Universitat Pompeu Fabra, Barcelona, Spain

Jameson Garland
Uppsala University, Sweden

Stephen Gilmore
King's College London, England

Laura María Giosa
Universidad Nacional de Centro de la Provincia de Buenos Aires, Argentina

Barbara Havelková
University of Oxford, England

Chih-hsing Ho
Academia Sinica, Taipei, Taiwan

Terry Sheung-Hung Kaan
University of Hong Kong, Hong Kong

Albert Lamarca Marquès
Universitat Pompeu Fabra, Barcelona, Spain

Athena Liu
University of Hong Kong, Hong Kong

Elisabeth McDonald
Victoria University of Wellington, New Zealand

Natalie Videbæk Munkholm
Aarhus University, Denmark

Yuko Nishitani
Kyoto University, Japan

Friedemann Pfäfflin
Ulm University, Germany

Walter Pintens
University of Louvain, Belgium, and Saarland University, Germany

Jens M. Scherpe
University of Cambridge, England, and University of Hong Kong, Hong Kong

María Victoria Schiro
Universidad Nacional de Centro de la Provincia de Buenos Aires, Argentina

Brian Sloan
University of Cambridge, England

Rachael Wallbank
Accredited Specialist Family Law Practitioner (LSNSW) and Principal of Wallbanks Legal, Australia

THE LEGAL STATUS OF TRANSSEXUAL AND TRANSGENDER PERSONS – AN INTRODUCTION

Jens M. Scherpe

Contents

I. AIM AND PURPOSE OF THE BOOK

The aim and purpose of this book is to make a contribution to the ongoing scholarly and political debates concerning the legal status of transsexual and transgender persons, both inside and outside of potential legislative reform processes. It is also intended as an aid to judicial and administrative decisions. That said, there of course already has been much – and often very fruitful – debate, and many leading academics, as well as transgender advocates (several of whom now contribute to this collection), have made tremendous contributions to this field. But so far, in terms of legal academic as opposed to policy-centred writing, a major comparative legal survey, particularly one which takes into account the most recent developments away from medicalisation and pathologisation towards self-determination, appeared to be missing, and it is this gap that the book hopes to fill. In doing so, there are not only 'legal' reports but also contributions from a medical/psychological and theological viewpoint. Law does not operate in a legal vacuum, and thus these additional chapters hopefully provide meaningful reference points for the legal debate.

The target audience for this book is not necessarily only specialists with previous in-depth knowledge in the field, but also in particular those who have not yet engaged in greater depth with the issues surrounding the legal status of transsexual and transgender persons. The book therefore offers a comparative basis to evaluate developments, existing legal rules and reform proposals.

II. TERMINOLOGY

One of the major difficulties this research/book project has faced was the question of appropriate terminology. The precise wording and terms used in debates surrounding gender identity often reflect the intensely personal views and feelings of the persons concerned, and often are an area of very intense disagreement. This is also reflected in the contributions in this volume; while the editor made suggestions as to which terminology he thought ought to be used (on which see below), the authors were of course free to decide which terminology they wanted to adopt. In many cases, the authors have decided to invoke the terminology which is currently being used in national debates, despite the fact that this terminology may be, at best, imprecise and, at worst, hurtful and insulting to transsexual or transgender individuals. It therefore needs to be noted that the terminology used in some chapters does not necessarily reflect the views of the authors concerned, but merely illustrates the current language being used in the courts/legal debates. However, in some cases the authors decided deliberately to move away from the terminology currently used (see especially the chapter by Rachael Wallbank). In any event, given the inherent difficulties in terminology, the language used in this project will not, and cannot, reflect the many different ways in which persons experience and express their preferred gender. In some cases, despite the best efforts of the authors, the terminology used may offend. With this in mind, it is important to reiterate, at the very outset of this collection, that the consensus of all authors, in the light of the aims and purpose of the book, was to be respectful. No offence or disrespect is intended. But the aim and purpose of the book also required that terminological choices had to be made.

Following the recommendation of the editor, the majority of the chapters (and indeed the book title) use the terminology coined by Professor Stephen Whittle OBE of Manchester Metropolitan University, one of the world's leading academics writing in this field. Professor Whittle has made an immense contribution to the scholarly debates, both nationally and internationally, and has also had an immeasurable impact on bringing about legislation for legal gender recognition in the United Kingdom. He also was President of the World Professional Association for Transgender Health (WPATH) between 2007 and 2009. His definitions not only have the benefit of the authority of someone immensely knowledgeable in the field but also, and perhaps crucially, of being accessible to the lay reader. In his highly acclaimed book *Respect and Equality: Transsexual and Transgender Rights* Professor Whittle defined 'transgender person' to indicate all persons who live, or desire to live, in the role of a gender which is not the one designated to that person at birth, while 'transsexual person' is meant to refer to those transgender persons who desire or have undergone gender reassignment treatment/surgery.[1]

1 S. Whittle, *Respect and Equality: Transsexual and Transgender Rights*, Routledge-Cavendish 2002, pp. xxii f.

III. CHOICE OF JURISDICTIONS

The aim of the book is to show developments concerning the legal status of transsexual and transgender persons around the globe, and thus jurisdictions were chosen where there have been such developments or that are on the cusp of such developments. Indeed, several jurisdictions were added during the project as there had been significant new legal activity. For Europe, the decisions of the European Court of Human Rights in *Goodwin v United Kingdom* (Application no. 28957/95) and *I v United Kingdom* (Application no. 25680/94) establish that all Contracting States of the European Convention on Human Rights must provide for the legal recognition of 'post-operative transsexual' persons. Neither decision, however, specifies particular modalities for recognition which are consequently for each Contracting State to decide. Further challenges to the existing systems therefore are inevitable, and indeed have begun already as the cases of *Hämäläinen v Finland* (Application no. 37359/09) and *YY v Turkey* (Application no. 14793/08) show. The existence of a supranational human rights court therefore makes European jurisdictions particularly interesting for comparison. Europe is thus looked at in the first part of the 'legal' section. The choice of European jurisdictions is briefly explained below.

Sweden was the first country in Europe to legislate on the legal change of gender in 1972 (Lag (1972:119) om fastställande av könstillhörighet i vissa fall). It only very recently modernised its legal rules, with further amendments to follow in 2016.

Germany was the second country in Europe to enact legislation on the change of legal gender as early as 1980 (Gesetz über die Änderung der Vornamen und die Feststellung der Geschlechtszugehörigkeit in besonderen Fällen (Transsexuellengesetz – TSG) (Bundesgesetzblatt I 1980, p. 1654)). Since then, many of the provisions have been successfully challenged in the Constitutional Court,[2] forcing legal progress and effectively a modernisation of the law. It also is a fascinating example of how human rights arguments can be used to bring about change. The successful judicial challenges have left Germany with a relatively progressive model for the legal recognition of preferred gender, but since these changes were often brought about through court decisions, there has not been a comprehensive reform and thus many issues are left unresolved, particularly with regard to parentage.

By contrast the United Kingdom (in this volume represented by *England and Wales*) was essentially forced to enact comprehensive legislation as a result of the above-mentioned decisions in *Goodwin v United Kingdom* and *I v United Kingdom* and the subsequent House of Lords decision in *Bellinger v Bellinger* [2003] UKHL 21. The Gender Recognition Act 2004 at that time represented the most modern approach, including the absence of any surgery requirement. However,

[2] See e.g. BVerfGE 60, 123 ff.; BVerfGE 88, 87 ff. and BVerfG, FamRZ 2006, 1818.

in the light of recent global reforms, the UK's status as a global leader has been increasingly undermined. In addition, even in 2014, the Gender Recognition Act 2004 leaves open related issues, such as parentage.

Italy is generally perceived to be a rather conservative country (for example with regard to unmarried cohabitation and same-sex relationships), but it introduced its statute on the change of legal gender in 1982 (Norme in materia di rettificazione di attribuzione di sesso, Legge 14 aprile 1982, no. 164).[3] Furthermore, there are a number of interesting court decisions, particularly from tribunals in northern Italy,[4] and recently the Court of Trento[5] questioned the constitutionality of Article 1 of the Act, under which surgical intervention is a necessary condition for obtaining a legal gender identity change.

Belgium is one of the countries where a change of legal gender has been possible for a long time, simply on the basis of a legal action to change one's status and as a result of the (unsuccessful!) challenge of the Belgian law in *van Oosterwijck v Belgium* (Application no. 7654/76) and the powerful dissenting and convincing opinion of the Belgian judge Ganshof van der Meersch. Nevertheless, in 2007 Belgium enacted a statute to regulate this area of law, to ensure legal certainty and consistency.[6] The continued requirements for surgery and sterilisation, however, make the current Belgian system a significant outlier among Western European jurisdictions which are increasingly moving away from medicalisation.

Spain, in a way which is quite similar to Belgium, has long taken a rather pragmatic approach to change of legal gender but also legislated on the matter in 2007 (Ley 3/2007, de 15 de marzo, reguladora de la rectificación registral de la mención al sexo de las personas).[7]

The Netherlands was the fourth jurisdiction in Europe to legislate on change of legal gender in 1985. Generally perceived to be a liberal country, the State's willingness to offer legal gender recognition was, in the mid-1980s, a comparatively liberal position. However, the Dutch rules as a general rule required significant, invasive medical interventions, a position which was only amended in 2013.

It might appear surprising that *Turkey* as a predominantly Muslim country had legislation on change of legal gender in place a long time before many Western European jurisdictions, namely in 1988 (originally Article 29, now Article 40 Turkish Civil Code). The provisions have been subject to reform and much criticism – and recently to successful challenges in the European Court of Human Rights in *YY v Turkey* (Application no. 14793/08). Reform debates in Turkey therefore are inevitable.

---

3 Gazzetta Ufficiale n. 106, del 19 aprile 1982, p. 2879.

4 Esp. Tribunale di Milano Sez. IX, 17 July 2000, Famiglia e Diritto (2000), 608 ff.; Tribunale di Milano, 14 July 1997, Rivista di diritto internazionale privato e processuale 1998, 508.

5 19.08.2014, n. 228, www.dejure.it.

6 Moniteur Belge, 11.07.2007.

7 Boletín official del estado (BOE) No. 65, 16.03.2007.

The *Czech Republic* was chosen as a 'representative' of the Eastern European jurisdictions which only very recently had to engage with issues of concerning the legal status of transsexual and transgender persons, particularly since ascending to the European Convention on Human Rights.

During the research/book project *Denmark* introduced very progressive legislation and therefore was added as a jurisdiction at a late stage.

Finally, the chapter on *Ireland* had to be updated several times during the project in order to keep on top of the legislative developments (or indeed delays); given the position the Irish courts took in *Foy v An t-ÁrdChláraitheoir (No. 1)* [2002] IEHC 116 and the decision, inevitable after *Goodwin v United Kingdom* and *I v United Kingdom*, in *Foy v An t-ÁrdChláraitheoir (No. 2)* [2007] IEHC 470 that Irish law was in violation of the European Convention on Human Rights. As a result, Ireland recently enacted the Gender Recognition Act.

The *Hong Kong Special Administrative Region*, which is the first of the jurisdictions looked at in the part of the book that contains the Asian jurisdictions, has been on the cusp of reform since the Court of Final Appeal decision in *W v Registrar of Marriages* [2013] HKEC 716. In that decision the applicant had undergone full gender affirmation surgery and wanted to be legally recognised as female so that she could marry her male partner, which the Registrar refused; the Court of Final Appeal held that this non-recognition of the preferred gender was a violation of the Basic Law of Hong Kong and gave the Legislative Council a year to implement legislation. However, for a variety of reasons the proposed (and very narrow) Bill failed to become law and thus at the time of writing Hong Kong remains 'on the cusp' of reforms'.

By contrast, *Japan* and *Singapore* have enacted legislation; but due to the restrictive requirements the laws of these countries have long been criticised by activists and human rights groups.

That can no longer be said of the law of *Taiwan* since the recent reforms, which, *inter alia*, have removed any requirement for gender affirmation surgery – as the first jurisdiction in Asia.

The next jurisdictions to be included are *Australia* and *New Zealand*. For the former, a slightly different approach was taken and there are two reports, neither of which are 'country reports' in the way the other chapters are. In the first, the judge who decided the seminal case of *Re Kevin: Validity of Marriage of Transsexual* (2001) 28 Fam LR 158, Richard Chisholm, offers his personal reflections on deciding the case. *Re Kevin* was a landmark case for the common law world[8] as it was one of the most high-profile cases to move away from the – now rightly largely rejected – English precedent of *Corbett v Corbett (otherwise*

[8] And was upheld on appeal: *Attorney-General for the Commonwealth v Kevin and Others* (2003) 30 Fam LR 1.

Ashley) [1971] P 83. Then one of the leading Australian advocates in the field, Rachael Wallbank, who not only represented Kevin but also the clients in many of the following seminal cases, offers her views on the legal status of people who experience difference in sexual formation and gender expression in Australia, while also giving an account of the current legal position in Australia. *New Zealand* also broke away from the precedent of *Corbett* in *Attorney-General v Otahuhu Family Court* [1995] 1 NZLR 603 and has seen some very interesting developments since.

The final 'part' comprises North and South America. *Argentina*, as the first jurisdiction in South America, recently enacted what has been described as one of the most progressive statutes on the legal status of transsexual and transgender persons, and this book includes one of the first full academic accounts of the new law in the English language. The *United States* of course comprise many jurisdictions which invariably have very different positions on issues like the legal status of transsexual and transgender persons; on top of that there is a division of powers between states and the federal government. Given this particular setting and also duties to recognise legal and administrative decisions of other US states, the United States was of great interest from a comparative perspective (although to most people working in the field writing the chapter was perceived to be a daunting task, which Jameson Garland mastered with great aplomb).

IV. THE BOOK COVER

A final word on the picture chosen for the book, 'Eight Heads' by Maurits Cornelis Escher. Apart from the fact that the editor always has liked M.C. Escher's work, there is a deeper reason for choosing this particular piece of artwork.

The notion of 'male' or 'female', *i.e.* the gender binary, is often used to impose 'normative' standards and behaviour patterns on people in general, but particularly on transsexual and transgender persons. All this is based on the patently absurd idea that there is something like 'the real male' and 'the real female', and that there are certain behaviours and physical characteristics which precisely define gender. In legal terms, this often finds expression in the so-called 'real life test' where a person is required to 'live in' a specified gender for a certain period of time in order to be allowed to change the current legal gender and gain recognition of their preferred gender. This is not only, as will be discussed in the final chapter of the book, an absurd requirement (after all, what exactly is 'male' or 'female' behaviour, and how does 'a man' or 'a woman' live?) but can often be extremely harmful for the individual concerned who has to conform with certain gender preconceptions of the decision-makers.

So the depictions of the 'male' and 'female' persons in 'Eight Heads' are almost caricatures, intended to make a mockery of harmful ideas about rigid 'gender'; also, the 'male' and the 'female' invariably are parts of each other and 'flowing into one another', rendering any clear-cut distinctions between them meaningless. So for the purposes of this book the artwork should be understood to ask questions about, and indeed challenge, strict societal and legal perceptions about gender, as well as the preconceptions on which they are based. Moreover, the picture (and this book) can also be understood as a challenge to the binary legal gender system and the very notion of a 'legal gender' itself, suggesting that it is the individual person who matters and not their appearance.

PART I

MEDICAL/PSYCHOLOGICAL VIEWS

TRANSGENDERISM AND TRANSSEXUALITY: MEDICAL AND PSYCHOLOGICAL VIEWPOINTS

Friedemann PFÄFFLIN

Contents

I. HISTORICAL SKETCH

1.1. THE DEVELOPMENT OF CLINICAL TERMINOLOGY

The first two clinical cases of the phenomenon later termed transsexualism were described in 1838 by the French psychiatrist Étienne Esquirol,[1] and in 1853 by the German psychiatrist Hieronymus Fränkel.[2] At that time, however, the cases did not attract much public attention. It was only at the end of the 19th century, with the advent of Forensic Psychiatry and Sexology in Austria, Germany and some other European countries, that the phenomenon was studied more closely, and that medical doctors began to think about how they could help their patients. A very influential case study by Carl Westphal, a German psychiatrist, published in 1870, classified his patient as suffering from a delusion.[3] At that time, patients with delusions were usually treated in closed psychiatric hospitals. Persons who would today be classified as male-to-female transsexual individuals, and who engaged in sexual interaction, were – depending on the country in which they were living – at risk of being criminalised for homosexual behaviour and of being sentenced to a term of imprisonment. In Germany, laws against male homosexuality were only revoked at the end of the 1960s, and I have met a number of transsexual persons who served prison sentences for having engaged in sexual partnerships with men before being finally accepted for appropriate treatment, not easily available in Germany in the 1950s.

The first sex change operation, as it was then called, was performed in 1912 in Berlin on a female-to-male transsexual individual. However, it was some years before Magnus Hirschfeld, a pioneer in sexology, referred to the case in the scientific literature.[4] It is my assumption that this delay in reporting may have been due to the fear of the surgeon involved being accused of inflicting grievous bodily harm on a healthy person, which was, and still is, a crime. At that time, the terms transsexualism and transgenderism had not yet been coined and were unknown. A number of further sex reassignment surgeries were performed in Prague (then Czechoslovakia), Berlin and Dresden (Germany) in the 1920s. The application of synthetic sex hormones became available only in the 1950s, *i.e.* at a time when most doctors still favoured psychotherapy as the treatment of choice for persons with gender identity problems, and there were waves of heated debate

---

1 É. Esquirol, *Des maladies mentales considérées sous les rapports médical, hygiénique et médico-légal, Volumes 1–12* [Mental illness as considered in medical, hygienic and medico-legal reports, Volumes 1–2], J.-B. Baillière, Paris 1838.

2 H. Fränkel, 'Homo mollis' (1853) 22 *Medicinische Zeitung (Berlin)* 102–103.

3 C. Westphal, 'Die conträre Sexualempfindung, Symptom eines neuropathischen (psychopathischen) Zustands' [Adverse sexual desire. Symptom of a neuropathic (psychopathic) condition] (1870) 2 *Archiv für Psychiatrie und Nervenkrankheiten* 73–108.

4 M. Hirschfeld, *Sexuelle Zwischenstufen. Das männliche Weib und der weibliche Mann. Sexualpathologie Bd. 2* [Intermediate sexual states. The male woman and the female man. Sexual pathology, Volume 2], A. Marcus & E. Webers Verlag, Bonn 1918.

about the legitimacy of sex reassignment operations both within and outside the psychotherapeutic communities in Germany, Switzerland, Austria, and the USA, cumulating in the phrase that a doctor is not God, thus qualifying surgical intervention not only as malpractice, but even as a kind of blasphemy. Apart from Switzerland, where the individual judge could permit the legal recognition of preferred gender, in all other European countries such legal recognition was impossible until the early 1970s, even after the patient had submitted to sex reassignment surgery.

In 1905, there was a major scandal at the court of the German emperor Wilhelm II after two of his close friends had engaged in homosexual activity, and the furore created by this scandal brought the gay liberation movement into great difficulties. The members of this movement feared that their fight for the abolition of anti-homosexual legislation would be put at risk. This caused Magnus Hirschfeld to create a new category, *transvestites*, including all effeminate homosexuals, to save the 'straight' homosexuals, as it were, who had managed to hide behind a heterosexual façade of married life.

Thus in 1910, when Magnus Hirschfeld published his two-volume monograph on transvestites, *transvestite* became the first specific name for a transsexual person.[5] In 1928, the English sexologist Havelock Ellis called such individuals *eonists,*[6] alluding to the Marquis d'Eon who lived from 1728 to 1810 and served as a diplomat of the King of France at the court of Catherine the Great, the Empress of Russia, in St. Petersburg, and who spent half of his long life living as a woman (of course with no specific treatment, as this was not available in those times).[7]

It was again Magnus Hirschfeld who, in 1923, first incidentally used the word *transsexual,*[8] which later became the leading term, first in the publications of Harry Benjamin (see below section 1.3), and then in the medical diagnostic classification systems, the 9th edition of the International Classification of Diseases, edited by the World Health Organization in 1978,[9] the 3rd edition of the Diagnostic and Statistical Manual of Mental Disorders of the American Psychiatric Association, published in 1980,[10] and the 10th edition of the International Classification

---

5 M. Hirschfeld, *Die Transvestiten - eine Untersuchung über den erotischen Verkleidungstrieb mit umfangreichem casuistischem und historischem Material* [The transvestites – a study of the erotic desire to cross-dress, with extensive casuistic and historical examples], Medicinischer Verlag, Berlin 1910.

6 H. Ellis, *Studies in the Psychology of Sex. Volume VII: Eonism and Other Supplementary Studies,* Davis, Philadelphia 1928.

7 M. Steinkühler, 'Geschlechtswechsel in nichtklinischer Zeit: Der Chevalier d'Eon' [Sex change in pre-clinical times. The Chevalier D'Eon] in F. Pfäfflin and A. Junge (eds.), *Geschlechtsumwandlung. Abhandlungen zur Transsexualität* [Sex change. Treatises on transsexualism], Schattauer, Stuttgart/New York 1992, pp. 45–54.

8 M. Hirschfeld, 'Die intersexuelle Konstitution' [The intersexual constitution] (1923) 23 *Jahrbuch für sexuelle Zwischenstufen* 3–27.

9 World Health Organization, *International Classification of Diseases. 9th ed.*, Geneva 1978.

10 American Psychiatric Association, *Diagnostic and Statistical Manual of Mental Disorders. 3rd ed. (DSM-III),* American Psychiatric Association, Washington, DC 1980.

of Diseases, edited by the World Health Organization in 1992.[11] In 1973, the American psychiatrist Norman Fisk introduced the term *gender dysphoria*.[12] In 1978, Virginia Prince coined the term *transgenderism*, which later became an umbrella term for all kinds of gender variant behaviours.[13] The 4th edition of the Diagnostic and Statistical Manual of Mental Disorders, published in 1994, deleted the word transsexualism and introduced the diagnosis *gender identity disorder*.[14] Finally, the 5th edition of the Diagnostic and Statistical Manual of the American Psychiatric Association, published in May 2013, has replaced gender identity disorder with *gender dysphoria*.[15]

1.2. TREATMENT OPTIONS

Treatment options developed slowly. In the late 19th century they consisted mainly of isolating the affected persons in psychiatric hospitals or criminalising and imprisoning them. The first sex reassignment surgery was performed in Germany in 1912. Synthetic hormones became available from the 1950s. From the 1950s until the 1970s most doctors preferred psychotherapy as the treatment of choice, and were very sceptical of surgical intervention. In 1931, a Swiss judge permitted the first legal recognition of an individual's preferred gender. In 1972, Sweden passed the first specific law for gender recognition or 'sex change' as it was then termed.

1.3. FAMOUS CASE EXAMPLES AND FIRST MONOGRAPH ON TRANSSEXUALISM

This section considers two exceptional and very influential case studies. The first one is the amended autobiography of the Danish painter Einar Wegener who, in the early 1930s, submitted to sex reassignment surgery in Dresden, Germany, and lived under the (female) name Lili Elbe (Elbe is the name of the large river leading from Bohemia via Dresden and Hamburg to the North Sea). She also hoped that she would be able to receive female reproductive organs in order to give birth to

---

11 World Health Organization, *The ICD-10 Classification of Mental and Behavioral Disorders. Clinical Descriptions and Diagnostic Guidelines*, Geneva 1992.

12 N. Fisk, 'Gender Dysphoria Syndrome. (The How, What, and Why of a Disease)' in D. Laub and P. Gandy (eds.), *Proceedings of the Second Interdisciplinary Symposium on Gender Dysphoria Syndrome*, University of California Press, Stanford 1973, pp. 7–14.

13 R. Ekins and D. King (eds.), 'Virginia Prince. Pioneer of Transgendering' (2005) 8(4) *International Journal of Transgenderism* XV-60.

14 American Psychiatric Association, *Diagnostic and Statistical Manual of Mental Disorders. 4th ed. (DSM-IV)*, American Psychiatric Association, Washington, DC 1994.

15 American Psychiatric Association, *Diagnostic and Statistical Manual of Mental Disorders. 5th ed. (DSM-5)*, American Psychiatric Association, Washington, DC 2013.

a child, but died following this hazardous intervention when doctors attempted to transplant a uterus. Although the English translation of the book states, in its subtitle, *The first sex change*, it was not in fact the first sex reassignment operation.[16]

The second case study is the autobiography of former George, later Christine Jorgenson,[17] an American soldier who was not able to find adequate treatment in the USA and went to Copenhagen, Denmark, from where his ancestors had emigrated. Initially, the objective of the patient and the team of three specialists at the University Clinic of Copenhagen, in whose care she was placed – a psychiatrist, an endocrinologist and a surgeon – was to provide the individual with relief from his effeminate homosexuality. On no account was it their intention to carry out surgical intervention. On the contrary, they first offered the patient male hormones so that she would experience more male feelings. Jorgenson rejected this offer. The team then applied female hormones, as they expected that this would lower Jorgenson's sexual drive. Actually, the female hormones intensified the feelings of being female. As a next step, the medical team suggested that the individual submit to surgical castration, hoping that this would bring relief. When this also did not occur, the team finally acceded to the individual's wish to have her penis amputated. On returning by ship to the USA, the press in New York announced that Jorgenson had undergone treatment for 'a sex change operation'. Jorgenson adapted to this new role and it was only in the following years that she finally located a surgeon in the USA willing to perform plastic surgery to construct her female genitalia.[18]

After Christine Jorgenson's story had been made public, she received more than one thousand letters from all over the world from individuals who claimed that they were suffering from the same condition, and asking her for advice. As she was not a doctor, and being unable to deal with all these requests, she contacted Harry Benjamin, a medical doctor and expert in sex hormones, and subsequently Benjamin's private practice became a special treatment centre for transsexual persons. From the 1950s Benjamin published a number of scientific papers on transsexualism.

1.4. FIRST GENDER IDENTITY CLINIC

The first Gender Identity Clinic was established in 1963 at the Johns Hopkins University Clinic in Baltimore, Maryland, USA. Apart from both the sociological

16 N. Hoyer (ed.), *Lili Elbe: Ein Mensch wechselt sein Geschlecht*, Carl Reissner, Dresden 1932 [Man into Woman. The First Sex Change. A Portrait of Lili Elbe. The true and remarkable transformation of the painter Einar Wegener, Jarrolds, Norwich 1933].

17 C. Jorgenson, *A Personal Autobiography*, Paul S. Erikson, New York 1967.

18 P. Hertoft and T. Sörensen, 'Transsexuality: Some Remarks Based on Clinical Experience' in *Ciba Foundation Symposium 62*, Amsterdam/Oxford/New York 1979, pp. 165–181.

studies initiated by Alfred Kinsey and his colleagues[19] and the physiological studies initiated by William Masters and Virginia Johnson regarding sexual dysfunction,[20] the study of gender identity disorders became the third cornerstone of the expanding sexology sphere in North America and other countries. Within a short time, 40 additional gender identity clinics were established in the USA. In 1966, three years after the establishment of the first Gender Identity Clinic in Baltimore, Harry Benjamin published his monograph *The Transsexual Phenomenon*.[21] Starting in the 1950s, and expanding rapidly in the 1960s, knowledge about transsexualism was popularised on a worldwide scale, and an increasing number of patients began to seek adequate treatment.

1.5. PSYCHOLOGY ENTERING THE SCENE

With the establishment of the Gender Identity Clinic at the Johns Hopkins University Hospital in Baltimore in 1963, psychology entered the scene in the person of John Money. He was a psychologist and the head of the Psycho-Endocrinology Department at Johns Hopkins. Previously, he had worked with children with intersex conditions,[22] and had developed theories explaining the differences and connections between sex and gender,[23] gender role and gender identity and the pathways leading to gender transposition.[24] As already mentioned, within a short time more than 40 Gender Identity Clinics were founded in the USA, and in a number of European countries the demand for sex reassignment grew rapidly. Before 1980, when transsexualism was included in the 4th edition of Diagnostic and Statistical Manual of the American Psychiatric Association, the diagnosis was not yet generally accepted, and doctors providing treatment were at risk of being sued for malpractice, especially when their treatment did not lead to satisfactory results. It was therefore paramount to develop Standards of Care.

---

19 A.D. Kinsey, W.B. Pomeroy and C.E. Martin, *Sexual Behavior in the Human Male*, W.B. Saunders, Philadelphia 1948; A.D. Kinsey, W.B. Pomeroy, C.E. Martin and P.H. Gebhard, *Sexual Behavior in the Human Female*, W.B. Saunders, Philadelphia 1953.

20 W.H. Masters and V.E. Johnson, *Human Sexual Inadequacy*, J. & A. Churchill Ltd, London 1970.

21 H. Benjamin, *The Transsexual Phenomenon*, Julian Press, New York 1966.

22 J. Money, 'Hermaphroditism, gender and precocity in hyperadrenocorticism: Psychological findings' (1955) 96 *Bulletin of the Johns Hopkins Hospital* 301–319.

23 J. Money, 'Gender: History, theory and usage of the term in sexology and its relationship with nature/nurture' (1985) 11 *Journal of Sex and Marital Therapy* 71–79.

24 J. Money, 'Zur Geschichte des Konzepts Gender Identity Disorder' [History of the concept of Gender Identity Disorder] (1994) 7 *Zeitschrift für Sexualforschung* 20–34.

1.6. STANDARDS OF CARE

The formulation of Standards of Care had three purposes: (1) to protect the treatment providers against accusations of malpractice; (2) to protect patients against malpractice and to guarantee the integrity of treatment programs; and (3) to guide the health care system in differentiating between proper and inappropriate methods of treatment.

The first Standards of Care were formulated in 1979 at an international Gender Dysphoria Symposium held in the USA. Some years later, when the Harry Benjamin International Gender Dysphoria Association, Inc. (HBIGDA, Inc.) was founded, one of its tasks was to ensure that Standards of Care were regularly updated. Again, some years later the Harry Benjamin International Gender Dysphoria Association changed its name to the World Professional Association for Transgender Health (WPATH) which now ensured the actualisation of the text. Currently, the 7th edition of the Standards of Care, published in 2011,[25] is the appropriate guideline for treating persons who suffer from gender dysphoria. Apart from these international standards of care, there are a number of countries in which scientific associations, e.g. sexological or psychiatric associations, as well as health care suppliers, have developed their own standards, many of them, although by no means all of them, referencing the Standards of Care of the World Association for Transgender Health.

II. MEDICAL AND LEGAL CONTROVERSIES

This book, and the conference from which it originated, deal with the question of how legal systems manage and mismanage sex and gender diversity. What had started with the first sex reassignment operation in 1912 as a seemingly purely medical procedure naturally had great legal impact. Following such an operation, a person was still socially restricted as he or she was unable to obtain legal recognition of his or her preferred gender. As already mentioned, as early as the 1930s Switzerland was the first country that allowed individuals to change their legal sex status after the person had submitted to surgical intervention. The first country to pass a specific law for the recognition of a transsexual person's preferred sex was Sweden in 1972. Germany was the second country with such a law, passed in 1980. Many other countries followed (e.g. Italy in 1982, Austria in 1983, Turkey in 1988, Finland in 2002, and the UK in 2004), and most of these laws have been revised at least once if not several times since they were passed. This will be discussed in more detail in other contributions to this book. Here

25 World Professional Association for Transgender Health, *Standards of Care for the Health of Transsexual, Transgender, and Gender-Nonconforming People, Version 7*, World Professional Association for Transgender Health 2011.

we will focus on only one example; the legal controversies discussed in Germany before and after the Law for Transsexuals was passed.

2.1. CONTROVERSIES ABOUT GENDER RECOGNITION IN GERMANY

The first major legal controversy in Germany related to whether hormone treatment and sex reassignment surgery should be regarded as regular medical treatments or malpractice when applied to a person with a healthy body. There were quite a few medical doctors who, at the end of the 1960s and in the early 1970s, would have opted for the second alternative, *i.e.* malpractice. In 1971, however, a patient won her case before the Federal Supreme Court. Seven years later, in 1978, another patient who had submitted to sex reassignment surgery, and who was denied recognition of her preferred gender by administrators, won her case at the Federal Constitutional Court, thus resolving the second major legal controversy. The court obliged the legislator to finally provide a legal response to the question of transsexualism, resulting in the Law for Transsexuals, passed in 1980. The third major question was whether health insurance providers, along with the welfare system, had to fund treatment for medical transitions. There were many doctors who claimed that sex reassignment treatment should be forbidden, or, if it was allowed, should be classified as a cosmetic procedure, a treatment of choice which the patient should pay for out of his or her own pocket. There were numerous court cases with differing outcomes, sometimes in favour of the patient, sometimes in favour of the health care supplier who did not want to pay for treatment. From the time the Law for Transsexuals came into force, it took 17 years until the Federal Social Security Court ruled that health insurance should pay – thus resolving the fourth major controversy – but only, however, when certain standards of care had been met and when the patient's suffering could not be diminished by other means, e.g. psychotherapy.

When the German Law for Transsexuals was being prepared, I was consulted, together with other psychiatrists and sexologists, by the heads of all those parliamentary committees which had to contribute to the formulation of the law. There were many aspects of the draft of the law on which the experts had dissenting opinions, e.g. whether there should be a minimum age for recognition, and, if yes, whether it should be 18 or 21. Another area of disagreement was whether a married applicant should have to divorce before accessing recognition, or should the marriage be dissolved automatically in the course of the recognition process. Again, does an applicant need one or two expert opinions for his or her diagnosis when he or she applies for recognition? These are just three examples of many more controversial issues.

In 1980, the German Law for Transsexuals seemed to be a progressive move and a good example for other countries. Now, thirty years later, it looks more like a fossil, an antiquated document, overloaded with regulations that do not meet the needs of transgender persons. In the past thirty years, the world of sex and gender has changed rapidly and tremendously.[26]

III. BROADENING THE SCOPE OF GENDER VARIANCE

In recent years, the narrow world of transsexualism, with the focus on sex reassignment surgery as a prerequisite of legal recognition of preferred gender, has opened up into the world of transgenderism. This process was initiated by Virginia Prince in the late 1970s. It was Virginia Prince, herself formerly a transvestite, who appears to have coined the term *transgenderism* which soon became an umbrella term for transvestites, transsexuals and a new category, transgenderists, who moved between the sexes and genders and did not necessarily insist on specific medical treatment; possibly cross-sexual hormone treatment, but no sex reassignment surgery. Ethnological reports from various parts of the world described lifestyles going beyond the binary division into the two sexes or genders, male and female, and claiming that there are third, fourth and possibly many other genders.

3.1. TYPES OF TRANSGENDERISM

The British sociologists Richard Ekins and Dave King have followed up on this development.[27] They differentiate between four types of transgenderism, the first one being the traditional transsexual who exclusively wants to be transformed from male to female or vice versa in terms of role behaviour, bodily outfit and legal recognition. The second type oscillates between variably long phases of living a male or a female social life. A third type fundamentally negates the gender dichotomy and wants to belong to neither category, neither male nor female, but to an alternative third sex and gender. Finally, there is a fourth type, wanting to escape sex and gender categories. Richard Ekins and Dave King define their attitude as *transcending*, which may be best defined as an attempt to overcome

[26] M.R. Will, '"... ein Leiden mit dem Recht." Zur Namens- und Geschlechtsänderung bei transsexuellen Menschen in Europa' ['... suffering from law.' The change of names and legal status for transsexuals in Europe] in F. Pfäfflin and A. Junge (eds.), *Geschlechtsumwandlung. Abhandlungen zur Transsexualität* [Sex change. Treatises on transsexualism], Schattauer, Stuttgart, New York, 1992, pp. 113–147. M.R. Will, 'Europarat und Transsexuelle – eine facettenreiche Wirkungsgeschichte' [Council of Europe and Transsexuals – A thorny modern legal history] *Recht & Psychiatrie* 29, 4, pp. 215–229 (part I) and *Recht & Psychiatrie* 30, 1, pp. 21–30 (part II).

[27] R. Ekins and D. King, *The Transgender Phenomenon*, Sage, London, Thousand Oaks, New Delhi 2006.

the gender question altogether. These persons do not want to be called male or female, transsexual or transgender, but only *trans* or *per*, derived form the word person.

3.2. IDENTITY, IDENTITIES AND NEO-SEXUALITIES

From the 1950s to the 1980s, when gender identity was a central point of discussion in sexology, psychiatry and psychotherapy, the word *identity* implied the sameness of a person in the course of time on the one hand, and belonging to a group of other people on the other hand, be it family, village population, nation or other group with common denominators. Since the 1990s, sex and gender, formerly focusing on two alternatives, male and female, have started to pluralise, to become sexualities or, as Volkmar Sigusch, a German sexologist, wrote in 2005, neo-sexualities, losing their affiliation with group contexts and becoming solipsistic, generating more and more new identities.[28] In her book *Gender Circuits. Bodies and Identities in a Technological Age*, the American sociologist Eve Shapiro goes even further:[29] she talks about permanently changing identities, including even transgender men who give birth to children post-transition. There are more than twenty such cases in the USA (personal communication Dr Heino Meyer-Bahlburg, Columbia University, New York) and, since autumn 2013, one such case in Germany (press release, 10 September 2013).

IV. PRESENT MEDICAL AND PSYCHOLOGICAL VIEWPOINTS, DSM-5

So far, a very condensed review has been presented of the development of the medical, psychological and sociological discussion of transsexualism, transgenderism and neo-sexualities from the beginning of this discourse almost a hundred and fifty years ago. Turning now to the medical and psychological view of transsexualism and transgenderism, this can be simplified in a few statements.

4.1. REVISION OF DIAGNOSTIC CRITERIA

The most up-to-date summary of the medical and psychological discourse on the two subjects can be found in the new edition of the Diagnostic and Statistical Manual of the American Psychiatric Association (DSM-5), published in May

---

28 V. Sigusch, *Neosexualitäten. Über den kulturellen Wandel von Liebe und Perversion* [Neosexualities. Cultural shifts of love and perversion], Campus, Frankfurt am Main, 2005.

29 E. Shapiro, *Gender Circuits: Bodies and Identities in a Technological Age*, Routledge, New York 2010.

2013.[30] The author was part of the workgroup preparing this text and will focus on the major changes as compared to previous editions of the DSM and the International Classification of Diseases, 10th edition, edited by the World Health Organization (1992). As regards the diagnosis *Transsexualism*, this was used only in the DSM-III (1980)[31] and the DSM-III-R (1987).[32] In the DSM-IV (1994) it was replaced by the diagnosis *Gender Identity Disorder*,[33] and in the 5th revision of the DSM, the DSM-5 (2013), this diagnosis was replaced by the diagnosis *Gender Dysphoria*.

The diagnosis *transsexualism* had been dropped earlier in the DSM, as it was considered to be too narrow and too closely linked to hormonal and surgical sex reassignment, and not sufficiently reflecting the needs of all those persons suffering from transgender problems without wanting to undergo the full surgical intervention treatments that transsexual persons would usually want to receive.

Compared to the DSM-IV, there are eleven substantial changes in the DSM-5. Here, I will mention only the seven most important ones:[34]

(1) The diagnosis is now *gender dysphoria*, emphasising the subjective suffering (dysphoria), and not so much the possible aims of treatment as is implied in the ICD-10 diagnosis of transsexualism.
(2) The diagnosis gender identity *disorder* was dropped because many transsexual and transgender persons protested against being diagnosed as having a *psychiatric disorder*. Apart from the desire of such persons to be acknowledged as a member of the other sex – or some other sex – they do not feel disordered.
(3) This is now the third important change: the DSM-5 takes into account that there may be more than just the two genders, male and female. The first criterion for the new diagnosis *gender dysphoria* now reads as follows: 'A strong desire to be of the other gender or an insistence that one is the other gender (*or some alternative gender different from one's assigned gender*)' (DSM-5, p. 452).
(4) The diagnosis *gender dysphoria* was placed in a separate chapter, separate from the *paraphilias* and the *sexual dysfunctions*.

30 American Psychiatric Association, *Diagnostic and Statistical Manual of Mental Disorders. 5th ed. (DSM-5)*, American Psychiatric Association, Washington, DC 2013.
31 American Psychiatric Association, *Diagnostic and Statistical Manual of Mental Disorders. 3rd ed. (DSM-III)*, American Psychiatric Association, Washington, DC 1980.
32 American Psychiatric Association, *Diagnostic and Statistical Manual of Mental Disorders. 3rd ed. revised (DSM-III-R)*, American Psychiatric Association, Washington, DC 1987.
33 American Psychiatric Association, *Diagnostic and Statistical Manual of Mental Disorders. 4th ed. (DSM-IV)*, American Psychiatric Association, Washington, DC 1994.
34 For a closer discussion of the changes, including additional changes, see: K. Zucker, P. Cohen-Kettenis, J. Drescher, H. Meyer-Bahlburg, F. Pfäfflin and W. Womack, 'Memo outlining evidence for change for Gender Identity Disorder in the DSM-5' (2013) 42 *Archives of Sexual Behavior* 901–914.

(5) The sexual attraction specifier, used in DSM-IV, was dropped. This specifier asked whether a person was mainly attracted to males, females, both or neither. We did not think that this information enhanced the diagnostic accuracy or contributed to treatment decisions.
(6) We included a subtype pertaining to the presence or absence of a disorder of sex development, including what was formerly called an intersex condition, although going beyond that.
(7) We included a post-transition specifier, *i.e.* allowing the diagnosis to be given even when somebody has had sex reassignment treatment. The purpose of this inclusion was so that anybody who receives hormone treatment can continue with this treatment and be reimbursed for it by his health insurance supplier, even though he or she no longer experiences him- or herself as dysphoric.

Although there was a large movement against the inclusion of *gender dysphoria* or a related diagnosis into the DSM-5, arguing that a psychiatric diagnosis is discriminatory per se, we opted for the inclusion of the diagnosis, mainly to guarantee that treatment options will be available for those suffering from the condition, even if they are convinced that they are not suffering from a psychiatric condition.

4.2. ETHIOLOGY

There are many theories which attempt to prove that transsexualism and transgenderism are inborn or acquired somatic conditions, and should therefore be included in the somatic sections of diagnostic manuals, not in psychiatric manuals. The workgroup of the American Psychiatric Association in charge of the revision of the diagnostic criteria found no evidence for such a conclusion. It remains to be seen how the committee presently preparing the revision of ICD-10 to ICD-11 will decide.

4.3. THE ROLE OF PSYCHOLOGISTS IN THE REVISION PROCESS AND IN TREATMENT

So far, psychologists have played only a minor role in this chapter. In the workgroup for the revision of the DSM, they played a central role. The group for the revision of sexual and gender identity disorders, including the revision of the diagnoses for sexual dysfunctions, paraphilias and gender identity disorders, was headed by Dr Ken Zucker, University of Toronto; the sub-working group for the revision of gender identity disorders was headed by Dr Cohen-Kettenis, Free University of Amsterdam, the Netherlands. They are both psychologists. Together with Dr Heino Meyer-Bahlburg, Columbia University, New York, another expert in the diagnosis and treatment of children and adolescents with gender dysphoria, 50% of the sub-working group for the revision of the former diagnosis gender identity disorder to the present diagnosis gender dysphoria were psychologists. Apart from that, psychologists play a major role in the psychotherapeutic support of children and adolescents, as well as adults, with gender dysphoria in many western countries.[35]

4.4. COERCION

Until the 1950s, and in some instances up into the 1970s and 1980s, medical doctors often felt coerced by their patients' suicidal threats to give in to their demand to access sex reassignment surgery. 'Either you perform the sex change on me, or I will kill myself', was a sentence often uttered by patients to their doctors. In the meantime, this situation has been totally reversed. Many transgender persons just want to be accepted in their desired gender role and receive legal recognition without accessing hormone treatment or surgical interventions. They claim to be urged by doctors, and forced, or coerced in turn, by the law of their country, to first undergo sex reassignment surgery before they can receive legal recognition of their preferred gender. In its decision of 1 January 2011, the German Federal Constitutional Court[36] ruled that sex reassignment surgery is no longer a prerequisite for legal recognition of gender. There are some other European countries that have drawn the same conclusion.

V. CONCLUSION

In summing up, the conclusions are (1) that the treatment of persons with transsexualism, transgenderism and gender dysphoria is rewarding and contributes greatly to the reduction of their distress;[37] as a large number of follow-up studies have demonstrated, patients having regrets are very rare; and (2) that the threshold for legal recognition of preferred gender should be lowered. The German Law for Transsexuals, celebrated in 1980 as very progressive, as well as some other laws for transsexuals in other countries, has demonstrated that the diagnostic, bureaucratic and legal requirements for achieving such recognition are unnecessarily high. It is time for smoother solutions.

---

35 See e.g. P. Cohen-Kettenis and F. Pfäfflin, *Transgenderism and Intersexuality in Childhood and Adolescence. Making Choices*, Sage, Thousand Oaks, London, New Delhi 2003; B.P.C. Kreukels, T.D. Steensma and A.L.C. De Vries, *Gender Dysphoria and Disorders of Sex Development. Progress in Care and Knowledge*, Springer Science & Business Media, New York 2014.

36 1BvR 3295/07.

37 U. Ruppin and F. Pfäfflin, 'Long-term follow-up of adults with Gender Identity Disorder' *Archives of Sexual Behavior 2015*. DOI 10.1007/s10508-014-0453-5.

PART II

CHRISTIAN VIEWS

TRANSGENDERISM AND THE CHRISTIAN CHURCH: AN OVERVIEW

Duncan Dormor

Contents

I. INTRODUCTION

Transgenderism[1] is a relatively rare, complex and genuinely perplexing phenomenon. It is poorly understood by the majority of most populations, challenges commonly held ideas about sexed difference and can generate powerful feelings of unease. It is particularly challenging to religious traditions that vest the differences between the sexes with great theological significance, as is the case for the major branches of Christianity, Roman Catholicism and Eastern Orthodoxy, and the conservative Protestant churches. As a consequence, the overwhelming majority of the 2.1 billion Christians in the world belong to churches which are officially unsympathetic to the claims of transgender people. However, over the last couple of decades there has been a very significant increase in the number of liberal and mainstream Protestant denominations which welcome transsexual and transgender Christians as congregational members and affirm their ministry as leaders and teachers. So, 35 years after Sky Anderson became the first transgender person to be a Christian minister, a growing number of Protestant churches in Europe and the United States of America ordain transgender people as pastors and teachers of the faith and conduct weddings for post-operative transsexual people in their confirmed gender.

Like all religions, Christianity is actively engaged with the moral and spiritual formation of persons and communities. As such, it has both a more holistic character and a more intimate influence in shaping personal identity and meaning than other forces that seek to influence or regulate the character of social life – like the law. The matter of gender identity and more specifically the issues raised by transgenderism are complex for religious authorities and churches in the modern world, in part because the implications are not simply

[1] The issue of terminology is particularly challenging when we consider the attitudes and institutional responses of the churches to transgenderism and transsexualism. This is inevitable for a number of reasons. The first is that within this area the linguistic field of meaning has evolved rapidly, so that what is meant by, for example, 'transgender' has changed over the last couple of decades, i.e. it has not always been an 'umbrella' term; see D. Valentine, *Imagining Transgender: An Ethnography of a Category*, Duke University Press, Durham 2007, pp. 32–33. The second is that the understandings of gender identity which these terms seek to convey are heavily contested by many Christian churches, especially those which operate with a strong understanding of the gender binary rooted in theological axioms. As a consequence, theological engagement with the issues raised has been dependent, in part, on the assessment of the underlying philosophical and theological claims. So, for example, the notion of gender identity associated with our contemporary understanding of transgender stands in opposition to the gender binary, whereas transsexualism has been, and can still be, construed in a fashion that affirms that binary. In practice, this chapter will employ terminology in a way which is consistent with the volume as a whole; however, in case studies 1 and 3, where the discussion is focused on particular texts which refer exclusively to 'transsexuality' and 'transsexual persons', and where it is not clear that this usage does in fact cover all transgender people, these terms will be used. It should also be noted that because transsexuality also involves radical medical intervention, including surgery and hormone treatments, it raises specific concerns within the well-established field of medical ethics to which Christian thinkers have made a profound contribution.

restricted to the rights of particular individuals or those of a minority group. Rather, inevitably, they have an impact upon communities, relationships between believers, and upon shared understandings of the sacred. The phenomenon of transgenderism and the presence of transgender and transsexual persons within churches have raised three related questions for Christian thinking and practice: Should transgender persons be able to participate as members of Christian congregations, and if so, on what terms? Can people be married in a confirmed gender? Can transgender persons be ordained or licensed as ministers or priests?[2] Responses to these questions have varied significantly between, and in some cases within, different Christian traditions and denominations.

Whilst there has always been gender variance within human populations, its contemporary manifestation in transgender identity and the possibility of gender confirmation surgery (GCS) is relatively recent, and very few, if any, major Christian denominations can be said to have produced anything approaching a definitive theological analysis. However, institutional and theological responses have not been formed in a vacuum; rather they have been profoundly shaped by the different attitudes to campaigns for the rights of women and sexual minorities that have been articulated since the 1960s. In the wake of that tumultuous decade, serious divisions emerged within mainstream Christian denominations, with the ordination of women as priests and bishops, and the status and legitimacy of same-sex relationships, becoming the key battlegrounds for theologically infused debates about gender and sexuality. Issues relating to transgender experience have, in the main, sat in the margins of these broader discussions about gender and sexuality, although stances taken by Christian groups with respect to transgenderism, from affirming to hostile, have been broadly congruent with those on sexual minority (LGB) issues.

In this chapter, I will begin by touching upon the key issue of theological anthropology, before providing a broad-brush sociological survey of Christianity, locating churches in their ecclesial, political and cultural settings. After this initial mapping exercise, the main focus of this chapter will be a description of three approaches to transgenderism and transsexuality, the conservative, radical and moderate, and their constitutive theologies, attitudes and practices. This description will draw upon a range of materials including official church documents, but also journalistic accounts, websites, news stories and ethnographic accounts of Christian congregations. This broad typology will then be brought into sharper focus through detailed case studies of the single most influential examples in each category: the Roman Catholic Church, the Universal Fellowship of Metropolitan Community Churches, and the Church of England, respectively.

Intellectually, the fundamental issue at stake is one of theological anthropology. That is the Christian understanding of the human condition, and in particular

2 V.S. Kolakowski, 'Toward a Christian Ethical Response to Transsexual Persons' (1997) 6 *Theology and Sexuality* 10–31.

the significance of sexed difference. Theological ideas about sexual anthropology vary significantly between Christian traditions and have a profound influence on whether transgenderism is considered a 'real' phenomenon or an unfortunate 'delusion'. In the main, judgments rooted in *a priori* theological anthropology have determined the ways in which the scientific and medical evidence has been assessed and appropriated. The moral acceptability, or otherwise, of GCS has flowed as a consequence of such assessments.

There is a rich and varied tradition of Christian ethical reflection, and within 'the West' this has drawn upon an extensive philosophical as well as theological heritage. Christians thus share with others debts to different schools of ethical reflection. However, in broad terms the primary sources of ethical or moral knowledge drawn on within Christianity by the churches are usually described as the Bible, tradition, experience and reason. The differential treatment of a particular moral issue across the spectrum of Christian thinking reflects not just the relative priority of these sources of moral knowledge, which itself differs significantly between churches, but also critically 'the recognition, hermeneutic, and prioritization of, and dialectic between, these sources' and the broader framing of the theological worldview.[3] So, for example, Roman Catholic Church thinking is very heavily influenced by the writings of Thomas Aquinas (1225–1274) and the Natural Law tradition. By contrast, Protestant traditions place a much greater emphasis on the principle of *sola scriptura*; that is, that the Scriptures contain all things necessary for salvation and the Christian life. Within this broad tradition, liberal Protestants give greater weight to the idea that all forms of human knowledge are historically contingent and are more attentive to scientific developments. Nevertheless on a range of ethical issues, especially in the area of gender and sexuality, there are revisionist Catholics who, faithful to their Thomist roots, arrive at very similar conclusions to those of liberal Protestants. Equally there are conservative Protestants whose interpretations of the Bible lead them to concur wholeheartedly with the Vatican.

There are two further general points to note at this stage. The first is that Christian ethical teaching seeks to be universal in its scope, that is, it is not understood to be for believers only, but rather to assist all individual human persons to flourish and live the 'good life' in the widest sense, which includes seeking the common good for all people. Secondly, the mature Christian theological traditions all acknowledge that ethical and doctrinal thinking can develop over time, most obviously in response to new knowledge or understanding, for example of a scientific nature.

More broadly, however, churches do not exist in isolation from the world; their identities and worldviews are inevitably shaped by political and cultural realities. So before embarking on a more detailed consideration of the views and

---

[3] T.A. Salzman and M.G. Lawler, *The Sexual Person: Towards a Renewed Catholic Anthropology*, Georgetown University Press, Washington, DC 2008, p. 671.

practices of particular churches in relation to transgender and transsexual people, we need to set contemporary Christianity in its historical and social context.

II. MAPPING CHRISTIANITIES

Within Christianity, there is a spectrum of views and ecclesial responses to transgender people. In his research within faith communities in the USA, Justin Tanis stresses the breadth of experience 'from acceptance and affirmation of a trans identity to intolerance and excommunication to humiliation and mockery'.[4] Tanis further observes that a great deal depends on the individual involved and that even amongst conservative congregations, there are some pastors who, for example, regard transsexuality as a purely medical problem with a medical solution, as well as those who may even regard transsexuality as essentially blasphemous – a 'decisive complaint or rebellion against God'.[5] Nevertheless, it is useful to group Christian responses into three broad categories – conservative, radical and moderate. This categorisation is based on a sociological mapping that considers three overlapping factors: historic ecclesial traditions and identities within the major branches of Christianity and significant denominations; church–state relationships, that is the way in which power, cultural influence and legal privileges are enshrined within national structures; and finally the ways in which churches and Christian groupings have responded to the important cultural changes in our understanding and acceptance of gender roles and sexual identities that have occurred since the 1960s, some of which can be seen as construed as conservative, others as more progressive in character.

The first, and most obvious, influence on attitudes to transgenderism flow as a consequence of the historical and theological differences between and within the major divisions within the Christian tradition. The most significant division within Christianity is that between its Western Catholic and Eastern Orthodox branches, which formally dates to the 'great schism' of 1054. The second significant fracture which led to the division of Western Christendom into Catholic and Protestant branches was initiated by the Reformation that began in 1517. Today these three major branches of Christianity – the Roman Catholic Church, the Protestant churches (including Pentecostalism) and the Orthodox

4 J. Tanis, *Transgendered: Theology, Ministry and Communities of Faith*, The Pilgrim Press, Cleveland 2003, p. 86. Justin Tanis notes that a minority conservative position often found in the Assemblies of God involves an acceptance of transsexuality combined with a condemnation of homosexuality. The New Apostolic Church International, another Pentecostal denomination, produced a clear statement on transsexuality in 2007 arguing that 'sex adaptation falls into the domain of self-responsibility'. Whilst transsexual persons cannot discharge ministerial or teaching functions they are in the language of the church to 'receive soul-care without any reservation'. See <www.nak.org/news/naci-news/article/14676/> accessed 12.09.2013.

5 R.A.G. Gagnon, 'Transsexuality and Ordination' 2007 <www.robgagnon.net/articles/TranssexualityOrdination.pdf> accessed 06.03.2013, p. 3.

churches – have a membership numbering 1,100 million, around 800 million and 260 million members respectively.[6]

The distribution of power and authority between a central hierarchy, national or regional bodies, and local congregations differs considerably between these three major traditions. At one end of the spectrum there is the Roman Catholic Church with authority clearly vested in the Pope and the teaching office of the Vatican, the magisterium. By contrast, Eastern Orthodoxy exists as a family of self-governing autocephalous churches with a fairly united set of beliefs, although each church is strongly tied to a national identity (e.g. the Russian Orthodox, the Greek Orthodox, the Romanian Orthodox etc.).[7] Protestantism is considerably more devolved and diverse with over 30,000 independent Protestant denominations or groupings ranging in size from single congregations, through small networks and alliances to denominations, communions and federations. The largest Protestant groupings, the World Communion of Reformed Churches, the World Methodist Council and the Lutheran World Federation range between 80 and 67 million members each.[8] Whilst there are characteristically Lutheran, Reformed or Anglican patterns of thinking or worship, Protestant Christianity is marked by significant levels of devolved authority and considerable differences exist between congregations and denominations within these wider federations especially on issues of gender and sexuality.[9] Such pluralism is, in part, the consequence of the highly variegated ways in which Christian bodies relate to national cultures and political power.

The second factor to consider then is the relationship between churches and political power or influence within states, and regional or national cultures. In many European and Latin American countries particular Christian denominations have exerted a powerful influence and enjoyed significant legal privileges and political protection. In some cases they have been officially recognised as state churches. This has been the case for Lutheranism in much of Scandinavia; Eastern Orthodoxy in Greece and some of the post-Soviet states; Roman Catholicism in a number of Latin American and European countries; and the Church of England within the United Kingdom. Such churches therefore remain 'highly significant players' in many countries, informing different visions, patterns of thinking and

---

6 Pew Research Center, 'Global Christianity: A Report on the Size and Distribution of the World's Christian Population' (2011) *The Pew Forum on Religion & Public Life* <www.pewforum.org/files/2011/12/Christianity-fullreport-web.pdf> accessed 09.04.2014.

7 Four in ten Orthodox Christians belong to the Russian Orthodox Church that numbers 101 million. Other large Orthodox churches include the Ethiopian Church (36 million), the Ukrainian Church (35 million), the Romanian Church (19 million) and the Greek Orthodox Church (10 million). Pew Research Center, above n. 6, p. 31.

8 The Anglican Communion is slightly larger with 85 million members however it has been shaped by both Catholic as well as Protestant theologies and practices.

9 So, for example, the largest Lutheran body in Australia, the Evangelical Lutheran Church in Australia is conservative in its approach, whilst that of the USA, the Evangelical Lutheran Church in America, is more progressive.

sensibilities.[10] The influence does however work in both directions, for even if inclined to, state churches simply cannot avoid or ignore major legal and cultural developments. So for example in Eastern Europe the principle of *cuius regio, eius religio* has prevailed, rendering the respective Orthodox churches 'ethno-nationalistic' in character.[11] In a similar vein, there are intimate links between the Scandinavian political cultures of social democracy that place a strong emphasis on equality, solidarity and universalism and enshrine a commitment to inclusionary and equal citizenship and the progressive Protestant Lutheran monopolies of those countries, to which an overwhelming proportion of their populations retain membership, albeit on a largely nominal basis. To a significant degree within such countries, the relationship between the state and 'its' church has a major impact on how such religious bodies respond to key issues including those pertaining to transgender persons.

The situation is quite different in the USA, where the constitution upholds a radical separation of church and state. Whilst historians rightly emphasise its Puritan inheritance, the USA, which has the largest population of Christians in the world, is characterised by a vibrant and highly pluralistic religious market.[12] Individual Christian congregations in the USA tend to be more associational in character with shared characteristics (ethnicity, class, lifestyles) and similar views rather than relating primarily to their immediate geographical territory, a pattern much more characteristic in Europe.[13] Thus congregations, networks and even denominations within a particular Protestant tradition (e.g. Lutheran, Episcopalian, Baptist etc.) may well have very different views on issues of sexuality and gender.[14] Despite very significant tensions with their respective ecclesial

---

10 P. Berger, G. Davie and E. Fokas, *Religious America, Secular Europe: A Theme and Variations*, Ashgate, Farnham 2008; G. Davie, *Religion in Modern Europe: A Memory Mutates*, Oxford University Press, Oxford 2000, p. 38.

11 Davie, above n. 10, p. 38.

12 The USA has the largest Christian population of any country (247 million) followed by two other nations in the Americas, which are predominantly Roman Catholic: Mexico (176 million) and Brazil (108 million). Pew Research Center, above n. 6, p. 11.

13 See, for example, Krista McQueeney's ethnographic description of a predominantly black, working-class, lesbian, evangelical congregation in the South of the USA: K. McQueeney, '"We are God's Children. Y'all:" Race, Gender, and Sexuality in Lesbian- and Gay-Affirming Congregations' (2009) 56(1) *Social Problems* 151–173.

14 USA Protestantism is highly diverse and variegated. The most commonly drawn distinction is that between mainstream, sometimes referred to as 'mainline', denominations that have deep historic roots and a long-standing influence on American culture, and the evangelical denominations established within the last 100–150 years. The latter include more fundamentalist, charismatic and conservative evangelical manifestations of Protestantism, primarily Baptist and Pentecostal including the largest African American churches denominations. The most important 'mainline' denominations are the United Methodist Church (UMC) (7.7 million members); the Evangelical Lutheran Church in America (ELCA) (4.3 million); The Episcopal Church (TEC) (2.0 million); the Presbyterian Church (USA) (PCUSA) (2.7 million); the American Baptist Churches (ABC) (1.3 million); and the United Church of Christ (UCC) (1.3 million). In terms of theological outlook these mature denominations tend to be theologically moderate and include within its membership both liberal and conservative individuals and congregations. They will be considered in some

hierarchies, there are also well-established LGBT support and advocacy groups with Roman Catholic or Orthodox identities.[15]

The third factor that has become increasingly important since the 1960s has been the growing division between progressive, liberal forms of Christianity and those of a more conservative, traditional, or frequently neo-traditional character.[16] To a very significant degree this growing division amongst Christians reflects a broader divide generated by the cultural upheavals of the 1960s. However, from an historical perspective, it is extraordinary to find fundamentalist Protestant Christians arm-in-arm with traditional Roman Catholics galvanised by their shared opposition to emancipatory movements for women and sexual minorities. In the face of what is perceived as an unholy and corrosive 'liberalism', there has been a convergence of thinking and the building of networks among conservatives of quite different provenance.

Whilst there has been a complex interaction between the three factors, Christian responses to transgenderism can be grouped into three broad categories – conservative, radical and moderate.

The dominant response, in terms of the Christian presence worldwide, has been conservative. Those holding such views can be divided into three constituencies: the Roman Catholic Church, conservative Protestant denominations (e.g. the Southern Baptist Convention (SBC) and the Church of God in Christ (CGC) in the USA) and the Orthodox churches. There are some differences between these. The first two might be regarded as neo-conservative in that such churches have to present arguments and articulate opposition in the face of strong cultural opposition, Christian as well as secular, at least in Europe and the USA, where there has been significant developments in LGBT-friendly equality, employment and marriage legislation over the last two decades. As a consequence, traditional arguments have, at least to a degree, been re-formulated to meet the new challenges with opposition to women in roles of leadership and

detail in section V below. The dominant tradition within the emergent family of evangelical denominations, which have come to particular prominence in the late twentieth century, are the Baptists. This includes the largest Protestant denomination in the USA, the Southern Baptist Convention (SBC) (16.1 million) and three predominantly African-American Baptist denominations that have arisen schismatically from the National Baptist Convention founded in 1895, The National Baptist Convention (NBC) USA, Inc. (5.2 million); the National Baptist Convention of America, (NBCA) Inc. (3.5 million); and the Progressive National Baptist Convention (PNBC) (1.0 million). The other main tradition in this grouping is Pentecostal and includes the Church of God in Christ (CGC) (5.5 million), a predominantly African-American denomination, and the Assemblies of God (AOG) (3.0 million). These denominations can all be regarded as conservative Protestant in orientation and advocates of a traditional approach to gender and sexuality. E.W. Lindner, *Yearbook of American and Canadian Churches – 2012*, Abingdon Press, Nashville 2012.

15 The most established group with a Roman Catholic identity is DignityUSA, founded in 1969: <www.dignityusa.org> accessed 15.10.2013. The most prominent Orthodox group, Axios, was founded in 1980: <www.eskimo.com/~nickz/axios.html> accessed 15.10.2013.

16 H. McLeod, *The Religious Crisis of the 1960s*, Oxford University Press, Oxford 2007, pp. 207–212.

same-sex marriage becoming totemic issues in a battle over what are understood to be the essential truths of Christianity. By contrast, the position of the Orthodox churches is, broadly speaking, congruent with the more traditional nature of the national populations they serve, largely in Russia and Eastern Europe. All of these conservative or neo-conservative churches have an exclusively male leadership or priesthood and, where it is clearly articulated, their opposition to transgenderism generally flows from an unshakeable belief in an essentialist account of gender difference.

The strongest contrast to such conservativism lies with those churches, denominations, associations and congregations, who not only welcome and affirm transgender Christians, celebrate and bless their marriages and unions, and encourage transgender candidates for ministry, but also actively campaign for their rights more widely within society and amongst other churches. Unsurprisingly such radical groups tend to have their origins outside of the mainstream Christian denominations and have been strongly influenced by the counter-culture and emancipatory movements of the 1960s. However, over time their advocacy has borne significant fruit, not least in their influence on more mainstream Protestant denominations.

Finally then, sitting closer to the mainstream of contemporary western society, there are the moderates: large Protestant denominations that, in seeking to serve a large proportion of the population, strive to represent or contain a spectrum of views. Some of these mainstream denominations could perhaps be described as 'polarised', as they continue to struggle with significant internal tensions over issues relating to sexuality and gender. In such churches, the ministry and marriage of transgender Christians has as often been grudgingly accepted as positively embraced, mostly within the last decade, and frequently in the face of significant unease or internal opposition. Nevertheless, there is growing momentum for change; for acceptance and welcoming of transgender Christians. Although a large number of Protestant churches across many nations could be identified within this broad category, two main types in 'the West' can be identified: the Protestant state churches of, for example, Lutheran Scandinavia or, in the UK, the Church of England, whose identity is firmly tied to the state and its legislature; and the mainline Protestant denominations (Lutheran, Episcopal, Presbyterian) characteristically found in the USA which have been described as embodying 'Golden Rule Christianity'.[17]

---

17 The sociologist and ethnographer, Nancy Ammerman coined 'Golden Rule Christianity' to describe a large segment of American Christianity which could be described as liberal and which places 'a high value on tolerance and diversity'; involves practices that demonstrate 'the pursuit of caring relationships and doing works of comfort'; and focuses primarily on the family and church but also extends to the larger community and world. In Ammerman's assessment, Golden Rule congregations are 'generally low-commitment congregations who favor opportunities to serve people in need, dynamic worship, and attractive activities for their children'. N.T. Ammerman, 'Golden Rule Christianity: Lived Religion in the American

However, we begin by considering in more detail the conservative approach and in particular the ideas and influence of the Roman Catholic Church.

III. CONSERVATIVE: 'MALE AND FEMALE HE CREATED THEM'[18]

3.1. THE 'ORDER OF CREATION' ARGUMENT

It is possible to identify a theological anthropology that is broadly shared by all those who hold the conservative position. It can be expressed in what might be called the 'Order of Creation' argument[19] and summarised as follows: God the Creator has made humanity in two distinct forms, male and female; these sexed identities are an essential characteristic of what it means to be considered a proper human being; and men and women find their purpose, that is they realise their destiny, through erotic attraction to persons of the 'opposite' sex, with whom they may procreate. Furthermore God does not make mistakes, or at least, given that disorders of sexual development (DSD) are irrefutable, not often.[20]

This view is clearly articulated by the eminent Evangelical Anglican ethicist, Oliver O'Donovan:

> 'Human beings come into existence with a dimorphically differentiated sexuality, clearly ordered at the biological level towards heterosexual union as the human mode of procreation. It is not possible to negotiate this fact about our common humanity; it can only be either welcomed or resented.'[21]

Within the conservative worldview, it is assumed that this understanding of male and female is timeless and representative of *the* Christian tradition as revealed in

---

Mainstream' in D.D. Hall (ed.), *Lived Religion in America: Toward a History of Practice*, Princeton University Press, Princeton 1997, p. 196.

18 Genesis 1:27. All biblical references are from the New Revised Standard Version.

19 D.J. Dormor, 'Rebellious Bodies and Disordered Desires: The Challenge of Transsexuality to Influential Christian Theologies of Creation' in N. Reilly and S. Scriver (eds.), *Religion, Gender, and the Public Sphere*, Routledge, London 2014, pp. 120–130.

20 It is a noteworthy feature of conservative commentary on transsexualism that the proportion of the population which is intersexed (DSD) is consistently downplayed. For example, Mathew Staver argues that 'true intersexuals only account for .0018% of the population': M. Staver, 'Transsexualism and the Binary Divide: Determining Sex Using Objective Criteria', *Working paper 1756, Bepress Legal Series*, 2006 <http://law.bepress.com/cgi/viewcontent.cgi?article=8309&context=expresso> accessed 21.11.2013, p. 40. See also Gagnon, above n. 5, p. 2.

21 O. O'Donovan, 'Transsexualism and Christian Marriage' (1983) 11(1) *Journal of Religious Ethics* 141. This highly influential article reproduces arguments first set forth in O. O'Donovan, *Transsexualism and Christian Marriage*, Grove Booklets Ltd, Bramcote 1982. They are re-stated in O. O'Donovan, *Begotten or Made?*, Oxford University Press, Oxford 1984, pp. 15–30 and in O. O'Donovan, *Transsexualism: Issues and Argument*, Grove Booklets Ltd, Cambridge 2007.

the Scriptures and known to the Church down the centuries.[22] This theological anthropology finds its clearest scriptural root, its *locus classicus*, in a text from the first book of the Bible: 'So God created humankind in his image, in the image of God he created them; male and female he created them.'[23]

The implications of such an account are that those behaviours that are perceived to transgress this objective ordering of creation are not 'normal'; rather they are acts against nature. Such acts are the consequence of disordered desires on the part of the individuals in question who are at best deluded and at worst wilfully immoral. The range of 'disordered desires' created by this fixed, binary model of two 'opposite' sexes varies between ecclesial communities but is likely to include minimally same-sex erotic attraction; the aspiration to certain roles belonging properly to one sex; and the desire to change sex/gender. Transgenderism and homosexuality are thus both deviations from this norm; that one refers to gender identity and the other to same-sex erotic attraction is from this perspective a detail, for both transgress and distort God's plan for the life of man and woman together. Transgenderism is therefore a moral 'problem' akin to homosexuality, and the advocacy of rights for transgender persons a manifestation of a secular 'gender agenda'.[24] This can be seen in the official statement issued by the General Presbytery of the Assemblies of God in 2014, 'Homosexuality, Marriage and Sexual Identity', which contains a clear condemnation of homosexuality and includes the following statement about gender identity:

> 'The Fellowship supports the dignity of individual persons affirming their biological sex and discouraging any and all attempts to physically change, alter, or disagree with their predominant biological sex – including but not limited to elective sex-reassignment, transvestite, transgender, or nonbinary "genderqueer" acts or conduct. (Genesis 1:26–28; Romans 1:26–32; 1 Corinthians 6:9–11).'[25]

One of the most comprehensive statements of the conservative position can be found in another recent resolution,[26] that 'On Transgender Identity' (2250) of

22 This is a highly contestable claim. As Thomas Laqueur has cogently argued this rigid binary understanding of gender, the 'two sex' model has its origins in the Enlightenment period, prior to this a more flexible understanding of gender dominated. T. Laqueur, *Making Sex: Body and Gender from the Greeks to Freud*, Harvard University Press, Cambridge, Mass. 1990. Also Dormor, above n. 19, pp. 126–128.

23 Genesis 1:27.

24 M.A. Case, 'After Gender: The Destruction of Man? The Vatican's Nightmare Vision of the "Gender Agenda" for Law' (2012) 31(3) *Pace Law Review* 802–817; J. Samson, W. Jansen and C. Notermans, '"The Gender Agenda": New Strategies in Catholic Fundamentalist Framing of Non-Heterosexuality in Europe' (2011) 4 *Journal of Religion in Europe* 273–299.

25 The General Council of the Assemblies of God, 'Homosexuality, Marriage, and Sexual Identity', 4–5 August 2014 <www.ag.org/Beliefs/Position_Papers/pp_4181_homosexuality.pdf> accessed 07.02.2015.

26 A number of large conservative denominations have produced clear statements condemning homosexuality and same-sex marriage, but to date have not issued statements about

the Southern Baptist Convention, passed overwhelmingly on 10 June 2014 at its meeting in Baltimore.[27] The preamble includes a clear axiomatic statement of theological anthropology: 'the creation of two distinct and complementary sexes' designates 'the fundamental distinction that God has embedded in the very biology of the human race'. Indeed it goes further, noting that 'distinctions in masculine and feminine roles as ordained by God are part of the created order and should find expression in every human heart'.[28] The preamble acknowledges a number of developments in wider society, including the fact that the American Psychiatric Association removed gender identity disorder from its lists of disorders in 2013, and the efforts by LGBT activists to 'normalise the transgender experience'. It further identifies a number of sites of socialisation and practices in its broader depiction of 'cultural currents' of which Southern Baptists should be aware. In particular, it observes that in some public schools teachers and parents are encouraged to 'affirm the feelings of children whose self-perception of their own gender is at variance with their biological sex' and to permit access to restrooms and locker rooms on that basis.[29] In its resolution, the delegates (known as messengers) to the SBC reaffirm their clear commitment to a theologically underpinned gender binary, the 'Order of Creation' argument. It is important to note that the statement clearly avoids placing direct moral responsibility on transgender persons, but rather locates the 'problem' in the 'brokenness and futility' that exist in the world as a consequence of a cosmic event, what Christians term 'the Fall'. Hence, the statement can speak of both intersexuality and transgenderism simultaneously: 'we grieve the reality of human fallenness which can result in such biological manifestations as intersexuality or psychological manifestations as gender identity confusion and point all to the hope of the redemption of our bodies in Christ'. This clear theological statement is then followed by an expression of compassion towards the transgender neighbour and an unequivocal condemnation of any bullying or abuse of transgender persons. Finally, unsurprisingly, there is a clear statement of opposition to all 'efforts to alter bodily identity, … all efforts by any governing official or body to validate transgender identity as morally praiseworthy, … all cultural efforts to validate claims to gender identity'.[30]

Compared with other articulations of the 'Order of Creation' argument, the SBC resolution is relatively sophisticated and it is also supported by clear pastoral

transgenderism, including the permissibility of transgender ordination, these include the CGC and the NBC USA Inc.

27 The original resolution was submitted jointly by Professor Denny Burk, of Boyce College, part of the Southern Baptist Theological Seminary, Louisville, and Andrew Walker, the director of policy studies of the Ethics and Religious Liberty Commission of the SBC. Southern Baptist Convention (SBC), 'On Transgender Identity Baltimore MD – 2014', Resolution 2250 <www.sbc.net/resolutions/2250/on-transgender-identity> accessed 30.01.2015.

28 SBC, above n. 27.

29 SBC, above n. 27.

30 SBC, above n. 27.

guidance for congregational members in a document entitled *10 Ways to Love Your Transgender Neighbour.*[31]

Arguments deployed in support of the conservative position vary significantly, but despite the historical gulf in patterns of thinking, there is a remarkable similarity between the Protestant and Roman Catholic versions.[32] To demonstrate how such thinking might work in practice we will turn to our first case study, that of the largest Christian body, the Roman Catholic Church (RCC), or more precisely the teaching of the Vatican.

3.2. CASE STUDY 1: THE VATICAN AND 'THE RICH REALITY OF THE HUMAN PERSON'

In the office of the Pope and the institutions of the Vatican, the Roman Catholic Church possesses a central teaching authority, the magisterium, which disseminates authoritative and authentic teaching to the faithful. It is important, however, to acknowledge the complex, diverse and heterogeneous nature of the RCC and that there exists very considerable dissent from the 'official view' of the magisterium, not least in matters of sexuality and gender. The widespread use of contraception amongst lay Catholics is one clear example, but it is also evident in the significant intellectual dissent to be found amongst Catholic intellectuals and theologians.[33] Nevertheless, whilst it would be misleading to equate the official position with 'the mind' of the worldwide church, the Vatican's pronouncements on gender and sexuality are highly influential and can clearly be identified as the official Roman Catholic position.

The Vatican has not produced an official statement specifically on transsexuality or gender confirmation surgery, although it is widely understood that a *sub-secretum* document was circulated in 2000 providing guidance to all

---

31 For example, this accompanying pastoral advice includes a clear condemnation of the bullying of transgender persons: D. Burk, '10 Ways to Love Your Transgender Neighbour' <http://erlc.com/documents/pdf/20140612_IA_TenWays.pdf> accessed 30.01.2015.

32 For example, there are significant parallels between the writings of Robert Gagnon, an ordained elder in the Presbyterian Church (USA), and the lay Catholic writer, Gabriele Kuby. See Gagnon, above n. 5, and G. Kuby, 'Gender Mainstreaming – the Secret Revolution' 2008 <www.lifesitenews.com/ldn/2008_docs/GenderMainstreaming.pdf> accessed 05.01.2014. For an assessment of Kuby's contribution, see also Case, and Samson, Jansen and Notermans, above n. 24.

33 Amongst Catholic scholars, including those who have been deprived of their teaching office but who continue to identify as Catholics, assent to official magisterial teaching in certain areas is a minority position: 'Within the Catholic theological community all recognize that the great majority of Catholic moral theologians writing today support revisionist positions in general, but a strong minority defends the positions of the hierarchical Magisterium': Salzman and Lawler, above n. 3, p. xiv.

Catholic bishops.[34] Aside from this, a modest reference within the Catechism[35] and the response of the Catholic Bishops' Conference of England and Wales (CBCEW) to the UK Gender Recognition Act (GRA) 2004,[36] there is very little by way of publicly available RCC documentation which directly states the church's position. Nevertheless it is not difficult to establish the Vatican's approach to the issue based on its broader understanding of the significance of sexual difference and its integrationist approach to the human body.

Although Roman Catholic theology is rich and varied, and different schools of thought can be identified, it is profoundly shaped by a tradition of thinking, usually described as Natural Law, rooted in the teachings of Thomas Aquinas that, in turn, is deeply indebted to Aristotelian thinking. This tradition of moral thinking known as Thomism, asserts that human persons are rational beings and able to participate, by virtue of that rationality, in the higher 'natural law' established by the Creator God.[37] Humans possess an inclination towards happiness and well-being which is ultimately rooted in union with God and they, we, also possess free will which, whilst often mis-directed, makes us capable of active choices for the good. This capacity for moral action is universal in character and does not rest upon divine revelation, although Christian faith is clearly thought to deepen understanding and increase the capacity to act for good in the world.

---

34 J. Norton, 'Vatican says "sex-change" operation does not change person's gender', 14 January 2003, *Catholic News Service*, p. xxxi. It is believed that the text of the *sub-secretum* document was prepared by Fr. Urbano Navarette, a former canon law professor at Rome's Gregorian University and that it was based upon an article published in 1997 in a journal of the *Pontificia Universitas Gregoriana:* U. Navarrete, 'Transexualismus et ordo canonicus' (1997) 86 *Periodica de re Canonica* 101–124. For an English translation, U. Navarrete, 'Transsexuality and the Canonical Order' <https://docs.google.com/file/d/0B5MCZqcy5eWjVDYwME11N2M0V2M/edit> accessed 21.11.2013. See also: E. Bucar, 'Bodies at the Margin: The Case of Transsexuality in Catholic and Shia Ethics' (2010) 38(4) *Journal of Religious Ethics* 601–615.

35 Catholic Church (CC), *Catechism of the Catholic Church* (1994) (English ed.) <www.vatican.va/archive/ccc_css/archive/catechism/p3s2c2a5.htm> accessed 04.01.2014, No. 2297.

36 Catholic Bishops' Conference of England And Wales (CBCEW), 'CBCEW Briefing note on the Gender Recognition Bill from a Catholic perspective', 8 January 2004 <http://catholic-ew.org.uk/Catholic-News-Media-Library/Archive-Media-Assets/Files/Department-of-Christian-Responsibility-and-Citizenship-files/Briefing-Papers/Gender-Recognition-Bill-Bishops-Conference-briefing-note> accessed 23.11.2013.

37 'It is only because matter is structured intelligently that our mind can interpret and actively refashion it. The fact that this intelligible structure comes from the same Creator Spirit who also gave us our own spirit, brings with it both a duty and a responsibility.' Catholic Church (CC) and Benedict XVI, 'Address of his Holiness Benedict XVI to the Members of the Roman Curia for the traditional exchange of Christmas greetings', 22 December 2008 <www.vatican.va/holy_father/benedict_xvi/speeches/2008/december/documents/hf_ben-xvi_spe_20081222_curia-romana_en.html> accessed 21.11.2013.

Several characteristic emphases that have a bearing on transsexuality flow from the ways in which Aquinas' thought have been appropriated and understood within contemporary Roman Catholicism.[38]

The first of these concerns the approach to science and other forms of human knowledge. This is expressed with particular clarity in the Vatican's statement on homosexuality, *Homosexualitatis Problema* (*HP*), written by Cardinal Ratzinger, later Pope Benedict XVI, when he was head of the Congregation for the Doctrine of the Faith in 1986:

> '[T]he Catholic moral viewpoint is founded on human reason illumined by faith and is consciously motivated by the desire to do the will of God our Father. The Church is thus in a position to learn from scientific discovery but also *to transcend the horizons of science* and to be confident that her more global vision *does greater justice to the rich reality of the human person* in his spiritual and physical dimensions, created by God and heir, by grace, to eternal life.'[39]

This understanding of the possibility of an enlightened reading of human knowledge makes it entirely reasonable and consistent for Ratzinger unselfconsciously to assert: 'The Church, *expert in humanity*, has a perennial interest in whatever concerns men and women'.[40]

So, turning to transsexuality, by way of illustration, in its response to the UK GRA 2004, the CBCEW stated in its description of the phenomenon that: 'it is as yet unproven whether it has a physiological basis; rather research suggests it is psychological and sociological elements that are the key factors'. It also noted that the incongruity experienced by the transsexual person 'stems from *believing* that they ought to have bodies with sexual characteristics of the opposite sex from those they were born with'.[41] That assessment is supported by the quotation of expert testimony that transsexual persons suffer from 'gender dysphoria syndrome that is an anxiety, sometimes reaching suicidal depression, as the result of an obsessive feeling'.[42] The experts in question, Benedict Ashley and Kevin O'Rourke are, as

---

38 For an alternative reading of scholarship on Aquinas, see, for example: E.F. Rogers Jr., *Aquinas and the Supreme Court: Biblical Narratives of Jews, Gentiles and Gender*, Wiley-Blackwell, Chichester 2013.

39 Catholic Church (CC) and Congregation for the Doctrine of the Faith (CDF), 'On the pastoral care of homosexual persons, *Homosexualitatis Problema*, Letter to the Bishops of the Catholic Church' 1 October 1986 <www.vatican.va/roman_curia/congregations/ccatheduc/documents/rc_con_ccatheduc_doc_19861001_homosexual-persons_en.html> accessed 10.03.2013, para. 2 (emphasis added).

40 Catholic Church (CC) and J. Ratzinger and A. Amato, 'Letter to the Bishops of the Catholic Church on the Collaboration of Men and Women in the Church and the World', 31 May 2004 <www.vatican.va/roman_curia/congregations/cfaith/documents/rc_con_cfaith_doc_20040731_collaboration_en.html> accessed 22.11.2013, para. 1 (emphasis added).

41 CBCEW, above n. 36, p. 2 (emphasis added).

42 CBCEW, above n. 36, p. 2 quoting from: B.M. Ashley and K.D. O'Rourke, *Healthcare ethics: A Theological Analysis*, 4th ed., Georgetown University Press, Washington, DC 1997, p. 342.

Dominican professors of moral theology, exactly those in the Vatican worldview most eminently qualified to do 'greater justice to the rich reality of the human person'.[43]

A second characteristic of the Thomist tradition is the idea of a natural teleology; that something is good because it helps to bring about a greater perfection; that it has a function to aid a higher purpose. Moral obligations are therefore tied to specific goods or purposes which themselves can be identified as a result of a proper understanding of the human condition, its capabilities and functions. These identified 'goods' exist in a hierarchy and Aquinas identifies the preservation of life, procreation, knowledge, society and reasonable conduct as those which are pre-eminent. As a consequence, a good deal of emphasis is placed within Thomism upon our creaturely existence, and upon procreation and marriage. Whilst a number of prominent Catholic theologians, as well as a large number of revisionists,[44] have argued for the importance of socio-historical factors in understanding the human condition, not least family life and sexuality, the teaching of the Vatican has tended to favour a 'rule-based, act-centred, authoritarian, classicist approach to ethical method and sexual anthropology'.[45] Roman Catholic sexual ethics are perhaps best understood then as '*essentially* marital morality', in that marriage is the only context in which human genital acts (within certain constraints) can legitimately take place.[46] The papal teaching on contraception of *Humanae Vitae* in which each and every act of sexual intercourse must remain open to the transmission of life is perhaps the clearest example of the dominance of this strongly physicalist interpretation of the natural law tradition.[47]

A third related characteristic of the Thomist tradition can be found in its approach to the relationship between mind and body. Unlike dualist accounts that stress the distinction and prioritise the mind, the natural law tradition is highly integrationist. As a consequence, great moral value is placed in the Catholic tradition on the significance of the body. In the main, applied to most parts of human anatomy, the legs or arms, heart or liver, this is entirely uncontroversial. However, when applied to the sexual organs or the secondary sexual characteristics which distinguish men from women, it leads to stark conclusions which seem to subject complex phenomenon to rather reductionist

43 CC and Benedict XVI, above n. 37, para. 2.

44 Prominent Catholic theologians like Karl Rahner (1904–1984) and Bernard Lonergan (1904–1984) both of whom might be described as Transcendental Thomists, and contemporary Catholic married lay theologians and ethicists like Florence Caffrey Bourg, Richard Gaillardetz, David Matzo McCarthy and Julie Hanlon Rubio. For a helpful review of recent Roman Catholic reflections on marriage: L.S. Cahill, 'Marriage: Developments in Catholic Theology and Ethics' (2003) 64 *Theological Studies* 78–105.

45 Salzman and Lawler, above n. 3, p. 56.

46 Salzman and Lawler, above n. 3, p. 46.

47 Catholic Church (CC) and Paul VI, 'On the Regulation of Birth: Encyclical, *Humanae Vitae*', 25 July 1968 <www.vatican.va/holy_father/paul_vi/encyclicals/documents/hf_p-vi_enc_25071968_humanae-vitae_en.html> accessed 20.09.2013.

readings stressing the significance of biological anatomy. So, to return to *HP*, it is only in marriage 'that the use of the sexual faculty can be morally good' and to engage in homosexual acts is to annul 'the goals of the Creator's sexual design'.[48]

It should be clear, given this intellectual framework, not only that transsexualism constitutes a fundamental challenge to Thomist thinking, but also how it is seen in a similar light to homosexuality. Let us now turn to consider this in more detail by looking at the implications of the Vatican's construal of gender for transsexuality, and at its assessment of GCS.

3.2.1. *The Essential Complementarity of 'Man and Woman Together'*

Superficially, the sexual anthropology of the Vatican is unchanging, and indeed the appearance of continuity is clearly very important to the institution of the Roman Catholic Church. To acknowledge otherwise might potentially concede ground to historicist accounts of sexuality and gender. Nevertheless there is clear acknowledgement that eternal truths may need to be re-stated and re-presented for different generations. Over the last thirty years the most influential ideas in Roman Catholic moral theology have originated from the very heart of the Vatican with papal documents from John Paul II (1978–2005) and Benedict XVI (2005–2013). At the heart of these documents has been a robust and authoritative account of the essential complementarity of male and female, man and woman, husband and wife, mother and father. The two sexes have been described as possessing an 'integral complementarity' and being 'two significantly different ways of being persons in the world'.[49] This complementarity is understood primarily as ontological in character but it is also quite clear that this binary is underpinned by a biological and psychological complementarity. It finds its defining expression in the relationship of marriage which is understood 'as a primordial sacrament' intimately connected to 'the creation of man and woman in the image and likeness of God'.[50]

---

48 'As in every moral disorder, homosexual activity prevents one's own fulfillment and happiness by acting contrary to the creative wisdom of God. The Church, in rejecting erroneous opinions regarding homosexuality, does not limit but rather defends personal freedom and dignity realistically and authentically understood.' CC and CDF, above n. 39, para 7.

49 P. Allen, 'Man-Woman Complementarity: The Catholic Inspiration' (2006) 9(3) *Logos: A Journal of Catholic Thought and Culture* 97.

50 CC and John Paul II, 'On the Dignity and Vocation of Women on the occasion of the Marian Year: Apostolic Letter, *Mulieris Dignitatem*', 15 August 1988 <www.vatican.va/holy_father/john_paul_ii/apost_letters/documents/hf_jp-ii_apl_15081988_mulieris-dignitatem_en.html> accessed 21.11.2013, para 29. Similar ideas can be found in a number of papal documents, for example: 'The obscuring of the difference or duality of the sexes has enormous consequences on a variety of levels. This theory of the human person, intended to promote prospects for equality of women through liberation from biological determinism, has in reality inspired ideologies which, for example, call into question the family, in its natural two-parent structure of mother and father, and make homosexuality and heterosexuality virtually equivalent, in a new model of polymorphous sexuality': CC, Ratzinger and Amato, above n. 33. Also, Catholic Church and John Paul II, 'On the Family: Apostolic Exhortation,

Such a vision of the complementarity of the sexes is, very largely, a consequence of the influence of Pope John Paul II's own thinking and writing, although his anthropology resonates very powerfully with what have been described as the 'nuptial hermeneutics' of the prominent theologian Hans Urs Von Balthasar (1905–1988) for whom, in the words of one commentator, sexuality has 'nearly become a religio-metaphysical category'.[51] Despite a somewhat curious intellectual provenance in various early twentieth-century thinkers,[52] this strongly personalist theological anthropology has dominated the Vatican over the last few decades.

An indication of just how important such thinking has become can be found in *HP*, where Ratzinger writes that: 'Human beings therefore, are nothing less than the work of God himself; and in the complementarity of the sexes they are called to reflect the inner unity of the Creator.'[53] To root the significance of sexual difference in one of the central doctrines of the Christian Church, the very nature of the Triune God, is both innovative and bold, not least because it is quite patently in significant tension with traditional mainstream thinking about God as Trinity.[54] Indeed, a clearer demonstration of the extraordinary influence of the symbolism of sexual difference within contemporary Roman Catholic theology is difficult to imagine.

One aspect of this new 'equal but complementary' teaching has been an effusive set of statements about the distinctive nature, vocation, dignity and even 'genius' of women,[55] again primarily at the instigation of John Paul II. This extraordinary elevation of the female is a world away from official Roman Catholic teaching of the first part of the twentieth century,[56] when Pope Pius XI, in his

---

Familiaris Consortio, of His Holiness Pope John Paul II to the Episcopate, to the Clergy and to the Faithful of the Whole Catholic Church Regarding the Role of the Christian Family in the Modern World', 1982 <www.vatican.va/holy_father/john_paul_ii/apost_exhortations/documents/hf_jp-ii_exh_19811122_familiaris-consortio_en.html> accessed 23.11.2013.

51 E.C. Vacek, 'Feminism and the Vatican' (2005) 66 *Theological Studies* 160.

52 John Paul II's thinking about complementarity was clearly influenced by a number of thinkers (mostly converts to Catholicism) who were disciples of the founder of phenomenology, Edward Husserl. In particular, the Catholic convert from Lutheranism, Dietrich von Hildebrand (1889–1977), and the Catholic convert from Judaism, St Edith Stein (1891–1942) as well as Jacques and Raissa Maritain and Emmanuel Mournier. For a fuller account, see: Allen, above n. 49, pp. 87–108.

53 CC and CDF, above n. 39, para 2.

54 Dormor, above n. 18, pp. 127–128. Also, G. Moore, *A Question of Truth: Christianity and Homosexuality*, Continuum, London 2003.

55 '[A] *woman represents a particular value by the fact that she is a human person,* and, at the same time, this particular person, *by the fact of her femininity* ... The Church gives thanks *for all the manifestations of the feminine "genius"* which have appeared in the course of history ...: she gives thanks for all *the fruits of feminine holiness*' (original italics), CC and John Paul II, above n. 50, para. 3.1.

56 'Before Vatican II, popes assumed and explicitly taught women's inequality and subordination to men, as well as condemned advocates of both women's equality and public roles for women.' C. Gudorf, 'Encountering the Other: The Modern Papacy on Women' in C.E. Curran (ed.), *Change in Official Catholic Moral Teaching, Readings in Moral Theology no 13*, Paulist Press, New York 2003, p. 270.

encyclical *Casti Connubi* wrote in December 1930 (in response to the Lambeth Conference's acceptance of contraception) of the harmful possibilities residing in the idea that there could be equality between husband and wife:

> 'This is no true emancipation of woman, nor is it the reasonable and exalted liberty which is due to the high office of a Christian woman and wife. On the contrary it is a degradation of the spirit of woman and of the dignity of a mother; it is a total perversion of family life, depriving the husband of his wife, the children of their mother, and the home and family of their ever-watchful guardian. The wife cannot but suffer damage from this unnatural equality with her husband ... Such demands for equality of rights between husband and wife are pretentious and exaggerated.'[57]

However, the female 'genius' of John Paul II lies in the capacity of women to accept and love others, a capacity 'linked to women's physical capacity to give life' and whether a woman becomes a mother or not, 'this capacity is a reality that structures the female personality in a profound way'.[58] Ultimately, then, such high language merely conceals a disguised form of biological reductionism.[59]

One consequence of this invention of complementarity is that certain categories, most obviously gender, simply do not 'make sense'. A dramatic indication of this can be found in an address by Benedict XVI in which he argues that humanity's responsibility to care for the earth as God's creation includes also a stewarding of the human condition:[60] He draws his ecological metaphor to a close with a comment on the category of gender:

> 'What is often expressed and understood by the term "gender" ultimately ends up being man's attempt at self-emancipation from creation and the Creator. Man wants to be his own master, and alone – always and exclusively – to determine everything that concerns him. Yet in this way he lives in opposition to the truth, in opposition to the Creator Spirit ... Rain forests deserve indeed to be protected,

---

57 Pius XI, 'On Christian Marriage: Encyclical, *Casti Connubii*', 31 December 1930 <www.vatican.va/holy_father/pius_xi/encyclicals/documents/hf_p-xi_enc_31121930_casti-connubii_en.html> accessed 23.11.2013, paras 75–76.

58 CC, Ratzinger and Amato, above n. 40, para. 13.

59 In her assessment of the related theology of Hans von Balthasar, the Catholic feminist theologian Tina Beattie comments that, it is 'the same old story of the same old sameness, fetchingly disguised in the masks of femininity and not averse to the occasional bit of cross-dressing'. T. Beattie, 'A Man and Three Women – Hans, Adrienne, Mary and Luce' (1998) 79 *New Blackfriars* 98.

60 'What is needed' he said, 'is something like a human ecology, correctly understood'; just as we need to protect the environment from destruction, so too we need 'to listen to the "language" of creation'. So: 'If the Church speaks of the nature of the human being as man and woman, and demands that this order of creation be respected, this is not some antiquated metaphysics'. Rather, he continued, 'To disregard this would be the self-destruction of man himself, and hence the destruction of God's own work'. CC and Benedict XVI, above n. 37.

but no less so does man, as a creature having an innate "message" which does not contradict our freedom, but is instead its very premise.'[61]

For the Vatican, promoting this vision of male and female as distinct but complementary in nature is not simply a matter for its teaching office, the magisterium, to instruct the faithful or seek to persuade the world through argument and exhortation. For the Vatican is also a political body with a voice and a vote in a number of international arenas.

3.2.2. *The Holy See and the 'Gender Agenda'*

Within both official documents, and other writings that express loyalty to the Vatican,[62] there is a clear depiction of a secularising 'Gender Agenda' that, through the auspices of the European Union, the United Nations and other bodies, seeks to oppose the views of the RCC root and branch. The construction of gender imputed to these international bodies in such documents is radically social constructionist in character. Within such a framing anything seems possible, hence the refrain that its advocates seek to redefine human nature itself. The destruction of the 'natural' differences between men and women as a consequence of the advancement of such a secular ideology are perceived to entail not just the extension of legitimacy to same-sex partnerships and marriages, or gay parenting, but also the erosion of traditional family life, including: the promotion of contraception and abortion, the devaluation of motherhood and the destruction of traditional marriage. So in the place of the false and distorting idea of 'gender', the official language of the RCC speaks consistently of 'man and woman together'.

However, the Vatican is not 'just' a religious centre, it is also, as a state, a political player, and in the battle against the 'Gender Agenda', the Vatican acts 'first and foremost as a state actor, the Holy See'.[63] As the Holy See, the Vatican seeks to influence the European Union as an 'insider, stressing the importance of its Christian contribution to European heritage and values'.[64] It seeks then to build alliances with other political actors against the widespread enshrinement of anti-discrimination legislation and the bestowal of rights upon women and sexual minorities, developments it views as part of a progressive de-Christianisation of Europe. At the global level, however, the Holy See is frequently allied with members of the Organization of the Islamic Conference in its opposition to

61 CC and Benedict XVI, above n. 37.

62 See, for example the writings of the conservative German activist, Gabriele Kuby, e.g. Kuby, above n. 32. Also Case, above n. 24, and Samson, Jansen and Notermans, above n. 24. A perspective similar to Kuby can also be found in D. O'Leary, *The Gender Agenda: Redefining Equality*, Vital Issues Press, Lafayette 1997.

63 Case, above n. 24, p. 807; Also Samson, Jansen and Notermans, above n. 24.

64 Case, above n. 24, p. 808.

'gender language' and the advancement of the rights of women and sexual minorities.[65] However, as Mary Ann Case points out, somewhat ironically, the Vatican's perception of a unitary and integrated 'Gender Agenda' far surpasses the reality in organisations like the UN where 'silo-ing' tends to prevent the development of such coherence.[66] Within these large-scale political and cultural contests, in which the Holy See seeks to oppose a wide range of developments including challenges to traditional sex roles, the acceptance of homosexuality, the recognition of a diversity of family forms, new reproductive technologies and family law reform, the advancement of transgender rights is generally treated as yet one more example of the secularising ideology of gender. Occasionally, however, it emerges as the paradigm for excessive deviancy on a slippery rhetorical slope that envisages the moral acceptability of bestiality, incest and paedophilia at its base.[67] The reason for this heightened concern is that transsexualism and GCS are particularly challenging to those who see themselves as guardians of a rigid binary distinction between men and women.

3.2.3. Gender Confirmation Surgery: 'A Misdirection of Surgery'

Not all transgender persons seek GCS but a significant number do and this presents further ethical challenges. GCS requires the destruction of healthy sexual and reproductive organs, creates permanent sterility and carries significant ongoing health risks. Given that its aetiology is not clearly understood, it is unsurprising that there is some disquiet about surgical intervention, including among some medical practitioners.[68] Within the Catechism of the RCC, 'directly intended amputations, mutilations, and sterilisations performed on innocent persons are against the moral law' except when 'performed for strictly therapeutic medical reasons'.[69] Given the Church's elevated view of the body and its strong emphasis on the good of procreation it is entirely unsurprising that the threshold for 'strictly therapeutic medical reason' will be high, in reality prohibitively so.

Throughout a range of Catholic writings on transsexuality, including textbooks on moral theology, journalism and commentary by Catholic health

---

65 This conflict between the Vatican and the overwhelming majority of the international community is a recurring theme in the work of the UN Commission on the Status of Women. See <https://www.un.org/womenwatch/daw/csw/> accessed 12.12.2013.

66 Case, above n. 24, p. 809.

67 See Gabriele Kuby, quoted in Samson, Jansen and Notermans, above n. 24, p. 291.

68 D. Benatur (ed.), *Cutting to the Core: Exploring the Ethics of Contested Surgeries*, Rowman & Littlefield, Oxford 2006, pp. 79–112.

69 CC, above n. 35. It should be noted that it comes in a section in which the primary reference is to kidnapping and hostage-taking. This is not necessarily made clear when 2297 is quoted in relation to GCS, see, for example: W. Saunders, 'Surgery that destroys Bodily Integrity', *Catholic Herald*, 01.11.2001 <www.catholicherald.com/stories/bSurgery-That-Destroys-Bodily-Integrityb,4684?sub_id=4684> accessed 04.01.2014.

professionals, two assertions are frequently repeated.[70] Both can be found exemplified in the official response of the CBCEW to the proposed UK GRA 2004 legislation. First, that 'there is at present only limited knowledge and understanding of the aetiology of transsexuality'. Second, that 'research suggests it is psychological and sociological elements that are the key factors'.[71] There is a clear inconsistency between these two statements. Many would concur with the first. However the second seems determined by *a priori* anthropological assumptions and is in conflict with the growing evidence that transsexuality may have a biological basis.[72] Despite a lack of evidence about its efficaciousness it is therefore commonplace to find in Catholic literature the assertion that 'transsexualism should be treated with psychotherapy'[73] or psychiatry.

Among the most authoritative Catholic voices is Paul McHugh who as psychiatrist-in-chief at the John Hopkins Hospital from 1975 until 2001 succeeded in closing its pioneering gender identity clinic in 1979. The views of Professor McHugh are entirely congruent with those of the Vatican, for whom he is an advisor, and in a recent statement he describes GCS as 'a misdirection of psychiatry', arguing that the strong desires of the pre-operative transsexual are best understood as being akin to those of an alcoholic.[74] He concludes a recent apologia by arguing that his own profession has been seriously misled:

> 'As for adults who came to us claiming to have discovered their "true" sexual identity and to have heard about sex-change operations, we psychiatrists have been distracted from studying the causes and natures of their mental misdirections by preparing them for surgery and for a life in the other sex. We have wasted scientific and technical resources and damaged our professional credibility by collaborating with madness rather than trying to study, cure, and ultimately prevent it.'[75]

[70] Ashley and O'Rourke, above n. 42; Saunders, above n. 69; P. McHugh, 'Surgical Sex', (November 2004), *First Things* <www.firstthings.com/article/2004/11/surgical-sex> accessed 06.11.2012; R.P. Fitzgibbons, P.M. Sutton and D. O'Leary, 'The Psychopathology of "Sex Reassignment" Surgery: Assessing its Medical, Psychological, and Ethical Appropriateness' (2009) 9(1) *National Catholic Bioethics Quarterly* 97–125.

[71] CBCEW, above n. 36, para. 10.

[72] See, for example, the assessment of the eminent neuroscientist, Dick Swaab: 'All the data indicates that gender problems arise in the womb' and 'So everything indicates that the early development of sexual differentiation in the brains of transsexuals is atypical and that they aren't, in fact simply psychotic, as ... a Dutch psychiatrist was impertinent enough to claim recently'. Swaab probably overstates the strength of his case nevertheless it is clear that the biological is significant. D. Swaab, *We are our Brains: From the Womb to Alzheimer's*, Allen Lane, London 2014, pp. 69, pp. 70–72.

[73] W. Saunders, above n. 69; also W. Saunders, 'Straight Answers: The Morality of "Sex Change" Operations', *Catholic Herald*, 10.20.2005 <www.catholicherald.com/stories/Straight-Answers-The-Morality-of-Sex-Change-Operations,1997?sub_id=1997> accessed 04.01.2014. It is essentially the same article as that published in 2001, but for one further paragraph recounting a story about someone who had undergone GCS and the hypothesised devastating impact upon family relationships: 'Couldn't a child say in this story, "My father killed himself to be someone else?" Therein lies the tragedy of this heinous act'.

[74] McHugh, above n. 70, p. 1.

[75] McHugh, above n. 70, p. 9.

To understand more fully this approach to transsexuality, it is worth considering a more detailed Catholic exposition of the 'psychopathology' of GCS. Like McHugh, Richard Fitzgibbons, Phillip Sutton and Dale O'Leary are clear that GCS 'violates basic medical and ethical principles and is therefore not ethically or medically appropriate', and is a 'category mistake' in that 'it offers a surgical solution for psychological problems'.[76] Their account focuses primarily on male-to-female transsexuals and is framed by the controversial typology[77] of Ray Blanchard, for whom the key to understanding the phenomenon of transsexuality is not gender identity, but rather sexuality. Blanchard argues that male-to-female transsexuals fall into two categories: 'homosexual transsexuals' (HT), that is men who transition in order to be able to 'pass' as real women to attract heterosexual 'masculine' men to whom they are erotically attracted; and autogynephilic transsexuals (AT), who transition because they are sexually aroused by the idea or image of themselves as women.[78] Fitzgibbons, Sutton and O'Leary also employ the work of Kenneth Zucker and Susan Bradley,[79] who have argued that an insecure mother–child relationship is implicated in young boys with gender identity disorder (GID), to generalise about the possibility that inadequate parenting and insecure attachment may play a significant role in GID. So, for example, Fitzgibbons, Sutton and O'Leary suggest that: 'Fathers with creative or artistic sons need to learn how to support and affirm these interests as authentically masculine', and that boys who lack eye-hand coordination or the ability to 'properly kick a soccer ball' may, in their sense of rejection by male peers, come to hate their sexual identity.[80] The authors' 'solution' to the challenge of GID is then to improve support for effective parenting; to help children with GID 'to identify with the goodness of their masculinity or femininity'; and to improve the quality of therapeutic intervention to address the serious emotional conflicts which those with GID suffer.[81]

In a progressively speculative account, Fitzgibbons, Sutton and O'Leary go on to identify child sexual abuse, same-sex attraction and masochism as contributing causes to the desire for GCS. These factors, so the authors argue, alongside experiences of 'abuse or neglect and of peer or parental rejection' which begin in early childhood, result in insecure attachments to the same-sex parent and peers and the creation of an erotic script 'in which, as persons of the other sex, they are able to overcome all difficulties'. As a consequence the male-to-female

---

76 Fitzgibbons, Sutton and O'Leary, n. 63, p. 99.

77 McHugh also relies on Blanchard's understanding, arguing that HT males are 'conflicted and guilt-ridden homosexual men who (see) a sex-change as a way to resolve their conflicts over homosexuality by allowing them to behave sexually as females with men'. McHugh, above n. 70, p. 3.

78 Clearly this classification aligns such individuals very closely with transvestic fetishism.

79 K.J. Zucker and S.J. Bradley, *Gender Identity Disorder and Psychosexual Problems in Children and Adolescents* Guilford Press, New York 1995.

80 Fitzgibbons, Sutton and O'Leary, above n. 70, p. 104, 105.

81 Fitzgibbons, Sutton and O'Leary, above n. 70, p. 106.

transsexual quest is 'a narcissistic one rather than a normal feminine sexuality'.[82] In the view of the authors then, the desire for GCS is the result of 'an array of psychological disorders'.[83]

Within Catholic writings then, the aetiology of gender dysphoria is consistently presented as psychogenic or sociogenic. Fitzgibbons, Sutton and O'Leary provide one of the starkest and most detailed expositions of this approach through a combination of their highly selective reading of the scientific and medical evidence and their own speculations.[84] Within assessments in this vein it is quite evident that the scientific evidence is made to fit the pre-existing anthropological axioms. Furthermore, it is assumed, given this aetiology, that psychiatric treatment is, and can be, the only solution despite the fact that, as one conservative commentator makes clear, transsexualism 'has so far proved intransigent to every mode of psychiatric treatment'.[85]

3.3. THE CONSERVATIVE VIEW: A SUMMARY

The conservative view is that the Scriptures and enlightened reason concur: God created humanity as sexually dimorphic and heterosexually procreative; ontologically distinct as male and female. In this view, transgender persons can be construed as the victims of a dangerous cultural development that has had the 'harmful effect of engendering an understanding of sexuality and personhood that is fluid',[86] of being deluded, or in thrall to fantasy and engaging in the impersonation of those of the 'opposite sex'. Transgenderism is therefore a manifestation of sin; of that which separates humanity in general and individual persons in particular, from true fulfilment. Thus for the majority of conservatives, such persons are sad and misguided individuals who suffer from a psychological or psychiatric condition that has been misdiagnosed and mistreated. For others, such individuals are seen in a harsher light as 'notorious sinners', engaged in 'a conscious and sacrilegious attempt at overriding the structure of maleness and

---

82 Fitzgibbons, Sutton and O'Leary, above n. 70, p. 119, 123.

83 Their account of these disorders is as follows: 'there is substantial evidence that the defense mechanism of rationalization serves to cover up serious emotional and personality conflicts and the underlying sexual motivation, namely, the desire by some to live out their sexual fantasies. At the very least, health professionals should evaluate the role that strong anger towards oneself, with self-destructive impulses and intense anger toward others, depression, self-pity, childhood trauma, addiction to masturbation and fantasy, and envy, plays in the development of HT and AT. These persons should be evaluated for personality disorders, particularly narcissistic and borderline types': Fitzgibbons, Sutton and O'Leary, above n. 70, p. 125.

84 For example, the section on masochism (pp. 117–118) which relies upon one scientific article from 1974 and the controversial writing of the radical feminist Janice Raymond: J. Raymond, *The Transsexual Empire: The Making of the She-Male*, Teachers College Press, Columbia 1979.

85 O' Donovan, above n. 21, p. 136.

86 SBC, above n. 27.

femaleness created by God' and in 'a decisive complaint or rebellion against God for having created oneself as male or female.'[87] The fact that such individuals are given encouragement and support by health services, psychiatrists and surgeons who provide medically sanctioned mutilation, and that such individuals have their rights enshrined by legal systems and governments, is testimony to the power of malign cultural influences – like relativism, consumerism, liberal individualism and love of technological innovation for its own sake – which are aligned in a secular assault upon traditional Christianity.

Returning to the opening set of questions about whether transgender persons are able to participate as members of Christian congregations, be married in an confirmed gender, or be ordained or licensed as ministers or priests, it is quite clear that for churches who do not regard transgenderism as a real phenomenon but as a manifestation of delusion, marriage and ordination are simply not viable options. For conservative churches, post-operative transsexual persons are judged to be ineligible for marriage in their confirmed gender because that identification is seen as a lie. Their post-operative state also raises significant questions about their mental stability and therefore their capacity for forming a marital relationship. In addition to this, especially for the RCC, there is the further issue of their biological incapacity to have children in line with their birth assigned gender. Conservative churches are therefore most likely to accept the marriage of a transsexual person only if they 'repent' of their 'rash' decision, seek to return to their former state and marry someone of the opposite sex to that of their birth assigned gender. In terms of ordination, priesthood or authorised ministry is of course already restricted within conservative churches to men. Transgender men however are still excluded on the grounds that the Christian priest or minister, having an exemplary role, cannot be a source of scandal to the Christian community, nor can a priest or pastor be licensed for ministry if it is believed that they are mentally unstable.

Participation as an ordinary member in the life of a church may be possible, though the individual's experience is quite likely to be determined as much by the local minister and the dynamics of particular congregations as by the official stance of the church in question. It is possible that some transgender and transsexual persons may well receive a warm welcome at their local Catholic or Orthodox Church, although discrimination and prejudice is also a common experience. In some cases, however, transgender persons are not welcome or no longer welcome as part of the Christian fellowship, so unless they renounce their identity, they face excommunication. Explicit policies on membership are rare; however, the SBC draws a clear policy line: in addition to extending 'love and compassion to those whose sexual self-understanding is shaped by a distressing conflict between their biological sex and their gender identity', the SBC resolves to love its transgender neighbours and 'welcome them to our churches and, *as they*

---

87 Gagnon, above n. 5, p. 4.

repent and believe in Christ, receive them into church membership', *i.e.* attendance is acceptable, but formal membership is not unless the individual renounces their 'mistaken' identity.[88]

The overwhelming majority of Christians belong to churches that articulate a conservative or neo-conservative theological anthropology which place a great emphasis on the differences between men and women, male and female. In the RCC, Eastern Orthodoxy and conservative Protestant churches, birth assigned gender is God-given, and transgenderism is regarded as an aberration, or in a more theological register, as sin, something that separates the human person from a greater realisation of the person God has called or intended them to be.

There are however Christian communities and theologians who do not share such a binary understanding of gender, who think along very different lines and take a quite different stance to the issue of inclusion. It is to these we now turn.

IV. RADICAL: 'THERE IS NO LONGER MALE AND FEMALE ... IN CHRIST'[89]

Given that transgenderism is rare and may be viewed, by those unacquainted with transgender persons, as a perplexing phenomenon that challenges widely held assumptions about sex difference, it is unsurprising that it is transgender Christians themselves who have been at the forefront of arguing for full acceptance within the Christian churches. Such individuals have shared their experiences of being both transgender and Christian; sought to articulate and bear witness to how they understand their gender identity in relation to their faith; and engaged in advocacy or provided resources for Christian leaders and congregations.[90] In speaking of their experience, they have risked rejection and often encountered hostility from those Christians and Christian bodies that do not acknowledge the existence of a certain degree of natural variation within the human condition with respect to gender and sexuality. However transgender Christians have also been received, welcomed and affirmed by many believers, congregations and churches.

Such welcome and affirmation is in many ways a natural consequence of the imperatives that lie at the very heart of the Christian worldview, namely those of compassion and justice.[91] Christianity is quite clear that all human beings are

---

88 SBC, above n. 27 (emphasis added).

89 Galatians 3:28.

90 Including various contributions in M. Althaus-Reid and L. Isherwood (eds.), *Trans/formations*, SCM, London 2009; C. Beardsley, *The Transsexual is my Neighbour: Pastoral Guidelines for Christian Clergy, Pastors and Congregations*, 2nd ed., The Gender Trust, Brighton 2007; Tanis, above n. 4; Kolakowski n. 2; and Beardsley in this volume, pp. 77–100.

91 Biblical justice, *tsedaqah*, is a central category of the Hebrew scriptures and the defining characteristic of God, see: D.C. Maquire, *A Moral Creed for All Christians*, Fortress Press, Minneapolis 2005, p. 41.

made in the image of God (*imago Dei*) and, as such, possess a fundamental value and dignity that must be respected.[92] That respect involves, among many other things, charity and open-mindedness in paying real attention to the experience of others. The Bible repeatedly condemns a refusal to engage properly with others as a profound moral shortcoming, a failure of charity in love towards one's neighbour that is indicative of a 'hardness of heart'.[93] Clearly transgenderism presents a new and powerful challenge to many people's understanding of sex difference, but many Christians would recognise and fully acknowledge their responsibility to respond in compassion and with justice. Those Christian groups and churches which might be deemed 'radical' are simply those who have been prepared to listen to the experience of transgender persons and, respecting the integrity of their testimony, have discerned it to be 'of God', rather than a manifestation of sin. Perhaps unsurprisingly, many, but not all, such communities have a greater experience of working with marginal groups or managing diversity within their congregations, including of course sexual minorities.

Theologically, the claims of transgender Christians to full inclusion have powerful resonance within the Christian tradition, especially in the life and teaching of Jesus Christ himself. In the gospel's accounts of Jesus' ministry we are presented with a person who does not conform to contemporary cultural expectations, but rather constantly challenges them. Again and again, Jesus looks past the righteous, the respectable, those at the religious 'centre' and reaches out to welcome and embrace those on the margins: those ignored, despised and stigmatised by society – the blind, the deaf, the tax-collector, the prostitute and the leper. Because of their status and position in society such people are frequently invisible to others: they are not seen; they are not heard. Within Jesus's ministry then we have a pattern of someone who pays serious attention to individuals who are voiceless and who recognises them for what they really are, namely the beloved of God.[94] In the context of such a pattern, the idea that 'God is love' is not a sentimental reality, but a concrete and powerful one with transformative capacity. Whilst it is inevitable that churches, like all social groups, including even LGBT communities, will tend to build exclusive communities of the like-

---

92 Although there are tensions between the modern concept of human rights and the Christian gospel, as there are between many Christian groups and the advocates of certain human rights, it is important to remember that there was 'a decisive Christian input to the United Nations Declaration on Human Rights in 1945'. G. Newlands, *Christ and Human Rights*, Ashgate, Aldershot 2006, p. 2. See also J. Nurser, *For All Peoples and All Nations – The Ecumenical Church and Human Rights*, Georgetown University Press, Washington DC 2005.

93 D.J. Dormor, 'Religious perspectives on intersexual and transgender identity and relationships', (2010), unpublished paper <https://cambridge.academia.edu/DuncanDormor> accessed 03.02.2014.

94 'No other teacher that we know of addressed his teaching to the poor and not the well-to-do, consorted with the disreputable in preference to the morally correct, challenged the virtuous by comparison with the capacity for generosity and heroic self-sacrifice latent in those generally regarded as sinners.' A.E. Harvey, 'Eunuchs for the Sake of the Kingdom', 1995 <www.biblicalstudies.org.uk/pdf/eunuchs_harvey.pdf> accessed 23.11.2013, p. 24.

minded, there is a very strong case for arguing that a radical inclusivity lies at the very heart of Christianity.[95] In addition to the many examples from Jesus's teaching and ministry which support this, the key biblical text for radical and liberal Christians (which inevitably itself becomes totemic and potentially excluding of conservative Christians) comes from the Apostle Paul, in a letter which tackles those Christians who would place barriers to Gentiles becoming part of the people of God:

> 'There is no longer Jew or Greek, there is no longer slave or free, there is no longer male or female; for all of you are one in Christ Jesus.'[96]

4.1. EUNUCHS FOR THE KINGDOM OF GOD

Perhaps, a little surprisingly, there are parts of the Christian Scriptures that do have some direct bearing on a group of gender-variant individuals. The biblical texts in question do not relate directly to transgender people but rather to eunuchs. Such castrated men were not uncommon in the ancient world and experienced both a shift in gender role and physical modification. Their joyful inclusion within the people of God has been actively appropriated by transgender Christians. According to the law of Moses, that is the teaching of the first five books of the Bible, known as the Pentateuch, eunuchs stand outside the definition of the people of God.[97] However, this excluding tradition is radically overturned by the prophet Isaiah:

> 'Do not let the foreigner joined to the Lord say, "The Lord will surely separate me from his people"; and do not let the eunuch say, "I am just a dry tree." For thus says the Lord: To the eunuchs who keep my sabbaths, who choose the things that please me and hold fast my covenant, I will give, in my house and within my walls, a monument and a name better than sons and daughters; I will give them an everlasting name that shall not be cut off.'[98]

Isaiah's vision of who is to be included in the people of God involves a rejection of the Mosaic limitations and a radical inclusivity that re-draws the boundary to include foreigners and other marginal groups, including eunuchs. Membership is based therefore on the faithfulness with which people live their lives rather than on the particularities of their bodies. The Isaianic prophecy in which the faithful eunuch is accepted within the community beloved of God and given the honour

---

95 R.A. Burridge, *Imitating Jesus: An Inclusive Approach to New Testament Ethics*, Eerdmans, Grand Rapids 2007.
96 Galatians 3:28.
97 Deuteronomy 23:1; Deuteronomy 22:5.
98 Isaiah 56:3–5. Also the Wisdom of Solomon 3:14.

due a head of a family strikes a strong note of graceful inclusion, and is powerfully reinforced by the two most relevant texts in the New Testament. In the first of these, from the Gospel of Matthew, Jesus adds to a traditional twofold distinction between eunuchs 'who have been so from birth' and those 'made eunuchs by others', a further group – those 'who have made themselves eunuchs for the sake of the kingdom of heaven'.[99] Although this Gospel saying is extremely interesting, its meaning has proved highly elusive. The traditional Christian reading assumes metaphorical intent to denote a purity of commitment to God that runs to celibacy. Thus, 'eunuchs for the sake of the kingdom' is a reference to those who 'for God's sake' reject the scriptural injunction to 'be fruitful and multiply'.[100] As Anthony Harvey has pointed out, this is a highly problematic interpretation.[101] Nevertheless, however the text is interpreted, it is clear that Jesus does not hold with the Mosaic prohibition, and indeed it is a distinct possibility that Jesus, himself an anomaly as an unmarried man who may well have been subject to name-calling as a 'eunuch', is placing himself and his disciples in direct solidarity with this category of outsider. Whatever the best interpretation of this contested passage, its powerful note of inclusivity, even solidarity, is strongly reinforced by the dramatic story of the conversion of the Ethiopian eunuch in the Acts of the Apostles.[102]

Acts relates the story of a minister to the Queen of Ethiopia who is a eunuch. He is reading the Book of Isaiah and puzzling over a passage (53:7–8), just three chapters earlier than the passage quoted above, when Philip the Evangelist, under divine instruction, appears by his side to assist and explain the significance of Jesus Christ. As a consequence the eunuch is converted and baptised. Given that under the Mosaic law such a man would have been excluded from the 'assembly of the Lord' this is a dramatic, far-reaching, even shocking development. The fact that the man is a foreigner and a eunuch is of central significance to the story, yet there is no special repentance, no miraculous making whole of his condition. Rather, he is simply and fully accepted as he is into the Christian community. This is a dramatic statement of inclusion and one that has been rightly appropriated by transgender communities, as one commentator, in neologising vein, puts it: 'The Ethiopian Eunuch is our most famous transcestor'.[103] In light of this, and notwithstanding the weight that conservatives place upon a complementarian reading of the creation narratives, one theologian in assessing the biblical evidence as a whole summarises it thus: 'there is at least as much biblical support for the full inclusion of even post-operative transsexuals in the community of

[99] Matthew 19:12.
[100] Genesis 9:7.
[101] Harvey, n. 94.
[102] Acts 8:26–40.
[103] L. Reay, 'Towards a Trangender Theology: Que(e)rying the Eunuchs' in M. Althaus-Reid and L. Isherwood, above n. 90, pp. 148–167.

faith as there is negative judgment'.[104] As Beardsley[105] so clearly demonstrates, transgender Christians are able to appropriate the broader Christian themes of journeying, transformation and *metanoia* very positively into their experience as Christian believers.

Before turning to look at ecclesial manifestations of inclusive Christianity, it is important to note some of the key theological ideas that have been influential in shaping welcoming and affirming communities, in particular, the development of Queer Theology.

4.2. CHALLENGING THE POWER OF THE BINARY

All fields of intellectual discourse are historically contingent and subject to shaping by a range of powerful forces. Theology is no exception. In the second half of the twentieth century a family of theologies, which have been described as 'particularising', were established that deliberately and self-consciously acknowledge this by 'standing up' for particular groups of marginalised or excluded individuals[106] and giving voice to a strong critique of certain social and political institutions (e.g. colonialism or patriarchy) as manifestations of what can be described as 'structural sin'. In so doing a challenge is laid down to mainstream, dominant Christian theology. The most far-reaching of these have been Liberation Theology,[107] which has sought to articulate a powerful solidarity with the poor, and Feminist Theology, which has sought to 'unmask' the ways in which traditional theologies have assisted with the project of patriarchy and the oppression of women. Inevitably such theologies place a strong emphasis on participation and activism, rather than mere observation, and privilege the experience of individuals within groups marginalised by manifestations of economic, political and cultural power.

One of the drawbacks to some of these particularising theologies lies in their contribution to generating defensive ghettos of essentialised identities. However, in the early 1990s from within this broad tradition of critical theology, but also influenced by philosophers like Michel Foucault and Judith Butler and the development of queer theory, emerged Queer Theology. Queer Theology builds upon the critique of patriarchy, and the denigration of the erotic highlighted by

---

104 J. Childs, 'Transsexualism: Some Theological and Ethical Perspectives' (2009) 48(1) *Dialog: A Journal of Theology* 30–41, 36.

105 See Beardsley, above n. 90.

106 R. Muers, 'Feminism, Gender and Theology' in D. Ford and R. Muers (eds.), *The Modern Theologians: An Introduction to Christian Theology since 1918*, Blackwell, Oxford 2005, p. 429.

107 In the past Liberation theology has been strongly condemned by the Vatican; however something of a rapprochement is occurring under the new Pope. See: Francis, 'The Joy of the Gospel: Apostolic Exhortation, *Evangelii Gaudium*', 24 November 2013 <http://w2.vatican.va/content/francesco/en/apost_exhortations/documents/papa-francesco_esortazione-ap_20131124_evangelii-gaudium.html> accessed 03.01.2014.

feminist and gay and lesbian theologies, to articulate a powerful critique of the 'naturalness' of heterosexuality, of the disguised biologism in much mainstream theology and the potential idolatry of the family and normative heterosexuality.[108] Crucially, it calls all stable identities and categorisations of people, including the gender binary, into question and seeks to make strange, or to 'queer', and relativise traditional theological readings and interpretations. As one theologian puts it, 'Queer seeks to outwit identity', which is perhaps evident, not least, in its appropriation of the insult 'queer' itself.[109]

There is a growing appreciation amongst contemporary theologians[110] of the capacity for Queer Theology to engage creatively with older, pre-Enlightenment theological traditions but also to re-engage Christian theology with the human body, a central focus for Christianity given the centrality of the incarnation – the idea that God in Jesus Christ took on flesh and became 'fully and truly' human. The central ideas of Queer Theology have thus had a significant impact on academic theology. However, Queer Theology has also had a very positive influence on transgendered Christians and affirming communities, helping them to avoid the potential difficulties associated with particularising theologies, *i.e.* an inadvertent over-identification with gender identity. It is to the emergence and development of these trans-friendly Christian communities that we now turn.

4.3. THE EMERGENCE OF TRANS-FRIENDLY CHRISTIAN COMMUNITIES

The 1960s were a period of massive social and cultural change in many 'Western' countries, not least the USA. In the wake of the emergence of the Gay Liberation Front, a handful of LGBT religious groups were founded within mainstream Christian denominations including Dignity in the Roman Catholic Church in 1969 and Integrity within the USA Episcopal Church in 1974.[111] Over the last couple of decades there has been a burgeoning of similar groups with networks of individuals and congregations within particular denominations, such that almost

---

108 Muers, above n. 106, p. 445.

109 G. Loughlin (ed.), *Queer Theology: Rethinking the Western Body*, Blackwell, Oxford 2007, p. 9.

110 See: Rogers, above n. 38; M. Althaus-Reid, *Indecent Theology: Theological Perversions in Sex, Gender and Politics*, Routledge, London 2000; M.D. Jordan, *The Invention of Sodomy in Christian Theology*, University of Chicago Press, Chicago 1997.

111 The mission statement of Dignity, now DignityUSA: 'DignityUSA envisions and works for a time when Gay, Lesbian, Bisexual and Transgender Catholics are affirmed and experience dignity through the integration of their spirituality with their sexuality, and as beloved persons of God participate fully in all aspects of life within the Church and Society.' <www.dignityusa.org/> accessed 14.10.2013. That for Integrity, now IntegrityUSA: 'to inspire and equip the Episcopal Church, its dioceses, congregations, and members to proclaim and embody God's all-inclusive love for LGBTQ persons and those who love them.' <www.integrityusa.org/> accessed 14.10.2013.

all mainstream or liberal denominations within the USA have such a group.[112] In addition, there are a whole host of Christian groups that seek to reach across denominational boundaries either as para-church agencies or campaigning groups, many of which provide pastoral and other resources.[113] In recent years there has also been a growth in groups specifically for transgender persons or tackling transgender issues.[114] Finally, the last decade has seen a diversification of LGBT-friendly churches and their liturgical and theological sensibilities, such that all major Christian traditions now have individual congregations or associations which are explicitly LGBT-friendly and affirming – including Orthodox, Roman Catholic and Pentecostal[115] groups. In the development towards a greater acceptance of transgender persons over the last few decades, a number of individuals and groups have played an important catalytic or even prophetic role. We now turn to consider the role of one denomination which has played a particularly key role in these developments.

4.4. CASE STUDY 2: THE PROPHETIC WITNESS OF THE UFMCC

The most distinctive pro-LGBT Christian development to emerge from the late 1960s was the Universal Fellowship of Metropolitan Community Churches

112 For example, the Association of Welcoming and Affirming Baptists founded in 1986: <www.awab.org/> accessed 14.10.2013.

113 In the United Kingdom, the Lesbian and Gay Christian Movement (LGCM), a 'UK-based international Charity which challenges homophobia and transphobia, especially within the Church and faith based organisations' was launched in 1976: <www.lgcm.org.uk/> accessed 14.10.2013; Changing Attitudes, an Anglican group founded in 1995, 'works for the full inclusion of gay, lesbian, bisexual and transgender people in the life of the Anglican Communion' <http://changingattitude.org.uk/> accessed 14.10.2013. There are also websites to help Christians find LGBT-friendly congregations, see: <www.gaychurch.org/find_a_church/> or <http://changingattitude.org.uk/find-a-church> accessed 14.10.2013.

114 For example, since 2004 there has been a group within The Episcopalian Church in the USA: TransEpiscopal <http://blog.transepiscopal.com> accessed 14.10.2013. Within the UK, there is Sibyls, a Christian spirituality group for transgendered people in the UK, <www.sibyls.co.uk>, accessed 14.10.2013.

115 The largest affirming Pentecostal association is the Global Alliance of Affirming Apostolic Pentecostals founded in 2007. In its statement on 'Gender, Gender Identity and Sexual Orientation', it declares: 'It is our conviction that the Scriptures understood in their historical and cultural context with the light of scientific, psychological and medical advancements do not support the religiously and culturally based discriminatory views long held to exclude minority groups. We believe that in Christ, gender, socio-economic status, political affiliation, race and sexual orientation have no bearing on a person's value, the condition of his or her soul, nor should they limit their involvement in the Church of God. God is no respecter of persons in Christ and what He hath cleansed, we should not call common or unclean. Both the laity and clergy should include persons who meet the Scriptural, discipleship and moral standards for salvation and service involvement in Christ's body. We believe God's ideal for sexual expression is that it only occurs between two monogamous individuals, united in love and partnership' <www.gaaap.net/our-constitution-and-bylaws.html> accessed 02.02.2014.

(UFMCC) founded in September 1968 in Los Angeles by a former Pentecostal minister, the Revd Troy Perry.[116] The UFMCC began life as one of the thousands of experimental communities founded in California in the 1970s, most of which have died out. However the UFMCC has prospered and is now a small international Protestant denomination with 222 congregations and more than 43,000 members in 37 countries. It has also successfully pressed for inclusion in larger Christian bodies: In 1991 it was granted 'observer status' at the World Council of Churches, an umbrella organisation whose membership represents over 500 million Christians, and within the US it is now represented on a number of ecumenical councils. The church has been performing same-sex ceremonies since the late 1960s, and the UFMCC was the first church to ordain a transgender minister, Sky Anderson, at its General Conference in 1979. In 1995 the Revd Elder Wilhelmina Hein (previously Willem) was re-elected to the Governing Board of the UFMCC. In addition, the UFMCC has developed a dedicated transgender ministry and actively seeks to promote the position, activities and ministries of transgender people within other denominations.[117]

Back in 1968, Troy Perry did not intend to found a new Christian denomination, but rather thought of himself as creating an inclusive church that simply had a special mission to gays and lesbians. So from the beginning in its celebration of monogamous relationships and its encouragement of disciplined and moderate lifestyles (e.g. in relation to alcohol) the UFMCC saw itself as having a role 'in bringing a Christian standard of morality to the chaotic gay male world of the late 1960's'.[118] The church thus functioned as a key religious base within the emergent gay movement and has continued over the last forty years to occupy a particular place within gay and lesbian sub-culture.[119]

Attentive to the needs of people from diverse religious backgrounds, Perry anticipated that the UFMCC would fade away in time as mainstream churches become more welcoming. However, in the wake of the Stonewall Riots and the emergence of the Gay Liberation Front, the church grew swiftly and with five congregations it established itself as a small Protestant denomination at an inaugural general conference in 1970. From its foundation, the UFMCC was strongly influenced by the civil rights movement which, given Perry's understanding of homosexuality as innate or God-given rather than chosen, is unremarkable. As a consequence it has been a church that has placed a particular emphasis on the unconditional love and acceptance of God of all his children

---

116 <http://mccchurch.org> accessed 24.10.2013.

117 <http://mccchurch.org/ministries/transgender/transformative-church-program/> accessed 24.10.2013.

118 M.W. Wilcox, 'Of Markets and Missions: The Early History of the Universal Fellowship of Metropolitan Community Churches' (2001) 11(1) *Religion and American Culture: A Journal of Interpretation* 101.

119 J.W. Paris and R.E. Anderson, 'Faith-based Queer Space in Washington DC: The Metropolitan Community Church-DC and Mount Vernon Square' (2001) 8(2) *Gender, Place & Culture: A Journal of Feminist Geography* 149–168.

irrespective of their differences, including those of sexual orientation and gender identity. Campaigning for social justice has remained a central focus of the church's activities.

Local UFMCC churches are self-governing and legally autonomous with a great deal of freedom of expression of both belief and practice;[120] however, there is a central list of authorised clergy who can serve as congregational leaders, and members are required to affirm the basic Christian creeds, use gender-inclusive language in worship and to celebrate the Eucharist once a week. Whilst styles of worship vary extensively the UFMCC has since its inception had a distinctively Pentecostal emphasis to its theology. There is then a strong emphasis on individuals having a personal relationship with Jesus Christ; on the inspired nature of the Bible (to be interpreted within its historical context); on evangelism; and on the charismatic gifts. The characteristic Pentecostal emphasis on the renewing activity of the Holy Spirit has also assisted the UFMCC to be open to embracing new theological movements like liberation theology as well as responding to other developments.[121] So although individual members of the Church come from a range of different Christian backgrounds, bringing a strongly ecumenical flavour to church life, its Pentecostal provenance has made it a natural home for LGBT 'refugees' from conservative Christian childhoods.[122] Ironically, the fact that the UFMCC has its roots in a more evangelical and conservative tradition within Christianity has had the effect of providing a particularly potent kind of religious affirmation for LGBT Christians. Originally dominated by its male gay members, the UFMCC swiftly embraced feminist concerns in the early 1970s and started to use gender-inclusive language in its services. Perhaps as a consequence, the proportion of its female members and pastors increased rapidly.

Throughout its history, the UFMCC has been at the forefront of campaigning for LGBT rights and as a consequence has experienced strong opposition, or what would now be described as 'hate crimes', from a number of quarters. Seventeen churches were vandalised in the early 1970s and in 1973 the Mother Church in Los Angeles was burnt to the ground. In the same year tragedy struck when thirty-two church members of the New Orleans congregation were killed in an arson attack on their meeting-place, the Upstairs Lounge. Despite the existence of a leading suspect, no one was convicted and there was no official response from the city government as would be expected in such tragic circumstances. The one Christian minister, an Episcopalian the Revd William Richardson, who held

120 D.G. Bromley, 'Universal Fellowship of Metropolitan Community Churches (MCC)' <www.has.vcu.edu/wrs/profiles/MetropolitanCommunityChurch.htm2011> accessed 12.12.2013.

121 Wilcox, above n. 118, p. 90.

122 For example, most members of the Faith Church, a predominantly black LGBT church in the deep South of the USA and a member UFMCC were brought up in conservative Black Baptist churches: McQueeney, above n. 13, p. 154.

prayers for the victims was subjected to a reprimand from his bishop and received a significant amount of hate mail.[123]

Although the character of the UFMCC is undoubtedly shaped by the events of the 1960s and its Californian provenance, it is securely rooted in the Christian evangelical tradition. Its commitment to inclusion and social justice is certainly not restricted to LGBT people, though its advocacy in this area could quite properly be described in the Christian tradition as prophetic in character. Like other Pentecostal pastors, Troy Perry, and the UFMCC itself, is ecumenical in spirit and does not attach great weight to institutional affiliation. As a consequence, the church has not prevented individual congregations from having multi-denominational affiliations.[124] In some cases congregations have even switched, as was the case with the Dallas congregation that moved to the United Church of Christ in 2006. This lack of institutional propriety has assisted the UFMCC in promoting and disseminating its welcoming and affirming ethos to other Christian denominations.

4.5. THE RADICAL VIEW: A SUMMARY

A small number of Christian communities have been at the forefront of social change in accepting and affirming transgender people alongside gay, lesbian and bisexual Christians since the 1970s. Some of these, like Dignity, have operated within conservative churches; others like the UFMCC have created their own denominations. Such pioneering groups have listened to the experience of transgender people, accepted that transgenderism is a 'real' phenomenon rather than a delusion, ordained and conducted weddings for post-operative transsexual persons and developed resources of advocacy and support. In so doing they have drawn on ideas that lie at the heart of the Christian faith: that all people are made in the image of God, that God demands of his people a profound commitment to social justice, and that the poor and those on the margins of society are central to the teaching and ministry of Jesus Christ. Unsurprisingly, such groups have encountered significant external opposition, but they have also had to wrestle with the challenges generated by the dynamics of identity politics within congregations.[125]

It is difficult to imagine a greater contrast than that between the Vatican, articulating the official position for 1.1 billion Roman Catholics worldwide, and those who identify with the much smaller UFMCC; between the complementarian

123 <http://walkingwithintegrity.blogspot.co.uk/2013/08/cloud-of-witnesses-rev-bill-richardson_9.html> accessed 04.01.2014.

124 Although the defection of one of the largest MCC congregations, that of the Cathedral of Hope in Dallas to the United Church of Christ in 2007, was largely a response to a mis-managed investigation into allegations of fraud on the part of the Senior Pastor.

125 Beardsley, above n. 90; McQueeney, above n. 13, p. 170; and Tanis, above n. 4, p. 87.

theology of John Paul II and Benedict XVI and Queer Theology; or between a conservative vision founded upon the 'Order of Creation' argument and that formulated by 'welcoming and affirming' congregations in light of the gospel imperative towards the inclusion of the marginalised. Unsurprisingly however, many Christians and churches sit somewhere between these two poles, and between the political cultures that support them, be that right-wing Catholic conservatism or the progressive Californian counter-culture of the 1960s. It is then to this centre ground that we now turn as we consider the developing attitudes and practices of moderate, or in many cases polarised, Protestant churches as they engage with the issues raised by transgender and transsexual persons.

V. MODERATE: FAITHFUL DISCIPLES AND MINISTERS OF THE GOSPEL

All of the Christian churches within this category can be described as mainstream or liberal Protestant denominations. Most of them have a membership of at least one million people and tend to be in the cultural mainstream of their respective societies. In the case of the formal state churches like the Lutheran churches of Scandinavia or the Church of England, their identity is also firmly tied to national culture and they may well be involved or implicated in a variety of ways in national legislation. In terms of their institutional ethos such churches tend to have an antipathy towards both the dogma of traditionalism and the identitarian tendencies of LGBT lobbying groups. Such churches are marked by a pastoral orientation with a practical emphasis on the love of neighbour, a tolerance of difference and a high view of individual conscience. Pragmatic and fairly democratic in nature, they have a broad appeal and, in the case of the state churches, they seek to include and relate to the entire population. Indeed, with a parish-based structure, ministers may have clear obligations to those in their parish irrespective of their religious commitments.[126]

In terms of ethical formulation, liberal Protestantism takes personal experience and scientific understanding seriously and the latter on its own terms, rather than filtering it through a prism like the natural law tradition of the RCC. Indeed it is not uncommon to find Protestant leaders with a significant scientific background.[127] As a consequence, ethical assessments of transsexuality tend to acknowledge the complexity of the phenomenon and urge an approach

126 For example, in England everyone is entitled to a burial service or to have their ashes buried in the churchyard of their Church of England parish church: <www.churchofengland.org/weddings-baptisms-funerals/funerals.aspx> accessed 12.02.2014.

127 For example, the Presiding bishop of The Episcopal Church (TEC) in the USA, the Rt. Revd Katharine Jefferts Schori, has a PhD in oceanography. The former Archbishop of York, the Rt. Revd and Rt. Hon. John Habgood (1983–1995) was a Fellow of King's College, Cambridge and taught pharmacology at the University.

that is open-minded, cautious and charitable.[128] However the broad appeal and inclusive reach of such churches means that they are frequently polarised, with advocates of both conservative and radical theologies and worldviews. In some cases those holding strongly conservative views are relatively small in number; in others there are significant internal divisions and even schisms.

Active inclusion and affirmation of transgender Christians including recognition of marriage in the affirmed gender and the possibility of transgender ordination has, in the main, been a fairly recent development within mainstream liberal Protestant denominations and dates from around 2000. In the case of the European state churches this development has in part been tied to the introduction of national legislation, partly in the wake of European legislation, most notably the European Court of Human Rights (ECtHR) decision in *Goodwin v United Kingdom*. The situation in the USA has been more varied, although similar patterns can be identified within different Protestant denominations. In such mainstream denominations, the issue of the ordination or authorisation of individuals as congregational leaders or pastors is a key indicator of the level of acceptance of transgender and transsexual Christians more widely as they are called to be exemplars of Christian living and entrusted to embody and teach the Christian faith.

5.1. PIONEERING DEVELOPMENTS IN THE USA

The first, or at least the first public and clearly documented, case of a mainstream denomination in the USA directly addressing the question of whether one of its ordained members could remain in their role as a religious leader following GCS was that of the Presbyterian church in Atlanta in 1996. After a rigorous investigative process and on the unanimous recommendation of their Committee on Ministry which was required to consider the matter, the Greater Atlanta Presbytery agreed by a narrow majority, 186–161, that the Revd Erin Svenson could continue in her post as an ordained minister, having served the church (as Eric) for the previous 23 years.[129] In that process the dominant concerns of the Church authorities appear to have been pastoral, focusing on the potential impact of her actions on the unity and health of the Church, or in scriptural terms whether her continuance as an ordained minister might prove to be a 'stumbling block' for other Christians.[130] It is quite evident that during the process, Erin

128 F.N. Watts, 'Transsexualism and the Church' (2002) 9(1) *Theology and Sexuality* 63–85; and J.M. Childs, 'Transsexualism: Some Theological and Ethical Perspectives' (2009) 48(1) *Dialog* 30–41.

129 For an account of the decision see Tanis, above n. 4, pp. 102–110. Swenson's own accounts can be found at: <www.transfaithonline.org/fileadmin/TFexplore/Swenson-HRC-WhileOrdained.pdf> and <www.transfaithonline.org/articles/other/tos/bodyandsoul/> accessed 12.02.2014.

130 I Corinthians 8:9 'Only take care lest this liberty of yours somehow become a stumbling block to the weak'. The idea is that Christians should not engage in behaviour which whilst

played a key role convincing the Committee on Ministry, which was initially very divided, through a succession of one-to-one meetings. In promulgating their decision the Atlanta Presbytery noted that there were no clear authoritative sources within scripture or historic Christian doctrine upon which to make a judgement about transsexualism. In what was a very public process, there was a clear focus on Erin's own actions, namely whether she had conducted herself throughout in a manner consistent with a position of exemplary leadership. The church concluded: 'in her relationship with other people in her personal life and ministry, she shows herself to be a faithful disciple of Jesus Christ and minister of the Gospel'.[131]

The process by which Svenson was affirmed in her role as an ordained woman is a powerful illustration of how important democratic and devolved decision-making can be within Protestant denominations and therefore how crucial particular individuals or small groups can be in bringing about significant change.

At the national rather than regional level, the General Synod of the United Church of Christ (UCC) within the Reformed tradition, numbering some 1.3 million people, has been particularly progressive in its approach. From the mid-1980s, it has positively affirmed its lesbian and gay members, and in 2003 it passed a resolution to affirm the participation and ministry of transgender people within the Church. Whilst not all individual congregations are supportive, the resolution encouraged all within the UCC to 'welcome transgender people into membership, ministry, and full participation' and the Church, among other activities, through various agencies:

> 'to learn about the realities of transgender experience and expression, including the gifts and callings and needs of transgender people ... to encourage the participation and ministry of transgender people in the life of the church and to prepare individuals and churches to receive such participation and ministry ... to develop appropriate resources, in consultation with a representative group of transgender people within the United Church of Christ ... and to provide leadership in advocating for the human and civil rights of transgender people.'[132]

permissible in itself might have a negative impact upon the faith of other 'weaker' Christians.

131 Quoted in Tanis, above n. 4, p. 107–8.

132 General Synod of the UCC, 'Affirming the participation and ministry of transgender people within the United Church of Christ and supporting their civil and human rights', 15 July 2003 <www.ucc.org/assets/pdfs/2003-AFFIRMING-THE-PARTICIPATION-AND-MINISTRY-OF-TRANSGENDER-PEOPLE-WITHIN-THE-UNITED-CHURCH-OF-CHRIST-AND-SUPPORTING-THEIR-CIVIL-AND-HUMAN-RIGHTS.pdf> accessed 12.01.2014.

5.2. LGBT INCLUSION: ACCEPTANCE AND POLARISATION

However, most of the larger Protestant denominations in the USA have been more internally divided and moves towards the acceptance of same-sex blessing and LGBT ministers have often resulted in conservative breakaway groups. So, for example, in an attempt to remain both faithful to scripture, tradition and the historic confessions of the Lutheran Church,[133] but also to affirm LGBT clergy in faithful monogamous relationships, issues of human sexuality and gender have been extensively debated over the last twenty years within the largest Protestant church in the USA, the Evangelical Lutheran Church of America (ELCA). Following the adoption of a new statement on sexuality,[134] in 2009 the ELCA amended its policies to embrace LGBT clergy and re-admit to its roster those who had been forced out or had to resign including the Revd Megan Rohrer, who thus became the first openly transgender Lutheran pastor in the ELCA. This momentous change was in part the consequence of long standing campaigning by groups like Lutherans Concerned,[135] but also of the actions of the Extraordinary Lutheran Ministries (ELM).[136] Evoking the tradition of extraordinary ordinations performed by Martin Luther himself at the Reformation, the ELM created its own roster of clergy separate from the official rosters of the ELCA and the Evangelical Lutheran Church in Canada. In 2009 those 'extraordinarily ordained' by ELM were reconciled to the ELCA and joined the official roster. However, this development came at a price, and in the following year a conservative dissenting group called North American Lutheran Church (NALC), with a membership of around 130,000 Lutherans, left the parent body, the ELCA, a denomination with an active membership of more than four million. In an account of these developments theologian Brent Hage points out that:

> 'the ELCA is not a denomination on the far-left fringes of American Protestantism; it is a traditionally moderate, left-of-center body whose historic heartlands are

133 The historic confessions of the Lutheran Church are made up of ten creedal documents known as the Book of Concord, they were published in 1580. For a contemporary English translation: P. McCain (ed.), *Concordia: The Lutheran Confessions*, Concordia Publishing House, St. Louis, MO 2005.

134 ECLA, *Human Sexuality: Gift and Trust*, 19 August 2009 <http://download.elca.org/ELCA%20Resource%20Repository/SexualitySS.pdf> accessed 13.01.2014.

135 Founded in 1974, Lutherans Concerned was subsequently renamed ReconcilingWorks. At its assembly in 2000 it approved a resolution adding transgender inclusion to programming and materials, and in 2012 it affirmed the formation of the TransLutherans affinity group in 2012. See <www.reconcilingworks.org> accessed 13.02.2014.

136 <www.elm.org> accessed 14.02.2014.

> the Mid-Atlantic and the Upper Midwest. If this denomination is making moves toward full inclusion, other Protestant bodies can't be far behind.'[137]

And, indeed, they are not. The Presbyterian Church (USA) also voted for full inclusion of LGBT clergy in 2010 and in 2012 The Episcopal Church (TEC) welcomed the ordination of transgender clergy having already affirmed gay and lesbian clergy. In a parallel development to the formation of the NALC, another conservative splinter group representing around 5% of TEC membership, the Anglican Church in North America (ACNA), was formed in 2009.

However the largest of the mainstream Protestant denominations in the USA, the United Methodist Church (UMC), presents a more curious case: it is the only significant mainstream denomination to have maintained the clear view that homosexuality is incompatible with Christianity, and to have opposed the affirmation of same-sex partnerships and the ordination of LGB individuals. This is primarily a consequence of the recent internationalisation of the composition of its governing body, the General Conference. For, whereas in 2004 only 19% were international delegates, by 2012 this had increased to 38%. The *status quo* has thus been maintained, despite increased support for LGB inclusion amongst American Methodists, through an alliance of (overwhelming conservative), overseas delegates and a small but significant US opposition.[138] However, transgender ministers are in a different situation, for unlike the case of homosexuality, there is no prohibition against a change in gender identity within the *Book of Discipline*,[139] which contains the doctrine and law of the UMC. So, when in 2007, the Revd Drew Phoenix, previously the Revd Ann Gordon, sought to minister under a new name having undergone GCS, the Judicial Council of the UMC took the clear view that it was in no position to oppose the change in name or gender identity.[140] This in turn provoked an attempt to deny ordination to transgender persons, but it failed to gain sufficient support at the General Conference of 2008. The visibility of transgender issues was further raised within the UMC when in 2009, another of its ministers, the Revd David Weekley, revealed his transgender status to his congregation and the wider church, having undergone GCS in 1975.[141]

---

137 B.A.R. Hege, 'A Reforming Tradition Struggles with Change: The Evangelical Lutheran Church in America's Historic Vote on LGBT Ordination, One Year Later' (2010) *Religion Dispatches* <http://digitalcommons.butler.edu/facsch_papers/149/> accessed 14.02.2014, p. 4.

138 R.W. Holman, *Queer Clergy: A History of Gay and Lesbian Ministry in American Protestantism*, The Pilgrim Press, Cleveland 2013, pp. 455–556.

139 United Methodist Church, *The Book of Discipline of the United Methodist Church 2012*, United Methodist Pub. House, Nashville 2013.

140 Judicial Council Decisions, Decision No. 1074 <www.archives.umc.org/interior_judicial.asp?mid=263&JDID=1156&JDMOD=VWD&SN=1001&EN=1088> accessed 07.09.2015.

141 N. Haught, 'Methodist minister confides to congregation that he is a transgender man', 30 August 2009 <www.oregonlive.com/living/index.ssf/2009/08/methodist_minister_confides_to.html> accessed 07.09.2015.

5.3. DEVELOPMENTS IN SCANDINAVIAN STATE CHURCHES

Parallel developments in the authorisation of ministers have also occurred within the Protestant state churches of Europe. In addition, as a consequence of their official status, changes in national marriage law have also had a direct impact upon church practices. These developments can be seen quite clearly in the 'purest' form of the state church found within Scandinavia, where the national populations are relatively homogenous and the nations are amongst the most progressive in the world in terms of gender equality and the inclusion and visibility of LGBT persons, including transgender persons. The majority of the population in each of these nations, Denmark, Finland, Iceland, Norway and Sweden are members of their respective national Lutheran churches – even if in most cases on a nominal basis. Although such churches seek to minister to all, including the more conservative constituencies within their national populations, the Evangelical Lutheran churches of Scandinavia are among the most inclusive on issues of sexuality and gender, with those in Sweden and Iceland the most progressive, closely followed by those of Denmark and Norway and then the more conservative Evangelical Lutheran Church of Finland. So, for example, within Sweden the ordination of LGBT clergy has been permitted since 2006 and same-sex marriage in churches since 2009, although clergy have a 'conscience clause', whereas the Lutheran church in Finland does not yet permit the ordination of non-celibate LGBT persons, nor same-sex blessings or marriage. Perhaps as an inevitable consequence of the small size of these national populations there has been limited vocalisation of transgender issues within the churches. Across the North Sea, significantly more discussion, albeit within limited circles, has taken place in another state church, one which, as the Mother Church of the 85 million strong Anglican Communion, has significant global influence. Furthermore, as the following case study demonstrates, leaders within that church, the Church of England, can play a significant role in determining the shape of legislation for the United Kingdom.

5.4. CASE STUDY 3: THE CHURCH OF ENGLAND: 'LIKE GENDER, ORGANISED RELIGION IS A COMPLEX MATTER'

The Church of England does not have a clear theological position or a consistent policy in relation to transgender people[142] and the matter has not been properly

[142] There is an excellent summary of the situation in J. Barrett, *Transsexual and Other Disorders of Gender Identity*, Radcliffe Publishing, Oxford 2007, p. 278: 'The mainstream Church of England does not seem to have a doctrinal position on change of gender role. It should be noted, though, that ordained Church of England priests have changed gender role and

debated by its governing body – the General Synod. There has been some academic discussion of the issues[143] but the dominant approach might be described as one of 'theological pragmatism'[144] on the part of the House of Bishops, which has clearly acknowledged that there is no consensus. That members of the Church of England disagree strongly is also evident from a study guide issued in 2003.[145] However, the clearest manifestation of the church's attitude to the issue can be found in its approach, as a state church, to the GRA 2004, which will be considered in more detail below.

According to Beardsley, whilst there are rumours of female-to-male priests serving in the Church of England, there are eight male-to-female clergy with a known transsexual history, of whom six were ordained prior to transition. Their experience has been mixed, but six remain in priestly ministry.[146] Within the Church of England, both in principle and in practice, there is a high view of episcopal authority, and bishops have a great deal of individual freedom to act. Unsurprisingly then, the experience of transgender clergy and ordinands[147] has been largely determined by the response of their bishops. So in 2001 a parish priest, the Revd Carol (previously Peter) Stone, transitioned whilst in active parish ministry with the support of both her congregation and bishop, the Rt. Revd Barry Rogerson, who stated clearly that there were no ethical or ecclesiastical objections.[148] Similarly in 2005 the Revd Sarah Jones was given strong support by her bishop, the Rt. Revd Anthony Priddis.[149] However such episcopal support is by no means universal and others have not received such warm encouragement, as Beardsley herself notes.[150]

The clearest statement about the official position of the Church of England on transsexualism comes from a residential meeting of the House of Bishops in January 2003.[151] It was one of sixteen items of business which also included a discussion of the reform of the House of Lords and most significantly a statement

---

remained in their occupation. This is not necessarily well accepted by the evangelical wing of the Church of England, and it seems fair to say that the Church of England contains within a multiplicity of opinions and managed to contain these by having no rigid doctrinal position'.

143 Anglican contributors to the debate include Oliver O'Donovan, Frazer Watts and Rodney Holder. See O'Donovan, above n. 21; Watts, above n. 128; and R. Holder, 'The Ethics of Transsexualism' (1998) *Crucible: The Christian Journal of Social Ethics* 89–99, 125–136.

144 C. Beardsley, 'Nudging towards Serendipity: The Church of England and Transsexual People' (2013) *Crucible* 19.

145 The Archbishops' Council, *Some Issues in Human Sexuality: A guide to the debate*, Church House Publishing, London, 2003.

146 Beardsley, above n. 144, p. 21.

147 Beardsley, above n. 144, p. 22.

148 BBC News, 'Sex change vicar back in Pulpit', 03.12.2000 <http://news.bbc.co.uk/1/hi/uk/1052786.stm> accessed 06.11.2012.

149 BBC News, 'Bishop defends transsexual curate', 24.09.2005 <http://news.bbc.co.uk/1/hi/england/hereford/worcs/4277176.stm> accessed 06.11.2012.

150 Beardsley above n. 144, p. 21.

151 House of Bishops, 'Summary of Decisions', 31 January 2003 (HB(03)M1). I am grateful to the General Synod office of the Church of England for granting me access to this document.

arguing against military intervention in Iraq. The episcopal discussion and statement followed the European Court of Human Rights (ECtHR) decision in *Goodwin v United Kingdom*[152] and anticipated the public and parliamentary debates associated with the GRA 2004. In its summary of decisions, the bishops were very frank in acknowledging strong disagreement within the Church as a whole and within the House of Bishops itself:

> 'The House recognised that there was a range of views within the Church on transsexualism and accepted that (as matters stood at present) both the positions set out below could properly be held:
> a) some Christians concluded on the basis of Scripture and Christian anthropology, that concepts such as 'gender reassignment' or 'sex change' were really a fiction. Hormone treatment or surgery might change physical appearance, but they could not change the fundamental God-given reality of 'male and female He created them'.
> b) others, by contrast, whilst recognising that medical opinion was not unanimous, were persuaded that there were individuals whose conviction that they were 'trapped in the wrong body' was so profound and persistent that medical intervention, which might include psychiatric, hormone, and surgical elements, was legitimate and that the result could properly be termed a change of sex or gender.'[153]

In recognising that both views could be 'properly held' within the Church of England, or to put it another way, as 'gender reassignment *may be* inconsistent with the doctrine',[154] of the Church, the House of Bishops agreed that discussions with the government should continue with a view to safeguarding the position of bishops unwilling to ordain transgender candidates and, once marriage of transgender persons became possible in law, securing an exemption for clergy not willing to solemnise such marriages.

The resulting legislation, the GRA 2004, strikes a delicate balance. It protects the privacy of a person who applies for an official recognition of gender by protecting the confidentiality of that information. It also makes it clear that a Church of England minister is not required to officiate at the wedding of a person she or he reasonably believes to be living in an 'acquired gender.'[155] However, under s. 22 of the GRA 2004, a criminal offence is created if someone who has obtained a person's gender history in an official capacity discloses that information. A subsequent order outlines specific circumstances under which disclosure

---

152 *Goodwin v United Kingdom* (2002) 35 EHRR 447.
153 House of Bishops, above n. 151, p. 2.
154 M. Hill, 'Rent Asunder: Westminster's war on Marriage', 2008 <www.parliament.uk/documents/lords-committees/merits-statutory-instruments/Professor-Mark-Hill-QC-Legal-Opinion-to-Merits-Committee-on-Marriages-and-Civil-Partnerships-(Approved-Premises)-(Amendment)-Regulations%202011.pdf> accessed 09.06.2013, p. 4 (emphasis added).
155 Gender Recognition Act (GRA) 2004, section 22; Schedule 4, Part 1, para. 3.

for 'religious purposes' is permitted. So, information can be shared between ministers to enable a decision about officiating at a wedding.[156] Disclosure is also permitted in relation to the appointment or employment of individuals to specific roles within organised religion 'or to determine whether the subject is eligible to receive or take part in any religious sacrament, ordinance or rite, or take part in any act of worship or prayer, according to the practices of an organised religion'.[157] However in this second scenario it is necessary, to comply with the legislation, that 'the person making the disclosure reasonably considers that that person may need the information in order to make a decision which complies with the doctrines of the religion in question or avoids conflicting with the strongly held religious convictions of a significant number of the religion's followers'.[158]

At the end of the legislative process the Church of England was able, plausibly, to claim some success:

> 'The Church of England has successfully sought provision to protect the personal consciences of clergy opposed to solemnising such marriages, but it has also sought to balance the personal rights of individual members of the clergy with the rights of transsexual parishioners to use their parish church.'[159]

In short, a pragmatic compromise was arrived at between the state and its established church over an issue affecting a small number of people. It did not exacerbate internal divisions over gender within the Church of England and in the process the Church did not contest the authority of the state nor take issue with the state's need to comply with the European Court's judgment.

However, it is worth delving a little deeper into the issue to illuminate the complex role of religion and the various players involved by considering the debates in the upper house of the United Kingdom: the House of Lords. As the established church, twenty-six of forty-four diocesan bishops are members of the House of Lords, the 'Lords Spiritual'. As such they participate in debates and have the ability to influence and shape legislation.

From the outset, it was clear that the GRA would pass with relative ease in the House of Commons where the issue split the Conservative party but all other major parties voted in favour, producing a clear majority. It was widely and correctly anticipated that the Bill would have more difficulty within the House of Lords, and 'religious' objections were raised repeatedly in that chamber. Certain religious groups had been vociferous in opposing the legislation and

---

156 Gender Recognition (Disclosure of Information) (GR DOI) (England, Wales and Northern Ireland) (No. 2) Order 2005, 4 Disclosure for religious purposes (2) a).

157 GR DOI, above n. 156, (2) c)–e).

158 GR DOI, above n. 156, (3).

159 Church of England, 'The Gender Recognition Act and the Church – what the Law says: A note from the Church of England's Mission and Public Affairs and Legal Divisions', April 2005, p. 4.

two in particular had submitted strongly worded submissions in line with the 'Order of Creation' arguments characteristic of the conservative position outlined above. These were The Christian Institute, a conservative evangelical lobbying organisation with a fairly modest level of support, and the Evangelical Alliance, an umbrella group to which most British evangelical churches are affiliated and which claims to represent up to two million Christians. Conservative Christian opposition to the Government's proposal had thus been made loud and clear. As a consequence a number of amendments were put forward with the intention of protecting churches and faith communities from some of the consequences of the new Act.

One of those who put forward a number of amendments was Baroness O'Cathain, a lay Christian woman and a patron of the Christian Institute. In moving an amendment (subsequently withdrawn) which would have allowed a church to refuse employment to a person who would not consent to the disclosure of any entry in the gender recognition register, she stated:

> 'Churches teach us that our sex is decided by God. They also teach that your sex is a matter of absolute truth, not personal choice. I ask, how could a Church employ a transsexual who effectively believes that God got his sex wrong? How can they employ a person who, in their eyes, lives a lie by impersonating the opposite sex?'[160]

A second vociferous objector to the Act was Lord Tebbit who made repeated and trenchant interventions expressing his clear beliefs about the biological basis of sexual difference in line with the decision of Ormerod in *Corbett v Corbett*. The Bill was in his view 'an objectable farce', 'wretched legislation' and would require the state to lie and ask its civil servants to lie.[161] Throughout his speeches Lord Tebbit made extensive reference to religious constituencies: 'I wonder what His Holiness the Pope thinks' or 'It is a great pity that, neither in this debate or earlier debates, have we heard the voice of Islam in this House.'[162] However, Lord Tebbit, a former government minister under Margaret Thatcher, was in a difficult position as a self-proclaimed agnostic, for despite his attempts to play up 'religion' as an important consideration, the Church of England bishops in the House of Lords did not support the position that he thought all right-thinking religious people should adopt.

A number of bishops spoke in the debate, including the bishops of Winchester, Chester, Southwell and Worcester, but their contributions were in the main sympathetic and constructive to the Government's intentions. Their primary concerns, consistent with the statement from the House of Bishops, were that religious ministers of whatever faith who refused to marry a transgender

---

160 House of Lords (HL), Hansard (Debate) 3 February 2004, 657, col. 635.
161 HL Deb 18 December 2003, 655, col. 1304.
162 HL Deb 10 February 2004, 657, col. 1067.

person would not be liable to prosecution and that churches could exercise the right to appoint as authorised ministers those whom they thought it appropriate to appoint. The general approach of the bishops was probably best summed up by the Bishop of Chester, the Rt. Revd Peter Forster:

> 'I am broadly in favour of the Bill and am among a minority, perhaps, of Christians and church people who are willing to go with the Bill and recognise that it is a way in which to deal with a genuine issue.'[163]

In short, no bishop of the Church of England voted against the Bill in the House of Lords (it was passed by 155 to 57), and no bishop spoke with any great passion against it or indeed voted for an amendment which would substantially have changed the Bill, although one bishop, the Rt. Revd Michael Scott-Joynt of Winchester, expressed clear sympathy for those who held the conservative Christian position on transsexuality.[164] Indeed it was the active intervention of several Church of England bishops, two of whom (Worcester and Winchester) spoke against, which led to the narrow defeat (149–144) of an amendment, introduced by Baronness O'Cathlain, giving religious bodies greater power and autonomy, which:

> 'would have allowed religious organisations to prohibit or restrict participation, by people with an acquired gender, in its religious activities or ceremonies, if the prohibition was necessary to comply with the doctrines of the religion or to avoid offending the religious susceptibilities of a significant number of the religion's followers.'[165]

One bishop went further and felt that the 'conscience clause' which enabled Church of England clergy to refuse to conduct a marriage for someone they reasonably believed to be a transsexual was already a step too far. Acknowledging that without a conscience clause the Bill would have faced stronger opposition he wished to place on record his 'considerable discomfort':

---

163 HL Grand Committee 13 January 2004, 656, col. GC 21.

164 Both the bishops of Winchester and Chester were clearly regarded as conservatives within the Church of England. For example, they were united in opposition to the nomination of Jeffrey John, an openly gay priest in a long-term relationship, as Bishop of Reading in 2003. The Bishop of Winchester, in particular, was a strong advocate for traditional sexual morality and an outspoken opponent of the increasing extension of rights to gay, bisexual and lesbian persons, not least through his opposition in the House of Lords to the Equality Act (Sexual Orientation) regulations in 2007.

165 C. Fairburn, 'The *Gender Recognition Bill* [HL]: Bill 56 of 2003–4', 17 February 2004, Research Papers 04/15, Home Affairs Section, House of Commons Library, p. 61.

'The clause, for all its right protection of the consciences of some clergy, actually troubles the consciences of many others of us by what it puts certain people through in their request to be married.'[166]

As the same individual, the Rt. Revd Peter Selby, the Bishop of Worcester, perceptively remarked: 'As we debate the matters, a picture is being built up in which organised religion always takes one view of the question.' Instead, as he pointed out, 'like gender, organised religion is a complex matter'.[167]

5.5. THE MODERATE VIEW: A SUMMARY

Small radical groups are naturally self-selecting and can easily generate consensus and momentum to make swift progress in advancing their concerns; however, the speed of change in large historic and mainstream denominations, which contain a much greater diversity of views, is inevitably much slower. In addition, not many Christians have much experience of transgenderism and it is therefore unsurprising that the issue has not found itself quickly onto the internal agendas of many churches.[168] Nevertheless, over the last twenty years, there have been significant developments within mainstream Protestant denominations in both the USA and Europe. This change has come about as institutions and their leaders have responded to three particular challenges.

The first of these have been ministers or priests who have transitioned or expressed the intention to do so. In approaching their respective religious leaderships, individuals like Erin Swenson and Carol Stone have sought not just pastoral support, but also clear validation about their continuing public role as Christian teachers and leaders. Such cases have been catalytic, challenging individual Christian leaders or representative decision-making bodies to think through their response and 'go on record'. Inclusive and welcoming responses to transgender Christians have often been articulated in response to such occasions. A second source of change, most evident within Council of Europe Member States as a consequence of the *Goodwin* decision, has been prompted by the requirement for churches to respond to newly introduced legislation which gives transgender people certain marriage and employment rights. Finally, change has come about through the consciousness-raising of a growing number of advocates and lobbying groups within the churches. As a consequence there has been slow but steady progress in the acceptance of transgender people within the Christian community across the spectrum of mainstream Protestant denominations, both as congregational members and leaders, with major denominations like the

166 HL Deb 3 February 2004 c626–7.
167 HL Deb 3 February 2004 c642–3.
168 Although as Christina Beardsley points out intersexuality, which is much more common, receives considerably less attention: Beardsley, above n. 144, p. 17.

ELCA and Church of England following only a few years behind the less diverse and more liberal UCC and the Church of Sweden.

VI. CONCLUSION AND FUTURE PROSPECTS

Returning to the opening questions about whether transgender persons are able to participate as members of Christian congregations, be married in a confirmed gender, or be ordained or licensed as ministers or priests, it is quite clear that in those churches which regard transgenderism as contradicting God's created order, marriage and ordination are simply not viable options. In 2014 two large USA Protestant denominations, the Southern Baptist Convention and the Assemblies of God, both produced clear statements denying the validity of the transgender experience and condemning GCS.[169] Whilst some participation in the life of conservative denominations may be possible, the nature of that experience will be determined as much by the local priest or minister and the congregational dynamics as the official stance of the church in question. Some transgender individuals may well receive a warm welcome at their local Catholic or Orthodox church or SBC congregation; just as others may not receive the welcome they anticipate within a more liberal denomination. However, within a growing number of liberal Protestant denominations, attitudes and practices, and most significantly policies, have changed significantly particularly over the last decade with churches allowing transgender Christians to be ordained and married in their affirmed gender. It is highly likely that such developments will continue. Indeed, given the emphasis that many Protestant denominations place upon congregational autonomy, it is possible that transgender people will become welcome in an increasing number of churches within more moderate conservative denominations as well.[170]

The issue of transgenderism takes us to the very heart of what is at stake in theological accounts of the significance of biological difference and gender. Although it is quite possible, in theory, to hold conservative religious views about gender and still accept the reality of the experience of the transsexual person,[171] Christians have tended to view both transsexuality and transgenderism within a broader understanding of the theological significance of gender and sexuality which has become highly polarised: the conservative, or in many cases, the neo-

---

169 Above nn. 25 and 27.

170 For example, within the large family of Baptist denominations in the USA, the Association of Welcoming & Affirming Baptists (AWAB), which offers support and affirmation of the LGBTQ community in the Church and beyond, have 'seen a growth in the desire of many churches that are a part of the Missionary Baptist Churches, Progressive National Baptist Convention and the National Baptist Convention' to become part of AWAB. They also have an increasingly number of affiliations from churches which see themselves as 'formerly Southern Baptist identified' <www.awab.org/about-awab.html> accessed 13.02.2015.

171 Bucar, above n. 34.

conservative view, being that God ordered creation with a rigid and strict sexual dimorphism into two distinct sexes, male and female. As Baroness O'Cathain speaking in the UK's House of Lords put it: 'our sex is decided by God' and is a 'matter of absolute truth'.[172] In such an account, transgender people are deluded narcissists, sad and misguided, or even notorious sinners. In the alterative liberal view, the theological significance of gender difference is regarded as secondary and subservient to the essential principle that all persons are equal in the sight of God, or 'before the Cross'. Such a view is rooted in a theological orientation that is more committed to respect for the integrity of human experience in the formulation of ethical judgments, and which acknowledges that the broad consensus of medical expertise understands the human condition to be characterised by a certain degree of natural variation with regard to gender and sexuality. These two opposed views align very closely with attitudes to homosexuality within and between churches.

Clearly there are dangers to the integrity and distinctiveness of any religious tradition that pays too much attention to contemporary thinking and weighs the claims of personal experience above all else, for it would simply enshrine and sanctify aspects of contemporary society. However there are also profound dangers associated with an uncritical reliance on the authority of the Scriptures, or what is understood to be received tradition. In reality, much contemporary Christianity, in common with other aspects of society, is blind to the provenance of its assumptions about human nature.[173] As Thomas Laqueur has amply demonstrated, the idea of 'two stable, opposite, incommensurable sexes' which underpins conservative accounts of theological anthropology can be historically situated within the dominant 'two sex/flesh' model of gender whose origins lie with the Enlightenment.[174] As a matter of historical record the 'two sexes' were not perceived as 'opposite' and 'polar' categories until the eighteenth century. There is clear evidence then that conservative, just as much as radical and liberal, forms of theology are continually reworked and renewed, and what constitutes an authoritative, natural or even 'literal' interpretation of a particular passage of scripture changes over time,[175] although this process is habitually disguised by the claims of continuity and the assertion of a timeless, unchanging tradition.

Broadly speaking, conservative Christian traditions are driven to interpret and condemn transgenderism as a psychic or moral disorder, against a growing medical consensus, as a consequence of their theological anthropology. This tendency is reinforced by the fact that, in the 'West' in particular, such Christian

---

172 HL Deb 3 February 2004 c635.

173 Dormor, above nn. 19 and 93.

174 Laqueur, above n. 22, p 6.

175 For example, Andrew Mein provides a clear critique of the idea, promoted by John Paul II and Benedict XVI, that Genesis 1:27 implies anything about the complementarity of men and women. A. Mein, '"Threat or Promise": The Old Testament on Sexuality' in D.J. Dormor and J.N. Morris (eds.), *An Acceptable Sacrifice? Homosexuality and the Church*, SPCK, London 2007, pp. 22–32. Also: M. Dawn, 'Whose Text is it anyway? Limit and Freedom in Interpretation' in Dormor and Morris, pp. 10–21.

identities have become entrenched in a pattern of 'cultural defence' against secular and liberal incursions, and issues of sexuality and gender have become central markers of identity in this cultural conflict. It is not certain that this pattern of cultural engagement will be maintained especially within the RCC under Pope Francis. It also remains a distinct possibility that in response to the careful and committed advocacy of groups representing transgender Christians, or a reassessment of the medical evidence, attitudes to transsexuality in particular could be reframed within some conservative Christian traditions.

METAMORPHOSIS AND (TRANS) MIGRATIONS: SPIRITUAL DIMENSIONS OF GENDER TRANSITION

Christina Beardsley

Contents

I. INTRODUCTION

In this chapter I explore two images to illuminate some spiritual dimensions of gender transition. By gender transition I mean the rite of passage by which a transgender person exchanges one mode of gendered living for another. Terms like 'female-to-male', 'male-to-female', or the notion of exchanging either a male or female presentation for a transgender or gender neutral one, are not simply crude, imprecise, and incapable of capturing the lived reality of that experience. They are also misleading. For example, transgender people often protest that they have never had a sense of belonging to their assigned gender, and that the 'journey', such as it was, hardly constituted a watershed. Indeed, they are more likely to view transition as the means to confirm and facilitate the recognition of their gender identity, which is an enduring aspect of their self-understanding, and not something that has been altered or amended by the process of transition.

Nevertheless, some changes will have occurred. For example, changing one's name to match one's own internal sense of gender identity, which might seem a minimal step, can feel momentous to some people. (At the Conference in Hong Kong it was explained that name change is not especially significant for local transgender people as Chinese first names tend to be gender neutral.) Transition may also involve what others may assume to be 'cross-gendered' dressing and behaviours, and so-called cosmetic procedures, such as electrolysis, or more extensive interventions, like hormone therapy and surgery. In some transgender people's narratives, these and other features of gender transition are often presented as life-changing – and frequently as life-saving.

They can also be portrayed as spiritually significant, especially in contrast to the earlier stages of the narrative, where the person is often oppressed by a negative spirituality associated with a sense of unease, or potential conflict with their environment, lack of self-awareness, denial, low self-esteem, or with feelings of entrapment. At some stage, though, spirituality can begin to assume a positive character with the emergence of an overwhelming need to challenge and overcome these limitations, however great a struggle that might entail, in order to be true to one's own sense of gender identity. As Chris Dowd observes, based on his research interviews into the spirituality of twelve transgender people:

> 'Several ... felt that their gender variance and their struggles to become themselves had been an important part of their spiritual journey. It had led them to places spiritually that they would not have found without the struggles they had experienced and the questions that they had to answer.'[1]

From the many metaphors that could be employed to illuminate the spiritual dimensions of gender transition, I have chosen two: metamorphosis and migration. Metamorphosis, because the term appears to succinctly encapsulate the external process of gender transition (though note my qualification of this above and in the following paragraph), and has both ancient and modern resonances; migration, because it is an established conceptual tool and metaphor for the transition journey, but not especially its spirituality, and I hope to rectify that here.

The disadvantage of drawing on these two dynamic metaphors is that they could suggest that transgender people actually 'change' gender identity when they transition, rather than finding affirmation and confirmation of their true

[1] C. Dowd, 'Transfaith: an investigation of Gender in the Church from the margins', University of Birmingham doctoral dissertation.

selves. The interpretation of metamorphosis in section 3.1, on (trans)migration, as a change of form rather than of essence, offers a helpful analogy in that transition could be said to constitute the formal change of gender role or presentation, while the person's gender identity remains essentially unchanged. Similarly, to describe gender transition as a migration could appear to prioritise these external shifts in presentation or role rather than the person's unwavering sense of gender identity which is more fundamental. Other critiques of the migration model are noted at section 3.2 alongside further examples of its rich imaginative possibilities, and the range of alternative narratives and images that have emerged in response to the increasing diversity of transgender people's lives. It is also important to state that 'metamorphosis' and 'migration' are deployed here metaphorically and are not to be taken literally. They are intended to function as images to illuminate the spiritual dimensions of gender transition and once they begin to obscure that they have lost their usefulness.

Although relatively abstract as concepts, my focus is the personal, and both metaphors relate to the person I have chosen for the concluding case study: the UK immigration lawyer, the late David Burgess, known latterly as Sonia. It seems especially fitting, in a volume devoted to the legal status of transsexual and transgender people, to take as my illustration a respected member of the legal profession.

1.1. SPIRITUALITY AND RELIGION

In what follows I am assuming the familiar, and occasionally contested, distinction between spirituality and religion, whereby spirituality refers to generic qualities, such as meaning, value, transcendence, connectedness, hope and purpose,[2] in contrast to the specific forms of spirituality associated with religion. Both perspectives will be explored here. Recent UK statistics indicate that while some people still prefer to define themselves as spiritual rather than religious, and 'religion' is perceived negatively, many are happy to identify with a specific religious tradition, but commitment to religious institutions is declining.[3]

Traditionally, spirituality has been understood as the personal appropriation of a religious tradition, and increasingly, in the modern era, human subjectivity has become the crucible in which religious teaching is refined, transformed and redefined by the exigencies of lived experience.[4] The latter development is helpful to

---

2 J. Swinton, *Spirituality and Mental Health Care: Rediscovering a 'Forgotten' Dimension*, Jessica Kingsley, London 2001/2006, pp. 36–38.

3 L. Woodhead, 'British faith today: open to the spirit, closed to religion', *The Conversation*, 27.11.2013 <http://theconversation.com/british-faith-today-open-to-the-spirit-closed-to-religion-20864> accessed 16.12.2013.

4 D. Cupitt, *The Sea of Faith*, British Broadcasting Corporation, London 1984, p. 153: 'Kierkegaard demythologised Christianity into spirituality, and did so quite naturally, without any special effort'.

transsexual and transgender people, who have often been condemned by religious traditions, including Christian churches,[5] and denied the opportunity to articulate their spirituality. Helen Savage's research among transgender and transsexual Christians, for example, demonstrated 'the vitality of [their] engagement with the Christian tradition' despite the Church's indifference to this kind of practical theology, and she recommended that the Church should 'listen before it dares to speak.'[6] The growing literature on transgender people's spirituality thus becomes a means of informing and expanding religious traditions.[7] Church of England priest-poet Rachel Mann underwent a Christian conversion post-transition, but her perception of God (discussed below) is shaped by her gender journey, as well as other experiences.[8]

For many transsexual and transgender people the Christian Church is regarded as a major obstacle to achieving legal status and human flourishing. Yet as Duncan Dormor's chapter acknowledges, there are several Christian perspectives on this matter, some of which are affirming. For example, the Church of England House of Bishops' study document, *Some issues in human sexuality*, presented two contrasting theological positions on transsexual people – one denying the reality of their experience, the other recognising its validity and the acceptability of gender transition from a Christian perspective – but refrained from deciding between them.[9] Later, the House decided that both positions 'could properly be held', but this is not well known,[10] and, as I have noted elsewhere,[11] there remains a sense of theological impasse.

Spirituality is one way of moving on the discussion, and hence my decision, which some may find puzzling in a chapter intended to express a 'Christian view', to start with a classical concept like metamorphosis. It is however a New Testament word as well, notably at Matthew 17:2 and Mark 9:3. The usual English translation is that Christ was 'transfigured', but the Greek Orthodox Church still speaks of Christ's 'metamorphosis' as well as the more familiar 'transfiguration'. I will look later at a more obviously biblical image, the concept of migration, but begin with the myth of metamorphosis to counteract the almost exclusive emphasis on the

---

5 e.g. Evangelical Alliance Policy Commission, *Transssexuality*, Paternoster Press, London 2000.

6 H. Savage, 'Changing Sex? Transsexuality and Christian Theology', University of Durham PhD dissertation 2005, p. 254 <http://etheses.dur.ac.uk/3364/1/185.PDF?DDD32+> accessed 25.11.2013.

7 L. McCall Tigert and M.C. Tirabassi, *Transgendering Faith: Identity, Sexuality & Spirituality*, Pilgrim Press, Cleveland, Ohio 2004.

8 R. Mann, *Dazzling Darkness: Gender, sexuality, illness and God*, Wild Goose, Glasgow 2012.

9 House of Bishops, *Some issues in human sexuality: A guide to the debate. A discussion document from the House of Bishops' Group on 'Issues in Human Sexuality'*, Church House Publishing, London 2003, pp. 247–249, 285–288.

10 C. Beardsley, 'Nudging Towards Serendipity: The Church of England and Transsexual People' (July–September 2013) *Crucible: The Christian Journal of Social Ethics* 18.

11 C. Beardsley, 'Love is a many gendered thing: gender roles, relationships and trans people' (2014) 55(2) *Modern Believing* 165.

Bible in contemporary Christian reflection on transsexualism – as on many other issues. Even the authors of *Some issues* concede 'there is general acceptance that there are no biblical texts that can be seen as addressing transsexualism as such.'[12] This makes the Bible a risky starting point, though attention is frequently given to analogous strands in the biblical sources, including genital mutilation and the priesthood, the Joseph narrative, biblical perspectives on eunuchs, the relevance, or otherwise, of Genesis 1:26–27 and, though to a lesser extent, Deuteronomy 22:5.[13] Each analogy has its limitations, and hence my decision to begin with the striking metaphor of metamorphosis, especially as the original classical text includes examples of gender transformation, which makes it directly pertinent to this topic.

1.2. CHRISTIANITY AND CLASSICAL CULTURE

No apology is needed, however, as much of Western Christian theology and culture has developed through the symbiosis of biblical revelation with classical philosophy and art. As recently as the nineteenth century in England, theological study was preceded by a thorough grounding in Greek and Latin languages and their literature. Pagan art and imagination, particularly its androgyny, were incorporated into Christian culture, and inhabit the unconscious and consciousness of the West.[14]

It is the attempt to isolate a biblical perspective from this rich amalgam of thought and art, with its suspicion of the imaginative world depicted in classical mythology, that renders gender transition 'a problem' for theology. One result of this attempted unpicking of the West's skilful weaving of intellectual and spiritual strands from both the 'goddess' cultures of the ancient world, and the more 'masculine' theology of the Bible, is the expectation that one must choose between them – thus replicating the gender binary – rather than interacting with both traditions. The mythological concept of metamorphosis, with its potential for dialogue, both with Christian concepts like transformation, transfiguration and resurrection, as well as an evolutionary understanding of life, provides a creative starting point for reflecting on the spiritual dimensions of gender transition.

---

12 House of Bishops, above n. 9, p. 228.

13 V.R. Mollenkott, *Omnigender: a trans-religious approach*, Pilgrim Press, Cleveland, Ohio 2001, pp. 95–97, 100–101, 108; House of Bishops, above n. 9, pp. 228–229; L. Reay, 'Towards a Transgender Theology: Que(e)rying the Eunuchs' in M. Althaus-Reid and L. Isherwood (eds.), *Trans/formations*, SCM Press, London 2009, pp. 148–167.

14 C. Paglia, *Sexual Personae: Art and Decadence from Nefertiti to Emily Dickinson*, Penguin, London 1991.

II. METAMORPHOSIS

2.1. OVID, *METAMORPHOSES*

Ovid's great Latin poem, *Metamorphoses*,[15] was completed in AD 7. Its Greek title means 'change of form', and its opening line states the poet's intent: 'My mind is bent to tell of bodies changed into new forms.'[16] A panegyric to the myriad examples of startling transformations contained in ancient mythology, beginning with the creation itself, Ovid's depiction of a universe in motion might seem more consistent with an evolutionary perspective on life than the biblical world view. The Bible, though, has its own share of almost magical transformations. For example, Lot's wife is turned into a pillar of salt,[17] and Aaron's rod transformed into a serpent;[18] Jesus turns water into wine,[19] and raises the dead to life,[20] while his own body is first transfigured[21] and then resurrected.[22] Jesus' parables too, in which tiny seeds develop into large trees or bumper harvests, [23] imply an organic, evolving perception of life and the spiritual world. Nor is gender fluidity limited to Ovid's poem: queer and transgender theologians argue that gender is strikingly destabilised in the New Testament.[24]

Ovid's text contrasts with the Christian scriptures because of the numerous changes of human beings into birds, animals, plants or inanimate objects. For instance, Lycaon is turned 'into a wolf, and yet retains some traces of his former shape',[25] Phaëthon's sisters become trees at his grave,[26] and Diana's nymph is turned into a bear.[27] Most, if not all, of these transformations are imposed on unwilling subjects, usually as punishment for moral failure, or breaking a taboo; like Narcissus who is punished for his rejection of Echo by being turned into a flower,[28] or Actaeon, changed into a stag by the goddess Diana for having glimpsed her bathing, and then hunted and devoured by his own hounds.[29] Indeed, the spiritual plight of Ovid's characters post-transformation tends to resemble that of transgender people *prior* to transition.

---

15 Ovid, *Metamorphoses*, trans. F.J. Miller, revised by G.P. Goold, 3rd ed. Books 1–8, 2nd ed. Books 9–15, Harvard University Press, Cambridge, Mass. 1977, 1984.

16 Ovid, Book I, line 1.

17 Genesis 19:26.

18 Exodus 7:10.

19 John 2:1–11.

20 Matthew 9:18–26; John 11:38–44.

21 Mark 9:2–8.

22 Luke 24:36–43.

23 Mark 4:26–32.

24 Mollenkott, above n. 13, pp. 105–107, 110–114; Reay, above n. 13, pp. 154–159.

25 Ovid, Book I, line 237.

26 Ovid, Book II, lines 346–355.

27 Ovid, Book II, lines 476–484.

28 Ovid, Book III, lines 344–510.

29 Ovid, Book III, lines 173–252.

One pre-transition experience on which the poem sheds unexpected light is the vexed notion of being 'trapped in the wrong body'. Although subjected to philosophical and theological critique in relation to transsexualism,[30] as a literary trope it has a long tradition. The early Latin novel *The Transformations of Lucius, or The Golden Ass,*[31] which owes much to Ovid's poem, and in turn influenced Shakespeare's *A Midsummer Night's Dream*, depicts the misery of a man trapped in the body of a donkey. A parallel example from *Metamorphoses* is Jove's transformation of Io into a white heifer to conceal his sexual indiscretion with her. Io's anguish, particularly her 'terror at her own voice' – her complaints emerge as a moo[32] – is reminiscent of a transgender person's anxiety at the incongruence between their voice and their gender identity.

Whatever its philosophical difficulties, the discomfort – dysphoria – of inhabiting a gendered body to which one has problems relating is a genuine form of spiritual distress. When Io's father discovers her plight, his pain that she will not bear him grandchildren[33] resembles a similar concern that can arise for the parents of childless transsexual people. Io's story has a happy ending, as her human body is restored, and her satisfaction and relief resemble transgender people's accounts of transition as the emerging of their 'true' or congruent physical identity: 'No trace of the heifer is left in her save only the fair whiteness of her body.' [34]

Camille Paglia calls *Metamorphoses* 'a handbook of sexual problematics', citing 'Iphis, a girl raised as a boy who falls in love with another girl and is relieved of her suffering by being changed into a man.'[35] The notion of gender transition as a heterosexual resolution of same-sex attraction would be strongly resisted by transsexual people who see their issue as one of gender rather than sexual orientation, but relationships complicate matters. With only slight modification, Ovid's tale of Iphis,[36] which hinges on male privilege, is a classic transgender man's narrative: a tomboy, who develops into a woman who loves women, and eventually transitions. It also highlights spiritual anxieties about deceit, including the defrauding of sexual partners: an accusation unfairly levelled recently at two transgender men,[37] and that misunderstands their quest for personal truth.

In the Iphis narrative transition is an outcome of prayer. Transsexual people's stories often include the detail that they have prayed nightly for their gender to

---

30 O. O'Donovan, *Transsexualism and Christian Marriage*, Grove Books, Nottingham 1982, reissued as *Transsexualism: Issues and Argument*, Grove Books, Cambridge 2007, pp. 12–20.

31 L. Apuleius, *The Transformations of Lucius, otherwise known as The Golden Ass*, trans. R. Graves, Penguin, Harmondsworth 1950.

32 Ovid, Book I, lines 637–639.

33 Ovid, Book I, lines 658–660.

34 Ovid, Book I, line 743.

35 Paglia, above n. 14, p. 132.

36 Ovid, Book IX, lines 666–797.

37 <www.queerty.com/scottish-man-found-guilty-of-fraud-for-not-telling-girlfriends-he-was-trans-20130307/> accessed 27.12.2013; <www.pinknews.co.uk/2013/03/22/uk-woman-jailed-for-obtaining-sexual-consent-of-another-woman-by-fraud/> accessed 27.12.2013.

be changed.[38] Iphis masculinises fully in direct response to her mother's prayer; modern transsexual people discover that they too are responsible for helping to make their prayers become a reality.[39]

An involuntary sex change in Ovid's poem – probably the most famous in ancient literature – happens to Tiresias, who goes from male to female and back again. It is sexual taboo – the sight of copulating snakes – that causes Tiresias's male-to-female transition, and again, seven years later, the transition from female-to-male.[40] Later, he is blinded by the goddess Juno for revealing that female sexual pleasure exceeds that of the male, but the god Jove shows pity, and transforms him into a wounded healer by granting him 'the power to know the future, lightening the penalty by the honour.'[41]

Like Tiresias, many transsexual people have lived first in one gender role and then, after transition, in another; while some transgender people oscillate – to use Ekins and King's term[42] – between the two. Typically, neither group will have identified with the gender they were assigned to at birth, but the experience of living in both genders, albeit one that was difficult to relate to, may bring unexpected insights. One transgender man, who had shared an ultra-feminist hostility to men when living as a woman, discovered a deep compassion towards men once he began to transition as a male.[43] This was a spiritual awakening. Likewise the wisdom of Tiresias (though formally conferred afterwards), is associated with his gender transitions: 'He knew both sides of love.'[44]

Tiresias was returned to his birth gender after living as a female, and although the numbers are small, some people do reverse their transition. This can sometimes follow a religious conversion, especially in conservative Christian circles[45] where gender transition is discouraged or considered impossible. In these religious cases, spirituality, in the form of prayer, counselling and Christian companionship, is deployed to re-adjust the person's sense of gender identity so that it aligns with that of their phenotype. While this may work for some people it can also be highly manipulative and harmful. For example, one member of the Sibyls, the UK Christian spirituality support group for transgender people,[46] underwent a series of metamorphoses reminiscent of Ovid's poem. First they

---

38 J. Morris, *Conundrum*, Penguin, London 1997, p. 25.

39 McCall Tigert and Tirabassi, above n. 7, p. 45.

40 Ovid, Book III, lines 316–331.

41 Ovid, Book III, lines 332–338.

42 R. Ekins and D. King, *The Transgender Phenomenon*, Sage Publications, London 2006, pp. 97–108.

43 G. Israel and D.E. Tarver, *Transgender Care: Recommended Guidelines, Practical Information and Personal Accounts*, Temple University Press, Philadelphia 1997.

44 Ovid, Book III, line 323.

45 Mann, above n. 8, p. 49.

46 See C. Beardsley, M. O'Brien and J. Woolley, 'Exploring the Interplay: The Sibyls' "Gender, Sexuality and Spirituality" Workshop' (2010) 16(3) *Theology and Sexuality* 260–262 for a brief history of the Sibyls and its founding principles. See also <www.sibyls.co.uk/> accessed 21.12.2013.

transitioned from male-to-female; then under pressure to conform to conservative Christianity, back to male; and finally, after prayerfully attending to their own heart, back to female again.[47] The taboo around gender transition in certain Christian circles is often justified by a peculiarly modern reading of Genesis 1:26,27: 'Let us make man in our own image ... So God created man in his own image; in the image of God he created him, male and female he created them.' A rigidly polarised, complementary idea of men and women, which emerged at the Enlightenment, becomes the lens on an ancient text, reducing gender to either/or rather than both/and,[48] even though the verses suggest that God is both male and female.

In Ovid's poem, gods like Mercury and Bacchus (Dionysus) are androgynous and frequently change form.[49] Gender transition, or oscillation, often suspected as signs of instability, or of leading inevitably to decline and destruction, finds divine approval in the shape-shifting of these gods. Bacchus's first appearance in the poem, as 'a little boy, with form as beautiful as a girl's'[50] confirms 'his role as a shape-shifter', and illustrates the deity's own gender transition as matrilineal social patterns were replaced by patriarchal ones. Feinberg's suggestion that Bacchus, marginal in his own myth, is god of the weak and oppressed, especially women and opponents of established order,[51] is one that would resonate with the many transgender people who experience social exclusion. They are characteristics too of Jesus in the gospel narratives.

Gender nonconformity can indeed be dangerous, and there is an alarmingly higher than average suicide risk among transsexual people, particularly prior to transition. Yet for all the spiritual hazards of Ovid's tragic tales, his poem's celebration of the malleability of human nature has inspired playfulness and experiment around gender, not least in its influence on Shakespeare's plays. It also reframes gender variance as godly, and potentially as a divine gift, rather than divine punishment, a perspective that contemporary transgender people are increasingly keen to embrace.[52]

2.2. FRANZ KAFKA'S *METAMORPHOSIS*

Kafka's novella, *Metamorphosis*, the most famous modern literary exposition of the concept, also depicts an involuntary transformation into another form, that

---

47 D. Batty, 'Mistaken Identity', *Guardian: Society*, 31.07.2004 <www.theguardian.com/society/2004/jul/31/health.socialcare> accessed 28.11.2013.

48 Beardsley, above n. 11, p. 169.

49 Ovid, Book II, lines 697–698, 846–851.

50 Ovid, Book III, line 607.

51 L. Feinberg, *Transgender Warriors: Making History from Joan of Arc to Rupaul*, Beacon Press, Boston 1996, p. 57.

52 V.R. Mollenkott, 'We Come Bearing Gifts: Seven Lessons Religious Congregations Can Learn From Transpeople' in Althaus-Reid and Isherwood, above n. 13, pp. 46–58.

of Gregor Samsa who becomes 'a monstrous insect'. Recent interpretations have suggested that Gregor's metamorphosis is a feminisation of sorts.[53] No longer 'the bread winner',[54] and removed from public view – characteristics associated with older, conventional ideas of gender – even his voice assumes a higher register: 'with a persistent horrible twittering squeak behind it like an undertone'.[55] The pleasure Gregor feels in his 'new' body [56] has also been noted. In Arthur Pita's dance-theatre adaptation,[57] the contortions of the semi-naked dancer Edward Watson, whose white body is gradually covered in dark oil, conveys this sensual, animal enjoyment of Gregor's metamorphosis. There is a parallel here to transgender people's experience: gender transition usually requires a shift of attention to bodily needs and feelings, and being 'at home in one's own skin'[58] is a familiar post-transition catchphrase.

Gregor's transition, from salesman and provider to insect, is Kafka's satire on the dehumanising effects of modern mass employment. Gregor morphs into an insect, like a giant ant or worker bee, because he is already depersonalised, and rendered 'other', just as transgender persons can be. Even in faith community settings, where one would expect personhood to be fore-grounded, the insect metaphor can arise spontaneously. As Jay Walmsley, the founder of the Sibyls, observed[59] disappointedly, in 2004, after meeting with a Church of England bishop: 'He views transsexual people with all the detachment and curiosity of an entomologist.' In other words, they were seen as interesting theological/ethical specimens rather than as human persons.

Almost more disturbing than Gregor's transformation is his rejection by his family. This is partly because they are shocked and ashamed at his transformation. His initial eagerness 'to find out what the others ... would say at the sight of him'[60] resembles the transgender person's desire for affirmation from significant others. In Gregor's case, although he has the sympathy of his mother and sister, they cannot bear to look at him, and he hides under the sofa when they enter his room, taking on their sense of shame at his altered appearance. A similar exchange can operate for transgender people, but sometimes it can work in their favour, as therapist Anne Boedecker notes: 'Those who accompany the transgender person on his or her journey share the pain, the fear, the hurt, the social ostracism, and the high emotional cost of leading a closeted or marginalized life.'[61]

---

53 D. Glover and C. Kaplan, *Genders*, 2nd ed., Routledge, Abingdon 2009, p. 111.

54 F. Kafka, *Metamorphosis and Other Stories*, trans. W. and E. Muir, Penguin Books, Harmondsworth 1963, pp. 27, 32–34.

55 Kafka, above n. 54, p. 11.

56 Kafka, above n. 54, pp. 36–38.

57 L. Marsh, 'Dancing Kafka', *The New York Review of Books*, 21.09.2013 <www.nybooks.com/blogs/gallery/2013/sep/21/metamorphosis-dancing-kafka/> accessed 28.11.2013.

58 McCall Tigert and Tirabassi, above n. 7, p. 45.

59 Conversation with the author.

60 Kafka, above n. 54, p. 18.

61 McCall Tigert and Tirabassi, above n. 7, p. 17.

In the novel, Gregor's room is literally and metaphorically the closet to which he is confined by his family's fearful, sometimes angry, responses. On the one occasion he 'comes out' of his room, he is said to have 'broken loose'.[62] Transgender people too delay or curtail their coming out, or their transition, to 'spare' their family's feelings, or because they are uncertain and anxious at how they might react, and this can lead to spiritual anguish and turmoil. At one point Gregor's mother expresses a hopeful response: 'that Gregor was a member of the family, despite his present unfortunate and repulsive shape, and ... family duty required the suppression of disgust and the exercise of patience, nothing but patience.'[63] A person-centred approach, supported by loyal family relationships, and the withholding of judgement, is also helpful to transgender people. Sadly, it fails to prevail in Kafka's text, where it is overwhelmed by societal responses. First the cook resigns, and later the three lodgers, who were taken on to supplement the family's income when Gregor was unable to work and support them financially.

The loss of family, or job, are still risks when someone transitions, and can occasion the most serious soul searching, as well as gouging the deepest emotional wounds. Dzintra Alksnitis writes, 'My experiences with my family have been the most painful of all.'[64] In response, some transgender people adopt the role of victim, while others discover that they are 'transgender warriors',[65] as courageous as any of Ovid's heroes and heroines.

Like Gregor's transformation, gender transition can feel chaotic, compared to the routine and order of the transgender person's former life, but with its own momentum, often experienced as irresistible, and inevitable. Gregor's bourgeois family resists, afraid of the animal, the primitive, the unconscious. Yet from these arise the powerful energies that precipitate, motivate and animate gender transition, which is why artistic accounts of metamorphosis, ancient and modern, are helpful pointers to its spiritual dimensions.

III. MIGRATION

3.1. (TRANS) MIGRATION

In the final book of *Metamorphoses* Ovid places a speech in the mouth of Greek polymath Pythagoras summarising the poem's thesis concerning the dynamic, evolving nature of life. Famed for his contribution to geometry, Pythagoras was also a leading exponent of the transmigration of souls (metempsychosis), or reincarnation, a doctrine he expounds in this speech, which advocates vegetarianism on the ground that former human souls inhabit the bodies of

62 Kafka, above n. 54, p. 42.
63 Kafka, above n. 54, pp. 44–45.
64 McCall Tigert and Tirabassi, above n. 7, p. 37; see also pp. 35–37, 69.
65 Feinberg, above n. 51.

animals, birds and fish. Although common to many religions and philosophies, reincarnation is not a Christian doctrine and is not investigated further here, except to note the striking image Pythagoras adopts in the speech:

> 'And, as the pliant wax is stamped with new designs, does not remain as it was before nor preserve the same form, but is still the selfsame wax, so do I teach that the soul is ever the same, though it passes into ever-changing bodies.'[66]

This theme underlies Ovid's poem. Applying it specifically to the spiritual dimensions of gender transition, one could argue that any physical changes that occur are a matter of form rather than essence, and therefore, that the person remains essentially the same, despite their gender journey. However, while the transgender person may be conscious that their gender identity and personality remain unaltered by transition, families and spouses may struggle with that, especially if there is a dramatic contrast with the person's previous gender presentation or gender role. For example, Ella Matheson found that she needed to ritualise her grief for the husband she felt she had 'lost,'[67] while Dzintra Alksnitis discovered that her church fellowship needed time to adjust to her transition: 'Slowly people learned that I was still pretty much the same person who had been worshipping in their midst since 1980.'[68]

Notwithstanding these continuities, for some transgender people transition denotes a radical new beginning and the language of rebirth is occasionally used to express this in relation to gender confirmation surgery. For instance, I once heard someone describe their experience of 'going under the knife' as a rite of passage by which they felt reborn on the 'sacrificial altar' of the operating table. Such hyperbolic language conveys how momentous and ongoing spiritual changes can find their symbolic 'moment' in gender confirmation surgery.

Christian metaphors of rebirth, which are rooted in the dialogue between Jesus and Nicodemus in St John's gospel about the necessity of being born again,[69] hold in tension the physical and the spiritual, the climactic and the progressive. The rite of baptism and conversion experiences are manifestations of an inner transformation that some may wish to assign to a particular moment in time, while others prefer to stress its unfolding over a lifetime. For some transgender people, surgery can be the dramatic turning point when they are 'reborn' in their true gender, but for others this 'rebirth' occurs over months, or even years, with various peaks and troughs, and encompasses a range of experiences – physical, emotional, psychological and spiritual – which are often described as a journey.

However, the main point of my punning reference to (trans)migration here is to emphasise that the metaphor of migration, which will be considered next,

---

66 Ovid, Book XV, lines 169–172.
67 McCall Tigert and Tirabassi, above n. 7, pp. 71–76.
68 McCall Tigert and Tirabassi, above n. 7, p. 34.
69 John 3:1–21.

concerns human souls in transit, as much as human bodies in motion. Many transgender people prefer to describe their transition in spiritual terms, in contrast to the medical and legal frameworks which they are often expected to adopt,[70] and some reference the shamanistic role of so-called 'transcestors'.[71] The notion of the soul's transmigration also provides a link from the mythic realm of metamorphosis to the apparently pedestrian one of migration.

3.2. A MIXED METAPHOR?

If metamorphosis is a minor theme in the Bible, migration is a major one, classically expressed in the exodus of the children of Israel and their settlement in the Promised Land. It is also the most controversial, touching on the presence of displacement, ethnic cleansing and cultural assimilation in the Old Testament narratives, albeit that the 'conquest' described in the Books of Joshua and Judges is a later theological construct with little historical foundation. By contrast, the exodus tradition is the paradigm for Jesus' own journey in the Gospels, whereby God's people are set free, and which in turn, and especially in recent times, has inspired a whole series of theologies of liberation which has brought hope to those who live on the margins of Church and society.[72] Later books and redactions of the Old Testament narrate the Jewish people's experience of exile and return to their homeland, and the Jewish dispersion is both a significant background to the New Testament and a factor in the spread of Christianity in the ancient world.

Migration is currently a contentious matter. Modern means of transportation, the end of colonialism and the rise of globalisation have led to the increasing movement of people across national boundaries. This has brought immense benefits, but has also 'rendered problematic clear notions of citizenship, national identity and belonging'[73] Currently, for example, the unrestricted movement of people within the European Union is being questioned by the British government, and there are calls for the stronger policing of national borders and the repatriation of illegal immigrants, as well as mounting concern about the scale of human trafficking and the rise of modern forms of slavery.

Theologically and culturally then migration offers rich potential both as a metaphor and a sociological framework for gender transition and the analogy has

---

70 T. Day, 'Spiritual Care as a Part of the Transgender Continuum of Care', *Transfaith*, 2013 <www.transfaithonline.org/display/article/spiritual-care-as-a-part-of-the-transgender-continuum-of-care/?no_cache=1&tx_ttnews%5BbackPid%5D=1368> accessed 16.12.2013.

71 Reay, above n. 13, p. 149.

72 T. Bohache, *Christology from the Margins*, SCM Press, London 2008, reviews Black African and Asian, Latin American Liberation, Feminist and Women of Colour Christologies prior to outlining a Queer Christology.

73 Ekins and King, above n. 42, p. 43: summarising Castles and Davidson.

been well explored.[74] Sociologists Richard Ekins and Dave King suggest that we are living in an age of gender, as well as general, migration, given that 'unknown numbers of people have left their assigned genders behind and migrated "over the border", raising interesting questions about what it means to be a man or a woman.'[75] Others go further, arguing that, just as world travel and the inhabiting of border territories symbolises the inadequacy of national, cultural, and ethnic categories, so transgender people's experiences symbolise the limitations of our sex/gender system.[76]

In fact, 'migrating' is just one of four categories of transgender stories identified by Ekins and King. For them it implies a 'single', or one-way, journey, in contrast to the other three categories – 'oscillating', 'negating' and 'transcending' – which open up the possibility of temporary border crossings, attempts to eliminate the boundary, or to move beyond it altogether.[77] These alternatives relate to the critique of the migrating metaphor, which will be considered shortly, but it requires further elaboration. Here is an exposition by Dave King:

> 'Both gender and geographical migrants often see themselves as beginning a new life; social membership and identity has to be reworked and negotiated; a new way of life has to be learnt; the old one has to be left behind. Migrants of both kinds are often regarded as undesirable and threatening; the legitimacy of settlement in the new country/gender may be denied; the granting of citizenship and other rights may be refused. The consequence may be that the migrant permanently occupies a position of marginality rather than full integration.'[78]

The analogy between geographical and gender migration arises from the idea of borders: the physical and political boundaries that define nation states, and the boundary between male and female, man and woman, that pertains under the binary system of gender in contemporary Western culture. Increasingly elusive even in the West, the gender boundary is configured differently elsewhere, as it has been in the past. Thomas Laqueur, for example, has distinguished the pre-modern one-sex/flesh model of humanity, with its insight into the similarity of male and female bodies, from the two-sex/flesh model that has dominated since the eighteenth century, and which conceives men and women as polar opposites.[79]

The sharply defined boundaries, whether geographical or gendered, encountered by modern migrants, presumably contribute to the negative

[74] R. Alsop, A. Fitzsimons and K. Lennon, *Theorizing Gender*, Polity Press, Cambridge 2002; Ekins and King above n. 42; T.T. Cotten (ed.), *Transgender Migration: The Bodies, Borders, and Politics of Transition*, Routledge, Oxford 2012.

[75] Ekins and King, above n. 42, p. 43.

[76] Alsop, Fitzsimons and Lennon, above n. 74, p. 213.

[77] Ekins and King, above n. 42, p. 34.

[78] D. King, 'Gender Migration: A Sociological Analysis (or The Leaving of Liverpool)' (2003) 6(2) *Sexualities* 173.

[79] Glover and Kaplan, above n. 53, p. 35.

possibilities King outlines. Yet as Alsop, Fitzsimons and Lennon point out, in their aptly titled chapter, 'Borderlands and gendered homes', the dichotomy between 'home' and 'borderland' has been resisted in post-colonial studies, and is destabilised when people choose to inhabit the borderlands, as is apparent since the advent of queer theory, the rise of the 'gender outlaw', and the emergence of a diverse range of gendered identities.[80] These developments are increasingly the subject matter of spiritual reflection, and suit the liminal character of spirituality with its locus on the boundaries between the self and (an)other, the mundane and the numinous or transcendent, and ultimately between life and death.

For example, Susannah Cornwall's striking parallel between the 'unknowingness' of transgender and the apophatic or negative theology of the Christian mystical tradition[81] neatly avoids notions of gendered identity or 'homes', and highlights a neglected spiritual tradition with potential resonance for transgender people. Though they did not use the actual term, many of Chris Dowd's interviewees reached what he regards as an apophatic view of God, 'a God ... too large to be constricted into a single image', and which they attributed to 'their growing understanding of their own identities.'[82] It is evident too in Rachel Mann's fondness for Henry Vaughan's image of God as 'dazzling darkness', though, like Dowd's respondents, she also embraces a positive, affirming theology, which in her case means that aspects of her own identity – 'trans, lesbian, disabled, chronically ill person' – are true, metaphorically, of God.[83]

An important dimension that religious and spiritual traditions can add to the meaning of migration is the sense of a divine call or prompting. It is evident in that paradigmatic biblical migration when God asks Abraham, then in old age, to leave his home, and journey with Sarah his wife, and his kindred, to a land where God will bless him and make him a blessing to others.[84] Interpretation of people's decision to transition, or to live as a transgender person, often overlooks this dimension of call, focusing instead on the ethical implications of these choices rather than their origin. Contrastingly, in the Sibyls' sponsored workshop, 'Gender, sexuality and spirituality', some people noted that 'being trans can involve serving God in specific ways and may be a unique or particular calling'.[85]

Virginia Ramey Mollenkott's essay, 'We Come Bearing Gifts: Seven Lessons Religious Congregations Can Learn from Transpeople',[86] explores that calling, especially in relation to diversity, gender and justice within spiritual traditions. Just as geographical migration can be a source of cultural enrichment and energy, rather than a problem, so transgender people can contribute to the transformation

---

80 Alsop, Fitzsimons and Lennon, above n. 74, pp. 204, 210, 211, 213.

81 S. Cornwall, 'Apophasis and Ambiguity: The "Unknowingness" of Transgender' in Althaus-Reid and Isherwood, above n. 13, pp. 13–40.

82 Dowd, above n. 1.

83 Mann, above n. 8, pp. 82, 84.

84 Genesis 12:1–3.

85 Beardsley, O'Brien and Woolley, above n. 46, p. 278.

86 Mollenkott, above n. 52.

of religious communities – as long as their gifts are welcomed rather than feared or rejected.

Abraham's call, like the call of Moses at the exodus, was not simply to an individual, but to a whole community, and this corporate vision was emphasised in twentieth century Roman Catholicism influenced by the documents of the Second Vatican Council, which envisaged the Church as 'the pilgrim people of God'. Many transgender people have lonely journeys, but numerous support networks exist so that no one need walk alone. For some people their religious community will be a source of affirmation and encouragement, and it is increasingly common for transgender people to request a rite of passage to mark what they see as a significant stage on their pilgrimage.

Just as becoming a citizen of another state can involve a ceremony, however simple, so too a change of gendered name or gender status can be celebrated with a ritual. Name changes often occur in the Bible to indicate or precipitate growth, or changing circumstances: Sarai becomes Sarah; Jacob becomes Israel; Naomi becomes Mara; Simon becomes Peter; Saul becomes Paul. All are people on a journey, literally and metaphorically; Sarah, Jacob and Naomi were migrant people. Although the context is different, these biblical examples can illuminate the spiritual significance of coming out as transgender, or key stages of gender transition, and Christian worship resources are available for their public or private celebration.[87]

3.3. COLONISATION AND THE PURSUIT OF JUSTICE

The most contentious term associated with migration is 'colonisation' with its attendant notions of infiltration, invasion, subjugation, and even obliteration. The Biblical material is illustrative of this. What starts in the Book of Exodus with the freeing of slaves from oppression – and has inspired rich traditions of liberation theology during the twentieth century and beyond – seems to degenerate into the worst excesses of ethnic cleansing in the Books of Joshua and Judges. Despite appearances, the latter are not historical narratives, and describe a momentum observed in other revolutions which have begun with the cry of liberty and ended in tyranny.

The accusation of colonisation was levelled at transgender women in particular in Janice Raymond's *The Transsexual Empire: The Making of the She-Male*, published in 1979, which 'represents male to female transsexuals as agents of a medical empire sent out to colonise women's community'.[88] Raymond's thesis has been extensively critiqued,[89] not least because it does not account for

87 McCall Tigert and Tirabassi, above n. 7, pp. 116, 118, 136–143.

88 Alsop, Fitzsimons and Lennon, above n. 74, pp. 202–203.

89 P. Califia, *Sex Changes: The Politics of Transgenderism*, Cleis Press, San Francisco 1997, pp. 92–108.

transgender men, but it still survives as a slur in some feminist circles, and even today transgender women can be excluded from certain women-only spaces.

Exclusion of this kind is increasingly challenged by faith groups on the basis of the intersecting nature of oppression. In January 2012, for example, the Cutting Edge Consortium, a UK collaborative of faith and secular organisations, formed to combat homophobia and transphobia, and especially its religious manifestations, held a Women's Group Public Meeting in central London entitled 'Feminism, Faith & LBGTQ Women: Is Anybody Listening?'[90] Shocked to learn that transgender women were still being turned away from some women-only events, the steering committee pointedly invited a transgender woman to join the panel, and the poster for the event emphasised that it was open to 'anyone who identifies as a woman'.

IV. METAMORPHOSIS AND MIGRATION: A CASE STUDY

4.1. MORPHING AND MIGRATION: MEETING SONIA – KNOWING DAVID

The subject of this case study, Sonia Burgess, was a friend, and it was spirituality that brought us together. We met in January 2009 at a Rainbow Space (the LGBT group) event at St Anne's Church, Soho, London, which she was attending then, and where I witnessed her ability to connect with the young people who were leading the session with me. I encouraged her to join the Sibyls[91] and had the pleasure of meeting her at the bi-monthly London meetings when Sibyls gather for prayer followed by a meal. The last time we met was at one of these occasions, and once again I saw her rapport with the young: a new member who was also disabled.

Sonia was somewhat apologetic about the fact that she still worked in male mode 'as a human rights lawyer', but was otherwise unforthcoming about her work. It was only after her death that I learned about her professional life as David Burgess 'one of the finest immigration lawyers of his generation, … responsible for a series of trailblazing judgements in the House of Lords and the European Court of Human Rights.'[92] The most notable was in 1991 when David brought contempt proceedings against the then Home Secretary for failing to stop the deportation of 'M', a Zairean asylum seeker. Upheld in the House of Lords, Sir William Wade described this victory as 'the most significant constitutional case

90 <https://sites.google.com/site/cuttingedgeconsortium1/cec-campaignsandevents/feminism_faithlbtqwomen1> accessed 30.12.2013.

91 Beardsley, O'Brien and Woolley, above n. 46.

92 E. Day, 'A life less ordinary', cover story, *The Observer: The New Review*, 09.01.2011, p. 8 <www.theguardian.com/uk/2011/jan/09/david-burgess-sonia-lawyer-death> accessed 28.12.2013.

for more than 200 years.'[93] As a result, asylum seekers in the UK are allowed to appeal against refusal of asylum prior to having to leave the country.

An expert on immigration, David was equally well acquainted with the discrimination experienced by gender 'migrants', having represented two transgender men at the European Court of Human Rights. These too were landmark cases. Mark Rees's application for the right to privacy and the right to marry was heard on 14 March 1984.[94] Rees was the first transsexual person to take legal action against the British government for refusing to update and alter the gender on people's birth certificates following transition; but the Commission did not rule in his favour. In 1992 David took on the case of legal academic, Stephen Whittle, who claimed the right to be legally recognised as the father of his first child (and subsequent children), and also began a decade as lawyer for Press for Change, the UK lobbying group for transgender people's rights.[95] Whittle, who in his obituary of Sonia, prioritises her female persona, recalls her brilliance and intuition in her legal work, and also – and highly relevant to her spirituality – 'her mission' as a lawyer, which she described as 'a job that she had just been given': 'to rescue the earth's dispossessed.'

These high profile cases were rarely, if ever, disclosed to the people who knew her only as Sonia. The European Court cases, for example, would have been especially interesting to her transgender friends, and there has been speculation about her reticence to mention these aspects of her past. An innate modesty probably played a part, but perhaps she was also conscious of starting a new life as Sonia, and more focused on present and future opportunities than on David's past achievements. Previously inclined to push at boundaries, transition may have necessitated circumspection, not least because, although she was migrating, she was also 'oscillating', retaining David as her work persona while being Sonia the rest of the time. Similarly, although she engaged in some gender blending at work – growing out her hair, wearing an earring – and colleagues were aware of her private life, few of them had met Sonia.

Sonia's story, though, is not untypical for a transgender woman. Ian Baker, a friend from university, recalls David being 'quite physical, quite macho' as a student – which sounds like standard compensating hyper-masculinity. Later, when they were both working, and David asked him to take him out for the evening dressed *en femme*, Baker found this 'very awkward and very uncomfortable because he was not at all a convincing woman at that time. But it was clearly something he needed and wanted to do.'[96] (This contrasts somewhat with Whittle's recollection

93 Day, above n. 92, p. 9.
94 Califia, above n. 89, p. 182.
95 S. Whittle, 'Sonia (David) Burgess (1947–2010): An obituary. Angelic Inspiration: Human Rights Lawyer Dies in Tragic Circumstances' 02.11.2010 & 12.2012 <http://whittlings.blogspot.co.uk/2010/11/sonia-david-burgess-1947–2010-obituary.html> accessed 30.12.2013.
96 Day, above n. 92, p. 10.

that '"David" looked like someone of neither sex'.)[97] David also explored homosexuality at one point, but eventually married (having told his Nepalese wife beforehand about his female persona/identity), and had children. David was a workaholic: a well-known coping strategy among transgender people.

Gender transition came in middle age – forty-two is the median age of transition in the UK[98] – but Sonia was not yet full-time, so there was an element of shape-shifting too. A mutual friend has described his surprise on passing in the street a man who resembled Sonia, and how he realised afterwards that it must have been David, who he was aware of, but had never actually met. As her photographs confirm, Sonia was an attractive looking woman. Baker, who visited her in 2010, felt that she had finally found 'a resolution of what had obsessed or troubled' her from the beginning, and then, using a metaphor worthy of Ovid, he adds, 'I think he was in his chrysalis stage for a long time and I think Sonia was the butterfly that emerged.'[99]

4.2. THE FINAL FRONTIER

Like the butterfly, Sonia's life would be relatively short. On the evening of Monday 25 October 2010 she intended to travel on the Piccadilly Line. Confusingly, the press reports differ. Some say that she was on the eastbound, others on the westbound platform. If it was the latter then she was probably on her way to a lecture at St Martin-in-the-Fields, the church she had migrated to. I think it is very likely that she had attended the previous talks in a series entitled 'Bible Opened for All'. On this occasion, the Reverend Lucy Winkett was due to speak about 'Being Biblical, Being a Woman'. The topic would have been of particular interest to Sonia, for obvious reasons; but she was not to hear it.

Sonia was seen arriving on the underground platform at Kings Cross Station just prior to 6.30pm, accompanied by a younger woman. They were talking animatedly. Within minutes Sonia fell to her death in the path of the arriving train. Her companion, Nina Kanagasingham, a Sri Lankan national, who at the time was undergoing gender reassignment, was arrested at the scene on a murder charge and taken to a male prison. Later, at the trial, the accused, who said he wished to be referred to as a man, and by his male name, was cleared of murder, but jailed for a minimum of seven years for manslaughter, on the grounds of diminished responsibility, having completed treatment for paranoid

97 Whittle, above n. 95.
98 Gender Identity Research & Education Society (GIRES), 'The Number of Gender Variant People in the UK – Update 2011' <www.gires.org.uk/assets/Research-Assets/Prevalence2011.pdf> accessed 21.12.2013.
99 Day, above n. 92, p. 11.

schizophrenia.[100] Immediately prior to the fatality, Sonia had accompanied Nina, whom she met in 2009, to a GP appointment, because of increasing concern for her friend's mental state.

That Sonia should die at the hands of another transgender person, and a foreign national, is hugely ironic given David's dedication to improving the legal status of transgender people and of immigrants to the UK, but Sonia's befriending of Nina was consistent with David's practical care and compassion for his clients. According to Robert Winstanley, with whom David co-founded the legal firm Winstanley-Burgess, this 'was over and above what was necessary to conduct their case. He was very pastoral with his clients. … If they needed a kindly word at 2am, they would get it from David.'[101] In 1991 David even put up a client in his own home for several weeks until he was granted asylum. As David's former colleague Chris Randall observes, 'In many ways, he was something of an outsider himself; his was a position of empathy with the client, not sympathy. He did not do "professional detachment."'[102]

It is known that Sonia had offered Nina financial help as well as support and friendship, but David's blurring of personal boundaries, although unorthodox, had proved highly effective as a professional strategy pushing the limits of UK immigration policy. It would be fatal for Sonia. This may be due to genuine gender differences: perhaps it is easier for men, or in David's case, someone operating in the male mode, to take risks of this kind than it is for women, who may be more vulnerable in similar circumstances. On the other hand, it can be equally perilous for men and women when a mental health issue is involved, as was the case here; and Sonia's position was already a precarious one.

As Elizabeth Day has noted (though I am adapting her resume to make Sonia, rather than David, the protagonist): on the day Sonia died, she 'was living as a woman and yet working as a man.' She was open about her transition to anyone who asked, but 'had separate groups of friends' – those who knew her as David, and those who knew only Sonia. Only Sonia's closest confidants were allowed to see her as both Sonia and David, and rather than mentioning David's achievements, she preferred 'to draw out the person to whom she was talking.'[103]

4.3. LIMINAL LIVING AND ITS FULLNESS

Although Sonia's life appears to embody several contradictions, for me they are all examples of the liminal quality of many transgender people's lives, which arise

100 P. Walker, 'Man who pushed solicitor under tube train jailed for life', *Guardian*, 22.12.2011 <www.theguardian.com/uk/2011/dec/22/man-pushed-solicitor-under-tube-train-jailed> accessed 16.12.2013.

101 Day, above n. 92, p. 10.

102 Day, above n. 92, p. 10.

103 Day, above n. 92, p. 10.

from the need to inhabit several margins at the same time, while pushing at, or crossing, the border of binary gender. Historically, this liminality has meant that transgender people were often the priests and shamans of their communities,[104] and it is no surprise that spirituality became increasingly important to Sonia. In 2004 she had spent a year in Tibet, studying Lamaism (Tibetan Buddhism) and learning the language, but latterly she had found her spiritual home in two central London churches.

Nowhere, apart from her family and colleagues, was the grief surrounding her death more deeply felt than by the congregation at St Martin-in-the-Fields, where a meeting was called shortly after the news broke, and a large number gathered to share their memories of Sonia – and of David. At St Martin's she had been known only as Sonia, but on this occasion, with some of her family and colleagues present, both her names were used, as were male and female pronouns. According to a friend who was present, terms and labels seemed irrelevant as people expressed their love and admiration for this remarkable person.

Later, at her funeral, attended by over 600 people, the most moving tributes came from her children, to whom she was both Sonia and father; and her spirituality lives on in them. In Chris Dowd's research project, transgender people's ability to forgive is one of several key spiritual outcomes or attributes,[105] and it is apparent in the response of Sonia's children who associated themselves with Sonia's lack of desire for retribution and her concern for the whole person:

> 'This was not what our father wanted. She was trying to help Nina. Ideally we would like Nina to recognise the harm she has done to many lives, but we hope that she can one day reach such a place so she can live life in fullness as our father would have wanted.'[106]

Though they did acknowledge and lament that this quality of life had been denied to them, her family, as well as to Sonia, whose metamorphosis was not fully complete when she died:

> 'We miss the possibility of being able to watch Dad evolve into the person she wanted to be'.

[104] Mollenkott, above n. 13, pp. 130–160.
[105] Dowd, above n. 1.
[106] Walker, above n. 100. Nina would not enjoy the fullness they envisaged. On 8 April 2013 she was found dead in her cell at Her Majesty's Prison Belmarsh, a men's prison in Thamesmead, south-east London. An inquest into her death followed in February 2015.

4.4. AFTERLIFE

Early reports of Sonia's death referred to her correctly as 'a woman'; it was only when the police discovered documents on her person that related to her male identity that crude headlines began to appear in the press about a 'man in a dress', or a 'transvestite', who had (allegedly) been '"pushed" under Tube train'. Never for a moment did I guess that they were referring to Sonia. To her many friends she was a woman: kindly and vivacious – Sonia. With its long-standing habit of misrepresenting transgender people and sensationalising their lives, the British press was unable to comprehend the subtleties of Sonia's metamorphosis, but on this occasion there was a huge outcry in protest, led by Trans Media Watch, which had only recently been formed to improve the portrayal of transgender people in the media. While this came too late for Sonia, the press coverage of her story became the focus for a campaign for greater sensitivity and respect when discussing transgender people's lives.

To die, as Sonia did, with her transition almost, but not quite, complete, probably made her appear more of an enigma than she actually was, intensified by the very public and violent nature of her death. Journalist Elizabeth Day's article was the best account in the print media to address the complexity of her story, and director Kip Loades, who has already documented his own reaction to the transition of his friend Meg,[107] is currently making a film about Sonia. Interviewed both for the article and for the film pilot, I was very conscious, on both occasions, that Sonia was unable to comment on the narrative that would emerge, but I felt moved to speak of her as I knew her, and not least about her spirituality. In this chapter I have drawn on Sonia's story to illustrate my chosen themes of metamorphosis and migration. Both metaphors appear to illuminate the spiritual dimensions of her journey, but she may well have preferred other categories.

V. FAREWELL

With its roots in classical mythology, 'metamorphosis' offers a dynamic, imaginative perspective on the spiritual dimensions of gender transition, and draws on the integration of classical and biblical themes and imagery in the Western Christian tradition. 'Migration' has emerged as a sociological metaphor for gender transition, and its long biblical history, and current connotations, conflate around the intricacies of border crossings and the image of 'the journey', an archetype of the spiritual quest.

The shape-shifting of metamorphosis, like the perils of the migrant journey, can provoke anxiety in both protagonist and beholders, and spiritual darkness

[107] K. Loades, 'Me, Doug & Meg – Trailer' <vimeo.com/43843470> accessed 16.12.2013.

and conflict are often present in gender transition (as they are in most of life). Yet even their apparent triumph, as on the day Sonia died, could not overwhelm the compassion, forgiveness, love and resilience of her life. Nor can they negate all the other spiritual qualities transgender folk embody as they 'emerge from the chrysalis', or inhabit the borderlands of gender, or attempt a border crossing to reach their own gendered 'homes', however stable or elusive the latter may turn out to be.

PART III
LEGAL VIEWS

THE LEGAL STATUS OF TRANSSEXUAL AND TRANSGENDER PERSONS*

Questionnaire for National Reports

The purpose of the questionnaire approach is to ensure that the same areas and problems are covered in each national report. Some of the points might not be of relevance in some jurisdictions – but that in itself can be valuable information from a comparative point of view.

The questionnaire is meant as a guideline and tool and not a straitjacket into which the information must fit. *The main aim is that each national report, while following roughly the same structure, is self-contained and readable.* Many of the legal rules can only be understood in their full legal, social and cultural context, and a contextual description should not be prevented by rigidly following the questionnaire. Please feel free to add any information you consider relevant. However, in order to make the book and the comparison accessible to readers, please follow the structure indicated with *Roman numbers* (that said, broadly following the Arabic numbering would presumably be very helpful, too!).

I. LEGAL FRAMEWORK AND STATISTICS

1. Are there/were there specific legal rules dealing with transsexual or transgender persons in your jurisdiction (especially: is there a specific statute or merely an administrative/court practice)?

   Please also describe the historic development leading up to the current law (and the general constitutional/legal framework where appropriate).

---

* There are a number of variously contested terms used in this area of law, and these terms have been chosen simply because they have enjoyed broad use and are broadly understood. In using these terms, the editor is expressly following Professor Stephen Whittle's definition (S. Whittle, *Respect and Equality: Transsexual and Transgender Rights*, Routledge-Cavendish 2002, pp. xxii f.). 'Transgender person' therefore is meant to indicate all persons who live, or desire to live in the role of a gender which is not the one designated to that person at birth, while 'transsexual person' is meant to refer to those transgender persons who desire or have undergone gender reassignment treatment/surgery. Certainly, no disrespect or offence is intended by the use of these terms.

2. Please state what the position of the national *health insurance* (or equivalent) and/or private health insurance is with regard to costs arising from medical/ psychological treatment where such is legally required/sought.

3. Please give (where available) *statistical information*, especially:
   - (estimated) number of transsexual and transgender persons in your jurisdiction and number of changes[1] of legal sex and/or legal gender[2] (if possible with breakdown of numbers of those persons affirming a female/ feminine and male/masculine legal identity);
   - number of persons changing their legal sex and/or legal gender that were in an existing formal legal relationship (such as marriage and/or civil/ registered partnership);
   - number of persons changing their legal sex and/or legal gender who had children at the time of the change (and, if possible, number of persons who became parents after changing legal sex and/or legal gender);
   - any other relevant/interesting statistical information.

II. CHANGING LEGAL SEX AND/OR GENDER – PROCEDURE AND REQUIREMENTS

1. *Legal Procedure*
   Please describe the legal procedure for changing one's legal sex and/or legal gender in general terms, including:
   - which authority is competent to deal with deal with the procedure;
   - whether it is administrative and whether an involvement of a court is required;
   - whether an appeal against a decision is possible.

2. *Official Documents*
   In which way are the relevant documents (such as birth certificates, passports etc.) changed/corrected/amended? How is the change of legal sex and/or gender recorded? Are these records accessible, and for whom?

---

1 The term of legal gender is used here for ease of exposition – and to make absolutely clear that the issue is not one (as it often is unhelpfully and rather insultingly misrepresented in uninformed/lay discussion) of changing gender, but rather of legal recognition of a person's preferred gender which they always have had.

2 The prefix 'legal' is added here to indicate that sex and/or gender are part of the legal identity record of a person in most jurisdictions, most often evidenced by the person's 'birth certificate' and/or other officially recognised identity documents. The terms 'legal sex' and 'legal gender', and indeed the terms 'sex' and 'gender', are used both independently and interchangeably in various jurisdictions.

3. *Legal Requirements*
   What are the legal requirements for changing one's legal sex and/or legal gender, particularly:
   - whether there is a minimum age;
   - whether there is a requirement to have undergone surgery and/or be infertile/submit to sterilisation (and, where appropriate, whether the gametes of a person stored before changing the legal sex and/or legal gender can be used for creating a child through artificial reproductive technology after the change of legal sex and/or legal gender);
   - whether there are restrictions with regard to the nationality and/or habitual residence;
   - whether there are restrictions with regard to the marital (or civil/registered partnership) status;
   - whether there is any requirement of a 'real life test'/having lived in the preferred sex and/or gender for a specific period of time;
   - whether there are any other medical/psychological requirements that need to be proved;
   - who other than the competent authority (court or administration) is involved in determining whether these requirements are met (e.g. medical boards, specialists panels); how the composition of these boards or panels is determined; whether there is the possibility to appeal against the findings of these boards and panels, and if so, what the procedural requirements are.

III. CONSEQUENCES OF THE CHANGE OF LEGAL SEX AND/OR LEGAL GENDER

1. *Future Rights, Duties and Entitlements*
   What are the legal consequences of a change of legal sex and/or legal gender? Is the person legally recognised as having their preferred gender for all intents and purposes or are there exceptions?
   Please consider particularly:
   - the right to enter into a marriage/civil or registered partnership or equivalent;
   - issues of parentage (*i.e.* being a genetic parent), parenthood (*i.e.* the legal position as mother/father, including adoption)[3] and parental responsibility/custody with regard to a child born after the change of legal sex and/or legal gender;

[3] In those jurisdictions where infertility/surgery is not a requirement for the change of legal sex and/or legal gender, it is possible that a legally male person/legally recognised masculine person gives birth to a child and a legally female person/legally recognised feminine person 'fathers' a child. What is the legal position of a person becoming a parent in this way?

- professional and amateur sports;
- penal system/prison regimes;
- peerages.

2. *Existing Rights, Duties and Entitlements*
   What is the impact on legal relationships/rights, duties and entitlements already established at the time of the change of legal sex and/or legal gender which are based on a specific sex and/or gender?
   Please consider particularly:
   - an existing marriage/civil or registered partnership or equivalent (if not already dealt with above);
   - issues of parentage (*i.e.* being a genetic parent), parenthood (*i.e.* the legal position as mother/father) and parental responsibility/custody with regard to a child born before the change of legal sex and/or legal gender;
   - existing family relations in general;
   - existing employment where the sex and/or gender is a specific requirement;
   - existing health and pension insurance rights and similar issues.

IV. LEGAL CHALLENGES OF THE EXISTING RULES

Unless already discussed above: Is or was the existing legal situation challenged in the courts? Have there been or are there Parliamentary initiatives or campaigns by pressure groups to change the law? If so, what were the outcomes/consequences?

EUROPE

THE LEGAL STATUS OF TRANSSEXUAL AND TRANSGENDER PERSONS IN BELGIUM AND THE NETHERLANDS

Walter PINTENS

Contents

I. INTRODUCTION

In Belgium and in the Netherlands the terms 'transgender' or 'transsexual' are used in different ways. In a strict sense the term is used for a person who cannot identify him or herself with one of the two sexes and who considers him or herself as belonging to both sexes or as between both sexes. In a broader sense, the term covers all persons having problems with the dichotomy male/female and includes not only intersex-affected persons but also transsexuals and cross-dressers. This paper focuses on transgender persons in a broad sense: persons identifying themselves with the gender opposite to the one assigned in their birth certificate. For the purposes of this chapter, transgender includes individuals who have already submitted to medical intervention, such as gender confirmation surgery.

Belgian and Dutch legislation do not use the term 'transgender' or 'transsexual' as such but describe transgender individuals as persons having the constant and irreversible conviction of belonging to the gender other than the one stated on their birth certificate. In practice, the terms 'transgender', 'transperson', 'transwoman' (for male-to-female transgender persons) and 'transman' (for female-to-male transgender persons) are increasingly used in the place of 'transsexual', especially in the Netherlands. Therefore, the term 'transgender' will be used instead of 'transsexual' in this overview.

II. LEGAL FRAMEWORK AND STATISTICS

2.1 STATUTE

2.1.1. Belgian Law

Until 2007 Belgian law did not provide a legal framework for the legal recognition of an individual's preferred gender. This did not mean, however, that gender identity recognition was excluded from Belgian law. As far back as the 1960s, a Brussels court had acquitted a medical doctor who performed gender confirmation surgery.[1] From then on, gender therapy, including surgery, was considered as normal medical therapy. It cannot be deduced from this judgment that transgender persons have an absolute right to recognition of their preferred gender.[2] The final decision lies with the medical doctor who has to decide what medical treatment is appropriate.[3] The right to the legal recognition of preferred gender is nowadays seen as an application of the principle of personal autonomy

1 Criminal Court Brussels 27 September 1969, Journal des Tribunaux (JT) 1969, 635, Pasicrisie (Pas.) 1969, III, 115.

2 Comp. Swennen, *Het personen- en familierecht*, 3rd ed., Antwerp, 2014, pp. 163 ff.

3 Balthasar, 'Transseksualiteit in het Belgisch recht' in T'Sjoen, Van Trotsenburg and Gijs (ed.), *Transgenderzorg*, Leuven, 2013, p. 244.

protected by the right to respect for private life as guaranteed under Art. 8 of the European Convention on Human Rights (ECHR). In the *Goodwin v United Kingdom* and *van Kück v Germany* cases, the European Court of Human Rights underlined that the very essence of the ECHR is respect for human dignity and human freedom. Under Art. 8 ECHR in particular, where the notion of personal autonomy is an important principle underlying the interpretation of its guarantees, protection is given to the personal sphere of each individual, including the right to establish details of his or her identity as an individual human being.[4] The right to a legal gender in accordance with the individual's gender identity is seen as a personality right and a human right.[5]

Several decades passed, however, before individuals gained the right to have the legal recognition of their preferred gender reflected on their birth certificates in Belgium.[6] A first approach was an application to the court for the rectification of the birth certificate. However, since it could not be shown that, at the moment of birth registration, the civil-status registrar had committed a mistake, the dominant opinion in the case law rejected those applications, even if the transgender person had already submitted to gender confirmation surgery and hormone treatments.[7] There were exceptions. In some cases the notion of rectification was broadly interpreted with the motivation both that the registrar had to limit himself to the morphological criterion and not take the psychological criterion into account, as well as the recognition that society had an interest in the conformity of the birth certificate with reality.[8] In 1980, the partial concurring opinion of the Belgian judge, Ganshof van der Meersch, in the Van Oosterwijck case (the first case on this subject pending before the European Court of Human Rights) opened another possibility. Judge Ganshof van der Meersch underlined that an application for a change of status was the only possible way of solving the problem. Since it was possible to apply for a change of status in the case of contestation of a status, it should also be possible to apply for a change of status if a person wanted the recognition of a new status. Even if Belgian law offered no specific legal ground, such an application could be declared admissible on the basis of a general principle of law, stating that every person has a right to

---

4 ECtHR 11 July 2007 *Goodwin v United Kingdom*, no. 28957/95, § 90; 12 June 2003 *van Kück v Germany*, no. 35968/97, § 69.

5 Resolution of the European Parliament of 12 September 1989 on discrimination of transsexuals, OJ C 256/34 of 9 October 1989. See also Todts, 'Le droit à l'orientation sexuelle et à l'identité de genre: un droit fundamental?' (2013) *Annales de droit de Louvain* 133 ff.

6 Pintens, 'Belgien', in Basedow and Scherpe, *Transsexualität, Staatsangehörigkeit und internationales Privatrecht*, Tübingen, 2004, pp. 22 ff.

7 Court of Appeal Brussels 7 May 1974, JT 1974, 713; Court of First Instance Mechelen 17 June 1975, Rechtskundig Weekblad (RW) 1975–76, 870, Anm. *Pauwels*.

8 Court of First Instance Ghent 24 May 1978, Revue Trimestrielle de Droit Familial (RTDF) 1979, 413.

recognition of his gender.[9] In 1985, the Brussels Court of First Instance applied this principle in the Van Oosterwijck case and accepted a change of status.[10] The Court confirmed that a person had to belong to one or the other gender, but that this was not a matter of law but rather of medical science. The change of status did not violate the general principle of invariability of this status, since a change of status was possible by a juristic act (e.g. recognition of a child, marriage) or by judgment (e.g. divorce). Admitting such a change of status did not mean that the status was at everyone's disposal, since it was only the result of a natural development and surgical interventions with a therapeutic aim. This judgment initiated a development leading to full acceptance of the recognition of gender identity by means of a change of status,[11] although some case law still used the rectification procedure.[12] A change of forename was possible by decree of the Minister of Justice, but only neutral forenames were admitted. The result was that transgender persons had to follow a judicial procedure for the recognition of their preferred gender and an administrative procedure to modify their forename.

In order to avoid legal uncertainty and a costly and time-consuming procedure, the Law of 10 May 2007 was enacted.[13] This law introduced two procedures. The first one is restricted to the change of the forenames, the Law of 15 May 1987 on names and forenames being amended for this purpose. The second procedure concerns the legal recognition of preferred gender. It includes the change of forenames. The civil and judicial codes were amended for this purpose and an administrative procedure before the civil-status registrar was introduced.

2.1.2. Dutch Law

The Dutch lower courts have traditionally favoured the rectification of birth certificates. However, the Hoge Raad, the Dutch Supreme Court, adopted a restrictive approach and focused on the morphological characteristics at birth.

---

9 ECtHR 6 November 1980 *Van Oosterwijck v Belgium*, no. 7654/76, partly concurring opinion of Judge Ganshof van der Meersch, § 20 ff. See Pintens, in Basedow and Scherpe, above n. 6, pp. 22 ff.

10 Court of First Instance Brussels 23 January 1985, RTDF 1987, 283 and 16 April 1986, RTDF 1987, 290. See Meulders-Klein, 'La vérité et le sexe. A propos du transsexualisme' (1989) *Revue générale de droit civil* 12 ff.; Pintens, in Basedow and Scherpe, above n. 6, pp. 23 ff.

11 Court of Appeal Antwerp 27 April 1988, RW 1988–89, 614, note A.V.; Court of Appeal Antwerp 29 June 1988, Pas. 1989, II, 12, note A.K.; Court of Appeal Ghent 26 March 1992, Pas. 1992, II, 44; Court of Appeal Brussels 7 April 1992, Pas. 1992, II, 49. Anm. A.V.

12 Court of Appeal Liège 15 June 1987, Jurisprudence de Liège, Mons et Bruxelles (JLMB) 1987, 994; Court of Appeal Mons 13 June 2000, JLMB 2000, 1736.

13 Belgisch Staatsblad 11 July 2007. See Balthazar, 'Transseksualiteit in het Belgisch recht' in T'Sjoen, Van Trotsenburg and Gijs, above n. 3, pp. 243 ff.; Cap, 'La loi du 10 mai 2007 relative à la transsexualité' (2009) *RTDF* 59 ff.; Senaeve and Uytterhoeven (ed.), *De rechtspositie van de transseksueel*, Antwerp, 2008.

Therefore, the rectification of the birth certificate was excluded.[14] As a result of this case law, the legislature was required to intervene. Together with Germany and Italy, the Netherlands was among the first group of European legal systems to introduce legislation in the field of gender identity recognition. The Law of 24 April 1985 amended the Civil Code and introduced a judicial procedure for the legal recognition of preferred gender. [15] This procedure required sterilisation and, in principle, also mandated that applicants submit to surgical intervention. The competent court was also permitted to change the applicant's forenames and, indeed, a person was entitled to restrict his or her application to such a change of forename. Previously, individuals were required to use the specific judicial procedure for the change of forename. [16]

Recently, the Law of 18 December 2013 took the Yogyakarta Principles into account and abolished the requirements of sterilisation and surgical intervention.[17] Furthermore, the judicial procedure was replaced by an administrative regime which takes place before the civil-status registrar.[18]

2.2 HEALTH INSURANCE

Hormone treatment and surgery are covered by health insurance like any other comparable treatment. They are considered a normal medical treatment. Sometimes transgender persons who have submitted to medical intervention complain that they are required to pay more for private supplementary hospital insurance, because they are considered to be a higher risk group.

---

14 Hoge Raad 13 December 1973, Nederlandse Jurisprudentie (NJ) 1975, 130, note EAAL, quashing Court of Appeal Amsterdam, 22 May 1973, NJ 1973, 331; Hoge Raad 3 January 1975, NJ 1975, 187, note EAAL, quashing Court of Appeal The Hague 7 June 1974, NJ 1975, 51.

15 Art. 28 Dutch Civil Code. See Gommers and Jansen, 'Transseksualiteit in Nederland' in T'Sjoen et al., above n. 11, pp. 251 ff.

16 Art. 4, para. 4 Dutch Civil Code.

17 Yogyakarta Principles of 26 March 2007 on the application of International Human Rights Law in relation to sexual orientation or gender identity <www.yogyakartaprinciples.org>. The Principles recommend that legal recognition of gender identity should not depend on medical procedures, including sex reassignment surgery, sterilisation or hormonal therapy. See also Recommendation R(2010)5 of the Committee of Ministers of the Council of Europe on measures to combat discrimination on grounds of sexual orientation or gender identity.

18 Staatsblad van het Koninkrijk der Nederlanden 2014, 1. The Act entered in force on 1 July 2014. See Jansen, 'Rechtspositie transgenders' (2012) *Tijdschrift voor Familie- en Jeugdrecht (FJR)* 62 ff.

2.3 STATISTICAL INFORMATION

2.3.1. *Belgium*

There are no official statistics in Belgium regarding the transgender community. In a study from 2012, an analysis of the national citizens register was made.[19] The statistics in that study do not reflect the total number of transgender persons since only those who have completed a process of transition and meet the statutory criteria can be registered in the registers of civil status. After registration, a transgender person's national registration number is changed from a legal male gender to a legal female gender and vice versa. Between 1993 and 30 June 2012, 631 persons obtained the legal recognition of their preferred gender in Belgium, 68% of whom identified as male-to-female and 32% of whom identified as female-to-male.[20] Those figures do not reflect the total number of transgender persons, however, because only those who obtain the legal recognition of their preferred gender are counted. On the basis of the number of persons who sought help or medical assistance, the number of transgender individuals in Belgium is estimated at 1:13,000 for men and 1:34,000 for women. Since not every transgender person seeks help and medical assistance, these figures may underestimate the actual size of Belgium's transgender community.

2.3.2. *The Netherlands*

Between 1995 and 2009, 900 people obtained legal recognition of their preferred gender in the Netherlands. Sixty-two per cent of these individuals transitioned from a male legal gender to a female legal gender. Thirty-eight per cent transitioned from a female legal gender to a male legal gender. The total number of transgender in the Netherlands persons is estimated at 1:11,500 for men and 1:32,000 for woman.[21]

III. CHANGING LEGAL GENDER – PROCEDURE AND REQUIREMENTS

Transgender persons in Belgium and the Netherlands can use different procedures to obtain the legal recognition of their preferred gender. The first procedure is restricted to a change of forename. The second procedure concerns the legal recognition of gender identity.

---

19 Van Hove, *Transseksuele personen in België – 2012* <http://transgenderinfo.be/f/pers/cijfers/>.

20 Based on the registration in the national citizens register and elaborated by the Institute for the equality of men and woman.

21 Kuyper, 'Transgender in Nederland: prevalentie en attitudes' (2012) *Tijdschrift voor Seksuologie* 130 with further references.

3.1 CHANGE OF FORENAMES

3.1.1. *Belgian Law*

In Belgium, the competent authority for the change of forename is the Minister of Justice. The application to change a forename is subject to the following cumulative requirements:

(a) The applicant has to have a constant and irreversible conviction that he or she belongs to the gender other than the one stated on his or her birth certificate;
(b) The applicant has adopted the corresponding gender role;
(c) A psychiatrist and endocrinologist have to state that the applicant has a constant and irreversible inner conviction that he or she belongs to the gender other than the one stated on his or her birth certificate, that the applicant has undergone hormone replacement therapy in order to induce the physical gender characteristics of the gender to which he or she believes he or she belongs and that the change of forenames is an essential part of the change of role.[22] Gender confirmation surgery is not required.

If those requirements are fulfilled, the applicant has a right to a forename which corresponds to the new gender role.[23] He or she can adapt the forename to that gender role (e.g. from *Leo* to *Leona*), but can also freely chose a completely new forename. The Minister of Justice can refuse the application only if the chosen forename could lead to confusion or could be detrimental to the applicant or third persons.

If the requirements, especially those concerning hormone treatment, are not fulfilled, the applicant can opt for the general procedure for a change of forenames. In the general procedure, the applicant does not have a right to a new forename, the change of forename being qualified as a favour.[24] Initially, the Minister of Justice accepted only neutral forenames (e.g. Dominique), but nowadays any forename can be chosen provided that it does not lead to confusion and is not detrimental to the applicant or third persons. The general procedure is more expensive than the specific one.

3.1.2. *Dutch Law*

In the Netherlands the District Court is competent to order a change of forename.[25] There is no specific procedure for an application to change forenames

---

22 Art. 2, para. 3 Law of 15 May 1987 as amended by law of 10 May 1987.

23 Wuyts, 'De voornaamwijziging van de transseksueel' in Senaeve and Uytterhoeven, above n. 13, pp. 129 ff.

24 Pintens, *Naam*, Ghent, 1982, p. 55.

25 Art. 4, para. 1 Dutch Civil Code (*arrondissementsrechtbank*).

by transgender persons. Transgender individuals must apply under the general procedure.[26] The law does not require specific and detailed conditions for a change of forenames, but the Court has to decide if the applicant has a sufficient substantial interest. The chosen forename may not be inappropriate or correspond to a family name, unless this family name is also used as a common forename.[27]

In the past, courts were reluctant to permit changes of forename. They required that the applicant had the conviction of belonging to the opposite legal gender and had adopted that corresponding gender role. However, ongoing medical treatment was also frequently required.[28] Since, under the Law of 18 December 2013, transgender individuals can obtain the legal recognition of their preferred gender, including a change of their forename, without any requirement of medical treatment, the requirement of ongoing medical treatment for a mere forename change makes no sense.

3.2. LEGAL RECOGNITION OF PREFERRED GENDER

3.2.1. Competent Authority

The competent Belgian authority for recognising the preferred gender of Belgian citizens is the civil-status registrar for the place of registration in the population register.[29] If transgender persons are not registered in the population register, the registrar for the place of birth is competent. If a transgender individual was not born in Belgium, the registrar for the City of Brussels is competent.[30] Foreigners have to be registered in the Belgian population register, with the civil-status registrar for the place of that registration.[31]

In Dutch law, the legal recognition of preferred gender was previously a matter for the courts. However, under the new law introduced in 2013, competence has been transferred to the civil-status registrar. This transfer was strongly criticised by the First Chamber of Parliament,[32] because it meant that a birth certificate could be modified only through a judicial procedure.[33] The administrative solution has the advantages that the applicant does not depend on the sovereign appreciation of the judge, that a lawyer is not necessary and that long procedures are avoided. If the birth certificate of a foreigner is not registered in the Netherlands, the declaration has to be made before the civil-status registrar of The Hague.

---

26 Art. 4, para. 4 Dutch Civil Code.
27 Art. 4, para. 2 Dutch Civil Code.
28 Court of Appeal Amsterdam 9 March 2010, no. 200.048.143/01.
29 Art. 62*bis*, § 1, para. 3 Belgian Civil Code.
30 Art. 62*bis*, § 1, para. 4 Belgian Civil Code.
31 Art. 62*bis*, § 1, para. 3 Belgian Civil Code.
32 The Upper House.
33 See JANSEN, above n. 18, pp. 64 ff.

3.2.2. *Applicants*

Under Belgian law, the following persons can apply for the legal recognition of their preferred gender: a Belgian adult without any age restriction; a Belgian emancipated minor; a Belgian non-emancipated minor assisted by his mother, father or legal representative; a foreign adult, registered in the population or aliens register; a foreign emancipated minor, registered in the population or aliens register; and a foreign non-emancipated minor registered in the population or aliens register assisted by his mother, father or legal representative.[34] The minor is not represented by his parent or legal representative. He has to make the application himself, but he is assisted by them. In practice an application by a minor is rather rare, given that in principle gender confirmation surgery is required and that, in most cases, this is not completed before the age of 18 years.[35]

In the case of a non-national, the national law of that individual's country of citizenship applies. Provisions of the person's national law excluding gender confirmation procedures are not applicable because there are seen as contrary to Belgian international public policy and Belgian law applies instead.[36] If a foreign law does not exclude the legal recognition of preferred gender, but has no specific provisions, Belgian law applies to the substantial and procedural requirements. If specific provisions exist, substantial requirements – concerning, for example, age, consent and gender adaptation – are governed by the national law of the applicant, but procedural requirements, for example the doctors' attestation, are governed by Belgian law.[37]

Under the former Dutch law, any Dutch citizen, in principle even a minor, could apply for the legal recognition of their preferred gender. However, having regard to the fact that most non-adult applicants would not have satisfied the medical intervention requirements before they achieved the age of majority, the legal recognition of a minor's preferred gender was extremely rare. Since, under the Netherlands' new gender recognition laws, it is no longer required that individuals submit to medical intervention, an age limit of 16 years has been prescribed.[38] A minor acts without the consent, or assistance, of his parents or legal representative.[39]

Dutch private international law differs from Belgian law. A person who is not of Dutch nationality may file a request for the legal recognition of his preferred gender if he has a valid residence permit and has been domiciled in the

---

[34] Art. 62*bis*, § 1 Belgian Civil Code and art. 35*bis* Belgian PIL Code.

[35] Uytterhoeven, 'De aangifte van de innerlijke overtuiging te behoren tot het andere geslacht' in Senaeve and Uytterhoeven, above n. 13, pp. 168 ff.

[36] Art. 35*ter* Belgian PIL Code. See Cap, above n. 13, pp. 76 ff.

[37] Circulaire betreffende de transseksualiteitswetgeving of 1 February 2008, Belgisch Staatsblad 2008, 10764.

[38] Art. 28, para. 1 Dutch Civil Code.

[39] Art. 28, para. 4 Dutch Civil Code.

Netherlands for at least one year.[40] Dutch law, not the applicant's national law, applies. The applicant must meet all the requirements of Dutch law.

3.2.3. *Requirements*

In Belgium, the applicant for legal recognition of preferred gender must prove, through a statement from a psychiatrist and a surgeon, that the following conditions have been met:

(a) The applicant has a constant and irreversible conviction that he or she belongs to the gender opposite to the one stated on his or her birth certificate;
(b) The applicant has undergone gender reassignment, if this is possible and justifiable from a medical standpoint;
(c) The applicant is not capable of producing children in accordance with his or her previous gender.[41]

The list of conditions indicates that, in principle, submitting to either surgical intervention or hormone treatments is necessary to obtain the legal recognition of one's preferred gender. This condition is not in accordance with the Yogyakarta Principles. The Belgian legislature has, however, introduced an exception which operates as a form of escape clause. Gender confirmation surgery or hormone treatments are only prescribed insofar as this is possible and justifiable from a medical point of view. This means that the legal recognition of preferred gender without medical intervention is possible if a risk for health exists. Examples of such a risk include the age of the person concerned or a risk of medical complications, such as embolism. There is some discussion as to whether this exception for medical reasons also covers psychological reasons, such as the applicant having an extreme fear of surgery. Although this is not explicitly foreseen, the exception is broad enough to cover such a scenario. There is no indication that the expression 'from a medical standpoint' is restricted to physical situations.[42] However, part of the legal doctrine has interpreted this first condition very strictly and excluded psychological reasons.[43] The requirement of infertility is absolute, with no exceptions. This does not mean, however, that surgical intervention is always necessary since infertility can have other causes. But this rule of principle is contrary to the Yogyakarta Principles.

Under the old Dutch law, any person who self-identified with a gender which was other than the legal gender on his or her birth certificate, and who had physically transitioned to their preferred gender as was possible and 'acceptable' from a medical and psychological perspective, could ask the District Court to

40 Art. 28, para. 3 Dutch Civil Code.
41 Art. 62*bis*, § 2 Belgian Civil Code.
42 Cap, above n. 13, p. 83, n. 106.
43 Uytterhoeven, in Senaeve and Uytterhoeven, above n. 13, p. 158.

order a change of the gender marker on his or her birth certificate. In order to obtain the legal recognition of one's preferred gender on a birth certificate, the applicant had to satisfy the District Court that he or she was no longer capable of playing a role in the conception of a child which corresponded with the biological sex indicated on the applicant's original birth certificate.

The 2013 law in the Netherlands has adapted the criteria for the legal recognition of preferred gender to the Yogyakarta Principles and has abolished any requirement concerning gender confirmation surgery and sterilisation. The applicant has to declare that he or she is convinced that he or she is of a gender other than the one indicated on his or her birth certificate.[44] The application has to be accompanied by a report of an expert designated among the gender teams from the university hospitals in Amsterdam, Groningen and Leiden,[45] issued at the latest six months before the date of the application. The report has to mention that the applicant has declared before the expert that he or she holds the conviction that he or she is of a gender other than the one indicated on his or her birth certificate. The applicant has to show before the expert that he or she understands his or her transgender status and that the application is deliberate.[46] The expert must be able to check whether the application is due to a mental disorder or to a caprice.[47] The expert must refuse to issue the report if he has serious reasons to doubt that the applicant's conviction is genuine.[48] The applicant may ask for a second opinion.

In both the Belgian and Dutch legal systems, there is no condition that any marriage should be dissolved. The Netherlands opened marriage to same-sex persons in 2000 and Belgium in 2003. Where a spouse obtains the legal recognition of his or her preferred gender, the couple's marriage is simply transformed from a marriage between persons of different sex into a marriage between persons of the same sex.[49] But the law does not distinguish between the two kinds of marriage. If gender recognition leads to an irretrievable breakdown of the marriage, then in both legal systems each spouse can apply for a divorce.

3.2.4. Procedure

Under Belgian law the civil-status registrar has no discretionary power. He can only verify his territorial competence and the satisfaction of the legal requirements. This implies that the registrar can verify that the prescribed

44 Art. 28 para. 1 Dutch Civil Code.
45 See Jansen, above n. 18, p. 65.
46 Art. 28a, para. 2 Dutch Civil Code.
47 Jansen, above n. 18, p. 65.
48 Art. 28a, para. 2 Dutch Civil Code.
49 Wuyts, 'De gevolgen van de juridische geslachtsaanpassing op familierechtelijk vlak' in Senaeve and Uytterhoeven, above n. 13, p. 217.

documents are formally in conformity with the law but he cannot verify the content of the doctors' declarations.

If the legal requirements are fulfilled, the registrar has to draw up a certificate acknowledging the newly recognised legal gender. The certificate contains the name and (new) forenames, place and date of birth and the newly recognised legal gender. The certificate also mentions the new affiliation with the parents, *i.e.* specifies that the person concerned is the daughter or the son of his mother and father in accordance with the newly recognised legal gender.

Within three days, the registrar has to notify his decision to the public prosecutor. In cases of fraud or doubtful content of the doctors' declarations, the public prosecutor can appeal and start proceedings in the Court of First Instance. In practice, such appeals are extremely rare. Other persons with an interest can also appeal,[50] including the spouse, the registered partner, the children and the parents. These persons each have an interest in not being confronted with a legal gender recognition that is not in accordance with the law.[51] Such interested parties have a period of 60 days to appeal.[52] The Court can only verify that the legal criteria have been respected and cannot take into account the interests of other parties. The fact that they can appeal only means that they can ask the Court to verify that the legal requirements have been fulfilled.[53]

If there has been no appeal, and at the earliest thirty days after the period of 60 days has expired, the registrar has to register the certificate in the register of births by way of a transcription.[54] The registrar must also mark the newly recognised legal gender in the margin of the birth certificate. On the request of the person concerned, the newly recognised gender can also be marked in the margin of other civil-status certificates.[55]

If the requirements are not fulfilled, the registrar refuses to draw up the certificate. He has to give reasons for his decision and inform the interested party and the public prosecutor.[56] Only the applicant can appeal, within 60 days, to the Court of First Instance.[57]

Under Dutch law, the civil-status registrar will amend the birth certificate if the requirements are fulfilled.[58] He may, if so requested, also order a change of the forenames of the applicant.[59]

---

50 Art. 1385*duodecies*, § 1, para. 1 Belgian Judicial Code.

51 Senaeve, 'Het verhaalsrecht bij de rechtbank' in Senaeve and Uytterhoeven, above n. 13, p. 186 ff.

52 Art. 1385*duodecies*, § 1, para. 2 Judicial Code.

53 Senaeve, in Senaeve and Uytterhoeven, above n. 13, p. 194.

54 Art. 62*bis*, § 4, para. 3 Belgian Civil Code.

55 Circulaire, above n. 37, p. 8.

56 Art. 62*bis*, § 6, para. 1 Belgian Civil Code.

57 Art. 62*bis*, § 7, para. 1 Belgian Civil Code and Art. 1385*duodecies*, § 1, paras. 1 and 2 Belgian Judicial Code.

58 Art. 28b, para. 1 Dutch Civil Code.

59 Art. 28b, para. 2 Dutch Civil Code.

IV. CONSEQUENCES OF LEGAL GENDER CHANGE

4.1 FORMER TIES OF AFFILIATION

In Belgian and Dutch law, the legal recognition of preferred gender has only constitutive effects.[60] Recognition is not declaratory and operates ex nunc. As a consequence, recognition does not affect existing filiation ties and their consequences. Therefore, gender recognition does not affect the legal relationship between a transgender parent and his or her children. In relation to those children, the transgender parent is seen to retain his or her previous previously recognised legal gender. A male-to-female transgender individual remains the legal father of a child and vice versa. The children can still request an extract of their birth certificate mentioning the previously recognised gender of their parent.[61]

The rights and duties resulting from a former relationship are not affected. This means, for example, that transgender parents continue to exercise parental responsibility. All applications concerning such existing legal family relationships can still be introduced after the legal recognition of preferred gender.

4.2 NEW TIES OF AFFILIATION

Under Belgian law, it is in principle not possible for an individual to produce offspring after he or she has obtained the legal recognition of his or her preferred gender. Belgian law requires that an individual must submit to a process of sterilisation before they can obtain recognition. In practice, however, it may happen that a transgender individual freezes sperm or ova and engages in artificial procreation through insemination or embryo transfer.[62]

After a legal change of gender, new affiliation ties can only be established in accordance with the newly recognised legal gender.[63] This means that in case of a male-to-female transgender person, maternal filiation rules apply and vice versa. A male-to-female transgender individual cannot become a father by application of the presumption of paternity; neither can she become a father by recognition of the child or by a successful paternity claim. This rule also applies to a child who was conceived but not recognised before the legal recognition of preferred gender. Only a man can become a father. This last solution has been criticised. If a transgender person can still be the father of a child whose legal family ties have been established before the legal recognition of preferred gender, there is no reason why in those exceptional cases, where children are conceived

---

60 Art. 62*bis*, § 8 Belgian Civil Code; Art 1:28c Dutch Civil Code.

61 Circulaire, above n. 37, p. 8.

62 See De Sutter and Wierckx, 'Vruchtbaarheid' in T'Sjoen, Van Trotsenburg and Gijs, above n. 3, p. 173 ff.

63 Art. 62*bis*, § 8, para. 2 Belgian Civil Code.

but not recognised before gender recognition, that an individual should be denied paternal affiliation. Such a rule seems not to be in accordance with Art. 8 ECHR. That Belgium has introduced adoption by same-sex persons is a further argument against such a rule. The same arguments, however, can be used for children exceptionally conceived after gender recognition.[64]

The criticisms of the current Belgian law were taken into account in creating the new Dutch legislation. Procreation after the legal recognition of preferred gender is here much more a real possibility since gender confirmation surgery and sterilisation are no longer required. In those circumstances, a transman can give birth to a child and a transwoman can still procreate. Transgender men will be legally considered as the mother of the child, because otherwise the child would have no mother.[65] Transgender women who conceive a child or consent to the procreation of a child with their own semen can become a mother through adoption.[66] However, the Law of 25 November 2013 allows the female partner of the mother to recognise the child, so that an adoption is not necessary.

V. PRIVATE INTERNATIONAL LAW

5.1. JURISDICTION AND APPLICABLE LAW

For jurisdiction and applicable law see section II above.

5.2. RECOGNITION OF FOREIGN DECISIONS

In Belgian law, the civil-status registrar and other competent authorities have to recognise foreign decisions. The Code on Private International Law distinguishes between the recognition of a foreign judgment and the recognition of a foreign authentic instrument.

A foreign judgment will be recognised in Belgium without the need for any procedure.[67] Some conditions have to be met, the most important being the absence of manifest incompatibility with public policy.[68] Since Belgian law accepts the legal recognition of preferred gender, this condition presents no problem, even if no surgical intervention has taken place. Under no circumstances can the foreign judgment be reviewed on the merits.[69]

A foreign authentic instrument will be recognised by the civil-status registrar and any other Belgian authority without the need for any procedure if its validity

---

64 Swennen, above n. 2, p. 167.
65 Art. 28c, para. 3 Dutch Civil Code.
66 Art. 28c, para. 3 Dutch Civil Code. See Jansen, above n. 18, p. 67.
67 Art. 22, § 1, para. 2 Belgian PIL Code.
68 Art. 25, § 1 Belgian PIL Code.
69 Art. 25, § 2 Belgian PIL Code.

is established in accordance with the law applicable by virtue of the Belgian Code on Private International Law.[70] This means that the Belgian competent authority has to verify whether the application of foreign private international law has led to the same result as if Belgian international private law had been applied.

In Dutch law, foreign decisions and authentic instruments are recognised by the courts.[71] Recognition can be refused on public policy grounds, but the application of a law other than the law that would have been applicable pursuant to the provisions of Dutch private international law is not incompatible with Dutch public order.[72]

The Netherlands and Spain have ratified the International Commission of Civil Status Convention of 12 September 2000 on the recognition of decisions recording a sex reassignment (ICCS Convention).[73] A decision by a competent authority in the Netherlands or Spain shall be recognised in the other contracting state if, at the time when the application was made, the person concerned was a national of, or habitually resident in, the state in which the decision was taken.[74] Recognition of the decision may be refused when:

(a) the physical adaptation of the person concerned has not been carried out and has not been recorded in the decision in question;
(b) such recognition is contrary to public policy in the contracting state in which the decision is relied on;
(c) when the decision has been obtained by fraudulent means.[75]

Having regard to the new Dutch legislation and in the light of the Yogyakarta Principles, the Netherlands and Spain will interpret the ICCS Convention by means of the teleological method and will not make use of the possibility to refuse recognition if gender confirmation surgery, hormone treatment or sterilisation have not been carried out.[76]

VI. CONCLUSION

That the existing rules have been challenged in the Netherlands is clear. This is the reason why the government introduced a proposal for a new law. Also in Belgium initiatives were taken in Parliament to adapt the law to the Yogyakarta Principles, but until now they have not been successful due to reforms in other fields.

---

70 Art. 27, § 1 Belgian PIL Code.
71 Art. 431, para. 2 Dutch Code on Civil Procedure.
72 Vonken, *Internationaal privaatrecht*, Deventer, 2013, pp. 6 ff. and 33 ff.
73 See Massip, Hondius and Nast, 'International Commission on Civil Status (ICCS)', in Pintens (ed.), *Family and Succession Law*, Int. Enc. Laws, Alphen aan den Rijn, 2014, p. 52.
74 Art. 1 ICCS Convention.
75 Art. 2 ICCS Convention.
76 See Massip, Hondius and Nast, above n. 73, p. 52.

THE LEGAL STATUS OF TRANSSEXUAL AND TRANSGENDER PERSONS IN THE CZECH REPUBLIC

Barbara HAVELKOVÁ*

Contents

I. INTRODUCTION

This chapter argues that although the legal recognition of *transsexuality* came early in the Czech Republic, the social and legal understanding and recognition of *transgender* identity and transgender people's rights has been and continues to be limited. I understand transsexuality as the desire to undergo (or having undergone) 'gender reassignment treatment/surgery'[1] and consider legal provisions that are exclusively tied to physical transition as addressing transsexuality. I understand

* The author would like to thank Eliška Toužimská and Petr Šnoknous for research assistance, Dita Jahodová for fruitful discussions, and Tomáš Holčapek and Lenka Šatrová for useful comments to earlier drafts. All mistakes are the author's.

1 S. WHITTLE, *Respect and Equality: Transsexual and Transgender Rights*, Routledge/Cavendish 2002, p. xxii.

transgender to be a wider concept, which includes but goes beyond transsexuality, and entails the desire to live in (or living in) the role of a gender which is not the one designated at birth.[2] The chapter's main argument is that while Czech law has to some extent addressed concerns of those who wish to 'fully transition' – such as the possibility of a name change and birth-record change connected to sex/gender confirmation surgery – it has not paid attention to those transgender people who do not wish to do so.

The law is based on a heteronormative, biological, and dualistic understanding of sex (rather than gender). First, its heteronormative character manifests itself in the requirement that a marriage be dissolved before a person can submit to sex/gender confirmation surgery.[3] It continues to be unthinkable for Czech law that two persons of the same sex could be married. Second, the biological attachment to 'sex' is apparent in the requirement of surgical intervention for any legal recognition of a person's preferred sex/gender. The law recognises the possibility that 'biological sex' and 'psychological sex' are misaligned. And it now enables their 'realignment', medically and legally. What it does not recognise is the possibility that gender identity can be different from biological sex, without a person wishing to physically modify their body, including their sex characteristics. The law does not accept that it might be called to recognise such a situation and enable some legal recognition of a person's preferred legal sex/gender or allow for a name change without that person first having submitted to gender confirmation surgery. Czech law can thus be said to address transsexual rather than transgender issues. Third, the law is incapable of transcending the sex binary. This is true for gender identities non-confirming to the clear male-female binary – a part of the required Real Life Test is the 'proven ability to live in the opposite sex role'.[4] It is also apparent with regard to reproduction. The law continues to require sterilisation as part of legal recognition, thus normatively ensuring the biological reproductive binary of men and women. All three underlying gender assumptions of the law impact the ability of transgender people to self-determine in ways recognised by the law.

The fact that the Czech law is solely concerned with a person's sex characteristics, and the term 'transsexuality' is overwhelmingly used by the Czech medical community, threw up terminological challenges for this chapter. The reader will notice that throughout the chapter I occasionally use the language of transsexuality rather than transgender. I do so when referencing or discussing the primary materials, mainly in order to highlight the lack of concern with gender and transgender in the Czech discourse. I use the term transgender in my

---

2 Ibid., p. xxii.

3 Or, as the new Civil Code subsidiarily stipulates, in cases where the marriage has not been dissolved, the marriage ceases to exist *ex lege*.

4 Czech Ministry of Health, *Doporučený postup při provádění chirurgických zákroků směřujících ke změně pohlaví u transsexuálních pacientů* [The recommended procedure for surgical interventions of sex change in transsexual patients] No. 29991/2012.

own analysis, however, in order to be respectful of those in the Czech Republic who do identify as transgender, whether or not they wish to undergo surgery. To reflect both these angles, I therefore also speak about legal sex/gender and sex/ gender confirmation surgery.

Aside from the limiting conceptualisation of transgender issues as relating to sex, the legal framework can moreover hardly be considered as guaranteeing 'rights'. Access is very much in the hands of the medical establishment (with regard to determining suitability for surgical intervention), at the mercy of administrators (especially with regard to name change), and at the discretion of family courts (with regard to care of children of transgender parents). I believe that both observations can be understood as legacies of the Czech Republic's socialist past: the country's intellectual isolation up until the 1990s prevented it from reaching a critical understanding of gender as a social construct when this happened in the West. I therefore dedicate particular attention to historical developments leading up to the current framework.

References to legislation in this chapter are valid as of March 2014, unless otherwise stated. All translations from Czech are mine unless otherwise indicated.

II. LEGAL FRAMEWORK AND STATISTICS

2.1. 'TRANSSEXUALITY'[5] UNDER STATE SOCIALISM (PRE-1989)

The Czech sexologist institutes which cater to transsexual 'patients'[6] have the first records of a diagnosis of transsexuality in 1942.[7] A maximum of two patients a year would come to the institute between 1942 until the late 1960s. The numbers rose slightly after 1968,[8] possibly in connection with the political thawing following the Prague Spring. But even in the 1970s and the 1980s, the numbers of 'patients' diagnosed every year as transsexual remained in single

[5] The term 'transgender' only emerged after the Velvet Revolution of 1989 in Czechoslovakia. During the state socialist period, only the term 'transsexual' was used.

[6] I keep the term 'patient' as used in the cited text (P. Weiss, H. Fifková and I. Procházka, 'Vývoj v oblasti transsexuality v České republice' [The development of transsexuality in the Czech Republic] in H. Fifková et al. (eds.), *Transsexualita a jiné poruchy pohlavní identity* [Transsexuality and other disorders of sexual identity], Grada 2008, p. 19). The term is indicative of the medical discourse which frames the issue of 'transsexuality' in the Czech Republic – Dita Jahodová argues that transsexual and transgender persons are seen as patients, *i.e.* objects of treatment, rather than as clients, *i.e.* subjects seeking care (D. Jahodová, 'Konceptualizace transsexuality v českém medicínském diskurzu a dokumentárním filmu po roce 1989' [Representations of transsexuality in the Czech medical discourse and documentary films after 1989] (2011) 7 *Dějiny, teorie, kritika* 289, 307).

[7] Weiss, Fifková and Procházka, above n. 6, p. 19.

[8] Ibid.

digits.[9] The first sex/gender confirmation surgeries seem to have taken place in mid-1960s.[10] Dita Jahodová notes that while in the 1970s surgical intervention was largely discouraged, in 1980s it started to be accepted as part of the 'cure' for transsexuality.[11]

A legal change of name was possible under general regulations, although not specifically for transsexual persons and not as a matter of right.[12] The legal recognition of preferred sex/gender (in birth records) was long opposed by the medical establishment. The Final Resolution from a medical symposium, which took place in 1969 in Bouzov, concluded that 'it is impossible, from a medicinal and natural science perspective, to accept that an operation can change a person's sex'.[13] Recognition was eventually made possible in 1980,[14] but only through an Internal Instruction of the Czech Ministry of Health, which did not have a character of a legal instrument and was thus not legally binding. The Instruction set guidelines for recommendations to the Register Offices (*matriční úřady*) to amend records where a person had submitted to sex/gender confirmation surgery. Changing one's name and birth records (with an *ex nunc* effect) was possible under the general legal provisions, and informally addressed through the non-binding Instruction. The mid-1980s were also the time when limited legal issues relating to transsexuality started to be discussed by legal scholars.[15] Other legal issues connected with transsexuality, addressed today in some legal systems – regarding marriage, relationships with children or discrimination in the workplace – were not specifically treated. Although the law, being agnostic to transsexuality, did not seem to discriminate on the basis of a person's gender identity, specific instances of the prosecutions of transsexuals under the criminal provisions[16] setting different

---

9 Ibid.

10 Working Group for the Issues of Sexual Minorities, *Analysis of the Situation of Lesbian, Gay, Bisexual and Transgender Minority in the Czech Republic*, 2007 <www.vlada.cz/assets/ppov/rlp/vybory/sexualni-mensiny/EN_analyza_web.pdf> p. 28.

11 Jahodová, above n. 6.

12 Sec. 2 Act No. 55/1950 Coll., on the Use and Change of Name and Surname and its implementing Ordinance No. 479/1950 Coll.

13 Final Resolution – Katedra soudního lékařství Lékařské fakulty University Palackého a krajské soudně lékařské oddělení FN v Olomouci, 'Symposium o soudně lékařských otázkách transsexualismu' [Symposium on the forensic and medicinal aspects of transsexualism] (Bouzov, 17 September 1969).

14 Internal instruction of the Czech Ministry of Health, No. 114-270-27.12.1979.

15 A. Brzek, *Soudní psychiatrie a sexuologie pro právníky*, Univerzita Karlova, 1985; J. Haderka, 'Jaký právní přístup k otázkám transsexualismu?' [What legal approach to transsexualism?] [1986] *Právník* 213.

16 The 1950 Criminal Code criminalised 'sexual intercourse between persons of the same sex' (the provision was gender neutral, *i.e.* lesbians were formally subject to it, as well as gays) (Sec. 241 Act No. 86/1950 Coll.). The 1961 Criminal Code decriminalised sexual intercourse between persons of the same sex but kept different ages of consent – 15 for heterosexual and 18 for homosexual sex (Sec. 244 Act No. 140/1961 Coll.).

ages of consent for same-sex intercourse have been noted in the literature.[17] To my knowledge, no research exists as to the actual practice of the Register Offices (*matriční úřady*), other public authorities, employers or family courts and their treatment of transsexuals during the period of late state socialism.

I have argued elsewhere that the concept of gender – as a socio-cultural construct – was unknown in state socialist Czechoslovakia.[18] This had consequences for women and men. For example, allowing or facilitating women to live lives not defined by their traditional gender roles as mothers, or the redefinition of the male norm, were unthinkable as policy and legal agendas of the socialist state. It also had consequences for transgender persons. The socio-cultural embeddedness of the male/female binary, as well as the dichotomy of heterosexuality/homosexuality, was neither realised nor critically evaluated and was thus unreflectively perpetuated by the medical practice and the law.[19] The strict division between the sexes, with their ascribed gender roles and heterosexuality[20] meant that a transgender identity was not comprehensible. Transgender issues were reduced to transsexuality.

Transsexuality was seen as a medical-psychological problem[21] of an 'inborn' 'discordance' between the 'biological and psychological'.[22] As such, it was reconcilable with the binary and biological understanding of men and women as two sexes with natural roles and heterosexual orientation. This can be illustrated for example by the fact that the Internal Instruction of the Ministry of Health, as regards doctors' recommendations for name-change, set as a condition that one conformed to the gender-appropriate behaviour of their new 'sex'. Post-operative transsexual persons had to have a 'sufficiently persuasive appearance as a person of the opposite sex'.[23] Their 'reproductive function' was mandatorily 'disabled'.[24]

Another aspect of the discourse was the pathologisation of transsexuality. In 1969, a transsexual person's rejection of his or her body and the desire for the

---

17 O. Pechová, V. Raichlová and I. Procházka, 'Transsexualita a právo' [Transsexuality and the law] in H. Fifková et al. (eds.), *Transsexualita a jiné poruchy pohlavní identity* [Transsexuality and other disorders of sexual identity], Grada 2008, p. 142.

18 I have previously discussed the missing understanding of gender as a social construct, and a lack of feminist awareness during the state socialist period in Czechoslovakia in B. Havelková, 'The legal notion of gender equality in the Czech Republic' (2010) 33 *Women's Studies International Forum* 21; B. Havelková, 'Gender in Law under and after State Socialism: The Example of the Czech Republic', DPhil thesis, University of Oxford 2013; and B. Havelková, 'The three stages of gender in law' in H. Havelková and L. Oates-Indruchová (eds.), *The Politics of Gender Culture under State Socialism: An Expropriated Voice*, Routledge 2014.

19 For a similar analysis of the medical discourse, see Jahodová, above n. 6.

20 Marxism was unambiguously heteronormative. Marx wrote that 'the relation of a man to a woman is the most natural relation of human being to human being'. From *The Economic and Philosophic Manuscripts of 1944* by Karl Marx, cited in A.M. Jaggar, *Feminist politics and human nature*, Rowman & Allanheld 1983, p. 69. And Engels expressed disgust with sodomy when discussing ancient Greece. In Engels' *Origin*, cited in ibid., p. 69.

21 Haderka, above n. 15, p. 213.

22 Ibid., pp. 213–214.

23 Internal instruction of the Czech Ministry of Health No. 114-270-27.12.1979.

24 Ibid.

legal recognition of preferred sex/gender was described as 'infantile', 'narcissistic', 'hypochondriac', 'pathetic' and 'spastic' by a leading psychiatrist.[25] When sex/ gender confirmation surgery became available from the 1980s, it was dealt with under the rubric of 'treatment of serious sexual disorders', together with operations on intersex individuals ('hermaphrodites') and 'deviants' (such as sadists, paedophiles, etc.).[26] A 1986 legal article described transsexual persons as 'unfortunates'[27] and medical experts overwhelmingly considered transsexuality as a 'sexual deviation'.[28] Paradoxically, probably because of this pathologisation of transsexuality, and the idea that a hormonal and especially an operative solution can cure and normalise the 'patient', the 'treatment' has since its inception been fully paid for from the public health insurance.[29]

2.2. TRANSGENDER IN TRANSITION (AFTER 1989)

The first explicit legal provision addressing the legal recognition of sex/gender appeared in 1991 in the Act on Popular Health-Care.[30] Section 27a(1) stipulated that:

> 'castrations, stereotactical operations and surgeries for transsexuals are only performed based on request by the person on which they are to be performed, and only after approval from an expert committee, which shall consist of a lawyer, at least two medical specialists in the relevant area, and two other doctors which will not carry out the medical treatment.'

Section 27a(2) specifically stipulated that the 'patient' needed to be informed about the risks and possible negative effects of submitting to treatment. The particulars of the surgical treatment were not legally specified. This provision governed medical procedures for almost 20 years.[31]

The rules relating to surgery were complemented by the legally guaranteed possibility of a name change in 2000.[32] These provisions are still in force today and I discuss them in greater detail below. The same year legal provisions were adopted allowing an *ex nunc* amendment to birth records and a change in

25 MUDr. Libuše Widermannová, presenting at Symposium Bouzov.

26 Communication of the Czech Ministry of Health No. LP-267–16.9.1970. The view of transsexuality as a 'sexual deviation' was also repeatedly mentioned in medical texts. Jahodová, above n. 6.

27 Haderka, above n. 15, p. 226.

28 Jahodová, above n. 6, pp. 294–295, and references therein.

29 This paradox is well explored by J. Butler, 'Undiagnosing gender' in P. Currah, R.M. Juang and S. Price Minter (eds.), *Transgender Rights*, University of Minnesota Press 2006.

30 Act No. 20/1966 Coll. on Popular Health-Care, as amended by 548/1991.

31 See also A. Baršová, 'Skalpel a duše. Ke změně pohlaví podle nového občanského zákoníku' [Scalpel and soul. The provision on legal sex change in the new Civil Code] (2013) 3 *Časopis zdravotnického práva a bioetiky* <www.ilaw.cas.cz/medlawjournal> no numbering.

32 Act No. 301/2000 Coll., on Register Offices, Name and Surname.

birth number, which is the unique identification number of each Czech citizen containing numerical information about that person's legal sex/gender.[33]

The legal regulation of transsexuality has experienced several recent developments. The surgery was addressed by the new Act on Specific Health Services[34] which came into force in 2012. The Act is more detailed in its definition of what constitutes sex/gender confirmation surgery than was previously the case. For example it makes the 'disabling of the reproductive function' an integral part of the procedure. While it has even previously been the practice of authorities to require proof of sterility for the purposes of changes in birth records, the statute has now made this a legal requirement.

A further legal specification which might in practice mean more stringent conditions for legal recognition of preferred sex/gender came into force on 1 January 2014 via the new Czech Civil Code. Unlike the previous Civil Code which was silent on the issue,[35] the new Civil Code explicitly addresses 'sex change' (*změna pohlaví*).[36] It stipulates in Section 29(1) that that the 'sex change' occurs 'through surgery with the simultaneous disabling of the reproductive function and the transformation of sexual organs' (*přeměna pohlavních orgánů*). The provision further ties the date of the legal change to the date of the 'confirmation (of operative change) issued by the health care provider'.[37] Andrea Baršová has criticised the provision for 'going beyond the requirements of the previous regime of the Act on Specific Health Services, especially with regards to the requirement of "transformation of sexual organs". Previously … only operative sex change was required and in practice, a partial change was deemed sufficient.'[38] Ondřej Frinta, the author of one of the leading commentaries on Section 29 of the new Civil Code, notes that the term 'transformation of sexual organs' was not part of the original proposal of the Civil Code, but was inserted during parliamentary proceedings. The term is not defined elsewhere in the legislation and thus requires interpretation. Frinta suggests, and I agree, that interpreting the term *stricto sensu*, as requiring fully completed surgical transition, would lead to serious compromises to transgender persons' rights to dignity and privacy. He thus considers that the previous practice – of considering hysterectomy (for FtM) and orchidectomy (MtF) sufficient – should be continued.[39]

This points to possible negative implications of the enshrining of the medical and legal aspects of the legal recognition of preferred sex/gender in statute. From many lawyers' perspective, the setting of clearer legal rules would be seen

---

33 Act No. 133/2000 Coll., on Population Records.

34 Act No. 373/2011 Coll., on Specific Health Services.

35 Act No. 40/1964 Coll., Civil Code.

36 Act No. 89/2012 Coll., Civil Code.

37 Although this is a refutable legal construction – the transgender person could prove otherwise. See also O. Frinta, '§ 29 (Section 29)' in J. Švestka, J. Dvořák and J. Fiala (eds.), *Občanský zákoník. Komentář. Svazek I* [Civil Code. Commentary. Part I], Wolters Kluwer 2014, p. 152.

38 Baršová, above n. 31.

39 Frinta, above n. 37, pp. 150–151.

as positive: it makes the regime clearer and more predictable, it makes it more obviously subject to judicial review, which means that statutory interpretation becomes a matter for courts, and individual rights can arguably be derived from these provisions. On the other hand, while some provisions merely codified previous practice (the requirement to dissolve an existing marriage), the changes in wording (from 'operative sex change' to 'transformation of sexual organs') and the new specific addressing of parental rights in the Civil Code, which I discuss below, allow, if not encourage, a stricter interpretation which could regress the rights of transsexual and transgender persons.

In terms of attention and attitudes to transsexuality and transgender, the former has increased and the latter improved, especially in the 2000s. Two collective monographs have been dedicated to transsexuality, one in 2002[40] and one in 2008.[41] They are largely written by doctors, and despite a more sympathetic approach to transsexuality than was previously the case in the medical community, they tend to medicalise and pathologise the issue. The title of the 2002 book speaks of 'treatment' and the title of the 2008 book of a 'disorder'. This attitude to transsexuality has obvious advantages but serious disadvantages too. On the one hand, it 'legitimises' transsexuality as a serious 'problem' the medical and legal establishment needs to deals with, and the treatment of which should be paid for by the health insurance. Indeed, any medical attention given during the supposed six phases of transition (referred to as the six stages of 'sex change') identified by Czech sexologists[42] – (1) diagnostics, (2) decision-making, (3) real-life test and real life experience, (4) hormonal therapy, (5) operation and (6) post-operative stage – is paid for by public health insurance.[43] Those who seek to transition are only required to contribute to the costs of hormonal treatment and pay for 'cosmetic treatment' which includes epilation, breast augmentation, insertion of prosthetic testes,[44] voice therapy, and thyroid eminence elimination.[45] On the other hand, this approach continues to pathologise transgender persons. As Judith Butler notes, the diagnosis singles transgender persons out as 'ill, sick, wrong, out of order, abnormal',[46] and leaves them open to stigmatisation.

---

40 H. Fifková et al. (eds.), *Transsexualita. Diagnostika a léčba* [Transsexuality. Diagnostics and Treatment], Grada 2002.

41 H. Fifková et al. (eds.), *Transsexualita a jiné poruchy pohlavní identity* [Transsexuality and other disorders of sexual identity], Grada 2008. Two years later, a textbook on Sexology also dedicated considerable attention to the issue: P. Weiss (ed.), *Sexuologie*, Grada 2010.

42 H. Fifková, 'Základní etapy procesu přemeny pohlaví' [The major stages of a sex change] in H. Fifková et al. (eds.), *Transsexualita a jiné poruchy pohlavní identity* [Transsexuality and other disorders of sexual identity], Grada 2008.

43 V. Raichlová and I. Procházka, 'Právní aspekty (Legal aspects)' in H. Fifková et al. (eds.), *Transsexualita. Diagnostika a léčba* [Transsexuality. Diagnostics and Treatment], Grada 2002, p. 110.

44 Ibid., p. 110.

45 I thank Dita Jahodová for this information.

46 Butler, above n. 29, 275.

In 2007, the Working Group for the Issues of Sexual Minorities of the Minister for Human Rights and National Minorities published a report entitled 'Analysis of the Situation of Lesbian, Gay, Bisexual and Transgender Minority in the Czech Republic'.[47] The document showed greater understanding for the difficulties encountered by lesbian, gay, bisexual, transgender and queer/questioning (LGBTQ) persons in the Czech Republic and was very comprehensive. Unfortunately, it has not been updated by subsequent governments. The legal aspects of transsexuality, as well as *transgender* issues, have recently been the subject of a workshop and consequent special issue of the Czech *Journal of Medical Law and Bioethics*.[48] The articles in this monothematic issue focused on transgender issues, sexual identity and related legal discourse. Their approach – looking at the legal issues starting from transgender people's needs[49] – is a welcome departure from the otherwise paternalistic approach of the medical establishment which has regarded them as patients.

2.3. STATISTICS

In the following, I rely on the statistical data presented in the 2008 monograph *Transsexuality and other disorders of sexual identity*.[50] The authors point out that, historically, there were two increases in the numbers of transsexual persons (whom the authors refer to as 'patients'), as well as those accessing sex/gender confirmation surgery (referred to as 'operative sex changes'). One increase occurred around 1968,[51] and the second, more significant increase, came after the regime change in 1989. Interestingly, the Velvet Revolution brought with it another change – to the 'direction' of the transitions. Before 1989, requests for female-to-male (FtM) transition dominated. There were around four times as many FtM transitions as there were male-to-female (MtF). That trend, however, has evened out since 1989 and now seems to have even reversed itself. According to the authors, the new situation appears to correspond to the ratios in other European countries.[52] The atypical composition of transsexual persons seeking sex confirmation surgery before 1989 has to my knowledge not been satisfactorily explained. One could perhaps tentatively suggest that women desiring transition (FtM) would tend to have less difficulty living in 'the male role'[53] before surgery, and they therefore might have been more willing to come forward. Men desiring

47 Working Group for the Issues of Sexual Minorities, *2007 Analysis*.
48 Vol. 3, No. 1 (2013).
49 Esp. Baršová, above n. 31.
50 Weiss, Fifková and Procházka, above n. 6.
51 When a period of political thawing was followed by the invasion of Czechoslovakia by the armies of several Warsaw Pact states.
52 Weiss, Fifková and Procházka, above n. 6, p. 20.
53 Unlike those desiring a MtF transition, those wishing for a FtM transition tend to approach their sexologist already living in their preferred 'sex role'. Frinta, above n. 37, p. 148.

a transition (MtF), on the other hand, might have felt particularly daunted by the possible judgment passed on them during the real-life-experience period before the sex confirmation surgery by the relatively uninformed and close-minded state socialist society.

Among other post-1989 developments was the shortening of treatment, from 55 months to 34 months on average. The time continues to decrease.[54] It also seems that those who 'had resigned themselves to their situation in the past'[55] came forward after 1989 – older individuals as well as those with children sought help in greater numbers. The following table shows the number of transsexual persons who were in an existing formal legal relationship (marriage or registered partnership) or had children at the point that they accessed sex/gender confirmation surgery. [56] It shows that those seeking MtF transition are more likely to be in a formal legal relationship and have children – there are more husbands and fathers seeking transition and recognition than wives and mothers.

Due to the focus on transsexual persons, and moreover transsexual individuals as 'patients', data on transgender persons is not readily available in the Czech Republic. Nor is information available regarding how many of those who have undergone sex/gender confirmation surgery have requested and been granted legal recognition – both of their preferred name and their preferred sex/gender.

Table 1. Numbers of transsexual with and without sex/gender confirmation surgery before 2008 (divided by MtF and FtM and pre-1989 and post-1989)[57]

Type of transsexuality		With 'operative sex-change'	Without 'operative sex-change'	Total
MtF	Before 1989	41	9	**50**
	After 1989	151	68	**219**
	Total	192	77	**269**
FtM	Before 1989	102	83	**185**
	After 1989	136	171	**307**
	Total	238	254	**492**

54 Ibid., pp. 22–23.

55 Ibid., pp. 22–23. The average age at the beginning of therapy was 23 years before 1989; it increased to 27 years after 1989.

56 The table includes all patients registered in the Czech Republic, both before and after 1989.

57 Table 3 in Weiss, Fifková and Procházka, above n. 6, p. 21.

Table 2. Marital/partnership status and parenthood by 2008 (divided by MtF and FtM)

Type of transsexuality		Relationship status		Total
		Single	**Other**	
MtF	Children – No	189	15	**204**
	Children – Yes	0	65	**65**
	Total	189	80	**269**
FtM	Children – No	445	18	**463**
	Children – Yes	4	23	27
	Total	**638**	**121**	**759**

III. CHANGING LEGAL SEX/GENDER – PROCEDURE AND REQUIREMENTS

As the legal recognition of sex/gender is highly dependent on medical procedures in the Czech Republic, I discuss these first, before turning to the legal procedure for recognition and the question of amending legal documents.

3.1 LEGAL REQUIREMENTS

Sex/gender confirmation surgery, which is the basis for legal recognition, is governed by the Act on Specific Health Services.[58] It defines surgical intervention (termed 'sex change') in the following terms:

> 'The term sex change in transsexual patients is to mean the medical operations, whose aim is to change sex operatively with the *concurrent disabling of the reproductive function*. A transsexual patient is a person who is affected by a *permanent discordance* between psychological and physical sex ("sexual identification disorder").'[59]

I consider the obligatory sterilisation to be a serious intrusion into the bodily integrity of those seeking sex/gender confirmation surgery. I believe it to interfere with a range of human rights,[60] such as the prohibition of inhumane or degrading treatment,[61] the right to respect of human dignity and private life,[62] and the right

58 Act No. 373/2011 Coll.
59 Sec. 21(1) ibid.
60 See also Baršová, above n. 31.
61 Art. 3 Convention for the Protection of Human Rights and Fundamental Freedoms, 3 September 1953, 213 UNTS 222 (ECHR); Art. 7(2) Act No. 2/1993 Coll., Charter of Fundamental Rights and Freedoms (Czech Charter).
62 Art. 8 ECHR; Art. 10 Czech Charter.

to health.[63] I consider the provision to be ripe for a constitutional challenge.[64] None has to my knowledge been brought, however. Aside from the diagnostic requirement and mandatory sterility, the Act also sets a 'real-life test' and civil status conditions for surgery:

> 'Surgical operations leading to a sex change can be performed on persons a) in whom the sexual identity disorder has been definitively diagnosed and who *have proven the ability to permanently live as a person of the opposite sex*, and b) who have *never been married or entered into registered partnership* (or a foreign equivalent), or prove that their marriage or registered partnership has *ended*.'[65]

The minimum age for sex/gender confirmation surgery is 18 years.[66] The Act does not regulate the minimum age for hormone treatment, but the common medical practice appears to require a minimum age of 16 years.[67] Surgical intervention cannot be performed on prisoners or persons otherwise in custody,[68] but, somewhat surprisingly, can be performed on persons with limited legal capacity,[69] upon request of their legal guardian with assent of a family court.[70]

The treatment is in principle not limited to Czech nationals or Czech residents, but foreigners might be disadvantaged with regards to financial coverage. 'Third country nationals', *i.e.* foreigners who are not EU citizens, can only avail themselves of the system of public health insurance if they are permanently resident in the Czech Republic or work for a Czech employer. Other foreign residents have to rely on private insurance providers, who often offer only limited coverage. Asylum seekers and those guaranteed asylum are treated as permanent residents and can therefore avail themselves of the system of public insurance.[71]

The surgical procedure – aside from a written request by the transgender person – requires an approval from an expert panel (*odborná komise*).[72] The panel is established by the Ministry of Health, and consists of a medical professional employed by the Ministry, a sexologist, a psychiatrist, a clinical psychologist, an expert in diabetology and endocrinology, an obstetrician-gynaecologist, and a

---

63 Art. 31 Czech Charter.

64 Among other things, it would press the government to justify the measure – it would be interesting to see whether there are any evidence-based medical arguments for it, or whether the obligatory sterilisation is merely an expression of a traditional binary understanding of sex and gender.

65 Sec. 21(2) Act No. 373/2011 Coll.

66 Sec. 21(3) ibid.

67 Fifková, above n. 42.

68 Sec. 21(5) 373/2011.

69 Although the Act speaks of persons deprived of legal capacity (*zbavení způsobilosti*), this now needs to be interpreted as 'limited legal capacity' (*omezení svéprávnosti*) under the new Civil Code.

70 Sec. 21(4) Act No. 373/2011 Coll.

71 Sec. 53c and 88 Act No. 325/1999 Coll.

72 Secs. 21(3)(a), (b) Act No. 373/2011 Coll.

lawyer with medical law expertise.[73] These experts must not be employed by the health care provider and must not be the doctor directly treating the 'patient'. The transgender person is invited to meetings of the panel,[74] his/her personal doctor might be invited to join the panel's meeting. The doctor is not to be present during the panel's interview of the transgender person.[75] After deliberation, the panel adopts a position. A positive position, recommending surgical intervention, requires the consent of all panel members.[76]

According to the Ministry of Health,[77] the panel meets three to four times a year. Between the entry into force of the Act on Specific Health Services in 2012 and October 2014, 148 requests were discussed.[78] 87 of them were presented in 2014 alone, 37 by men and 50 by women, which shows a marked recent increase.[79] In 2014, only one of the 87 decisions was negative.[80]

The positive position of the expert panel is one of the documents, alongside the 'patient's' request,[81] which are then the basis on which the health care provider proceeds to surgery.[82] The 2012 Recommendation of the Ministry of Health,[83] which implements the Act on Specific Health Services and while not legally binding has the force of setting *lege artis* standards, contains further specifications and adds the following requirements: (1) an unequivocal diagnosis of 'full sexual identity disorder – transsexuality'; (2) a real life test lasting at least 12 months; (3) use of hormonal treatment in the past 12 months; (4) being unmarried and not in a registered partnership; (5) being 18 years of age; and (6) awareness of the character and possible complications of the surgery.

The expert panel does not appear to be an administrative body, nor is its decision an administrative decision. As a consequence, it does not seem to be possible to appeal – the Act on Specific Health Services certainly does not foresee that possibility. I am unaware of any judicial challenge on the matter.[84] What appears to be possible, however, is a resubmission of the case to the panel at a later date.

---

73 Sec. 22(1) ibid.
74 Sec. 22(4) ibid.
75 Sec. 22(7) ibid.
76 Sec. 22(6) ibid.
77 E-mail communication with the Press Secretary, Štěpánka Čechová, on 14 May 2014.
78 Ibid.
79 L. Silný, 'Žádostí o změnu pohlaví je v Česku rekordní počet' [Record numbers of requests for sex change in the Czech Republic] <www.novinky.cz/domaci/351246-zadosti-o-zmenu-pohlavi-je-v-cesku-rekordni-pocet.html> accessed 09.02.2015.
80 Ibid.
81 Or that of the legal guardian.
82 Sec. 21(3) Act No. 373/2011 Coll. In the case of persons with diminished capacity, the consent of a court is also required. In that case, the health care provider applies to a court to attain consent with the surgery. Sec 22(10) ibid.
83 Czech Ministry of Health, *Recommendation*.
84 The Ministry of Justice full-text search database on higher court decisions contains no cases regarding 'sex change' or relating to 373/2011. I also thank Tomáš Holčapek, a medical law expert, for consultation on the issue.

3.2. LEGAL PROCEDURE

The legal procedure to obtain recognition of one's preferred sex/gender consists of an amendment to the birth records and the issuance of a new birth number.[85] The change in birth records is regulated by the Act on Population Records[86] and the Act on Register Offices.[87] The change is recorded on the basis of a written confirmation by the health provider about the surgical intervention (termed the 'sex change'). The health provider is obliged to inform the Register Office within three working days of this 'sex change'.[88] The Act on Register Offices also regulates name change. In general, the Act prohibits a man to change his name to a woman's name and vice versa.[89] In the Czech language, most first names as well as surnames[90] easily identify a person as male or female. There are, however, names and surnames which are neutral, and the Act enables persons who transition to the use a neutral name, on the basis of their request and a certificate from the health provider, where the person is being treated.[91] This change of legal name is done for free.[92] There are three problems with the process. First, anecdotal evidence suggests that the willingness of the individual Register Officers to perform the change and to accept the chosen neutral name varies.[93] Indeed, the office of the Czech Public Defender of Rights (*Veřejná ochránkyně práv*), the Czech equality body under EU directives, has addressed a complaint by a transgender person regarding narrow interpretation of 'neutral name'.[94] The problem is often linguistic and can be addressed via a Czech language expert statement,[95] which however means delays and additional costs. The second problem is that the change is entirely dependent on the assessment of the doctor. While 'undergoing sex change' can be interpreted extensively to include hormonal treatment, it seems to exclude transgender people who have no desire to eventually undergo surgery, but have a gender identity not corresponding to their birth-assigned sex. Even more so, it excludes transgender people who do not seek treatment. Indeed, personal stories suggest that some transgender persons have undergone sterilisation merely to be able to change their name.[96] The possibility of a change to a gender-neutral name merely

85 Sec. 17(2)(d) Act No. 133/2000 Coll.
86 Ibid.
87 Act No. 301/2000 Coll.
88 Sec. 17a ibid.
89 Sec. 72(3) ibid.
90 Most commonly, the suffix 'ová' is added to a man's surname. For example the author's surname Havelková is the feminine version of the male surname Havelka.
91 Sec. 72(5) Act No. 301/2000 Coll.
92 Item 11 Act No. 634/2004 Coll., on Administrative Fees.
93 Fifková et al., above n. 6, p. 197.
94 E-mail communication with Petr Polák, Head of Department of Equal Treatment in the Office of the Public Defender of Rights, 9 February 2015. The details of the case are unfortunately not publically available.
95 Fifková et al., above n. 6, p. 197.
96 I thank Dita Jahodová for this information.

on the basis of a request by the transgender person would be welcome. Third, the Act explicitly states that a 'change of name will not be allowed if a male person requests a change to a female first name and vice versa'.[97] It is not entirely clear whether, after surgery, a transgender person can change from a neutral name to a name which corresponds to their newly recognised legal sex/gender. A generous interpretation of the Act could allow for a change of first name, as the Act sets no conditions for it,[98] as well as of surname – the 'weighty reason' required by the Act should be seen as existing by virtue of the sex/gender confirmation surgery.[99] These decisions would, however, be at the discretion of the Register Office and a change would not have to be performed as a matter of right.[100] And a transgender person who is not undergoing treatment would most probably not be allowed to change their name to that of their preferred gender at all.

As I mentioned above, the Czech birth number is a unique identification number containing numerical information about a person's sex/gender. In order for a transgender individual to live in their new identity after transition without their history being immediately disclosed, he or she must obtain a change in the birth number. The Act on Population Records explicitly allows for a change of birth number.[101] As above, with regard to name change, while this provision caters for those who have undergone surgery, it does not address people who do not conform to their birth sex or to a gender binary in their identity, appearance and behaviour. Eliminating the information about sex from the birth number entirely would be a recommendable change to the current legal regime. It would not only help transgender persons who do not wish to undergo sex/gender confirmation surgery, but also those who did undergo surgery, but who – although they can avail themselves of a new number – often have to disclose their old birth number and thus the previous legal sex/gender to prove legal continuity of their person to a range of public and private subjects.

3.3. OFFICIAL REGISTERS AND DOCUMENTS

The legal recognition of an individual's sex/gender is entered into the Register (*matrika*) and a new birth certificate can be supplied. A new passport can be issued, although recognition is not explicitly mentioned in the relevant legislation as a mandatory reason.[102] The same is true for Personal Identification Cards[103] and other personal documentation. It might be beneficial for the issuance of

---

97 Sec. 72(3) Act No. 301/2000 Coll.
98 Sec. 72(1) ibid.
99 Sec. 72(2) ibid.
100 In Sec. 72(5), the change is mandated by the Act.
101 Sec. 17(2)(d) Act No. 133/2000 Coll.
102 Act No. 329/1999 Coll., on Travel Documents.
103 Act No. 328/1999 Coll., on Personal Identification Cards.

new documentation to be expressly included in the statutes as a matter of right, without an additional fee.

Information about the legal recognition of a person's sex/gender is recorded in the 'agenda information system of population records', administered by the Ministry of the Interior. A range of public institutions have access to the information, including other ministries[104] and the social security administration.[105] While it might be necessary to obtain this information to secure legal continuity for a transgender person who has undergone sex/gender confirmation surgery whose birth number has changed, it also means that the privacy of the person as regards surgery is diminished. A sex-neutral birth number, which I argued for above, would eliminate this problem.

There are a range of other non-legal documents which contain information about a transgender person's pre-transition identity. Alterations to only some of these documents has thus far been addressed and mostly in non-binding guidelines. In terms of educational diplomas, for example, Article 5 of the Guidelines of Education Ministry 29 210/98–20 stipulates that new documentation should be issued. In practice, however, this stipulation appears to be often disregarded.[106] Indeed the office of the Czech Public Defender of Rights has received a complaint by a transgender person who has had difficulties obtaining a new secondary education final examination transcript (*maturitní vysvědčení*).[107]

With regard to other documents, such as records of previous employment, there are no guidelines at all. The possibility of these being reissued with the new identity will depend entirely on the goodwill of the individual employer. The lack of such supporting documentation can have negative repercussions for transgender people in the labour market (I return to the question of discrimination below).

IV. CONSEQUENCES OF THE CHANGE OF LEGAL SEX/GENDER

4.1. FUTURE RIGHTS, DUTIES AND ENTITLEMENTS

Following sex/gender confirmation surgery, a person is considered, in law, as having their newly recognised 'sex'. Those who have undergone sex/gender confirmation surgery are not barred from entering into a marriage or a registered partnership. They are not legally barred from becoming a parent, but the

104 For example the Ministry of Employment and Social Affairs, Sec. 147c Act No. 435/2004 Coll., on Employment.

105 Sec 11a Act No. 582/1991 Coll., on the Organization and Implementation of Social Security.

106 I thank Dita Jahodová for this information.

107 E-mail communication with Petr Polák, Head of Department of Equal Treatment in the Office of the Public Defender of Rights, 9 February 2015. The details of the case are unfortunately not publically available.

requirement of 'disabling of the reproductive function' contained in the Civil Code[108] in practice means that they will not be able to become biological parents.

As far as assisted reproduction is concerned, it is frequently of little assistance to transgender individuals. Men and women can have their sperm or eggs frozen for future use, but assisted reproduction is then available only to 'infertile couples' consisting of a man and a woman.[109] A post-operative female would thus be left with frozen sperm and a post-operative man with frozen eggs, which will be of no help if they subsequently tried to avail themselves of assisted reproduction with a partner of the opposite sex. Same-sex couples cannot use assisted reproduction in any case. Loosening the rules on assisted reproduction is, in my opinion, to be recommended, especially the opening of procedures to single women. This would not just benefit the transgender community, but also lesbian-identified women and single heterosexual women.

As for surrogate motherhood, such arrangements are made difficult by the unequivocal rule that the mother of a child is the woman who gave birth to it.[110] While there are occasional media reports on surrogate motherhood happening in the Czech Republic (though not for transgender people), the situation of the would-be parents is extremely precarious, as any contract against the surrogate mother would be unenforceable.[111] Any subsequent adoption – the only option for parenthood to pass from the biological and legal mother – would thus be uncertain.

As for adoption, it is available to married couples as well as single persons, but it is explicitly excluded for same-sex registered partners.[112] There is no legal obstacle for transgender persons after transition to adopt a child. The court, in deciding on adoption, assesses the possible parent(s), their 'personal characteristics and lifestyle'.[113] While I am unaware of any adoption proceedings relating to transgender persons, whether successful or unsuccessful, I believe there to be scope for discrimination, based on societal prejudice.

4.2. EXISTING RIGHTS, DUTIES AND ENTITLEMENTS

Section 29(2) of the Civil Code states that 'the sex change does not affect the personal status of an individual, nor his[114] personal or proprietorial status'. The 2007 Analysis by the Working Group for the Issues of Sexual Minorities of the Minister for Human Rights and National Minorities mentioned that although

108 Sec. 29(1) 89/2012. The requirement of sterilisation has always been part of the operative procedure, even though it was only legally codified recently.
109 Secs. 3–11 Act No. 373/2011 Coll.
110 Sec. 775 Act No. 89/2012 Coll.
111 Explanatory memorandum to Sec. 775 ibid.
112 Sec. 13(2) Act No. 115/2006 Coll., on Registered Partnership.
113 Sec. 799 Act No. 89/2012 Coll.
114 The generic masculine is used in Czech legal provisions.

'the legal continuity of transsexual people is generally recognised in the Czech Republic; there still exist though a number of situations where this right is not respected by public or private subjects.'[115] Because of the change of birth number, many public and private institutions see post-operative transgender persons as new individuals. The Analysis mentions, for example, problems which the transgender community faces with banks: '[post-operative transsexuals] have to pay fees for services (mainly fees for registration or for holding an account), which they had already paid once, or they are denied advantages to which they had legal entitlement up until that time (e.g. banking and insurance services bound to the previous client history).'[116] Problems also arise for transgender entrepreneurs who run businesses as individuals. The tax identification number (*DIČ*) for self-employed persons is created using a birth number. Difficulties with having this change implemented following the change in birth number, yet still maintaining legal continuity, have been reported.[117]

As for the impact of recognition on pre-existing familial relationships, historically a proof of unmarried status has always been required by doctors.[118] The requirement is now contained in the Act on Specific Health Services[119] and the expert committee requires proof of divorce or dissolution of registered partnership before they contemplate a case.[120] Moreover, in cases where the marriage or registered partnership has not been dissolved, the new Civil Code stipulates that the marriage or registered partnership ceases to exist *ex lege* as a consequence of the transition process.[121] The explanatory memorandum to the Civil Code explains that this subsidiary provision is meant to catch cases where the divorce or dissolution was meant to happen abroad but has not taken place. The legislator is thus clearly very (heteronormatively) concerned to prevent a situation where two people of the same sex find themselves married.[122]

As for parental rights, historically doctors were reluctant to start treatment in parents of young children.[123] In 2002, Vlasta Raichlová and Ivo Procházka remarked that 'surgery is not as a rule performed on parents or adoptive parents of small children'.[124] Baršová notes that transgender parents who want to undergo surgery have usually been required to 'arrange' their relationship with their

115 Working Group for the Issues of Sexual Minorities, *2007 Analysis*, p. 38.
116 Ibid., p. 39.
117 I thank Dita Jahodová for sharing the anecdotal evidence with me.
118 Raichlová and Procházka,above n. 43, p. 109.
119 Sec. 21(2)(b) Act No. 373/2011 Coll.
120 O. Pechová, *Transsexuální lidé v kontaktu s veřejnou správou* [Transgendered people in contact with public authorities] Multikulturní centrum Praha <www.mkc.cz/uploaded/antidiskriminace/MKCA4korekturaIII.pdf>, 2007, p. 61.
121 'Marriage or registered partnership shall cease to exist.' Sec. 29(2) Act No. 89/2012 Coll.
122 It is true that the situation where two people of the opposite sex find themselves in a registered partnership is equally illegal under Czech law. It is, surely, however, of less concern to gender traditionalists.
123 Raichlová and Procházka, above n. 43, p. 109.
124 Ibid., p. 109.

children.[125] Although Czech law does not allow parents to relinquish 'parental responsibility',[126] a court can strip them of their rights and obligations. Parents can agree to, and the court can also minimise, parental involvement – custody and visitation rights – in connection with divorce proceedings. The practice, by doctors and social workers, to require transgender persons who decide to transition to curtail their contact with children has no basis in law, but continues to be reported.[127]

The relationship with children is now explicitly addressed by the Civil Code. With regard to a parent's rights and obligations to his or her children (including 'financial'), the provisions governing divorce should apply – *i.e.* parental rights and obligations are not adversely affected by the legal recognition of preferred sex/gender. However, the provision specifically mentions that a 'court will decide *ex officio*' as to the care of children. This could be understood to imply that parents who have transitioned are removed from the general regime of family law as far as the care for children is concerned. This could mean that courts are given greater discretion with regard to awards of custody and visitation rights to transgender parents, although such an interpretation should be seen as breaching the principle of equality. The relative novelty of the provision means that there has not yet been relevant case law.

In terms of the impact of legal recognition on other existing relationships, discrimination has been reported to occur most often in the area of services, but also in employment relationships.[128] According to the 2007 Analysis, the most vulnerable individuals are those who are currently undergoing treatment, when their documents do not correspond with their appearance and identity, as well those transgender people who do not want to, or cannot undergo, a full process of medical and physical transition.[129] Olga Pechová[130] reported a 2004 case of discrimination against an MtF post-operative transsexual woman in accessing employment in the Czech Army. Although the job applicant, J.B., fulfilled all the job criteria, when the potential employer discovered that the individual had submitted to sex/gender confirmation surgery, she was not given a contract. While originally the explanation given by the Army was 'transsexuality', a later appeal decision of a military health commission cited 'health problems'. Unfortunately, the applicant eventually decided against pursuing a discrimination claim before the courts.[131] Anecdotal evidence suggests that there is also widespread prejudice against transsexual and transgender people working with children,

125 Baršová, above n. 31.
126 Sec. 858 Act No. 89/2012 Coll.
127 Pechová, Raichlová and Procházka, above n. 17, p. 142; see also Working Group for the Issues of Sexual Minorities, *2007 Analysis*, p. 40.
128 Working Group for the Issues of Sexual Minorities, *2007 Analysis*, p. 38.
129 Ibid., p. 38.
130 Pechová, above n. 120.
131 Ibid., p. 15.

including employment discrimination in the education sector.[132] Unfortunately, to the author's knowledge, no cases against discrimination on the basis of gender identity have yet been brought before the Czech courts.

V. LEGAL CHALLENGES TO THE EXISTING RULES

There have been no court challenges to the existing legal framework.[133] The office of the Czech Public Defender of Rights has registered on average two submissions a year related to mistreatment of transgender persons since 2012, which is well below the average for other grounds for discrimination. Petr Polák, the Head of Department of Equal Treatment in the Office of the Public Defender of Rights, thus speaks of serious under-reporting in relation to transgender issues.[134]

The lack of legal challenges before courts or of submission against discrimination or human-rights-incompatible treatment of transgender people may relate to the fact that some of the legal rules are quite new. It may also reflect the relative novelty of the LGBT movement in the Czech Republic, especially as regards transgender persons,[135] and the lack of framing of their concerns in terms of rights. There has been some community organising among transgender people. The NGO, TransForum, active since the late 1990s, is dedicated to 'supporting its members in all phases of their life, fighting against discrimination towards transgender persons in the workplace and life in general, and awareness-raising'.[136] Transgender issues are also addressed by the LGBT umbrella organisation, PROUD.[137] PROUD made it part of their agenda in 2012 to attempt to change the legislation as regards mandatory sterilisation and divorce.[138] The organisation comments, however, that although several communities of transsexual and transgender people exist in the Czech Republic, they have so far not been involved in activism and even less so in campaigning for legal change.[139]

The reasons for the reluctance to engage publically in trans rights advocacy are probably similar to those which transgender communities have experienced in

132 Ibid., p. 15.

133 The Constitutional Court database <http://nalus.usoud.cz/Search/Search.aspx>, the Supreme Court database <www.nsoud.cz/>, the Supreme Administrative Court database <www.nssoud.cz/main0col.aspx?cls=JudikaturaExtendedSearch> and the Ministry of Justice database containing other higher courts decisions <www.nsoud.cz/Judikaturans_new/judikatura_vks.nsf/webSpreadSearch> were searched for 'sex change', 'transsexual' and 'transgender'.

134 E-mail communication with Petr Polák, Head of Department of Equal Treatment in the Office of the Public Defender of Rights, 9 February 2015.

135 The gay and lesbian communities are better established, and considerably more scholarly attention has been paid to them.

136 Its websites <translide.cz> and <transsexualita.cz> offer practical tips about the transition process, among other things.

137 <www.proudem.cz>.

138 PROUD, 'Výroční zpráva PROUDu 2012' [PROUD annual report 2012] <www.proudem.cz/component/attachments/download/17.html> accessed 09.02.2015.

139 <www.proudem.cz/trans-lide.html>.

other European countries: the prevailing social prejudices mean that transgender rights trailblazers can expect to pay a heavy personal price for their advocacy. But there probably are some Czech – or even more generally post-communist Central European – specifics as well. First, debates about how to deal with heterogeneity in society (be it gender, ethnic, etc.) have been delayed compared to Western Europe because of the intellectual isolation of these countries during the state socialist period. Second, the transgender community might be fragmented by the current legal regime and medical attitudes, which by and large caters to those who want to undergo surgical transition. For this part of the community a challenge to the heteronormative, sex-binary based current approach might not be as urgent as for those who wish to live in ways not conforming to traditional gender expectations without undergoing treatment.

A debate on the human rights compliance, and thus constitutionality, of the 2012 framework, set up by the Act on Specific Health Services and the 2014 Civil Code, is probably not imminent. And it might be a while before any challenge to requirements such as mandatory sterilisation and dissolution of marriage or registered partnerships reaches the courts, or before a change is seriously considered in the political arena.

LEGAL STATUS OF TRANSSEXUAL AND TRANSGENDER PERSONS IN DENMARK

Natalie VIDEBÆK MUNKHOLM

Contents

I. LEGAL FRAMEWORK AND STATISTICS

1.1. SPECIFIC LEGAL RULES DEALING WITH TRANSSEXUAL OR TRANSGENDER PERSONS

1.1.1. The General Constitutional Framework of Denmark

Denmark is a small Scandinavian country with a population of approximately 5.6 million (2014).[1] Denmark is characterised by a high standard of living, the highest taxes in the world, democracy, and universal welfare services, such as free health care and free education. The labour market is flexible, the Danish Model, and men and women work almost the same number of hours. Around 11% of the population are immigrants or their descendants. Denmark is a member of, *inter alia*, the European Union (EU), the United Nations (UN), the North Atlantic Treaty Organization (NATO), the Organization for Economic Co-operation and Development (OECD), the World Trade Organization (WTO) and the International Monetary Fund (IMF). Denmark is reported to have the lowest levels of corruption in the world,[2] and Danish people are supposedly the happiest individuals.[3]

The legal foundation in Denmark is the Constitution.[4] Denmark is a constitutional monarchy, and the powers of state are divided between three institutions.[5] The legislative power rests with the Parliament and the king (the government), the executive power belongs to the king (the government), and the

---

1 <http://denmark.dk> accessed 05.05.2015.

2 e.g. Denmark ranked world first in the 2014 World Justice Project Rule of Law index <http://data.worldjusticeproject.org/#/index/DNK> accessed 23.07.2014.

3 Since 1973 Denmark has been at the top of the Eurobarometer on well-being and happiness. In 2012 Denmark was ranked the happiest nation in the world in the World Happiness Report commissioned by the UN, *cf.* <http://denmark.dk> accessed 05.05.2015.

4 *Grundloven* (the Constitutional Act of Denmark) 5 June 1953, available in English at <www.eu-oplysningen.dk/euo_en/facts/constitution/> accessed 05.05.2015.

5 The Constitution §§ 2 and 3.

judicial power is invested in the courts, who interpret and apply legislation and regulations.

Statutory laws – in the form of Acts – are passed by the Parliament. Parliament can, and does, delegate rulemaking competencies to administrative bodies (the Ministries) through Acts. The Ministries issue Administrative Orders,[6] which cannot expand or derogate from the delegated mandate. Administrative orders are binding, whereas Administrative Guidelines,[7] issued according to Administrative Orders, are binding for public authorities only, not private citizens. Lower level rules cannot derogate from or expand upper level rules – a distinct hierarchical system of regulation. Public authorities administrate the rights and obligations of citizens, and manage the everyday application of rules in real life. The authorities must apply their discretionary powers in accordance with the procedures and within the framework of the rules (Acts, Administrative Orders, Administrative Guidelines, and the recognised principles of public administration, such as the principle of equality). The rule of law is a fundamental principle in the Danish legal system.

Statutory Acts with associated Administrative Orders and Guidelines are the foundation of rules establishing the legal framework around transsexual or transgender persons in Denmark.

1.1.2. Specific Legal Rules Dealing with Transsexual or Transgender Persons in Denmark

The Danish language does not distinguish between the terms sex and gender, as the generic term '*køn*' refers to social and biological aspects alike. The term '*transseksuel*' (transsexual) is used as a clinical diagnostic term referring to the World Health Organization (WHO) diagnosis classification of gender identity disorder (GID).[8] The term '*transkønnet*' (transgender) refers to a person's experience of discrepancy between the biological gender and the gender with which the person identifies.[9] A person can be transgender without being transsexual. Transgender is politically viewed as a gender identity issue, not a

---

6 The Danish term is '*Bekendtgørelser*'.

7 The Danish term is '*Cirkulærer*' or '*vejledning*'. The Administrative Guidelines contain examples and detailed descriptions in an everyday explanatory language.

8 WHO diagnosis classification ICD-10, transsexuality is in the group 'gender identity disorders'. The diagnosis F64.0 Transsexualism is characterised by 'the desire to live and be accepted as a member of the opposite sex, usually accompanied by the wish to make one's body as congruent as possible with one's preferred sex through surgery and hormonal treatment' <www.who.int/classifications/icd/en/GRNBOOK.pdf> accessed 05.05.2015. The administrative orders concerning access to medical treatment for transsexuals are in the process of being amended.

9 *Rapport fra arbejdsgruppen om juridisk kønsskifte, JustitsMinisteriet*, 27.02.2014 (Report of the working group on change of legal gender, Ministry of Justice), p. 6.

sexual orientation issue.[10] In some types of legislation, gender identity is still protected under the umbrella term 'sexual orientation'.[11] The term transgender entered Danish legislation in May 2005, but without a specific legal definition.

A major amendment to Denmark's laws concerning the legal gender of transgender persons was passed by Parliament in June 2014.[12] The amendment established that, as of 1 September 2014, the legal gender of a person is distinguished from biological gender, and, in many areas of law, congruence between legal gender and biological gender is no longer a requirement.

In Denmark, the key to a person's legally recognised gender is their CPR number. According to the Act on the Central Person Registry (*CPR-loven*),[13] all citizens are issued with a ten-digit personal identification number (CPR number). The last digit indicates whether the person has a female gender (even numbers), or a male gender (uneven numbers).[14] Thus, gender is immediately recognisable from the CPR number. The amendment made it possible to change the legal gender indicated in the CPR registry without requiring a change of biological gender.[15]

Acts establishing rights and obligations on the basis of legal gender refer back to the CPR number. This is the case for the Passport Act (*Pasloven*)[16] and the Name Act (*Navneloven*).[17] The Name Act states that a first name cannot indicate the opposite gender of the person carrying the name,[18] and, to this end, the Ministry of Social Affairs publishes a list of pre-approved girls' and boys' names.[19] With the amendment, a transgender person can gain access to a name and a passport corresponding to the gender the person identifies with, without having to involve any health authorities.

Other areas of law continue to refer to the biological characteristics of a person, such as access to certain health programmes established in the Health Act (*Sundhedsloven*).[20] Likewise, the regulations in the Children's Act (*Børneloven*),[21] which establish parental roles, continue to use the biological gender as reference.

---

10 Ministry of Justice Answer to the Parliament Committee on Equality, Question 2, B 28, 2012–13, of 27.05.2013.

11 e.g. *Straffeloven* (The Criminal Act) no. 871 of 04.07.2014, it is considered aggravating circumstances if a criminal act is motivated by another person's sexual orientation 'or the like', *cf.* §81 nr. 6 and §266b, *cf.* the Minister of Justice Answer to the Parliament Legal Committee, B 50, question 2, 2009–10, 19.02.2010, stating that gender identity is covered by 'the like'.

12 *Lovforslag L 182 and L 189* (Amendment Acts L182 and L189) proposed 30.04.2014, passed by Parliament on 11.06.2014.

13 *Lov om Det Centrale Personregister, Lovbekendtgørelse nr. 5 af 09.01.2013.*

14 *Bekendtgørelse om folkeregistrering mv., nr. 1153 af 23.11.2006*, § 1 stk. 2 (Administrative Order under the CPR Act).

15 *Lov om ændring af lov om Det Centrale Personregister, lov nr. 752 af 15.06.2014* (Amendment Act to the CPR Act) § 1 no. 1.

16 *Lov om pas til danske statsborgere m.v., Lovbekendtgørelse nr. 900 af 08.09.2008.*

17 *Navneloven, Lovbekendtgørelse nr. 392 af 01.05.2012.*

18 The Name Act § 13 stk. 2.

19 The Name Act § 14 stk. 1.

20 *Sundhedsloven, Lovbekendtgørelse nr. 913 af 13.07.2010.*

21 *Børneloven, Lovbekendtgørelse nr. 18 af 10.01.2014.*

Legislation relating to medical treatment and procedures for transsexualism is likewise regulated in the Health Act and the Administrative Order and Guidelines issued accordingly. These rules will be adjusted as a consequence of the amendments to change of legal gender in June 2014. Finally, the Danish equality and anti-discrimination legislation, *i.e.* the Equality Act (*Ligestillingsloven*)[22] and the Equal Treatment Act (*Ligebehandlingsloven*),[23] protect against discrimination on the basis of gender, including gender identity.

The legal rights and protections will be further elaborated on below.

1.1.3. Historic Development Leading up to the Current Legal Framework

Transgender/transsexual rights have developed within society over a period of years, primarily being advanced by interest groups,[24] a number of political parties[25] and certain legal scholars.[26]

The issue has received increasing focus in Parliament in recent years.[27] In 2007, a proposal to Parliament aimed at ensuring transgender persons access to a list of rights, and at revising the process for obtaining access to gender confirmation treatments, was submitted but not adopted.[28] A similar proposal in 2008[29] was

22 *Lov om ligestilling af kvinder og mænd, Lovbekendtgørelse nr. 1678 af 19.12.2013.*

23 *Lov om ligebehandling af mænd og kvinder med hensyn til beskæftigelse mv., Lovbekendtgørelse nr. 645 af 08.06.2011.*

24 Primarily LGBT Denmark, Trans-Danmark, Foreningen af Transpersoner I Danmark (FATID, the Organization of Transpersons in Denmark), as well as individual activists.

25 Primarily left-wing party *Enhedslisten* (EL, the Unity List).

26 Legal publications on the issue of '*kønsskifte*' (change of gender) in the leading Danish legal periodicals *Ugeskrift for Retsvæsen* (UfR, the Weekly Law Review) and *Juristen* (The Lawyer) count merely seven articles in twenty years (1987–2006) most of which take an international human rights approach; one book, M. Holdgaard and B.L. Kristiansen, *Kønsskifte – juridisk set* (Change of gender – a legal view), DJØF, Copenhagen 2004; one book-chapter, M. Holdgaard and B.L. Kristiansen, '*Kap. 4 – Retspolitiske aspekter af fysisk kønsskifte*' (Legal political aspects of physical change of gender) in J. Evald and S. Schaumburg-Müller (eds.), *Om retspolitik* (On legal politics), DJØF, Copenhagen 2002; one article in English by M. Holdgaard, 'Family Life and Transsexuals – Developments in the light of changes in 'present-day conditions', 2003 (*EU-ret & Menneskeret)* 2, 70–80; and one country report in English for the European Agency for Fundamental Rights, B.K. Olsen, 'Legal Study on Homophobia and Discrimination on Grounds of Sexual Orientation – Denmark' including a section on transgender issues, February 2008 <http://fra.europa.eu/sites/default/files/fra_uploads/318-FRA-hdgso-NR_DK.pdf> accessed 18.08.2014.

27 See e.g. a search on the Parliament's webpage on the term '*transkønnede*' revealing an increasing frequency of proposals and questions <www.ft.dk/search.aspx?q=transk%C3%B8nnede&sf=&msf=&SortBy=SortDate&pageSize=&pageNr=3#search> accessed 20.08.2014.

28 B142 of 30.03.2007 <www.ft.dk/samling/20061/beslutningsforslag/b142/index.htm> accessed 20.08.2014, rendering 42 questions to the Minister of Health and Domestic Affairs.

29 B65 of 26.02.2008 <www.ft.dk/samling/20072/beslutningsforslag/b65/index.htm> accessed 20.08.2014, rendering 5 questions to the Minister. The view furthered by the then majority in the Parliament Health Committee, included that transsexual persons already had access to a change of name without a change of biological gender, that free choice of gender identification in the CPR registry would be too complicated to manage from a practical point of view as females might get drafted for the army, and males would receive invitations to mammography. The gender indication X in the passport was promoted instead of free choice of gender.

likewise not passed. In 2009, the issue of transgender identity being categorised as a mental disorder was raised. In 2010, general questions and contentions were lodged, and a proposal[30] was again forwarded but not passed.

A change of government occurred in 2011 and transgender and transsexual issues were part of the new government's Policy Scheme.[31] The Policy Scheme included a section on Equality and Diversity,[32] with a subsection on Sexual Equality. In this section, the government undertook to examine the regulation on gender confirmation measures, including the possibility of obtaining legal gender recognition without submitting to surgical intervention.[33]

In 2011, a range of national and international interest organisations, national and international health personnel, and national private persons put forward a five-page manifesto[34] to the Parliamentary Health Committee. The manifesto concerned the issue of transgender identity not being an illness. In 2012, a total of 19 questions were posed to different ministries, and a total of five requests were lodged by interest organisations. The Parliamentary Health Committee participated in a public, live-streamed consultation on gender identity and sexual orientation held by LGBT Denmark[35] in Christiansborg, the Parliament building.[36] The year 2013 saw one new proposal.[37] In addition, five requests were lodged by interest groups, and three additional questions posed to the ministers. In 2014, Parliament, for the first time, received contentions on the treatment of transgender rights from international entities, Amnesty International and the European Council.

The proposals, questions and contentions from 2007 to 2014 by and large focused on: (1) categorisation of gender identity as a mental disorder, (2) the right to decide one's legal gender, including the right to choose an appropriate first name, (3) procedures in the Clinic of Sexology, and (4) equal access to services, e.g. adoption.

The new government established a working group in 2013, consisting of representatives from the Ministry of Justice, the Ministry of Health, the Ministry of Equality and Church, the Ministry of Economy and Domestic Affairs, and the Ministry of Social, Children's and Integration Affairs. The working group's assignment was to examine the current legal protection of transgender persons in

---

30 B168 of 26.03.2010 <www.ft.dk/samling/20091/beslutningsforslag/b168/index.htm> accessed 20.08.2014, rendering 4 questions to the Minister.

31 *Regeringsgrundlaget: Et Danmark der står sammen, Oktober 2011*, <http://stm.dk/publikationer/Et_Danmark_der_staar_sammen_11/Regeringsgrundlag_okt_2011.pdf> accessed 14.07.2014.

32 Ibid., pp. 65–66.

33 Ibid., p. 66.

34 <www.ft.dk/samling/20111/almdel/suu/bilag/137/1062581.pdf> accessed 20.08.2014.

35 LGBT Denmark, The Danish National Organisation for Gay Men, Lesbians, Bisexuals and Transgender persons, <lgbt.dk/english/> accessed 19.01.2015.

36 Available at <www.ft.dk/webtv/video/20111/suu/tv.1301.aspx> accessed 05.05.2015.

37 B116 of 10.04.2013 <www.ft.dk/samling/20121/beslutningsforslag/b116/index.htm> accessed 20.08.2014, rendering 7 questions. The proposal was withdrawn in June.

Denmark, to consider international experiences, and to propose models for access to the legal recognition of preferred gender.

In its 77-page report,[38] the working group suggested that any procedure involving treatment as a prerequisite for recognition of legal gender would place Denmark in breach of international obligations, and that an amendment of the existing legislation was necessary. The report resulted in two amendment proposals in April 2014,[39] passed by Parliament in June 2014.

The legal situation for transgender persons in Denmark, until the amendments were passed in June 2014, had been subject to strong criticism over the years.

1.1.3.1. Outline of the Legal Framework before the 2014 Amendments

Before September 2014, a new CPR number with a changed gender marker could only be obtained after a full set of gender confirmation procedures had been completed.[40] This included removal of both testicles (orchiectomy) and penis (penectomy) for male-to-female transgender persons, and the removal of the uterus (hysterectomy) and both ovaries (bilateral oophorectomy) for female-to-male transgender individuals.[41] Reconstructive surgery was not, however, a pre-condition for legal recognition.

The Health Act, the former Administrative Order on Sterilisation and Castration[42] and Administrative Guidelines on Castration[43] established the criteria for access to gender confirmation surgery and other treatments within the public health system in Denmark.

In order to receive treatment a person had to be diagnosed with 'transsexualism'. The Clinic of Sexology, a highly specialised department at the National Hospital in Copenhagen, is the only entity in the public health system approved to observe, diagnose and recommend treatment for transsexual and transgender persons.[44]

The diagnosis of transsexualism was obtained via an observation programme at the Clinic of Sexology. The programme involved the expertise of a multi-disciplinary team of psychiatric, psychological, gynecological and plastic surgery professionals with knowledge about transsexualism. The observation programme

---

38 Report of 2014, above n. 9.

39 Above n. 12.

40 *Vejledning nr. 85 af 23.11.2006 om folkeregistrering* (Administrative Guideline no. 85 of 23.11.2006 on Person Registration), section 2.1.3.

41 *Vejledning om kastration med henblik på kønsskifte, nr. 1077 of 17.11.2006* (Administrative Guidelines on Castration for the purpose of change of gender), sec. 4. The Guidelines are repealed and are awaiting amendment, September 2014. See discussion of the proposed amendments below nn. 98 and 99.

42 Former *Bekendtgørelse nr. 14 af 10.01.2006 om sterilisation og kastration, herunder med henblik på kønsskifte.* Now replaced with *Bekendtgørelse om sterilisation og kastration, nr. 957 af 18.08.2014* (Administrative order on sterilisation and castration).

43 Above n. 40.

44 Report 2014, above n. 9, p. 9.

consisted of interviews with the applicant, interviews with parents or close relatives, psychological and psychiatric tests, accounts of the applicant's social history, measuring hormone levels and analysing chromosomes.[45] When a diagnosis of transsexualism was reached, the applicant was referred to initial treatment by local medical doctors and hospital departments, who administered hormones. Gender confirmation surgeries short of castration could likewise be carried out. The observation programme lasted approximately two years[46] from the initial meeting to the point when treatment could commence. The Clinic of Sexology did receive complaints about the behaviour of health personnel towards transgender persons,[47] the views expressed about transgender persons[48] and about undue delays in the programme.

If, after completing the programme of observation, a person wished to access full gender confirmation surgeries, including the removal of reproductive organs, the approval of the Danish Health and Medicines Authority (*Sundhedsstyrelsen*) had to be obtained.[49] Only persons whose current gender caused 'considerable mental torment or social deterioration',[50] and who was above the age of 21,[51] could be approved. The Clinic of Sexology likewise performed an evaluation of the person's level of torment as a legal criterion for approving full gender confirmation

45 Report 2014, above n. 9, pp. 11–12.

46 Report 2014, above n. 9, p. 8.

47 See e.g. question to the Minister of Health, question 199 of 18.12.2012 <www.ft.dk/samling/20121/almdel/SUU/spm/199/index.htm> accessed 16.07.2014, on the behaviour of the personnel at the Clinic of Sexology towards transgender persons, including the fact that in 2012 8 out of 15 persons had complained about demeaning behaviour of the personnel.

48 Commentary of Lisa Andersen to the Parliament Health Committee, November 2013, on the Health Minister's answer to the Parliament Health Committee on 26 November 2013, p. 2 <www.ft.dk/samling/20131/almdel/suu/bilag/167/1306872.pdf> accessed 16.07.2014, stating that the majority of men referred to the Clinic of Sexology with as wish to undergo MtF gender-correcting surgery are rejected with the diagnosis F65.1 in ICD-10, fetishistic transvestism, and are referred to by the health personnel as 'formerly transvestite men', a demeaning and insulting term.

49 Administrative Order on Castration § 5, *cf.* Health Act § 115, sec. 1 i.f. before the 2014 amendment.

50 The Danish term is '*betydelig sjælelig lidelse eller social forringelse*'. The term is the original term from 1935, which was added to the former Act on Castration. The Act on Castration was primarily aimed at minimising sex crimes by offering castration to the offenders. The addition in 1935 enabled non-criminals to gain approval for castration. It was the view, that castration would aid in easing the considerable mental torment and social deterioration a person wishing a different gender was experiencing, *cf.* Kristiansen and Holdgaard 2004, above n. 26, pp. 87–88. As part of an amendment to the Health Act, L 74 of 16.06.2005, the Act on Castration was repealed, and the section on access to castration was transferred to the Health Act. The terminology was however not updated and the condition of 'considerable mental torment' was upheld until the 2014 amendment. The term was changed in the 2014 Amendment to the Health Act, § 115, 1 now stating that a person can obtain approval for castration as part of a change of gender, if the applicant has the diagnosis transsexualism, has a permanent wish to be castrated, and can comprehend the consequences.

51 Health Act § 115, sec. 3 before the 2014 amendment.

surgery. If approval was given, the surgery was carried out at specialised surgical departments in Denmark or abroad.[52]

Some transgender persons instead chose to consult local or private doctors or hospitals in Denmark for treatments and surgeries short of removal of the reproductive organs, privately financing the costs.[53] However, in the view of the Danish Health and Medicines Authority's Disciplinary Board, any surgical procedures aimed at changing the gender appearance of a person should not be carried out without consulting the Clinic of Sexology.[54]

In practice, some people chose to travel abroad for full gender confirmation treatments and financed the costs privately.[55]

After surgery, the Danish Health and Medicines Authority acknowledged the 'change' of biological gender and informed the CPR office at the Ministry of Economy and Domestic Affairs. The CPR office registered the 'new' gender in the CPR registry and issued a new CPR number.

The Name Act regulates which last names, middle names and first names a person can have, stating that 'a first name cannot indicate the opposite gender of the person carrying the name'.[56] A list of pre-approved names, categorised as boys' or girls' names, is published by the Ministry of Social Affairs and Integration.[57] The Name Act uses the gender indicated in the CPR registry as the reference gender.[58] In reality, under the earlier framework, a person had to go through a full removal of the reproductive organs in order to change his or her first name to a preferred name. Likewise the passport, driver's licence, birth certificates and other official documents referred to the CPR registry to determine gender markers.

A few improvements were made regarding first name and passport gender indication. In 2005 an amendment to the Name Act made it possible for transgender persons with a diagnosis of transsexualism to change their first name

---

52 Some surgical performances have been carried out at highly specialised clinics in Belgium, paid by the Danish state, Report of 2014, above n. 9, p. 14.

53 Report 2014, above n. 9, p. 19.

54 In 2011, a surgeon at a private plastic surgery clinic in Denmark removed the breasts of a 15-year-old person, without consulting the Clinic of Sexology. The procedure was performed after many consultations with the person and the person's parents who all consented. This was criticised by the Danish Health and Medicines Authority's Disciplinary Board, underlining that surgical procedures with an aim to change the biological gender of a person is not cosmetic surgery but gender changing surgery. In carrying out the procedure without a full evaluation performed by competent sexology experts, the doctor had not acted in concordance with 'the norm for a widely recognized professional standard'. The doctor should have ensured an evaluation by a fully competent sexology expert, particularly with a view to the person's young age. <www.patientombuddet.dk/Afgoerelser_og_domme/Afgoerelser_fra_Sundhedsvaesenets_Disciplinaernaevn/Afgoerelser_med_navn/2012/1294528.aspx> accessed 11.07.2014.

55 Report 2014, above n. 9, p. 19. The number of persons obtaining gender changing surgery abroad is unknown, as not all apply for a change of legal gender upon returning to Denmark.

56 The Name Act § 13, 3.

57 The Name Act § 14, 1.

58 *Lovbekendtgørelse nr. 900 af 08.09.2008 af lov om pas til danske statsborgere, mv.*, and *Bekendtgørelse nr. 1337 af 28.11.2013, om pas mv., § 4, 5* (Administrative Order on Passports).

to the gender with which they identified. Surgery was no longer a requirement. In 2009, this option was extended to persons 'completely similar'[59] to transsexuals, likewise assessed by the Clinic of Sexology. The assessments required a minimum of 2–3 meetings, where the applicant had to prove that he or she lived and expressed him or herself in the gender opposite to the current legal gender.[60] Similar amendments in 2009 and 2010 enabled persons diagnosed as transsexuals or 'completely similar' by the Clinic of Sexology to obtain the gender indication 'X' in their passports.

The status before 2014 in effect placed the transgender person in a position where full gender confirmation surgery was necessary to amend their legal gender marker in the CPR registry. For treatments in the Danish health system, the person had to be diagnosed with transsexualism and assessed as experiencing 'considerable mental torment or social deterioration' by the Clinic of Sexology. A transgender person could change his or her first name and/or obtain the gender indication 'X' in his or her passport, with a diagnosis of transsexualism or with a certification that he or she was 'completely similar' to a person with a diagnosis of transsexualism.

1.1.3.2. Evaluation of the Legal Framework by the Working Group

In the public debate two overall approaches were prominent:[61] the basic rights approach – declaring that an adult person should have the right to make decisions about his or her own body, freedom and autonomy – and the nature approach – stating that gender is decided by nature or by God, and it should not be interfered with by legislation. In addition, it seems that the relatively small number of persons concerned was a valid argument against examining the issue in earlier years.[62]

The governmental working group of 2013 adopted a purely rights-based approach. International human rights obligations were used as the reference point, particularly the developing scope of protection for the right to respect of private life in Article 8 in the European Convention on Human Rights (ECHR).[63]

---

59 Amendment to the Name Act in 2009. The Danish term is *'ganske må ligestilles hermed'*.

60 *Navnebekendtgørelsen* (Administrative Order on Names), *nr. 1324 of 27.11.2013*, § 13, 1.

61 Kristiansen and Holdgaard 2004, above n. 26, p. 95.

62 Statement of the Ministry of Justice in the Minister of Health and Domestic Affairs' answer to question 161, alm. Del. Bilag 167, 2002–03, that 'according to the view of the Ministry of Justice, there was no reason to examine the current legislation on the issue of change of gender, and points out that less than 20 applications are received per year for approval of change of gender'.

63 European Convention on Human Rights as amended by Protocols Nos. 11 and 14, entering into force 1 June 2010, supplemented by Protocols Nos. 1, 4, 6, 7, 12 and 13 <www.echr.coe.int/Documents/Convention_ENG.pdf> accessed 02.09.2014.

Since 1980[64] the European Court of Human Rights (the Court), in a number of cases, has established that gender identity is protected as part of private life,[65] and that states are obliged to engage in positive actions to ensure the individual's personal development.[66] In 1992, the Court, for the first time, in a case against France, concluded that the lack of legal recognition of preferred gender post-confirmation surgery was a violation of Article 8.[67] At the same time, in cases against the United Kingdom, in 1986, 1990 and 1998, a lack of legal recognition of a person's preferred gender, post-surgery, was found not, per se, to breach Article 8.[68] In 2002, however,[69] the Court changed course. Owing to a continuing international trend towards increased social acceptance of transsexuals (the terminology used by the Strasbourg judges) and towards legal recognition of preferred gender for post-operative transsexuals, the Court stated that such legal recognition is a protected right under Article 8. Since 2002, 'the government could no longer claim that the matter falls within their margin of appreciation, save as regards the appropriate means of achieving recognition of the right protected under the Convention.'[70]

The matter of appropriate means was left within the margin of discretion of the Contracting Parties, as long as the legal rights of the new gender were secured after treatment. The Strasbourg Court has not taken a position on whether medical or surgical treatments, as pre-conditions for legal gender recognition, violate Article 8.

The margin of discretion is dynamic and developed by the Court in step with the development of society, attaching importance to the clear and uncontested evidence of a continuing international trend.[71] The working group of 2013 argued that international developments since 2002 have, in all probability, narrowed the margin of discretion for Contracting Parties:

In 2006 the Yogyakarta Principles on the Application of International Human Rights Law in Relation to Sexual Orientation and Gender Identity were developed by 29 human rights experts from 25 different countries.[72] Principle no. 3 concerns the right to legal recognition, stating that 'each person's self-defined sexual orientation, and gender identity is integral to their personality and is one of the most basic aspects of self-determination, dignity and freedom, and that no one

64 *Case of Van Oosterwijck v Belgium* of 06.11.1980, which was dismissed as domestic remedies had not been exhausted (4 dissenting judges).

65 e.g. *Case of Van Kück v Germany* of 12.06.2003, and *Case of Schlumpf v Switzerland*, of 08.01.2009.

66 e.g. *Case of B. v France* of 25.03.1992.

67 *B. v France.*

68 *Case of Rees v the United Kingdom* of 17.10.1986, *Case of Cossey v the United Kingdom* of 27.09.1990, and *Case of Sheffield and Horsham v the United Kingdom* of 30.07.1998.

69 *Case of Christine Goodwin v the United Kingdom* of 11.07.2002, and *Case of I. v the United Kingdom* of 11.07.2002.

70 *Goodwin* para. 93.

71 *I.* para. 65.

72 <www.yogyakartaprinciples.org/> accessed 14.07.2014.

shall be forced to undergo medical procedures including reassignment surgery, sterilisation or hormonal therapy, as a requirement for legal recognition of their gender identity.'

In 2009, the Human Rights Commissioner of the Council of Europe, Thomas Hammarberg, referred to the Yogyakarta Principles in his Issue Paper of Human Rights and Gender Identity.[73] The paper recommends the Member States to abolish sterilisation and other compulsory medical treatment as necessary requirements to recognise a person's gender identity in laws regulating the processes for name and sex change.[74]

In 2013 the Committee of Social Affairs, Health and Sustainable Development of the European Council passed the resolution 'Putting an end to coerced sterilisations and castrations'.[75] The resolution states that the concept of coercion is evolving in human rights law, and a situation can be viewed as coercion even if written consent is given.[76] The Assembly urged the Member States to revise their laws and policies as necessary to ensure that no one can be coerced into sterilisation or castration in any way for any reason.[77] In the report on the resolution, the chairperson mentions gender-correcting treatment being a condition for obtaining change of legal gender as an example of illegal coercion by the state.[78]

Even when gender-reassignment surgery is solely initiated by application, the substantial discrepancy experienced between the biological gender and the experienced gender can create a level of emotional pressure forcing the person to undertake surgical treatment in order to obtain a change of legal gender.[79] From this perspective gender-reassignment surgery is not voluntary, and therefore constitutes a violation of Article 8.

Finally, looking at national developments, the number of Member States no longer requiring physical procedures as conditions for change of legal gender is rising.[80] This could be evidence of an international trend, which would narrow the margin of discretion of the Member States.

International tendencies hence point towards viewing a requirement of surgery as an expression of indirect force towards the person. In the view of the working group, the Court could easily find that a requirement for surgical

---

73 T. Hammarberg, Council of Europe Commissioner for Human Rights, 'Issue Paper on Human Rights and Gender Identity', Strasbourg 29.07.2009, CommHD/IssuePaper (2009) 2 <https://wcd.coe.int/ViewDoc.jsp?id=1476365> accessed 14.07.2014.

74 Ibid., p. 44.

75 Parliamentary Assembly, Council of Europe, 'Putting an end to coerced sterilisations and castrations', Report, Doc. 13215, 28.05.2013 <http://assembly.coe.int/ASP/Doc/XrefViewPDF.asp?FileID=19755&Language=EN> accessed 11.09.2014.

76 Ibid., sec. 2.

77 Ibid., sec. 7.

78 Report of 2014, above n. 9, p. 30.

79 Ibid., p. 29.

80 Ibid., p. 31.

intervention would now constitute a violation of Article 8 and no longer lie within the margin of appreciation of Contracting Parties.[81]

Article 8(2), states that interference with the right to private life can only be legitimate if necessary in a democratic society in the interests of national security, public safety or the economic well-being of the country, etc. The Court assesses the proportionality between the interests of society in para. 2, and the right to private life in para. 1, on a case-by-case basis.[82] States have a margin of appreciation in the evaluation of which interferences are fair. In 2002, the Court stated that it must be taken into consideration that the conflict between social reality and law places the transsexual in an anomalous position, in which he or she may experience feelings of vulnerability, humiliation and anxiety.[83] In a 2007 ruling[84] a transgender person had gone through partial gender-correcting surgery, but the law did not regulate access to full gender confirmation procedures. This legislative gap had left the applicant in a situation of distressing uncertainty with regard to his private life and the recognition of his true identity. A delay of more than four years in adopting the relevant legislation was not a fair balance between the public interest and the applicant's rights.[85] In the 2002 and 2007 rulings, the Court put considerable weight on the applicant's rights, even pointing to feelings of distressing uncertainty, vulnerability, humiliation and anxiety. The level of distress could be the same for post-operative and non-operative transgender persons alike.[86] In balancing the individual's rights against the public interest, the working group suggested that it could not be said with certainty that societal interests can justify physically intrusive and irreversible surgical or medical treatments as a condition for recognising change of legal gender.[87]

The working group concluded that a change of existing Danish legislation was necessary, as failing to do so would – presumably – render Denmark in breach of international obligations, particularly Article 8 ECHR.[88] The working group proposed three new models for gaining access to recognition of legal gender: the declaration model[89] – legal gender can be amended on the basis of a declaration by the applicant; the assessment model[90] – legal gender can be amended on the basis of an assessment of a psychiatrist (not the Clinic of Sexology) that the person is transsexual or 'completely similar'; and the diagnosis model[91] – legal gender can be corrected on the basis of a diagnosis of transsexualism by the Clinic of

[81] Ibid., p. 34.
[82] Kristiansen and Holdgaard 2004, above n. 26, p. 72.
[83] *Goodwin* para. 77.
[84] *Case of L. v Lithuania* of 11.09.2007.
[85] *L.* para. 59.
[86] Report of 2014, above n. 9, p. 32.
[87] Ibid., p. 34.
[88] Ibid., p. 77.
[89] Ibid., p. 46.
[90] Ibid., p. 49.
[91] Ibid., p. 49.

Sexology. In the view of the working group, any framework involving medical or surgical treatment procedures would render Denmark in breach of international regulation.[92]

The results were fully embraced by the government, which chose to follow the most progressive of the three models, the declaration model. The government stated[93] that persons experiencing a discrepancy between their birth-assigned gender and the gender with which they identify should not be met with unnecessary barriers for legal gender recognition. By implementing the declaration model, the Danish regulation achieves the highest degree of consideration of personal freedom without compromising consideration for the rest of society. The model recognises and appreciates the wish of transgender persons for legal recognition of preferred gender, and gives the individual the complete competency to carry out the legal and social aspects of recognition. The amendment maintains a role for health professionals in the subsequent question of accessing irreversible and risky procedures, such as hormone treatments and surgery.[94] The terminology around access to gender confirmation procedures was likewise amended, replacing the criterion of 'considerable mental torment and social deterioration' with 'a diagnosis of transsexualism, an enduring wish of castration and being able to comprehend the consequences of this'.[95] Likewise, the legal age for castration was lowered from 21 years to 18 years of age.[96]

The amendments were adopted by Parliament, signifying a change to an official Danish individual rights approach, strongly inspired by international obligations, developments in the European Court of Human Rights, and developments in international human rights fora.

The procedures for access to medical or surgical processes within the public health system have likewise been amended. The Danish Health and Medicines Authority issued a revised Administrative Order on Sterilisation and Castration.[97] Draft Guidelines for Examining and Treating Transgender Persons

---

92 Ibid., pp. 52–53.

93 *L 182, Fremsat den 30. april 2014, bemærkninger til lovforslaget, 2.3. Regeringens begrundelse for valg af erklæringsmodellen med refleksionsperiode.*

94 Opposing views were forwarded in the Parliament Equality Committee Report on L182, *Betænkning afgivet af Ligestillingsudvalget den 28.05.2014, Til lovforslag nr. L 182, Folketinget 2013–14*, p. 2, maintaining there was nothing to gain from attempting to legislate away from the biological fact of one's gender, which could only be changed by surgery, that practical issues such as use of changing rooms were not resolved by the amendment, and that lack of correspondence between the biological gender and the gender indicated in the passport put the general public at a security risk.

95 *Lov om ændring af sundhedsloven og lov om assisteret reproduktion i forbindelse med behandling, diagnostik og forskning mv., lov nr. 744 af 15.06.2014* (Amendment Act to the Health Act) § 1 no. 19. Also see above n. 49.

96 Ibid., § 1 no. 20.

97 *Bekendtgørelse om sterilisation og kastration, nr. 957 af 28.08.2014.*

were submitted for public consultation in July to August 2014.[98] Responses to the draft Guidelines were mixed.[99] The transfer of the issue of transgender rights from the political legal sphere, passing the Amendment Acts, to the administrative medical sphere, publishing the Administrative Orders and Guidelines, has proven difficult. The amended Administrative Guidelines were published in their final form in December 2014.[100]

98 Danish Health and Medicines Authority, '*UDKAST – høringsversion, vejledning om udredning og behandling af transkønnede*', 02.06.2014 <www.ft.dk/samling/20131/lovforslag/l189/bilag/8/1376608.pdf> accessed 19.08.2014.

99 The draft received criticism for continuing to be patronising, stigmatising, paternalistic and complicating, for not being aligned with the International Standards of Care and the modern, international approach and recognition of the gender-dysphoric person's situation and needs, for still being based in Danish treatment practice which has not changed considerably over the last 50 years, and for continuing to treat transgender persons as having an illness and being incapable of managing his or her own affairs, referring to elements such as involving the parents (or other relatives) of the patient irrespective of the patient's age, continuing to require a diagnosis, using gender stereotypes to assess a patient's 'Real Life Experience', *cf.* Prof. Emer. L. Andersen's response <www.ft.dk/samling/20131/almdel/suu/bilag/509/1385865.pdf> accessed 16.07.2014, and <www.thranesen.dk/artikler/LGBT-DK_20140808_Hoeringssvar_SST_Vejl.pdf> accessed 19.08.2014. LGBT Denmark rejected the draft guidelines in full, and submitted alternative guidelines. The Committee of Ethics <www.etiskraad.dk/da-dk/Hoeringssvar/~/media/hoeringssvar/2014/2014-06-20-udredning-og-behandling-af-transkoennede.pdf> accessed 19.08.2014, was less critical, suggesting an increased focus on the involvement of the patient, dialogue with the patient, support and counselling when the patient is not approved for treatments, basic public administration rules of giving the reasons for a denial including information on complaints procedures. Even less critical was the Danish Institute of Human Rights <http://menneskeret.dk/files/media/hoeringssvar/hoeringssvar_afgivet_i_2014/juni_2014/juni%202014%20tilg%C3%A6ngeligt/68_b_vejledning_udredning_og_behandling_transkoennede.pdf> accessed 19.08.2014, but it did point out the need for clarifying that transsexuality is not a somatic or psychiatric illness. The National Council for Children <www.boerneraadet.dk/hoeringssvar/hoeringssvar-2014/hoeringssvar-til-udkast-til-aendring-af-bekendtgoerelse-og-vejledning-om-sterilisation-og-kastration> accessed 16.01.2015, criticised the draft for allowing sterilisation of minors (under 18), for not clarifying the involvement of the child, and for not ensuring that the child's opinion and views are expressed or that the requirements for consent of minors are strengthened.

100 *Vejledning om udredning og behandling af transkønnede, nr. 10353 af 19. december 2014* (Administrative guidelines on diagnosis and treatment of transgender persons). The final guidelines took into consideration many of the criticism, albeit not as far as LGBT Denmark would have preferred. The guidelines specifically state that transgender is not a somatic or psychiatric illness, that the condition of the patient must be the starting point for any processes, that all personnel have an individual responsibility to display diligence and awareness when interacting with patients, that the evaluation process must be performed in close dialogue with the patient and the patient has a right to be informed before and during the process, that involvement of relatives requires the consent of the patient, that the patient must receive an explanation as to the reasons for not being approved for treatment including information about a complaints procedure, and that the multidisciplinary team does not need to agree unanimously on recommendations of treatment. The guidelines clarify the roles of the entities involved, creating a floor as well as a ceiling for the processes and criteria that are valid in the evaluation process. However, still a multidisciplinary team must be involved before any treatment can commence, making access to e.g. hormonal treatment more complicated than before the amendments in 2014. The guidelines still leave the health personnel at the multidisciplinary team a generous margin of discretion, and it remains to be seen to what extent the guidelines succeeds in improving the situation and experience for persons consulting the Clinic of Sexology.

1.2. POSITION OF THE NATIONAL HEALTH INSURANCE AND/OR PRIVATE HEALTH INSURANCE COSTS

In Denmark national health insurance is on the state budget, financed via taxes. All persons have access to free medical treatment in the public health system, which is the primary health and medical services provider in Denmark. Alongside the free public hospitals and doctors, some private hospitals and specialised private clinics offer privately financed services. Private health insurances are, however, on the rise and are almost entirely financed by employers.[101] The main purpose of private health insurance is to get employees back to work as fast as possible, as the public health system suffers from long waiting lists. Private health insurance is primarily used to finance services by private health professionals, private hospitals or clinics,[102] where the waiting lists are not long.

When a person is diagnosed as a transsexual by the Clinic of Sexology, the person will be offered a number of treatments within the public health system, including medical and surgical procedures. All treatments are free,[103] financed by the state, and carried out either by the family doctor, at state hospitals or at highly specialised hospitals abroad, depending on the type of treatment.

If a person prefers not to use the public health system, or is not authorised for treatments by the Clinic of Sexology, the private health system or health providers in other countries can be used, in which case treatment must be financed privately.

101 Statistics show a significant rise in the number of private health insurances from the level in 2003 of approx. 228,000 insurances, to the level in 2013 of approx. 1,850,000 insurances: <www.forsikringogpension.dk/presse/Statistik_og_Analyse/statistik/forsikring/antalpolicer/Sider/Sundhedsforsikring_Antal_forsikrede_praemier_erstatninger.aspx> accessed 03.09.2014.

102 <www.forsikringogpension.dk/presse/Statistik_og_Analyse/statistik/forsikring/erstatninger/Sider/SundhedsforsikringFordelingaferstatninger.aspx> accessed 03.09.2014.

103 Publicly financed services include all tests and procedures involved in the observation process, counselling and therapy during the evaluation process as well as treatment with stop-hormones in case of a negative evaluation, treatment with gender hormones, breast-reduction surgery or breast implants, removal of ovaries, uterus, vagina and reconstructing neo-penis and neo-scrotum, removal of the testicles, penis, and reconstructing neo-vagina, voice and speech-training by audiologist, and, if necessary, surgery on the Adams' apple and vocal chords, epilation of hair growth, and a wig. Under the regulation on assisted reproduction, a person can be referred to deposit or freeze spermatozoon with a view to assisted reproduction at a later point in time, and deposit egg cells with a view to placing these back in the same woman at a later point in time. Follow-up procedures include pre-emptive measures for persons in continuing hormone treatment, including risk areas such as increased cardio-vascular risks, brittle bones and certain types of cancer, *cf.* Administrative Guideline 10353 of 19.12.2014, pp. 2–6.

1.3. STATISTICAL INFORMATION

1.3.1. Number of Transsexual and Transgender Persons

There are no official statistics on the number of transgender persons in Denmark. No official surveys have been carried out. Public registrations are not exhaustive, as not all transgender or transsexual persons have chosen to register for medical treatment, a change of first name or recognition of preferred legal gender on their passport.

The estimates available vary greatly. In the absence of reliable surveys on transgender persons, the 2013 working group looked at international estimates on transsexual persons, which indicate a maximum of 560 male-to-female transsexual persons and 187 female-to-male transsexual persons in Denmark; this corresponds with the estimate of the number of transsexual persons offered by a domestic interest group.[104] Another domestic interest group claims that up to 1% of the population, *i.e.* 56,000 persons, is transgender.[105] The civil authorities earlier received approximately 15 applications per year for a change of first name, on the basis that the person had been diagnosed as transsexual or 'completely similar'.[106] During the first seven days of the new procedure for change of legal gender, the authorities received 123 applications.[107] Perhaps with an easier access to change of legal gender, a more accurate estimate of the number of transgender persons in Denmark can soon be advanced.

1.3.2. Number of Gender Confirmation Procedures

Likewise, there are no official statistics on the number of people who submit to gender confirmation treatments in Denmark, as some persons receive treatment outside the public health system, and may not apply for the legal recognition of their preferred gender afterwards.

Under the former regime, applicants for gender confirmation surgery in the form of castration had to obtain a statement from the Legal Medical Council.

---

104 International estimates for Danish MtF range between 1 in 30,000 and 1 in 10,000, and for FtM between 1 in 100,000 and 1 in 30,000: Report of 2014, above n. 9, p. 7. The Danish activist group Gender Pioneers at <http://gender-pioneers.dk/?p=490> accessed 10.07.2014, estimates the same level, a little less than 1,000 transsexuals in Denmark, based on indexes in countries with comparable legislation.

105 T-group, a social subgroup of LGBT Denmark, estimates that approx. 1% of the population is transgender <http://transperson.dk/index.html> accessed 10.07.2014.

106 Report of 2014, above n. 9, p. 25.

107 Statement of the CPR registry to a newspaper <www.etik.dk/danmark/2014-09-08/123-personer-har-s%C3%B8gt-om-f%C3%A5-juridisk-k%C3%B8nsskifte> accessed 10.09.2014.

Statistics from the Legal Medical Council on the number of applications considered per year:[108]

Year	Applications for castration	Year	Applications for castration
1988	8	2001	6
1989	5	2002	6
1990	5	2003	6
1991	7	2004	7
1992	3	2005	5
1993	5	2006	7
1994	2	2007	4
1995	4	2008	2
1996	9	2009	4
1997	7	2010	6
1998	7	2011	7
1999	10	2012	10
2000	15	2013	7

The National Hospital in Copenhagen has performed a number of gender confirmation surgeries. The 2013 working group received the following statistics on[109] the number of gender confirmation surgeries performed at the National Hospital.

Year	Surgeries performed	MtF	FtM
2007	3	1	2
2008	2	0	2
2009	1	0	1
2010	3	1	2
2011	6	0	6
2012	6	1	5
2013	8	1	7

The Danish Health and Medicines Authority formally acknowledges that a person has undergone a medical gender confirmation process by application, and they provided these numbers for the working group.[110]

[108] Statistic provided by Gender Pioneers <http://gender-pioneers.dk/?p=493> accessed at 19.01.2015, based on the annual reports of the Legal Medical Council <www.retslaegeraadet.dk/%C3%85rsberetninger> accessed at 19.01.2015.

[109] Report of 2014, above n. 9, p. 14.

[110] Report of 2014, above n. 9, p. 19.

The number of 'change of biological gender' procedures (*i.e.* people who have submitted to a medical gender confirmation process) acknowledged by the Danish Health and Medicines Authority is given below:

Year	Total acknowledged	MtF	FtM	Performed abroad
2007	5	3	2	N/A
2008	4	3	1	N/A
2009	7	3	4	N/A
2010	1	1	0	N/A
2011	16	8	8	N/A
2012	15	8	7	7
2013	12	6	6	7

The three sets of statistics do not correspond, as the application for castration is considered before surgery is performed, as an application of acknowledgment does not need to be filed in the same year as the surgery, as not all post-operative transsexuals apply for acknowledgement, and as some applications are based on surgery performed abroad.

1.3.3. Other Statistics

There are no official statistics on the marital or parental status of persons applying for legal gender recognition or for access to gender confirmation procedures.

II. CHANGING LEGAL SEX AND/OR GENDER – PROCEDURE AND REQUIREMENTS

2.1. LEGAL PROCEDURE

A new administrative procedure for obtaining legal gender recognition is laid out in the remarks of the Minister of Economy and Domestic Affairs to the proposed Amendment Act to the CPR Act.[111] The CPR registry published corresponding guidelines on 25 August 2014.

The legal recognition of preferred gender in Denmark starts with an application for a new CPR number. The Amendment Act sets out a very simple procedure. A person wanting a new CPR number must accordingly:

---

111 The Minister of Economy and Domestic Affairs, remarks to the proposed Act. *Lovforslag L 182, Folketinget 2013–14, Fremsat 30.04.2014, Bemærkninger til lovforslaget, section 3.2 Lovforslagets indhold pp. 5–6.*

(1) submit a written application to the Ministry of Economy and Domestic Affairs,
(2) state in the application that the wish is based on an experience of belonging to the other gender, and
(3) reaffirm the application after a period of reflection of no less than six months.

A change of CPR number is a right when the person fulfils the above criteria. The competent authority is the Ministry of Economy and Domestic Affairs' CPR administration office. The office issues a new CPR number as an administrative decision.

The new CPR number is recorded in the CPR registry. As is always the case when a change of CPR number is granted, the original CPR number is retained in the registry, referring to the new CPR number. The new CPR registration will contain a reference to the original number. All information in the CPR registry from the original number will be transferred to the new number, which will from then on be the basis for all new registrations.[112]

The records are accessible only to public authorities or private persons who have been granted this right by law, by administrative order according to law, or have been authorised by the Ministry of Economy and Domestic Affairs.[113] The access to the personal information data registered in the CPR registry is regulated in the Act on Personal Data,[114] implementing the European Council Directive 95/46/EC of 24 October 1995.

2.2. OFFICIAL DOCUMENTS

The applicant will automatically receive a new National Health Card (*sundhedskort*) with the new CPR number. The person will be required to change his or her first name in order to comply with the regulation in the Name Act. A change of first name involves an application to the local person registry authority, and includes a small fee. An applicant wishing to renew additional personal documents, such as a passport, driver's licence, birth certificate, etc., must take the initiative for this. New personal documents will be issued according to the normal procedures laid out in the individual statutes, including potential fees. The issuer will access the information in the CPR registry, and the new document will be updated with the correct gender and new first name.

112 Remarks above n. 106, section 3.1. *Gældende ret*, p. 5.
113 CPR Act § 34, 1.
114 *Lov om behandling af personoplysninger, Lov nr. 429 af 31.05.2000.*

2.3. LEGAL REQUIREMENTS

All persons eligible for a CPR number can apply for a change of CPR number. The CPR Act covers all persons who are registered as residing (intended residence of more than three months) or born in Denmark, work for a Danish employer and make payments to the Public Pension Fund (*ATP*), or become part of a taxation review by the Danish tax authorities.[115] The personal scope of the Act is not limited regarding access to legal recognition of preferred gender.

It is a condition that the person is 18 years of age at the time of application.[116]

The only substantive condition is the reason for the application. The person must declare that the application is made out of an experience of belonging to the opposite gender. The personal declaration suffices. The statement is not tested, no health professionals are involved, and the person's mental or physical health is not assessed.

A reflection period of six months is established in order to minimise the risk of impulsive applications, and minimising the risk of a person regretting the decision. The person will be able to use the six months to live in his or her preferred gender, but it is not a legal requirement. Six months after the time of application, the person must re-affirm his or her wish in writing to the CPR office, who then issues the new CPR number.

If the Ministry of Economy and Domestic Affairs in some way becomes aware that the declaration is false, normal public administration principles allow the CPR administration to withdraw approval and to re-issue the person with the original CPR number. Under certain circumstances, the action of false declaration could result in a penalty according to § 163 of the Criminal Act.[117]

III. CONSEQUENCES OF THE CHANGE OF LEGAL SEX AND/OR LEGAL GENDER

3.1. FUTURE RIGHTS, DUTIES AND ENTITLEMENTS

As mentioned above, legal gender is the gateway to all rights and obligations based on formal legal gender, including new identification documents and change of first name.

115 CPR Act § 3, 1, (1)–(3).
116 *Lov om ændring af CPR-loven, nr. 752 af 25.06.2014*, (Amendment Act to the CPR Act) § 1, 1.
117 The Criminal Act § 163 includes penalties or up to four months' imprisonment.

3.1.1. *Military Conscription*

The Danish Constitution[118] states that every male person able to bear arms must do mandatory military service. Danish males are drafted for military inspection around their 18th birthday.[119] Males and females are both invited to volunteer as well.[120] The conscription of males is carried out on the basis of the CPR registry. Legal males will be conscripted for military service, even if they have female reproductive organs, and will be obliged to serve if otherwise found fit for service. A legal female will not be conscripted, even if she has male reproductive organs, but will, on an equal footing with other women, be able to volunteer for service. Concern was expressed by the Parliament Equality Committee during the debates that males would abuse legal gender recognition to escape military service. The Ministry of Defense considers such a risk to be minimal and very unlikely, and the Minister of Economy and Domestic Affairs agrees with the working group that in the event of abuse, the situation would be sufficiently covered by the false declaration provision in the Criminal Act.[121]

3.2. EXISTING RIGHTS, DUTIES AND ENTITLEMENTS

Not all existing rights are cancelled as a result of legal gender recognition. A person who obtains legal gender recognition will still be treated in the Danish legal system according to the purpose of each type of legislation, sometimes as having their legal gender and sometimes as having their birth-assigned gender. This fact was debated intensively in Parliament during debates on the proposals and the passage of the two amendment acts.[122]

3.2.1. *Health Care*

The Health Act regulates access to health services and care. As part of the 2014 amendments, the gender references in the Health Act were adjusted, clarifying that health services are offered to persons according to their birth-assigned

---

118 The Constitution § 81: Every male person able to bear arms shall be liable with his person to contribute to the defence of his country under such rules as are laid down by statute.

119 *Værnepligtsloven Lovbekendtgørelse nr. 225 af 13.03.2006* (Act on Military Duty) § 1.

120 Act on Military Duty § 21a.

121 Answer by the Minister of Economy and Domestic Affairs to question no. 7 of the Parliament Equality Committee on 26.05.2014 <www.ft.dk/samling/20131/lovforslag/l182/spm/7/svar/1139333/1373562.pdf> accessed 19.01.2015.

122 Parliament debate on 30.04.2014 on the proposals of L 182 and L 189 <www.ft.dk/samling/20131/lovforslag/l189/beh1/forhandling.htm?startItem=-1#alleindlaeg> accessed 16.07.2014.

gender.[123] The Health Act offers services referring to biological features, e.g. persons with female breast tissue are offered free mammography screenings,[124] a pregnant person has a right to receive pregnancy care and guidance, as well as abortion or multifetal pregnancy reduction if the criteria are met,[125] and cervical screening tests are offered to persons with a uterus. The Health Authorities send out invitations to screenings based on gender in the CPR registry, and legal males will not receive automated invitations. Instead, legal males with female biological features will have to contact the hospital at their own initiative to participate in medical programmes. It remains to be seen whether legal males making appointments for cervical smears or mammography scans will encounter barriers. The Ministry of Economy and Domestic Affairs recommend that a transgender person with a legal gender not corresponding with their birth-assigned gender (or with a legal gender not usually associated with the individual's biological characteristics) inform all health personnel about this, in order to minimise the risk of wrong treatments.[126]

3.2.2. *Assisted Reproduction*

The Act on Assisted Reproduction gives access to free assisted reproduction for single women or childless couples, not distinguishing between same-sex or opposite-sex couples. As part of the 2014 amendments, the definition in the Act was clarified so the term 'woman' now signifies a person with a uterus or ovarian tissue, and the term 'man' signifies a person with at least one testicle.[127] A legal male with female reproductive organs retains the right to enter into an assisted reproduction scheme, in order to become pregnant and give birth to a child, and vice versa a legal female with male reproductive organs can enter into an assisted reproductive scheme, and can father a child. The Amendment Act clarified that the right to assisted reproduction is attached to the biological gender of a person, not the legal gender.

---

123 *Lov om ændring af sundhedsloven og lov om assisteret reproduktion i forbindelse med behandling, diagnostik og forskning, mv., lov nr. 744 af 15.06.2014* (Amendment Act to the Health Act and Act on Assisted Reproduction, etc.).

124 The Health Act § 85, stk. 1.

125 Ibid., section VII, chapters 25–28.

126 *Vejledende information til personer, som har søgt om nyt personnummer begrundet i en oplevelse af at tilhøre det andet køn* (guidelines for persons having applied for a new CPR number), Ministry of Economy and Domestic Affairs, CPR office, 01.09.2014 <https://cpr.dk/media/218378/vejledende_information_til_brug_for_bekr_ftelse_af_ans_gning_om_juridisk_k_nsskifte.pdf> accessed 04.09.2014.

127 Amendment Act to the Health Act, above n. 118, § 2.

3.2.3. *Marriage*

The right to enter into marriage is regulated in the Marriage Act.[128] In 2012, the Marriage Act was amended in order to allow persons of same legal gender to marry on an equal footing as persons of opposite gender.[129] The rights and obligations are now the same for same-sex marriage as for opposite-sex marriage, and access to enter into marriage is not influenced by the legal recognition of preferred gender. The generic Danish term for a party in the marriage, '*ægtefælle*', is used to denote male and females alike in legislation.

The legal effects of marriage are regulated in the Act on Legal Consequences of Marriage,[130] which sets out the rights and obligations of the spouses. The Marriage Consequences Act was likewise amended in 2012, stating that rights and obligations that are specific to one gender in a marriage are not applicable in same-sex marriages.[131] One such example is the broader right of the wife to enter into legally binding agreements on behalf of her husband.[132] Parties in a same-sex marriage can only enter into legally binding agreements on each other's behalf within the specific areas of maintaining a usual household or the needs of the children.

The right to enter into or to remain in a marriage is not affected by the legal recognition of preferred gender.

3.2.4. *Parental Roles and Responsibilities*

The Children's Act[133] sets out the rules for allocation of legal parenthood (*i.e.* fatherhood, motherhood and co-motherhood, and the legal relationship between child and parent). The Children's Act is strongly founded in a principle that every child has a right to two parents. The civil authorities take an active role in allocating two parents for every child in Denmark.

An amendment to the Children's Act in 2013 extended the concept of legal parenthood to include co-motherhood. The two legal parental roles allocated by the Children's Act are (1) the birth-mother as the mother, and (2) a father or a co-mother (the woman married to, or partner of, the birth-mother).

Family patterns in Denmark are quite varied.[134] Under the former set of rules, parenthood was not a legal barrier for approval of gender-correcting surgery. A father who received gender-correcting surgery would remain the

128 *Ægteskabsloven, Lovbekendtgørelse nr. 1052 af 12.11.2012.*
129 Ibid., § 1.
130 *Lov om ægteskabets retsvirkninger, lovbekendtgørelse nr. 1053 af 12.11.2012.*
131 Ibid., § 53a.
132 The Marriage Act § 11 stk. 1.
133 *Børneloven, Lov nr. 460 af 7.6.2001.*
134 Statistics Denmark, the official Danish statistics bureau, issue regular reports on family life, available in English at <www.dst.dk/en/Statistik/emner/husstande-familier-boern.aspx> accessed 04.09.2014.

father in the view of the Children's Act, even if she (referring to the individual's preferred gender) had a female legal gender and physical characteristics which were typically associated with the male gender.

In relation to the Children's Act, the allocation of fatherhood and motherhood refers only to the biological reproductive capacities of the person, and does not use legal gender. Guidelines for allocation of parenthood include:

- the person giving birth is the child's mother, even if the mother is a legal male;
- if the mother is married to an individual who was assigned to the male gender at birth (due to biological characteristics), that individual is registered as the father without investigating the genetic fatherhood,[135] even if she has a female legal gender;
- if the mother is unmarried, the mother and a person who has male biological characteristics can agree to allocate fatherhood to the latter person,[136] even if she has a female legal gender;
- if the mother is married to an individual who has female biological characteristics, and the sperm donor is unknown or does not want to be the legal father of the child, the spouse or partner is registered as the co-mother,[137] even if he has a male legal gender;
- if the mother is unmarried, and a sperm donor is unknown or does not want to be the legal father of the child, the mother and an individual with female biological characteristics can agree to allocate co-motherhood to the latter individual,[138] even if he has a male legal gender;
- if the child is conceived via assisted reproduction, and the sperm donor is unknown or does not wish to be the father, the partner of the birth-mother is registered as the legal father if that person has male biological characteristics. This is so even where the partner has a female legal gender;[139]
- a sperm donor can be registered as the legal father, even if she has a female legal gender.[140]

The Act on Provisions for Children[141] establishes responsibilities for the financial provision of children. The Act corresponds with the Children's Act. With regard to economic provision for a child, a person will be given rights, duties and entitlements according to the parental role defined in the Children's Act,[142] based on the biological gender.

135 The Children's Act § 1.
136 Ibid., § 2.
137 Ibid., § 3a.
138 Ibid., § 3b.
139 Ibid., §§ 27 and 27a.
140 Ibid., §§ 27b and 27c.
141 *Lov om børns forsørgelse, lovbekendtgørelse nr. 1044 of 29.10.2009.*
142 Report of 2014, above n. 9, p. 69.

The Parental Responsibilities Act[143] allocates custody over children under the age of 18 years. The primary rule is shared custody between the two parental roles according to the Children's Act. In the case of separation and divorce, the Act likewise sets out the principles for continued shared custody, residence and visitation rights, as well as criteria for applications for single custody. The terminology in the Parental Responsibilities Act is gender neutral, referring only to the parent or parents of the child, as one parental role under the law has no formal preference over the other.

3.2.5. Adoption

Single persons and couples can apply for adoption under the Act on Adoption.[144] Since 2010 the Act has not distinguished between the gender of the applicants, and does not discriminate between same-gender and opposite-gender couples with regard to approval for adoption. The Act does not base the right to adopt on the gender of the applicants, and men and women can apply as single parents and couples alike. The amendment in 2010 provided for anonymous adoptions, in order to ease adoptions for same-gender couples.

The Act requires that couples are married at the time of approval,[145] marriage being available to same-gender and opposite-gender couples alike. If applicants are not married, the application is considered an application for adoption as a single parent.

Adoption of the child of a spouse does not require approval. Since 1999, this right has been gender neutral in Denmark, and same-gender couples hold the same rights as opposite-gender couples.[146] As no approval is needed, transgender persons are on a formal equal footing with other persons.

If a person or a couple wishes to adopt an unknown child, they have to be approved as adopting parents. When adopting as a couple the legislation does not refer to the genders of the applicants.[147] Adoptions from within Denmark are possible for all couples. International adoptions can be more difficult, as most donor countries do not approve of adoptions by same-gender couples. In July 2014, the first Danish gay couple succeeded in an international adoption,[148] proving that the option is real, not only a formal recognition.

143 *Forældreansvarsloven, Lovbekendtgørelse nr. 1073 af 20.11.2012.*

144 *Adoptionsloven, lovbekendtgørelse nr. 392 af 22.04.2013.*

145 The Act on Adoption § 5 stk. 2.

146 Ibid., § 5a.

147 By July 2012 only one domestic unknown adoption by a same-gender couple had been completed: <www.b.dk/globalt/mange-homoseksuelle-par-maa-opgive-adoption> accessed 05.09.2014.

148 <http://politiken.dk/forbrugogliv/livsstil/familieliv/ECE2347377/foerste-danske-homopar-adopterer-fra-udlandet/> accessed 05.09.2014.

Single persons can be approved as an adopting parent as well. The conditions for being approved as a single adopting parent are considerably stricter than those for a couple.[149]

Persons with mental illnesses are not allowed to adopt.[150] A transgender person wishing to obtain legal gender recognition would, before 2014, have had to obtain a diagnosis of transsexualism (hindering adoption) and also have his or her reproductive organs removed (hindering reproduction). In reality, the person would have to choose between the right to have children or the recognition of preferred legal gender. With the 2014 amendment, recognition in itself no longer pre-excludes a person from adopting or reproducing children.

3.2.6. Equality

Protection against discrimination at the workplace is regulated in the Equal Treatment Act (*Ligebehandlingsloven*),[151] which implements EU Directive 2006/54/EC (Equal Treatment Directive).[152] The Court of Justice of the European Union (CJEU)[153] in cases from 1996[154] and 2003[155] established that gender identity is protected under the gender classification within the Equal Treatment Directive.[156] Danish courts have not yet reviewed complaints about gender identity discrimination at the work place, and the Board of Equal Treatment has yet to assess a complaint.[157] However, as Danish courts are obliged to interpret national implementing legislation in observation of the interpretations by the CJEU, the Equal Treatment Act is viewed as protecting against discrimination on the basis of gender identity at the workplace.

---

149 *Adoptionsbekendtgørelsen, nr. 807 af 21.06.2013* (Administrative Order on Adoption), § 6a.

150 *Vejledning om vurderingen af adoptionsansøgerens fysiske og psykiske helbredsforhold, nr. 9316 of 17.06.2013* (Administrative Guidelines for the assessment of the applicant's physical and psychological health), chapter 4. An amendment to these guidelines in 1999 enabled persons with disabilities to be approved as adoptive parents, mainly aimed at persons with physical disabilities.

151 *Lov om ligebehandling af mænd og kvinder med hensyn til beskæftigelse, mv., lov nr. 645 af 08.06.2011.*

152 Directive 2006/54/EC of the European Parliament and of the Council of 5 July 2006 on the implementation of the principle of equal opportunities and equal treatment of men and women in matters of employment and occupation (recast), OJ L 204/23.

153 Then Court of Justice of European Communities (CJEC), since the 2009 Treaty of Lisbon the European Court of Justice (ECJ).

154 *Cornwall Case* C-13/94 from 1996.

155 *KB Case* C-117/01 from 2003.

156 Both cases referred to the earlier version of the Equal Treatment Directive, Council Directive 76/207/EEC, Art. 5(1), continued in the 2006 Directive as Art. 5.

157 The Board of Equal Treatment (*Ligebehandlingsnævnet*) is an administrative organ assessing all types of discrimination complaints. One case on alleged discrimination at the work place on the basis of gender identity has been filed, but the Board did not assess the complaint, below n. 173. Decisions of the Board of Equal Treatment are accessible online at <www.ligebehandlingsnaevnet.dk/naevnsdatabase/default.aspx> accessed 11.07.2014. The annual reports of the Board have in later years included a section in English, e.g. <http://ast.dk/publikationer/arsberetning-ligebehandlingsnaevnet-2012> accessed 11.07.2014.

Outside the workplace, the Equality Act (*Ligestillingsloven*)[158] aims to promote equality between women and men in all of society's functions, and to counteract direct or indirect discrimination, harassment and sexual harassment on the basis of gender.[159] The Equality Act implements EU Directive 2004/113/EC (Equal Opportunity Directive).[160] Although the terminology used is 'women and men', complaints about discrimination on the basis of gender identity have been assessed by the Board of Equal Treatment.[161] Although the Board has not yet rendered any of the situations in breach of the Equality Act, the assessments carried out recognise that transgender identity is a protected criterion under the Equality Act.

In the view of the working group of 2013, the protection against discrimination under Danish law does not depend on a certain diagnosis or whether hormonal/surgical intervention has been accessed. The issue is whether a person is being treated differently on the basis of the personal expression or appearance.[162]

3.2.7. *Existing Practical Issues*

The new legislation solves some of the problems experienced by transgender persons in their daily activities, but of course not all. The legislation enables correspondence between the person's preferred gender and the legally recognised gender.

The amendment legislation does not specifically take into consideration a number of situations, where discrepancy between the legal gender and the biological gender creates practical challenges. The issue of access to participate in sports on the basis of legal gender or biological gender is not mentioned, neither are practical everyday challenges relating to the use of changing rooms in public sports facilities,[163] or sleeping quarters when in the military,[164] in hospital or in prison.[165] Such issues were addressed in many of the questions of the Parliament Committees.[166] Likewise, the amendments have not touched on subjects such as existing employment on the basis of a certain gender (when legitimate).

---

158 *Lov om ligestilling af kvinder og mænd, Lovbekendtgørelse nr. 1678 af 19.12.2013.*

159 Equality Act § 1.

160 Council Directive 2004/113/EC of 13 December 2004 implementing the principle of equal treatment between men and women in the access to and supply of goods and services, Journal of the European Union, L 373/37.

161 See below under section IV.

162 Report of 2014, above n. 9, p. 67.

163 Question no. 4 of the Parliament Committee of Equality <www.ft.dk/samling/20131/lovforslag/l182/spm/4/svar/1139324/1373548.pdf> accessed 19.01.2015.

164 Question no. 5 of the Parliament Committee of Equality <www.ft.dk/samling/20131/lovforslag/l182/spm/5/svar/1139320/1373541.pdf>.

165 Question no. 3 of the Parliament Committee of Equality <www.ft.dk/samling/20131/lovforslag/l182/spm/3/svar/1139304/1373516.pdf>.

166 A list of all the questions by the committee and answers by the Minister are available online in Danish at <www.ft.dk/samling/20131/lovforslag/L182/spm.htm#dok> and <www.ft.dk/samling/20131/lovforslag/L189/spm.htm#dok> accessed 16.07.2014.

The solutions will unfold over the next years, as the Minister refused to give specific guidelines on these issues. The answers of the Minister of Economy and Domestic Affairs convey the current governmental view that the practical challenges already exist, and as such the amendments are not creating new problems. The Minister states that today no legislation regulates these situations, and further:

> 'the proposed amendment do not change, that these situations – as today – must be resolved amicably. I hold the view that these conditions are not fit for regulation by legislation. It is my belief, that persons using the option of obtaining a legal change of gender, as well as the surrounding society, appreciate that the community must function in consideration of each other. Therefore, as is the case today, it must be assessed in the individual situation, how one in the best possible way is considerate of the transgender person as well as of other persons e.g. regarding visits to the public swimming pool, where perhaps there is the option of using a separate changing room, or in hospitals, etc., where perhaps there is the option of screening around a bed, or allocating a single room, etc. The same is the case in relation to e.g. imprisonment in Danish prisons, where an amicable solution must be found in consideration of the transgender person and the other prisoners alike, as well as the particular conditions of this area'.[167]

As is evident, the Minister does not give much guidance to the personnel faced with decisions in everyday activities. The responsibility for finding a solution in practice is placed in the hands of the front personnel in prisons, swimming pools, etc., but without any clear guidance as to what is considered non-discriminating treatment of transgender person in the situation. Likewise, no guidance is offered on the weight the consideration of the surrounding society (the other prisoners, the other hospitalised persons or the other women in changing facilities for women) – if at all – can be given in the balancing of considerations. The terminology of mutual consideration poses the question of who should adjust and in consideration of what. Whether transgender persons are expected to adjust their behaviour in order not to upset the surrounding society, or whether surrounding society is expected to adjust in situations that in practice rather than in words will then reinforce one view over the other, is left open by the Minister.[168]

As the modern view of transgender persons' rights is only just unfolding in Danish society, and as the Minister leaves the matter in the hands of front personnel without specific guidance, it seems essential to support the development of public views with information or educational campaigns along

[167] The Minister's answer to question no. 3 <www.ft.dk/samling/20131/lovforslag/l182/spm/3/svar/1139304/1373516.pdf accessed 19.01.2015.

[168] The issue is far from trivial, as some of the other contributions in this book reveal. The Danish politicians chose to close the subject with guidance in terms of 'mutual consideration' and 'amicable solutions', which really does not give the front personnel any substantial aid in how to treat transgender persons on an equal footing.

with the amendments to legislation. Even politicians, who are informed on quite a detailed level,[169] and medical authorities, who work with transgender persons in their professional capacity,[170] apparently struggle with embracing a modern, respectful and dignified approach.

IV. LEGAL CHALLENGE OF THE EXISTING RULES

4.1. COURTS

Issues of gender identity, medical transition and legal transition have not been challenged in the courts. Persons having undergone gender confirmation surgery have used the court system on an equal footing to others.[171]

4.2. ADMINISTRATIVE ORGANS

In an administrative statement from the Department of Civil Affairs in 2000,[172] the marriage of a man and a male-to-female transgender individual, who had accessed gender confirmation surgery, was deemed valid. The Danish regulation at that time would have deemed a same-gender marriage null and void. The Department stated that, as the woman had undergone full gender confirmation procedures, she would fulfil the criteria under Danish law for recognition in her preferred legal gender. It had no influence on the validity of the marriage that she still retained a male legal gender, that the laws of Thailand did not recognise her transition or that she had used a false female name and a false passport.[173]

---

169 Respectful and dignified treatment of transgender persons has been an issue of dispute at the political level over the last years, lately expressed as the opposition of the right wing members of Parliament to pass the 2014 amendments to the CPR Act and the Health Act, the Minister of Health in the debate on the proposal of the amendment to the Health Act exclaiming 'Shame on you' to the right-wing parties voting against the amendment act, question 13 to L 189 at <www.ft.dk/samling/20131/lovforslag/l189/spm/13/svar/1140446/1375232.pdf> accessed 16.07.2014.

170 Above n. 98.

171 e.g. *TfS 1998.457* (Tax Law Weekly, 1998 p. 457). The complainant had undergone gender changing surgery from male to female; the court addressed the complainant as 'she'.

172 *TFA2000.227, CRD2000.1999-510-62, Civilretsdirektoratets udtalelse af 5. april 2000, vielse med kønsskiftet mand, der havde anvendt falsk navn, anset for gyldig* (Family and Succession Law Weekly, 2000 p. 227).

173 The Authority stated that the man could possibly have applied for a repeal of the marriage on the basis of false pretences, as the woman did not inform him of her gender changing surgery, but the three-year limit for such applications had passed.

4.3. THE BOARD OF EQUAL TREATMENT

The Equal Treatment Act and the Equality Act recognises gender identity as a gender.

The Board of Equal Treatment (*Ligebehandlingsnævnet*) is the administrative assessment board reviewing complaints about discrimination on the basis of all protected criteria, and in all types of situations.[174] The reviewed complaints about discrimination on the basis of gender identity show an inconsistent approach.

In 2001,[175] the (then) Equality Board ruled on a complaint about discriminatory statements made by a nurse and a doctor to a transsexual person in connection with a gender confirmation surgical procedure. The Equality Board stated that transgender identity is part of the competency of the Board, referring to EU case law on gender identity.[176] In cases where the parties disagree on the evidence, the Board will not assess the case, but refer it to review by the courts. In this case, the persons involved did not agree on the contents of the statements, the complainant intended to complain to the Minister of Health and the Civil Authorities as well, and the Board decided not to assess the complaint. Surprisingly the Board then in fact ruled that the complaint was not sustained. The Board could instead have dismissed the case on the basis of disagreement over the facts of the case, and referred further disputes to the civil courts.

In 2005[177] the Equality Board reviewed a complaint about discriminatory treatment on grounds of 'transsexualism'. A theatre school ran a three-year acting course with annual participation reviews. The school, after one year, recommended that a transgender student take a leave of absence and reconsider his future in theatre, due to inconsistencies between the aims of the school and the wishes of the student. The student perceived that the school's recommendation was an effective termination of his education, that the termination was motivated by his gender identity and that the school thought transgender persons were incapable of sustaining an acting career. In gender discrimination cases the burden of proof is shared. In this case, the Board assessed that the complainant had not established the basic facts making it presumable that the recommendation of the school was based on the sexuality of the complainant.[178] The Board using the terms 'sexuality of the complainant' and 'a transsexual student' in the ruling is inconsistent with the terminology used by the student and also with the protected criterion 'gender'

[174] The Board was established in 2009, a procedural improvement creating one administrative procedure for all types of discriminations. Before 2009, gender discrimination cases were assessed by the Equality Board (*Ligestillingsnævnet*), racial discrimination cases by the Complaints Committee for Ethnic Equality (*Klagekomitéen for Etnisk Ligebehandling*), whereas other types of discrimination complaints could only be assessed in the court system.

[175] Case no. 23/2001 of 21.11.2001.

[176] *Cornwall Case* C-13/94.

[177] Case no. 32/2005 of 19.12.2005.

[178] *'Nævnet finder ikke, at klageren har sandsynliggjort, at henstillingen fra indklagede om at overveje det videre forløb på skolen skyldes klagerens seksualitet.'*

in the Act, but it is representative of the lack of distinction in the public debate at the time.

In a case from 2011[179] the complainant was referred to in the transcript as 'transsexual'.[180] The complainant held a male CPR number and a female first name, and rented a room in the house of her ex-wife. The complainant felt discriminated on grounds of gender identity by the local authority's assessment, that she was in fact 'sharing a household' with the former wife, resulting in reduced pension payments. Further, she felt discriminated against by a case worker's behaviour. The local authorities stated that the assessment of 'household' was not based on the gender or gender identity of the persons,[181] that all citizens should be treated decently, including 'transsexuals', and that they regretted the complainant had felt hurt and humiliated by the case worker, the incident not abiding by normal standards. At staff meetings, it was subsequently pointed out that all citizens must be treated equally, and discussions as to which behaviours constitute decent and equal treatment had been held. The Board found that the complainant had not established facts giving rise to a presumption that discrimination on the basis of gender identity had occurred, as the gender identity had not influenced the review of the case. The Board also stated that cases of harassment on grounds of gender do not fall under its competency, only cases of discrimination on the basis of gender do. The view on harassment was corrected in a ruling in 2013 – see below.

In 2012[182] the Board ruled on a complaint from a 'transsexual'[183] tenant and her partner against the letting organisation. The person felt discriminated against because of the passivity of the letting organisation towards her complaints of harassment and discrimination by persons in and around the buildings. The letting organisation stated they had received twelve complaints, had reacted to all of them with an assessment of the situation, had sent letters to the persons involved including information to the complainant. The letting organisation had received three complaints from the complainant about the handling of the cases, and had also received complaints from other residents about the complainant and her partner. The Board found that the complainant had not established factual circumstances giving rise to a presumption that the complainant had been discriminated on grounds of gender identity. In the view of the Board,

179 Case no. 166/2011 of 11.11.2011.

180 The terminology of the ruling does not distinguish between transgender and transsexual persons, and the facts of the case cannot be used to determine whether the complainant was in fact transgender or transsexual. The lack of distinction is representative of the public debate at the time.

181 The complaints board later overruled the assessment of the local authorities, and the complainant received her full pensions.

182 Case no. 418/2012 of 21.11.2012.

183 The terminology of the ruling again does not distinguish between transgender and transsexual persons, and the facts of the case cannot be used to determine whether the complainant was in fact transgender or transsexual. The lack of distinction is representative of the public debate at the time.

nothing indicated that the gender identity of the complainant had influenced the assessment of the situations.

In 2013[184] the Board received the first complaint about discrimination in the workplace on the basis of gender identity. The complainant was assigned a male legal gender at birth but lived as a woman. She had submitted to medical intervention, including chemical castration. Interestingly the Board again referred to the complainant as a 'transsexual' person, whereas the complainant self-identified as being 'transgender'. She was in job-testing as a forklift operator in a supermarket storage area. On the third day, the employer instructed her not to continue. Both parties agreed that the complainant had done a good job operating the forklift. The complainant perceived that the decision to discontinue was based on her gender identity, especially her female appearance. This view corresponded with the notes of her supervising colleague, referring to discussions about her level of make-up, that she should use a hairband, that she should try to 'pack it up' during working hours between 4.30 am and 9.30 am, and that the employer was worried about customers' reactions. Also, the complainant explained that they had discussed the clothing regulation of the work place, a jacket and safety shoes, which the complainant had agreed to follow; however the complainant was only supplied with safety shoes, not a jacket, and thus the complainant continued to wear her own clothes. The employer stated that the decision to discontinue was based solely on the complainant's refusal to wear appropriate work attire as set out in the personnel handbook. The employer argued that,[185] even if the decision was based on the complainant's female appearance, she was not protected by the Equal Treatment Act, the Anti-Discrimination Act or the Equality Act, as the wish to dress in women's clothes is not an expression of sexual orientation, and as the gender of the complainant is irrelevant as long as the person has not undertaken gender confirmation surgery. The Board decided that the case could not be assessed by the Board as the parties fundamentally disagreed on the facts of the case. The case was dismissed by the Board and referred to judicial review instead.[186]

In 2013[187] the Board corrected their view on harassment as put forth in the 2011 ruling, now stating that harassment on the basis of gender is prohibited by the Equality Act and thus is within the competency of the Board.

Later in 2013,[188] the Board reviewed a case where the complainant had undergone gender confirmation surgery (female to male) and had obtained a new CPR number. The taxation information was not transferred to the new CPR number, and a tax case worker subtracted the highest level of tax from payments

---

184 Case no. 171/2013 of 28.08.2013.

185 The employer's arguments could indicate that the public is still in need of education about gender identity and equality.

186 By January 2015, the case had not yet appeared before ordinary court.

187 Case no. 241/2013 of 27.11.2013.

188 Case no. 249/2013 of 27.11.2013.

forwarded to the complainant over a period of months. The case worker did not access the relevant taxation information, or use the documentation supplied by the complainant. The complainant tried to reach the case worker via telephone and email several times, and only managed two conversations in a matter of three months. The complainant felt discriminated against because the case worker had not solved the problem, causing reductions in the monthly payments. The Board assessed that the local tax authorities were not in breach of the Equality Act, as the facts of the case did not indicate that the treatment was based on gender or legal gender recognition.

In 2014[189] the Board stated that an organisation was not in breach of the Equality Act. In a web-based questionnaire, the participants could indicate gender as 'male', 'female', 'transgender' and 'do not want to disclose'. It was not considered a breach of the Equality Act not to offer the option 'transsexual' as a separate gender indicator.

The Board has not yet held that any of the complaints in situations regarding gender identity were in breach of the Equality Act or the Act on Equal Treatment. The frequency of complaints is slowly increasing, and the complaints concern a greater variety of discriminative behaviours.

4.4. PRESSURE GROUPS

It is quite common in the democratic process in Denmark to invite activist groups to participate in the legislative processes and in the developments of the welfare state, a participation primarily carried out via dialogue.[190]

The interest groups LGBT Denmark, Trans-Denmark[191] and the Organisation of Transgender Persons in Denmark (FATID) have all been actively involved in the democratic process by influencing Parliament, submitting written responses, submitting letters and statements to the Parliamentary Committee of Health, visiting parliamentary committees for interviews, and by organising a public live-streamed hearing in the Parliament building. Some of the interest groups also have well-organised and informative websites, such as the LGBT[192] and privately maintained websites.[193]

---

189 Case no. 106/2014 of 14.05.2014.

190 S. Bengtsson and D.L. Stigaard, *Aktuel Skandinavisk og Britisk Handicap-forskning – en kortlægning af miljøer*, 11.44, The Danish National Centre for Social Research, Copenhagen 2011, p. 20.

191 The national organisation for transvestites and transsexual persons, presumably closed on 28.09.2013 <www.thranesen.dk/trans-danmark/> accessed 19 January 2015.

192 <LGBT.dk/english> accessed 19.01.2015.

193 <thranesen.dk> accessed 19.01.2015.

The experiences of the persons involved in the personal interactions, such as visits by invitation to parliamentary committees, were however quite varied,[194] and the process towards the June 2014 amendments proved long and bumpy. Many issues still remain unresolved in the pursuit of real equality for transgender persons in Denmark.

194 e.g. Report of visit to the Parliament Health Committee on 14.09.2007 by Jytte Witt <www.thranesen.dk/b-142-jytte-witt-og-elisabeth-japsen-i-foretraede-for-sundhedsud_valget/> accessed 19.01.2015.

THE LEGAL STATUS OF TRANSSEXUAL AND TRANSGENDER PERSONS IN ENGLAND AND WALES

Stephen Gilmore

Contents

I. LEGAL FRAMEWORK AND STATISTICS

1.1. THE GENERAL LEGAL FRAMEWORK

In England and Wales the principal sources of law are statutes of the United Kingdom Parliament and decisions of the courts of England and Wales. The law is subject to a human rights framework enacted by the Human Rights Act 1998, which incorporates into English law, in a freestanding way, many of the articles of the European Convention for the Protection of Human Rights and Fundamental Freedoms 1950 (Convention rights).[1] Courts are required to take into account decisions of the European Court of Human Rights,[2] legislation must be interpreted, so far as it is possible to do so, in a way which is compatible with Convention rights,[3] and no public authority (which includes a court or tribunal) may act in a way which is incompatible with a Convention right.[4] If a law cannot be interpreted as compatible with a Convention right, a court may make a declaration of incompatibility,[5] whereupon the expectation is that Parliament will address the problem. As we shall see below, this human rights framework has been influential in shaping the law of England and Wales with respect to the status of transsexual and transgender persons.

1.2. THE PRINCIPAL LEGAL SOURCES ON THE LEGAL STATUS OF TRANS PERSONS

The legal status of transsexual and transgender persons in England and Wales is regulated in statute principally by the Gender Recognition Act 2004, which was enacted on 1 July 2004[6] and largely implemented on 4 April 2005.[7] The recent enactment of the Marriage (Same Sex Couples) Act 2013, which, as its title suggests, permits same-sex marriage, has necessitated several consequential amendments to the 2004 Act, in particular to address the impact of a change of

1 As set out in sch 1 to the Human Rights Act 1998. The Convention rights are Articles 2–12, 14, 16, 17, and 18, Articles 1, 2 and 3 of the First Protocol, and Article 1 of the Thirteenth Protocol.
2 Human Rights Act 1998, s 2.
3 Ibid., s. 3.
4 Ibid., s. 6.
5 Ibid., s. 4.
6 Date of Royal Assent.
7 SI 2005/54.

gender on an existing marriage or on a civil partnership (which in English law is a status confined to same-sex couples).[8]

In the absence of the applicability of the Gender Recognition Act 2004, the law with regard to a person's legal gender is to be found in judicial decisions (the common law). Interestingly, both the context in which the modern English common law position was established, and also that which provided the final impetus for the enactment of the 2004 legislation, was the issue of whether a transgender person should be able to marry.

1.2.1. The Common Law

The common law is set out in the longstanding High Court decision in *Corbett v Corbett (Otherwise Ashley).*[9] In that case Ormrod J held that a purported marriage between a man (Mr Corbett) and a fully post-operative male-to-female 'transsexual'[10] person (April Ashley) was void, and granted Mr Corbett a decree of nullity of marriage.[11] Ormrod J also stated, *obiter*, that a transsexual person is incapable of consummating a marriage.[12]

Expert medical opinion presented to the judge had accepted at least four criteria for assessing a person's sex, namely: '(1) chromosomal factors; (2) gonadal

8 Civil Partnership Act 2004. As we shall see, the law has had to consider whether such a partnership should be capable of conversion to a marriage where one party changes gender, or whether the original civil partnership continues to exist where both parties change gender simultaneously.

9 [1971] P 83. For a detailed assessment, see S. Gilmore, '*Corbett v Corbett (Otherwise Ashley)* – Once a man, always a man?' in S. Gilmore, J. Herring and R. Probert (eds.), *Landmark Cases in Family Law*, Hart Publishing, Oxford 2011, pp. 47–72. *Corbett* was not the first case in the United Kingdom to address the issue of transsexualism: see the judgment of Lord Hunter in the Scottish Court of Session in *In Petition of John Alexander Cumnock Forbes-Sempill and the Honourable Ewan Forbes-Sempill,* Judgment 29.12.1967, National Archives of Scotland, reference CS258/1991/P892 (discussed in Gilmore, above). For a useful account of the background to this case, see Z-J. Playdon, 'The Case of Ewan Forbes', published at <www.pfc.org.uk/legal/the-case-of-ewan-forbes>; and see for another earlier Scottish case *X Ptr* 1957 SLT (Sh Ct) 61, cited in L.-A. Barnes, 'Gender Identity and Scottish law: the Legal Response to Transsexuality' (2007) 11(2) *Edinburgh Law Review* 162, 169.

10 In his judgment, Ormrod J referred to April Ashley as a transsexual person and so that terminology is adopted here in discussing the case. There was no discussion in *Corbett* as to whether April Ashley adopted either the terminology of transsexual or transgender because she put her case on the basis that she was an intersex-affected person.

11 *Corbett* was decided on common law principles prior to the Nullity of Marriage Act 1971, which put the law of nullity in statute, *inter alia* providing in s 1(c) of the Nullity of Marriage Act 1971 that the parties to a marriage must be respectively male and female. The provision was later consolidated in the Matrimonial Causes Act 1973, s. 11(c), which will be repealed by the Marriage (Same Sex Couples) Act 2013.

12 [1971] P 83, 107F, distinguishing *SY v SY (Otherwise W)* [1963] P 37 (anatomical woman whose vagina was surgically enlarged, was capable of consummating marriage). It is debatable whether these *obiter* comments would now be followed after enactment of the Gender Recognition Act 2004, which now makes possible a valid marriage between a man and a male-to-female transsexual person. For discussion, see R. Probert, 'How would *Corbett v Corbett* be decided today?' [2005] Fam Law 382.

factors (ie presence or absence of testes or ovaries); (3) genital factors (including internal sex organs); and (4) psychological factors'[13] but also agreed that 'the biological sexual constitution of an individual is fixed at birth (at the latest)'.[14] Ormrod J drew from this that 'the law should adopt in the first place, the first three of the doctors' criteria, ie the chromosomal, gonadal and genital tests, and if all three are congruent, determine the sex for the purpose of marriage accordingly, and ignore any operative intervention.'[15] Ormrod J held that for the purpose of marriage a person's 'true sex' is fixed at birth, and a male-to-female transsexual person cannot 'reproduce a person who is naturally capable of performing the essential role of a woman in marriage'.[16]

The *Corbett* decision has been endorsed in some cases in other jurisdictions,[17] while rejected in others,[18] and its reasoning has on occasions been severely criticised.[19] Of particular note is the powerful criticism in the Australian Family

13 *Corbett v Corbett (Otherwise Ashley)* [1971] P 83, 100. Some of the experts would have added hormonal factors or secondary sexual characteristics.

14 [1971] P 83, 104D–E.

15 Ibid., 106C–E.

16 Ibid., 106.

17 In South Africa, see *W v W* (1976) (2) SALR 308, Nestadt J ('Imitation cannot be equated with actual transformation', at p. 314E–F). For criticism, see M.L. Lupton, 'The Validity of Post-operative Transsexual Marriage' (1976) 93 *South African Law Journal* 385. In Canada, see *M v M (A)* (1984) 42 RFL (2d) 267. In New Zealand, see the *obiter* comments of McMullin J in *Re T* [1975] 2 NZLR 449. Several US courts have also held that, for the purpose of marriage, a person's sex is biologically determined at birth, see *In re Ladrach* 513 NE 2d 828 (1987), Ohio Probate Court; *Littleton v Prange* 9 SW 3d 223 (1999) Court of Appeals of Texas, Fourth District, San Antonio, cert denied 531 US 872; *In the Matter of the Estate of Marshall G. Gardiner, Deceased* 42 P3d 120 (2002), Supreme Court of Kansas; *Kantaras v Kantaras* 884 So. 2d 155, Court of Appeal of Florida, Second District.

18 Rejected in *MT v JT* (1976) 335 A 2d 204 (Appellate Division of the Superior Court of New Jersey); strong criticism in *R v Harris and McGuiness* (1988) 17 NSWLR 158; rejected in *M v M* [1991] NZFLR 337, Family Court, Otahuhu ('the evidence may lead to a finding that the cumulative effect of the changes that have occurred is to have brought about a change of sex in a real sense'), and *Attorney-General v Family Court at Otahuhu* [1995] 1 NZLR 603. For comment, see R. Mackenzie, 'Transsexuals' Legal Status and Same Sex Marriage in New Zealand: *M v M*' (1992) 7 *Otago Law Review* 556. *Corbett* was rejected in *Re Kevin: validity of marriage of transsexual* [2001] FamCA 1074. For the view that even in cases in which *Corbett* has been rejected, its spectre may still be seen, see A. Sharpe, 'English Transgender Law Reform and the *Spectre* of Corbett' (2002) 10 *Feminist Legal Studies* 65–89, especially at 71–80 and A.N. Sharpe, 'Endless Sex: The Gender Recognition Act 2004 and the Persistence of Legal Category' (2007) 15 *Feminist Legal Studies* 57–84.

19 For example, Ormrod J's use of the phrase 'essential role of a woman in marriage'. If this referred to the respondent's ability to have sex as a woman it was contradicted by the medical evidence. If it referred to the ability to procreate, it ignored the law of nullity which does not make such ability a condition of a valid marriage. If it referred to an ability to look and act like a woman, it was contradicted by Ormrod J's finding that April Ashley lived as a female. See *R v Harris and McGuiness* (1988) 17 NSWLR 158, which was highly critical of the reasoning in *Corbett*. For commentary, see M. Otlowski, 'The Legal Status of A Sexually Reassigned Transsexual: *R v Harris and McGuiness* and Beyond' (1990) 64 *Australian Law Journal* 67. And see also I.M. Kennedy, 'Transsexualism and Single Sex Marriage' (1973) 2 *Anglo-American Law Review* 112, 124; and D.K. Smith, 'Transsexualism, Sex Reassignment Surgery and the Law' (1971) 56 *Cornell Law Review* 963, 1006 ff.

Court in *Re Kevin: validity of marriage of transsexual*[20] in which, calling into question the logic of the reasoning, it was observed that Ormrod J's use of the term 'true sex' 'creates the false impression that social and psychological matters have been shown to be irrelevant' when 'they have simply been assumed to be irrelevant.'[21]

Despite the criticisms, and although Ormrod J made clear that he was determining 'legal sex' in the context of marriage, not at large,[22] the *Corbett* approach to sex determination has been consistently applied in English law in other contexts.[23] It was adopted by the Court of Appeal in *R v Tan and Others*[24] in the context of the offence of living off the earnings of prostitution,[25] for reasons of 'common sense and the desirability of certainty and consistency'.[26] *Corbett* was also applied in *Re P and G (Transsexuals)*[27] where the Divisional Court dismissed applications for judicial review of the Registrar General's refusal to alter the birth register to reflect the applicants' 'reassigned' sex. Similarly, in *S-T (Formerly J) v J*[28] the correctness of *Corbett* was not questioned in a case addressing issues of public policy with regard to financial provision following annulment of a

---

20 [2001] FamCA 1074. Discussed in this volume in Richard Chisholm's chapter. For commentary, see M. Otlowski, 'What is the harm in it anyway?: *Re Kevin* and the recognition of transsexual marriage' [2002] AJFL LEXIS 12 and J. McConvill and E. Mills, '*Re Kevin* and the Right of Transsexual Persons to Marry in Australia' (2003) 17 *International Journal of Law, Policy and the Family* 251.

21 Ibid., paras. 78 and 84. Chisholm J upheld the validity of a marriage between a woman and a female-to-male transsexual person, determining sex at the date of the marriage, having regard to all relevant factors, including life experiences and self-perception. The decision was subsequently upheld by the Full Court of the Family Court of Australia in *Attorney-General for the Commonwealth v Kevin and Others* [2003] Fam CA 94 (Nicholson CJ, Ellis and Brown JJ).

22 *Corbett v Corbett (Otherwise Ashley)* [1971] P 83, 106. Nearly twenty years later, Sir Roger Ormrod wrote in correspondence with an Australian academic, Dr Henry Finlay: 'The real issue in Corbett was the meaning of the word "marriage". It is agreed that it means the formal union of a man and a woman. The only question, therefore, was one of construction! Giving the word "woman" its natural and ordinary meaning, could April Ashley be described as a woman? The answer must be No!'. See H. Finlay, 'Corbett to Kevin: Legal Recognition of Transsexualism in England and Australia', paper presented to the Society of Legal Scholars conference in Oxford, 2003.

23 For a discussion of why the decision has had a strong *de facto* precedent status, see S. Gilmore, above n. 9, pp. 47–72 (e.g. the expertise of the judge who was medically qualified, the eminence of experts, and the margin of appreciation afforded to the UK by the European Court of Human Rights over the following years).

24 [1983] QB 1053. In barely a paragraph referring to *Corbett* the court did not engage at all with its reasoning, and the result was based in part on a concession by counsel. For commentary, see P.J. Pace, 'Sexual Identity and the Criminal Law' (1983) *Crim LR* 317 (fallacious to seek consistency between civil and criminal law). Compare, however, the Crown Court decision of Hooper J in *R v Matthews* (unreported) 28 October 1996 that it was possible for a male to female transsexual person to be raped vaginally (seemingly question *R v Tan*).

25 Sexual Offences Act 1956, s 30.

26 [1983] QB 1053, 1064C.

27 [1996] 2 FLR 90 (Kennedy LJ, Forbes J), albeit acknowledging that point might come when the *Corbett* criteria on their own have become so out of date that to continue to use them would be irrational' (ibid., p. 97F–G).

28 [1998] Fam 103, 122 (Potter LJ and Sir Brian Neill; Ward LJ dissenting).

marriage between a woman and a female-to-male transsexual person.[29] Indeed, in the House of Lords in *Bellinger v Bellinger (Lord Chancellor intervening)*[30] Lord Hope of Craighead commented:

> 'There is much to be said for the view that the words "male" and "female" should each be given a single, clear meaning that can be applied uniformly in all cases. That was achieved by the decision in *Corbett v Corbett (orse Ashley).*'[31]

Corbett was distinguished, however, in *W v W (Physical Inter-sex),*[32] a case in which the legal issues were similar to *Corbett* except that the respondent's biological indicia of sex were not congruent at birth. Charles J held that in the case of an intersex-affected person, sex was to be determined at the time of the marriage, having regard to the person's development and all of the indicia of sex listed in *Corbett*, that is biological, psychological and hormonal factors, as well as secondary sexual characteristics. Furthermore, in such a case the capacity to consummate a marriage was a relevant but not decisive factor.[33] Having found on the facts that the respondent was female at the time of the marriage (unlike in *Corbett*) the judge refused a decree of nullity.

1.2.2. Gender Recognition Act 2004 and its Background

Not surprisingly, given the inflexible and formalistic approach in *Corbett*, human rights challenges were pursued before the European Court of Human Rights, alleging breaches of Article 8 (right to respect for private and family life) and Article 12 (right to marry and found a family) arising out of the state's failure to accord transgender persons legal recognition in various spheres of their lives.[34]

---

29 Although Ward LJ commented that he was 'unable lightly to dismiss' the reasoning of Ellis J in *Attorney-General v Family Court at Otahuhu*, and that *Corbett* might 'bear re-examination at some appropriate time' (ibid., p. 122A–B). He added that the words 'male' and 'female' in section 11(c) of the Matrimonial Causes Act 1973 may have 'left the way open for a future court, relying on developments of medical knowledge, to place greater emphasis on gender than sex' (at p. 124F–H), a view which Sir Brian Neill acknowledged was arguable: ibid., p. 153C.

30 [2003] UKHL 21, [2003] 2 AC 467.

31 Ibid., para. [58].

32 [2001] Fam 111, reassured by Ormrod J's own appreciation that the respondent's inter-sex condition might require a different approach: see his Lordship's extra-judicial statements at (1972) 40 *Medico-Legal Journal* 78, especially at p. 86. For comment, see A. Barlow, 'A new approach to transsexualism and a missed opportunity?' [2001] *Child and Family Law Quarterly* 225. See also P.-L. Chau and J. Herring, 'Defining, Assigning and Designing Sex' (2002) 16 IJLPF 327; and J. Herring and P.-L. Chau, 'Assigning Sex and Intersexuals' [2001] Fam Law 762; and J. A. Greenberg, 'Defining Male and Female: Intersexuality and the Collision Between Law and Biology' (1999) 41 *Arizona Law Review* 265.

33 Preferring the Court of Appeal decision in *SY v SY (Otherwise W)* [1963] P 37, which had been distinguished in *Corbett*.

34 *Rees v United Kingdom* [1987] 2 FLR 111 (refusal of Registrar General to alter birth certificate of female-to-male transsexual person); *Cossey v United Kingdom* (1990) 13 EHRR 622 (similar claim in respect of male-to-female transsexual person); *X, Y, and Z v United Kingdom* [1997]

Initially, the claims were unsuccessful,[35] the European Court of Human Rights concluding that there was little common ground between contracting states and therefore this was 'an area in which the parties enjoy a wide margin of appreciation',[36] albeit also recognising the seriousness of the problems affecting transgender persons and the 'need for appropriate legal measures' to be 'kept under review having regard particularly to scientific and societal developments'.[37]

By 1998, in *Sheffield and Horsham v United Kingdom,*[38] the ECtHR was reiterating that view, whilst also noting 'that there is an increased social acceptance of transsexualism and an increased recognition of the problems which post-operative transsexuals encounter'.[39] The court in the *Sheffield and Horsham* case had also referred to the European Court of Justice (ECJ) decision in *P v S and Another (Case C-13/94)*[40] which had held that the Equal Treatment Directive (76/207/EEC) extended to protect transsexual persons from discrimination on the basis of gender reassignment, and which subsequently led to amendment of domestic anti-discrimination legislation.[41]

A change in the European Court of Human Rights' approach came with the Grand Chamber judgments in *Goodwin v United Kingdom; I v United Kingdom*[42] in which the Court unanimously upheld allegations of violations of Articles 8 and 12 of the ECHR in respect of the UK's failure to recognise the legal status of transsexual persons in the spheres of employment, social security, pensions and marriage. The court now attached more significance to an 'emerging consensus within contracting states' and a 'continuing international trend towards legal

---

2 FLR 892 (refusal to register female-to-male transsexual as the legal father of children conceived through assisted conception: for commentary, see C. Lind, 'Perceptions of sex in the legal determination of fatherhood: *X, Y and Z v UK*' [1997] *Child and Family Law Quarterly* 401); *Sheffield and Horsham v United Kingdom* (1998) 27 EHRR 163 (failure to recognise postoperative reassigned gender on, for example, social security and police records, and for the purpose of marriage).

35 Albeit over time by slimmer majorities. In *Rees* a majority of 12 to three found no breach of Article 8 and unanimously no breach of Article 12, whereas in *Cossey* the votes were only 10 to 8 on Article 8; and 14 to 4 on Article 12. In the latter case there was also a strong dissenting opinion of Judge Martens focusing on the transsexual person's right of self-determination.

36 See *Rees v United Kingdom*, above n. 34, para. 37. For criticism of this approach to human rights protection, arguing that it should not depend on convergence of views in states, see C. Lind [1997] *Child and Family Law Quarterly* 401, 406.

37 *Rees v United Kingdom*, above n. 34, para. 47.

38 (1998) 27 EHRR 163.

39 See *Sheffield and Horsham v United Kingdom*, para. 60. This judgment also saw a strong dissenting opinion of Judge Van Dijk, which continued the theme of Judge Marten's dissenting judgment in *Rees*, of respect for a transsexual person's right of self-determination.

40 [1996] ICR 795.

41 Sex Discrimination (Gender Reassignment) Regulations 1999 (SI 1999/1102), which amended the Sex Discrimination Act 1975. The relevant protections are now contained in the Equality Act 2010.

42 (2002) 35 EHRR 18. For comment, see C. Bridge [2002] Fam Law 738; J. Sawyer, '*Goodwin v UK*' [2002] IFL 123; and J. Sawyer, 'Providing the Catalyst for Change' (2002) 152 (7041) NLJ 1089. For discussion, see C. Bessant, 'Transsexuals and Marriage after Goodwin v United Kingdom' [2003] Fam Law 111.

recognition',[43] than to lack of evidence of a common European approach. The court saw the 'coherence of administrative and legal practices' in domestic law as relevant to assessment of Article 8, commenting that where a state has authorised medical treatment, 'it appears illogical to refuse to recognise the legal implications of the result to which the treatment leads';[44] and that given the 'level of commitment and conviction required to achieve a change in social gender role' the ongoing debate surrounding the aetiology of transsexualism is 'of diminished relevance'. The court was not convinced that the terms 'man' and 'woman' must 'refer to determination of gender by purely biological criteria'[45] and held that 'a test of congruent biological factors can no longer be decisive in denying recognition to the change of gender of a post-operative transsexual.'[46] However, the Court did not set down any particular conditions for legal recognition of preferred gender, which has been a source of significant difficulty across European countries, including the UK, in the struggle to determine the most appropriate criteria for legal gender recognition.

Following the European Court of Human Rights' warnings in the late 1990s as to the precariousness of the state's margin of appreciation, the Home Office had set up an Interdepartmental Working Group on Transsexual People 'to consider, with particular reference to birth certificates, the need for appropriate legal measures to address the problems experienced by transsexual people, having due regard to scientific and societal developments, and measures undertaken in other countries to deal with this issue'. Its report, published in April 2000, identified three options for reform: '(a) to leave the current situation unchanged; (b) to issue birth certificates showing the new name and possibly, gender; and (c) to grant full legal recognition to the new gender subject to certain criteria and procedures'.[47] Anticipating the decision in *Goodwin*, the Working Group on Transsexual People was reconvened in 2002 with wider terms of reference, and the Government subsequently announced[48] it would introduce legislation to reflect the decision in *Goodwin*. This would require a shift from a person's gender being determined simply by reference to a person's sex attributed by reference to biological criteria and, as we shall see later in this chapter, the legislation represents a movement away from the terminology of the domestic case law, and now the law predominantly refers to 'gender' rather than 'sex'.

The final impetus for change, if indeed it were needed, was the claim, advanced in *Bellinger v Bellinger*,[49] that the marriage of Elizabeth Bellinger, a

---

43 Ibid., para. 84, citing the evidence provided by Liberty at paras. 55–56 of the judgment.
44 (2002) 35 EHRR 18, para. 78.
45 Ibid., para. 100.
46 Ibid.
47 Para. 5.5.
48 R. Winterton MP, 'Government Announcement on Transsexual People', 13 December 2002: see <www.lcd.gov.uk/constitution/transsex/statement.htm>.
49 [2003] UKHL 21, [2003] 1 FLR 1043. For comment, see S. Gilmore, '*Bellinger v Bellinger* – Not quite between the ears *and* between the legs – Transsexualism and marriage in the Lords'

post-operative male-to-female transsexual person, to Mr Bellinger in 1981 was valid at its inception and subsisting. When the case reached the House of Lords, it was argued, in light of *Goodwin v United Kingdom*, that the failure legally to recognise the marriage was incompatible with Articles 8 and 12 of the ECHR.[50] Because of the impending legislation, the House of Lords did not see this case as a suitable occasion on which to change the law and did not engage with the common law in *Corbett*. The court thus declined to declare that the Bellingers' ceremony of marriage was valid but, in the light of *Goodwin*, declared pursuant to section 4 of the Human Rights Act 1998 that the requirement in section 11(c) of the Matrimonial Causes Act 1973 that parties to a marriage be 'respectively male and female' was incompatible with Articles 8 and 12 of the ECHR, as scheduled to the 1998 Act. The Government subsequently dealt with this declaration of incompatibility by producing a Draft Bill,[51] which was the subject of pre-legislative scrutiny by the House of Lords and House of Commons Joint Committee on Human Rights.[52] Following scrutiny, a Bill was laid before Parliament and eventually enacted as the Gender Recognition Act 2004.[53] In brief, the Act allows a person to obtain a Gender Recognition Certificate recognising for all purposes[54] what the law describes as 'acquired gender'. The details of the process for, and consequences of, acquiring a gender[55] under the Act are set out below at Part II.

1.3. STATISTICS

Before turning to the detail of the Act, it is convenient first to try to indicate the likely number of persons affected by this change in the law. A study in Scotland in 1998 reported an incidence of transsexualism in 1 in 12,400 persons, which at the time translated to estimates of 2,000 male-to-female transsexual persons,

[2003] *Child and Family Law Quarterly* 295; and A. Bradney, 'The Lords and Transsexual Marriages' [2003] *Family Law* 585.

50 The Lord Chancellor intervened and through counsel conceded that, in the light of Goodwin, the law would have to change, but resisted the declaration on the ground that it would serve no useful *purpose*. Arguing that the minister's powers had already been triggered by the Human Rights Act 1998, s. 10(1)(b). See at para. [54].

51 Cm 5875, July 2003.

52 Nineteenth Report of Session 2002–03, HL Paper 188-I, HC 1276-I, 20 November 2003.

53 For a brief overview of the Act, see S. Gilmore, 'The Gender Recognition Act 2004' [2004] *Family Law* 741.

54 Subject to provisions of the Gender Recognition Act 2004.

55 It is appreciated that the use of the term 'acquired gender' has been subject to significant criticism. For transgender persons, the term 'acquired gender' suggests that the process of gender recognition permits individuals to adopt a new gender when, in reality, the law is simply recognising a person's true, self-identified gender. The term 'acquired gender' is used here only because it is the term used in the Gender Recognition Act 2004.

and 400 female-to-male transsexual persons in the UK.[56] It is likely, however, that this represents an underestimate.[57]

A report in 2009[58] by the Gender Identity Research and Education Society, a UK charity, indicated an incidence of referrals to treatment centres of 3 in 100,000 persons as of 2008, but also showed that the trend has been of a rapid growth in referrals. The report also estimated, by applying survey findings to data concerning Gender Recognition Certificates, that by 2007 close to 10,000 persons had presented with gender dysphoria, a prevalence in the UK of 20 per 100,000 persons aged 16 and over.

Statistics relating to Gender Recognition Certificates provide an accurate picture of the number of persons applying for, and receiving, a Gender Recognition Certificate, but of course not all transgender persons will have sought legal recognition of their preferred gender in this way. In some cases, as we shall see, this may be because legal recognition would require the dissolution of an existing marriage which the person concerned does not desire. The Gender Recognition Certificate statistics are discussed below (section 2.4), after an account of the Gender Recognition Act, since an understanding of the breakdown of the statistics requires some comprehension of the workings of the Act.

II. CHANGING LEGAL SEX AND/OR GENDER – PROCEDURE AND REQUIREMENTS

2.1. LEGAL PROCEDURE

The Gender Recognition Act 2004 puts in place a procedure whereby an application can be made to a tribunal known as the Gender Recognition Panel[59] for a Gender Recognition Certificate. The Gender Recognition Panel is thus part of HM Courts and Tribunals Service.[60] The Panel consists of legal members who have a relevant legal qualification,[61] and medical members, who must be either a registered medical practitioner or a registered psychologist.[62] Applications are

56 See *Report of the Interdepartmental Working Group on Transsexual People* (Home Office, 2000), para. 1.3.

57 It should also be noted that the language used is misleading since the figures spoke more generally in terms of individuals who self-identify with a gender other than their legal gender rather than those who had submitted to gender confirmation surgery or hormone treatments.

58 B. Reed, S. Rhodes, P. Schofield and K. Wylie, *Gender Variance in the UK: Prevalence, Incidence, Growth and Geographic Distribution* (June 2009).

59 Ibid, s. 1(3) and sch. 1.

60 Details of the panel, its procedure, and forms used for applications can be found at <www.justice.gov.uk/tribunals/gender-recognition-panel>.

61 A seven-year general qualification within the meaning of s. 71 of the Courts and Legal Services Act 1990: see Gender Recognition Act 2004, sch. 1, para. 1.

62 Gender Recognition Act 2004, sch. 1, para. 1.

determined in private, with no hearing unless the panel considers one necessary. Reasons for the decision must be communicated to the applicant.[63]

The applicant 'may appeal to the High Court on a point of law against a decision to reject the application'.[64] If rejected, another application may not be made 'before the end of the period of six months beginning with the date on which it is rejected'.[65] There is also power, where the Secretary of State considers the decision to grant an application[66] was secured by fraud, to refer the case to the High Court [67] which must quash the decision (and revoke the certificate), or confirm the decision.[68]

2.2. LEGAL REQUIREMENTS

An application may be made by a person of either legal gender who is at least 18 years old, on either of two bases: living in the other legal gender (under section 1(1)(a)) or having 'changed gender' under the law of a country or territory outside the UK (section 1(1)(b)). The former is referred to by the Ministry of Justice as the (domestic) 'standard track' and the latter as the 'overseas track'. A Gender Recognition Panel considering an application under section 1(1)(a) must consist of at least one medical and one legal member[69] but applications under section 1(1)(b) (in which no medical issues are usually raised) require only one legal member.[70] Each Panel has a presiding legal member who, where necessary, has a casting vote. The gender in which the person is living or, as the case may be, to which the person has 'changed' under the law of another country or territory, is referred to in the Act as 'the acquired gender'.[71]

An application under section 1(1)(a) must be granted if the Gender Recognition Panel is satisfied that the applicant:

> '(a) has or has had gender dysphoria,[72]
> (b) has lived in the acquired gender throughout the period of two years ending with the date on which the application is made,

---

63 Sch 1, para. 6.
64 Gender Recognition Act 2004, s. 8(1).
65 Ibid., s. 8(4).
66 Under ss. 1(1), 5(2) or 6(1): see further discussion of these provisions below.
67 Gender Recognition Act 2004, s. 8(5).
68 Ibid., s. 8(6).
69 Sch. 1, para. 4(2).
70 Sch. 1, para. 5. The same applies to applications under ss. 5(2) and 6(1) of the Act.
71 Ibid., s. 1(2).
72 In the first two years from commencement of the Act, the following words were added to s. 2(1)(a): 'or has undergone surgical treatment for the purpose of modifying sexual characteristics'. In the case of any application based on such surgical treatment within that two year period, or in the case of any application made within the first six months from commencement of the legislation, the two year period in s. 2(1)(b) was increased to six years. See Gender Recognition Act 2004, s. 27.

(c) intends to continue to live in the acquired gender until death, and
(d) complies with the requirements imposed by and under section 3.'[73]

An application under section 1(1)(b) must be granted if the country or territory has been approved by order of the Secretary of State and the applicant complies with the requirements imposed by and under section 3.[74] The requirements in section 3 relate to evidence supporting the application. An application under section 1(1)(a) must include:

- a report by a registered medical practitioner or registered psychologist who practises in the field of gender dysphoria, together with a report by another medical practitioner, who need not necessarily be such a specialist. The report must include details of the diagnosis of the applicant's gender dysphoria,[75] and details of any treatment undergone, prescribed or planned;[76]
- a statutory declaration concerning the matters in section 2(1)(b) and (c), *i.e.* that the applicant has lived in the acquired gender for two years preceding the application and intends to live in the acquired gender until death;[77]
- a statutory declaration as to whether or not the applicant is married;[78]
- further evidence supplied as required by the Secretary of State, the Gender Recognition Panel, or according to the wishes of the applicant.[79]

It can be seen that there is no requirement that the applicant submit to medical intervention, such as gender confirmation surgery or hormone treatment. The Joint Committee on Human Rights viewed this as a 'sensitive and sensible compromise',[80] given the safeguard of scrutiny by a Gender Recognition Panel. It 'would avoid discriminating against people who for some medical reason unconnected with their gender are unsuitable for particular kinds of surgical, hormonal or other treatment'.[81] However, such treatment is recognised for the purpose of National Health Service treatment and must be available on the basis of clinical need.[82] It is recognised, however, that there is a need for health trusts to prioritise resources, and not all treatment may therefore be funded. It has been held, for example, that it was not irrational for a health care trust to refuse to fund

73 Ibid., s. 2(1).
74 Ibid., s. 2(2).
75 Ibid., s. 3(2).
76 Ibid., s. 3(3).
77 Ibid., s. 3(4).
78 Ibid., s. 3(6).
79 Ibid., s. 3(6).
80 Joint Committee on Human Rights, above n. 52, para. 29.
81 Ibid., para. 28.
82 See *R v North West Lancashire Health Authority ex parte A* [2000] 1 WLR 977.

breast augmentation surgery for a transgender woman whose hormone treatment had left her with breasts of a size normally found in females of 11–13 years old.[83]

There is also no requirement in English law that a person be infertile before obtaining a Gender Recognition Certificate. The fact that a person intends to seek the legal recognition of his or her preferred gender does not prevent that person from storing gametes prior to recognition. There is no law which would prohibit that person from subsequently using those gametes to produce a child through artificial reproductive technology.

An application under section 1(1)(b) requires 'evidence that the applicant has changed gender under the law of an approved country or territory'[84] and there must also be a statutory declaration as to whether or not the applicant is married. A 'person's gender is not to be regarded as having changed by reason only that it has changed under the law of a country or territory outside the United Kingdom'.[85]

If the application is successful, the applicant must be issued with a Gender Recognition Certificate.[86] There are, however, further requirements in the case of an applicant who is married or a party to a civil partnership.

2.2.1. *Cases in which the Applicant is Married or a Civil Partner*

Schedule 5 to the Marriage (Same Sex Couples) Act 2013 amended the Gender Recognition Act 2004 to address the implications for a change of gender[87] of the legal recognition of same-sex marriage in English law. Prior to this change, the legal position was that, in the case of a married person or party to a civil partnership, a full Gender Recognition Certificate could only be issued if the existing marriage or civil partnership had been dissolved.[88] In such a case, the Gender Recognition Panel issued an Interim Gender Recognition Certificate.[89] The Interim Certificate then became a ground for annulment of the marriage,[90] and a court making absolute a decree of nullity on this ground would issue a full Gender Recognition Certificate.[91] An Interim Certificate could also be 'upgraded' to a full certificate by application to a Gender Recognition Panel within six months of dissolution or annulment of the marriage or civil partnership (on

83 *R (on the application of AC) v Berkshire West Primary Care Trust* [2011] EWCA Civ 247.

84 Gender Recognition Act 2004, s. 3(5).

85 Ibid., s. 21(1).

86 Ibid., s. 4(1).

87 Schedule 5 specifically uses the language of 'change of gender' and is headed 'change of gender of married persons or civil partners'.

88 The Joint Committee on Human Rights (above n. 52) remained to be satisfied that this requirement 'would be proportionate to a pressing social need so as to be "necessary in a democratic society"' (para. 87). For an unsuccessful challenge to the law, see ECtHR, *Parry v United Kingdom* (Application No. 42971/05h).

89 Ibid., s. 4(3).

90 Matrimonial Causes Act 1973, s. 12(g). Proceedings must be instituted within six months of issue of the Interim Certificate: Matrimonial Causes Act 1973, s. 13(2A).

91 And send a copy to the Secretary of State: see Gender Recognition Act 2004, s. 5(1).

a ground other than the issue of an Interim Certificate), or the death of the applicant's spouse/civil partner (unless the applicant is again married or party to another civil partnership). The Panel would grant the application if satisfied that the applicant is no longer married or in a civil partnership, as the case may be. Although the law has now changed, the above brief account of the previous law provides important background against which the changes effected by the 2013 Act can properly be understood.

2.2.1.1. Changes Effected by the Marriage (Same Sex Couples) Act 2013

The 2013 Act introduces additional evidence requirements into section 3 of the Gender Recognition Act 2004 relating to the applicant's existing marriage. New subsections (6A)–(6C) are inserted. Section 3(6A) requires a statutory declaration as to whether the marriage is a marriage under the law of England and Wales, of Scotland, of Northern Ireland, or of a country or territory outside the United Kingdom. This provision is required because the Marriage (Same Sex Couples) Act 2013 extends marriage to same-sex couples in England and Wales, but not in other parts of the United Kingdom. The Act thus excludes from its definition of marriages whose continuity may be protected, those in Scotland and Northern Ireland. It does so by defining some marriages and civil partnerships as 'protected' by the Act. Under the Act a 'protected civil partnership' means a civil partnership under the law of England and Wales, and a 'protected marriage' means (a) a marriage under the law of England and Wales, or (b) a marriage under the law of a country or territory outside the United Kingdom. Section 3(6B) then goes on to provide that if the applicant is married, and the marriage is a protected marriage, an application under section 1(1) must also include:

> '(a) a statutory declaration by the applicant's spouse that the spouse consents to the marriage continuing after the issue of a full gender recognition certificate ("a statutory declaration of consent") (if the spouse has made such a declaration), or
> (b) a statutory declaration by the applicant that the applicant's spouse has not made a statutory declaration of consent (if that is the case).'

Section 3(6C) clarifies that if an application includes a statutory declaration of consent by the applicant's spouse, the Gender Recognition Panel must give the spouse notice that the application has been made.

New subsections (2) and (3) are also inserted into section 4 of the Gender Recognition Act 2004. Section 4(2) provides that the Panel may grant a full Gender Recognition Certificate where the applicant is single, or is a party to a protected marriage and the applicant's spouse consents to the marriage continuing. In the latter case, a new section 11A of the Gender Recognition Act 2004 provides that the continuity of the marriage is not affected by the change of gender. A full

Gender Recognition Certificate may also be granted where the applicant is party to a protected civil partnership and the Gender Recognition Panel has decided to issue the other party with a full Gender Recognition Certificate too. The insertion of section 5B into the Gender Recognition Act 2005 provides that in such a case the certificates must be issued on the same day. A new section 11B provides that the continuity of a civil partnership is not affected by the issuing of full gender recognition certificates to both civil partners. Thus, for example, where there are two individuals with a male legal gender in a civil partnership, both of those individuals can now obtain the legal recognition of their preferred female gender at the same time and continue an existing civil partnership.

By section 4(3), a Gender Recognition Certificate will be an interim certificate where the applicant is in a protected marriage and the spouse has not consented to continuation of the marriage, or in the case of applicants who are in non-protected marriages or non-protected civil partnerships.

A new section 4A is inserted into the Gender Recognition Act 2004 providing that if an Interim Gender Recognition Certificate has been made and within six months of its issue the applicant's spouse subsequently consents to the continuation of his or her marriage to the applicant, then the Interim Certificate can be 'upgraded' to a full Gender Recognition Certificate. There is a similar possibility of 'upgrade' where a civil partnership is converted to a marriage within six months. The conversion of a civil partnership into a marriage is permitted by section 9 of the Marriage (Same Sex Couples) Act 2013.

As noted earlier, the former requirement to dissolve an existing marriage or civil partnership may have inhibited some persons from seeking the legal recognition of their preferred gender. Recognising such persons, who may have lived in their preferred gender for many years, the Marriage (Same Sex Couples) Act 2013 introduces into the Gender Recognition Act 2004 new sections 3A and 3B, which provide alternative grounds and evidence requirements in such cases. Section 3A sets out several conditions: that the applicant was a party to a protected marriage or a protected civil partnership; was living in the 'acquired gender' six years before the commencement of section 12 of the Marriage (Same Sex Couples) Act 2013;[92] continued to live in the acquired gender until the date the application was made; intends to continue to live in the acquired gender until death; has or has had gender dysphoria, or has undergone surgical treatment for the purpose of modifying sexual characteristics; and is ordinarily resident in England, Wales or Scotland. Section 3B provides that in such cases only one medical report is required to evidence the gender dysphoria or the treatment as the case may be, and a Gender Recognition Panel need only have one legal member. Of course, the applicant's spouse's consent to the continuation of the marriage is also required.

---

92 That is, the commencement of the provisions in Schedule 5 to the Act, amending the Gender Recognition Act 2004.

2.3. RECORDING THE ACQUIRED GENDER – THE GENDER RECOGNITION REGISTER

Schedule 3 to the Gender Recognition Act 2004 enjoins the Registrar General to maintain a Gender Recognition Register, which is not to be open to public inspection or search. Where a full Gender Recognition Certificate has been granted the Secretary of State must send a copy of it to the Registrar General.[93] On receipt, the Registrar makes an entry in the Gender Recognition Register, marks the birth register, and makes traceable the connection between those entries. It is then possible to obtain certified copies of entries in the Gender Recognition Register, and short certificates of birth compiled from it, both of which must not disclose that the entry or compilation is from the Gender Recognition Register. It is an offence for a person to disclose information, acquired in an official capacity, concerning the application or the person's previously recognised legal gender.[94]

2.4. STATISTICS RELATING TO GENDER RECOGNITION CERTIFICATES

The statistics relating to Gender Recognition Certificates are collected and reported by the Ministry of Justice on a quarterly basis and financial year basis (April to March). Some general statistics are available for completed financial years beginning with the year 2004/5 and ending with the final quarter of 2012/13 (*i.e.* January to March 2013). During those nine years 3,877 applications were received by the Gender Recognition Panel, of which 3,739 (96%) were dealt with.[95] After an initial surge of applications shortly after implementation of the Act,[96] the number of applications received annually has levelled off at around 300.[97] Of the 3,739 applications dealt with, 3,344 (89%) resulted in a full Gender Recognition Certificate. In 158 cases (4%) an Interim Gender Recognition Certificate was granted. One hundred and sixty applications (4%) were refused, and in 77 cases (2%) the applications were withdrawn.

A bulletin of statistics relating to gender recognition certificates has been compiled since the second quarter of 2009/10 with a more detailed breakdown of applications. At the time of writing, breakdowns were available for three full financial years, namely 2010/11, 2011/12 and 2012/13. Of the applications received in those years (a total of 924), 883 (96%) were on the standard track, and 41 (4%)

---

93 Gender Recognition Act 2004, s. 10(1).

94 Ibid., s. 22, subject to defences in s. 22(4).

95 Ministry of Justice Statistics Bulletin (4 April 2013), *Gender Recognition Statistics October to December 2012,* Table 1, p. 2, with figures for the fourth quarter of 2012/13 added in.

96 In the years 2004/5, 2005/6 and 2006/7 the figures for applications received were respectively 395, 1,007, and 693. See ibid.

97 2007/8 294, 2008/9 278, 2009/10 303, 2011/12 320, 2012/13 301.

on the overseas track.[98] Of the 759 full Gender Recognition Certificates granted in those three years, 570 (75%) were to persons who were assigned a male legal gender at birth and 189 (25%) to persons who were assigned a female legal gender at birth. [99] There was a wide spread of dates of birth of applicants. Eight per cent of applicants were born in the years up to 1949, 24% in 1950–59, 25% in 1960–69, 20% in 1970–79, 19% in 1980–89, and 3% in 1990 onwards.[100]

III. CONSEQUENCES OF THE CHANGE OF LEGAL SEX AND/OR LEGAL GENDER

3.1. FUTURE RIGHTS, DUTIES AND ENTITLEMENTS

3.1.1. General

The effect of a full Gender Recognition Certificate is that 'the person's gender becomes for all purposes the acquired gender.'[101] According to section 9(1) of the 2004 Act, if a person's acquired gender is male, the person's sex becomes that of a man, and if the acquired gender is female, the person's sex is that of a woman. This followed the view of the Joint Committee on Human Rights that the legislation should 'be cast in the clearest terms possible'[102] to indicate that any question of a person's sex must be answered in accordance with the acquired gender.[103]

3.1.2. Marriage

There is thus no restriction on entering into a marriage or civil partnership in the acquired gender, except that no clergyman 'is obliged to solemnise the marriage of a person whose gender has become the acquired gender'.[104] However, controversially, the fact that a person has an acquired gender is of itself a ground for having a marriage annulled.[105] Proceedings must be instituted within three years of the marriage,[106] and the court must be satisfied the other party to the marriage entered the marriage without knowledge of the spouse's acquired gender.[107]

98 Ministry of Justice Statistics Bulletin (4 April 2013), *Gender Recognition Statistics October to December 2012,* Table 2, p. 3, with figures for the fourth quarter of 2012/13 added in.
99 Ibid., Table 4, p. 5, with figures for the fourth quarter of 2012/13 added in.
100 Ibid.
101 Gender Recognition Act 2004, s. 9(1).
102 Note 51 above, para. 33.
103 Ibid., para. 34.
104 Marriage Act 1949, s. 5B, inserted by the Gender Recognition Act 2004, sch. 4, para. 3.
105 Matrimonial Causes Act 1973, s. 12(h). For criticism, see A. Sharpe, 'Transgender Marriage and the Legal Obligation to Disclose Gender History' (2012) 75(1) *Modern Law Review* 33–53.
106 Matrimonial Causes Act 1973, s. 13(2).
107 Ibid., s. 13(3).

3.1.3. Parenthood/Parental Responsibility and Post-Separation Parenting Disputes

Section 12 of the Gender Recognition Act 2004 provides that the acquired gender does not affect 'the status of the person as the father or mother of a child'. The wording of this provision is ambiguous but the better view is probably that this provision is aimed at parental status which existed prior to recognition of the acquired gender. Thus it does not affect a person's ability to acquire legal parenthood in the acquired gender.[108] For example, pursuant to section 35 of the Human Fertilisation and Embryology Act 2008,[109] where a female-to-male transgender person is lawfully married to a woman who is artificially inseminated, he will be the father of the child unless it is shown that he did not consent to the artificial insemination.[110] Although section 35 applies to a void marriage, it is unlikely that this provision would be held to apply to a marriage void under section 11(c) of the Matrimonial Causes Act 1973 by reason that the parties are not respectively male and female.[111]

Even if not married to the child's mother, if the mother's transgender partner has obtained legal recognition of his male gender at the time of the insemination,[112] he may be the father if the artificial insemination is carried out at a clinic licensed by the Human Fertilisation and Embryology Authority and the relevant conditions for his becoming the father of the child are complied with.[113] These provisions mean, of course, that if the transgender person has previously given birth to a child, that person could be the mother of one child and the father of another.

Whether the person of the 'acquired gender' has parental responsibility for a child will depend on the person's parental status and the rules relating to allocation and acquisition of parental responsibility.[114] All mothers, and parents who are either married to the mother or in a civil partnership with the mother, have parental responsibility. If a parent does not have parental responsibility automatically, he or she can acquire it in various ways set out in the Children Act

108 See *J v C (Void Marriage: Status of Children)* [2006] EWCA Civ 551, [2006] 2 FLR 1098, in which this possibility was not doubted, although finding on the facts of that case that the applicant was not the father of the child because he was not a man at the time of artificial insemination.

109 And previously under the Human Fertilisation of Embryology Act 1990, s. 28(2).

110 Human Fertilisation and Embryology Act 2008, s. 35.

111 See *J v C (Void Marriage: Status of Children)* [2006] EWCA Civ 551, [2006] 2 FLR 1098, which so held in relation to an earlier, similar but not identical, provision in section 27 of the Family Law Reform Act 1987.

112 A Gender Recognition Certificate does not have retrospective effect, a point made in this context by the Court of Appeal in *J v C (Void Marriage: Status of Children)* [2006] EWCA Civ 551, [2006] 2 FLR 1098.

113 Human Fertilisation and Embryology Act 2008, ss. 36 and 37.

114 Children Act 1989, ss. 2, 4 and 4ZA.

1989 (through birth registration, agreement with the mother, or by obtaining a court order).[115]

There are no specific rules with regard to post-separation disputes between parents about a child's residence, or contact with a child, in cases in which one parent identifies as a transgender individual. Such disputes are determined applying the child's welfare as the paramount consideration,[116] guided by a checklist of factors.[117] A court must give due regard to the child's ascertainable wishes and feelings in the light of his or her understanding. In the case of older children, this might be a significant factor if the child reacts badly to the legal recognition of his or her parent's preferred gender, as in *Re F (Minors) (Denial of Contact)*.[118] In that case, the Court of Appeal held that a judge had been right not to compel boys aged 12 and 9 to see their father when they became distressed and did not wish to see their father as a female. Of course each case must be decided on its own facts, and it has been said that the court should take a medium-term and long-term view of the child's welfare and not be too influenced by what may be short-term or transient problems surrounding change on the breakdown of parents' relationships.[119] It has also been said that children 'have to know the parents that they have' and that it is 'generally not considered to be in the best interests of children to wish that they had different parents from those that they have.'[120]

3.1.4. *Criminal Law/Penal System/Prison Regimes*

The 'acquired gender' does not prevent the commission or attempted commission of a gender-specific offence which involves the accused engaging in sexual activity.[121] A gender-specific offence is defined as one which can be committed only by, or only on or in relation to, a person of a particular gender.[122] Thus a person whose acquired gender is now female, but who still has a penis, can commit the *actus reus* of rape.

The Secretary of State for Justice has devised a policy to address the care and management of transgender prisoners.[123] The essential feature of the policy is that

115 See in relation to a father, Children Act 1989, s. 4. Similar ways of acquiring parental responsibility can be found in s. 4ZA of the Children Act 1989 for a female partner of the mother who is a legal parent under s. 43 of the Human Fertilisation and Embryology Act 2008, following assisted conception together with the child's mother.

116 Children Act 1989, s. 1(1).

117 Ibid., s. 1(3).

118 [1993] 2 FLR 677.

119 See *Re O (Contact: Imposition of Conditions)* [1995] 2 FLR 124, CA.

120 *Re L (Minors)*, CA (10 June 1998).

121 Gender Recognition Act 2004, s. 20.

122 Ibid., s. 20(3).

123 *The Care and Management of Transsexual Prisoners PSI 07/2011* which came into force on 2 March 2011. As is evident, the name and language used for the guidelines refer specifically to 'transsexual' persons. However, in reality, the guidelines do not limit their reach to individuals

any prisoner who considers himself or herself to be transgender is permitted to live permanently in the acquired gender role.[124] Such persons are to be provided with assistance to allow them to live in their acquired gender, such as cosmetics and appropriate clothing, including for example padded bras and prostheses. Items can 'only be prohibited' if 'it can be demonstrated that they present a security risk which cannot be reasonably mitigated.'[125]

Once a transgender prisoner has obtained a Gender Recognition Certificate, it may be the prisoner's expectation that he or she is transferred to another prison which holds prisoners of the same gender as the acquired gender. However, this may give rise to tensions where the Gender Recognition Certificate has been obtained without gender confirmation surgery. In *R (on the application of AB) v The Secretary of State for Justice, The Governor of HMP Manchester*[126] a pre-operative transgender woman sought judicial review against the Secretary of State to challenge a decision to keep her within the male prison estate and not to transfer her to a female prison. The prisoner was serving a sentence for offences committed whilst a male, which included attempted rape of a female. It was also significant, however, that the Gender Identity Clinic treating her would not consider her for surgery unless she had spent two years living in her preferred gender in a women's prison. On these facts, the High Court quashed the Secretary of State's decision and held that her continued detention in a male prison breached Article 8 of the ECHR. The court concluded that the risk she posed in a female prison could be managed and the Secretary of State's decision was not a proportionate response given the serious interference with the personal autonomy of the prisoner, who would thereby be prevented from qualifying for the possibility of surgery.[127] In the case of transgender persons who have not obtained a Gender Recognition Certificate, their placement in the prison estate of their preferred gender is considered on an individual case basis, following a case conference in which a range of factors is considered, including the risks from the individual to other prisoners and the risks to the individual from other prisoners in the current and potential establishments.[128]

---

to have submitted to gender confirmation surgery. Rather, according to para. 1.1, 'transsexual' individuals include each person who 'lives or proposes to live in the gender opposite to the one assigned at birth'. Therefore, it would appear that a more appropriate expression would be 'transgender' individuals. The UK Border Agency also has policies: see Detention services order 11/2012 *Care and management of transsexual detainees.*

124 *The Care and Management of Transsexual Prisoners PSI 07/2011*, para. 3.2.

125 Ibid., Annex B, at B6. See, for example, *R (on the application of Green) v Secretary of State for Justice* [2013] EWHC 3491 (Admin) in which the decision of the Governor of HMP Frankland to deny a trans-woman a wig, tights and prosthetic breasts and vagina were held not to be unlawful, being justified for security reasons.

126 [2009] EWHC 2220 (Admin).

127 Ibid., paras. [57] and [58]. Compare *R (on the Application of DB) v Secretary of State for the Home Department and Ashworth Hospital Authority* [2006] EWHC 659 (Admin), Davis J (detention of pre-operative male-to-female transsexual prisoner on male ward of high security psychiatric hospital not unlawful).

128 *The Care and Management of Transsexual Prisoners PSI 07/2011*, Annex D.

3.1.5. *Sports Activities*

As discussed in more detail below, the Equality Act 2010 generally makes unlawful discrimination on the basis of a person's 'gender reassignment'. However, section 195(2) of the 2010 Act provides that such anti-discrimination provisions are not contravened 'only by doing anything in relation to the participation of a transsexual person as a competitor in a gender-affected activity if it is necessary to do so to secure in relation to the activity (a) fair competition, or (b) the safety of competitors.' A gender-affected activity is:

> 'a sport, game or other activity of a competitive nature in circumstances in which the physical strength, stamina or physique of average persons of one sex would put them at a disadvantage compared to average persons of the other sex as competitors in events involving the activity.'[129]

3.2. EXISTING RIGHTS, DUTIES AND ENTITLEMENTS

The issue of a Gender Recognition Certificate 'does not affect things done, or events occurring, before the certificate is issued', although the acquired gender operates 'for the interpretation of enactments passed, and instruments and other documents made, before the certificate is issued (as well as those passed or made afterwards)'.[130]

3.2.1. *Parenthood and Parental Responsibility*

As noted above, the acquired gender does not affect 'the status of the person as the father or mother of a child'.[131] Thus, for example, if a person with a legal female gender gives birth to a child and then obtains legal recognition of his preferred male gender, the person is recognised in law as having a male gender but remains the legal mother of the child. In this example, the man concerned will have parental responsibility automatically by operation of law as the mother of the child.[132]

3.2.2. *Succession*

The acquired gender does not affect the disposal or devolution of property under a will or other instrument made before 1 July 2004,[133] nor the descent of any peerage

---

129 Equality Act 2010, s. 192(3).
130 Gender Recognition Act 2004, s. 9(2).
131 Ibid., s. 12.
132 Children Act 1989, s. 2.
133 Gender Recognition Act 2004, s. 15, and see also s. 26 for the 'appointed date'.

or dignity or title of honour, or the devolution of property limited to devolve with the same (unless there is a contrary intention in a will or other instrument).[134] The High Court is granted power to redistribute property 'where the disposition or devolution of any property under a will or other instrument (made on or after 1 July 2004) is different from what it would be but for the fact that a person's gender has become the acquired gender'.[135]

3.2.3. Discrimination in Employment and Provision of Services, etc.

The Equality Act 2010 provides that gender reassignment is a characteristic which attracts the protection of its anti-discrimination provisions.[136] A person has this protected characteristic if he or she 'is proposing to undergo, is undergoing or has undergone a process (or part of a process) for the purpose of reassigning the person's sex by changing physiological or other attributes of sex.'[137] Subject to very few exceptions, therefore, it is unlawful to discriminate against a person, either directly[138] or indirectly,[139] or harass[140] a person, on the basis of gender reassignment. Specifically protected under the 2010 Act is discrimination on the basis of a transsexual person's need to be absent from work because of the process of gender reassignment when compared with others' absence from work because of sickness or injury.[141] In the sphere of employment, a person does not contravene relevant provisions of the 2010 Act by applying in relation to work a requirement not to be a transsexual person if it is shown that, having regard to the nature or context of the work, (a) it is an occupational requirement, (b) the application of the requirement is a proportionate means of achieving a legitimate aim, and (c) the person to whom the requirement applies does not meet it (or there are reasonable grounds for not being satisfied that the person meets it).[142] There are also some general exceptions for the protection of national security, the efficiency of the armed forces, the work of charities and religious sensitivities.[143]

3.2.4. State Benefits and Pension Rights

The effects of the acquired gender on state pensions and social security benefits are set out in Schedule 5 to the 2004 Act. The acquired gender will affect a

134 Ibid., s. 16.
135 Ibid., s. 18.
136 Equality Act 2010, s. 7.
137 Ibid., s. 7(1).
138 Ibid., s. 13.
139 Ibid., s. 19.
140 Ibid., s. 26: (1) A person (A) harasses another (B) if – (a) A engages in unwanted conduct related to a relevant protected characteristic, and (b) the conduct has the purpose or effect of – (i) violating B's dignity, or (ii) creating an intimidating, hostile, degrading, humiliating or offensive environment for B.
141 Ibid., s. 16.
142 Ibid., schedule 9, para. 1(1) and 1(3)(a).
143 Ibid., Part 14, and schs. 22 and 23.

state benefit which is paid on the basis of a person's gender. So, for example, a female-to-male transgender person's previous entitlement to a widow's pension ceases upon change of gender.[144] In relation to payment of the state retirement pension, an issue arises concerning the date of entitlement because English law, for some age groups, makes a distinction between men and women as to the age at which the pension becomes payable. A woman born before 6 April 1950 attains pensionable age at 60 years, whereas a man born before 6 April 1959 attains pensionable age when he attains the age of 65 years.[145] In order to deal with this difference in the context of the legal recognition of preferred gender, paragraph 7 of Schedule 5 to the 2004 Act provides that a person's entitlement after a Gender Recognition Certificate has been issued is 'to be decided as if the person's gender had always been the acquired gender.' So, if immediately before the certificate is issued the person has a female legal gender and is entitled to a retirement pension, but has not attained the age of 65, the person ceases to be so entitled when the certificate is issued. Conversely, if the person has previously been assigned a male legal gender and has attained the age at which women of the same age attain pensionable age, but she has not attained the age of 65, the person is to be treated as attaining pensionable age when the certificate is issued. In *Richards v Secretary of State for Work and Pensions*[146] the Court of Justice of the European Communities held that EEC Directive 79/7 on equal treatment of men and women in the field of social security applied to discrimination arising from gender reassignment. In *Timbrell v Secretary of State for Work and Pensions*[147] the Court of Appeal held that English law was in breach of the Directive in failing to put in place a means of legally recognising for social security purposes the gender of a post-operative transsexual person prior to the Gender Recognition Act 2004. Accordingly, Christine Timbrell, a male-to-female transsexual person, who had surgery in 2000 and reached her 60th birthday in 2001 (prior to implementation of the 2004 Act) was entitled to a retirement pension from her 60th birthday.[148] It has been held, however, that following implementation of the Gender Recognition Act 2004, such a claim cannot be based solely on gender reassignment surgery; the 2004 Act now provides the criteria by which a person's preferred gender can be legally recognised,[149] and therefore the national law by which equal treatment required by the Directive is to be achieved.

144 Gender Recognition Act 2004, schedule 5, para. 4.

145 Pensions Act 1995, sch 4. The pensionable age for a woman is increased to 65 for those born after 5 April 1955.

146 [2006] 2 CMLR 49.

147 [2010] EWCA Civ 701.

148 See also *Grant v United Kingdom* (2007) 44 EHRR 1, which held that the denial of legal recognition of an individual's gender reassignment on any date since the Court's 11 July 2002 judgment in *Goodwin v United Kingdom* constituted a breach of Article 8 of the ECHR.

149 See, for example, *MB v Secretary of State for Work and Pensions (RP)* [2013] UKUT 0290 (AAC), and *M v The Commissioners for Her Majesty's Revenue and Customs* [2010] UKFTT 356 (TC) (Judge Paines).

IV. SUMMARY AND CONCLUDING COMMENTS

Except in the case of intersex-affected individuals, a person's legal gender in England and Wales is initially determined at birth by reference to congruent biological factors, as set out in *Corbett v Corbett*. The common law is, however, now subject to the provisions of the Gender Recognition Act 2004, which permits a person to acquire a legal gender different from that assigned at birth (an 'acquired gender'). Upon evidence that, *inter alia,* the applicant has lived in the acquired gender and is suffering or has suffered from gender dysphoria, a Gender Recognition Panel may grant a Gender Recognition Certificate to the effect that the person's legal gender is thereafter the 'acquired gender'.

The Act can, of course, be criticised on several grounds, for example for its use of the notion of 'acquired gender' as opposed to 'validation of persistent sense of gendered self-identity',[150] its medicalisation of the transgender 'condition',[151] and exclusion of that which does not conform to a binary model of gender.[152] In addition, the 2004 Act, as initially enacted, did not permit a party to a marriage (or, subsequently, a civil partnership) to acquire a gender without an existing marriage/civil partnership being dissolved. However, the recent enactment of the Marriage (Same Sex Couples) Act 2013 permitting same-sex marriage, and the consequential amendments to the Gender Recognition Act 2004 by Schedule 5 to the 2013 Act have now largely eliminated that criticism.

Overall, while recognising some of the shortcomings of the Gender Recognition Act 2004, it is clear that it was a landmark statute,[153] de-legitimising involuntary surgery and hormone treatment as a requirement for legal recognition of a preferred gender, and emboldening the cause for change in other jurisdictions. The protections afforded to transgender persons by the Equality Act 2010, and by the Marriage (Same Sex Couples) Act 2013 Act represent further 'legal jumps' in the right direction. However, over a decade since enactment of the Gender Recognition Act 2004, some of its provisions, such as the requirements regarding 'lived experience', age limits, and diagnosis of gender dysphoria, are now seen as subjects for reform, particularly having regard to recent European reforms in the Netherlands and Denmark.

---

150 Ibid., p. 250.

151 See e.g. S. Cowan, 'Looking Back (To)wards the Body: Medicalization and the GRA' (2009) 18 *Social & Legal Studies* 247, 248–249.

152 R. Sandland, 'Running to Stand Still' (2009) 18 *Social and Legal Studies* 253, 254.

153 A. Sharpe, 'Gender Recognition in the UK: a Great Leap Forward' (2009) 18 *Social and Legal Studies* 241, 244.

THE LEGAL STATUS OF TRANSSEXUAL AND TRANSGENDER PERSONS IN GERMANY

Anatol DUTTA

Contents

I. GENDER AND TRANSGENDERISM AS LEGAL CONCEPTS – THE FRAMEWORK

Under German law, the gender of human beings is relevant right from the beginning of their lives. Once a child is born, the civil status registrar is required by the Personenstandsgesetz (PStG), the German Civil Status Act, to certify in the birth register not only the child's name, place, day, hour and minute of birth and the parents' names, but also the legal gender of the child (see § 21(1) No. 3

PStG). The gender to be registered – which can only be either female or male,[1] although the wording of the Civil Status Act is actually silent on that point[2] – is solely determined by the biological sex characteristics of the child and by the fact whether those characteristics conform to either the female or male legal gender. Any personal identification is irrelevant. Indeed, at such a young age, it would simply not be possible to ascertain such an identification.

Once documented by the registrar, the legal gender of a person is part of his or her civil status for life, mainly with consequences for family law where the legal gender of a person is still relevant. Just two examples: According to the Bürgerliche Gesetzbuch (BGB), the German Civil Code, the mother of a child can only be a *woman* who has given birth to the child, see § 1591 BGB ('*Mutter eines Kindes ist die Frau, die es geboren hat.*'). Similarly, the father of a child can only be a *man* who meets the conditions for his legal fatherhood, see § 1592 BGB ('*Vater eines Kindes ist der Mann …*'). Additionally, only a female and a male person can conclude a marriage,[3] whereas only persons of the same legal gender can enter into a registered partnership under the Lebenspartnerschaftsgesetz (LPartG), the German Registered Partners Act, see § 1(1)1 LPartG.

Yet what happens if, after the birth of a child, the legal gender of the child *cannot be determined* because the child's body shows ambiguous sex characteristics? In the past, the parents, doctors and midwives had – often prematurely – to decide on the child's male or female legal gender. This situation has now – after criticism *inter alia* of the German Ethics Council[4] – been changed. Since the end of 2013, a new provision in the Civil Status Act (the new § 22(3) PStG) permits the civil status officers to refrain from certifying a child's legal gender in the birth register if (because of an intersex condition) the child cannot be assigned a male or female legal gender at the time of birth ('*Kann das Kind weder dem weiblichen noch dem männlichen Geschlecht zugeordnet werden, so ist der Personenstandsfall ohne eine solche Angabe in das Geburtenregister einzutragen*'). That newly created civil status of an uncertain legal gender can persist until the death of the person. The person can, however, at any time notify the registrar that a male or female gender should be registered. The notified legal gender must then be certified subsequently in the birth register, as the new § 27(3) No. 4 PStG stipulates in its first alternative. Although the new civil status of a person having an uncertain legal gender gives

[1] See No. 21.4.3 of the Allgemeine Verwaltungsvorschrift zum Personenstandsgesetz (General Administrative Regulations for the German Civil Status Act), which states: '*Das Geschlecht des Kindes ist mit „weiblich" oder „männlich" einzutragen*'.

[2] See, however, the principle of equality regarding sex enshrined in Art. 3(2) of the German Basic Law which suggests that there is only a male and a female sex.

[3] See notably the case law of the German Constitutional Court (e.g. in BVerfG 17 July 2002, BVerfGE 105, 313, 345) which consistently held that the institution of marriage is reserved for the relationship between a man and a woman. – See also § 1355(2), § 1362(1), § 1363(2), § 1366(2), § 1416(1), § 1421, § 1459(1) BGB which assume that a marriage consists of a man and a woman.

[4] See the statement of the Deutscher Ethikrat, *Intersexualität – Stellungnahme*, 2012, p. 177 ff.

rise to many legal questions (e.g. can such a person conclude a marriage or register a partnership? Can such a person be legally the mother or the father of a child?), questions which are discussed in German currently,[5] the German legislator has at least opened the possibility that a person, and more particularly his or her parents can decide on assigning the legal gender without time pressure after birth – a fact which might help to avoid, at least partly, the conflict to be discussed in in the present book, *i.e.* the conflict which arises where the legal gender assigned to a person at birth, generally on the basis of their biological sex characteristics, diverges from the individual's self-identification and preferred gender, so that a legal process of recognising the person's preferred gender is required.

The introduction of the new civil status of an uncertain legal gender does not, of course, cater for all situations where a person's legal gender and his or her self-identified gender differ. A person may, at his or her birth, exhibit sex characteristics which are fully consistent with the sex characteristics typical of a particular legal gender. In such cases, doctors and parents do not have the option of invoking the new law. Similarly, a person may have been born long before the new civil status was available and was therefore unable to take advantage of its terms. In order to permit a person to obtain legal recognition of his or her preferred gender, the German legislator, as far back as 1980, after an earlier decision of the German Bundesverfassungsgericht, the Federal Constitutional Court, allowing such recognition on constitutional grounds,[6] adopted the Transsexuellengesetz, the Transsexuals Act (TSG). The Act provides a statutory basis for the change of the (male or female) first name and the recognition of preferred gender in certain situations. Under the Act, both forms of recognition require a court decision and, hence, a formal court procedure (see § 1(1) and § 8(1) TSG).

II. STATISTICS

The number of court proceedings under the Transsexuals Act has increased over the years, as the statistics of the German Federal Office of Justice illustrate. However, against a total German population of approximately 81 million persons, the number of people seeking gender recognition actually appears quite

[5] See, for example, W. Sieberich, 'Das unbestimmte Geschlecht' [2013] *FamRZ (Zeitschrift für das gesamte Familienrecht)* 1180; J. Theilen, 'Intersexualität, Personenstandsrecht und Grundrechte' [2014] *StAZ (Das Standesamt)* 1; T. Helms, 'Personenstandsrechtliche und familienrechtliche Aspekte der Intersexualität vor dem Hintergrund des neuen § 22 Abs. 3 PStG' in I. Götz, I. Schwenzer, K. Seelmann and J. Taupitz (eds.), *Familie – Recht – Ethik, Festschrift für Gerd Brudermüller*, 2014, p. 301; R. Hepting and A. Dutta, *Familie und Personenstand*, 2nd ed., 2015, p. 398 ff.; from a private international law perspective see S. Gössl, 'Intersexuelle Menschen im Internationalen Privatrecht' [2013] *StAZ (Das Standesamt)* 301.

[6] BVerfG 11 October 1978, BVerfGE 49, 286, where the Constitutional Court recognised the constitutional right of a transgender individual to change his or her sex entry in the birth register; the Court based its decision on the general right of personality guaranteed in Art. 2(1), Art. 1(1) of the Grundgesetz (GG), the German Constitution.

low. It must be noted that the case numbers also include applications where the transgender individual is merely seeking a legal name change, without asking for full recognition of his or her preferred gender.

Table 1. Proceedings under the Transsexual Act before the first instance courts (Amtsgerichte)[7]

Year	Number of proceedings
1995	400
1996	457
1997	447
1998	507
1999	541
2000	722
2001	772
2002	758
2003	767
2004	886
2005	791
2006	644
2007	799
2008	903
2009	992
2010	1,118
2011	1,657
2012	1,277

7 Source: Bundesamt für Justiz, *Zusammenstellung der Geschäftsübersichten der Amtsgerichte für die Jahre 1995 bis 2012* (21 February 2014), available at <www.bundesjustizamt.de>. See also the response of the Federal Government to a parliamentary inquiry which counts 265 cases in 1991, 311 cases in 1992, 389 cases in 1993 and 435 cases in 1994, source: Antwort der Bundesregierung auf die Kleine Anfrage der Abgeordneten Christina Schenk und der Fraktion der PDS, BT-Drucksache 14/9789, p. 4 (2002). An earlier statistical review can be found in C. Weitze and S. Osburg, 'Transsexualism in Germany: Empirical data on epidemiology and application of the German Transsexuals' Act during its first ten years' (1996) 25 *Archives of Sexual Behavior* 409.

III. LEGAL RECOGNITION OF PREFERRED GENDER – REQUIREMENTS AND PROCEDURES

3.1. SUBSTANTIVE REQUIREMENTS FOR RECOGNISING PREFERRED LEGAL GENDER – LEGISLATOR VERSUS CONSTITUTIONAL COURT

The conditions for obtaining legal recognition of preferred gender are laid down in § 8 of the Transsexuals Act. The story of the Transsexuals Act, particularly of its § 8, is notable for the initially harsh conditions which the legislator imposed for recognised the preferred gender being gradually overturned by the German Federal Constitutional Court. That Court has the power to decide on the constitutionality of legislative acts in Germany, in particular whether such acts violate human rights.

The German legislator, in the original version of the Act, had required an applicant

- to be unmarried (original version of § 8(1) No. 2 TSG),
- to be infertile (original version of § 8(1) No. 3 TSG),
- to have modified his or her secondary sex characteristics through surgery to the other sex[8] (original version of § 8(1) no. 4 TSG: '*sich einem ihre äußeren Geschlechtsmerkmale verändernden operativen Eingriff unterzogen hat, durch den eine deutliche Annäherung an das Erscheinungsbild des anderen Geschlechts erreicht worden ist*'),
- and to have reached the age of 25 (§ 8(1) No. 1, § 1(1) No. 3 TSG in its original version).

Over the years since the 1980s, these requirements have been declared unconstitutional by the Federal Constitutional Court,[9] mainly based on the principle of equality (Art. 3(1) of the Grundgesetz (GG), the German Basic Law, the constitution) and on a right to sexual self-determination ('*sexuelle Selbstbestimmung*') and to individual gender identification ('*das Finden und Erkennen der eigenen geschlechtlichen Identität*') flowing from the general right of personality (Art. 2(1) in connection with Art. 1(1) GG).

---

8 The costs of such a gender confirmation surgery are covered by the statutory health insurance, insofar transsexualism is regarded as an 'illness', *cf.*, for example, the decision of the German Federal Social Court in BSG 28 September 2010, NJW 2011, 1899, para. 15; BSG 11 September 2012, BeckRS 2012, 75488, para. 10 seq.

9 BVerfG 16 March 1982, BVerfGE 60, 123 (both as to the age requirement); BVerfG 27 May 2008, BVerfGE 121, 175 (as to the non-marriage requirement); BVerfG 11 January 2011, BVerfGE 128, 109 (as to the infertility and surgical-measures requirement). *Cf.* also BVerfG 26 January 1993, BVerfGE 88, 87; BVerfG 15 August 1996, NJW 1997, 1632; BVerfG 6 December 2005, BVerfGE 115, 1 (all as to the requirements to change the first name, the so-called 'small' solution, see below section V).

3.1.1. *Age Requirements*

The Federal Constitutional Court first considered the substantive requirements of the Transsexuals Act only a short period of time after the law was introduced. In 1982, the Court held that the age requirement stipulated by the original Transsexuals Act violated the equality principle laid down in Art. 3(1) GG, which guarantees that all persons shall be equal before the law.[10] The case concerned a male-to-female (MtF) transgender individual who had, at the age of 21, submitted to gender confirmation surgery, also resulting in her infertility. After those surgical measures, the applicant sought to obtain recognition of her preferred legal gender, even though she had not yet reached the statutorily required age of 25 years.

Reviewing the Transsexuals Act, the Federal Constitutional Court first concluded that the purpose of the age requirement was, in general, permissible under German constitutional law. By restricting legal recognition to applicants who had attained the age of 25, the legislator tried to avoid a situation where gender confirmation surgery, a statutory condition for obtaining recognition, would be undertaken prematurely. Nevertheless, the Court held that the age requirement constituted a discrimination for transgender persons below the age of 25 years because the legislator had only restricted the right of legal recognition, but not access to surgery. Transgender persons under the age of 25 were still allowed to submit to surgical interventions. Thus, a transgender person would not be entitled to claim legal recognition of his or her preferred gender even where that person had fulfilled all the other substantive conditions for such recognition, in particular the surgical measure requirement. Such differentiation based on the age of the applicant could not be constitutionally justified because it did not fulfil the legislative aim it claimed to pursue. The legislator could only have reached its stated aim if it had, in addition to restricting legal recognition, also limited the right of young transgender individuals to access gender confirmation surgery. In that context, the Court emphasised that the legislator has to be particularly careful in the sensitive area of sexual self-determination, which is protected by the Grundgesetz as part of the general right of personality in Art. 2(1) in connection with Art. 1(1) GG.

Following the decision of the Constitutional Court, the legislator dropped the age requirement (see as to the representation of minors *infra* section 3.3).

3.1.2. *The Non-Marriage Requirement*

In a second decision[11] from 2008, the Constitutional Court held that the non-marriage requirement stipulated in the German Transsexuals Act (*i.e.* the

[10] BVerfG 16 March 1982, BVerfGE 60, 123.

[11] BVerfG 27 May 2008, BVerfGE 121, 175.

requirement that applicants for legal recognition be either single or divorced) violated the constitutional protection of marriage, laid down in Art. 6(1) GG, because it forced married transgender persons to divorce. The non-marriage requirement also contravened the general right of personality, based on Art. 2(1) in connection with Art. 1(1) GG, which included the constitutional obligation upon the state to recognise a person's own gender identification.

The 2008 case concerned an application by a MtF transgender person who was married for more than fifty years. The applicant had three children with her spouse. In 2002, the applicant submitted to a process of medical transition, including gender confirmation surgery. Although she – or, from a legal point of view, still he – was married, the applicant sought legal recognition of her preferred female gender.

The Federal Constitutional Court stressed that the non-marriage requirement of the Transsexuals Act put married transgender individuals in a situation in which they had to decide whether to retain their marriage, but also maintain their non-preferred legal gender, or to divorce and obtain legal recognition of their preferred gender (on the presumption that divorce was legally possible at all because a spouse's transgender identity was not necessarily capable of creating a ground for divorce, in particular an irretrievable breakdown of the marriage, see § 1565(1) BGB). Under the German Transsexuals Act, married transgender persons were not able to achieve two aims: the recognition of their preferred gender and the continuation of their legal relationship with their married partner. This situation was – according to the Court – constitutionally unacceptable.

At first, the Federal Constitutional Court noted that the non-marriage requirement only partly fulfils its purposes, in particular to avoid same-sex marriages. There is no restriction on married transgender individuals submitting to gender confirmation surgery. Furthermore, a married transgender individual can even change his or her first name (as to the so-called 'small' solution – which does not require the applicant not to be married – see *infra* section V). The non-marriage requirement therefore only provides a *de jure* prohibition on same-gender marriages. The reality is that, under the current law, transgender individuals were able to live in what, for all intents and purposes, are marriages with two people of the same gender (even though the law has not yet recognised the preferred gender of one of the spouses).

The main reason that the Constitutional Court regarded the non-marriage requirement as violating the Constitution related to the high constitutional value which the Grundgesetz confers upon the marriage institution, see Art. 6(1) GG. That protection would, in practice, be denied to married transgender persons if the law required them to divorce in order to obtain recognition of their preferred gender. In cases where there is no breakdown of the relationship, the transgender person (and his or her spouse) may, under the non-marriage requirement, have even been encouraged to present false facts in the divorce proceedings in order to dissolve the marriage and obtain recognition of legal gender. The Constitutional

Court emphasised the need to protect the applicant's spouse, who had to be able to rely upon the legal continuity of the marriage as long as the spouses lived together and mutually took care of each other.

In 2009, the legislator abandoned the non-marriage requirement in the Transsexuals Act, reacting to the decision of the Constitutional Court. However, the legislator did not explicitly address the fate of marriages (and registered partnerships) after the legal recognition of preferred gender (see *infra* section IV).

3.1.3. The Infertility and Surgical Measures Requirement

The Federal Constitutional Court most recently considered the Transsexuals Act[12] in 2011 when it reviewed the infertility and surgical measures requirement. Once again, the Court held that such requirements violated the Constitution, specifically the general right of personality protected by Art. 2(1) in connection with Art. 1(1) GG. Therefore, both requirements were no longer applicable to the application for legal recognition of preferred gender without any further legislative action being needed.[13]

The 2011 case illustrates how highly the Constitutional Court values the individual right of sexual self-determination and gender identification. The requirements of infertility and surgical intervention were both found to be unconstitutional because they prevented a lesbian-identified MtF transgender person (who had not yet obtained legal recognition of her female gender and, therefore, was legally still regarded to be male) from entering into a registered partnership with her female partner, which is restricted – as already mentioned (see *supra* section I) – to same-sex couples. Hence, the couple were, under German law, 'only' entitled to enter a traditional – opposite-sex – marriage, for which the same-sex registered partnership is considered a substitute.

The Constitutional Court concluded that both alternatives for the transgender individual to establish a legal relationship with her partner – entering into a marriage or obtaining legal recognition of her female gender under the present Transsexuals Act – were constitutionally not justified, because both violated her right to sexual self-determination.

On the one hand, the Court regarded marriage as an unacceptable solution for the partners. The German legislator had intentionally restricted marriages to couples with different legal genders and registered partnerships to same-gender couples. The legislator had, therefore, attributed to both marriage and registered partnerships certain gendered connotations. German society understood registered partnerships as being formed exclusively between two same-gender persons. Requiring the applicant to enter into a marriage was, hence, 'wrong',

---

12 BVerfG 11 January 2011, BVerfGE 128, 109.

13 Clarified in BVerfG 27 October 2011, NJW 2012, 600.

both from the perspective of the applicant's gender but also in relation to the applicant's sexual orientation.

On the other hand, the Constitutional Court concluded that the legal recognition of the preferred legal gender was similarly not an option as long as it imposed high and unacceptable requirements. The requirement of infertility and surgical measures was found to be unacceptable because it amounted to a massive impairment of the applicant's bodily integrity (which is constitutionally protected by Art. 2(2) GG). The Court stressed that, in particular, according to existing scientific understanding, altering one's sex characteristics to conform to the sex characteristics of the opposite gender is not a valid indicator of a stable and irreversible self-identification with that gender. In terms of the infertility requirement, the Constitutional Court emphasised that, in principle, the aim of that requirement – to avoid legal males giving birth or legal females fathering children, which would contradict gender concepts and would have far-reaching implications for the legal system – is within the permissible constitutional boundaries. Yet the Court pointed to the fact that the means of modern reproductive technique limit the effectiveness of the infertility requirement considerably. A MtF transgender person can still, in certain circumstances, father a child even after obtaining legal recognition through a process which required her sterilisation. The individual may have preserved sperm before submitting to sterilisation. Furthermore, according to the Constitutional Court, there are much more moderate ways of avoiding difficulties in the parent–child context, for example by providing that legal recognition of preferred gender has no impact on parent–child relationships (see *infra* section IV).

3.1.4. Legal Requirements which Remain Untouched by the Constitutional Court

The Constitutional Court has left in place some substantive requirements for the legal recognition of preferred gender. These requirements are laid down in § 8(1) No. 1, § 1(1) No. 1 & 2 TSG. The applicant must still show (1) that he or she feels as though not belonging to his or her current legal gender but rather to the opposite legal gender, (2) that he or she has felt a compulsion to live according to his or her perceived gender for at least three years, and (3) that there is a high probability that the applicant's sense of belonging to the opposite gender will not change in the future.

3.2. INTERNATIONAL SCOPE

There is a further condition for the legal recognition of preferred gender which should not be overlooked. The Transsexuals Act has a limited international scope. Not everyone is entitled to apply for recognition in Germany. Rather, the Transsexuals Act, in § 8(1) No. 1, § 1(1) No. 3 TSG, requires applicants to have a certain connection to Germany, whether by being a German national, in the sense envisaged by the German constitution (§ 1(1) No. 3 lit. a TSG), by being a stateless or displaced person having his or her habitual residence in Germany (§ 1(1) No. 3 lit. b TSG), or by being a person who is entitled to a grant of asylum or is a foreign refugee domiciled in Germany (§ 1(1) No. 3 lit. c TSG). In addition, other foreign nationals may make applications under the Transsexuals Act if the law in their country of nationality does not contain provisions comparable to the German Transsexuals Act and the foreign national has legal status under German immigration law. In such cases, the foreign national must either have an unlimited right of residence in Germany or a renewable residence title, and he or she must reside permanently and lawfully in Germany, § 1(1) No. 3 lit. d TSG).

The Transsexuals Act, hence, in general, still follows, in terms of its international scope, the nationality principle. The law shifts responsibility for legal gender recognition mainly onto the state of nationality. This approach is, in principle, quite sensible as it is the home state of the applicant which is in charge of his or her identification documents (which should always conform to the legal status that person has). But the Transsexuals Act grants foreigners a kind of *forum necessitatis* in Germany. It applies only where the home country of an applicant does not permit the applicant to obtain legal gender recognition and in cases where the applicant is strongly connected to Germany. This *forum necessitatis*, like many of the most important developments in this area, was not introduced by the German legislator but rather again by the Constitutional Court. The Constitutional Court came to the conclusion, based *inter alia* on an expert opinion of the editor of this volume, Jens Scherpe,[14] that, in particular, the Constitution's equality principle, enshrined in Art. 3(1) GG, would be violated if Germany refused to recognise the preferred gender of foreigners who legally, and not merely temporarily, reside in Germany and whose home-country laws do not provide for the legal recognition of preferred gender.[15]

3.3. PROCEDURE

The proceedings before the competent Amtsgericht (§ 2, § 9(3)1 TSG), the first instance court, are generally conducted under the Gesetz über das Verfahren in Familiensachen und in den Angelegenheiten der freiwilligen Gerichtsbarkeit (FamFG), the Act on Family Proceedings and Matters of Non-Contentious Jurisdiction (§ 4(1), § 9(3)1 TSG). That Act ensures, for example, that the court investigates the facts of legal gender recognition *ex officio* (see § 26 FamFG)

14 See J. Basedow and J.M. Scherpe, *Transsexualität, Staatsangehörigkeit und internationales Privatrecht,* 2004.

15 BVerfG 18 July 2006, BVerfGE 116, 243.

and that the court proceedings are not open to the public (see § 170 of the Gerichtsverfassungsgesetz, the Judicature Act).

The procedural provisions of the Transsexuals Act do not establish any limitations regarding the age of an applicant. Persons having no full capacity are represented in the proceedings by their statutory representative (§ 3(1)1, § 9(3)1 TSG, see also *supra* section 3.1.1). Children are notably represented by their parents (see § 1626, § 1629 BGB). An application under the Transsexuals Act by a statutory representative always requires approval by the competent family court (see § 3(1)2, § 9(3)1 TSG).

The only parties in proceedings under the Transsexuals Act are the applicant and a so-called representative of the public interest (*Vertreter des öffentlichen Interesses*), see § 3(2) & (3), § 9(3)1 TSG. Family members of the applicant are not party to the proceedings, even though family relationships might be affected by the legal recognition of gender and although family members might have sought to become parties under the general procedural provisions, see § 7(2) No. 1 FamFG.

The Transsexuals Act requires the court to hear the applicant personally (§ 4(2), § 9(3)1 TSG). It is notable that a court may only grant an application for legal recognition after obtaining two opinions of experts who are – based on their education and their professional experience – sufficiently familiar with the specific problems of transgenderism ('*zwei Sachverständigen ..., die auf Grund ihrer Ausbildung und ihrer beruflichen Erfahrung mit den besonderen Problemen des Transsexualismus ausreichend vertraut sind*', § 4(3)1, § 9(3)1 TSG). The experts are required to deliver their opinions independently and they have to address the question of whether the applicant's self-identification with the opposite gender is unlikely (with a high degree of probability) not to change, § 4(3)2, § 9(3)1 TSG.

The parties can appeal against the decision of the court, § 4(4), § 9(3)1 TSG, §§ 58 seq. FamFG. The applicant can, at any time after the decision permitting legal recognition of his or her preferred gender, apply for an annulment of that decision if he or she subsequently self-identifies with his or her birth assigned gender, § 6, § 9(3)1 TSG.

3.4. SUPPORT BY PRIVATE ASSOCIATIONS

Obtaining legal gender recognition is a time consuming process in Germany. During the three-year period in which the applicant has to show that he or she is compelled to live in the opposite legal gender (§ 8(1) No. 1, § 1(1) No. 1 TSG), a decision of the court cannot be obtained. In order to facilitate the day-to-day life of potential applicants during this period of transition, the German Association for Transidentity and Intersexuality (Deutsche Gesellschaft für Transidentität und

Intersexualität e. V.), a private association, offers a document[16] supplementing the official identity card or passport by describing – in three languages – the situation of the person and explaining why the person's gender expression might not conform with the current legal gender displayed in his or her official documents.

IV. CONSEQUENCES OF THE LEGAL RECOGNITION OF PREFERRED GENDER

The Transsexuals Act stipulates, in § 10(1) TSG, that, once the decision to legally recognise preferred gender is *res iudicata*, all *legal rights and obligations* which are dependent on the legal gender of the applicant follow *ex nunc* the newly recognised gender, save where otherwise provided for by statute. In terms of past rights and obligations, the applicant is treated in law as having had the legal gender assigned to him or her at birth.

An exception to the general principle rule is found in the Transsexuals Act itself. According to § 12(1)1 TSG, the legal recognition of preferred gender does not impact existing rights to pensions or other periodic benefits. Recognition does not, however, oblige the transgender person to agree with an alteration of existing insurance contracts even if the insurance premium is calculated in a manner related to the legal gender of the insured party,[17] as far as such a differentiation between the sexes regarding insurance premiums is admissible at all.

However, the Transsexuals Act, under § 11 TSG, clarifies that the legal recognition of preferred gender does not affect existing *parent–child relations*. Following recognition, the applicant remains the father or mother of a child even though he or she has now obtained legal recognition of his or her male or female gender. This provision also applies to children born after recognition, such as those who are born through artificial reproduction.[18] Yet the relevance of the provision is mainly restricted to one's civil status. Regarding the rights and duties of parents and children, § 11 TSG is really only of symbolic nature as the parent–child relationship under German law does not depend on the gender of the parties to that relationship.[19] It is therefore confusing that the legislator in the second sentence of § 11 TSG extends the scope of that provision to relationships between

16 See <www.dgti.org/index.php?option=com_content&view=article&id=10> accessed 10.05.2014).

17 See BGH 9 May 2012, NJW 2012, 2733.

18 See OLG Köln 30 November 2009, NJW 2010, 1295 (for a male-to-female transgender person who is regarded as the *father* of the child born after legal recognition of preferred gender); KG 30 October 2014, FamRZ 2015, 32 (for a female-to-male transgender person who is regarded as the *mother* of the child born after legal recognition of preferred gender). The latter case is currently pending before the German Federal Court of Justice, the supreme court in civil matters (case no.: XII ZB 660/14).

19 See M.S. Augstein, *Transsexuellengesetz*, 2012, § 11 TSG para. 1.

the issue of the applicant's children and the applicant, leaving aside, however, the relationship of the applicant to the parents of his parents.

In terms of other family relationships, in particular *a marriage or registered partnership of the applicant* which, as we have seen, does not exclude an application under the Transsexuals Act anymore (see *supra* section 3.1.2), the Constitutional Court has held that those relationships must be protected after the legal recognition of preferred gender.[20] By discarding the non-marriage requirement for the legal recognition of gender, the legislator decided to keep a marriage or registered partnership as a marriage or registered partnership even after recognition.[21]

The Transsexuals Act also strives to protect the *privacy* of the applicant, his or her '*Recht auf informationelle Selbstbestimmung*', the so-called right of informational self-determination. The Act provides, in § 5(1), § 10(2) TSG, that no German public authority is allowed to disclose or to investigate the previous name or legal gender of the applicant after the court decision under the Act has become *res iudicata*. However, that prohibition of disclosure and investigation does not apply if special reasons of public interest require disclosure or investigation of the previous name or legal gender or if a legal interest is shown. This exception applies, for example, to creditors which have obtained a judgment against the applicant and now have to change the wording of the enforceable title.[22] An interesting special provision is contained in § 5(2) and (3) TSG. The family members of the applicant are only obliged to specify the new name and legal gender of the applicant as far as this is necessary for public books and registries.

V. CHANGE OF FIRST NAME – 'SMALL' VERSUS 'MAJOR' SOLUTION

The Transsexuals Act does not only allow the recognition of legal gender but also provides in §§ 1 seq. TSG for a change of the person's first name. The change of name is often referred to as the 'small solution' (*kleine Lösung*) whereas the recognition of legal gender is regarded as the 'major solution' (*große Lösung*). However, since 2011, the distinction between the small and major solution – at least regarding the preconditions of both solutions – has really only existed on paper. As the Constitutional Court found the additional requirements for the recognition of legal gender to be unconstitutional,[23] the preconditions for

[20] BVerfG 27 May 2008, BVerfGE 121, 175.

[21] M.S. Augstein, *Transsexuellengesetz*, 2012, § 8 TSG para. 4 seq. See as to the possible legislative options to protect the marriage BVerfG 27 May 2008, BVerfGE 121, 175, 202 ff., where the Court held that the legislator could (1) transform the marriage into a civil partnership, (2) create a legal relationship *sui generis* or (3) to keep the marriage as it is.

[22] See M.S. Augstein, *Transsexuellengesetz*, 2012, § 5 TSG para. 1.

[23] See the references above in n. 9.

recognition and for amending a first name are, at the moment, the same[24] (as the Constitutional Court has also stressed).[25] The only precondition the Court left standing was § 8(1) No. 1 TSG which refers to the conditions for changing one's name, § 1(1) TSG. Considering this rapprochement between the requirements for both 'solutions', it is surprising that expert opinions on the applicant (*cf. supra* section 3.3) obtained for the purposes of the 'small solution' shall – according to court practice – not be admissible in 'major solution' proceedings.[26] If the applicant, however, applies for the legal recognition of preferred gender, he or she also has to change his or her first name, see § 8(2), § 9(3)2 TSG.

The Constitutional Court has, in the past, also been invited to consider the constitutionality of the preconditions for the 'small' solution. As far back as 1993, the Court removed the age requirement[27] which was not only relevant for the 'major' solution (see *supra* section 3.1.1) but also for the 'small' solution. The Court held that the age requirement for a change of first name violated the equality principle in Art. 3(1) GG. The Court stressed that young transgender persons should have the possibility of changing their first name before they start their professional careers.

The Constitutional Court has also ruled on the consequences of the 'small' solution. A MtF prison inmate, who had changed her male-orientated first name to female name, was still addressed by the prison staff in the male form '*Herr*' ('Mr'). The prison administrators were of the opinion that the individual had only changed her first name and had not obtained legal gender recognition (which alone was decisive in determining the way in which prisoners were addressed). The Constitutional Court held that, flowing from the right to gender identification, the prisoner was entitled to be addressed according to her gender identification in the female form.[28]

A legal change of first name becomes invalid according to § 7(1) TSG if the applicant produces a child, which is conceived after the change (No. 1 and 2), or if the applicant marries (No. 3). The legislator presumed that, in this situation, the transgender person implicitly shows that he or she now identifies with his or her assigned legal gender. The latter cause of invalidity of the name change – a subsequent marriage – was again limited by the Constitutional Court in a case similar to that regarding the infertility and surgical measures requirement for the 'major' solution (see *supra* section 3.1.3). In 2005, the Court held that § 7(1) No. 3 TSG cannot lead to a loss of a new first name if a lesbian-identified MtF transgender person (who still retains a male legal gender) enters into a marriage

[24] S. Wielpütz, 'Die neue große Lösung ist vor allem eins: klein – Die Reform des TSG durch das BVerfG' [2011] *Neue Zeitschrift für Verwaltungsrecht* (NVwZ) 474.
[25] BVerfG 27 October 2011, NJW 2012, 600.
[26] See OLG Hamm 8 December 2012, StAZ 2013, 218.
[27] BVerfG 26 January 1993, BVerfGE 88, 87.
[28] BVerfG 15 August 1996, NJW 1997, 1632; confirmed in BVerfG 27 October 2011, NJW 2012, 600.

with her female partner.[29] In particular, the Court points to the fact that for a homosexual couple the entering into a marriage as such does not indicate a re-identification with the legal gender. Entering into a registered partnership – which presupposes the same legal gender of the partners – is not an option. The loss of the first name would thus violate the sexual self-determination of the transgender person protected by Art. 2(1) in connection with Art. 1(1) GG.

VI. LEGAL CHALLENGES TO THE EXISTING RULES

Where does the law in Germany currently stand? It appears that the battle between the legislator and the Bundesverfassungsgericht, the Federal Constitutional Court, is over – a battle which has created a fairly liberal system for the legal recognition of preferred gender. The driving force behind that development has clearly been the Constitutional Court and not the legislator which most of the time has only reacted to the decisions of the Court. It is now time that the legislator puts the old Transsexuals Act (from which only the torso is left) into the museum of legal history and reformulates the whole Act[30] – which had been promised by the former conservative-liberal government of Angela Merkel in 2009,[31] but not accomplished, and which appears, unfortunately, not to be prioritised on the agenda of the current coalition government.[32]

---

29 BVerfG 6 December 2005, BVerfGE 115, 1.

30 See e.g. already M. Grünberger, 'Ein Plädoyer für ein zeitgemäßes Transsexuellengesetz' [2007] *StAZ (Das Standesamt)* 357, 368.

31 See *Wachstum. Bildung. Zusammenhalt. – Koalitionsvertrag zwischen CDU, CSU und FDP* 2009, p. 108: '*Das geltende Transsexuellengesetz ist in seinen wesentlichen Grundzügen inzwischen fast dreißig Jahre alt. Es entspricht nicht mehr in jeder Hinsicht aktuellen medizinisch-wissenschaftlichen Erkenntnissen. Wir werden das Transsexuellengesetz deshalb unter Berücksichtigung der Rechtsprechung des Bundesverfassungsgerichts auf eine neue zeitgemäße Grundlage stellen, um den betroffenen Menschen ein freies und selbstbestimmtes Leben zu ermöglichen*'.

32 See the rather vague formulation in *Deutschlands Zukunft gestalten. – Koalitionsvertrag zwischen CDU, CSU und SPD*, 2013: '*Die durch die Änderung des Personenstandrechts für intersexuelle Menschen erzielten Verbesserungen werden wir evaluieren und gegebenenfalls ausbauen und die besondere Situation von trans- und intersexuellen Menschen in den Fokus nehmen*'.

THE LEGAL STATUS OF TRANSSEXUAL AND TRANSGENDER PERSONS IN IRELAND

Brian SLOAN*

Contents

* The author is extremely grateful to Peter Dunne and Alison Fynes for their helpful comments on an earlier draft.

I. LEGAL FRAMEWORK AND STATISTICS

1.1. BACKGROUND AND OVERALL LEGAL FRAMEWORK

At the time of writing, there is no mechanism by which a transgender person can have his or her preferred gender comprehensively recognised in Irish law.[1] The general legal position remains that biological indicators present at the time of birth 'continue to act as the governance in the determination of sex'.[2] In his 2007 judgment in the High Court case of *Foy v An t-Árd Chláraitheoir*, McKechnie J declared that Ireland was in breach of Article 8 of the European Convention on Human Rights[3] in the light of the European Court of Human Rights' judgment in *Goodwin v United Kingdom*[4] because of the 'absence of any provision which would enable the acquired identity of [the applicant] to be legally recognised in this jurisdiction'.[5]

Nevertheless, the Government's Gender Recognition Advisory Group (the 'GRAG' or the 'Group') did not report until 2011 (following the Government's decision to abandon a surprising attempt to appeal the decision in the *Foy* case[6]),[7] and the 'General Scheme' of a Gender Recognition Bill was finally published only in July 2013.[8] A relevant report of the parliamentary Joint Committee on Education and Social Protection was then published in January 2014, recommending a number of changes to the anticipated Bill.[9] Following discussion of the Committee's recommendations by the Cabinet,[10] a Revised General Scheme (containing few major changes) was published in June 2014,[11] and a Bill based on it was published only in December 2014.[12] Indeed, the Minister for Social

1 See, generally, O. O'Sullivan (ed.), *Equality and Identity: Transgender and Intersex Experience in Ireland,* Transgender Equality Network Ireland, Dublin 2013, ch. 2. *Cf.* Gender Recognition Act 2015 (GRA), which became law in July 2015 but is not in force at the time of writing.

2 *Foy v An t-Árd Chláraitheoir* [2002] IEHC 116, at [121] (McKechnie J).

3 See European Convention on Human Rights Act 2003, s. 5.

4 Appl. no. 28957/95 [2002] 35 EHRR 447 (ECtHR).

5 *Foy v An t-Árd Chláraitheoir* [2007] IEHC 470, at [102]. See T. Ní Mhuirthile, 'Declaring Irish Law Incompatible with the Law of the ECHR – Where to Now?' (2008) 4 *Independent Law Review* 2 for discussion.

6 Transgender Equality Network Ireland, 'Dr Lydia Foy's Case' <www.teni.ie/page.aspx?contentid=588> accessed 25.03.2015. In 2014, Dr Foy reached a settlement with the state as regards its failure to recognise her female gender: Transgender Equality Network Ireland, 'Press Release: TENI Welcomes News of Settlement in Lydia Foy Case', 28.10.2014 <www.teni.ie/news-post.aspx?contentid=1160> accessed 18.08.2015.

7 Gender Recognition Advisory Group, *Report to Joan Burton, TD, Minister for Social Protection*, 2011.

8 Department of Social Protection, *General Scheme of Gender Recognition Bill 2013*, 2013 (the 'original General Scheme').

9 Joint Committee on Education and Social Protection, *Report on the General Scheme of a Gender Recognition Bill 2013*, ESP31011, 2014.

10 Dáil Deb 9 May 2014, vol. 840, no. 4, p. 629.

11 Department of Social Protection, *(Revised) General Scheme of Gender Recognition Bill 2014*, 2014 (the 'Revised General Scheme').

12 Gender Recognition Bill (No. 116 of 2014) <www.oireachtas.ie/viewdoc.asp?DocID=27835&&CatID=59&StartDate=01%20January%202014&OrderAscending=0> accessed 18.08.2015.

Protection has admitted that gender recognition was an issue that has been 'left unaddressed for far too long'.[13] By the time the General Scheme was published, two Private Members' Bills had been propagated, by Aengus Ó Snodaigh TD[14] and Senator Katherine Zappone[15] respectively. This chapter will focus on the Government Bill (GRB)[16] that became the Gender Recognition Act (GRA) in July 2015 after considerable amendment and debate. It is apparently expected to be commenced by the end of August 2015.[17]

Ireland has a written constitution. However, in a 2002 judgment relating to earlier proceedings in *Foy*, McKechnie J rejected the submission that the applicant's inability to have the register of births amended to reflect her preferred female identity violated her constitutional 'rights of privacy, of dignity, [or] of equality',[18] or her right to marry, in spite of his recognition that those constitutional rights did exist. Indeed, it will become clear that Ireland's (pre-amendment) constitutional protection of heterosexual marriage and the marital family had the potential to limit the effectiveness of any scheme of gender recognition.[19]

It should be noted, however, that Ireland's Equality Tribunal has recognised that the existing gender ground in Ireland's anti-discrimination employment legislation[20] applies to a transgender individual.[21] This has been used as a justification not to include a ground relating to transgender or intersex status,[22] but the Joint Committee recommended that '[c]onsideration should be given to amending Equality legislation to add "gender identity" to the existing nine grounds under which discrimination is illegal'.[23]

1.2. MEDICAL TREATMENT

The Gender Recognition Advisory Group, perhaps oddly composed entirely of representatives from government departments and without any trans members, engaged in some discussion of medical provision for those with gender identity

13 Department of Social Protection, 'Minister for Social Protection Publishes Revised General Scheme of the Gender Recognition Bill 2014' (17.06.2014) <www.welfare.ie/en/pressoffice/Pages/pr180614.aspx> accessed 18.08.2015.

14 Gender Recognition Bill (No. 56 of 2013) <www.oireachtas.ie/viewdoc.asp?DocID=23558&&CatID=59> accessed 18.08.2015 (the 'Ó Snodaigh Bill').

15 Legal Recognition of Gender Bill (No. 75 of 2013) <www.oireachtas.ie/viewdoc.asp?DocID=23950&&CatID=59> accessed 18.08.2015 (the 'Zappone Bill').

16 Gender Recognition Bill (No. 116b of 2014) <www.oireachtas.ie/viewdoc.asp?fn=/documents/bills28/bills/2014/11614/b116b14s.pdf> accessed 18.08.2015 (the 'GRB').

17 Transgender Equality Network Ireland, 'Legal Gender Recognition in Ireland' <http://www.teni.ie/page.aspx?contentid=586> accessed 18.08.2015.

18 *Foy v An t-Árd Chláraitheoir* [2002] IEHC 116, at [132] (McKechnie J).

19 See e.g. Gender Recognition Advisory Group, above n. 7, at [5.5.1]. *Cf.* Thirty-fourth Amendment of the Constitution (Marriage Equality) Bill 2015.

20 Employment Equality Act 1998 as amended, s. 6(2)(a).

21 DEC-E2011-066 (Equality Tribunal).

22 Joint Committee on Education and Social Protection, above n. 9, at [5.7].

23 Joint Committee on Education and Social Protection, above n. 9, p. 38.

disorder in Ireland. It generally did so, however, without referring specifically to its sources of information. In its 2011 report, it asserted that there were 'two principal clinics operated by mental health professionals for GID patients in Ireland', but that no specific psychiatric or psychological clinics were publicly funded via the Health Service Executive (HSE).[24] It did report that '[a] HSE consultant endocrinologist operates a hormone treatment clinic'.[25] However, it was clear that '[g]ender re-assignment surgery is not available in Ireland', albeit that a small number of Irish patients 'are known to have had surgery in the United Kingdom and in other countries such as Thailand'[26] and this has on occasion been funded by the HSE.[27] The Ó Snodaigh Bill would impose a specific but light obligation on the state to 'facilitate re-entry visas for non-EU nationals who travel abroad' for such treatment, where it is 'necessary and practicable' to do so.[28]

A 2009 report of a HSE mapping exercise asserted that 'there are significantly limited tailored healthcare services to meet the needs of Transsexual people in Ireland'.[29] In spite of the setting up of a transgender health working group in 2011, it has been said that '[a]ccess to healthcare is one of the most urgent issues facing the trans community'.[30] In a document published in March 2013 (but seemingly written in 2012), the Government asserted that 'a National HSE Strategy and Action Plan for LGBT people' was 'in preparation and expected to be published shortly'.[31] That said, the GRAG felt unable to make any recommendations on 'access to health and support services for transsexuals',[32] and no such specific provision appears to have been made in the GRA.

As regards private health insurance, coverage depends on the particular insurance contract, although the Health Insurance Act 1994 (Minimum Benefit) Regulations 1996 mandate a minimum level of provision. The Government has pointed out that those regulations exclude 'cosmetic services or treatment

24 Gender Recognition Advisory Group, above n. 7, at [2.5.1].
25 Gender Recognition Advisory Group, above n. 7, at [2.5.1]. See also C. De Gascun, J. Lucey, J. Kelly, N. Salter and D. O'Shea, 'Gender Identity Disorder' (2006) 99(5) *Irish Medical Journal* 146.
26 Gender Recognition Advisory Group, above n. 7, at [2.5.1]. See also Health Service Executive, *LGBT Health: Towards Meeting the Health Care Needs of Lesbian, Gay, Bisexual and Transgender People*, 2009, p. 33.
27 See e.g. Equality Authority, *Equality Authority Submission to the Gender Recognition Advisory Group*, 2010, p. 11; Joint Committee on Education and Social Protection, *General Scheme of Gender Recognition Bill 2013: Discussion (Resumed)*, 24.10.2013, p. 14.
28 Ó Snodaigh Bill, cl. 15(2).
29 Health Service Executive, above n. 26, p. 283.
30 Transgender Equality Network Ireland, *Presentation: Oireachtas Committee on Health and Children*, 2013, p. 2. See, generally, O. O'Sullivan, above n. 1, ch. 5, and Transgender Equality Network Ireland, 'Press Release: New Survey Reveals nearly 80% of Trans People have Considered Suicide' (02.12.2013) <www.teni.ie/news-post.aspx?contentid=970> accessed 18.08.2015.
31 Steering Committee For Human Rights, *Follow-up to Committee of Ministers' Recommendation CM/Rec(2010)5 on measures to combat discrimination on grounds of sexual orientation or gender identity: Member States['] replies*, CDDH(2013)004FIN, 2013, p. 283.
32 Gender Recognition Advisory Group, above n. 7, at [5.18].

except the correction of accidental disfigurement or significant congenital disfigurement',[33] and asserted that insurance cover would be provided for procedures such as hysterectomy and breast reduction only if 'deemed medically necessary'.[34] It also claimed, however, that measures such as hormone treatment 'can be conducted on an outpatient basis and may be covered depending on the health insurance policy held'.[35]

The Ó Snodaigh Bill provides specifically that '[w]here a person under 18 is seeking access to total and partial surgical interventions and/or comprehensive hormonal treatments to adjust their bodies, including their genitalia, to their self-perceived gender identity, the normal age of medical consent of 16 shall apply having regard to the rights of children'.[36] Where such a person is refused the relevant treatment, the Bill would allow him or her to apply to the District Court for consent to the treatment,[37] and the Court would be required to 'take into account the evolving capacities, best interests and welfare of the person as outlined in the UN Convention on the Rights of the Child'[38] (as it would be on an application by a non-adult for legal recognition of gender identity) and deliver a decision within 60 days of the application.[39]

1.3. STATISTICS

The Gender Recognition Advisory Group estimated that there were around 300 adults with gender identity disorder in Ireland.[40] That said, it also recorded that this was the approximate number of patients registered with the principal clinics for those with GID, suggesting that the actual number is likely to be higher. The campaigning organisation Transgender Equality Network Ireland goes as far as to say that there are 'tens of thousands' of 'trans or intersex people … living their lives in Ireland today'.[41] The 2011 Census suggested that the total Irish population is approximately 4.6 million people.[42] The GRAG claimed that 90% of people with GID wished to transition from male to female.[43]

As stated above, it is not currently possible for a transgender individual to have his or her gender identity comprehensively recognised in Irish law.

33 Steering Committee for Human Rights, above n. 31, p. 283. See Health Insurance Act 1994 (Minimum Benefit) Regulations 1996, SI No. 83/1996, r. 3.
34 Steering Committee for Human Rights, above n. 31, p. 283.
35 Steering Committee for Human Rights, above n. 31, p. 283.
36 Ó Snodaigh Bill, cl. 13(1).
37 Ó Snodaigh Bill, cl. 13(2).
38 Ó Snodaigh Bill, cl. 14(a).
39 Ó Snodaigh Bill, cl. 14(b).
40 Gender Recognition Advisory Group, above n. 7, at [2.5.1].
41 Transgender Equality Network Ireland, *TENI Presentation to Fine Gael Committee on Justice, Equality and Defence*, 2013, p. 1.
42 Central Statistics Office, *Census of Population 2011 Preliminary Results*, 2011.
43 Gender Recognition Advisory Group, above n. 7, at [2.5.1].

Nevertheless, and again without citing independent research or indeed specific evidence of any kind, the Group confidently asserted that '[f]or the majority of transgender persons who were married in their former gender but have since transitioned to the opposite gender, the marriage will have broken down by the time the transgender spouse wishes to apply for gender recognition'.[44] It will be seen that this assertion was frequently used to justify a restriction on the legal recognition of gender identity to those who are neither married nor in a civil partnership before it became relatively clear that same-sex marriage would be introduced in Ireland.

II. RECOGNISING THE PREFERRED LEGAL SEX AND/OR GENDER OF A TRANSGENDER/ TRANSSEXUAL PERSON – PROCEDURE AND REQUIREMENTS

2.1. LEGAL PROCEDURE

The GRAG proposed a 'scheme whereby the State recognises the changed gender of persons who are living full-time in the gender that is opposite to that shown in the birth register entry of the person'.[45] It should be noted that the Group's scheme was not designed to include intersex persons,[46] though the Government hoped that it had made adjustments sufficient to facilitate applications by such individuals when it published even the original General Scheme.[47]

The Group's scheme would have worked via an application for a gender recognition certificate made to a statutory (administrative) independent three-person Gender Recognition Panel including a medical expert and a legal expert, chaired by 'a lay person representing wider civil society'.[48] The Group recommended that '[u]nsuccessful applicants should be allowed to appeal to the Circuit Court sitting as the Family Court',[49] and also that there should be 'a revocation and correction process'.[50]

---

44 Gender Recognition Advisory Group, above n. 7, at [5.5].

45 Gender Recognition Advisory Group, above n. 7, at [6.1.1].

46 Gender Recognition Advisory Group, above n. 7, at [5.8.3].

47 Department of Social Protection, 'Minister for Social Protection Publishes General Scheme of the Gender Recognition Bill 2013' (17.07.2013) <www.welfare.ie/en/pressoffice/Pages/pr170713.aspx> accessed 18.08.2015.

48 Gender Recognition Advisory Group, above n. 7, at [5.11.1]. See A. Fynes, *A Comparison of the UK and Irish Approaches to Transgender Legislation*, unpublished LLM thesis, Cambridge, 2013, pp. 37–39 for discussion.

49 Gender Recognition Advisory Group, above n. 7, at [6.4].

50 Gender Recognition Advisory Group, above n. 7, at [6.1.2].

The Ó Snodaigh Bill would simply require a (proven) adult to submit a 'request to amend the sex recorded on their birth certificate in the records',[51] along with any new name under which the applicant wishes to be registered.[52] Only those under 18 would be required to apply 'through their legal representatives or Guardian ad Litem to the District Court' for a new birth certificate.[53] The Zappone Bill would also involve a direct application to the Registrar General to 'record and recognise the person's gender identity'.[54] Its requirements are slightly more onerous than the Ó Snodaigh Bill, since it requires a statutory declaration *inter alia* that it is the relevant person's 'intention to live permanently as a person of [the relevant] gender identity',[55] with 'permanently' meaning 'for the remainder of the life of the person'.[56] But it is also less onerous in another respect, since even those under 18 but who are at least 16 could make a direct application with the consent of at least one guardian,[57] and the guardian or guardians themselves could make an application for a younger child.[58]

In formulating its Bill, the Government chose a method closer to that in the Ó Snodaigh and Zappone Bills, which the Minister hoped would be a 'more progressive and less cumbersome approach' than that proposed by the Group.[59] The GRA provides that the Minister for Social Protection herself will receive and adjudicate upon applications.[60] There will therefore be no need for a Gender Recognition Panel, though the Minister would be able to 'request further information from the applicant regarding any information furnished by the applicant on his or her behalf'.[61] The GRA is less clear than the General Scheme on the Minister's obligation to issue the certificate if 'the application meets all the qualification requirements',[62] but the Explanatory and Financial Memorandum to the Bill makes clear that such an obligation is intended.[63] As we will see, those requirements are more onerous than those imposed by the two Private Members' Bills. No application fee would be payable, although it is implied that the applicant would be responsible for the costs of obtaining and submitting the required evidence.[64]

51 Ó Snodaigh Bill, cl. 4(b).
52 Ó Snodaigh Bill, cl. 4(c).
53 Ó Snodaigh Bill, cl. 6(1).
54 Zappone Bill, cl. 2(2).
55 Zappone Bill, cl. 2(3)(b).
56 Zappone Bill, cl. 1.
57 Zappone Bill, cl. 2(5).
58 Zappone Bill, cl. 2(4).
59 Department of Social Protection, above n. 47.
60 GRA, ss. 8(1), 2; see also Revised General Scheme, Head 4(1).
61 GRA, s. 8(4). *Cf.* GRB, cl. 8(4)(b); see also Revised General Scheme, Head 4(4).
62 Revised General Scheme, Head 4(2).
63 Department of Social Protection, 'Gender Recognition Bill 2014: Explanatory and Financial Memorandum' <www.oireachtas.ie/viewdoc.asp?fn=/documents/bills28/bills/2014/11614/b11614d-memo.pdf> (12.2014) accessed 18.08.2015, p. 2.
64 GRA, s. 8(2); *cf.* Revised General Scheme, Head 4(5).

If an application does not meet the requirements, the Minister would be required to issue the person concerned with a written notice setting out the reason(s) why the application is not being approved and advising that person of his or her right to appeal the decision and the fact that the decision will be suspended until the deadline for appeals has passed or an appeal has been disposed of.[65] The appeal[66] would lie to the Circuit Family Court,[67] and would have to be made within 90 days of the refusal to issue the certificate, although the court could apparently grant an extension.[68] Provision would also be made for the correction of certificates.[69] Revocation of a certificate would be possible if it is subsequently established that the applicant concerned did not meet the requirements[70] or if the person to whom it was issued wishes to revert to their original legal gender.[71] The level of evidence would effectively equal that needed for the original application, and the Revised General Scheme's Explanatory Notes asserted that the intention behind the gender recognition scheme is that 'revocations due to "a change of mind" would be extremely rare'.[72]

The Zappone Bill provides for an appeal to the High Court against the refusal to record an applicant's true gender identity within three months of the refusal.[73] An appellant may seek an order 'directing An tArd-Chláraitheoir [the Registrar General] to record and recognise the person's gender identity in the Gender Recognition Register'.[74] No specific right of appeal appears to be included in the Ó Snodaigh Bill, perhaps because there are so few bases upon which an application could possibly be refused in the first place in light of its requirements.

2.2. OFFICIAL DOCUMENTS

2.2.1. Current Position

Even under the pre-GRA law in Ireland, a person's preferred gender can be recognised for the purposes of passports. The Passports Act 2008 allows a person who 'has undergone, or is undergoing, treatment or procedures or both to alter [that person's] sexual characteristics and physical appearance to those

65 GRA, s. 8(5); see also Revised General Scheme, Head 4(3).
66 GRA, s. 17, which also covers appeals regarding correction and revocation; see also Revised General Scheme, Head 18.
67 GRA, s. 17(1); *cf.* Revised General Scheme, Head 18(1). See Irish Human Rights Commission, *Observations on the General Scheme of Gender Recognition Bill 2013*, 2013, at [37]–[38] on the importance of the ready availability of legal representation in such proceedings.
68 GRA, s. 17(1); see also Revised General Scheme, Head 18(3).
69 GRA, s. 16; see also Revised General Scheme, Head 19.
70 GRA, s. 14; see also Revised General Scheme, Head 20(1)(i).
71 GRA, s. 15; see also Revised General Scheme, Head 20(1)(ii). *Cf.* original General Scheme, Head 19.
72 Revised General Scheme, Head 20 Explanatory Notes.
73 Zappone Bill, cl. 2(12).
74 Zappone Bill, cl. 2(12).

of the opposite sex'[75] to apply for a passport to be issued in the 'new sex'[76] and in a name that is different from the one shown on the applicant's birth certificate, from one on another document used to prove evidence of Irish citizenship or previous passport, or from the applicant's married name.[77] If the applicant produces 'evidence (including medical evidence from a registered medical practitioner) to the satisfaction of the Minister [of Foreign Affairs[78]] to confirm that the applicant has undergone, or is undergoing' the relevant treatment,[79] together with, 'if appropriate, evidence to the satisfaction of the Minister of the use by the applicant of the new name',[80] the Minister 'may … issue a passport to the applicant in the new name, if appropriate, and in which the new sex of the applicant is entered'.[81] Significantly, the procedure under the Passports Act 2008, while onerous and difficult to use in itself,[82] is expressed not to 'confer any right or entitlement' on the successful applicant that is 'not connected with the purposes' of the Act,[83] or to 'affect any right, entitlement, duty or obligation arising under statute or otherwise'.[84] The 2008 provisions will be softened by the GRA and may nevertheless be of some use to transgender people in a marriage or civil partnership, or some 16- and 17-year-olds, even once the GRA as currently drafted is commenced.[85]

A transgender individual could also change his or her name by enrolment of a deed poll, which contains an affidavit to the effect that the applicant is 'abandoning the use' of the former name, will use the new name at all times and requires others to do the same.[86] The use of a deed poll means that 'a record of the change is kept for future identification'.[87] The record can be attached to an individual's birth certificate and 'is acceptable for most administrative procedures'.[88] The applicant in *Foy v An t-Árd Chláraitheoir* changed her name via this method, with the result that she was 'described as "female" bearing her chosen name of Lydia Annice in

75 Passports Act 2008, s. 11(1)(a).
76 Passports Act 2008, s. 11(1).
77 Passports Act 2008, s. 11(1)(b). See s. 10 for details of how the applicant's name is otherwise determined for these purposes.
78 Passports Act 2008, s. 2.
79 Passports Act 2008, s. 11(2)(a).
80 Passports Act 2008, s. 11(2)(b).
81 Passports Act 2008, s. 11(2).
82 See e.g. Transgender Equality Network Ireland, *Human Rights Violations in Ireland on the Basis of Gender Identity and Intersex Identity: Submission to the Country Report Task Forces, 109th Session of the Human Rights Committee*, 2013, p. 4.
83 Passports Act 2008, s. 11(3)(a).
84 Passports Act 2008, s. 11(3)(b).
85 GRA, s. 38; Department of Social Protection, above n. 63, p. 9.
86 <www.citizensinformation.ie/en/birth_family_relationships/problems_in_marriages_and_other_relationships/changing_your_name_by_deed_poll.html>; see also Civil Registration Act 2004, s. 25 on changes to the forename of a child.
87 Citizens Information Board, 'Changing your Name by Deed Poll' <www.citizensinformation.ie/en/birth_family_relationships/problems_in_marriages_and_other_relationships/changing_your_name_by_deed_poll.html> accessed 18.08.2015.
88 Citizens Information Board, above n. 87.

documents such as her passport, driving licence, car registration records, medical card, medical card records and tax and social security documents'.[89] A passport can be issued in a new name (without the legal recognition of gender identity) if the applicant simply 'produces evidence to the satisfaction of the Minister of the use by him or her of the new name for a period of not less than 2 years prior to the date of the application'.[90]

The fundamentally significant document for the purposes of legal gender, however, is the birth certificate, and in the 2002 judgment in *Foy* (reaffirmed in 2007 but with a declaration of incompatibility with the ECHR) it was held that the Registrar had made no relevant error by registering the transgender applicant as a male with the male name supplied by her parents shortly after birth and therefore had no power to 'correct' the entry notwithstanding the applicant's subsequent gender reassignment surgery and adoption of a feminine name. As McKechnie J acknowledged, there were a 'limited number of occasions' on which the applicant had to produce that birth certificate containing her originally recorded gender, causing 'distress and embarrassment' as well as 'a loss of dignity and privacy'.[91]

2.2.2. New Legislation

Under the GRA, a successful applicant to the Minister would be entitled to a new birth certificate or entry in the foreign birth register recognising their preferred gender,[92] which on the GRAG's view would be 'indistinguishable in content, style and design from the original that would have been issued to the same person'.[93] The GRA provides that 'any requirement of law for the production of a certificate of birth shall be satisfied by the production of the certified copy' of an entry in the register of gender recognition.[94]

The GRA specifically states that '[t]he person to whom the gender recognition certificate is issued shall not be required to produce it as proof of gender or identity for any purpose save as required by law',[95] albeit that he or she 'may produce it to provide proof of gender or identity, if he or she so chooses'.[96] The person to whom a gender recognition certificate is issued 'may contact [the Registrar General] and request that the required particulars relating to the recognition of the gender of the person are entered in the register' of gender recognition, though

89 [2007] IEHC 470, at [64(2)].
90 Passports Act 2008, s. 10(4).
91 [2007] IEHC 470, at [64(2)].
92 Department for Social Protection, above n. 63, p. 5; *cf.* Revised General Scheme, Head 10(3). See also Gender Recognition Advisory Group, above n. 7, at [5.12.1], and Ó Snodaigh Bill, cl. 7.
93 Gender Recognition Advisory Group, above n. 7, at [5.14.1].
94 GRA, s. 27, inserting Civil Registration Act 2004, s. 30D(3); see also Revised General Scheme, Head 10(2).
95 GRA, s. 18(4); *cf.* Revised General Scheme, Head 9(6)–(7). See also Gender Recognition Advisory Group, above n. 7, at [6.2].
96 GRA, s. 18(5); see also Revised General Scheme, Head 9(5).

this is perhaps odd since the Minister must inform the Registrar of the decision.[97] When informed and sufficiently 'satisfied', the Registrar would record details of the gender recognition certificate in a new register of gender recognition,[98] whose index would not be open to public inspection or search and would be searchable only by the subject of the entry or by various surviving relatives in the event of the death of that person.[99]

The Registrar would be obliged to 'maintain an index to make traceable the connection between each entry in the register [of gender recognition] and the corresponding entry in the register of births or the Adopted Children Register'.[100] That index would 'not be open to public inspection',[101] and 'no information from that index [would] be given to any person except by order of a court'.[102] Necessity for the purposes of a criminal investigation had previously been given as one example of a circumstance in which such disclosure would be appropriate,[103] although this is not apparently mentioned in the GRA and it specifically provides that a '[a] court shall not make [a relevant] order where the person to whom the information relates is a child of less than 18 years of age, unless satisfied that it is in the best interest of the child'.[104]

In rather less depth than the GRA, the Ó Snodaigh Bill states that it will be 'prohibited to refer to the current law', by which it apparently means the Bill itself, 'in the amended birth certificate or any new identity documents issued on foot thereof'.[105] It provides that '[o]nly those persons authorised by the document holder, or provided with written consent, or consent of the District Court, may access an original birth certificate once it has been amended',[106] which implies that the original birth record would still exist. It also contains a general prohibition on 'publishing details of an amendment of recorded sex and name or names save where the explicit consent of the document holder has been given'.[107] It would be a specific offence for a person who 'acquired protected information in an

97 GRA, s. 27, inserting Civil Registration Act 2004, s. 30B(1); GRA, s. 13; *cf.* Revised General Scheme, Head 9(4).

98 GRA, s. 27, inserting Civil Registration Act 2004, s. 30B(2); see also s. 33 for equivalent provisions relating to those who have been the subject of intercountry adoption; Revised General Scheme, Head 11(1), Gender Recognition Advisory Group, above n. 7, at [5.14.1].

99 GRA, s. 27, inserting Civil Registration Act 2004, s. 30B(2); see also s. 28; *cf.* Revised General Scheme, Head 11(5).

100 GRA, s. 27, inserting Civil Registration Act 2004, s. 30D(1); see also Revised General Scheme, Head 13(1)(c); Gender Recognition Advisory Group, above n. 7, at [5.14.1]; Steering Committee For Human Rights, above n. 31, p. 279.

101 GRA, s. 27, inserting Civil Registration Act 2004, s. 30D(2); Revised General Scheme, Head 13(2).

102 GRA, s. 27, inserting Civil Registration Act 2004, s. 30D(2); *cf.* original General Scheme, Heads 11(3), 12(3); Revised General Scheme, Heads 13–14.

103 Gender Recognition Advisory Group, above n. 7, at [5.14.1].

104 GRA, s. 27, inserting Civil Registration Act 2004, s. 30D(4).

105 Ó Snodaigh Bill, cl. 8.

106 Ó Snodaigh Bill, cl. 11(1).

107 Ó Snodaigh Bill, cl. 11(2).

official capacity' to 'disclose the information to any other person'.[108] 'Protected information' is defined to mean 'information which relates to a person who has had their recorded sex changed, or made an application to have it changed', and concerns the application, the 'information changed' or 'the person's previous recorded sex'.[109] A wide definition of 'official capacity' is employed, which includes the acquisition of information in the course of 'the conduct of business or the supply of professional services',[110] but the Bill also specifies a number of circumstances in which the offence would not in fact be committed.[111]

A linking method is also employed in the Zappone Bill. The Registrar General would 'record and recognise the [applicant's] gender identity in the Gender Recognition Register and … attach a note to the entry concerning that person in the registry of births indicating that there is now an entry concerning the person in the Gender Recognition Register'.[112] There is then a rather general provision to the effect that 'access to the entry in the register of births shall be restricted to a person authorised under the [Civil Registration Act] 2004'.[113] The Bill also provides that any legal requirement for the production of a birth certificate 'shall be satisfied by the production of a copy of a certificate of birth containing the particulars entered in the gender recognition register'.[114] Similarly, any application for a certification of birth concerning someone with an entry in the Gender Recognition Register would, 'unless otherwise specified and duly authorised, be deemed' to be a request 'for a copy containing the particulars from that Register'.[115] The Registrar General would be placed under a specific obligation to 'ensure that it is not evident, from examination of any certificate of birth containing the particulars entered in the Gender Recognition Register, that such certificate is in any way distinguishable from a certificate containing particulars entered in the register of births',[116] and the Registrar, the Minister for Social Protection and 'their respective officers' would be required to ensure, '[s]ave where the law requires otherwise', that 'the identity of an applicant [for gender recognition] and all other particulars relating to the application are kept confidential'.[117]

As well as mandating the transfer of information to the Registrar General, the Revised General Scheme provided that the information 'may' be transmitted to 'facilitate changes to the Public Service Identity (PSI) dataset' held by the Department of Social Protection 'and promulgation to the wider group of public

[108] Ó Snodaigh Bill, cl. 16(1).
[109] Ó Snodaigh Bill, cl. 16(2).
[110] Ó Snodaigh Bill, cl. 16(3).
[111] Ó Snodaigh Bill, cl. 16(4)–(6).
[112] Zappone Bill, cl. 2(2).
[113] Zappone Bill, cl. 2(2).
[114] Zappone Bill, cl. 2(8).
[115] Zappone Bill, cl. 2(9).
[116] Zappone Bill, cl. 2(10).
[117] Zappone Bill, cl. 2(11).

agencies that are legally authorised to use the PSI data',[118] and to 'the Passport Office of the Department of Foreign Affairs and Trade for use in approving and issuing passports'.[119] This specific provision appears to have been omitted from the GRA. Under the Ó Snodaigh Bill, such details would be passed to 'the National Vetting Bureau and other bodies as determined by the Minister for Social Protection'.[120]

2.3. LEGAL REQUIREMENTS

The GRAG's recommendations, to a significant extent reflected even in the Revised General Scheme and the GRB, before it was amended to some extent, would have imposed a number of stringent conditions before the legal recognition of a transgender person's gender identity would be allowed, and indeed the Explanatory Memorandum to the Ó Snodaigh Bill describes the Group's requirements as 'unduly restrictive'.[121]

2.3.1. Birth/Adoption Registration and Ordinary Residence

Under the Revised General Scheme, the application for a gender recognition certificate would have been open only to a person whose birth was registered in Ireland (whether because he or she was born there or appears on the foreign births entry book or register) or who has been ordinarily resident there for at least a year.[122] The GRB expands eligibility to include those whose adoption (including intercountry adoption) is registered in Ireland,[123] but all of these criteria, *inter alia*, apply equally to applicants whose preferred gender was recognised abroad.[124] Applications from such people would succeed only if the foreign requirements can be shown to the satisfaction of the Minister to be 'at least equivalent' to the remaining Irish requirements, which sets a relatively high threshold.[125] As the Group recognised, however, many people who had their preferred gender recognised abroad 'would have no need to seek a gender recognition decision in Ireland as they would have entered Ireland in their new gender with all the relevant supporting personal documentation'.[126] Indeed, ironically the Government has

118 Revised General Scheme, Head 9(5)(a).
119 Revised General Scheme, Head 9(5)(b). *Cf.* Gender Recognition Advisory Group, above n. 7, at [5.15.1].
120 Ó Snodaigh Bill, cl. 12.
121 Ó Snodaigh Bill Explanatory Memorandum <www.oireachtas.ie/viewdoc.asp?fn=/documents/bills28/bills/2013/5613/b5613dmemo.pdf> accessed 18.08.2015, p. 3.
122 Revised General Scheme, Head 5(a)–(c). See also Gender Recognition Advisory Group, above n. 7, at [5.3.1].
123 GRA, ss. 2, 9.
124 GRA, s. 11(2); *cf.* Revised General Scheme, Head 6(a)(vii).
125 GRA, s. 11(2)(b)(i); *cf.* Revised General Scheme, Head 6 Explanatory Notes, Gender Recognition Advisory Group, above n. 7, at [5.9.1].
126 Gender Recognition Advisory Group, above n. 7, at [5.9].

announced in response to a questionnaire on the implementation of a Council of Europe recommendation[127] that 'the General Registrar Office ... will accept a birth certificate amended by another State where gender reassignment is recognised ... from a person born outside of Ireland' even under the current law for the purposes of notification of intention to marry or enter a civil partnership.[128]

2.3.2. *Age*

Under the original General Scheme, extremely cautiously, a gender recognition certificate could have been issued by the Minister only if the applicant were aged 18 or over.[129] The Group had decided not to recommend that gender identity could be recognised before the applicant reached the age of 18, on the basis of supposed and disputed 'evidence from the literature that minors who desire a gender change frequently change their minds as they reach adulthood'.[130] The Irish Human Rights Commission has doubted whether this requirement was human rights compliant and pointed out its inconsistency with the general age of consent for medical treatment.[131] It clearly contrasts with the Ó Snodaigh Bill, which provides that a court can consider an application for gender identity recognition by someone under 18, even in the absence of the consent of relevant adults,[132] taking into account the minor's 'evolving capacities, best interests and welfare' as well as his or her constitutional rights.[133] Under the Zappone Bill, moreover, court involvement is not a requirement of an application by or on behalf of a minor. Those between 16 and 18 could apply with the consent of at least one guardian,[134] while for those under 16 it is the guardian making the application on behalf of the relevant person (and not a court) who must 'in so far as is practicable, give due weight to the views of the child, having regard to the child's age and maturity',[135] and 'ensure the best interests of the child [are] the paramount consideration'.[136]

---

127 Recommendation CM/Rec(2010)5 of the Committee of Ministers to member states on measures to combat discrimination on grounds of sexual orientation or gender identity.

128 Steering Committee For Human Rights, above n. 31, p. 279.

129 General Scheme, Head 5(d). See also Gender Recognition Advisory Group, above n. 7, at [5.4.1].

130 Gender Recognition Advisory Group, above n. 7, at [5.4]; *cf.* Transgender Equality Network Ireland, *Legislation Based on Human and Civil Rights is Key to Equality for All*, 2014, pp. 5–6. Time spent living in the preferred gender between the ages of 16 and 18 would have been taken into account under the GRAG proposal, provided it was supported by medical evidence as to the applicant's capacity during that period (at [5.4.1]), but the minimum period was not in any case included in the General Scheme.

131 Irish Human Rights Commission, above n. 67, at [16]–[21]. See also Transgender Equality Network Ireland, above n. 130, pp. 4–6 for criticism.

132 Ó Snodaigh Bill, cl. 6(3), oddly describing such adults as 'legal representatives'.

133 Ó Snodaigh Bill, cl. 6(2).

134 Zappone Bill, cl. 2(5).

135 Zappone Bill, cl. 2(6)(a).

136 Zappone Bill, cl. 2(6)(b).

This would be an interesting application of the 'paramountcy' principle in the context of decision-making by private individuals rather than by a court.[137]

To some extent reflecting the concerns of its consultees concerning the rights of minor transgender persons, the parliamentary Joint Committee on Education and Social Protection recommended that the minimum age reflected in the General Scheme be lowered to 16.[138] The Government partially accepted this recommendation, since while the default minimum age remains 18 in the revised scheme and the GRA,[139] an exemption could be granted by court order for those who are 16 or 17.[140] This was by far the most significant change made in the Revised General Scheme. The court would be able to grant the order only if apparently each of a number of evidential criteria is met.[141]

The first evidential requirement is that 'the court is satisfied, that, as appropriate, the child's parents, surviving parent or guardian consent or consents'.[142] That said, the GRA would add a power of the court to 'make an order dispensing with the requirement of ... consent' where it is 'satisfied that the consent cannot be obtained because the person [whose consent would otherwise be required] cannot be identified or found or is failing or neglecting to respond to a request for consent', or that it 'should not be obtained because the nature of the relationship between the child ... and the person shows that it would not be in the interest of the safety or welfare of the child to contact the person'.[143] While this is a positive addition, it is a long way from a true application of a welfare principle[144] or self-determination for competent adolescents where consent is not given.

The second requirement is that in the opinion of the child's 'primary treating medical practitioner' the child 'has attained a sufficient degree of maturity to make the decision to apply for gender recognition' and 'is aware of, has considered and fully understands all the consequences', and that the applicant's decision was 'freely and independently made' without duress or undue influence.[145] The third requirement is that 'an endocrinologist or psychiatrist, who has no connection to the child', certifies that his or her opinion 'concurs' with that of the primary treating practitioner.[146] Finally, the GRA (unlike the Revised General Scheme) specifically provides that 'court shall not make an order under this section unless satisfied that it is in the best interest of the child'.[147] Once the exemption is granted

137 *Cf.* e.g. R. Hodgkin and P. Newell, *Implementation Handbook for the Convention on the Rights of the Child*, 3rd ed., Unicef, Geneva 2007, p. 39.
138 Joint Committee on Education and Social Protection, above n. 9, p. 37.
139 Revised General Scheme, Head 5(d); GRA, s. 8(2)(a).
140 GRA, s. 12; see also Revised General Scheme, Head 7.
141 GRA, s. 12(4)–(6); *cf.* Revised General Scheme, Head 7(2)(d).
142 GRA, s. 12(4)(a); *cf.* Revised General Scheme, Head 7(2)(d)(i).
143 GRA, s. 12(5).
144 *Cf.* Department of Social Protection, above n. 63, p. 3.
145 GRA, s. 12(4)(b)(i); *cf.* Revised General Scheme, Head 7(2)(d)(ii); see also GRA, s. 12(4)(c) for equivalent provisions for applications to revoke a gender recognition certificate.
146 GRA, s. 12(4)(b)(ii); *cf.* Revised General Scheme, Head 7(2)(d)(iii).
147 GRA, s. 12(6).

by the court, the application could proceed in the same manner as for those over 18, provided that the evidence of the court order is supplied to the Minister.[148]

The removal of the absolute bar on applications by those under 18 by the revised scheme and the GRA is welcome. That said, the apparent imposition of cumulative demanding criteria, in addition to the overall requirement of a court order (the criteria seemingly being necessary but not sufficient for such an order) is onerous by comparison with the Ó Snodaigh and Zappone Bills. The same could be said for the continuing bar on applications by those under 16. Moreover, the persisting need to secure a second medical opinion seems particularly harsh given the removal of the medical requirement for adults (considered below),[149] and might make the shortage of appropriate medical expertise in Ireland particularly problematic for 16- and 17-year-olds.

2.3.3. Declaration, 'Life Test' and Medical Requirements

Under the GRA, the applicant must make a statutory declaration that he or she has 'a settled and solemn intention of living in the preferred gender for the rest of his or her life'[150] (adjusting the terminology from that of the 'acquired' gender used in the General Scheme),[151] that he or she 'understands the consequences of the application',[152] and that he or she 'makes the application of his or her free will'.[153] The Group described a declaration of this sort as 'the foundation step for any person wishing to make the transition from one gender to the other'.[154] It has been seen that a similar declaration is required by the Zappone Bill,[155] but not the Ó Snodaigh Bill.

In its General Scheme (as revised and reflected in the GRA), the Government rejected the Group's recommendation of a 'life test' being imposed for a fixed period.[156] This would have required the applicant to prove that he or she has 'been living full-time in the new gender during the two years immediately preceding the application',[157] via 'independent evidence' such as a 'change of gender and name in official and other documentation' and 'statements of witnesses familiar with the applicant'.[158] This 'life test' with a fixed qualifying time period could legitimately

148 GRA, s. 12(1); *cf.* Revised General Scheme, Head 6(a)(vii).

149 Department of Social Protection, 'Government agrees self-declaration approach for Gender Recognition Bill', 03.06.2015 <http://www.welfare.ie/en/pressoffice/pdf/pr030615.pdf> accessed 18.08.2015.

150 GRA, s. 10(1)(f)(ii).

151 Revised General Scheme, Head 6(a)(v).

152 GRA, s. 10(1)(f)(iii); *cf.* Revised General Scheme, Head 6(a)(v).

153 GRA, s. 10(1)(f)(iv); *cf.* Revised General Scheme, Head 6(a)(v), Gender Recognition Advisory Group, above n. 7, at [5.6.1].

154 Gender Recognition Advisory Group, above n. 7, at [5.6].

155 Zappone Bill, cl. 2(3)(b).

156 Gender Recognition Advisory Group, above n. 7, at [5.7].

157 Gender Recognition Advisory Group, above n. 7, at [5.7.1].

158 Gender Recognition Advisory Group, above n. 7, at [5.7.1].

be regarded as excessive given the other requirements, and the rejection of it in principle by the Government is welcome even if it lives on in substance.

However, the Government did originally decide to carry forward the Group's recommendation that medical evidence be required, albeit in attenuated form. Under the Group's original proposal, the applicant would in addition have had to provide medical evidence taking one of two forms. The evidence could have consisted of 'a formal diagnosis' of gender identity disorder 'by one or more qualified mental health professionals'[159] 'together with confirmation that the person is not suffering from any other debarring mental disorder'.[160] This would also have been accompanied, if possible, by 'supporting relevant medical evidence such as details of treatments undergone or in progress'.[161] Alternatively, the applicant could provide 'proof that [he or she] has undergone gender reassignment surgery',[162] comprising 'a formal statement by a qualified medical practitioner' to that effect, 'based on a physical examination'.[163] In formulating its onerous requirements,[164] the Group aimed to ensure consistency with the evidence currently required under the Passports Act 2008, discussed above.

Under the GRB pre-amendment, rather more flexibly, a qualifying application would have required a certificate by the applicant's 'primary treating medical practitioner'[165] confirming that the applicant 'has transitioned' or 'is transitioning' to his or her 'preferred' gender[166] (*i.e.* the gender a person applies to have specified in a gender recognition certificate),[167] and that the practitioner is 'satisfied' that the applicant 'fully understands the consequences of his or her decision to live permanently in the preferred gender'.[168] The Minister regarded these diluted conditions, as well as the absence of a fixed life test, to be a 'more compassionate and understanding approach' that was 'central to the spirit of the Bill'.[169] The Bill as introduced required the certificate to be 'based on a medical evaluation of the applicant',[170] but this requirement was removed by the Seanad.[171] While the GRA defines a 'primary treating medical practitioner' as a 'primary treating endocrinologist or psychiatrist' at the time of writing, the Government announced its intention to delay the Dáil committee stage in order to consult with general practitioners on whether they should be included in the so-called

159 Gender Recognition Advisory Group, above n. 7, at [5.10].
160 Gender Recognition Advisory Group, above n. 7, at [5.8.4].
161 Gender Recognition Advisory Group, above n. 7, at [5.10].
162 Gender Recognition Advisory Group, above n. 7, at [5.8.4]. See Transgender Equality Network Ireland, above n. 41, p. 8 for criticism of any medical diagnosis requirement.
163 Gender Recognition Advisory Group, above n. 7, at [5.10].
164 See Fynes, above n. 48, p. 34 for criticism of the invasiveness of the examination-based criterion.
165 GRB, cl. 10(1)(g)(i); *cf.* Revised General Scheme, Head 6(a)(vi).
166 GRB, cl. 10(1)(g)(ii)(I); *cf.* Revised General Scheme, Head 6(a)(vi).
167 GRB, cl. 2; *cf.* Revised General Scheme, Head 2.
168 GRB, cl. 10(1)(g)(ii)(II); see also Revised General Scheme, Head 6(a)(vi).
169 Department of Social Protection, above n. 13.
170 Gender Recognition Bill as introduced, above n. 12, cl. 9(1)(g)(ii).
171 GRB, cl. 10(1)(g)(ii).

'validation' process.[172] The Cabinet came to the rather more dramatic conclusion that no medical statement should be required at all for adults, and the Government announced in June 2015 that the requirement would be removed from the Bill during the committee stage, and this is reflected in the GRA.[173]

The Minister expressed the hope that the approach even in the pre-amendment GRB would 'facilitate applications from people with intersex conditions should they wish to apply'.[174] The Joint Committee on Education and Social Protection (rather opaquely) recommended that the General Scheme's language be 'reconsidered to address the concerns ... that people not be stigmatised' by its evidential requirements.[175] The Minister, however, emphasised that intersex people would be within the scope of the legislation[176] and that the original General Scheme (substantially reflected in the revised version and the GRB) did 'not in any way stigmatise persons who wish to apply for a gender recognition certificate'.[177] Problems could nevertheless still have occurred given that the GRB appeared to remain premised on a 'transition' from one gender to another and the amendments in the GRA may have solved the difficulty.

The Irish Human Rights Commission said that the use of the word 'acquired' (used in both versions of the General Scheme) 'may not be appropriately sensitive to the reality of the experience of transgender persons or persons who are intersex' because it 'suggests that gender is a matter extraneous to the person, rather than an intrinsic part of a person's identity'.[178] The Joint Committee recommended that the word 'preferred' be considered as a replacement for 'acquired',[179] and it is a positive development that this suggestion was taken up in the GRB.[180]

Any medical requirement was burdensome and a significant fetter on self-identification,[181] particularly given the potential difficulties faced by some transgender individuals in accessing appropriate treatment discussed above.[182] Indeed, the Group conceded that '[t]he relatively small number of mental health and medical professionals who are active in treating GID patients in Ireland ... would seem to rule out the establishment of lists or panels of approved expert witnesses'.[183] The medical evidence requirement may in substance have introduced a version of the 'life test' that the Government expressly purported to reject, and

172 Department of Social Protection, 'Government to Engage with GPs on Gender Recognition Bill' (10.03.2015) <www.welfare.ie/en/pressoffice/Pages/pr100315.aspx#> accessed 25.03.2015.
173 Department of Social Protection, above n. 149; GRA, s. 10.
174 Department of Social Protection, above n. 13.
175 Joint Committee on Education and Social Protection, above n. 9, p. 37.
176 Dáil Deb 9 May 2014, vol. 840, no. 4, p. 629.
177 Dáil Deb 9 May 2014, vol. 840, no. 4, p. 630.
178 Irish Human Rights Commission, above n. 67, at [11]–[12].
179 Joint Committee on Education and Social Protection, above n. 9, p. 37.
180 Revised General Scheme, Head 2.
181 Irish Human Rights Commission, above n. 67, at [35]–[36].
182 Transgender Equality Network Ireland, above n. 130, pp. 4–6.
183 Gender Recognition Advisory Group, above n. 7, at [2.5.1].

the Government's eventual embracing of a self-determination principle for adults is enormously progressive.

The Ó Snodaigh Bill went even further than the GRB by specifically providing that an applicant to the Registrar General 'shall not be required to provide evidence that any surgical procedure for total or partial genital reassignment, hormonal therapies, or any other psychological or medical treatment has taken place in order to have their recorded sex amended'.[184] No similar statement is made in the Zappone Bill, though it is clear that the same effect is intended,[185] and the Bill set out to avoid the need for gender recognition to depend on assessments by professionals.[186] This, like the eventual GRA, would create the possibility that a person could successfully change his or her legal gender even if he or she has not experienced gender identity disorder or any related medical condition at all. While the GRA contains an offence of 'knowingly or recklessly', in respect of an application for a gender recognition certificate, providing 'information to the Minister that is false or misleading in a material respect', the absence of a medical evidence requirement significantly reduces the scope for such an offence to be committed.[187]

That said, even the GRAG admitted that there would be no financial risks to the state if people not suffering from gender identity disorder made applications, and that, 'given the nature of the condition and the difficulties and distress experienced by individuals in making the transition from one gender to the opposite one, the probability of frivolous applications was extremely low'.[188] This itself casts doubt on the appropriateness of requiring an applicant to be assessed and adds weight to the Government's decision to abandon such a requirement.

2.3.4. Marital/Civil Partnership Status

The Group recommended that 'the criteria for legal recognition of an acquired gender should include a provision whereby the applicant cannot be married or in a civil partnership',[189] in spite of the fact that all individual respondents to its consultation exercise and 'almost all' organisational respondents had been opposed to such a requirement.[190] We have seen that the Group claimed that '[f]or the majority of transgender persons who were married in their former gender but have since transitioned to the opposite gender, the marriage will have broken down by the time the transgender spouse wishes to apply for gender

184 Ó Snodaigh Bill, cl. 5.
185 See e.g. Zappone Bill, cl. 2(7).
186 Zappone Bill Explanatory Memorandum <www.oireachtas.ie/viewdoc.asp?fn=/documents/bills28/bills/2013/7513/b7513s-memo.pdf> accessed 18.08.2015, p. 3.
187 GRA, s. 35(1)(a); *cf.* Revised General Scheme, Head 20.
188 Gender Recognition Advisory Group, above n. 7, at [2.3].
189 Gender Recognition Advisory Group, above n. 7, at [5.5.1].
190 Gender Recognition Advisory Group, above n. 7, at [3.4].

recognition'.[191] When announcing that the Group's recommendation would be carried forward into the General Scheme, the Minister similarly asserted that she wanted to 'legislate now for the majority of the people affected, who are single' even if that would be 'disappointing for the small number of transgender persons concerned who are already married and wish to remain married while having their changed gender recognised'.[192]

Both the Group and the Government were particularly wary of in substance allowing same-sex marriage or opposite-sex civil partnership via gender recognition in Ireland's current constitutional context, which was widely (but not universally) believed to require privilege for heterosexual marriage.[193] The outcome of the constitutional referendum on same-sex marriage that took place in May 2015 removed this difficulty,[194] and the Government announced that the marriage and civil partnership bars will be removed from the GRB during the committee stage.[195] Unfortunately, however, a court challenge to the referendum result caused the single status requirement to be retained in the GRA as enacted in July 2015.[196]

It was rather a pity that both the Group and (originally) the Government felt it necessary to impose an absolute bar on applications by people in subsisting formalised relationships,[197] rather than at least allowing the new gender to be recognised on an interim basis until the relevant relationship could be dissolved. That state of affairs would have been particularly unfortunate in situations where an applicant had been forced to dissolve a marriage or civil partnership in order to make an application for a gender recognition certificate that was ultimately unsuccessful. It also meant that a desire for gender identity recognition would not have been a ground for nullity or divorce in itself,[198] and that an applicant would have had to make use of Ireland's restrictive law on divorce/dissolution or nullity before having his or her preferred gender recognised. In order to obtain a divorce, a married couple must have lived apart for periods totalling at least four years in the previous five years.[199] The court must also be satisfied that there is no reasonable prospect of reconciliation between the spouses before the divorce

---

191 Gender Recognition Advisory Group, above n. 7, at [5.5].

192 Department of Social Protection, above n. 13.

193 See e.g. *Zappone and Gilligan v Revenue Commissioners* [2006] IEHC 404; and B. Sloan, 'The Changing Concept of "Family" and Challenges for Family Law in Ireland' in J.M. Scherpe (ed.), *European Family Law Volume II: The Chancing Concept of 'Family' and Challenges for Domestic Family Laws*, Edward Elgar, Cheltenham 2016 (forthcoming), and Joint Committee on Education and Social Protection, above n. 9, at [5.3], for discussion.

194 Referendum Ireland <http://www.referendum.ie> accessed 08.08.2015. *Cf.* Transgender Equality Network Ireland, above n. 130, p. 9.

195 Department of Social Protection, above n. 13.

196 Department for Social Protection, 'Legal Recognition for Transgender People' (15.07.2015) <http://www.welfare.ie/en/pressoffice/pdf/pa150715.pdf> accessed 18.08.2015; GRA, s. 9(2)(b).

197 See e.g. Irish Human Rights Commission, above n. 67, at [22]–[34].

198 *Cf.* Zappone Bill Explanatory Memorandum, above n. 186, p. 4 for a discussion of the possible relevance of transgender status to the current law of nullity.

199 Irish Constitution, Article 41.3.2(i)°.

can be granted,[200] by virtue of what has been described as 'the most restrictive' divorce law in Europe,[201] and of course that may not be an accurate representation of the parties' relationship. It had also been suggested that encouraging couples to divorce may itself be contrary to the Constitution.[202] Same-sex civil partners may obtain a dissolution more easily, since they have to show have lived apart for periods totalling two years in the previous three years[203] and the court is not required to inquire into any reasonable prospect of reconciliation. But the GRAG admitted that married couples who wished for their relationship to continue but also for one or more of the parties to be able to change legal gender would be placed in a 'very difficult position', and that its requirement would be 'very distressing' for them.[204] It is therefore heartening that the requirement will apparently be removed if the challenge to the referendum result is dismissed.

Neither of the Private Members' Bills were intended to allow a gender recognition decision to affect, or be affected by, a subsisting marriage or civil partnership of the applicant.[205] The Explanatory Memorandum to the Zappone Bill argues that marriages between an opposite-sex couple, one of whom later acquires a different legal gender, 'were contracted as valid opposite-sex marriages and thus are not legally same-sex marriages'.[206] There is a certain irony in the fact that gender recognition advocates found themselves arguing that marriages or civil partnerships founded on incorrect genders should nevertheless remain valid once gender recognition occurs.

2.3.5. *Alternatives*

In contrast to the relatively stringent overall requirements recommended by the Advisory Group, many of which were translated into the Government's General Scheme (even as revised) and the GRA at the time of writing, the Ó Snodaigh Bill requires that '[o]nce a request has been made'[207] by a proven adult,[208] 'the Office of the Registrar General shall, without any additional legal or administrative procedure, issue a new birth certificate incorporating the requested change reflecting the amended sex and the new name or names as recorded, if

200 Irish Constitution, Article 41.3.2(ii)°.
201 M. Antokolskaia, *Harmonisation of Family Law in Europe: A Historical Perspective. A Tale of Two Millennia*, Intersentia, Antwerp 2006, p. 351.
202 Ó Snodaigh Bill Explanatory Memorandum, above n. 121, p. 5; Joint Committee on Education and Social Protection, above n. 9, at [5.3].
203 Civil Partnership and Certain Rights and Obligations of Cohabitants Act 2010, s. 110(a). See generally M. Walls, 'Dissolution and Provision for Qualified Cohabitants' in *The General Scheme of the Civil Partnership Bill: Legal Consequences and Human Rights Implications*, Irish Council for Civil Liberties, Dublin 2009.
204 Gender Recognition Advisory Group, above n. 7, at [5.5].
205 Ó Snodaigh Bill Explanatory Memorandum, above n. 121, pp. 4–5; Zappone Bill Explanatory Memorandum, above n. 186, pp. 4–6.
206 Zappone Bill Explanatory Memorandum, above n. 186, p. 5.
207 Ó Snodaigh Bill, cl. 7.
208 Ó Snodaigh Bill, cl. 4.

applicable'.[209] Similarly, the Zappone Bill provides that the Registrar General 'shall as soon as practicable upon receipt of [the required] statutory declaration … record and recognise the applicant's preferred gender and as appropriate the preferred forename or forenames in the Gender Recognition Register and shall attach the appropriate note to the entry concerning the applicant in the register of births'.[210] Only an application by a minor seemingly involves any substantive evaluation (by the court in that instance) under the Ó Snodaigh Bill, and indeed it is the applicant on behalf of the child who conducts the relevant evaluation under the Zappone Bill.[211] Views will differ as to whether this extremely liberal approach is appropriate, but any substantive qualifying criteria risk excluding some deserving individuals and it is widely accepted that the risk of abuse of a gender recognition scheme is extremely low. It is therefore a largely positive prospect that the GRA will eventually be similarly liberal.

Other procedural details were considered above.

III. CONSEQUENCES OF RECOGNITION OF THE PREFERRED LEGAL SEX AND/OR GENDER OF A TRANSGENDER/TRANSSEXUAL PERSON

3.1. FUTURE RIGHTS, DUTIES AND ENTITLEMENTS

The Government has claimed that '[t]he acquired gender of transgender persons is currently recognised in many official dealings with the State … in social welfare, healthcare and revenue matters'.[212] Anecdotal evidence nevertheless suggests that individual experiences can be anything but straightforward,[213] and the Joint Committee highlighted that '[i]ssues faced by transgender youth within the school system were raised by some stakeholders' during its evidential hearings.[214] In *Foy* it was said that there was 'some uncertainty as to how [the applicant] would be treated if she had to endure a prison sentence',[215] and Transgender Equality Network Ireland has 'been contacted by a number of individuals who have been incorrectly assigned to detention centres which do not respect their gender identities'.[216] In her book *Sport and the Law* Donnellan does not appear to mention any jurisdiction-specific provision for athletes in the section on transgender rights in Ireland.[217]

---

209 Ó Snodaigh Bill, cl. 7.

210 Zappone Bill, cl. 2(7).

211 Zappone Bill, cl. 2(6).

212 Steering Committee For Human Rights, above n. 31, p. 279.

213 Transgender Equality Network Ireland, above n. 40, pp. 3–4; O. O'Sullivan (ed.), above n. 1.

214 Joint Committee on Education and Social Protection, above n. 9, at [5.5].

215 [2007] IEHC 470, at [64(2)] (McKechnie J). *Cf.* Steering Committee For Human Rights, above n. 31, p. 274.

216 Transgender Equality Network Ireland, above n. 81, p. 11.

217 L. Donnellan, *Sport and the Law*, Blackhall, Blackrock 2010, p. 136.

The granting of a gender recognition certificate under the GRA would in general mean that 'the person's gender shall from the date of that issue become for all purposes the preferred gender'.[218] That recognition, according to both the Group and the Explanatory and Financial Memorandum of the GRB, would take effect 'for all purposes, including dealings with the State, public bodies, and civil and commercial society',[219] though no further specific guidance on what this means for the purposes of peerages and other matters was provided by the Group. It expressly declined to make recommendations on 'supports for young people in schools and in sporting and other organisations' and 'the issuing of educational certificates by official bodies' in the light of its 'specific remit'.[220] For its part, the GRA currently provides expressly that '[a] person issued with a gender recognition certificate may only'[221] 'marry a person of the opposite gender to the preferred gender'[222] or 'be a party to a civil partnership registration with a person of the same gender as the preferred gender',[223] but it has been seen that this provision is expected to be removed. Rather more helpfully than the Group's proposal, the GRA contains a number of other provisions dealing with particular circumstances. For example, where 'the disposition or devolution of any property under a will or other instrument' made *after* the day the eventual Act comes into effect 'is different … from what it would be but for the fact that a gender recognition certificate is issued to a person',[224] a person 'adversely affected' by the difference would be able to apply for a High Court order.[225] The Court would have the power to make 'such order as it considers appropriate' in relation to 'any person benefiting' from the difference, 'if it is satisfied that it is just to do so'.[226] This is a pragmatic provision, though it is odd that the order it facilitates is focused on the *person* benefitting from the difference in disposition rather than the property itself.

The GRA would make an exception to the recognition of a preferred gender for gender-specific crimes committed both before and after the gender recognition decision. It provides that 'where … a relevant gender-specific sexual offence could be committed or attempted only if the gender of the person to whom a gender recognition certificate has been issued were not the preferred gender, the fact that the person's gender has become the preferred gender does not prevent the offence

218 GRA, s. 18(1); see also Revised General Scheme, Head 10(1), Gender Recognition Advisory Group, above n. 7, at [5.12.1].

219 Gender Recognition Advisory Group, above n. 7, at [5.12.1]; Department of Social Protection, above n. 63, p. 5.

220 Gender Recognition Advisory Group, above n. 7, at [5.18]. *Cf.* F. Black, 'Transsexual wins Plea to alter Gender on Exam Certs', Independent.ie, 01.06.2007 <www.independent.ie/irish-news/transsexual-wins-plea-to-alter-gender-on-exam-certs-26294405.html> accessed 18.08.2015.

221 GRA, s. 18(3).

222 GRA, s. 18(3)(a).

223 GRA, s. 18(3)(b); *cf.* Revised General Scheme, Head 9(2).

224 GRA, s. 22(1).

225 GRA, s. 22(2); see also Revised General Scheme, Head 24(2).

226 GRA, s. 22(3); see also Revised General Scheme, Head 24(3).

being committed or attempted'.[227] A 'relevant gender-specific sexual offence' is then defined[228] to mean a sexual offence that can be committed either only by someone of a particular gender, or only against or in relation to someone of a particular gender, or both.[229]

Finally, the original General Scheme would have allowed a 'body responsible for regulating the participation of persons' in events involving 'a gender-affected sport' to 'prohibit or restrict the participation as competitors' of people who have obtained legal recognition of their gender identity, if this is necessary to secure 'fair competition' or 'the safety of competitors'.[230] No distinction was apparently made between professional and amateur sport. The Irish Human Rights Commission expressed grave concern that the provision governing sport could 'allow for a most serious invasion of the individual's privacy, cause undue embarrassment regarding an intimate detail of a person's private life' and 'defeat the very recognition already granted to them by the State'.[231] The Joint Committee recommended that this aspect of the General Scheme 'should be reconsidered in consultation with stakeholders', and that 'Irish sporting regulatory bodies receiving public funding should develop comprehensive policies in relation to the participation of transgender people'.[232] The relevant head in fact appeared to have been omitted from the Revised General Scheme.[233] and indeed no equivalent clause appears in the GRA.

In the absence of specific provision governing other matters, one must presumably fall back upon the proposed Bill's general principle that a person's legal gender becomes his or her preferred gender on the date of the decision to issue a gender recognition certificate. On a practical level, the Joint Committee has at least recommended that '[g]uidelines on supporting the inclusion of transgender young people in schools should be developed in consultation with relevant stakeholders'.[234]

The Ó Snodaigh Bill explicitly confers the 'right' on 'each person' to 'the recognition of their gender identity', to 'the free development of their person according to their gender identity', and to 'have their recorded sex amended, along with changes in name or names and image, in accordance with their own self-perceived gender identity'.[235] 'Gender identity' is specifically defined in both the Ó Snodaigh and Zappone Bills using the Yogyakarta Principles on the Application of International Human Rights Law in relation to Sexual Orientation

227 GRA, s. 23(1); see also Revised General Scheme, Head 26(1).
228 GRA, s. 23(2)–(5); see also Revised General Scheme, Head 26(2)–(4).
229 GRA, s. 23(2)–(4); see also Revised General Scheme, Head 26(2)–(3).
230 Original General Scheme, Head 26(b).
231 Irish Human Rights Commission, above n. 67, at [39]–[41].
232 Joint Committee on Education and Social Protection, above n. 9, p. 38.
233 The table of contents of the Revised General Scheme nevertheless refers to a 'Head 27' with the title 'Sport'.
234 Joint Committee on Education and Social Protection, above n. 9, p. 37.
235 Ó Snodaigh Bill, cl. 3.

and Gender Identity[236] to mean 'each person's deeply felt internal and individual experience of gender, which may or may not correspond with the sex assigned at birth, including the personal sense of the body (which may involve, if freely chosen, modification of bodily appearance or function by medical, surgical or other means) and other expressions of gender, including dress, speech and mannerisms'.[237] The Ó Snodaigh Bill also provides that, subject to its own provisions, 'all laws and regulations adopted shall respect the person's right to their gender identity as well as ensuring that there is no limitation, restriction, exclusion or annulment of the exercise of the right to gender identity'.[238]

The Zappone Bill simply provides that '[s]ave where the context or law otherwise requires it, the gender entered and recorded in the Gender Recognition Register on foot of an application under [the Bill] be for all purposes the recognised gender of that person from the date of entry'.[239] No further detail is provided, and while the simplicity of its statement is admirable, the general exception for where the context or law requires that the person not be recognised in his or her preferred gender could cause significant difficulties.

3.2. EXISTING RIGHTS, DUTIES AND ENTITLEMENTS

Under the GRA, '[t]he issue of a gender recognition certificate' is expressed not to 'affect the rights or liabilities of a person or consequences of an action by the person in their original gender prior to the date of issue of the certificate'.[240] The Group explicitly stated that the fact that a person's changed gender has been recognised would 'not affect the status of the person as the father or mother of a child'.[241] It was unclear whether this merely confirmed the prospective nature of the gender recognition decision in respect of *existing* children, or whether it was intended to introduce a special rule so that, for example, a person who gives birth to a child is always the child's mother even if that person has obtained a gender recognition certificate and is a man for all other purposes at the time of birth. The Revised General Scheme used the same ambiguous wording.[242] Thankfully, the GRA makes clear that a gender recognition certificate 'shall not affect the status of the person as the father or mother' only 'of a child born prior to the date of the issue of the certificate'.[243]

236 Ó Snodaigh Bill Explanatory Memorandum, above n. 121, p. 2.
237 Ó Snodaigh Bill, cl. 2; Zappone Bill, cl. 1.
238 Ó Snodaigh Bill, cl. 15(1).
239 Zappone Bill, cl. 3(2).
240 GRA, s. 18(6); *cf.* Revised General Scheme, Head 10(4), Gender Recognition Advisory Group, above n. 7, at [5.12.1].
241 Gender Recognition Advisory Group, above n. 7, at [5.12.1].
242 Revised General Scheme, Head 22.
243 GRA, s. 19.

The GRA also provides that the issuing of a gender recognition certificate will 'not affect the disposal or devolution of property under a will (including a codicil) or other instrument executed before the date this Act comes into operation',[244] and the relevant provisions of the Bill are not intended to 'affect the right of a person to make a claim in respect of any property, other than where the property is sold to a purchaser for value in good faith and without notice.[245] That said, the Act would also relieve a trustee or personal representative of any duty to enquire 'whether a gender recognition certificate has been issued to any person or revoked' in carrying out their duties,[246] and from liability arising out of a failure to make such enquiries.[247]

The Ó Snodaigh Bill similarly, but perhaps less clearly, provides that '[a] change in the recorded sex of a person shall not change the legal entitlements, rights, and legal obligations that were afforded to persons before the recording of the amendments, nor those derived from relationships established under family law, including adoption and marital rights'.[248] The Zappone Bill's equivalent clause provides that '[s]ave where the context otherwise requires it, the making of an entry in the Gender Recognition Register does not affect the previous operation of anything duly done under law or affect any right, privilege, obligation or liability acquired, accrued or incurred, or affect any penalty incurred, or prejudice or affect any legal proceedings (civil or criminal) pending at the time of the making of the entry in the Gender Recognition Register concerning the person in question'.[249] This spells out matters rather more than the same Bill's complementary sub-clause on prospective matters, but leaves the parentage question open to doubt.

IV. LEGAL CHALLENGES TO THE EXISTING RULES

Imperfect as it currently is, it is to be hoped that the Gender Recognition Act 2015 will soon be brought into force. In spite of considerable pressure exerted on the Government by Transgender Equality Network Ireland *inter alia*, transgender individuals in Ireland have already waited far too long for comprehensive recognition of their preferred genders. There is some consolation in the fact that the Irish legislation appears likely to be among the more internationally progressive gender recognition statutes when it is eventually commenced. Legal position may not remain static for long after the GRA comes into force, however, since it obliges the Minister to 'commence a review' of its operation not more than two years after it comes into effect.[250]

244 GRA, s. 20(1); *cf.* Revised General Scheme, Head 23.
245 GRA, s. 21(3); see also Revised General Scheme, Head 24(3).
246 GRA, s. 21(1); see also Revised General Scheme, Head 24(1).
247 GRA, s. 21(2); see also Revised General Scheme, Head 24(2).
248 Ó Snodaigh Bill, cl. 9.
249 Zappone Bill, cl. 3(1).
250 GRA, s. 7.

THE LEGAL STATUS OF TRANSSEXUAL AND TRANSGENDER PERSONS IN ITALY

Maria Giovanna Cubeddu Wiedemann

Contents

I. LEGAL FRAMEWORK

There is currently no single, uniform law which regulates the status of transsexual or transgender persons in Italy.[1] Italian law does not define trangenderism and transsexualism. Italy first introduced legislation for the legal recognition of preferred gender in 1982.[2] The Sex Reassignment Act 1982 ('the 1982 Act') does not specifically regulate the status of transsexual or transgender persons, but

[1] M. Dogliotti, 'Transessualismo (profili giuridici)', *Nov. Dig. It. (Novissimo Digesto Italiano)*, vol. VII, UTET, Turin 1987, p. 790 ff.; P. Stanzione, 'Transessualità', *Enc. Dir. (Enciclopedia del diritto)*, vol. XLIV, Giuffrè, Milan 1992, p. 890; P.M. Vecchi, 'Transessualismo', *Enc. Giur. Treccani (Enciclopedia Giuridica Treccani)*, Ed. Enc. It., Rome 1994, p. 1 ff.; S. Patti, 'Transessualismo', *Digesto IV*, vol. XIX, UTET, Turin 1999, p. 416.

[2] The Sex Reassignment Act no. 164 of 1982 (the 1982 Act). The 1982 Act was amended in 2011 by Art. 31 of the Reform Act no. 150 of 2011.

rather establishes a set of requirements which an individual must satisfy in order to have their gender identity recognised in Italian law.

Italy has adopted legislation which prohibits discrimination on the basis of gender identity.[3] Under Article 3.1 of the Italian Constitution, all citizens have 'equal social dignity' and are 'equal before the law', without distinction as to 'sex, race, language, religion, political opinion, personal and social conditions'. Recognising that the right to privacy protects self-determination and that sexuality, as well as a person's sexual life, are at the core of private life, there has been a recent trend towards better protection for the identity of the person and, as a result, increased social integration of transsexual and transgender persons.[4] Various regional laws now expressly use the language of 'transgender'[5] and numerous draft laws have been published which would protect transgender persons against discrimination and sexual crimes.[6]

II. CHANGING LEGAL SEX AND GENDER – REQUIREMENTS AND PROCEDURE

Under Italian law, the registration of a new birth must always include the name and legal gender of the child.[7] The legal gender to be registered (female or male) is generally determined by the biological sex characteristics of the newborn. If, however, at the time of birth, the child exhibits ambiguous sex characteristics (intersex), doctors may, in consultation with the child's parents, assign a legal gender to the child. Where, at a later stage, it is apparent that the selection is inconsistent with the child's physical development, it is possible in certain circumstances to amend the birth certificate.[8]

Before 1982, gender confirmation surgery[9] was prohibited in Italy. Italian law adhered to the belief that sex is 'immutable' and that a person's body is 'inviolable'.[10] However, under the Sex Reassignment Act 1982, surgical treatments were finally

---

3 P.M. Vecchi, 'Transessualismo e divieto di discriminazioni' (2001) Familia, p. 343 ss.

4 S. Patti, 'Aspetti oggettivi e soggettivi dell'identità sessuale' (1984) Riv. crit. dir. priv. (Rivista critica di diritto privato), p. 335.

5 For example, Art. 2 l. rg. Tosc. 15.11.2004, no. 63.

6 A.C. no. 690, Norme contro la discriminazione motivata dall'identità di genere e dall'orientamento sessuale; A.C. no. 715, 12.06.2011.

7 Arts. 29, 35, D.P.R. 03.11.2000, no. 396, Regolamento per la revisione e la semplificazione dell'ordinamento dello stato civile.

8 According to Arts. 95 et seq., D.P.R. 03.11.2000, no. 396, Regolamento per la revisione e la semplificazione dell'ordinamento dello stato civile. S. Trib. Macerata, 12.11.1984 (1985) I, 2, Giur. it. (La giurisprudenza italiana), p. 195.

9 Gender Confirmation Surgery is a medical procedure by which an individual's physical and sexual characteristics are altered, typically to bring those characteristics into line with the stereotypical features of the individual's self-identified gender.

10 S.V. Sellaroli, 'La regolamentazione giuridica del cosiddetto cambimento di sesso' (1968) III Giust. Pen. (Giustizia penale), p. 1 ff.; P. Perlingieri, 'Note introdutive ai problemi giuridici del mutamento di sesso' (1970) Dir. Giur. (Diritto e giurisprudenza), p. 830 ff.; G. Petrina,

permitted and a court-order procedure for accessing medical intervention was introduced.[11] The 1982 Act has been criticised for its focus on creating consistency between an individual's social and physical identity rather than emphasising the right of persons to self-determine their gender. In a landmark 1985 decision, however, the Constitutional Court declared that the entire Sex Reassignment Act 1982 was constitutional, referring both to the inviolability of the body and the protection of personal identity.[12]

2.1. REQUIREMENTS

Since 1982, Italian law has allowed individuals to change their legal name and gender in the Civil Registry by amending the person's birth certificate. Under current practice, the court must ascertain the existence of the psychological and physical requirements of the person. An administrative authority is then charged, by Court order, with carrying out amendments to the individual's birth certificate.

The current procedures for obtaining legal recognition of preferred gender are hampered in a number of ways, most notably by the significant lack of clarity which runs through the system. It remains unclear what exact requirements a person must satisfy before they are entitled to recognition. It is not certain, for instance, whether applicants must observe a period of reflection before obtaining gender identity recognition or what role medical intervention plays in the process. Following the Reform Act no. 150 of 2011 ('the 2011 Reform Act'), the procedures for the legal recognition of preferred gender now include both a judicial and an administrative component. The 2011 Reform Act introduced a series of procedural, as well as substantive, changes, the most important of which are the jurisdiction of the Ordinary Court and the requirement that applicants for recognition must notify their spouses and children.

2.1.1. Nationality

The Sex Reassignment Act 1982 is silent on the question of nationality. According to Italy's Basic Law, any person, irrespective of nationality or residency status, can bring an action in the Italian civil courts. Italian judges have no discretion to refuse an application merely because the plaintiff is a non-national. However, the decided cases illustrate that the legal recognition of gender identity has only been available to those who are formally listed on the national population registry. In a landmark 2000 judgment, foreign citizens were finally permitted to apply for

Problemi giuridici del transessualismo, 1972, p. 353; P. D'Addino Serravalle, P. Perlingieri and P. Stanzione, *Problemi giuridici del transessualismo*, ESI, Naples 1981.

11 P. Palmieri and M. Venuti, 'Il transessualismo tra autonomia privata e indisponibilità del corpo', (1999) Dir. fam. pers. (Diritto della famiglia e delle persone), p. 1331 ff.

12 Constitutional Court of Italy, 24.05.1985, no. 161 (1985) I Foro it. (Il foro italiano), c. 2162.

gender recognition in Italy if they could show that they were legal residents.[13] Gender identity recognition is only permitted, however, in relation to documents which are issued by the Italian authorities. Italy cannot modify personal data on non-Italian passports, because that would require foreign legal systems to acknowledge and accept a decision taken by an Italian court.

2.1.2. *Age*

Italy's Basic Law provides that the legal recognition of gender is open to persons over 18 years of age where those persons have sufficient mental and intellectual capacity to act.[14] Legal representatives for minors may be authorised by the Tutelary Judge (*Giudice tutelare*) to consent on the minor's behalf to both the entire legal process and any medical intervention as treatment, if necessary. Where there are proceedings relating to the legal recognition of preferred gender for a person who is under 18 years of age, that child has a mandatory right to be heard during the proceedings. In the past, Italian courts have refused to grant applications made by minors through their parents, because such parental representation was considered to be inadmissible for the protection of personal rights.[15] However, more recent decisions show that gender confirmation surgery is increasingly considered as part of the medical treatment aimed at achieving a psychological and physical identity for the minor. In this way, when the interests of a minor are taken in account, the principle of parental (legal) representation can apply.[16]

2.1.3. *Medical Intervention (Surgery, Hormones, etc.)*

Until the 2015 decision of the Italian Constituional Court, the most controversial aspect of legal gender recognition in Italy was the question as to what extent applicants must submit to medical intervention, including hormone treatment, surgery or enforced sterilisation. There was significant uncertainty as to the exact form of medical treatment, if any, Italian law imposes upon applicants. As a first observation, it appeared that neither sterilisation nor infertility was a specific requirement under Italian law. Similarly, a 'psychological change' of identity was not expressly stipulated in any legislation, although, in practice, it was a requirement for recognition.[17] On the other hand, there was a body of case law which suggests that applicants for recognition must submit to some form

---

13 Court of Milan, 17.08.2000 (2000) Fam. Dir. (Famiglia e diritto), p. 6.

14 Caggia, *Atti di disposizione del corpo, Persona, famiglia e successioni* (Cuffaro ed.), IPSOA, Milan 2006, p. 171.

15 Court of Catania, 12.03.2004, 2005 I Giust. Civ. (Giustizia civile), p. 1107.

16 Court of Rome, 14.04.2011, 2011 Fam. Dir. (Famiglia e Diritto), p. 183.

17 See S. Patti, *Il transessualismo, Diritto della famiglia* (M.G. Cubeddu/S. Patti (eds.)) Giuffrè, Milan 2011 p. 944.

of surgical intervention.[18] Of particular importance, especially for female-to-male (FtM) applicants, was the question whether it sufficed that an individual modify their external sex characteristics or whether there was also a requirement to alter internal sex organs.[19] Additionally, it was not clear whether 'destructive' modifications were sufficient, or whether an applicant also had to undergo a 'reconstructive' procedure.[20]

In recent years, Italian courts have begun to adopt a wider interpretation, moving away from the emphasis on gender confirmation surgery. In 2011, the Court of Rome stated that surgical intervention is not an essential requisite for amending personal records in the Civil Registry.[21] Surgical treatment is necessary only where it is required to ensure that a person is physically and mentally stable.[22] The legal recognition of gender is granted only after completion of all necessary treatments, including non-surgical intervention, and the applicant has achieved a gender identity which differs from their legal sex.[23]

Under the current law, as set out in Article 31 of the Reform Act no. 150 of 2011, a court may authorise surgical intervention 'where it is necessary to adapt the sexual characteristics to be achieved by surgical treatment.'[24] A court will not permit medical interventions which can physically or psychologically affect the applicant.[25] The reforms of 2011 envisage a legal recognition regime where legal gender is not wholly dependent on sex characteristics. This is a welcome development, particularly having regard to the difficulties which applicants may face in accessing proper medical care and the physical inability of certain applicants to submit to medical intervention.[26]

Such trend also marks Order no. 228 by the Court of Trento,[27] which goes as far as questioning the constitutionality of Article 1 of Law no. 164/82, under which the surgical intervention is a necessary condition for obtaining a legal gender identity change. The Court of Trento argued that such a condition is clearly in contrast with both Article 8 ECHR and Article 2 of the Italian Constitution. In addition, submitting a person's right to choosing their gender identity to a

---

18 Court of Pavia, 02.02.2007 (2007) Fam. pers. succ. (Famiglia, persone, successioni), p. 25.

19 Court of Pavia, 02.02.2007 (2007) Fam. pers. succ. (Famiglia, persone, successioni), p. 25; Court of Benevento, 16.01.1986 (1986) I, 2, Giur it. (La giurisprudenza italiana), p. 470.

20 App. Bologna, 20.03.2013 (2013) <www.articolo29.it>.

21 Court of Rome, 14.04.2011 (2011) Fam. Dir. (Famiglia e Diritto), p. 183. See also Court of Rome, 18.10.1997 (1998) Dir. fam. pers. (Diritto della famiglia e delle persone), p. 1033; Court of Salerno, 05.03.1998 (1998) Dir. fam. pers. (Diritto della famiglia e delle persone), p. 1057; Court of Siena, 12.06.2013, no. 412 <www.dejure.it>. *Contra* Court Vercelli, 27.11.2014, no. 159, <www.dejure.it>.

22 Court of Rovereto, 03.05.2013 (2014) NGCC (La nuova giurisprudenza civile e commenatta), p. 1116.

23 Court of Rome, 14.04.2011, 2011 Fam. Dir. (Famiglia e Diritto), p. 183.

24 Article 31 of the Reform Act no. 150 of 2011, paras. 1, 2 and 3.

25 Court of La Spezia, 25.07.1987 (1987) Arch. Civ. (Archivio civile), p. 1233.

26 S. Patti, *Il transessualismo, Diritto della famiglia* (M.G. Cubeddu/S. Patti (eds.)) Giuffrè, Milan 2011, p. 947.

27 Court of Trento, 19.08.2014, no. 228 <www.dejure.it>.

potentially dangerous surgical intervention not only violates the right itself, but also clearly contradicts Articles 3 and 32 of the Italian Constitution. In 2015 the Italian Supreme Court followed this reasoning and held that medical intervention and sterilisation are not necessary prerequisites for the recognition of a person's preferred gender, and that 'medical treatment' in the 1982 Act must be interpreted accordingly.[28]

2.2. PROCEDURE

Under the Sex Reassignment Act 1982, the procedure for obtaining legal recognition of gender involves two distinct stages. During the first stage, the applicant may seek medical intervention where necessary and appropriate. As noted, a court may refuse medical treatment which would be detrimental to the applicant's health or which would have no physiological or psychological impact on the applicant.[29] In addition, an applicant need not apply for medical treatment if he or she has already submitted to such interventions abroad.[30] Having undergone court-authorised medical treatment, the individual must then submit another application for the Court to authorise amendments to the Civil Registry. While in principle applicants must observe both stages of the procedure, many individuals never make the initial application for court-ordered medical treatment. Instead, they simply apply for recognition having already submitted to treatment. This phenomenon may be explained by the cost involved in bringing two actions before the civil courts. Applicants frequently prefer to reduce their fees by seeking medical intervention outside of the court-ordered system.

Since 2011, the procedure for legally recognising preferred gender has been subject to the same civil procedure rules as the so-called ordinary judgment of cognition (*rito ordinario di cognizione*).[31] The competent court is the presiding court in whichever region the applicant is habitually resident. The President of that court designates the examining magistrate and sets both the date for the

---

28 Decision no. 15138 of 20 July 2015.

29 Court of Vicenza, 02.08.2000 (2001) Dir. fam. pers. (Diritto della famiglia e della persone), p. 220; Court of Milan, 05.10.2000 (2001) Fam. Dir. (Famiglia e diritto), p. 324; Court of Brescia, 15.10.2004 (2005) Corr. mer. (Corriere del merito), p. 505.

30 Court of Pisa, 15.01.2008 (2008) Dir. fam. pers. (Diritto della famiglia e della persone), p. 1288.

31 Art. 31 (Disputes relating to the rectification of attribution of sex):
'1. Disputes relating to the rectification of attribution of sex are, according to Article 1 of the Law of 14 April 1982 no. 164, governed by the ordinary rite of cognition, unless otherwise provided in this article;
2. The competent court is the court in the district where the acting person has his place of residence.
3. The writ of summons is sent to the spouse and children of the acting person and the prosecutor attends the judgment.
4. Where it is necessary to alter the sexual characteristics through medical and surgical treatment, the court authorises them with a final judgment. The procedure is governed by paragraphs 1, 2 and 3.

hearing and the deadline by which the applicant must notify his or her spouse and children. The Public Prosecutor attends the judgment. The examining magistrate may order an Official Technical Consultancy (OTC). In practice, the applicant must provide the court with sufficient documentation to show that he or she satisfies the psychological and physical prerequisites for legal recognition of his or her preferred gender.

III. CONSEQUENCES OF LEGAL GENDER RECOGNITION

Article 4 of the Sex Reassignment Act 1982 and Article 31 of the Reform Act no. 150 of 2011 state that the recognition of preferred gender in Italy has no retroactive effect. Following recognition in law, the applicant is considered as having their newly recognised gender for all purposes to the extent required.

3.1. OFFICIAL DOCUMENTS

As a result of legal recognition, the applicant may seek to amend his or her personal records and documents, including Italian passports and national security numbers, so that those records reflect the applicant's true identity.[32] The applicant may seek to rectify his or her birth certificate, which no longer remains a record of the legal sex 'with which [the applicant was] born.' The applicant may also seek to amend his or her first name.[33] Where, however, the applicant wishes to use a first name which is completely different from his or her original, the applicant will have to comply with the general rules relating to change of name.[34]

---

5. In the judgment granting the application for rectification of gender assignment the court orders the registrar of the town where the birth certificate was issued to make the correction in the respective register.
6. The judgment of rectification of attribution of sex has no retroactive effect. It determines the dissolution of marriage or termination of the civil effects consequent to a marriage celebrated by religious rite. The provisions of the Civil Code and the Act of 1 December 1970, no. 898 are applied.'

[32] The data related to the sex of the person are considered to be extremely sensitive data. (Art. 22, l. 31 December 1996, n. 675): the processing of sensitive data, the legitimacy of which, as a general rule (p. 1), requires the simultaneous presence of the written consent and authorisation of the Guarantor for the protection of personal data, and is allowed by the 'public' (p. 3), even in the absence of consent and authorisation, on condition that there must be: (a) a significant purpose of public interest, (b) an express provision of law authorisations, and (c) a specification of the legislative data types of the operations manageable and executable (see Cass., 8 July 2005, no. 14390).

[33] Court of Pisa, 15.01.2008 (2008) Dir. fam. (Diritto della famiglia), p. 1288.

[34] S. Patti, *Il transessualismo, Diritto della famiglia* (M.G. Cubeddu/S. Patti (eds.)) Giuffrè, Milan 2011 p. 951: Article 89 of Presidential Decree no. 396 of 3 November 2000. See also Luchini, 'Rettificazione di sesso e diritto al cambiamento del prenome: riflessioni in merito alla legge 164/82' (1997) Dir. fam. pers. (Diritto della famiglia e delle persone), p. 773. Contra

The right to amend documents does not cover criminal records and *in extenso* birth certificates. These documents can be accessed only by State or public bodies. The officer of the Registry may always see the complete records on the original birth certificate. There is, thus, no complete cancellation of the original data. Article 5 of the Sex Reassignment Act 1982 provides that, post legal recognition, certificates of civil status are issued, indicating only the new name and newly recognised legal gender.[35]

3.2. MARRIAGE

Italian law does not recognise same-sex marriage. There is no express prohibition of same-sex marriages in Italian legislation. However, the requirement that there be both a female bride and a male bridegroom is accepted in the case law on Article 107 of the Civil Code, which refers to the husband (*marito*) and wife (*moglie*).[36] Where a person obtains legal recognition of his or her preferred gender, that person is entitled to enter into a valid marriage with a person of the opposite legal gender.[37]

Where a person seeks legal recognition post-marriage, there is uncertainty as to what consequences that recognition has for the legal status of the marriage. In particular, there is a question as to whether recognition automatically dissolves a valid heterosexual marriage, or if recognition merely acts as a ground for divorce. The Sex Reassignment Act 1982 states that legal gender recognition gives rise to the automatic dissolution of a marriage.[38] The 1982 Act did not, however, specify whether the Registrar had to note *ex officio* the legal recognition of gender on the marriage register. In 1987, the question of the exact legal consequences of gender identity recognition arose again when reforms to Italy's divorce laws designated gender recognition as a ground for divorce (thus suggesting that dissolution

App. Firenze, 23.11.2007 (2008) NGCC (La nuova giurisprudenza civile e commentata), p. 1188.

35 In a recent statement, the Italian Privacy Authority has clarified that, where an individual is issued with a copy of his or her Bachelor's degree post-legal recognition, the relevant educational authority must not issue a document which discloses that the individual has obtained legal gender recognition Sent. no. 341 of 15.11.2012.

36 G. Palmieri, *Le condizioni per contrarre matrimonio, Il nuovo diritto di famiglia* (G. Ferrando (ed.)), vol. I, Zanichelli, Bologna 2010, p. 112 ff. See also Art. 64 d of the P. R. 3 November 2000, No. 396, Regolamento dello stato civile.

37 G. Ferrando, *Il matrimonio civile, Famiglia e matrimonio* (T. Auletta (ed.)), vol. I, Giappichelli, Turin 2010, p. 228.

38 Art. 4 of Law no. 164 of 14 April 1982. S. La Torre, *Le cause civili di divorzio, Famiglia e matrimonio* (Zatti (ed.)) Vol. 1, 2, Giuffrè, Milan 2011, p. 1599 ff. S. Patti, *Il transessualismo, Diritto della famiglia* (M.G. Cubeddu/S. Patti (eds.)) Giuffrè, Milan 2011, p. 955. See also Court of Rome, 03.12.1982, 1983 I Giust. Civ. (Giustizia civile), p. 996; Court of Fermo, 28.02.1996, 1997 I Foro it. (Il foro italiano), p. 1656.

was optional rather than automatic).[39] Under the 2011 Reform Act, the Italian Parliament appears to have now clarified that the legal recognition of preferred gender (a) triggers the dissolution of a marriage and (b) attracts the relevant consequences set out in the Civil Code and Law no. 898 of 1 December 1970.[40]

The forced dissolution of marriages has been subject to challenge in Italy's courts. The Court of Cassation[41] has previously held that an automatic dissolution of a valid marriage violates the Italian Constitution,[42] as well as the European Convention on Human Rights.[43] The automatic dissolution of a marriage is an unjustified interference with the right to respect for private and family life.[44] In a decision of 11 June 2014, the Constitutional Court held that such automatic dissolution of the marriage following legal recognition of one of the spouses' gender identity is not contrary to Article 29 of the Italian Constitution.[45] The protection afforded to the married couple under Article 29 of the Italian Constitution presupposes, in the same way as the Civil Code presupposes, that there are two parties of the opposite legal gender. Hence, the recognition of the individual's preferred gender transforms a valid heterosexual marriage into a union between two same-sex persons. On the other hand, the Constitutional Court calls for an amendment of the law, which in its current state simply deprives transgender persons and their spouses of all legal recognition, demoting such couples from a status of 'maximum legal protection' to 'absolute indeterminacy'.[46] Such automatic dissolution of the marriage, stripping the couple of all their legal rights following one of the spouses' gender identity recognition is a violation of their 'inviolable rights of man' as set out in Article 2 of the Italian Constitution. Just like the Constitutional Court had previously called upon the Italian legislator to introduce non-marriage-based recognition for same-sex couples, the Court once again pressed for the introduction of registered partnerships so that transgender persons wishing to remain legally bound to their same-sex former spouse will not

---

39 Article 31 of the Reform Act no. 150 of 2011 provides that the court order granting the applicant legal recognition of gender automatically brings about the dissolution of the marriage. The relevant provisions of the Civil Code and the Act of 1 December 1970, no. 898 are applied. S.M. Sesta, *Diritto di famiglia*, Cedam, Padua 2015, pp. 314–315; A.M. Benedetti, *Le cause di divorzio, Il nuovo diritto di famiglia* (G. Ferrando (ed.)), 168–169, vol. I, Zanichelli, Bologna 2010, p. 778.

40 Bonilini, 'Rettificazione di attribuzione di sesso e scioglimento automatico del matrimonio ai sensi dell'art. 31 d.lgs. n. 150/2001' (2011) Fam. pers. succ. (Famiglia, persone, successioni), p. 805.

41 Cass., 06.06.2013, no. 14329 (2013) Corr. giur. (Corriere giuridico), p. 1519.

42 Arts. 2, 3 and 29 of the Italian Constitution.

43 Arts. 8 and 12 of the European Convention on Human Rights.

44 S. Patti, 'Il divorzio della persona transessuale' (2012) Riv. crit. dir. priv. (Rivista critica di diritto privato), p, 163; Id, 'Un ben motivato rinvio alla Corte costituzionale in materia di divorzio "automatico della persona transessuale" (2013) Corr. giur. (Corriere giuridico), p. 1526.

45 Constitutional Court of Italy, 11.06.2014, no. 170 (2014) <www.cortecostituzionale.it/action SchedaPronuncia.do?anno=2014&numero=170> accessed 29.06.2014.

46 Constitutional Court of Italy, 11.06.2014, no. 170 (2014) <www.cortecostituzionale.it/action SchedaPronuncia.do?anno=2014&numero=170> accessed 29.06.2014.

be deprived of all legal recognition.[47] Nevertheless, the judgment is controversial for both neglecting the symbolic and social importance of marriage in Italy and for shifting the burden onto the Italian Parliament. Since the Constitutional Court's last statement on the issue of same-sex partnerships, the Italian Parliament has taken little action to remedy the existing illegality faced by same-sex couples (including couples where one partner has obtained legal recognition of his or her preferred gender).

However, this is very likely to change. In *Oliari and Others v. Italy*[48] the ECtHR held that that the legal protection currently available to same-sex couples in Italy did not only fail to provide for the core needs relevant to a couple in a stable committed relationship, but it was also not sufficiently reliable, and that a civil union or registered partnership would be the most appropriate way for same-sex couples like the applicants to have their relationship legally recognised. Therefore there now is considerable pressure to create a scheme for the legal recognition of same-sex relationships.

3.3. PARENTAL RIGHTS

A person does not automatically lose their rights and responsibilities as a parent merely because they access legal recognition of their gender identity. Under Italian law, a court will restrict or remove a parent's rights in relation to his or her child only where the parent poses a risk of prejudice to the child. There is, however, evidence in the case law which suggests that Italian judges have, in some instances, considered that accessing legal gender recognition may cause psychological harm to a child.[49] An individual who has obtained gender identity recognition is entitled to access adoption services.[50]

47 Constitutional Court of Italy, 11.06.2014, no. 170 (2014) <www.cortecostituzionale.it/actionSchedaPronuncia.do?anno=2014&numero=170> accessed 29.06.2014.

48 Application no. 18766/11 and 26030/11.

49 Minor's Court of Turin, 20.07.1982 (1982) Dir. fam. pers. (Diritto della famiglia e delle persone), p. 979. The Court of Naples (18 December 1984, in Dir fam., 1985, 229; in Dir Leg., 1984, 951) rejected the argument that the particular sexual tendencies of a child's parent should be an obstacle to that parent obtaining custody rights over the child during judicial proceedings.

50 Appeal Court of Perugia, 11.02.1998 (1999) Giur. it. (La giurisprudenza italiana), p. 1628. Minor's Court of Perugia, 22.07.1997 (1997) Rass. Leg. Umbra, p. 728, stated that, in deciding whether an individual should be entitled to apply for an international adoption, it was not the role of the Court to review the normalcy or adequacy of an applicant's sexuality. Rather, the Court was asked to review whether the applicant was capable of engaging in a loving, altruistic and self-sacrificing relationship with the adopted child. Once this is shown, the Court would allow the application of a female-to-male transsexual individual.

3.4. PROTECTION FROM DISCRIMINATION

Italian legislation prohibits sex discrimination and promotes equal opportunities, notably through the national Equal Opportunities Code and the Workers' Statute.[51] Article 8 of the Workers' Statute prevents employers, from the point of first interview, from investigating aspects of a job candidate's life which are irrelevant to the candidate's professional competency. An employer may not carry out checks into a prospective employee's private life in order to determine whether the employee is transgender-identified.[52] The Italian Constitutional Court has held that regional legislation which ensures equal opportunities, protects against social exclusion and promotes positive perceptions of transgender persons in the professional sphere is of discretionary competence in the field of education and training.[53]

A number of Italian prison facilities, such as San Vittore in Milan and the Roman Rebibbia, house special units for transgender persons. In 2011, a court in Spoleto ordered a Local Health Authority (LHA) to provide hormone treatments for a transgender inmate, where such treatment was considered necessary by the prison's health officers.[54] Such initiatives were aimed to provide special departments able to deal with the specific health needs of transgender inmates, as well as protect transgender persons, particularly male-to-female transgender persons, from the risk of sexual violence in prisons.

---

51 Act No. 300 of 20 May 1970.

52 Equal Treatment between Men and Women in matters of employment Act of 12 September 1977 No. 903; Act no. 125 of 4 October 1991, 'Positive actions for the realization of equality between men and women at work'; Act no. 300 of 20 May 1970 'Workers' Statute', and in particular Art. 15, which prohibits discriminatory behaviours; Act no. 108 of 11 May 1990 'rules of individual dismissals'.

53 Constitutional Court of Italy, 04.07.2006, no. 253 (2006) I Giust. civ. (Giustizia civile) 1974, regarding Art. 3, 4 l. reg. Tuscany no. 63 of 2004.

54 Court of Spoleto, 13.07.2011.

THE LEGAL STATUS OF TRANSGENDER AND TRANSSEXUAL PERSONS IN SPAIN

Josep FERRER RIBA and Albert LAMARCA MARQUÈS

Contents

I. LEGAL FRAMEWORK AND BACKGROUND

In 2007, Spain introduced a new statute-based system for permitting individuals to obtain legal recognition of their preferred name and gender. Act 3/2007 of 15 March, which regulates the amendment of one's gender marker in the Civil Registry,[1] allows a person whose gender identity does not match his or her assigned legal gender to modify the gender marker in the Civil Registry and

[1] Act 3/2007, of 15 March, *reguladora de la rectificación registral de la mención relativa al sexo de las personas* (State Official Bulletin BOE No. 65, of 16 March 2007).

change his or her name, provided that certain requirements have been met. The Act was passed during a period of left-wing, liberal reforms in Spain's family law, including the legalisation of same-sex marriage and the establishment of a regime of unrestricted divorce.[2]

Prior to 2007, in the absence of statutory regulation, courts had already begun to permit individuals to obtain legal gender recognition. However, this recognition could only be granted by a court. According to the jurisprudence of the Spanish Supreme Court, whose leading case in this period dates back to 1987, 'transgenderism' was defined as a psychological pathology consisting in 'an overwhelming feeling of belonging to the opposite sex, a rejection of one's own sex, and an obsessive desire to change the genital morphology'. The Supreme Court's decisions established a series of conditions which applicants for legal gender recognition were required to satisfy. Applicants were required to submit to hormone treatment and undergo gender confirmation surgeries (whether or not desired). These medical interventions were intended to suppress secondary sexual characteristics, remove primary sex characteristics and implant artificial sexual organs corresponding to those sex characteristics associated with the applicant's preferred gender.[3] Although the Supreme Court allowed for the recognition of preferred gender (on the basis that the applicant suffered from a psychological disorder and had altered his or her physical body), the Court nevertheless

[2] *Cf.* J. Ferrer Riba, 'Same-sex Marriage, Divorce Express and Related Developments in Spanish Marriage Law' (2006) *International Family Law* 139; A. Lamarca Marquès, 'The changing concept of "family" and challenges for family law in Spain and Catalonia' in J.M. Scherpe (ed.), *European Family Law Volume II: The Changing Concept of 'Family' and Challenges for Domestic Family Law*, Edward Elgar, Cheltenham 2016 (forthcoming).

[3] *Cf.* STS 02.07.1987 (RJ 5045), 15.07.1988 (RJ 5722), 03.03.1989 (RJ 1993), 19.04.1991 (RJ 2725) and 06.09.2002 (RJ 7180). The initial decisions were not unanimous and included dissenting opinions. In this case law, references can be found to the ECtHR decisions with the purpose of justifying the decision in the presence of a legal gap and distinguishing the outcome from the decisions *I. v UK* and *Christine Goodwin v UK*, both of 11 July 2002. This case law has been profusely analysed, see A. Gordillo Cañas, 'Comentario a la STS de 3 de marzo de 1989' (1989) 19 *Cuadernos Civitas de Jurisprudencia Civil* 322; M. Elósegui Itxaso, *La transexualidad. Jurisprudencia y argumentación jurídica*, Comares, Granada 1999, p. 127; J.R. de Verda y Beamonte, 'La transexualidad en la jurisprudencia del Tribunal Supremo' (1999) *Revista General de Derecho* 10689; J.V. Gavidia Sánchez, 'El matrimonio del transexual' (2002) *Revista de Derecho Privado* 526; M.C. Gómez Laplaza, 'Transexualidad' (2004) *Aranzadi Civil* 2.016; E. Rubio Torrano, 'Transexualidad y Registro Civil' (2007) *Revista Doctrinal Aranzadi Civil-Mercantil* 1826; J. Alventosa del Río, *Discriminación por orientación sexual e identidad de género en el derecho español*, Ministerio de Trabajo y Asuntos Sociales, Madrid 2008, p. 338; Y.B. Bustos Moreno, *La transexualidad (De acuerdo a la Ley 3/2007, de 15 de marzo)*, Dykinson, Madrid 2008, p. 159; M.I. de la Iglesia Monje, 'Transexualidad y el cambio de la mención de sexo y de nombre' (2008) *Revista Crítica de Derecho Inmobiliario* 367; M.R. Lloveras Ferrer, 'Una ley civil para la transexualidad' (2008) 1 *InDret* 10; I. Espín Alba, *Transexualidad y tutela civil de la persona*, Reus, Madrid 2008, p. 80; L. Vázquez-Pastor Jiménez, 'El transexualismo primario y su contemplación legal en el ordenamiento jurídico español' in S. Navas Navarro (dir.) / S. Camacho Clavijo and A. de Lama y Aymà (coords.), *Iguales y diferentes ante el derecho privado*, Tirant lo Blanch, Valencia 2012, p. 710; B. Sillero Crovetto, 'Del derecho a la identidad de género al tratamiento integral de la transexualidad (Normativa estatal y autonómica)', *Boletín del Ministerio de Justicia*, 2170/2014, p. 5.

maintained that such recognition was, in reality, 'a legal fiction'. Therefore, it did not result in the individual obtaining recognition for all legal purposes. The extent of the 'fiction' would be determined on a case-by-case basis. In particular, marriage with a person of the same 'chromosomal sex' remained prohibited.[4]

Before Act 3/2007, the Supreme Court's case law had already been partly challenged by a number of lower court decisions. Lower courts did not always require full gender confirmation surgery, especially where the applicant for gender recognition was a female-to-male (FtM) transgender individual.[5] The lower court decisions also authorised a number of marriages between transgender persons and a spouse who shared the same legal gender as that assigned to the transgender person at birth.[6] In introducing these liberalising trends, some lower courts invoked a prior amendment of the Spanish Criminal Code in 1983. That amendment had decriminalised gender confirmation surgery. Since then, such surgical intervention had been treated as an exception to the crime of injury in spite of the consent of the victim, provided that the consenting person had reached the age of majority and had given valid, free, conscious and express consent (Article 428.2 Criminal Code 1973, as amended in 1983; currently, Article 156 Criminal Code 1995).[7]

---

4 This reasoning was implemented by the Civil Registry authorities, which initially dismissed the applications for marriage authorisations (RDGRN 02.10.1991, RJ 8611). However, after some lower courts' decisions which embraced the opposing view, the General Directorate of Registries and Notaries (DGRN) also changed its criterion in 2001 and began to authorise those marriages, as in Resolutions of 08.01.2001 (RJ 2569), 31.01.2001 (RJ 5095) and 24.01.2005 (RJ 1954). The Directorate also issued a 'doctrinal note' on 21 March 2001 (published in the *Boletín de Información del Ministerio de Justicia,* No. 1890, p. 91), containing some rules which all the registries had to follow. On these developments, see also Gómez Laplaza, above n. 3, p. 2024; E. Arroyo i Amayuelas, 'Sexo, identidad de género y transexualidad' in S. Navas Navarro (dir.), *Matrimonio homosexual y adopción. Perspectiva nacional e internacional*, Reus, Madrid 2006, p. 173; J.M. Díaz Fraile, 'Identidad sexual y Registro Civil. Exégesis de la ley 3/2007, de 15 de marzo reguladora de la rectificación registral de la mención relativa al sexo de las personas' in M.T. Areces Piñol (coord.), *Estudios jurídicos sobre persona y familia*, Comares, Granada 2009, p. 109.

5 *Cf.* Order of the Court of First Instance (JPI) Melilla 10.01.2000 (AC 1999/2607); Judgment JPI Lleida 21.09.1999 (AC 1651); Order JPI Igualada 3.01.2001 (AC 915).

6 See SAP Pontevedra 27.09.2003 (JUR 2006/26139), SAP Barcelona 17.02.2004 (AC 893), SAP Madrid 15.07.2004 (JUR 243776), SAP Valladolid 23.05.2005 (AC 1549), SAP Jaén 09.10.2006 (JUR 145216), SAP Cádiz 15.05.2007 (JUR 359509) and SAP Burgos 12.06.2007 (AC 1910). In cases of male-to-female transsexuals, requiring surgery, see SAP Madrid 25.07.2001 (JUR 2002/10787), SAP Barcelona 07.04.2003 (JUR 200183), SAP Valencia 24.02.2004 (JUR 163839), SAP Madrid 23.12.2004 (AC 2005/109), SAP Barcelona 01.09.2005 (AC 2006/268), SAP Asturias 25.09.2006 (JUR 279071). In cases of female-to-male transsexuals, also requiring surgery, but with some exceptions, see SAP Toledo 10.04.2002 (AC 1192), SAP Barcelona 06.05.2002 (JUR 186509), SAP Asturias 30.09.2003 (AC 1630), SAP Valencia 30.12.2003 (JUR 164317); SAP Islas Baleares 01.09.2004 (JUR 276127). *Cf.* Arroyo i Amayuelas, above n. 4, p. 148; Lloveras Ferrer, above n. 3, p. 11; Espín Alba, above n. 3, p. 86.

7 See STS 02.07.1987 (RJ 5045), referring to the decriminalisation as a main justification for allowing the reconstructive surgery and consequent sex reassignment. See also J. López-Galiacho Perona, *La problemática jurídica de la transexualidad*, McGraw-Hill, Madrid 1998, p. 215; Gómez Laplaza, above n. 3, note 69 p. 2.014; Arroyo i Amayuelas, above n. 4, p. 118; Alventosa del Río, above n. 3, p. 334; Vázquez-Pastor Jiménez, above n. 3, p. 709.

Act 3/2007 contributed substantially to these liberalising trends. In establishing clear statutory requirements for legal gender recognition, the law has provided much needed clarity and certainty. Although the Act omits all reference to constitutional values and rights, the legal literature considers that the law is based on a number of fundamental rights and principles recognised in the Spanish Constitution (CE), notably the dignity of the person and the free development of personality (Article 10),[8] the right to health (Article 43.1),[9] the right to personal privacy and reputation (Article 18.1), and even the right to physical and moral integrity (Article 15).[10]

The 2007 Act is not, however, a fully comprehensive regulation.[11] Its scope is limited to the legal recognition of preferred name and gender in the Civil Registry. Once such recognition has been effected, the persons concerned can exercise all rights inherent to their new legal condition. Although legal recognition of preferred gender, particularly through rights-compliant procedures for rectifying the Civil Registry, was the central concern for the transgender community when lobbying for the law, the Gender Act has failed to satisfy many other key demands. In particular, Spain's transgender community has criticised the Act for failing both to promote public policies which are conducive to the social integration of transgender persons. The Act also fails to recognise and extend important government benefits, including state payment for gender-related health care. Six autonomous communities, out of the seventeen in Spain – Navarra (in 2009),[12] the Basque Country (in 2012),[13] Galicia,[14] Andalusia,[15] Catalonia[16] and the Canary Islands (in 2014)[17] – have passed laws which address these demands at the regional level.

8 Arroyo i Amayuelas, above n. 4, p. 141; A. Vaquer Aloy, 'Els drets de la personalitat' in A. Vaquer Aloy (coord.), *Dret civil. Part general i dret de la persona*, Atelier, Barcelona 2013, p. 254; R. Bercovitz Rodríguez-Cano, 'Transexualidad, matrimonio entre personas de un mismo sexo y nombre' (2007) *Revista Doctrinal Aranzadi Civil-Mercantil* 1829.

9 Bustos Moreno, above n. 3, p. 37.

10 Gómez Laplaza, above n. 3, p. 2.006; Gavidia Sánchez, above n. 3, p. 649; E. Belda Pérez-Pedrero, 'Transexualidad y Derechos Fundamentales: protección integral sin la utilización del factor sexo como diferencia' (2004) 21 *Cuadernos de Derecho Público* 139.

11 Alventosa del Río, above n. 3, p. 358; Espín Alba, above n. 3, p. 108; Vázquez-Pastor Jiménez, above n. 3, p. 708.

12 Regional Act (*Ley Foral*) 12/2009, of 19 November, on the non-discrimination on grounds of gender identity and the recognition of the rights of transsexual persons (BON No. 147, of 30 November 2009).

13 Act 14/2012, of 28 June, on the non-discrimination on grounds of gender identity and the recognition of the rights of transsexual persons (BOPV No. 132, of 6 July 2012).

14 Act 2/2014, of 14 April, on the equal treatment and non-discrimination of lesbian, gay, transsexual, bisexual and intersexual persons in Galicia (DOG No. 79, of 25 April 2014).

15 Act 2/2014, of 8 July, integral for the non-discrimination on grounds of gender identity and the recognition of the rights of transsexual persons in Andalusia (BOJA No. 139, of 18 July 2014).

16 Act 11/2014, of 10 October, for the safeguard of the rights of lesbian, gay, bisexual, transsexual and intersexual persons and for the eradication of homophobia, biphobia and transphobia (DOGC No. 6730, of 17 October 2014).

17 Act 8/2014, of 28 October, on the non-discrimination on grounds of gender identity and the recognition of the rights of transsexual persons (BOC No. 215, of 5 November 2014).

There are no reliable statistics with respect to the size of Spain's transgender community. Data usually provides estimated percentages based on the figures of other demographic variables. According to these estimates, there would be between 3,000 and 4,000 transgender individuals living in Spain.[18] Since the entry into force of Act 3/2007, official data shows that a total of 1,495 people have obtained the legal recognition of their preferred gender in the period from mid-March 2007 to December 2014.[19]

II. RECOGNITION OF PREFERRED GENDER – PROCEDURE AND REQUIREMENTS

2.1. LEGAL PROCEDURE

Act 3/2007 permits amendment of a person's legal gender marker in the Civil Registry. The law describes such an amendment as 'Registry rectification'. The Act is in line with other rules relating to data held within the Civil Registry. This Registry publishes relevant data concerning the identity and civil status of citizens. It must be 'rectified' if the data recorded does not conform to reality (Article 3, 92 ff Civil Registry Act 1957; Articles 90 and 91 Civil Registry Act 2011).[20] The person's legal gender is one of these relevant items, as it is considered as an essential component of a person's identity.

The reference to 'rectification' has, nevertheless, sparked some controversy because 'rectification' usually implies that there was an original mistake.[21] The term seems therefore more appropriate in intersex cases, where individuals are affected by a condition of sex development which may have led to an error in assigning legal gender at birth. Indeed, applications made by intersex-affected individuals for 'rectification' have usually been accepted as a case where there was discordance between the legal gender assigned at birth and the actual gender in which the person develops. These findings were made pursuant to Article 93.2 of the Civil Registry Act of 1957[22] and a well-settled jurisprudence of the General Directorate for Registries and Notaries (DGRN), the highest administrative

18 Cfr. Arroyo i Amayuelas, above n. 4, p. 116; Lloveras Ferrer, above n. 3, p. 4.

19 Information provided by the Spanish Ministry of Justice.

20 The Civil Registry Act of 1957 will be abolished as soon as the new Act of 2011 (Act 20/2011, of 21 July, on the Civil Registry, BOE No 175, of 22 July 2011) enters into force. According to its Final Provision No. 10, this should have happened three years after the date of publication. Nevertheless, the Final Provision No. 19 of the Royal Decree-Law 8/2014, of 4 July (BOE No. 163, of 5 July 2014) has prolonged the vacancy period until 15 July 2015.

21 Bustos Moreno, above n. 3, p. 119; Lloveras Ferrer, above n. 3, p. 7; J. Rams Albesa, 'Cambio de nombre y rectificación de la mención del sexo. Transexualidad y Derecho transitorio' in M. Yzquierdo Tolsada (coord.), *Comentarios a las sentencias de unificación de doctrina: civil y mercantil (2005/2007)*, Vol. I, Dykinson, Madrid 2008, p. 547; Díaz Fraile, above n. 4, p. 87.

22 López-Galiacho Perona, above n. 7, p. 97; Gavidia Sánchez, above n. 3, p. 521; M.P. Sánchez González, 'La intersexualidad como problema jurídico' in A. Cabanillas Sánchez et al.

body in this field.[23] In the case of transgender persons, however, the question has been more controversial, although from the perspective of the preferred gender there is clearly a discordance with the Registry which must be rectified. This is the line of reasoning which has finally prevailed. The new Civil Registry Act of 2011 (Article 91.2) upholds the traditional approach by considering legal gender recognition as an issue of rectification (*i.e.* correcting an original error), making explicit reference to the Act 3/2007.

Act 3/2007 has introduced fundamental innovations into the procedure for legally recognising preferred gender. Since 2007, proceedings for legal recognition have an administrative and not judicial character.[24] As a matter of principle, the law does not require an applicant to appear in court and obtain approval in ordinary judicial proceedings, as was the case in the past.[25] Given that the information regarding legal gender is recorded in the birth entry of the Civil Registry, a person who wishes to have the Registry rectified needs only file a petition to amend that entry. The proceedings before the Registry officer are simply aimed at checking whether the conditions for rectification, as set out in the Act, have been met.

The job of maintaining the Civil Registry in Spain has traditionally been assigned to the judiciary, although it is conceived as an administrative function and therefore judges, in this position, do not exert judicial power. Their powers are delegated by the executive branch and supervised by the Ministry of Justice. Applications for legal gender recognition are therefore handled and decided by a judge, following an administrative procedure which ends with a decree without the effect of *res judicata*. Unfavourable decisions can be appealed to the Directorate General of the Registries and the Notary. Ultimately, it is possible to appeal the Directorate's resolutions before a court of justice, as is normal for all decisions made by administrative authorities in Spain. What is peculiar about Civil Registry resolutions, however, is that appeals are not filed before administrative, but rather civil courts.

The handling and deciding of gender recognition cases has not been centralised.[26] The territorial competence does not lie with the judge in charge of the Registry at the applicant's birthplace, as it is common in Civil Registry proceedings, but rather with the judge at the applicant's place of residence (Article 3 Act 3/2007). If the Registry in this latter place is entrusted to a judge

(coords.), *Estudios Jurídicos en Homenaje al Profesor Luis Díez-Picazo*, Vol. I, Cívitas-Thomson, Madrid 2003, p. 924; Arroyo i Amayuelas, above n. 4, p. 161; Espín Alba, above n. 3, p. 25.

23 The DGRN established that only intersexuality warranted the correction of the Registry, although exceptionally admitted the rectification in case of transsexuals (RDGRN 02.03.1971, EDD 562; 12.06.1971, EDD 584). Several later resolutions stuck to the original doctrine that the only mechanism to achieve a change of legal sex was the judicial procedure (RDGRN 17.03.1982; 17.02.1983; 26.04.1984, EDD 6905; 06.05.1987, EDD 10002; 14.05.1991; 29.12.1994).

24 Sillero Crovetto, above n. 3, p. 12.

25 See case law cited above n. 3. *Cf.* Bustos Moreno, above n. 3, p. 181; Lloveras Ferrer, above n. 3, p. 12; Díaz Fraile, above n. 4, p. 101; F.J. Jiménez Muñoz, 'Unas notas sobre el tratamiento jurídico-civil de la transexualidad en España' (2012) *Revista de Derecho UNED* 491.

26 Bustos Moreno, above n. 3, p. 125.

of the peace by delegation – as may arise in small towns – then this type of application is not handled by the judge of the peace, who is a layperson in law, but rather by a superior first instance court judge.[27] Following the implementation of the new Civil Registry Act of 2011, the keeping of the Civil Registry will be likely transferred from the judiciary to another body of public officers, but will retain its administrative character.[28] Since the entry into force of Act 3/2007, there has been no evidence of persons who have been denied legal recognition of their preferred gender.

2.2. PERSONAL REQUIREMENTS – CITIZENSHIP, AGE AND CAPACITY

A person who applies for rectification of his or her gender marker in the Civil Registry must be a Spanish national, have reached the age of majority and enjoy sufficient capacity (Article 1 Act 3/2007). Interestingly, the law does not impose any conditions relating to the family status of the applicant or which might affect his or her ability to form or maintain family relations. Under the Act, an applicant need not be single or divorced. There is no requirement for an applicant to submit to prior sterilisation, nor is there any prohibition on an applicant, once he or she has achieved legal recognition of preferred gender, from using techniques of artificial reproduction in the future. This can be explained by the fact that Spanish law has allowed same-sex marriage and adoption by same-sex couples without any restriction since 2005. Thus, the decision to recognise an individual's preferred legal gender does not affect the creation and subsistence of family relationships from the perspective of Spanish law.

2.2.1. Citizenship

The Act requires the applicant to be a Spanish citizen. This complete exclusion of foreigners has been subject to criticism. The DGRN accepted, before 2007, the international competence of Spanish courts to recognise the preferred legal gender of non-citizens on grounds of the right to effective legal protection (Article 24 CE) and the competence of domestic courts in all questions concerning the validity of records made in public registries (included the Alien's Administrative Registry).[29]

---

27 Judges of the peace are competent, by delegation, to handle proceedings for marriage authorisation; more complex proceedings are entrusted to the delegating authority: see Díaz Fraile, above n. 4, p. 105.

28 According to the Final Provision No 20 of the Royal Decree-Law 8/2014, of 4 July (BOE No. 163, of 5 July), the keeping of the Civil Registry will be assigned to Land and Mercantile Registrars once the new Civil Registry Act of 2011 enters into force. The offices of the Civil and the Mercantile Registries will be merged into a single joint office.

29 RDGRN 24.01.2005 (EDD 11359).

In addition to this, confining recognition of legal gender to Spanish nationals implies a more restrictive policy than the one espoused by the ICCS – CIEC Convention No. 29, on the recognition of decisions recording a sex reassignment, ratified by Spain in 2011 (see also the chapter on Belgium and the Netherlands). According to the Convention, decisions taken in a contracting state shall be recognised in the other contracting states if, at the time of the application, the person concerned was a national of, or habitually resident, in the state in which the decision was taken (Article 1).[30] The exclusion of foreigners residing in Spain creates a situation where there is a serious lack of protection for the immigrant population.

On the other hand, it is noteworthy that the requirement of citizenship does not need to be coupled with legal residency in the Spanish territory. If a Spanish citizen lives abroad, the Act permits that individual to engage with the recognition process and confers competency on the local Spanish consulate.[31]

2.2.2. *Age*

The requirement for an applicant to have obtained the age of majority is intended to ensure that the individual has a sufficient degree of personal maturity to make his or her own decision. According to a number of experts, however, gender dysphoria is commonly diagnosed at an early age and it is not unusual for transgender persons to seek hormone treatment before adulthood ('primary transsexualism').[32] The need to comply with the requirement of legal age does not prevent a transgender young person from accessing any form of medical intervention before he or she is 18 years old. The conditions required for accessing these treatments depend on the rules regarding informed consent in medical interventions. Such rules make provision for young people to consent, on their own, from the age of 16, except in the case of gender confirmation surgery. From the age of 16, it is legitimate for a young person to consent to hormone treatment.[33] This makes it easier to apply for legal gender recognition immediately upon reaching the age of majority, because the Act establishes, as a precondition for recognition, that the applicant must have already received at least two years of medical treatment (Article 4.1.b).

---

30 For a critique of this requirement, considering the powers of the Spanish Civil Registry in relation to foreign nationals, see Díaz Fraile, above n. 4, p. 88; see also Espín Alba, above n. 3, p. 120.

31 From 2007 to 2014, twenty-four preferred gender recognitions have been made in Spanish consulates abroad.

32 Vázquez-Pastor Jiménez, above n. 3, p. 706.

33 Art. 9.3.c Act 41/2002, of 14 November, regulating patient's autonomy, rights and duties of information, and clinical documents. The same approach can be found in Art. 7.2.d of the Catalan Act 21/2000, of 29 December. See also Bustos Moreno, above n. 3, p. 68.

The age requirement also raises the question of whether it is possible to submit to gender confirmation surgery before the age of 18.[34] The Spanish Criminal Code prohibits both the giving of consent by minors and the replacing or supplementing of their consent by their legal representatives (Article 156). In very exceptional cases, however, judges have granted authorisation to minors to access surgical intervention pursuant to the judges' their broad powers of child protection (Article 158 No. 4 Civil Code).[35] But, even in those rare cases, the legal recognition of the child's preferred gender was postponed until he or she reached the age of majority.

The time lag existing between access to medical treatment and rectification of the Civil Registry raises a question (applicable both to minors and adults) of whether a transitional regime would have been advisable, perhaps with a right to access temporary documentation and permission to use a preferred legal name. Act 3/2007 does not foresee the possibility of taking this kind of measure. During the mandatory two-year period, where the individual must receive medical treatment before recognition, the patient has to use identification documents reflecting a legal gender and name which is not in accordance with his or her gender identity and, in many cases, gender expression.[36] More recent regional legislation has attempted to overcome this unsatisfactory situation by allowing the issuance of 'adequate administrative documentation' during this two-year period.[37]

2.2.3. Capacity

Article 1 of Act 3/2007 also requires that an applicant must enjoy 'sufficient capacity' to apply for rectification of the Civil Registry. This requirement is intended to prevent applications from adults with diminished capabilities of discernment, whether or not they have been declared legally incompetent. The standard of sufficient capacity requires less than full legal capacity, but implies that the person must be able to understand the meaning and consequences of obtaining gender recognition. The requirement of capacity does not mean that the person must act by him or herself. The applicant may resort to an authorised representative. However, the fact that the applicant has to enjoy sufficient capacity seems to imply that rectification of the Civil Registry cannot be sought by a tutor or another legal representative after a declaration of incompetence. This outcome is unsatisfactory. In those exceptional cases of incapacity arising after

---

34 Bustos Moreno, above n. 3, p. 61.

35 Vázquez-Pastor Jiménez, above n. 3, p. 722.

36 The possibility of adopting interim measures was raised during the congressional debates, but the final text omitted it. See Bustos Moreno, above n. 3, p. 227.

37 Art. 7 of the Basque Country Act 14/2012, Art. 2.4 of the Andalusian Act 2/2014, Art. 23.1 of the Catalan Act 11/2014, and Art. 14.2.c of the Canarian Act 8/2014, cited in notes 13 to 17. Of course, the application of the rule is confined to documentation issued by the regional authorities.

the completion of medical treatment, a legal representative should be able to act for the applicant.

2.3. MEDICAL REQUIREMENTS – GENDER DYSPHORIA AND MEDICAL TREATMENT

The legal regime regarding the status of transgender persons, introduced by Act 3/2007, fundamentally departs from the previous system of legal recognition in that it does not require submission to gender confirmation surgery. Article 4.2 of the Act states that 'for a Registry rectification of the person's gender marker to be granted the medical treatment will not require to include sexual reassignment surgery.'[38] The Act only requires that the applicant provide a diagnosis of gender dysphoria and evidence that he or she has undergone medical treatment so as to transition his or her physical characteristics to the characteristics typically associated with his or her preferred legal gender.

2.3.1. Diagnosis

The applicant must be diagnosed with gender dysphoria. The accreditation shall be done by means of a report issued by a doctor or clinical psychologist licensed in Spain or whose qualifications have been recognised or approved in Spain (Article 4.1.a).

Article 4.1.a, No. 1 states the diagnosing report must refer to the '[e]xistence of a dissonance between the morphological sex or the physiological gender originally recorded and the psychosocial sex or gender identity felt by the applicant, as well as to the stability and persistence of this dissonance'. In the definition of gender dysphoria, the Act recognises a duality: the physiological or morphological sex versus the psycho-social identity of the applicant. The discrepancy between both these concepts is said to constitute gender dysphoria. Along with this requirement, the report must confirm that the applicant does not suffer from personality disorders that may bear a decisive influence on the existence of the dissonance (Article 4.1.a, No. 2).

2.3.2. Medical Treatment

The applicant has to provide evidence of having been medically treated for at least two years in order to transition his or her physical characteristics to the

[38] The previous requirement of surgery had been incidentally questioned by the Supreme Court Courts, which wondered whether it was in conformity with the Constitution: *cf.* STS 17.09.2007 (RJ 4968) and particularly STS 06.03.2008 (RJ 4039), in a case where the life of the person could be at risk. See de la Iglesia Monje, above n. 3, p. 372.

characteristics associated with the preferred legal gender (Article 4.1.b).[39] Medical treatments which took place prior to the Act qualify for the purpose of compliance with the two-year period.

As has been explained, the law is aimed at correcting an inconsistency between the information recorded in the Civil Registry and the applicant's gender identity. The physical transition in the applicant's appearance becomes the common way of proving the discrepancy. In normal cases, in order to obtain recognition, it is neither sufficient that the applicant is willing to live persistently in his or her preferred gender nor that the applicant complies with a 'test of everyday life' which applies in other jurisdictions.[40] The law requires, in principle, that the applicant submits to a process which aims to modify personal appearance. Article 4.1.b of the Act does not require the treatment to have a particular intensity or produce irreversible effects, nor does it specify whether the applicant or a medical professional on his behalf must show that the treatment has been fully successful or what level of physical transition must be achieved. Evidence of compliance with the legal requirement takes the form of a medical report.

The need to alter one's physical characteristics in order to meet expectations regarding characteristics of the preferred legal gender has been questioned by transgender advocacy groups, who argue with good reason that the recognition of preferred gender through a process of living and experiencing that gender is the paramount concern and should be sufficient from the perspective of the legal requirements. Act 3/2007 only partially addresses these concerns when it establishes an exception to the requirement of medical treatment in cases where it cannot be expected. Article 4.2 limits the exception, however, by saying that the requirement of medical treatment will be dispensed with only 'if there are health or age reasons which make impossible the following-up of treatment and those reasons are certified by a doctor.' In these cases, the legal recognition of preferred gender is possible on the basis of the gender dysphoria diagnosis alone. By referring to age reasons, the provision shows an understanding of the position of many older transgender persons who were unable to transition in their earlier lives and who now wish to obtain legal recognition of the preferred gender. This is a particularly vulnerable group among the transgender population.

Act 3/2007 can be praised for removing the requirement that an applicant for legal gender recognition must first submit to surgical intervention.[41] Of course this surgery still qualifies as treatment which permits the rectification of gender markers in the Civil Registry. Where a person has submitted to gender confirmation surgery, the patient is still required to meet the two-year medical treatment requirement. Pursuant to the transitional provision of Act 3/2007,

---

39 Regarding the length of the treatment before the Act 3/2007, see López-Galiacho Perona, above n. 7, p. 206.

40 Bustos Moreno, above n. 3, p. 167; Espín Alba, above n. 3, p. 129.

41 Courts had denied the change of name and sex because of the lack or surgery, whether for health problems or for financial difficulties. See e.g. STS 06.09.2002 (RJ 7180).

transgender individuals who submitted to gender confirmation surgery before the passage of Act are released from meeting the conditions set out in Article 4 (*i.e.* diagnosis and two years of medical treatment).[42] The intensity and exact requirements relating to this surgery, which is a question of particular importance for female-to-male (FtM) applicants, is no longer a relevant issue from the entry into force of Act 3/2007, provided that the medical treatment is certified.

Applications that were pending before the courts prior to 2007 have subsequently been required to comply with the terms of the Act. This was the case of the Supreme Court judgment of 17 September 2007, and several later judgments which were issued in 2009.[43]

2.3.3. Reports on Diagnosis and Medical Treatment

The procedure for legal gender recognition requires the production of two medical reports, one of them dealing with a diagnosis of gender dysphoria and the other concerning the performance of medical treatment (or the exemption therefrom).

The diagnosis of gender dysphoria must be certified by a report from a medical doctor or a clinical psychologist. The law is not particularly demanding about the conditions of this certification. The report must be issued by a professional who is licensed in Spain or whose degree has been recognised or approved in Spain. There is no single centralised medical committee competent for this role, nor is there a requirement that the doctor belongs to a specific hospital unit specialised on these matters. Since the passage of the Act, there are no reported cases of an objection to certify.

In terms of medical treatment, the certificate must be signed by the licensed medical doctor under whose direction the treatment was performed or, failing this, by a forensic doctor (*i.e.* a doctor ascribed to judicial service). In those cases where there is an intention to forgo the medical treatment for age or health reasons, the law only requires a medical certification. It must be understood that the conditions set out in Article 4.1.a, concerning the medical license or the recognition of the professional title in Spain, will also apply.[44]

---

42 Díaz Fraile, above n. 4, p. 99.

43 Even though the transitional provision of Act 3/2007 does not deal with this situation, the courts have applied the general rules of the Civil Code on this issue. See STS 17.09.2007 (RJ 4968); 28.02.2008 (RJ 2932); 06.03.2008 (RJ 4039); 06.03.2008 (RJ 4040); 17.07.2008 (RJ 4383); 18.07.2008 (RJ 4484); 22.06.2009 (RJ 3408). See also A. Salas Carceller, 'La llamada disforia de género en la reciente jurisprudencia de la Sala Primera del Tribunal Supremo' (2008) *Repertorio de Jurisprudencia Aranzadi* 11; Alventosa del Río, above n. 3, p. 359; de la Iglesia Monje, above n. 3, p. 373; Rams Albesa, above n. 21, p. 550; M.D. Toldrà Roca, 'Solución jurisprudencial a los procedimientos incoados y no concluidos a la entrada en vigor de la ley 3/2007, de 15 de marzo' in M.T. Areces Piñol (coord.), *Estudios jurídicos sobre persona y familia*, Comares, Granada 2009, p. 277.

44 It must be noted that the law requires only one document certifying the diagnosis and another one the medical treatment, not two certificates being in agreement. *Cf.* Bustos Moreno, above n. 3, p. 131.

2.4. LEGAL RECOGNITION OF PREFERRED NAME

The recognition of the applicant's preferred gender also requires a change of name. In Spain, the Civil Registry Act, and its implementing Regulation, have traditionally established that names given to persons should not deceive as regards the holder's legal gender. Article 54 of the Civil Registry Act (1957) prohibited the attribution of a name which would 'make identification confusing' and be 'misleading about sex.' Pursuant to Article 1 of Act 3/2007, changing the applicant's name is intended to prevent any discordance between the legal name and legal gender markers in the Civil Registry.

However, the Act exceptionally allows a person to retain his or her original legal name so long as retention complies with the rules of the Civil Registry Act (Article 2.1 II). This provision is meant to apply when the applicant bears a non-gender-specific name. In this regard, it is relevant to note that recent trends tend to weaken the function of the name as a mechanism to ascertain the gender identity of its bearer. In fact, Article 51 of the new Civil Registry Act of 2011 eliminates the requirement that a person's name must not mislead as to that person's legal gender. As mentioned above, there is no transitional mechanism allowing for the use of a different name other than the original name prior to obtaining legal recognition of preferred gender and name.

III. CONSEQUENCES OF THE LEGAL RECOGNITION OF PREFERRED GENDER

3.1. RECTIFICATION OF THE REGISTRY AND PUBLICITY

If an application for legal gender recognition is successful, the competent public authority will issue a resolution which orders the rectification of the applicant's name (if appropriate) and gender markers in the Civil Registry. From the moment of rectification, the applicant is permitted, and required, to use his or her recognised legal gender and name whenever there is a need to provide this information.

The Act facilitates the identification by making provision for the issuance of new official documentation. Pursuant to its Article 6.2, the applicant assumes a legal duty to request the issuance of a new national identity card with the amended data. The card holder retains the original national identification number and does not have to pay any fee for obtaining the new card. With regard to official documents with a date earlier than the date of the resolution, the law allows the issuance of duplicates at the request of the applicant. Such duplicates reproduce all original data with the exception of the legal name and gender, which now appear in their amended form.

The rectification allows the applicant to make public his or her newly recognised status and to use the new name for all intents and purposes. However, the fact that the individual has obtained legal recognition remains confidential and is not publicised. Although, as a matter of principle, information recorded in the Civil Registry is public and open to any person having a legitimate interest in accessing it (Article 6 Civil Registry Act 1957; Article 15 Civil Registry Act 2011), some data is subject to a regime of 'restricted publicity'. In this regard, information concerning the legal recognition of a person's preferred gender is qualified as 'specially protected' (Article 83.1.d Civil Registry Act 2011). This means that only the applicant or a legal representative may access the information and may authorise access to third parties. Following the applicant's death, authorisation may be granted by a judge who first scrutinises whether the person who is applying for the information has a legitimate interest in its receipt (Article 84 Civil Registry Act 2011). In order to guarantee the highest level of privacy, Act 3/2007 provides for the possibility that the original registry folio might be cancelled (instead of being amended) at the request of the applicant and a new folio containing the rectified data be opened (Article 1.2).[45]

3.2. RIGHTS AND DUTIES

The decision to permit rectification of the gender marker in the Civil Registry produces constitutive effects from the date of registration (Article 5.1 Act 3/2007). The fact that the effects are constitutive rather than declaratory is a singularity in the Civil Registry legislation.[46] The underlying but indeed controversial rationale is that the decision to grant rectification of the legal gender marker does not correspond to the existence of an original mistake, but rather a mismatch between the newly recognised legal gender and the gender which was assigned to the applicant at the time of first registration (usually at birth).

Pursuant to Article 5.2, 'rectification will allow the person to exercise all rights pertaining to his or her new condition.' This means that transgender persons are considered for all purposes as having a legal gender which corresponds to their gender identity. These persons enjoy all the rights and duties, whatever their nature, attributed by law or by private regulations, to individuals of that legal gender. Nonetheless, the constitutive nature of the rectification excludes the acquisition of rights or the imposition of duties with retroactive effect.

Having regard to the fact that, to a large extent, Spain's laws of marriage and non-biological parentage have become independent from gender considerations, it is easy to understand that gender recognition does not bring about relevant

45 Díaz Fraile, above n. 4, p. 114. This possibility has been implemented by Art. 307 of the Administrative Regulation of the Civil Registry, as amended by the Royal Decree 820/2005, of 8 July.

46 Arroyo i Amayuelas, above n. 4, p. 158.

consequences in family relationships. Prior to 2005, the Spanish Supreme Court prevented individuals, who had obtained legal gender recognition, from marrying persons of the opposite legal gender. Thus, a transgender man would have been prohibited from marrying a person who was assigned a female legal gender at birth. Similarly, transgender women were traditionally prevented from marrying individuals who were assigned a male legal gender at birth. The introduction of same-sex marriage in 2005 effectively rendered these difficulties irrelevant.[47] In the same vein, the legal recognition of a preferred legal gender does not affect an existing marriage. Recognition neither requires automatic dissolution nor is it a specific ground for divorce (because, in Spain, divorce is free and does not depend on the existence of stated 'grounds').

Parentage and parent–child relationships are not affected by legal gender recognition. Intent-based parentage in Spain is gender neutral. On the one hand, adoption is accessible to single persons and to couples, including heterosexual and homosexual spouses or cohabitants. The right to adopt requires that the candidate(s) pass the suitability test carried out by the child protection public agencies, which cannot discriminate on gender grounds. On the other hand, techniques of assisted reproduction are available to women who are married to, or partnering with, men or with other women, as well as to single women (Articles 6.1 and 6.3 Act 14/2006, on techniques of assisted human reproduction). Considering that, under Spanish law, it is possible to have two fathers or two mothers, existing parent–child relationships remain unaltered where one parent obtains legal gender recognition.

In some cases of separation or divorce, transgender persons have seen their custody or contact rights restricted, either during the period of their medical treatment or even after its completion. A highly publicised case dealing with this problem reached the Spanish Constitutional Court in 2008 (Judgment 176/2008 of 22 December).[48] The case arose during divorce proceedings, where one parent sought to restrict the contact rights of the other parent. The civil court had severely curtailed the contact rights of the legal father, who was undergoing hormone treatment with the aim of seeking legal gender recognition. The civil court held

47 Gavidia Sánchez, above n. 3, p. 662, exposes the arguments on this issue before the 2005 legislation.

48 M.I. de la Iglesia Monje, 'Transexualidad y restricción del régimen de visitas' (2009) *Revista Crítica de Derecho Inmobiliario* 1518; M.D. Bardají Gálvez, 'Transexualidad y derecho de visita' (2010) *Revista Jurídica de Catalunya* 125; A.M. Romero Coloma, 'Transexualidad del progenitor y derecho de visitas. Sentencia del Tribunal Constitucional de 22 de diciembre de 2008 y las limitaciones al derecho de visitas' *La Ley* no. 7471/2010; M. Madriñán Vázquez, 'Restricción del régimen de visitas a un padre transexual: ¿discriminación por razón de orientación sexual o interés del menor? STC 176/2008 de 22 de diciembre' in S. Navas Navarro (dir.) / S. Camacho Clavijo and A. de Lama y Aymà (coords.), *Iguales y diferentes ante el derecho privado*, Tirant lo Blanch, Valencia 2012, p. 607; I. Espín Alba, 'Discriminación, orientación sexual y derecho privado' in S. Navas Navarro (dir.) / S. Camacho Clavijo and A. de Lama y Aymà (coords.), *Iguales y diferentes ante el derecho privado*, Tirant lo Blanch, Valencia 2012, p. 231.

that the legal father was emotionally unstable and that this would affect the child's educational and emotional development. The court stated that its decision should not be seen through the lens of discrimination, but rather as an example of judges prioritising the best interests of the child. The Constitutional Court dismissed the legal father's appeal (*recurso de amparo*) and held that there had been no violation of fundamental rights. The legal father subsequently brought an unsuccessful appeal before the European Court of Human Rights. In its ruling of 30 November 2010,[49] the ECtHR agreed that there had been no violation of the rights of the legal father. Following this decision, similar rulings have been handed down by lower courts, limiting or suspending the parental rights of transgender persons.[50]

In relation to the fundamental right to honour and privacy (Article 18 CE), there is extensive case law dealing with situations in which transgender persons argued that their rights had been violated because information had been disseminated about their condition or opinions had been expressed about it. The courts have decided these cases by applying the general criteria developed for the protection of honour and privacy, but also reconciling such rights with rights to free speech and freedom of information. Thus, if the transgender identity of a person is publicly known, the courts have tended to find that there was no privacy violation in disseminating information about that identity. Similarly, there is no rights violation if the disseminator's behaviour constitutes an exercise of free speech.[51] On the other hand, if the transgender identity of a person is being used to harm his or her reputation, courts usually hold that there has been a violation of the honour of the affected person.[52]

Regulations in some fields have shown sensitivity to the situation and needs of transgender persons who have not satisfied the legal requirements for recognising their preferred legal name and gender. This applies, for instance, to inmates under the surveillance and protection of prison authorities. Transgender prisoners who have obtained legal recognition of their preferred name and gender are treated in every way according to their preferred legal gender. The situation is more complex, however, where there are inmates whose legal gender does not correspond to their preferred and expressed gender. In those cases, the inmate may apply for recognition of his or her preferred gender with the help of supporting medical and psychological reports. If the petition is accepted, the person is entitled to separation from inmates of his or her birth assigned gender, may be called by his or her preferred name and offered medical treatment for the

49 Case *P.V. v Spain* (application no. 35159/09).

50 SAP Sevilla 28.12.2012 (JUR 179173): the contact between the transsexual parent, who was living in Switzerland, and the daughter was suspended by the court, which argued the potential negative effects on the girl's emotional health because she had to travel abroad to the country where the transsexual parent was residing and live with his or her new partner, also a transsexual person.

51 SAP Málaga 22.03.2002 (AC 1266); 16.01.2003 (AC 1298); STS 26.09.2008 (RJ 5579); STS 07.11.2011 (RJ 1364); SAP Asturias 02.12.2011 (JUR 438236).

52 SAP Málaga 24.04.2002 (AC 1269); SAP Madrid 03.10.2013 (JUR 2014/5764).

process of transition.[53] These measures do not constitute the legal recognition of the individual's preferred gender in the same way as under the Act. A person who seeks to obtain full legal recognition must still satisfy the conditions set down in the Act.

Spain's regulation on the right to asylum also shows concern for the personal condition of transgender persons. The Organic Act 3/2007 added a provision to Act 5/1984 of 26 March, regulating the right to asylum and the status of refugees, according to which asylum can now be granted to a woman who fears abuse or persecution in her country of origin on the basis of her gender. The reference to gender was understood as covering transgender persons seeking asylum out of fear of being persecuted because of their gender identity.[54] The asylum regulation was later replaced by Act 12/2009 of 30 October, which regulates the right to asylum and subsidiary protection. This later regulation specifically grants asylum or refugee status on those who have a well-founded fear of being persecuted because of their gender identity or sexual orientation (Article 3). The protection also extends to people who may be persecuted for belonging to a specific social group. The notion of group may include people having a common feature of gender identity (Article 7.1).

IV. LEGAL CHALLENGES TO THE CURRENT SITUATION

Act 3/2007 did not achieve complete consensus in Parliament (the conservative Popular Party did not vote for it) but it was not challenged before the Constitutional Court. The law's implementation has not proven to be overly problematic. In particular, the right to marry a person who has the same biological sex characteristics has not been called into question (no doubt because of the introduction in 2005 of same-sex marriage). Although Act 13/2005, which legalised same-sex marriage, was challenged before the Constitutional Court, that Court dismissed the challenge in November 2012 (Judgment 198/2012 of 6 November), creating certainty for transgender individuals who wished to marry.[55]

Advocacy groups continue to demand the enactment of comprehensive legislation on gender identity. The broad diversity and scope of questions which such legislation should address would require the involvement of both the central state and the autonomous communities. Two compelling reasons for more comprehensive legislation are (a) the need to fight discrimination in

[53] Circular (*Instrucción*) of the Directorate General of Penal Institutions I 7/2006 TGP of 9 March 2006, on the integration into the prison community of transsexual persons.

[54] Bustos Moreno, above n. 3, p. 118.

[55] *Cf.* A. Lamarca Marquès, 'Same-sex marriage in Spain: the decision of the Constitutional Court' (2013) 1 *International Family Law* 76.

employment[56] and (b) the need to guarantee access to appropriate healthcare, particularly in light of the cost of gender confirmation surgery. As previously noted, six autonomous communities – Navarra, the Basque Country, Galicia, Andalusia, Catalonia and the Canary Islands – have already taken action. The legislation enacted by these regions sets the stage for a public policy in this field, including the implementation of measures against transphobia, promoting the healthcare of transgender individuals, tackling discrimination in employment and raising awareness of transgender identities in the education system.[57]

As a matter of principle, the Spanish National Health Care Service does not fund gender confirmation surgery.[58] In the latest updates made to these services (2006), such surgical treatments were not included, despite repeated requests.[59] Act 3/2007 makes no reference to this issue. The autonomous communities, which are responsible for the provision of healthcare in their territory, have the option to assume coverage of additional healthcare benefits from their own budgets. To this date, at least ten autonomous communities have assumed the cost of gender confirmation surgery (Andalusia, Aragon, Asturias, the Basque Country, the Canary Islands, Catalonia, Extremadura, Madrid, Navarra and Valencia).[60]

56 Concerning the discrimination on the grounds of transsexuality, see, in the affirmative, SJS Barcelona 26.03.2007 (AS 1392), and in the negative, STSJ Madrid 27.06.2005 (JUR 186387) and STSJ Cataluña 19.01.2006 (JUR 84419). See also J.J. del Val Arnal, 'La argumentación razonable por la empresa en la extinción del contrato de trabajo de un transexual: el error en la persona; la defensa del trabajador: discriminación por razón de sexo' (2007) *Aranzadi Social* 2746; C. Chacartégui Jávega, *Discriminación y orientación sexual del trabajador*, Lex Nova, Valladolid 2001; Alventosa del Río, above n. 3, p. 299.

57 Cfr. Sillero Crovetto, above n. 3, p. 15.

58 Costs stand around 12,000–18,000 euros for a vaginoplasty and 24,000–36,000 euros for a phalloplasty. *Cf.* Bustos Moreno, above n. 3, p. 84.

59 The Royal Decree 1030/2006, of 15 September, which sets the portfolio of common services by the Health National System and the procedure for its updating, does not mention these treatments, unlike the former regulations, which explicitly excluded them (3rd Annex of Royal Decree 63/1995, of 20 January). Nevertheless, a subsequent Royal Decree (1207/2006, of 20 October), which regulates the management of the Health Cohesion Fund, mentions the 'care of transsexuality' among the pathologies covered in some Spanish centres. Accordingly, some courts have recently considered that sexual reassignment surgery might be covered by the National Health Care System (*cf.* STSJ Asturias 01.02.2013, AS 244). In this regard, see C. Grau Pineda, 'Nuevos horizontes para las personas transexuales: ¿fantasía o realidad?' (2007) *Revista Doctrinal Aranzadi Social* 1421; Sillero Crovetto, above n. 3, p. 14.

60 There are five public referral hospitals for the carrying out of these treatments in Barcelona, Bilbao, Madrid, Malaga and Valencia. See also Bustos Moreno, above n. 3, p. 100; Jiménez Muñoz, above n. 25, p. 495.

In view of the economic crisis currently facing Spain, it is difficult to foresee that the National Health Care System will take on responsibility for funding such high-cost treatments in the near future.[61] By contrast, however, surgical intervention for intersex-affected persons is included among the health benefits funded by the national system.[62]

---

61 Most judicial decisions deny that public funds should cover the reassignment surgery: STSJ Asturias 31.01.2003 (AS 1718), STSJ Madrid 23.09.2005 (AS 2900), STSJ País Vasco 21.06.2005 (AS 2428). To the contrary, however, see STSJ Cataluña 18.02.2003 (AS 1332) and STSJ Madrid 30.06.2005 (AS 3950), overturned by STS 29.05.2007 (RJ 6348). *Cf.* Arroyo i Amayuelas, above n. 4, p. 177; Alventosa del Río, above n. 3, p. 328.

62 Section 5 Annex III of the Royal Decree 63/1995, of 20 January, about the ordering of health care provision by the National Health Care System, which included the list of treatments not covered by the System or by other central government funds earmarked for health care, expressly stated: 'Sexual reassignment surgery, except for surgery treating of intersexual pathologies'. However, the later Royal Decree 1030/2006 (cited above n. 9), does not mention these pathologies; see Bustos Moreno, above n. 3, p. 92.

THE LEGAL STATUS OF TRANSSEXUAL AND TRANSGENDER PERSONS IN SWEDEN

Jameson Garland

Contents

1. LEGAL FRAMEWORK AND STATISTICS

1.1. OVERVIEW

In 1972, Sweden became the first country in the world to enact a national legislative scheme for changes of registered gender and legal gender status.[1] The Gender Classification Act[2] was also the first law of its kind to establish national rules for such changes for children with atypical sex development. On the surface, the current Act appears to be much the same statute today as it was when it came into force.[3] The criteria for changes of registered gender under the current law, as well as the provisions for governance of medical care, are strikingly similar to those in use for the last four decades. In 2012, however, the government began a series of reforms that recently culminated in a sweeping proposal to radically overhaul the Act – not only in its regulatory aims, but at its very conceptual foundations – recognising gender identity as a human right, rather than a medical condition or registered identity that would warrant only strictly controlled changes as a matter of law.[4] Even without these reforms, a comparison of the current Act to the original law underscores subtle, recent changes that resonate with substantive distinctions, influenced by the European Convention of Human Rights (ECHR), the Yogyakarta Principles, and the Convention on the Rights of the Child. If the proposed reforms take effect on schedule in 2016, this chapter may quickly become a mere historical chronicle of how one influential nation reconsidered its approach to conferring benefits and imposing hardships on transgender people, with the relative successes and failures of its legal scheme perhaps best measured by those whose lives are most directly affected by it.

At its inception, the Gender Classification Act integrated changes of registered gender with medical care. In part, this grew out of Sweden's universal health care system, which covers most of the costs of diagnosis and basic treatment associated with gender identity distress (clinically known as *dysphoria*).[5] As early as 1968, the government recognised that much of this stress arose, in fact, from incorrect legal registrations assigned at birth.[6] Thus, treatment for such stress was also

1 National Board of Health and Welfare, *Transsexuella och övriga personer med könsidentitetsstörningar: Rättsliga villkor för fastställelse av könstillhörighet samt vård och stöd* [Transsexuals and other persons with gender identity disorders: Legal conditions for determination of gender, as well as care and support] 2010, p. 13.

2 SFS 1972:119: *Lag om fastställande om könstillhorighet i vissa fall* (KtL). The original title translates most closely to the law 'on the establishment of gender belonging in certain cases'. In Swedish, the word '*genus*' was originally conceived to represent 'gender' distinct from '*kön*' to mean 'sex'; today the word '*kön*' is often used to mean sex and gender interchangeably. For the purposes of this chapter, I use 'gender' except where 'sex' is a clinical classification.

3 See sections 1.2 and 2 for details.

4 See *Juridiskt kön och medicinsk könskorrigering*, SOU 2014:91. For further details, see section 2.3, below.

5 See National Board, above n. 1, pp. 10–13 and 45–56.

6 *Intersexuallas könstillhörighet*, SOU 1968:28, pp. 33–34 and 38.

ratified as standard care in the Act,[7] which gives the National Board of Health and Welfare the authority to approve all genital and gonadal surgery connected with any application for a registered gender change, as well as the hospitals where certain procedures take place. The Board was also given the power to establish guidelines for changing registered gender – a process, until recently, based on extensive medical documentation.[8] Accordingly, both gender surgery and change of registered gender have taken place in Sweden under extensive supervision, both by the government and medical professionals. On the one hand, this centralised system has provided access to health care for individuals who seek relief from gender distress. On the other hand, the system has placed the gender identity of those seeking medical and legal assistance under extensive administrative control, as well as putting the force of law behind non-consensual gender therapies on children.

Sweden does not collect statistics on persons whose identities do not match their registered gender. Rather, the government considers the population register presumptively correct as its central mechanism for collection of data about the population.[9] As such, Sweden's statistical gender portrait is framed by the register and changes to it, both in individual years and over time. In turn, the National Board's data on the transgender population has focused on applications for changes of registered gender, which have steadily increased. From 1972 to 2002, the National Board reported that it received 426 applications for changes of registered gender, but received 439 applications from 2003 to 2011 alone, with most applications granted.[10] Through 2012, the National Board has estimated that approximately 50 to 70 individuals per year applied for change of registered gender, but in 2013, 170 persons applied for such changes.[11] The changes to registered gender from male-to-female historically represented roughly 60 per cent of all applications, with 40 per cent representing female-to-male registry changes,[12] but in 2011 those percentages reversed.[13] The National Board also estimated an average intake of 1,000 patients per year in the health care system with potential gender distress or dysphoria,[14] but by the end of 2014, 1,365 persons were in the 2013 patient register diagnosed as having some form of gender

7 See section 2.2.1, below.

8 For details, see section 2.1.

9 National Board of Health and Welfare, *Administrative problems for persons who change juridical gender* (Dnr. 5.3–51189/2012), 2014, p. 2.

10 Compare Prop. 2011/12:142, *Ändrad könstillhörighet*, p. 17–18 and National Board, above n. 1, p. 22.

11 National Board of Health and Welfare, *Nationellt kunskapsstöd för vård och behandling av personer med könsdysfori*, 2014, p. 17. According to the Board, 120 of 125 of these applications had been processed by February 2014. Ibid.

12 Compare the sources above, n. 10.

13 Prop. 2011/12:142, above n. 10, p. 18.

14 National Board, above n. 11, p. 12.

identity disorder.[15] While the government has offered no official explanation for these statistical changes, they may not be surprising given that in 2008 the government strengthened prohibitions on gender identity discrimination and in 2010 proposed significant reforms of the Gender Classification Act, removing burdens placed on those who sought to correct their gender identity.

Because confidentiality laws protect patients' medical records, only limited conclusions can be drawn from other available data. For example, of the adults in the health care register classified as diagnosed with a gender disorder in 2013, only 85 per cent were officially diagnosed with 'transsexualism', defined by the Board as wishing to live fully in a gender other than the one registered at birth.[16] Only 78 persons under 18 were similarly listed in the register, only half of whom were diagnosed with transsexualism.[17] Regarding medical treatment related to gender correction, government records show that, between 1972 and 2002, only approximately 70 per cent of applicants for changes in the registry received substantial surgery, with even lower percentages requesting surgery prior to 1985.[18] Beyond these general categories, much information remains elusive. For example, the most recent investigation of changes of registered gender for persons with atypical sex development indicated only one correction of registration per year for such persons, though 10 to 20 infants per year typically have received surgical gender assignment or gender conforming surgery.[19] Most of these gender surgeries have not been captured in the registry because most of the children affected have been surgically altered for planned gender assignment at birth. In sum, the available data challenges the notion that the number of changes in registered gender is coterminous with the number of gender assignment surgeries in Sweden. Illumination of the complexities of gender variance requires carefully considered outreach to the population, a project that the Swedish government has not yet undertaken.

1.2. LEGAL BACKGROUND AND EVOLUTION

1.2.1. Original Legislation

Prior to 1972, Swedish medical authorities offered certain treatments to persons who identified with a gender other than the one assigned at birth, typically when

---

15 National Board of Health and Welfare, *Snabb vård minskar lidande när könsidentiteten inte stämmer*, 2014.

16 Ibid.

17 Ibid.

18 See S. Olsson and A.R. Möller, 'On the Incidence and Sex Ratio of Transsexualism in Sweden' (2003) 32(4) *Archives of Sexual Behavior* 383; see also C. Dhejne, P. Lichtenstein, M. Boman, A.L.V. Johansson, N. Långström and M. Landén (2011) 6(2) *PLoS ONE (Public Library Open Source One)* 3.

19 See *Ändrad könstillhörighet – förslag till ny lag*, SOU 2007:16, pp. 41 and 111.

they came to the attention of specialists in the health care system diagnosing differential causes for gender distress.[20] These treatments consisted of hormonal therapies and eventually surgery, the latter becoming more prevalent in the late 1950s.[21] During this period, Swedish law formally served as an impediment to surgery, particularly for persons originally classified as males but expressing a female identity, to the extent that orchiectomy, for those who desired it, could not occur without the National Board's permission.[22] Castration had been available, however, for 'humanitarian' reasons, particularly for gay men, who were seen as individuals 'struggling' with sexual desire.[23] As such, surgery was accessible in some cases for persons seeking gender reassignment. Nevertheless, the law contained no formal mechanism for changing registered gender, which had been left to the discretion of various government departments. By 1968, at least 53 individuals in Sweden had applied to government officials for a change of their name or legal status from one gender to another, with most applications approved administratively, but with approximately 100 persons undergoing treatment of some kind for gender distress in a given year.[24]

Three key developments precipitated legal change. The first arose from governmental concerns about the lack of established criteria for changing registered gender, particularly in cases where the grounds for such change were not fully documented. Thus, in 1963, the Central Statistical Office requested legal advice from the Attorney General on such cases, with the Attorney General formally requesting a governmental investigation on these matters.[25] During this same period, the government had also tightened controls over medical care, formally requiring all treatments and diagnoses to be based on science and proven experience,[26] in addition to increasing penalties for risky procedures offered by unqualified medical personnel.[27] Finally, by the 1960s, surgical gender assignment and other gender treatment had become the standard of care for children with atypical sex development, in many cases affecting the registered

20 See J. Wålinder, 'Incidence and Sex Ratio of Transsexualism in Sweden' (1971) *British Journal of Psychiatry* 195–196.

21 See Olsson and Möller, above n. 18, p. 384.

22 See Wålinder, above n. 20, p. 195; see also Lag (1944:133) om kastrering (repealed 2013).

23 Prop. 2011/12:141, above n. 10, p. 161.

24 See SOU 1968:28, above n. 6, p. 34.

25 Ibid., pp. 12 and 36.

26 Allmänna läkarinstruktionen (1963:341), § 3, st. 1 (providing that each physician, whether in public or private service, is required to advise and treat the patient 'in accordance with science and proven experience'). The requirement became unqualified for the first time in 1963, removing 'so far as possible' from the prior instruction. See E. Axelsson, *Patientsäkerhet och kvalitetssäkring i svensk hälso- och sjukvård*, Iustus 2011, p. 229. The requirement has remained in the law since, currently found in the Patient Safety Act, SFS 2010:659, 6 kap, 1 §.

27 The joint reforms tightened qualifications for medical practice and licensure while strengthening penalties for non-scientific medicine. See SFS 1960:408 *om behörighet att utöva läkaryrket* and SFS 1960:409 *om förbud i vissa fall mot verksamhet på hälso- och sjukvårdens område.*

gender of children.[28] At the time, Sweden lacked clear mechanisms for correction of errors in classification at birth when these children's gender had not been carefully identified. The absence of such procedures made surgical alterations problematic after a child's gender had been registered. Medical and legal experts concluded that these children and others who wished to change registered gender were *intersexuals* – caught 'in between' a male-female assignment – dubbing those who were born with bodies typical for their assigned gender as *non-somatic intersexuals* ('transsexual'), with *somatic* used to describe persons with variant sex development. The government formally grouped these individuals as those whose conditions placed them in precarious circumstances because their gender identities conflicted with their legal status.

On 30 September 1966, the Justice Department formally called for the establishment of a committee of experts to investigate the issues surrounding requests for a change of registered gender, with an estimated 19 cases waiting to be decided pending that investigation.[29] In its report, *Intersexuals' Gender Belonging*, the experts detailed the state of medical knowledge at the time for persons with gender anomalies and distress. They concluded that gender is such a complex mix of physiology, psychology, and sexuality that science did not permit a strict formula for establishing categorical definitions of gender that could be applied to individuals.[30] Instead, the experts concluded, the true gender of many persons could only be determined on a case-by-case basis after extensive consultation.[31] Nevertheless, because Swedish law at the time differentiated certain rights, privileges, and other legal duties on the basis of gender, the expert committee warned that individuals who were born somatically atypical for their gender or otherwise experienced gender distress were suffering due to legal uncertainty surrounding their deeply felt gender identities.[32] As such, the committee recommended that the law should, as far as possible, recognise the gender identity for these individuals in a way that would, in most cases, be decisive and permanent. The government agreed, proposing that it would be more efficient to attempt a focused solution for what was perceived as a problem for a small class of persons, rather than attempt to reconstruct and redefine gender in the law, which the government concluded should be kept 'vague'.[33]

The government proposed a two-tiered system for gender reclassification, premised on the assumption that any registered gender was correct and required a determination of eligibility to change it. For *non-somatic intersexuals*, the proposal emphasised that careful psychological assessment was needed to ensure

---

28 See SOU 1968:28, above n. 6, pp. 24–25.
29 Ibid., pp. 24–25, 45–48 and 52–53.
30 Ibid., pp. 20–31 and 38–39.
31 Ibid., p. 39.
32 Ibid., pp. 33–38.
33 Prop. 1972:6: *Kungl. Maj:ts proposition med förslag till lag om fastställande av könstillhörighet i vissa fall, m.m.*, p. 18.

that any request for a change of gender identity was sincere and that any gender reassignment, particularly surgery, occurred only once.[34] The government required applicants to be unmarried to avoid transformation of male-female marriages to same-gender marriages. Its proposal also rested on the expectation that many applicants for gender change would seek surgery that would render them sterile.[35] While the government found that there was no reason to separate parents applying for such changes from their children, it questioned the commitment to a gender identity for any individual who wanted to retain reproductive capacity typical of the gender assigned at birth.[36] The government acknowledged that medical experts in Sweden criticised sterilisation as potentially dangerous and medically unnecessary, but nevertheless proposed requiring the procedure where it did not otherwise result from medical treatment, so as to preserve order in 'kinship relations'.[37] For *somatic intersexuals*, or persons with atypical sex development, the proposal focused on bodily appearance and standard medical treatments for eliminating physical anomalies, so that gender reclassification could be rapidly processed as long as the body of the person in question conformed to one typical for the requested gender. The proposal considered that most applicants who changed gender under this provision would be children[38] and presumed (incorrectly) that most children would be sterile or otherwise could be assigned a gender so that they could procreate according to their genetic sex.[39] Most significantly – acknowledging that medical experts were divided on whether science was advanced enough to ensure that gender assignment would be accepted by the affected children[40] – the government emphasised a need for a mechanism for a second gender reclassification of children who rejected the gender imposed on them.[41] The Gender Classification Act based on these requirements became law on 1 July 1972.

1.2.2. Significant Reform Measures

The first reforms with impact on the Gender Classification Act emerged from legislation not formally connected to it. In 2008, the government revised the Discrimination Act to extend protections against gender discrimination to all persons who changed registered gender or identified as transgender.[42] In 2009,

34 Ibid., pp. 15 and 23.
35 Ibid., pp. 14–15.
36 Ibid., p. 23.
37 Ibid., pp. 49–50; for experts' criticisms, see also ibid. at pp. 37–38.
38 Ibid., p. 25.
39 Ibid., pp. 11–14.
40 Ibid., p. 24.
41 Ibid., pp. 26 and 57.
42 SFS 2008:567, *Diskrimineringslag*, 1 kap. 5 § 1 st & 2 st; *See also* Prop. 2007/08:95, *Ett starkare skydd mot diskriminering* (2008), pp. 111–117.

the Swedish government also removed gender requirements for marriage.[43] Recognising this evolving gender neutrality through the lens of human rights, the National Board in 2010 proposed several reforms of the Gender Classification Act. The Board recommended that the requirement that an applicant for a change of registered gender could not be married to someone with the same (requested) gender was nullified and should be removed.[44] Moreover, while immigrants to Sweden had long since represented a significant number of applications for gender registry changes,[45] the government acknowledged that membership in the EU required reconsideration of the restriction of health care only to Swedish citizens, as EU citizens and others who resided and received health care in Sweden may be wrongly registered and entitled to receive corrective gender surgery.[46] Thus, the Board proposed that anyone so registered was eligible for legal and medical remedies under the law.[47] Finally, acknowledging international criticism on human rights grounds, the Board proposed removal of the sterilisation requirement from the Act.[48] Protracted controversy within the coalition government, however, delayed these reforms, with the requirements for applicants to be unmarried citizens removed in 2012,[49] and the sterilisation requirement removed a year later in 2013.[50]

While the lengthy legislative reform process was not unusual for Sweden, particularly regarding laws related to medical procedures,[51] the sterilisation debate was marred by transphobic sentiments from within the coalition government.[52] Göran Hägglund, the Social Department Minister with authority over reform of the Act, formally opposed the repeal in 2011, claiming that study was needed to assess the impact on children raised by parents who were treated for gender disorder.[53] As a result, Barbro Westerholm, the former director of the National Board and a

43 See SFS 2009:253, *Lag om ändring i äktenskapsbalken*.

44 Prop. 2011/12:142, pp. 45 and 59–60.

45 See Olsson and Möller, above n. 18, p. 385 (summarising numbers of applicants of foreign origin through 2002).

46 Prop. 2011/12:142, pp. 45 and 59–60.

47 National Board, above n. 1, p. 13.

48 Ibid.

49 SFS 2012:456.

50 SFS 2013:405.

51 Indeed, Swedish law did not require medical personnel formally to obtain informed consent from patients until 2015. See SFS 2014:821. The proposals for the law took two decades to result in legislation. E. Rynning, 'Still no Patient's Act in Sweden – reasons and implications', Nordic Health Law in a European Context – Welfare State Perspectives on Patient's Rights in *Nordic health law in a European context: welfare state perspectives on patients′ rights and biomedicine*, Nijhoff, Leiden 2012, pp. 122–132.

52 M. Bax, 'KD kan lamnas utanför beslut om konsbyte', *QX*, 1 August 2011 <www.qx.se/samhalle/18484/kd-kan-lamnas-utanfor-beslut-om-konsbyte> accessed 14.02.2015.

53 H. Sulaiman, 'Regeringen kör över KD om sterilisering', *Dagen*, 29 July 2011, <www.dagen.se/regeringen-k%C%B6r-%C3%B6ver-kd.om-sterlisering-1.124246> accessed 14.02.2015. Hägglund repeated these claims even when endorsing the repeal of sterilisation in February 2012. See G. Hägglund, 'Kravet på sterilisering vid könskorrigering bör avskaffas' <https://www.kristdemokraterna.se/Media/Nyhetsarkiv/Pa-besok-i-Indien/> accessed 15.02.2015.

member of the Riksdag, threatened to introduce legislation for the repeal unless the government committed to it.[54] The Social Department thus changed its position and began work on the proposal for the Board's recommended reforms.[55] While the proposal was finalised, the Administrative Court in Stockholm held that the sterilisation requirement could not be applied in an individual case, citing the National Board's concession that the requirement was unnecessary to changing gender registration.[56] Shortly thereafter, the government finally released its proposal to allow married persons and Swedish residents to change gender and also proposed repeal of the sterilisation requirement, with details to be introduced at a later date.[57] The Social Department completed its investigation of the legal consequences of sterilisation repeal, albeit without conforming legislation, in November 2012.[58] Relying on that report, the Court of Appeals in Stockholm upheld the lower court's decision in December 2012, holding sterilisation to be a radical, irreversible bodily intrusion no longer defended by the government and, thus, a violation of the Swedish Constitution and the ECHR.[59] The government let the decision stand, with the Riksdag finalising the repeal of sterilisation, taking effect on 1 July 2103.[60]

The reformed law that emerged from this controversy reflected the imperfect nature of the Swedish legislative process, but it also changed the discourse surrounding the Gender Classification Act. On the one hand, the failure to develop clear conforming legislation left many questions open, particularly regarding the gendered nomenclature still used to identify parents under Swedish law. On the other hand, the repeal of the sterilisation requirement meant that the

54 *Sterlisering kvar vid könsbyte*, SVT, 12 January 2012 <www.svt.se/nyheter/sverige/sterlisering-blir-kvar-vid-könsbyte> accessed 14.02.2015.

55 Hägglund publicly committed to repeal in February 2012. See Hägglund, above n. 51. Members of the coalition government, including Westerholm, confirmed that the government proposal recommended repeal in January. 'Oklar linje om tvångssteriliseringar', *Svenska Dagbladet*, 12 January 2012 <www.svd.se/nyheter/inrikes/oklar-linje-om-tvangssteriliseringar_6764915.svd>.

56 *Socialstyrelsen v NN*, Mål nr. 1968–12 (Kammarrätten 2012) at pp. 2 and 8 (describing the lower court's decision).

57 Prop. 2011/12:142, above n. 10, pp. 51–56.

58 *Avskaffande av steriliseringskrav som villkor för ändrad könstillhörighet*, Ds 2012:46, 2012, p. 20.

59 *See Socialstyrelsen v NN*, above n. 56, pp. 5–8. For further details, see section 4, below. Of note, the National Board appealed the administrative court's decision for reasons that remain unclear, given that the Board recommended repeal of sterilisation. In the appeal, the Board's primary argument appears to have been that the decision was unnecessary because the administrative court essentially ratified the Board's proposal. A more likely explanation is that damages are available in Swedish Court for violations of the ECHR. See NJA 2007 s. 584. Precedent already existed for compensation of victims of forced sterilisation in Sweden. See *Steriliseringsfrågan i Sverige 1935–1975: Historisk belysning*, SOU 2000:20. The Government passed special legislation for criteria for that compensation. See SFS 1999:332 (on compensation for sterilised persons in certain cases), which would not cover persons sterilised under the Gender Classification Act. In fact, the Government has so far refused to offer compensation to individuals sterilised under the Act.

60 SFS 2013:405.

Act no longer contained any mandatory medical procedure for gender registry changes, setting the stage for future investigations of the law's coupling of gender status with medical care. Perhaps of most importance, the courts' rebuke of the government's retention of the sterilisation requirement without justification ensured that the repeal was primarily justified on human rights grounds. For the first time in history, the government's 2013 proposal for reform of the Gender Classification Act committed to conforming the law not only to the ECHR[61] – which has the status of law in Sweden[62] – but the Yogyakarta Principles[63] and the Convention on the Rights of the Child,[64] to ensure that children should be heard, where possible, if subjected to change of registered gender without their consent. Indeed, shortly after the repeal of sterilisation, the government ordered a new investigation of the Act on human rights grounds, particularly to determine how the Act affects minors. The resulting reform proposals were released in early 2015, with public debate pending.[65]

II. CHANGING LEGAL GENDER – REQUIREMENTS AND PROCEDURE

2.1. LEGAL PROCEDURE AND OFFICIAL DOCUMENTS – OVERVIEW

The Gender Classification Act primarily governs the legal process associated with a request for a change of registered gender. The Act currently authorises the National Board to process all applications for change of registered gender,[66] as well as approvals of genital and gonadal surgery,[67] specifically restricting gonadal surgery to persons aged 23 and older, except with government approval.[68] The National Board's Legal Advisory Council ('the Council') – consisting of a forensic psychiatrist, three physicians, a behavioural scientist, and one additional staff member[69] – approves these applications.[70] Historically, the Act has also been linked to the more general Sterilisation Act, which governs all consensual surgery associated with elimination of reproductive capacity,[71] requiring that the patient

61 Prop. 2012/13:107, *Upphävande av kravet på sterilisering för ändrad könstillhörighet*, pp. 17–18.
62 SFS 1974:152 (*Regerinsformen*), 2 kap. 19 §.
63 Ds 2012:46, above n. 58, pp. 44–45 and 52.
64 Prop. 2012/13:107, above n. 61, pp. 55 and 73 and SOU 2007:16, *Ändrad könstillhörighet – förslag till ny lag*, pp. 143–144 and 267–268.
65 See section 2.3, below.
66 KtL 5 §.
67 KtL 4 § and 4a §.
68 KtL 4a §.
69 See Prop. 1972:6, above n. 33, p. 31.
70 Förordning (2009:1243) med instruktion för Socialstyrelsen, 16 §.
71 SFS 1975:580: *Steriliseringslag.*

must be fully informed of the implications and consequences of surgery,[72] as well as that the procedure is performed by specialists in approved hospitals.[73] Both the Gender Classification Act and Sterilisation Act impose penalties on any person who performs genital, gonadal, or other sterilisation surgery in violation of law.[74] Any adverse action by the National Board or the Council regarding an application may be appealed to the Stockholm Administrative Court, with further appeals in accord with ordinary rules for such appeals.[75] Applicants, however, may also apply directly to the Council for reconsideration of any denied application on the basis of new facts, and new approvals have been granted in such cases.[76]

Once an application has been granted, the Council's approval authorises the Tax Agency to issue a new *personnummer*, the identification number used by all citizens and most long-term residents in Sweden.[77] The number's ninth digit is gendered – an even number for females and an odd number for males – and must be regenerated.[78] The Tax Agency also has authority to issue a new ID card for use in Sweden.[79] All citizens request a passport or changes thereto through the Police Department.[80] Changes of name are made separately and often prior to the processing of an application for changes of registered gender.[81] The Council's approval of a change of registered gender may be used to support any of these requests, along with other changes of records. Once these changes are made, under the Gender Classification Act, all prior information must be kept private, subject to penalties, except in cases where anyone in public service needs to disclose the information to serve the health of the applicant.[82] This exception generally depends on whether the applicant is unable to consent to disclose necessary information.[83]

---

72 Ibid., 5 §.

73 Ibid., 6 §.

74 See KtL § 8 and *Steriliseringslag*, above n. 71, 8 §.

75 KtL 6 §.

76 National Board, above n. 1, p. 22.

77 See Prop. 2011/12:142, p. 22 (describing the process). The regulation authorising changes generally is *Förordning* (2001:589) *om behandling av personuppgifter i Skatteverkets folkbokföringsverksamhet*, 2 §.

78 Under Swedish law, each person's identification number in the registry consists of two parts, the first six digits indicating the date of birth, and the final four digits an informational code, in which the third digit is an odd number for male children and an even number for female children. See SFS 1991:481: *Folkbokföringslag* 24 §.

79 Förordning (2009:284) *om identitetskort för folkbokförda i Sverige.*

80 See *Passförordningen* (1979:664) 29 § 1 st (authorising the Police Department to issue passports) and *Förordningen* (2005:661) *om nationellt identitetskort och 13 § första stycket 1 förordningen*, 24 § 1 st (authorising the Police Department to issue national ID cards).

81 At this writing, the Swedish Names Act is administered by the Patent and Registration Office and Tax Agency. The Patent and Registration Office must approve requests to change the first name entirely, particularly when a person only has one first name. A government committee has proposed loosening the restrictions on name choices and vesting all authority in the Tax Agency, which is currently proposed to come into force in 2016. See SOU 2013:35, *En ny lag om personnamn.*

82 KtL 7 §.

83 See SFS 2009:400: *Offentlighets- och sekretesslag*, 25 kap. 1 § and 13 §.

While this system was designed to ensure that the approval of change of registered gender is operative across all aspects of Swedish law and may not be questioned by authorities, the administrative process has required significant time and effort to process each change through multiple agencies.[84] Government agencies have access to the Tax Authority's database, but only some automatically change records.[85] Universities, though publicly funded, have their own administrations and also require applicant-initiated corrections of records.[86] In 2014, the National Board has reported that many efforts to streamline the process are being made internally within each agency, but other reforms may require a formal government investigation and legislation to balance the interests of persons who wish to control disclosure of changes in the gender registry with those who wish more systemic changes to occur on their behalf.[87]

Treatment related to gender correction is governed by separate legislation. For patients who want treatment related to gender, the Health and Medical Services Act requires that all persons seeking it receive initial consultation in their municipality or county, unless a patient chooses to contact a private caregiver for such consultations.[88] The Patient Safety Act requires treatments to be offered in accordance with 'science and proven experience' related to diagnosis and treatment of the patients' condition.[89] These provisions account for the current medical process for gender treatments, as most patients are referred to one of six specialised sexology clinics after initial consultation for at least part of the investigation, particularly to authorise hormone treatments and non-surgical gender treatments (such as voice training and epilation), with surgery following, if the patients desire, at specialised surgical centres authorised to perform them under the Gender Classification Act. Some refinement procedures are subsidised only for those with severe dysphoria.[90] Otherwise, these costs are borne by the patient, notwithstanding government-supported treatment for all that is deemed necessary to enable the patients to live according to their gender identity. As a whole, this system is designed to ensure that treatment is offered with guaranteed access to expertise for essential care,[91] but questions linger as to whether the system imposes hardships on patients or permits even substandard care at the

---

84 See National Board, above n. 9, pp. 3–4.

85 The Transport Agency, National Agency for Social Insurance, and Pensions Agency automatically update their records through the State Person and Address Registry (SPAR), but the National Agency for Education and, ironically, the National Board of Health and Welfare do not. Thus, individuals licensed to teach or provide health care services must initiate changes in their licences in the event they need them for further employment, as well as to change their grades and degrees. See ibid., pp. 5–8.

86 Ibid., p. 5.

87 Ibid., pp. 11–14.

88 See SFS 1982:763: *Hälso- och sjukvårds lag* (HSL) §§ 3–26e. Patients may receive a second opinion for serious illness outside their county of residence. See SFS 2014:821, 7 §.

89 See SFS 2010:659: *Patientsäkerhetslag* (PSL) 6 kap. 1 §.

90 See section 2.2.1 and n. 103 below.

91 See Prop. 1972:6, above n. 24, pp. 14 and 29.

local level – matters that are currently expected to be improved by newly released Board guidelines for evidence-based care.[92]

2.2. LEGAL REQUIREMENTS

2.2.1. Legal Change of Gender Classification Based on Identity and Experience

For most individuals – those who do not qualify as having atypical sex development – a change of registered gender must take place under the first section (1 §) of the law. That section has four requirements that must be fulfilled before an applicant is eligible to request change of registered gender. The applicant must (1) feel that he or she belongs to the other gender and have had this feeling for a 'long time', (2) live according the requested gender identity for some time prior to applying for legal change, (3) expect to live in this gender identity in the future, and (4) be at least 18 years of age. These four requirements are the same principal requirements as those in place since 1972, with the primary exception that the original statute formally required that the feeling of identifying with the requested gender must have been 'since youth'. The government has acknowledged that when the law was originally enacted, the medical profession had already recognised that gender distress could emerge later in life and that disqualification for gender change for such persons was not in accordance with medical understanding of how some individuals come to terms with their gender identity.[93] The preparatory works to the current law make clear that 1 § should be open to those who come to accept their gender identity later in life.[94]

The plain language of 1 § provides that applicants may directly apply for a change of registered gender as long as they fulfil criteria set forth in that section, none of which refer to medical diagnosis or supervision. In April 2014, the National Board endorsed this view when it formally announced that applicants do not need to consult medical personnel for the application, provided that they can document their eligibility for the requested change.[95] Unfortunately, neither the statute nor its preparatory works provide any details as to how an applicant can individually document a longstanding feeling of gender belonging or having lived in the gender role. Rather, the preparatory works clarify that these requirements were drawn from medical standards of diagnosis and treatment of 'transsexualism', premised on the assumption that persons who wished to change registered gender would also seek medical care for genital and gonadal surgery.[96] The 1 § requirements were, in fact, intended to be a safeguard to ensure that future

---

[92] See n. 103, below. For concerns in this area, see National Board, above n. 1, pp. 36–55.
[93] Prop. 2011/12:142, above n. 10, pp. 32–33.
[94] Ibid.
[95] National Board, above n. 11, p. 21.
[96] See Prop. 2011/12:142, *Ändrad könstillhörighet*, p. 79.

surgery was suitable for the patient and would culminate in a singular change of registered gender that could not be undone.[97] Indeed, the final proviso of 1 § provides that the only persons who may receive a second change of registered gender are those whose gender was changed incorrectly under 2 §.

For those persons who seek both change of registered gender and corrective surgery, the merger of legal and medical procedures in practice was designed to be a lengthy process. Through 2013, the Legal Advisory Council's informal guidelines provided that applicants for these changes would enter the health care system to begin a medico-legal process, with (1) the first year to consist of psychiatric and physical examinations, followed by (2) a year of hormone therapy and other cosmetic therapies to enable the applicant to live for a year in the gender role with which the applicant identifies, before (3) applying for change of registered gender and surgery – with surgery expected two-and-a-half years from the start of the process.[98] The guidelines anticipated that the applicant could only apply to the Council for change of registered gender near the end of the process, with the application accompanied by a medical report summarising the proposed future medical treatments.[99] However, the Board's recent pronouncement that change of registered gender does not require medical documentation has effectively negated that timetable. In May 2014, the Stockholm Administrative Court also ruled that any requirement that all applicants follow the Council's guidelines could not be justified by the language of the Act.[100]

The former medicalisation of the process set forth in 1 § frequently made it difficult to determine which requirements in the law were truly medical and which were administrative. Patient advocates have warned that the medicalisation of the process also converted ostensible medical safeguards into restrictions on the right of persons to change registered gender, with some clinicians using patient reluctance for hormone therapy and surgery as grounds to question the patients' commitment to their gender identity and withhold support for the application to correct the population registry.[101] Moreover, as Swedish law requires medical

---

97 National Board, above n. 11, pp. 15 and 33. Indeed, in 1972, the government originally asserted that the conditions may seem harmful and unnecessary but are means of proof to the government and physicians that the person has the conviction to accept permanent medical and legal changes to gender. See Prop. 1972:6, above n. 33, pp. 15–23.

98 For the preparatory works, see n. 33, above. The Gender Classification Act authorises the National Board or other competent agency to issue guidelines for these criteria, see Gender Classification Act 8 §. To date, however, the Board's Legal Advisory Council has only issued informal, non-public guidelines – *Utredningsgång Könsbyte* [Investigative Pathway to Sex Change] – that have been made public through advocacy groups. For a summary, see the website for the Swedish Federation for Lesbian, Gay, Bisexual and Transgender Rights, *Könskorrigerande vård* <www.rfsl.se/?p=382> accessed 28.12.2013.

99 Ibid.

100 *NN v Socialstyrelsen*, Mål nr. 24931-13 23 (May 2014).

101 For extensive analysis, see S. Bremer, *Kroppslinjer: kön, transsexualism och kropp i berättelser om könskorrigering*, Makadam, Göteborg 2011. Indeed, Jan Wålinder, a member of the original 1968 expert committee on the law reform, opined in 1976 that patients who did not desire gender surgery should be questioned for their 'conviction' in belonging to the requested

professionals to base their care on their competence and expertise,[102] the basis for their ability to 'confirm' patients' feelings about their gender or commitment to it was always unclear. Nor was it ever certain that medical personnel could document how patients live in a gender role, apart from their visits to a clinic. Finally, because 1 § of the Act permitted an application for change of registered gender only at age 18, the Board's practice left in doubt that minors could begin treatment so that they would be ready to apply for change of registered gender when they reached the age of majority. The 2014 decisions of the both the National Board and the Administrative Court disapproving of these timetables have, at least officially, deemed all of these practices as being without legal foundation.

From a medical point of view, these recent reformulations have dovetailed with new governmental guidelines for treatment of persons with gender-related needs, which were finalised in April 2015.[103] The central focus in the new guidelines is that patients should not feel coerced in care, but rather that individualised treatments should be offered based on the best available knowledge and treatment options, wherever patients reside in Sweden. This includes ensuring patients the right to apply for registered gender change independent of any staged medical care.[104] To the extent that medical personnel work with the patients to document living in a gender role – either to change registered gender or receive further treatment – the Board's guidelines provide that this period may now run concurrently from immediate entry into the health care process, as well as before that entry, depending on the evidence in the individual case.[105] Consequently, medical assessments should not be focused on categorical timetables but on individualised needs, such that the period could be shorter or longer depending on the experiences of the patient.[106] The new guidelines also permit minors to receive counselling and may begin preliminary treatments so that they may begin their applications for more permanent changes at age 18.[107] Of course, any declaration of the success or failure of these reforms would be precipitate at this writing. The gains under these reforms may come with added uncertainty, as patients may no longer have concrete expectations of time frames for care, all of which may become more complicated as more patients enter the system, requiring, perhaps, more oversight. Nevertheless, if future legal reforms

---

sex. See J. Wålinder and I. Thuwe, 'A Law Concerning Sex Reassignment of Transsexuals in Sweden' (1976) 5(3) *Archives of Sexual Behavior* 256–257.

102 See HSL, above n. 88, §§3–3i and §§18–18d and PSL, above n. 89, 6 kap. §§1–3.

103 National Board of Health and Welfare, *Good care of adults with gender dysphoria: National knowledge support,* 2015. National Board of Health and Welfare, *Good care of children and youth with gender dysphoria: National knowledge support,* 2015.

104 National Board, above n. 11, p. 21.

105 Ibid., p. 33.

106 Ibid., pp. 13–15 and 32.

107 Ibid., pp. 58–59 (noting that further investigation into safety of certain treatments is warranted); see also SOU 2007:16, above n. 19, pp. 150–169 (surveying international standards on treatment of minors and finding no clear barrier to hormone treatments under age eighteen in the legislation).

disentangle change of registered gender from medical care, the individualisation of medical care would permit that care, at least, to be assessed in the same manner as care for all Swedish citizens, at least in terms of efficiency, access to care, and quality.

2.2.2. Legal Change for Persons with Atypical Sex Development

The Gender Classification Act's second section (2 §) provides an additional mechanism for change of registered gender where the applicant has somatic sex development that is deemed atypical for his or her genetic sex. Currently, this provision permits change of registered gender as long as the requested gender is compatible with 'the development of gender identity' and the applicant's 'physical condition'. The provision does not require any of the staged criteria to confirm gender identity required in 1 §. The provision also has no minimum age limit for an application. A person who is 18 may apply for reclassification under 2 §, but a guardian may apply on a minor's behalf, both for gender registry changes and surgery on the genitals or gonads to support that gender reclassification. If the child is aged 12 or older, the child must consent to the legal reclassification. Finally, the law provides that individuals addressed by 2 § may also apply for a second gender reclassification under 1 § if the first reclassification fails – particularly for minors – or if the applicant is otherwise ineligible under 2 §. Each of these unique conditions requires elaboration to clarify the purpose behind them.

As a whole, the provision was intended for a range of conditions where the gender classification at birth is complicated by the fact that the sex development of the child was atypical.[108] This includes a variety of conditions, for example where the child's external morphology appears to support a visual classification for one gender, but with genes or the internal morphology typical of the other gender.[109] This would also apply in cases where the external morphology changes over time, such as when a child's body appears more typical of one gender at birth but changes in puberty. More controversially, it has also included patients whose bodies are simply atypical, whom doctors in the last century routinely recommended to have their gender reassigned. For example, a young male child with undescended or malformed testicles and an atypically small penis might be reassigned as female – effectively given a new registered gender reinforced by a surgically constructed one – whereas a virilised female might be surgically altered to appear more typical for a female assignment.[110] Thus, while 2 § is available to adults who may have been misclassified because their gender was not medically ascertainable at birth, the primary focus in the preparatory works has been to

[108] Prop. 1972:6, above n. 33, p. 25.

[109] SOU 1968:28, above n. 6, pp. 24–25.

[110] A. Nordenström, A. Nordenskjöld, L. Frisén, A. Wendell and M. Ritzén, 'Pojke eller flicka – gissa aldrig! Diagnostik och behandling av tillstånd med avvikande könsutveckling' (2008) *Läkartidningen* 629–632.

provide physicians and parents a mechanism to control perceived gender variance in children.

Each of these conditions serves to explain the differences between the two mechanisms for gender reclassification. First, the law formally permits persons over 18 to apply for himself or herself if the gender distress is due to a somatic condition and thus avoid 1 § on the assumption that the distress is rooted in physically observable gender variance. It also, however, allows a guardian to apply for a minor where parents and physicians determine a different gender and possible appearance would be more optimal, in their view, for the child.[111] Second, the law requires no proof of gender identity under 2 § because the government has consistently assumed that there is some biological basis for the claim to the gender variance.[112] Indeed, because the government contemplated that infants and children under 3 years of age might be reclassified under the law, those individuals might be presumed too young to express a gender identity. While the current law expressly states that any gender reclassification must be compatible with the 'development' of the applicant's gender identity, the preparatory works to the law indicate that where gender identity is not formed, the appearance of the genitals may tip the balance in favour of the requested gender registration.[113]

The final key provisions related to 2 § are more complex, both directed at the concern that children are involved. The current law requires the consent of a child to reclassification only if the child is aged 12 or older. The age designation in this provision was not based on any medical assessment of the child's capacity to consent, but rather on the age where children's wishes are considered relevant under other matters under Swedish law.[114] The age limit overall is particularly controversial because the government expressed concern as early as 1968 that gender identity forms at very early ages, and that significant harm could be done to a child if gender assignment surgery proved harmful, particularly if it assigned the wrong gender to the child.[115] For these reasons, the law provides that a person with atypical gender development whose gender was reclassified in error under 2 § may apply for a second gender change under 1 §.[116] Such a person may also apply directly under 1 § if gender reclassification was refused under 2 §, on the grounds that her or his body did not support the requested gender, as body conformity is not required under 1 §. Since 2012, the law has required that the child's views shall be considered where possible under age 12, consistent with the Convention on the Rights of the Child, but does not require the child's consent.

Growing recognition that forced gender surgery and interference with gender identity are human rights violations has finally brought these procedures

111 SOU 1968:28, above n. 6, pp. 45–58.
112 Prop 1972:6, above n. 33, pp. 20–26.
113 Prop. 2011/12:142, above n. 10, pp. 38.
114 Prop. 1972:6, above n. 33, pp. 51–52; Prop. 2011/12:142, above n. 10, pp. 38–39.
115 SOU 1968:28, above n. 6, pp. 52–54, Prop. 1972:6, above n. 24, pp. 26–27.
116 Prop. 1972:6, above n. 33, pp. 26 and 57.

into the spotlight. Indeed, in 2012, the world's leading practitioners reviewed the evidence ostensibly supporting gender surgery in infancy and found that no studies confirmed that these procedures are medically necessary or safe for children, especially as they carry an unpredictable risk of surgically imposing the wrong gender on such children.[117] Recently, the Parliamentary Assembly of the Council of Europe, the UN Special Rapporteur for Torture, and Other Cruel, Inhuman and Degrading Treatment, and the World Health Organization have also formally called for an end to medically unnecessary, cosmetic, and gender conforming surgery on children with atypical sex development.[118] Most of these surgeries, of course, fall outside the Act, which requires the Legal Advisory Council's approval for genital or gonadal surgery on children *only* if the gender registry is to be changed[119] – in short, bypassing government review when the surgery is performed in infancy with a gender assignment in mind, or to conform the child's body to the registered gender. In light of the growing scepticism from medical and human rights authorities, the legality of even these provisions are now at least questionable, as authorisations by the government of invasive procedures on children without their consent.

2.3. IMPLICATIONS FOR FUTURE REFORM

Though premised on highly differentiated medical diagnoses, the current two-tiered system in the Gender Classification Act has been inconsistent in its gender logic, at best. For persons who were born with a physiology typical for their genetic and registered gender, the Act has not only required that a patient wait until she or he is 18 to apply for the correct legal identity, but in many cases, to wait even longer for gender surgery. In practice, applicants until recently endured two years or more of medical supervision to be approved to change registered gender, theoretically as a safeguard against inappropriate gender surgery – even though surgery is not required by the law for gender change. As a result, even though the Act has, since 1972, rested on the assumption that individuals diagnosed with gender dysphoria have experienced severe gender distress since youth, the Act has

---

117 P. Lee, J. Schober, A. Nordenström, P. Hoebeke, C. Houk, et al., 'Review of recent outcome data of disorders of sex development (DSD): Emphasis on surgical and sexual outcomes' (2012) *Journal of Pediatric Urology (J. Ped. Urol.)* 611–615; J. Schober, A. Nordenström, P. Hoebeke, P. Lee, et al., 'Disorders of sex development: Summaries of long-term outcome studies' (2012) *J. Ped. Urol.* 616–623; S. Creighton, S. Chernausek, R. Romao, P. Ransley, et al., 'Timing and nature of reconstructive surgery for disorders of sex development – Introduction' (2012) *J. Ped. Urol.* 602–610.

118 Juan E. Méndez, Report of the special rapporteur on torture and other cruel, inhuman or degrading treatment or punishment to the U.N. General Assembly, 1 February 2013 (A/HRC/22/53) at ¶¶ 77 and 88. Parliamentary Assembly of the Council of Europe, Resolution 1952 (2013) (Children's right to physical integrity). WHO, *Eliminating forced, coercive and otherwise involuntary sterilization*, UN, Geneva 2014, p. 14.

119 Ibid., pp. 28–29.

provided them only limited legal assistance before adulthood unless they could show a congenital physical anomaly and proceed for relief more rapidly under 2 §. In turn, for persons born with atypical gender development, no precautionary period exists for change of registered gender or surgical alteration. Indeed, the 'anomaly' in their development, as described in the current statute, was originally perceived as a 'malformation', suggestive of a birth defect, for which treatment was presumptive, performed on infants as early as possible,[120] even though the Act itself acknowledges that such surgery could have catastrophic consequences requiring a second change of gender and more corrective surgery. In short, while 1 § in the Act has been premised on caution for persons seeking relief on their own behalf, 2 § has permitted rapid and dangerous gender reassignment for children, by their parents and physicians, and without their input.

For children with atypical sex development, the logic in the Act has been particularly inscrutable. While genital and gonadal surgery are not required for a change under 1 § – so that persons may change registered gender without having a body typical for that gender – the law has restricted change of registered gender for persons with atypical sex development under 2 § unless the applicant's body is 'more typical' for the requested gender. Consequently, while children may receive a second gender change (under 1 §) to correct the first (under 2 §), they must not only wait until they are 18 for that correction, but currently must meet all the criteria under 1 § – including living in their true gender and proving that they have suffered an incorrect gender assignment for a long time – all to ensure that a second gender reclassification is not made in haste, even though the first was wrong, due in part to a lack of safeguards. Older children who reject gender conforming surgery under 2 § must wait for relief without surgery under 1 §, solely on the grounds that the law requires a genital match under 2 § but not under 1 §. While the 2012 reforms purport to ensure that the child has a right to be heard under 2 §, that protection is illusory for infants and young children.

In response to these problems, the government in February 2014 called for a formal investigation of the Gender Classification Act to determine the possibilities for young persons to change their registered gender, with any proposed legislation to be based on human rights and the best available scientific evidence.[121] As part of its investigation, the committee determined that neither human rights nor medical advances warranted any medical preconditions on changes of registered gender, with limited exceptions – a finding that challenged the original conception of the Act as a whole, not merely as it applied to minors.[122] Moreover, the committee determined that the abolition of the sterilisation requirement no longer warranted linkage of gender registration with the Sterilisation Act,[123] particularly as the restriction in that law to those aged 23 and older was medically

120 Prop. 2011/12:142, above n. 10, pp. 37–38.
121 Dir. 2014:20.
122 SOU 2014:91, above n. 4, pp. 17–18 and 25–26.
123 Ibid., pp. 191–192 and 307.

obsolete.[124] Thus, the final investigative report, *Juridical Gender and Medical Gender Correction*, proposed separation of the law for changes in registered gender for all persons from any legislation referring to medical care. Under the proposal, the Gender Classification Act would be replaced with two new laws, one for change of registered gender and the other for regulation of gonadal and genital surgery, both of which would take effect in 2016.[125]

Under the proposed *Act for Change of Juridical Gender*, the new law would lower the age for application of change of registered gender from age 18 to 15, permitting interested persons to apply for such changes directly to the Tax Agency, eliminating approval from the National Board.[126] For persons who are 15 or older but not yet 18, the proposed law provides that if the application is not endorsed by a legal guardian, the Tax Agency has no power to reject the application but must inform Social Services to ensure that the minor has access to any needed support or protection.[127] For these minors, the law also prevents parents from appealing to a court to stop changes of their registered gender.[128] For children with atypical sex development, the proposed law permits children aged 12 but not yet 15 to apply for change of registered gender, requiring their consent and permission of their parents or guardians.[129] For such children under age 12, the proposed law still permits parents to apply for a change of gender for the child but requires a specialist medical opinion to ensure that the change of gender conforms to the child's gender identity and takes into account the child's wishes, in accord with his or her age and maturity.[130] The Act imposes no other medical requirement or proof on applications for changes of registered gender, with no restrictions on the number of changes that can be made.

Under the proposed Act for Authorisation for Certain Operations on the Genitals and Removal of the Gonads, the proposed law provides that anyone aged 18 years or older may apply for removal of the gonads and genital surgery in connection with gender correction, provided that the standard of care for eligibility for surgery conforms to science and proven experience.[131] For persons aged 15 and older but not yet 18, the proposed law permits such minors to apply for these procedures with the guardian's permission.[132] The law further provides that these procedures for minors must not only be in accord with science and

124 Ibid., p. 291.
125 Ibid., pp. 18–24, 26–33 and 35–38.
126 Ibid., pp. 35–36. The proposed eligibility at age 15 is found in the new 2 § of the Act for Change of Juridical Gender.
127 Ibid., p. 35 (proposed 2 §, 2 st.).
128 Ibid., p. 36 (proposed 8 §).
129 Ibid., p. 35 (proposed 3 §).
130 Ibid., p. 35 (proposed 4 §).
131 Ibid., p. 37 (proposed 3 §).
132 Ibid., p. 37 (proposed 4 §). The Patient Act permits minors to participate in medical decisions and consent in some circumstances, but does not guarantee minors age 15 and older to consent to serious procedures on their own. See Prop. 2013/14:106, pp. 65–67.

proven experience but must be made with the assurance of the minor's consent.[133] The current version of the proposed law does not require any approval of the National Board of Health and Welfare for these procedures, but provides that the government may direct the agency to promulgate additional regulations.[134] For all remaining gender surgeries and medical treatment, the investigative committee's report directed the National Board to continue to develop national guidelines and treatment standards, particularly for children with atypical sex development.

If enacted, these two new laws would radically alter the design of the original legislative scheme, not only for the administration of registered gender and treatment related to gender, but also for the meaning of registered gender in Sweden. For all applicants under the original Gender Classification Act, changes in juridical gender historically depended on concepts of what constituted maleness or femaleness by requiring adults seeking gender correction under 1 § to negate their reproductive capacity as a vestige of belonging to the gender they rejected and, particularly for children under 2 §, to conform physically to a body typical for the gender of their identity. Under the proposed legislation, changes in registered gender would be determined solely by the applicants themselves and can be changed more than once. Clearly, these changes would broaden access to relief under the Gender Classification Act to all transgender persons, particularly transgender youth.

Nevertheless, while all of these reforms are likely to be beneficial to transgender persons, they not only fail to include needed oversight by the Board for non-consensual gender surgery on children with atypical sex development, but, rather, they remove the Board's only power to disapprove such procedures for those children whose bodies are changed by their parents without their consent. For the affected children, human rights authorities have called for *greater* governmental control and oversight, not less, to ensure protection of these children in their future gender identity and to halt irreversible and medically unnecessary removal of their genitals and gonads. To be sure, the Gender Classification Act has always left these children to the trust and care of physicians without substantial oversight. But by leaving the fate of these children to future reform, the children remain the most vulnerable persons whose identity and bodily integrity are not protected under Sweden's gender registration laws.

---

133 SOU 2014:91, above n. 4, p. 37 (proposed 4 §, 2 st.).

134 Ibid., pp. 38 (proposed 8 §).

III. CONSEQUENCES OF THE CHANGE OF LEGAL GENDER

3.1. EQUALITY

An individual's legally registered gender is a protected status, effective throughout Swedish law, and cannot be questioned by other authorities.[135] Today, of course, virtually all of the gender-based distinctions in Swedish law that motivated the original Gender Classification Act have been neutralised, such that gender is largely irrelevant in most circumstances.[136] Sweden's Constitution currently prohibits the government from subjecting individuals to differential treatment on the basis of gender unless that treatment is designed to ensure substantive gender equality.[137] The Discrimination Act prohibits discrimination against a person who has changed registered gender as discrimination against that person on the basis of sex,[138] a position that is also consistent with Sweden's incorporation of the ECHR into Swedish law.[139] The Discrimination Act further prohibits discrimination on the basis on transgender identity and expression.[140] These prohibitions extend broadly throughout the public and private sector, covering discrimination, harassment, and reprisals in employment, housing, social services, government benefits, and health care.[141] The one substantial clarification lacking in the Discrimination Act relates to access to gender-segregated changing rooms and toilets. The government has stated that the Act does not require creation of special, separate facilities for transgender persons, but has yet to affirm that the Act clearly permits transgender persons to choose a changing room or

135 See Prop. 1972:6, above n. 33, pp. 26 and 52.

136 A notable exception is for prisoners, other detainees and single asylum seekers, who are typically housed according to gender, although governing agencies have in practice worked to accommodate gender variant persons in these circumstances. The National Board has called for regulation in these areas. See National Board, above n. 9, pp. 7–9 and 13.

137 See Regeringsformen (Instrument of Government) 1 kap. 2 § and 2 kap. 13 §.

138 Diskrimineringslag (2008:567) 1 kap. 5 §, 1 st. and final proviso. Under the current law, through 2015 at least, the preparatory works have provided that 'sex discrimination' was intended to apply to 'transsexuals'. Prop. 2007/08:95, above n. 42 p. 113. Under the 2015 law reform proposal, the ability to change registered gender is designed to encompass transgender persons, which should mean that discrimination against such persons would also constitute sex discrimination.

139 The Instrument of Government provides that a law or regulation cannot operate in Sweden in violation of the ECHR. See Regeringsformen 2 kap. 19 §.

140 SFS 2008:567: *Diskrimineringslag* 1 kap. 5 §, 2 st.

141 Ibid., 2 kap.

toilet according to their gender identity.[142] Pending litigation may shed further light on this matter.[143]

A more detailed variance to the general requirement of equal treatment under Swedish law exists in provisions regarding health care and social services. The Discrimination Act permits medical treatments and social services to be based on the needs of the persons receiving the service.[144] Thus, in health care, for example, the starting point for determining whether differential treatment is permitted is whether it is necessary and appropriate – a determination expected to be made on the basis of science and proven experience.[145] For persons who have changed their registered gender, the exception is significant in that it allows ongoing treatment based on bodily conditions not typically associated with one gender. This is particularly true where a person, for example, has chosen not to have genital surgery, breast surgery, or removal of reproductive organs, which might require care more typical for someone of the patient's originally registered gender. Similarly, such persons may be eligible for assisted reproduction according to their actual reproductive capacity, rather than their current registered gender. In any event, the law should ensure that persons who have had a change of gender do not suffer discrimination in health care,[146] particularly on the basis of prejudicial assumptions about gender roles.

3.2. PARENTHOOD

Sweden follows certain legal presumptions, often unwritten, to define motherhood and fatherhood. Accordingly, the person who gives birth is presumed to be the mother.[147] That presumption has been statutorily codified in the cases of assisted reproduction when a woman gives birth using a donated ovum.[148] Similarly, the husband of the mother is presumed to be the father.[149] The same presumption extends to husbands in cases of assisted reproduction with the husband's consent, as well as spouses and cohabiting partners.[150] For these latter couples, particularly

---

142 Compare Prop. 2007/08:95, above n. 42, pp. 496 and 535. But see SOU:2007:16, above n. 19, p. 65 (taking the view that separate facilities for men and women are consistent with discrimination law while acknowledging that trans-youth, in particular, may suffer trauma from being required to change in a room inconsistent with their gender).

143 See 'Intergender DU-anmäler Stockholms stad', *Svenska Dagbladet*, 9 December 2013 <www.svd.se/nyheter/inrikes/intergender-du-anmaler-stockholms-stad_8782654.svd> accessed 28.12.2013.

144 SFS 2008:567: *Diskrimineringslag,* 2 kap. 13b §.

145 Prop. 2007/08:95, above n. 42, p. 255.

146 Diskrimineringslag (2008:567) 2 kap. 13b §; Prop. 2007/08:95, above n. 42, pp. 254–256.

147 For a description, see A. Singer, *Föräldrarskap i rättslig belysning,* Iustus, Uppsala 2000, pp. 365–366 and 424 (explaining reliance on Roman law as well as social custom).

148 See SFS 1949:381: *Föraldrabalk* 1 1 kap., 7 §, (Children and Parent's Code).

149 Ibid., 1 kap., 1 §.

150 Ibid.

outside the context of assisted reproduction, additional steps may be required for couples to confirm parenthood, such as through adoption.[151] Swedish law has further been revised for presumed or putative fathers to permit genetic testing as means for disavowing or claiming paternity for a particular child.[152]

All of these rules have, for many years, posed a risk for persons who have changed their registered gender and were parents before the change took effect. For these persons, their parenthood would have been registered according to the presumptions in Swedish law, using their registered gender. Thus, a person legally registered as a man would be presumed to be the father of a child if married to a woman who gave birth, who, in turn, would be considered the mother of the child. If either of these parents requested a change of registered gender, the change has only applied to their personal records. Further, on those records, their parental statuses would not be listed as mother or father but in code.[153] For the child's records, however, the original records remain as historic records of the circumstances at birth. Thus, under current regulations, in references on the child's birth certificate, the person who gave birth but is now registered as male may not be able to be registered as the child's father, while a person who is female but registered as a father of her child may not be able to be re-registered as the mother.[154] As a result, while many public records may be shielded in such a way that prevents general public exposure of a person's gender history, use of children's birth records may expose the medical and legal history of the parents or put parents in circumstances requiring explanation of any gender reclassification.

Today, the failure to revise these laws in the wake of removal of the sterilisation requirement for change of registered gender has posed new challenges for persons who become parents after such changes. This is especially true if they procreate utilising their biological reproductive capacity. As a result, a person who is legally classified as male but is capable of giving birth would, according to legal presumptions in Swedish legal practice, be classified as the mother, but under the Gender Classification Act, he should not have any facts about his gender history made public. For a person who is legally female who contributes sperm to the reproduction, no rule enables her to be assigned as the mother, as, by tradition and the Children and Parents Code, she only would have a claim of fatherhood – through presumptions in the law, affirmation at birth, or through genetic establishment of paternity.

The government's most recent proposal regarding establishment of parenthood proposed that government agencies reason by analogy when assigning a parental classification, pending any new legislation to govern the matter.[155] For

---

151 For unmarried fathers, confirmation is required, *Föräldrabalk*, 1 kap., 3 §, as is true for both marriages and cohabitation partnerships between two women who do not utilise ART in Swedish public hospitals as provided in 1 kap., 9 §.

152 *Föräldrabalk*, 1 kap. 2 §.

153 Ds 2012:46, above n. 58, pp. 34–36.

154 Prop 1972:6, above n. 33, pp. 23 and 53.

155 Ds 2012:46, above n. 58, pp. 70–71.

example, the government has indicated that, in the case of a couple where the parents are both legally female and one gives birth, the non-birth parent can be registered as a 'parent', drawing upon legislation permitting such registration for lesbian co-parents. Whether this will work across the board remains to be seen. For persons who were parents before reclassification, in at least some cases the Tax Agency has formally declined to change the status on their child's records from the original gendered registry. In 2014, however, courts began to nullify the categorical refusal of the Tax Agency to register a man who gives birth as the father of his child.[156] Regardless of the outcome in future litigation, guidance from the government is clearly needed in this matter.

3.3. ASSISTED REPRODUCTION

In Sweden, assisted reproduction technology (ART) is generally supported by the public health care system for couples who cannot have children, typically because of their health. Nevertheless, additional restrictions are placed on access to publicly funded ART, borne out of several government policies regarding adoption and parental rights, the rights of children to know their genetic origins, and perceptions of the best interests of the child. The most complex restriction in this regard is that a couple cannot have both gametes donated, such that an infertile couple can only receive donated ova or sperm, which ensures that at least one legal parent has a genetic connection to the child.[157] Subsidised ART is also not available for unpartnered women, primarily to ensure that the child has two active parents at birth.[158] Surrogacy is also not currently considered a legal means for parenthood in Sweden,[159] such that male couples, individual men, and partnered women who cannot bear children also do not have access to ART. The government has conceded that these restrictions have encouraged Swedish citizens to go abroad for ART, particularly in the EU. These restrictions are all currently under review, with new reform proposals expected in 2015.[160]

---

156 See section IV.

157 The Genetic Integrity Act specifically provides that a 'fertilised egg may be placed in a woman's body only if the woman is married or cohabiting and the spouse or partner written consent. If the egg is not the woman's own, the egg must have been fertilised by her husband's or partner's sperm.' SFS 2006:351; *Lag om genetisk integritet*, 7 kap. 3 §.

158 See ibid.; see also ibid., at 6 kap. 1 § ('Insemination may be provided only if the woman is married or *sambo*. For insemination, written consent of the husband or *sambo* is required'). '*Samboförhållande*', or a cohabitation relationship, in Swedish is not a licensed or registered partnership but rather is recognised under the Cohabitation Act to govern ownership and inheritance for unmarried couples, '*sambo*' meaning the person with whom one is cohabiting for the foreseeable future. See generally SFS 2003:376: *Sambolag*.

159 No specific legislation addresses surrogacy, but under Swedish law, the person who gives birth is the mother, and strict rules for adoption apply, without compensation. For extensive discussion, see J. Stoll, *Surrogacy Arrangements and Legal Parenthood: Swedish Law in a Comparative Context*, Uppsala University, Uppsala 2013, pp. 99 ff and 115 ff.

160 The Swedish Government has appointed investigators to study the impact of increased ART possibilities in Sweden, including surrogacy, access to ART for single persons, the definition of

Nevertheless, the Swedish government has indicated that individuals who have changed registered gender are generally eligible on equal terms for ART.[161] Thus, as the government has explained, such persons are eligible for ART not only if they are infertile due to anomalies in sexual development, but also if they are made so from medical conditions, such as cancer. The removal of sterilisation from the Gender Classification Act theoretically casts the decision of a person to remove her or his reproductive organs as a disqualifying choice rather than medical need. Indeed, while contemplating new parenthood configurations for persons whose gender has been reclassified without sterilisation, the government has indicated that it presumes that such persons may procreate without ART but, instead, in their own biological reproductive capacity.[162] It is unclear whether the government has emphasised this possibility because unassisted reproduction poses the greatest challenges for classifying parenthood under current Swedish law, or to question the medical necessity for ART in some cases for persons who have changed their registered gender. Nevertheless, the removal of reproductive organs as part of treatment associated with gender correction should be consistent with eligibility for ART, with clear support from medical authorities that such surgery was appropriate for the patient's gender.[163] In light of the government's clear comparison of persons undergoing gender transitions to cancer patients and endorsement of their equal treatment for ART, disqualifying such persons would be inconsistent with the Gender Classification Act and the Discrimination Act.[164] At a minimum, persons who lose their reproductive capacity in connection with treatment for gender correction should be eligible to freeze their gametes for future use in ART.

In theory, the Gender Classification Act would recognise all persons in their corrected gender role for reproductive purposes and, correspondingly, also treat their relationships similarly to any other partnerships, whether of the same or different gender. For the purposes of ART, however, the reproductive needs and abilities of persons whose registered gender has been changed may situate them, under the Discrimination Act, more similarly with their originally assigned gender. This is particularly true for those who were born with the reproductive organs of the gender atypical for someone with their gender identity. For example, a person born with female reproductive organs who identifies as male cannot

---

motherhood, and a review of legislation relating to children's interests. Dir 2013:70: *Utökade möjligheter av ofrivillig fertilitet*, 19 June 2013.

161 Ds 2012:46, above n. 58, p. 61.

162 Ibid.

163 Indeed, Swedish specialists have historically assumed that the desire for change of reproductive organs is a measure of a strong feeling of gender difference. See Wålinder and Thuwe, above n. 101, pp. 256–257.

164 Ds 2012:46, above n. 58, p. 24 ('Many people who suffer from transsexualism or other gender identity disorder will at some point want to be parents ... The practical management of assisted fertilisation and storage of gametes can be compared with patients with cancer, whose gonads have been harmed by radiation or chemotherapy') (author's translation).

produce sperm. He may, however, be able to produce ova or give birth. As a result, if he enters into a relationship with a cis-woman, donor sperm is required for the couple to have a child. Though their pairing would personally, socially, and legally constitute a couple of two different sexes, their procreative needs are more comparable to a lesbian couple and, thus, the couple may be eligible for ART. In contrast, a person born with male reproductive organs but who identifies as female cannot produce ova or give birth. If she enters into a relationship with a cis-man, the pair could not procreate without surrogacy, which is currently unavailable in Sweden. This couple – though personally, socially, and legally constituting a couple of two different sexes – is in the same medical and legal situation as a male-male couple and ineligible for ART.

In its most recent report on parenthood proposing the removal of sterilisation requirements, the government set forth five scenarios of potential couples who might become parents after any changes in registered gender, primarily without ART. The table below sets forth these scenarios, modified here to include ART.[165] The first column uses the gender of the couples to describe them as they identify (M or F) with any corrections in the gender registry, which are binding under Swedish law. To illustrate the complexity of these classifications for the purposes of parenthood and ART, additional notations on the table reflect where a person is cisgender (c) or has the reproductive capacity typical for a gender other than that for which he or she is registered (m or f). The second column sets forth the government's assumptions about the procreative capacity of each couple. Regarding ART, this column indicates 'potentially none' is needed if they are otherwise fertile and capable of reproducing without ART. The final column sets forth what should be possible under current Swedish law with ART.

Prospective parents (by gender)	**Assisted reproduction needed**	**Assisted reproduction possible**
$F1^{(m)}$ & $F2^{(c)}$	potentially none	ova from F2 and donor sperm *or* sperm from F1 and donor ova; F2 must currently give birth
$F^{(m)}$ & $M^{(c)}$	ova and surrogate needed	currently not possible
$M^{(f)}$ & $F^{(c)}$	sperm needed	ova from M *or* F with donor sperm; M or F must give birth
$M1^{(f)}$ & $M2^{(c)}$	potentially none	ova from M1 with donor sperm *or* sperm from M2 with donor ova; M1 currently must give birth
$M^{(f)}$ & $F^{(m)}$	potentially none	ova from M with donor sperm *or* sperm from F with donor ova; M currently must give birth

As the table indicates, if a same-gender couple consists of one member who has undergone change of registered gender, that couple may also have the reproductive

165 Ds 2012:46, above n. 58, pp. 61–65.

capacity of a fertile male-female pairing. A similar situation would exist if both partners in a male-female couple changed registered gender but retain the reproductive capacity associated with their former registered gender. In contrast, the couples who legally constitute male-female couples may have the reproductive capacity of a same-gender couple where one has a reclassified gender as a matter of law – that is, where one member had the same registered gender at birth as that of her or his current partner or spouse.[166] As explained in section 4.1, the Discrimination Act provides that in health care, strict treatment of a patient in his or her registered gender is not required where the medical needs of the patient warrant. Consequently, three of the pairings may be able to procreate in ways that are not typical for their registered gender but without ART. Equally, for all but one of the five pairings above, if any partner in the couple is infertile, either because of treatment associated with gender identity or other medical condition, that couple at a minimum should be able to receive ART – just as other couples would, depending on their true potential reproductive capacity as a couple.[167]

IV. LEGAL CHALLENGES TO EXISTING RULES

In 2009, the Supreme Administrative Court handed down its most significant decision for all transgender persons in Sweden, not under the Gender Classification Act, but under the Names Act.[168] In that case, a personal legally classified as male but who identified as female had been using the name 'Madeleine' for twenty years in close relationships. In the years leading up to the decision, she had used the name publicly to express her gender, then applied to formally change her first name from Jan-Olov to Madeleine, on the grounds that use of her birth name caused her great distress.[169] The Tax Agency refused the change on the grounds that the name Madeleine was not usual for a man.[170] Though the Names Act provides no authorisation to agencies to make such gendered considerations, the legislative preparatory works had indicated that the agencies could reject gendered names for a child to prevent the child being subjected to teasing and harassment. The Supreme Administrative Court held that the name Madeleine

166 For a general survey of the parenthood rights of same-sex couples in Sweden with ART, see C. Sörgjerd, *Reconstructing marriage: The legal status of relationships in a changing society*, Intersentia, Antwerp 2012, pp. 189–191. For more on ART for same-sex couples in Sweden, see E. Ryrstedt, 'The challenge of new families' (2010) *Col. Jrnl. of Gender and Law* 1076, 1079–1081.

167 As noted above, the fifth pairing – one in which both are born with the capacity to give sperm but not bear children – would be similarly situated with a same-sex couple and cannot access ART under current Swedish law, though this is under investigation and may change sometime in or after 2015.

168 *The names Q (I), A-C (II) together with the name Madeleine for a man (III) accepted as a forename*, RÅ 2009 ref. 55, s. 369–373 (2009).

169 Ibid., p. 369.

170 Ibid., p. 370.

was not particularly unusual, nor would it be likely to constitute embarrassment to the applicant, who was not a child, but, rather, an adult who suffered with the name given to her. The Court emphasised that a first name is 'so personal that considerable freedom must be recognised for individuals' in that choice.[171] As a result, the Names Act is no longer considered a barrier for any transgender person to change a name, a freedom independent of any process governed by the Gender Classification Act.

In 2012, the Stockholm Court of Appeals handed down the first significant decision in Sweden signifying future application of the ECHR to the Gender Classification Act.[172] Holding the sterilisation requirement unenforceable in individual cases, the Court held:

> 'The concept of forced bodily violation … is more than a mere operation that is forced in the sense that the individual cannot stop it. If the surgery is a condition to receive certain benefits or rights, it is usually considered to be forced. It has been established … that the requirement for sterilisation does not follow from prerequisites of certain physical conditions as criteria for establishing one's gender belonging.
>
> Sterilisation involves a very radical and irreversible physical operation for the individual. To justify a sterilisation requirement solely with reference to keeping order in familial relationships can hardly be permitted to be done in light of these types of intrusions and prevailing values. In addition, the requirement to undergo the surgery cannot be considered to be voluntary. In this Court's judgment, the sterilisation requirement is such an intrusive procedure that it cannot be considered consistent with Chapter 2, § 6 of the Swedish Constitution and Article 8 of the ECHR. Furthermore, the requirement is directed only toward transsexual persons. Establishment of such a far-reaching requirement for one certain group means that the requirements of the *könstillhörighetslag* must also be considered in conflict with the prohibition of discrimination in ECHR Article 14.'[173]

Most recently, the Stockholm Administrative Court invalidated a decision by the Tax Agency's registration of a man as the mother of his child, after he gave birth in his corrected legal identity.[174] The parent in the case had faced questioning by police about his parental identity when he tried to obtain a passport for his child. The Court found no law generally requiring registration of the person who gives birth as the mother. On the other hand, the Court held that Article 8 of the ECHR required respect for the parent's private life and supported by the confidentiality provisions of the Gender Classification Act, which the Tax Agency's registration defied and threatened to expose by registering his parental status as female. Invoking the Convention on the Rights of the Child, the Court further held

---

171 Ibid., pp. 372–373 (quoted text translation by author).
172 *Socialstyrelsen v NN*, Mål nr. 1968–12 (2012).
173 Ibid., pp. 5–6 (author's translation).
174 *NN v Skatteverket*, Mål nr. 24685–13 (14 April 2014) (non-public decision).

that the child's best interests weighed heavily in favour of family security and consistency of its parents' legal documents. The Court thus held the Tax Agency had an obligation to register the parent as the father. In July 2015, the Stockholm Court of Appeal upheld that decision.[175] While the case is on appeal at this writing, the decision not only documented the injuries transgender parents face from inconsistent legal treatment in their corrected legal identity, but affirmed the importance of human rights in this field to protect transgender individuals from discrimination by the government.

V. CONCLUSION

If Sweden can be viewed as a bellwether nation in laws regarding gender classification, its experiences may provide certain lessons about the strengths and weaknesses of a comprehensive administrative approach to medical and legal management of gender. In one respect, the Swedish system has ensured that significant numbers of its citizens and residents have access to medical treatment for significant gender distress, without bearing the brunt of the costs for surgery and continuous medical care. And yet, strict legal control over access to that treatment runs the risk of becoming administratively repressive, particularly when the government does not keep pace with medical science for good health care, or fuses medical care with legal concerns, often on the basis of assumptions about the gender typicality of a person's body. Even with a centralised system for gender registry changes, Sweden's complex administrative system for controlling legal identity has subjected persons to multiple agencies and procedures, all so that they can simply correct the many ways that their gender is recorded and used in the legal system.

Nearly 400 years ago, Linnaean taxonomy emerged from Sweden, leading the scientific world in classifying life forms on the basis of gendered ideas and sexual markers, even separating mammals from all other species on these very grounds.[176] Much as that taxonomy seems questionable today in retrospect, Sweden's pioneering legal scheme for managing gender no longer appears as progressive as it may have been viewed in the past. Instead, its humanitarian vision appears to have been compromised by conflicting motives for controlling gender typicality and nonconformity, rather than confronting the appropriateness of using gender as basis for assigning rights and privileges in law. Recently, Sweden has once again been hailed as a model for other nations to follow, particularly for its sweeping proscriptions against gender identity discrimination.[177] And yet, the

---

[175] *Skatteverket v NN*, Mål nr. 3201–14 (9 July 2015).

[176] See P. Fara, *Sex, Botany & Empire*, Icon, Cambridge 2003; L. Schiebinger, *Nature's Body: Sexual Politics and the Making of Modern Science*, Pandora, New York 1993.

[177] S. Agius, R. Köhler, S. Aujean and J. Ehrt, *Human Rights and Gender Identity: Best Practice Catalogue*, ILGA/TGEU, Brussels 2011, p. 37.

government's more compelling legacy, perhaps, may depend on its recognition that its priority is ensuring that its laws adhere to gender neutrality and global human rights standards, at the very least, so that future reforms can work toward maximising the health and minimising the harm imposed on persons who ask to be legally respected in their gender.

THE LEGAL STATUS OF TRANSSEXUAL AND TRANSGENDER PERSONS IN TURKEY

Yeşim M. Atamer*

Contents

* The author would like to thank Assoc. Prof. Dr Başak Baysal for presenting this paper in Hong Kong on 6–7 September 2013 at the conference on 'The Legal Status of Transsexual and Transgender Persons' organised by the Centre for Medical Ethics and Law, and making valuable comments while redrafting the paper.

I. DEVELOPMENT OF THE RELEVANT LEGAL RULES

The right of transgender persons to effect a change of their gender marker in the civil status register after gender confirmation surgery was accepted in Turkey by law in 1988. With this new provision, major Turkish research hospitals started to offer medical treatment, including surgical intervention, for transgender individuals. Even though there is no official statistical data, witness statements of surgeons indicate that, on average, more than 300 operations are conducted in Turkey per year.[1] Given that transgenderism is acknowledged as a medical condition ('gender identity disorder'), public and legal perceptions of transgender persons are more lenient than in comparison to, for example, homosexuality. Same-sex marriages are forbidden; any type of cohabitation except marriage between men and women is not recognised by Turkish law.[2] Even though public awareness of lesbian, gay, bisexual and transgender (LGBT) problems has risen throughout Turkey in recent decades, a strong tendency towards homophobia is still present and no change in the law has been discussed.[3] In fact, this attitude is also reflected in the provisions regarding transgender persons, given that such persons are totally neglected as a group and a change in the civil status register is only allowed if an individual submits to gender confirmation surgery, as prescribed by law.

The legal status of transgender persons in Turkey can be analysed in three phases. In the period before 1988, there was no special legal provision at all. However, the issue was debated in case law. The second phase was introduced

---

1 See: <www.haberevet.com/yasam/turkiye-her-yil-yuzlerce-insan-cinsiyet-degistiriyor-h677474.html> or <www.haberturk.com/yasam/haber/824452-cinsiyet-degistirme-hakkinda-her-sey>.

2 *Cf.* on this issue C. Yasan, *Milletlerarası Özel Hukukta Aynı Cinsiyetten Kişilerin Birliktelikleri* [Same Sex Partnerships in Private International Law], On Iki Levha, Istanbul 2013, pp. 57 ff.

3 *Cf.* e.g. A. Erol (ed.), *Anti Homofobi Kitabı* [Anti-Homophobia Book], Ankara 2009; *2012 Cinsel Yönelim ve Cinsiyet Kimliği Temelli İnsan Hakları İhlalleri İzleme Raporu* [Sexual Orientation and Sexual Identity Based Human Rights Violations Observation Report], SpoD, Istanbul 2013; A. Polat, S. Yuksel, A. Genc Discigil and H. Meteris, 'Family Attitudes Toward Transgendered People In Turkey: Experience From A Secular Islamic Country' (2005) 35 *Int'l J. Psychiatry in Medicine* 4, 383–393. According to the 'Value Atlas 2012' 87% of the Turkish population does not want to have a homosexual as neighbour. This is followed by 84% of extreme alcohol consumers and 76% of AIDS patients: Y. Esmer, *Degisimin Kültürel Sinirlari, Türkiye Degerler Atlası 2012*, Istanbul 2012, p. 67. A positive step forward was the 2008 decision of the Turkish Court of Cassation to reject the closure of an association of LGBT people based on immorality and to grant freedom of association, Y7HD 25.11.2008, E. 2008/4109, K. 2008/5196 (Kazanci database).

by a change to Article 29 of the Turkish Civil Code (TCC) in 1988, allowing for the change of the civil status register after gender confirmation surgery. The so far final phase started with the introduction of a new Turkish Civil Code[4] in 2002. Article 40 of the new code now stipulates the pre- and post-operative legal procedure to be followed in order to achieve a change in the gender marker in the civil status register.[5]

In the first phase, where no legal rule concerning transgender persons existed, the Turkish Court of Cassation was required to consider the application of a famous Turkish singer who had submitted to gender confirmation surgery abroad and wanted to amend the gender marker in the civil status register. The court rejected the application on the ground that the existing laws did not give individuals the freedom to choose their gender.[6] The Court concluded that nobody could 'change' his or her sex arbitrarily and then request an amendment to the civil status register. The Court explicitly refused to accept the view that Turkish law was silent on the subject, which would have meant that judges had the right to fill the legal gap according to Article 1 TCC (through the creation of a new type of action to amend the register).[7] According to the decision, only those who

---

4 The former Turkish Civil Code was mainly a translation of the Swiss Civil Code of 1907. It was put into force in 1926. In 2002 a new Civil Code was issued. However, this Code still follows in major parts the Swiss Civil Code and confines itself to adapting the legal reforms enacted in Switzerland in the last 80 years. But the provision on transsexuals is original. *Cf.* on the role of the Swiss Civil Code in Turkey, Y.M. Atamer, 'Rezeption und Weiterentwicklung des Schweizerischen Zivilgesetzbuches in der Türkei' (2008) 72 *RabelsZ (Rabels Zeitschrift für ausländisches und internationales Privatrecht)* 723–754.

5 In detail Y.M. Atamer, 'The Legal Status of Transsexuals in Turkey' (2005) 8 *International Journal of Transgenderism*, 65–71; Y.M. Atamer 'Laenderbericht Türkei' in J. Basedow and J.M. Scherpe (eds.), *Transsexualitaet, Staatsangehörigkeit und internationales Privatrecht – Entwicklungen in Europa, Amerika und Australien*, Mohr Siebeck, Tübingen 2004, pp. 74–79.

6 2nd chamber of the Turkish Court of Cassation (Y2HD), 21.01.1982, Yargitay Kararlari Dergisi (1982), pp. 323–326 and Y2HD, 27.03.1986, Yargitay Kararlari Dergisi (1986), pp. 1112–1126. For explanations regarding the first phase see A. Ozturel, 'Transseksualizm ve Hermafrodizmde Yasal, Tıpsal ve Adli Problemler' [Legal, Medical and Forensic Problems of Transsexualism and Hermaphroditism] (1981) 37 *AUHFD (Ankara Üniversitesi Hukuk Fakültesi Dergisi)* 1–4; N. Kocayusufpasaoglu, *Turk Hukuku'nda Transseksüeller Nüfus Kütüğündeki Cinsiyet Kaydının Düzeltilmesi için Dava Açabilir mi?* [Can Transsexuals File a Case to Change the Birth Register According to Turkish Law?], Filiz, Istanbul 1986; for a review of the publication of Kocayusufpasaoğlu see H. Burcuoglu, (1986) 60 *İBD (İstanbul Barosu Dergisi)* 7–9.

7 Art. 1 of Swiss and Turkish Civil Codes both have the following wording: 'The law regulates all matters to which the text or spirit of one of its dispositions relate. If the law is silent, the judge shall decide according to customary law and if this also lacks, he shall decide according to the rule he would have set had he been the lawmaker. While deciding, he shall make use of doctrine and jurisprudence.' It is interesting to know that most of the Swiss courts which were also confronted with the pleas to change the birth register after a sex reassignment surgery accepted these, even though they were working with the same Civil Code articles as in Turkey. In contrast to the Turkish courts, the Swiss courts concluded, that the law was silent on this subject and that a register change action of a *sui generis* type had to be created according to the right given to the judge in Art. 1 al. II of the Civil Code. See e.g. Bezirksgericht Laupen 17.02.1971, (1971) *ZZW (Zeitschrift für Zivilstandswesen)* 129–130; Bezirksgericht Vevey 09.05.1974, (1975) *ZZW* 181–185; Zivilgericht Kanton Basel-Stadt 08.05.1979, (1979) *ZZW* 281–285; For an analysis of these decisions see P. Aubert and H. Reich, 'Der Eintrag der Geschlechtsänderung

suffered from an intersex condition from birth were allowed to submit to gender confirmation surgery. The court concluded that since the litigant in question was not affected by an intersex condition prior to the surgery abroad, one could only pity the applicant for, in the words of the court, the loss of her 'male sexuality' without being able to 'transform' into a 'real' woman. The Court could not, however, give the applicant the right to change her legal gender markers in the civil status register according to her preferred gender.[8]

In 1988, the Turkish Parliament decided to amend the Turkish Civil Code in order to regulate the status of transgender individuals. According to updated version of Article 29, a person who was able to produce a report of a health commission[9] certifying that he or he has submitted to gender confirmation surgery could request the courts to order an amendment of the civil status register. Should this person be married, the spouse would be given due notice of the application, and upon the court ordering the amendment, the marriage would automatically come to an end. In the event that the couple in question had children, the court would also be required to decide which of the parents would be entitled to retain custody of the children.

Although this regulation was clearly a step forward with regard to the legal situation of transgender persons, it was strongly criticised in the legal doctrine.[10] As Turkish law only recognises marriages between people of different sexes, one of the main issues that came up for debate was the possibility of married people submitting to gender confirmation surgery. Another criticism raised was that Article 29 did not specify the preconditions for accessing surgery. Given the reality of widespread malpractice in connection with gender confirmation surgery in the 1980s, it was considered necessary to have stringent regulations for access to such surgery. It was hoped that medical practice would be controlled through strict laws.

---

in die Zivilstandsregister' (1987) *ZZW* 2–8. See also St. Gallen Bezirksgericht 26.11.1996, (1997) *SJZ (Schweizerische Juristenzeitung)* 442–443. For a comparison of the Swiss and Turkish court decisions on the subject see M.R. Will, 'Die Sängerin im Zivilgesetzbuch – zum neuen türkischen Transsexuellengesetz' in Pfister and Will (eds.), *Festschrift für Werner Lorenz zum siebzigsten Geburtstag*, Mohr Siebeck, Tübingen 1991, pp. 825, 832; M.R. Will and B. Oztan, 'Hukukun Sebebiyet Verdiği Bir Aci: Transseksüellerin Hukuki Durumu' [Pain Caused by Law: The Legal Status of Transsexuals] (1993) 43 *AUHFD* 244.

8 Ozturel and Will report of several decisions of lower courts which did accept the pleas for change in the birth register after gender confirmation surgery. However, until the change in the law, the Court of Cassation always rejected those lower court decisions which were appealed (see for these unpublished decisions: Ozturel (1981) 37 *AUHFD* 253, 268–273 and Will, above n. 7, p. 825, pp. 832–834.

9 For a Court of Cassation decision (Y2HD, 02.12.1993), accepting the report given by the Forensic Medicine Institute, stating that a gender confirmation surgery was carried out, see: O.U. Genccan, *Nüfus Davalari* [Personal Status Actions], Ankara 2000, p. 267.

10 N. Kocayusufpaşaoglu, 'La situation juridique des transsexuels en droit privé turc' in *Festschrift Deliyannis*, Thessaloniki 1991, pp. 255, 261 ff.; Will, above n. 7, pp. 825, 837 ff.; Will and Oztan, above n. 7, pp. 225, 237 ff.; K. Guven, 'Cinsiyet Değişikliği ve Hukuki Sonuçları' [Sex Reassignment and Its Legal Consequences] (1997) 1 *GÜHFD (Gazi Üniversitesi Hukuk Fakültesi Dergisi)* 45, 59 ff.

Under these circumstances, it is perhaps not surprising that, in the third phase, harsh regulations were introduced. This phase started with the new Turkish Civil Code, enacted in 2002. Article 40, which is found among the regulations concerning the civil status registers, follows Article 39 which concerns the need for a court decision to execute any change in the civil status registers. According to Article 40 TCC, there are now two stages to be completed before a person's preferred gender can be recognised in the civil status register. The first stage is prior to the operation; the second is subsequent to the operation. A candidate for recognition must first apply to a court for permission to submit to gender confirmation surgery. The aim of this provision is obviously to bring such surgical treatments under control. During the second stage, the applicant must provide the court with a report from the health board which attests that the applicant has undergone the required surgical procedure.

Until very recently, the Turkish Social Security Institution (SSI) did not classify gender confirmation surgery as being within the scope of national health insurance. This practice was criticised as violating the law, given that the Turkish Social Security and General Health Insurance Code[11] only excludes plastic surgery with beauty and slimming purposes. A public debate in 2013, following the gender confirmation surgery of a young Turkish actress, had a particularly important impact. On 23 October 2013, the Social Security Institution informed all social security directorates by letter to consider transgenderism as a medical condition and to cover all necessary medical interventions, including surgeries such as top surgery for transgender women.[12] Private insurance companies, however, continue to exclude coverage for gender confirmation surgery by way of standard insurance terms.[13]

II. CHANGING LEGAL SEX – PROCEDURE AND REQUIREMENTS

Article 40 of the Turkish Civil Code reads as follows:

> 'A person who wants to change his/her sex has to apply to the court personally and ask for permission for a sex reassignment. For this permission to be given, the applicant must have reached the age of 18 and must be unmarried. Besides he/she must prove with an official health board report issued by an education and research hospital that he/she is of transsexual nature, that the sex reassignment is

---

11 Sosyal Sigortalar ve Genel Sağlık Sigortası Kanunu (no. 5510), 31.05.2006, Resmi Gazete (OJ) 16.6.2006 no 26200.

12 Sosyal Güvenlik Kurumu Başkanlığı, 23.10.2013, 10463188/3878389-17074768 sayı ve "Cinsiyet Değiştirme Ameliyatı" başlıklı yazı [Letter from the Social Security Institution with subject 'gender confirmation surgery'].

13 *Cf.* e.g. Allianz Private Health Insurance General Conditions Art. 13/J <https://www.allianzsigorta.com/tr/v_1429202933000/tr/files/Diger_Saglik_Urunleri.pdf>.

compulsory for his/her mental health and that he/she is permanently deprived of the capacity of reproduction.

If it is confirmed by an official health board report, that a sex reassignment operation was effected based on the permission given and in accordance with the purpose and medical methods, the court will decide for the necessary changes to be made in the civil status register.'

Article 40 clearly designates the courts as the competent authority to permit gender confirmation surgery and also to order an amendment to a person's gender markers in the civil status register.[14] Article 40 differentiates between two phases and court decisions: pre- and post-operation phases, which both require a different procedure to be followed.

2.1. THE PRE-OPERATION COURT DECISION

An individual who would like to submit to gender confirmation surgery must first get the permission of the relevant court, which is the court at the place of residence of the applicant. The application must be made at a stage where a research hospital can, by official health board report, certify that gender confirmation surgery is required for the individual's mental health. In addition, the person must fulfil other objective criteria, such as reaching a minimum age and being unmarried. These requirements are considered below.

2.1.1. Official Health Board Report

A court which gives permission for gender confirmation surgery will do so only if a medical report supports such operation as necessary treatment. This report must testify on three different issues. First, that the applicant is a transgender individual (*i.e.* that the person self-identifies with a gender other than the legal gender assigned to him or her at birth). Second, that the applicant requires gender confirmation surgery for mental health reasons. Finally, that the applicant is permanently deprived of its capacity of reproduction. The court cannot examine the existence of these three conditions on its own. Rather, it makes a decision according to the expert opinion.

---

14 A decision of the Turkish Court of Cassation on 19.04.2012 seems to suggest that for intersex persons the procedure of Art. 40 TCC must not be followed. Even though very few details are given in the case, one can deduce that the operation of the intersex person was already conducted without prior permission. The decision of the lower court to apply the prerequisites of Art. 40 TCC was rejected based on the argument that the *Nufus Hizmeleri Kanunu* [Civil Registration Services Act (no. 5490), RG (OJ) 29.04.2006 no. 26153] is applicable which is providing for a correction in name and sex of the applicant. Y18HD, 19.04.2012, E. 2012/4125, K. 2012/4125 (Kazanci database).

2.1.1.1. Competence to Issue Such Report

The provision explicitly requires that the report be prepared by a health board of an education and research hospital.[15] The hospital, which may prepare this expert opinion, is defined very strictly so as to prevent the treatment of transgender persons, and issue of an expert opinion, by medical institutions which have inadequate expertise or inadequate procedures for prior medical examination. The requirement of a *board* report indicates that there has to be more than one specialist engaged in the procedure. In fact, most of the education and research hospitals providing gender confirmation surgery have already introduced 'gender identity councils' (*Cinsel Kimlik Konseyi*), which consist of specialists of different medical branches. The information letter of the Social Security Council of 23 October 2013 now expressly states which branches must be represented on the competent board (psychiatry, endocrinology, urology, gynaecology and reconstructive surgery). The Council also mentions that the view of a medical genetics expert has to be attached to the report.

In cases where the official health board concludes that the prerequisites for gender confirmation surgery are not satisfied, the board will issue a negative report. There is no official appeals mechanism against decisions of the medical board. However, given that it is not imperative that the transgender person obtain a report at the hospital of his or her place of residence, the individual may subsequently apply to another education and research hospital in order to access a positive report.

2.1.1.2. Content of the Report

The report issued by the official health board must testify first that the applicant is transgender. The law does not state how long a person must have identified with a gender other than his or her birth gender, and how exactly this identification issue has to become manifest. The criteria are established by medical experts. Turkish psychiatrists generally follow the standards of the World Professional Association for Transgender Health (WPATH – and previously the standards of HBIGDA).[16] An individual who would like to obtain recognition of preferred gender is

---

15 The Turkish Ministry of Health designates the education and research hospitals.

16 *Cf.* on the criteria e.g. S. Yuksel, I.B. Kulaksizoglu, N. Turksoy and D. Sahin, 'Group Psychotherapy with Female-to Male Transsexuals in Turkey' (2000) 29(3) *Archives of Sexual Behavior* 279–290; S. Yuksel, 'Transseksüellik ve Cinsiyet Değiştirmenin Standart Değerlendirme, Karar verme ve Bakım İlkeleri' [Standard Evaluation, Decision and Care Principles for Transsexuals and Sex Change], in *Anti Homofobi Kitabı* 2009, pp. 91–94; B. Özata, *Transseksüel Bireylerde Cinsiyet Dönüştürmenin Ruh Sagligi ve Yasam Kalitesi Uzerine Etkileri* [Effect of Sex Reassignment on the Wellbeing and Live Quality of Transsexuals], Thesis Istanbul University Medical Faculty, 2012, pp. 32–67.

observed by psychiatrists for a period lasting up to two years.[17] After extensive psychiatric sessions, the individual is prepared for the real life test, whereby he or she mostly begins hormone treatments. If, at the end of the observation period, the psychiatrist decides that the real identity of the person is the opposite legal gender, the case will be presented to the Board for the final decision. If the Board is to issue a positive report, it must come to the conclusion that gender confirmation surgery is necessary for the mental health of the applicant (*i.e.* meaning that the applicant would otherwise suffer lifelong distress).

However, the requirements set out in Article 40 TCC do not end at that point. There is a third, highly problematic, medical condition which the applicant must satisfy prior to accessing gender confirmation surgery: the applicant must be permanently deprived of the capacity of reproduction.[18] However, in many situations, a transgender person, before he or she submits to gender confirmation surgery, will be fertile and capable of bearing children. Turkish law requires that, as part of the recognition process, a transgender person must be deprived of this capacity. The main concern of the regulation is probably to prevent transgender men from 'mothering' children and transgender women from 'fathering' children. Given that the requirement of sterilisation, and indeed the entire process of making people submit to surgical intervention, has been increasingly criticised and rejected in countries such as Germany and Sweden, it would appear absolutely unacceptable that Turkish law requires infertility even before a person can access gender confirmation surgery.[19] The consequence of this requirement is that it is doctors who are actually forced to sterilise individuals, by surgery if necessary.[20] This constitutes an unnecessary physical and mental burden for the transgender community in Turkey. Besides, it is also unclear from the wording

---

17 *Cf.* for a critical evaluation of the therapy phase A. Zengin, 'Sex for Law, Sex for Psychiatry: Pre-Sex Reassignment Surgical Psychotherapy in Turkey' (2014) 56 *Anthropologica* 55–68, 59 ff.

18 Atamer (2005), above n. 5, pp. 66–67. In contrast, European laws that mention infertility require it as a condition for registering the sex change and do not see it as a condition for the gender confirmation surgery itself (see e.g. Dutch Civil Code Article 1:28a(c)). However, even this requirement was lately found unconstitutional for example in Sweden as well as Germany, on which see the chapters by Garland and Dutta in this volume.

19 Very critical also G. Turan Basara, 'Türk Medenî Kanunu'nun 40'inci Maddesi Kapsamında Cinsiyet Degisikliği ve Hukuki Sonuclari' [Legal Consequences of Gender Change According to Art 40 TCC] (2012) *TBBD (Türkiye Barolar Birliği Dergisi)* 245, 255–256 <http://tbbdergisi.barobirlik.org.tr/m2013-103-1234>; B. Erman, *Tibbi Mudahalelerin Hukuka Uygunlugu* [The Lawfulness of Medical Interventions], Ankara 2003, p. 215; M.R. Will, 'Allah Kimseyi Hekime, Hakime Muhtac Etmesin! – Das Menschenrecht auf Geschlechtsidentitaet im Normenwirrwarr: Tuerkei und Finnland – Pioniere im Europaeischen Familienrecht?', Prof. Dr Turgut Kalpsuz'e Armagan, Ankara 2003, pp. 741–773, 752; I. Saglam, 'Türk Medeni Kanunu Madde 40 Üzerine Bir Degerlendirme' [An Evaluation of Art. 40 of the Turkish Civil Code] (2004) *Atatürk Üniversitesi Erzincan Hukuk Fakültesi Dergisi* 455, 464 ff.; Atamer (2005), above n. 5, p. 67.

20 In fact, the Turkish Court of Cassation has remanded the decision of a first instance court allowing for sex change even though the report was expressing that the applicant was still fertile, Y2HD, 20.04.2006, E. 2005/20746, K. 2006/5916 (Kazanci database).

of the provision whether a transgender person must even be infertile from birth. Such an interpretation would obviously prevent transgender individuals who already have children from submitting to gender confirmation surgery and obtaining legal recognition.[21]

All these question marks have led to a challenge to Article 40 TCC before the European Court of Human Rights (ECtHR). The case of *Y.Y. v Turkey* (no. 14793/08) was triggered when a domestic court refused permission to a FtM transgender man to submit to gender confirmation surgery. The court held in 2005 that the applicant did not meet the statutory condition of being diagnosed as permanently infertile.[22] The decision was approved by the Turkish Court of Cassation in 2007. In his challenge, the applicant relied in particular on Article 8 of the European Convention on Human Rights (ECHR) which concerns respect for private and family life. The ECtHR decided on 10 March 2015 in favour of the applicant and held that Article 8 was violated. In its reasoning the court especially referred to the latest changes in the laws of Member States and also to the Resolution 1728 (2010) of the Parliamentary Assembly of the Council of Europe calling on Member States to issue official documents that reflect an individual's preferred gender identity, without any prior obligation to undergo sterilisation or other medical procedures such as sex reassignment surgery and hormonal therapy. The comparative analysis lead the Court to the conclusion that the requirement of being permanently deprived of the capacity of reproduction before gender confirmation surgery violates the Convention and that the applicant has suffered considerable distress due to the long period it had to wait until the right to surgery was finally granted in 2013.

2.1.2. Legal Age and Mental Capacity

An applicant who wants to undergo gender confirmation surgery must have reached the age of 18. However, there are suggestions with the academic literature that, in extraordinary circumstances where a delay in surgical intervention might cause serious problems, consent to gender confirmation surgery before the age of majority can be given by a court.[23] Although not mentioned in the relevant legal article (in the Civil Code), it is apparent that the applicant must also enjoy sufficient mental capacity. The Turkish Patients' Rights Regulation of 1998[24] states

21 Parallel Saglam, pp. 455, 461.

22 Paras. 7–21 <http://hudoc.echr.coe.int/sites/eng/Pages/search.aspx#{"itemid":["001-152779"]}>.

23 M. Kaya, 'Türk Hukukunda Cinsiyet Değişikliği ve Hukuki Sonuçları' [Sex Change under Turkish Law and its Legal Effects], *Ankara Üniversitesi Hukuk Fakültesi Öğrencilerinin Fakültelerine Armağanı*, Ankara 2008, p. 73 <http://auhf.ankara.edu.tr/auhf-yayinlari-arsivi/armaganlar/mecmua/03.pdf>; Turan Basara, above n. 19, p. 251; Will, above n. 19, p. 753; N. Tekin, 'Cinsiyet Değiştirme Kavramı ve Cinsiyet Değişikliği Ameliyatının Hukuki Açıdan Değerlendirilmesi' [Sex Reassignment and Legal Assessment of Gender Confirmation Surgery] (2009) 39 *THD (Terazi Hukuk Dergisi)*, p. 97, 108.

24 Hasta Haklari Yönetmeligi, Resmi Gazete (OJ), 01.08.1998, no. 23420.

that, for medical interventions on people under legal guardianship principally, the guardian must give consent. However, having regard to the highly personal nature of gender confirmation surgery, it is suggested that the applicant should decide for him or herself as long as the applicant enjoys sufficient mental capacity.[25]

2.1.3. *Requirement not to be Married*

In order to access gender confirmation surgery, an applicant must prove that he or she is unmarried. Even though Article 40 TCC does not expressly state whether this means that the applicant must never have been married, or if it suffices that there is no longer an existing marriage, the second interpretation should be favoured.[26] The only requirement therefore is that the applicant should not be married at the time of the application.

2.1.4. *Decision of the Court*

After evaluating the Official Health Board Report and checking the existence of the objective criteria, a judge may give permission for gender confirmation surgery, involving the modification of the applicant's physical and biological sex characteristics. However, according to Turkish procedural law, the Board's report is an expert opinion which is not binding on the judge (Article 282 of the Code of Civil Procedure). A judge can freely evaluate this evidence and ask for a new expert opinion where he or she considers that the existing report is unsatisfactory. Obviously, the reasons for doubt have to be explained very clearly. In cases where the Court of First Instance rejects the application of the transgender individual, an appeal to the Court of Cassation is possible. This is a general right according to the Turkish Code of Civil Procedure (Article 341, 361).

2.1.5. *Deficiencies in the Current Law*

There are several issues which are left open under the current regulation. One of them is the situation of people who have undergone gender confirmation surgery without prior court permission (e.g. surgeries conducted in a foreign country). As Article 40/2 TCC seems to allow changes to the birth register only for surgery performed with prior permission, it would appear that the court must technically reject all other applications, including those performed abroad. In reality, however, Turkish doctrine considers that, while it is established that unauthorised surgeries are illegal, the law must find a proper solution where individuals submit to such surgery. Transgender individuals who access unauthorised treatment should be

[25] Cf e.g. M. Dural and T. Oguz, *Türk Medeni Hukuku, Cilt 2 (Kisiler Hukuku)* [Turkish Civil Law, Law of Persons], Istanbul 2013, para. 629; Turan Basara, above n. 19, p. 252.

[26] Same as here Turan Basara, above n. 19, pp. 252–253. Will, above n. 19, pp. 753–754.

able to effect a change in the civil status register despite the absence of a prior court permission.[27] The Turkish Court of Cassation has expressed its opinion in favour of such transgender persons, at least for surgeries obtained abroad. In 2010, the Court overruled a decision of a lower court rejecting an amendment to the register where the applicant, a Turkish citizen, had accessed surgical intervention in Germany.[28] According to the Court of Cassation, the Court of First Instance must proceed according to Article 40 TCC and allow the applicant to deliver proof of gender confirmation surgery. In another decision from 2009, the applicant, a former Turkish citizen, who was not a German national, wanted the Turkish courts to validate Germany's recognition of preferred gender. The Court of Cassation set aside the lower court decision, which had held that it would violate public order for Turkey to recognise an individual's preferred legal gender even though the individual had not satisfied the conditions set out in Article 40. According to the High Court, it did not violate Turkish public order rules that the procedure in Article 40 was not followed in Germany.[29]

Another question is whether a court decision prior to gender confirmation surgery should remain indefinitely valid and subsisting, even if the person does not access surgical treatment within a reasonable time after the court order. Article 40 TCC is silent in this respect. If surgery is not carried out within a reasonable time, doctors would be well advised to ask for a new decision if there are doubts as to whether the condition for surgery still exists.

And lastly, the current law does not address the issue of the nationality of the applicant. Whether or not foreigners resident in Turkey or medical tourists fall under Article 40/1 TCC is unclear. According to the general principle of the Turkish Law on International Private and Procedural Law, all personal matters of a foreigner are subject to his or her own national law.[30] Therefore, it is submitted that the requirements mentioned in Article 40/1 TCC are not applicable to a non-national. However, the need to get a court decision allowing gender confirmation surgery is a procedural rule and procedure is *lex fori*. Turkish courts will have to decide according to the prerequisites of the foreign law whether or not gender confirmation surgery is allowed. In cases where the national law of the foreigner does not allow for surgical intervention, Turkish courts should find this as violating Turkish public policy and should permit the non-national individual to rely on Article 40 TCC.[31]

---

27 Dural and Oguz, above n. 25, para. 636. See also Atamer (2004), above n. 5, p. 78.

28 Y2HD 13.12.2010, E. 2009/19039, K. 2010/20942 (Kazanci database).

29 Y2HD 21.12.2009, E. 2009/9678, K. 2009/22090 (Kazanci database).

30 E. Nomer, *Devletler Hususi Hukuku* [International Private Law], 11th ed., Beta, Istanbul 2011, p. 223; C. Sanli, E. Esen and I. Ataman Figanmese, *Milletlerarası Özel Hukuk* [International Private Law], Vedat, İstanbul 2013, p. 112.

31 See also Atamer (2004), above n. 5, p. 79. *Cf.* Will, above n. 7, pp. 843–844 for the situation before 2002.

2.2. THE POST-OPERATION COURT DECISION AND CHANGE IN DOCUMENTS

After the court gives its consent for gender confirmation surgery, the applicant can have the surgery performed at any hospital he or she desires. It can also be performed abroad. After surgery, the person concerned needs to apply to court again, this time, to obtain a decision allowing him or her to gain recognised gender in the civil status register. The precondition for such a decision is a report issued by an official health board which states that the person has submitted to an authorised and proper gender confirmation surgery ('in accordance with the purpose and medical methods') (Article 40/2 TCC). Any official health institution can issue such a report. The stricter requirements, set out in Article 40/1 TCC, which mandate a report from an education and research hospital in relation to access to surgery, do not apply for the post-surgery report. However, like Article 40/1, the report must be issued by a board where the previously mentioned medical branches are represented. Frequently, such an inclusive medical board will only exist in education and research hospitals.

What is problematic about this provision is the requirement that gender confirmation surgery must be effected 'in accordance with the purpose and medical methods'.[32] What this means exactly has already been the subject of a decision by the Turkish Court of Cassation, and regrettably was resolved against the interests of transgender persons. In that case, the first surgery conducted on a FtM transgender person had removed the *labia minora* and closed the individual's vagina. However, male genitals had not yet been constructed. Even though the board's report testified that the second operation was going to be effected soon, the Court rejected the application for gender recognition in the birth register and decided that this is only possible after male genital reconstruction is finalised.[33] Until decided otherwise, this presumably means that full surgery is required for an individual to obtain legal recognition of preferred gender, which is quite out of sync with the developments in other jurisdictions (such as Germany, the Netherlands or Argentina) and also very questionable from a medical and human rights point of view.

Once the court allows an application, the relevant authorities must make the necessary amendment to the civil status register. In such cases, the reason for amendment of the gender marker in the register is displayed as 'sex reassignment surgery'. Even though the records are not open to the public, relatives, to a certain degree, may have access – which is certainly very problematic in light of information privacy requirements. Article 44(g) of the Civil Registration Services Act states that 'the registered person or their spouses, parents, guardians, lineal ancestors and descendants, or those who submit a power of attorney provided

[32] *Cf.* also WILL, above n. 19, pp. 754–755.

[33] Y2HD 13.02.2006, E. 2005/17485, K. 2006/1343 (Kazanci database).

by the registered person' are entitled to obtain a copy of the civil status register. Paragraph 4 of the same article prohibits any other person from obtaining information from the civil status register without the knowledge of the registered person.

After the changes in the birth register have been effected, the relevant authorities will also amend a birth certificate, passport and other personal documents on application by the individual.

III. CONSEQUENCES OF THE CHANGE OF LEGAL SEX

3.1. FUTURE RIGHTS AND ENTITLEMENTS

3.1.1. Name Change

After an individual obtains legal recognition of his or her preferred gender in the civil status register, he or she has the right to a name change. According to Article 27 TCC, a person has the right to file a suit in order to change name if there is a 'just ground'.[34] It is up to the judge to decide if the ground is just or not. Certainly gender confirmation surgery, and the recognition of legal gender in the civil status register, must be considered as such a 'just ground', as the previous name will not conform to the individual's newly recognised legal gender.

3.1.2. Marriage

Following amendment of the gender marker in the register, a transgender individual has the right to marry someone of the opposite legal gender (*i.e.* a person who has a legal gender which is the same as the legal gender assigned to the transgender person at birth). Under Turkish law, only a man and a woman can enter into a marriage. A transgender person who submits to surgery but has not obtained full gender recognition will not be entitled to marry a person of the opposite gender until he or she obtains full recognition. After recognition, there will be no legal obstacle to such a marriage.

Where a person's spouse is, before marriage, unaware that the individual had transitioned (both legally and medically), the spouse is permitted to annul the marriage under Articles 149 or 150 TCC. Article 149 gives the spouse the right to dissolve the marriage if the other spouse does not possess some major qualities

[34] *Cf.* for high court decisions allowing for name change in case of gender confirmation surgery: H.G. Babacan and K. Uslu, *Uygulamada Nüfus Davaları* [Personal Status Actions in Practice], Ankara 2013, pp. 216–217. See also Tekin, above n. 23, p. 110; Kaya, above n. 23, p. 81. *Cf.* on the right to change the name in general K. Oguzman, O. Selici and S. Oktay-Ozdemir, *Kisiler Hukuku* [Law of Persons], 13th ed., Filiz, Istanbul 2013, pp. 114–123.

without which it would be unbearable for him or her to live with this partner. Parallel to this, Article 150 stipulates the right of the spouse to annul the marriage if he or she was deceived by fraud about some major qualities of the other spouse. Both of these cases are subject to a six-month limitation period from the date where the spouse first becomes aware of the absent quality or the fraud, and in any case to an absolute limitation period of five years from the date of marriage. After this period, the only way to end the marriage is by divorce.

3.1.3. Children

Turkish law is very strict regarding the infertility requirement for legal recognition of preferred gender. As explained above, infertility is a requirement even to access gender confirmation surgery. Therefore, it is legally impossible that the person undergoing surgery will later be able to procreate. The person concerned cannot produce genetic children by storing gametes and then later using them for artificial reproduction. While the 2010 Regulation on treatments facilitating procreation[35] stipulates in Article 18/11 that patients who will undergo an operation or treatment which may end or harm the fertility of that person (like castration, chemotherapy, etc.) can store gametes, the later usage of these is only possible in a marriage and with the gametes of the spouse. Given that a FtM transgender male can only store his ova, and later will be married to a woman who also produces ova, it is technically not possible for that couple to have a child together. This reasoning also applies for a MtF transgender woman who subsequently marries a man. The Regulation expressly prohibits all couples from using gametes from any other human being (Article 18/5).

Therefore the only option for transgender persons, post-legal transition, is to adopt a child. According to Turkish law, a person who is single and 30 years or older can adopt a child on his or her own (Article 307).[36] If a married couple wants to adopt a child, then both spouses must be 30 years old or the couple must have been married for at least five years (Article 305). Only married couples can jointly adopt a child. Cohabitation outside marriage does not confer joint adoption rights because such relationships are not recognised in law. According to Article 305 TCC, the adopting person has to take care of the child for a period of at least one year and it is only after fulfilling this necessary precondition that an application to the court for an order to allow the adoption can be filed. Before allowing the adoption, the judge must make thorough investigations, especially with respect to the health of the adopting person and the adopted child, their mutual relationship, their economic situation, the educational qualifications of the adopting person, and his or her motives for the adoption,

---

35 Üremeye Yardimci Tedavi Uygulamalari ve Üremeye Yardimci Tedavi Merkezleri Hakkinda Yönetmelik, Resmi Gazete (OJ), 06.03.2010, no. 27513.

36 *Cf.* on adoption under Turkish law M. Dural, T. Oguz and A. Gumus, *Türk Özel Hukuku, Vol. III, Aile Hukuku* [Turkish Private Law – Family Law], 5th ed., Istanbul 2012, p. 286 ff.

as well as the family situation and developments during the one year period of care (Article 316/2 TCC). The judge is entitled to ask for professional assistance while taking this decision (Article 316/1 TCC). It is legally possible for any transgender persons who have undergone gender confirmation surgery to make an application under the above-mentioned preconditions.[37]

3.1.4. *Penal/Prison System*

The Centres for Observation and Classification of Prisoners use certain criteria in order to determine how to group prisoners.[38] These criteria include the length of the sentence, the type of crime committed and the age or health condition of the prisoner. Article 26 of the Regulation stipulates that prisoners may also be grouped according to their psychological or physical conditions. Criteria for this include disability, addictions or sexual orientation. This presumably means that transgender persons will be grouped in a way that ensures their safety and well-being.

3.1.5. *Military Service*

In principal, a FtM transgender male is obliged to fulfil his military service duty if he is younger than 40 years of age. However, it is widely known that LGBT people encounter problems in qualifying and also in being exempt from military service.[39] Health control for qualification is conducted according to the Turkish Armed Forces Health Control Regulation. This Regulation lists in its annexes on 'Illnesses and Defects' in Article 17/D/4 'gender identity and behaviour disorder' as a reason for disqualification. In the explanation given in the Regulation it is stated that 'one has to form a medical opinion on those falling under this subsection whether their gender identity and/or behavioural patterns are so express in their daily life that they would cause or are causing a unfavourable situation in military environment.' For exemption from military service, a person must be observed by a military doctor and obtain a new report testifying to his unsuitability for service.

---

37 Atamer (2005), above n. 5, p. 68.

38 Art. 26 of the Regulation on Centres of Observation and Classification (Gözlem ve Sınıflandırma Merkezleri Yönetmeliği) issued by the Ministry of Justice, Resmi Gazete (OJ), 17.06.2005, no. 25848.

39 Eşcinseller İçin Askerlik Broşürü (Military Service Brochure for Homosexuals), prepared by Kaos LG, 2013 <www.kaosgldernegi.org/resim/yayin/dl/kaosgl_askerlik_brosuru.pdf>.

3.2. EXISTING RIGHTS, DUTIES AND ENTITLEMENTS

3.2.1. *Existing Marriage*

The new regulation gives only unmarried persons the chance to obtain court permission for gender confirmation surgery. However, in practice, a married person may submit to surgery without court consent. In this case the question that arises is how the marriage should be treated. The 1988 provision in the Turkish Civil Code stipulated that the marriage would be automatically dissolved following a court decision giving the right to amend the gender marker in the birth register. But as the new code does not take into account the status of those transgender persons who do not have court consent prior to undergoing gender confirmation surgery, the resulting situation will be exactly one that the framers of the new code wanted to avoid. There will necessarily be couples of the same gender who will remain married, given that the reasons for annulment of a marriage are restricted and same-gender marriage is not listed among them. The better position, if one wanted to avoid same-gender marriages categorically, would be to leave the marriage intact and not to effect the legal recognition of gender change in the register until a divorce is sought by the partners.[40]

3.2.2. *Existing Family Relations*

Where a person who submits to gender confirmation surgery already has a child, the genetic parents of that child will remain as stated at time of birth. Parentage does not change because a person has transitioned. If this child were born out of wedlock, custody would normally be given to the mother (Article 337 TCC). In cases where the legal mother accesses gender confirmation surgery and obtains recognition of his preferred male gender, custody of the child might remain with the legal mother or the court might decide that the change in life circumstances justifies the transfer of custody to either the legal father or another person. The main concern here is the best interests of the child and there is no stated rule that a court must remove a child from a transgender parent. If the child is born in wedlock and the parents divorce because one partner wants to submit to gender confirmation surgery, the judge must decide to which parent custody of the child will be awarded. This will be the parent with whom the child is going to live (Article 336 TCC). The same principle is valid here. As long as it is in the best interests of the child to stay with the transgender parent, there is no legal obstacle

---

[40] Turan Basara, above n. 19, pp. 259–260; S. Ayan, *Evlilik Birliginin Korunması* [Protection of the Marital Union], Ankara 2004, pp. 153–154. However, the view that the marriage is dissolved immediately with the sex reassignment surgery is also expressed in doctrine, see e.g. Dural, Oguz and Gumus, above n. 36, p. 74, para. 406.

for the court to decide accordingly.[41] In any case, the parent not given custody has a right to a personal relationship with the child as long as this is not contrary to the well-being of the child.[42]

3.2.3. Existing Employment

Termination of an existing employment after the worker has accessed gender confirmation surgery would in principle violate Article 5 of the Code of Employment,[43] as well as Article 10 of the Turkish Constitution on equality before the law (*Anayasa*). Article 5 stipulates the principle of equal treatment in employment relations and expressly forbids every type of discrimination also in case of termination of an employment contract. There might certainly be some types of contracts where the gender of the person employed is crucial, such as a contract with a midwife or a model. A transgender woman might, pre-transition, work as an underground miner, a profession which is limited to individuals who have a legal male gender. Following transition, the woman may be removed from her employment, with a severance payment (Article 18 Code of Employment). However, one can expect that the moral concepts of Turkish society might lead to a discussion whether gender confirmation surgery constitutes a just ground according to Article 25 and thereby merits any severance payment at all.[44] This view should certainly be dismissed.

3.2.4. Social Benefits

Relating to all kind of social benefits, it has to be accepted that, where a person obtains legal recognition of his or her preferred gender, that person must be able to access those benefits in that gender. This means that, principally, the retirement age will be determined in line with a person's newly recognised legal gender and that all kinds of social payments will be assessed in the same way.[45] In a decision

---

41 Same Turan Basara, above n. 19, pp. 262–263; Tekin, above n. 23, pp. 111–112; Guven (1997) 1 *GÜHFD* 73. Yet the Court of Cassation had decided in 1982 that the custody of the daughter cannot be trusted to the mother who is homosexual given that this is an 'illness' and endangers the wellbeing of the child, Y2HD, 21.06.1982, E. 1982/5077, K. 1982/5531 (Kazanci Database).

42 Tekin, above n. 23, p. 112; Guven (1997) 1 *GÜHFD* p. 74.

43 Is Kanunu (no. 4857), 22.05.2003, Resmi Gazete (OJ) 10.06.2003 no. 25134. *Cf.* on this provision in detail G.B. Yildiz, *Isverenin Esit İslem Yapma Borcu* [Duty of the employer not to discriminate], Ankara 2008.

44 *Cf.* e.g. the case of H.I. Dincdag, a Turkish referee who acknowledged that he was homosexual in 2009 while he was an official in a lower division of the Turkish Football Federation (TFF). The TFF then unilaterally expelled him on the grounds that he had been exempted from military service due to his sexual orientation <www.hurriyetdailynews.com/turkeys-first-openly-gay-referee-gets-german-anti-homophobia-award.aspx?pageID=238&nID=74778&NewsCatID=339>. *Cf.* also on the problems of finding a job: 'I Was Reborn, Data Collection Report of the Counselling Centre for Transgender People Association', September 2014, pp. 35, 47.

45 Atamer (2005), above n. 5, pp. 68–69; Turan Basara, above n. 19, p. 257.

given by the Turkish Council of State in 1993, for example, it was accepted that the appellant, who was a MtF transgender woman, should continue to receive the orphan's pension, which, according to Turkish law, is paid only to female descendants after the age of 25 years. The court stated that the appellant who had obtained an amendment to her gender markers in the birth register had absolutely the same rights as any other woman in Turkey.[46]

IV. CONCLUSIONS AND EVALUATION

Looking at the developments of the last 25 years, one has to conclude that Turkish law still 'equates sex with genitals'[47] and denies rights to LGBT people. Even though public visibility and debates have raised awareness of LGBT people and their problems, homophobia is still deeply rooted in Turkish society. According to data available on the Internet, 69 LGBT individuals have been killed since 2002.[48] The factual situation is best summarised in the 2014 Turkey Progress Report issued by the European Commission:

> 'A draft law on the establishment of an Anti-discrimination and Equality Board remained pending at the Prime Ministry. References to discrimination on grounds of sexual orientation or gender identity were taken out of the initial draft. Respect for the fundamental rights of lesbian, gay, bisexual, transgender and intersex (LGBTI) persons needs to be improved. Regarding the right to life, 4 transgender people were killed as a result of suspected hate crimes. Court sentences for hate crime offenders were often reduced on the basis of "unjust provocation" by the victim and good behaviour. In addition, in numerous cases, crimes against people of a different sexual orientation or gender identity remained unpunished. Shortcomings in the investigation and prosecution of crimes were reported, as well as reluctance by LGBTI people to file complaints.
>
> A self-identified LGBTI person was elected to serve on a municipal council in Istanbul. However, there were cases of discrimination at the workplace. Cases were reported of civil servants being dismissed from their jobs due to the disclosure of their sexual identity, and three court cases on grounds of discrimination on sexual orientation have been on-going. A police officer's appeal against dismissal from his profession for his sexual orientation was awaiting a trial date.
>
> Transgender people faced bureaucratic difficulties after sex – change operations and discrimination in access to health services. LGBTI sex workers faced police violence, arbitrary administrative interventions, fines and discriminatory measures aimed at protecting "general morality" and "general health". A 2012

46 10th chamber of the Council of State, 27.12.1993, E.1992/4706, K. 1993/5536 (Hukukturk database).

47 ZENGIN, above n. 17, p. 66.

48 <http://tr.wikipedia.org/wiki/T%C3%BCrkiye%27de_nefret_cinayeti_kurban%C4%B1_LGBT%27ler>; see also <www.transrespect-transphobia.org/uploads/images/maps/TvT-TMM-Map-2008-12_EN.png>.

> ECtHR judgment, where the court upheld a complaint relating to sexual orientation by a gay man about the treatment he suffered while in detention, was not implemented (X v. Turkey case). The Turkish Armed Forces' disciplinary system continued to define homosexuality as "unnatural" and envisaged the discharge of "morally indecent" personnel. The military's Medical Competence Regulation continued to refer to homosexuality and transsexuality as illnesses.'[49]

Parallel to this, transgender persons are only heard so far as they accept that their condition is medical and needs to be cured by gender confirmation surgery. Other legal solutions are denied. No consideration is given to how the person self-identifies; an amendment in the civil status register without surgery is not possible. Discussion in Parliament or in the legal literature towards changing prevailing attitudes is non-existent. Whether or not the strict requirements regarding gender confirmation surgery will be revisited after the decision of the European Court of Human Rights remains to be seen.

---

49 <http://ec.europa.eu/enlargement/pdf/key_documents/2014/20141008-turkey-progress-report_en.pdf>.

ASIA

THE LEGAL STATUS OF TRANSGENDER AND TRANSSEXUAL PERSONS IN HONG KONG

Athena Nga-chee Liu *

Contents

---

* This is part of a series of four papers and some of the materials here appear in my earlier publications, see A. Liu, 'Gender Recognition: Two Legal Implications for Marriage' (2013) 43 *HKLJ* 407; 'Understanding *Goodwin*: *W v Registrar of Marriages*' (2012) 42 *HKLJ* 403; 'Exacerbating *Corbett*: *W v Registrar of Marriages*' (2011) 41 *HKLJ* 759.

I. LEGAL FRAMEWORK AND STATISTICS

The legal system of the Hong Kong Special Administrative Region (Hong Kong SAR) is comprised of two main parts. First, the pre-1997 colonial era which consisted of a mixture of customary law, the English common law, equity, and local statutes. Second, after 1 July 1997 (the People's Republic of China resuming sovereignty over the Hong Kong SAR), the Basic Law is the Constitution of the Hong Kong SAR. The Basic Law preserves the law previously enforced (*i.e.* the common law, rules of equity, ordinances, subordinate legislation and customary law).[1]

1.1. LEGAL RULES AND HISTORICAL DEVELOPMENT

Hong Kong ordinances use the term 'sex', 'male', 'female', 'man', 'woman' and 'gender',[2] but they are not defined.[3] Like many other jurisdictions, a person is assigned to either 'male' or 'female' at birth, and this is then recorded on the person's birth certificate.[4]

The first judicial decision on the meaning of the words 'male' or 'female', 'man' or 'woman' was the recent landmark judgment in *W v Registrar of Marriages.* In this case, the Court of Final Appeal recognised a post-operative male-to-female transsexual person's right to marry.

W v Registrar of Marriages involved Ms W, who was stated in the judgment to be a 'post-operative male-to-female transsexual person'.[5] Ms W sought judicial review to quash the Registrar of Marriages' refusal to allow her to marry her male partner. Her argument was premised on the ground that the Registrar misinterpreted the meaning of the words 'woman' and 'female' in

---

1 Article 8: 'The laws previously in force in Hong Kong, that is, the common law, rules of equity, ordinances, subordinate legislation and customary law shall be maintained, except for any that contravene this Law, and subject to any amendment by the legislature of the HKSAR.'

2 Section 7(1) of the Interpretation and General Clauses Ordinance (Cap 1) provides that: 'Words and expressions importing the masculine gender include the feminine and neuter genders.'

3 For instance, s. 56(3) of the Immigration Ordinance (Cap 115) provides that the power of search by an authorised public officer is limited to searching persons of the same sex. Section 59A(7) of the Police Force Ordinance (Cap 232) provides that an intimate sample of urine may only be taken from a person by a police officer of the same sex as that person.

4 Schedule 2 of the Birth and Death Registration Ordinance (Cap 174).

5 *W v Registrar of Marriages* [2013] 3 HKLRD 90, (2013) HKLFAR 112 (hereafter cited as 'CFA'), paras. 25, 52.

section 40(2) of the Marriage Ordinance (MO) (Cap. 181)[6] and section 20(1)(d) of the Matrimonial Causes Ordinance (MCO) (Cap. 179)[7] respectively. She sought a declaration that the Registrar had wrongly regarded her as male for the purposes of these provisions. She also sought a declaration that such an interpretation was inconsistent with Article 37 of the Basic Law and/or Articles 14 and 19(2) of the Hong Kong Bill of Rights (the equivalent of Arts. 17 and 23(2) of the International Covenant on Civil and Political Rights (ICCPR)).

The High Court (Andrew Cheung J)[8] dismissed both of Ms W's claims. It held that the meaning of 'man' and 'woman' was a matter of statutory interpretation. Having reviewed the relevant case law from other jurisdictions, Andrew Cheung J held that (following *Corbett v Corbett (Otherwise Ashley)*[9] or '*Corbett*') the determination of the gender (termed 'sex' in the judgment) of a person for the purpose of marriage was based on biological factors alone. The gender of a person was fixed at birth and immutable. Psychological factors were irrelevant. This is sometimes called the *Corbett* criteria. Andrew Cheung J also held that such an interpretation was not inconsistent with the human rights provisions. This decision was later upheld by the Court of Appeal.[10]

The Court of Final Appeal[11] (the highest appellate court) disagreed with the lower courts' decision. It held that the *Corbett* criteria were inconsistent with a post-operative transgender person's right to marry because such criteria ignore both the psychological and social aspects of a person's sexual identity, as well as the medical reality of 'sex reassignment surgery (SRS)' (a term used in the judgment).[12] The Court held that in deciding whether Ms W qualifies as a 'woman', so as to be entitled to marry a man, the law ought in principle to consider all the circumstances – biological, psychological, medical and social – relevant to assessing that individual's sexual identity at the time of the proposed marriage. Having held that the provisions in the MCO and the MO are (without remedial interpretation) inconsistent with the constitutional right to marry, the Court gave a remedial interpretation to them; this required that the provisions be read to include, within the meaning of the words 'woman' and 'female', a post-operative male-to-female transgender woman whose gender has been certified by an appropriate medical authority to have 'changed' as a result of surgical or

6 It provides that: 'The expression "Christian marriage or the civil equivalent of a Christian marriage" implies a formal ceremony recognised by the law as involving the voluntary union for life of one man and one woman to the exclusion of all others'.

7 It provides that: 'A marriage which takes place after 30 June 1972 shall be void on any of the following grounds only – ... (d) that the parties are not respectively male and female.'

8 [2010] 6 HKC 359. See A. Liu, 'Exacerbating *Corbett*: *W v Registrar of Marriages*' (2011) 41 *HKLJ* 759.

9 [1971] P. 83.

10 [2012] 1 HKC 88. See A. Liu, 'Understanding *Goodwin*: *W v Registrar of Marriages*' (2012) 42 *HKLJ* 403.

11 See above n. 5. A. Liu, 'Gender Recognition: Two Legal Implications for Marriage' (2013) 43 *HKLJ* 407.

12 CFA, para. 42.

medical intervention.[13] All the judges agreed that legislative reform on gender recognition would be desirable.

Prior to this landmark decision, a post-operative transgender woman, such as Ms W, had been issued with a replacement identity card and had been recognised as a person of the 'acquired gender' (or sometimes referred to as preferred gender) 'for a whole range of purposes'.[14] For instance, the person would be required to use the women's facilities in public toilets and swimming pool changing rooms.[15] Where the person was sent to prison, she would be housed in a women's detention facility.[16] The significance of being able to obtain from the Immigration Department a replacement identity card will be considered below. However, before the Court of Final Appeal's decision, a post-operative transgender woman could not have entered into a valid marriage, with her acquired gender, to someone of the opposite gender.

Read narrowly, the Court of Final Appeal's decision (or *W*'s case) only affects a post-operative transgender person's right to marry, and it has no impact on other areas where gender remains important in law. For instance, it remains true today that the gender marker on a person's birth certificate cannot be changed.

Now, a few words on the terminology used in this chapter. *W*'s case is the first judicial decision on the meaning of the words 'female' and 'woman'. It marks the beginning of the law's exploration of notions such as sex, birth sex, gender, gender identity, transgender and gender diversity. Gender remains an important area of legal development, and hence the discussion of gender recognition for all legal purposes and law reform. Robyn Emerton in her paper explained these terms well and I adopt her use of these terms.[17] Further, 'gender' as a term, in this chapter, refers to legal gender and so is gender recognition. Consequently, I shall not be using terms such as 'legal gender' or 'legal gender recognition' or 'gender recognition in law' as the reference to the law becomes otiose. This chapter is concerned with legal issues related to gender, even though gender raises non-legal questions such as whether an individual psychologically or self-identified to be of one gender or another, and whether such gender is socially accepted or not. As the need for comprehensive gender recognition for all legal purposes is a nascent awareness, the term 'gender recognition', when used, may be a reference to limited areas only, e.g. in the context of a transgender person's ability to marry in his or her acquired gender. However, it may also be a reference to a person's ability to obtain a new Hong Kong identity card. Other terminology used in this chapter follows closely those used in the Court of Final Appeal's decision, for instance, the term 'male-to-female transsexual person' and 'sex reassignment surgery

13 CFA, para. 123.
14 CFA, paras. 11, 17, 18, 94.
15 CFA, para. 51.
16 Ibid.
17 R. Emerton, 'Neither Here nor There: the Current Status of Transsexual and Other Transgender Persons under Hong Kong Law' (2004) 34 *HKLJ* 245.

(SRS)', although sometimes reference is also made to male-to-female transgender person, transgender person or transgender community and surgical or medical intervention more generally. The primary reason for doing so is that this chapter does not wish to embark on discussion as to what may be the more preferred (or more appropriate) terms, a topic which should be explored elsewhere. Thus, for the sake of convenience and clarity, I follow the terms used in the Court of Final Appeal's decision. Adhering to them also helps to shed light on the stage of legal development in Hong Kong on the question of gender awareness.

This chapter examines some of the immediate impacts of *W*'s case, highlights some of the legal challenges ahead and argues that comprehensive law reform is the only way to ensure the full integration of a post-operative transgender individual into the law. An example of comprehensive law reform is the United Kingdom's Gender Recognition Act 2004. Section 9(1) of the Gender Recognition Act 2004 stipulates that:

> 'Where a full gender recognition certificate is issued to a person, the person's gender becomes for all purposes the acquired gender (so that, if the acquired gender is the male gender, the person's sex becomes that of a man and, if it is the female gender, the person's sex becomes that of a woman).'

For Hong Kong, gender recognition resembling the Gender Recognition Act remains a journey to be undertaken. The reason why the Gender Recognition Act is mentioned here are twofold, first because Hong Kong's legal developments has traditionally been linked to the UK, and second, it is expressly mentioned by the Court of Final Appeal's decision. Although it covers only post-operative transgender persons, there is no reason why gender recognition should not be extended to pre-operative transgender persons.

1.2. HEALTH INSURANCE

There is no universal health insurance in Hong Kong. The majority of the population rely on the relatively inexpensive government funded medical service provided in public hospitals managed by the Hospital Authority.[18] The Hospital Authority offers a limited service for the treatment of gender identity disorder (GID).

Private health care operates in tandem with the government publicly funded medical service; however, private health care insurance may not cover the treatment of GID. For instance, the HSBC Hospital Insurance plan excludes

[18] Hospital Authority Ordinance (Cap 113).

'psychiatric condition'.[19] Consequently, a person seeking treatment for GID or looking to access SRS must either rely on the medical service provided in public hospitals or self-finance treatment locally or overseas.

1.3. STATISTICAL INFORMATION

In *W v Registrar of Marriages*, the Court noted that medical treatments were first made available to transgender persons in Hong Kong in 1980. The services were initially provided at Queen Mary Hospital, which was a public institution. The first documented surgical intervention was performed in 1981.[20]

Hong Kong medical professionals adopt the DSM-IV[21] as the diagnostic criteria for GID. However, there is no systematic collection of statistical information regarding the prevalence of GID (*i.e.* how many people have been diagnosed, how many have undergone SRS in government hospitals since 1981, and/or how many people have obtained a replacement identity card, etc.). According to Eleanor Cheung, 'between 1991 and 2001, 34 cases were referred for assessment relating to Gender Reassignment Surgery, and 28 of them were found to fulfil the DSM-IV diagnostic criteria for transsexual.'[22] The Court of Final Appeal writes that:

> 'From 1 October 2007 to 30 September 2009, there were 86 patients diagnosed with gender identity disorder. From January 2006 to September 2009, 18 patients underwent SRS in hospitals managed by the Hospital Authority. The practice is to confine SRS to persons who are at least 21 years old. The whole treatment, including SRS, is publicly funded. It has been suggested that "many more have undergone surgery privately, both in Hong Kong and, more commonly, overseas."'[23]

Recently, the Ming Pao Daily News reported that, as of February 2007, Dr Yuen Wai Cheung Albert, the Chief of the Department of Surgery at Ruttonjee Hospital, was the only doctor who conducted SRS in Hong Kong public hospitals. However, the Ruttonjee Hospital lacked sufficient facilities and staff for conducting such interventions.[24]

---

19 Clause 7 in Part 3 of the HSBC Hospital Insurance Policy, see <https://www.hsbc.com.hk/1/2/hk/insurance/health/hospital> accessed 28.03.2015.

20 CFA, para. 15.

21 Diagnostic and Statistical Manual of Mental Disorders (DSM I-V) <http://allpsych.com/disorders/dsm/#.VRZP2TuUdfY> accessed 28.03.2015. Its fifth edition was published in May 2013.

22 E. Cheung, 'GID in Hong Kong: A Critical Overview of Medical Treatments for Transsexual Patients' in C. Yau (ed.), *As Normal as Possible: Negotiating Sexuality and Gender in Mainland China and Hong Kong*, Hong Kong University Press, Hong Kong 2010.

23 CFA, para. 15.

24 袁維昌為病人圓變性願, *Ming Pao Daily News*, <www.mingpaohealth.com/cfm/news3.cfm?File=20070226/news/gwm3.txt> accessed 14.01.2014.

Another local Chinese newspaper reported that, as of 6 October 2010, there were approximately 200 transgender people in Hong Kong.[25] Dr Yuen Wai Cheung Albert has performed more than 60 SRS surgeries over the years. Around 20–30 people per annum seek surgical intervention in Hong Kong's public hospitals. However, only two to three procedures are actually performed each year. Those who cannot wait may undergo surgery in either private hospitals or overseas. In Thailand, for instances, surgery reportedly costs about HK$100,000.[26] According to another source, 26 patients had surgery in the Hospital Authority during the period 2005–2006 and 2009–2010.[27] The South China Morning Post noted that in Hong Kong, 'women undergoing sex change operations to become men now outnumber men wanting to become women.'[28]

The Transgender Resource Centre[29] suggests that the total number of people obtaining a replacement identity card showing their acquired gender is minimal. For instance, between January 1994 and June 2002 the Immigration Department received only 27 applications:

> 'According to the Director for Immigration, 27 applications were received from TSs [transsexuals] wishing to amend the details on their identity cards between January 1994 and June 2002. 12 of these applications were from MtF TSs, and 15 from FtM TSs. All applications were approved, and replacement identity cards issued.'[30]

Other figures show that in the years 2000–2012, the Immigration Department approved 72 requests for recognition of acquired gender.[31]

The fragmented statistics above suggest that those who seek recognition of their acquired gender represent a small proportion of the population. No doubt there is a need to systematically collect basic vital information to better understand the full scope of Hong Kong's transgender community, and to plan, manage and deliver services which address that community's needs.

---

25 年約30人要求做手術, 律敦治為逾60人變性, Hong Kong Daily News 新報, <www.hkdailynews.com.hk/news.php?id=125511>.

26 Ibid.

27 See <www.cmab.gov.hk/en/images/issues/22_12_10/SMFpaper3-2010.pdf> accessed 17.06.2013. Additionally, data from Now TV news in 2013: "醫管局表示，過去五個年度完成了16宗變性手術。而醫管局每年大約接獲五十多宗個案，要求改變性別。有精神科醫生指，要評估大約兩年才能判斷病人是否適合做變性手術。", see <http://news.now.com/home/local/player?newsId=67780> accessed 17.06.2013.

28 <www.scmp.com/news/hong-kong/article/1120895/sex-change-patients-getting-younger-and-are-more-likely-be-women> accessed 08.07.2013.

29 It is the leading Hong Kong Transgender NGO promoting a better societal understanding of transgender issues, see <www.tgr.org.hk/tgr.org.hk/index.php?option=com_content&view=article&id=1&Itemid=3&lang=en> accessed 14.01.2014.

30 See <www.transgenderasia.org/country_report_hk_legal.htm>accessed 14.01.2014.

31 See <http://orientaldaily.on.cc/cnt/news/20130514/00176_016.html> accessed 17.06.2013.

II. CHANGING LEGAL GENDER – PROCEDURE AND REQUIREMENTS

Unlike the Gender Recognition Act 2004 in the UK, there is currently no specific set of rules called 'gender recognition rules' in Hong Kong. As such it is difficult to outline the procedure or requirements of gender recognition. However, as can be seen in the Court of Final Appeal's decision, a person who has completed SRS is able to obtain:

- from the doctor who performs the surgery a certificate that the person's 'gender has been changed',[32] and
- a replacement identity card.

The identity card is a legal document issued by the Commissioner of Registration.[33] It is one of the most important, as well as the most often used, identity documents. It includes details such as the holder's name (in both Chinese and English), date of birth, sex, and information relating to place of birth.[34] Section 17C(1) and (3) of the Immigration Ordinance (Cap. 115) requires any persons aged 15 years or over, who is a holder of an identity card, to carry it with him or her at all times. It is an offence to fail to produce proof of identity on demand to a police officer or immigration officer, although in practice prosecutions for such an offence have not been pursued. A police officer has the power to stop, detain and search and ask for the identity card of a person who acts in a suspicious manner, whom he reasonably suspects of having committed, being about to commit or intending to commit any offence.[35] Additionally, an identity card is often used as proof of a person's identity when one interacts with governmental and non-governmental organisations, such as entering and leaving Hong Kong via immigration control points, booking leisure and sporting facilities, using bank or public library facilities, and admission into hospitals.

2.1. LEGAL PROCEDURE

The current practice of the Director of Immigration[36] is to accept a letter from the Hospital Authority certifying that a person's gender has been changed as a result of SRS. This letter is used, *inter alia*, for issuing a replacement identity card (as well as a passport) which reflects a person's acquired gender.[37] The Director of

32 CFA, para. 19.
33 Section 17B, Immigration Ordinance (Cap 115).
34 <www.gov.hk/en/residents/immigration/idcard/hkic/smartid.htm>.
35 Section 54, Police Force Ordinance (Cap 232).
36 Acting as the Commissioner of Registration under the Registration of Persons Ordinance.
37 CFA, paras. 16 and 17.

Immigration also accepts certificates where the surgical intervention has taken place privately, whether locally or overseas.[38]

The legal basis for a post-operative transgender person to obtain a replacement identity card is in the Registration of Persons Ordinance (RPO) (Cap. 177). Currently, a person holding a Hong Kong identity card issued under the RPO *must* report to the Immigration Department when the submitted particulars in the identity card have become incorrect. This can be done under the Registration of Persons Regulations (RPR) by filling in an application form and sending it to the Registration of Persons Office. Upon receipt of an application, that office requires the applicant to attend an interview and produce originals of the relevant supporting documents.[39] Regulations 14 to 18 deal with amending the registered particulars of an identity card. Regulation 14(1) states:

> '(1) Subject to subregulations (2) and (6), a holder of an identity card may apply to a registration officer –
> (a) for alteration of that card;'

Regulation 14(2) states:

> '(2) The registration officer shall only issue a replacement identity card –
> (a) …
> (b) after the production of such evidence, under oath or otherwise as he may require; and
> (c) after such investigation as he may consider necessary.'

In short, the registration officer shall only issue a replacement identity card after the production of 'such evidence, under oath or otherwise' and this underpins the current practice (as mentioned earlier above) of the Director of Immigration to accept a letter from the Hospital Authority, certifying that a person has completed SRS, as a basis for issuing a replacement identity card and passport.[40] Unlike the requirement under the Gender Recognition Act 2004, only one medical certificate is required.[41]

Regulation 18(1)(a) provides that where particulars of an identity card have become incorrect (e.g. as in the case of a person who has completed SRS and obtained a medical certificate, affirming alteration to the person's sex characteristics), this has to reported. Under Regulation 19(1), failure to report corrections as required by Regulation 18 is an offence. To that extent, there

38 CFA, para. 17.
39 See <www.gov.hk/en/residents/immigration/idcard/hkic/faq_hkic.htm#arp> accessed 17.06.2013.
40 CFA, para. 16.
41 See <www.gov.hk/en/residents/immigration/idcard/hkic/faq_hkic.htm#arp> accessed 17.06.2013.

is a legal obligation on post-operative transgender persons to report for the correction of their gender designation. Appeals against a decision of the Director of Immigration under the Registration of Persons Ordinance do not fall within the ambit of the Administrative Appeals Board Ordinance, so the only way to challenge a refusal to issue a replacement identity card is by way of judicial review.

In light of the current practice, and even prior to the Court of Final Appeal's decision in *W*, one might have safely assumed that obtaining an updated identity card is the only mechanism for gender recognition. However, in view of the Court of Final Appeal's decision, there appears to be an alternative mechanism for gender recognition. This is so because the Court of Final Appeal held that the meaning of the words 'woman' and 'female' are to be read to include 'a post-operative male-to-female transsexual person whose gender has been certified by an appropriate medical authority to have changed'[42] as a result of SRS. In other words, where a post-operative transgender person undergoes medical treatment and, as a result, obtains a certificate affirming a gender change (but has yet to obtain a replacement identity card) must be treated as having her acquired gender, at least for the purposes of marriage.

The challenges ahead must be to identify a single mechanism for gender recognition, as well as a point in time when a person's acquired gender will be comprehensively recognised in law, as it would be undesirable for a post-operative male-to-female transgender person to be regarded as a woman for the purposes of marriage and using public conveniences, and yet continue to be treated as having a male gender for the purpose of sexual offences in criminal law.

2.2. OFFICIAL DOCUMENTS

As mentioned above, a person who has obtained a medical certificate that the person's gender has changed must report for a correction of his or her gender marker on the identity card and passport.[43] Other government related documents are less of an issue; for instance, a Hong Kong driver's licence does not include information regarding gender.[44]

School reports or educational certificates can be important for job applications. In *W v Registrar of Marriages,* Ms W was successful in changing her gender to 'female' for all records from those education institutions in which she had studied.[45] Other examination certificates (the Hong Kong Certificate of Education Examination, the Hong Kong Advanced Level Examination and the Hong Kong Diploma of Secondary Education Examination) are issued by the Hong Kong

42 CFA, para. 150.
43 CFA, para. 94.
44 CFA, para. 135.
45 [2010] 6 HKC 359, para. 43.

Examination and Assessment Authority.[46] They contain the candidate's name, but not their gender. It is not possible for a certificate to be reissued, but a Statement of Results, having the same effect as a certificate, may be issued.[47] A person's Hong Kong birth certificate, containing information regarding the gender assigned to a person at birth, issued under the Birth and Death Registration Ordinance (Cap. 174) cannot be changed, as it records a historical fact.[48]

Another important travel document which many Hong Kong residents use is the 'Mainland Travel Permit for Hong Kong and Macau Residents' (sometimes called the 'Home Return Permit' 港澳居民來往內地通行證 或 回鄉證). It contains information on a person's 'sex' or 'gender' (性別). This document is issued by the Guangdong Provincial Public Security Department (廣東省公安廳) on behalf of the Ministry of Public Security of the People's Republic of China (中華人民共和國公安部),[49] not by the Hong Kong SAR.

2.3. LEGAL AND NON-LEGAL REQUIREMENTS

Currently, there are no legal requirements, although there are two non-legal (medical) requirements, a person must meet prior to undergoing treatment for GID or surgery. The first is the 'real life experience' test, which was explained in the Court of Final Appeal's decision as follows:

> 'the management of persons with the relevant symptoms begins with a full psychiatric assessment. If the diagnosis of gender identity disorder is confirmed, the patient is usually required to go through a "real life experience", living in the preferred gender for about two years while having hormones of the opposite sex administered to produce reversible physical changes in the body and to ease the patient's psychological discomfort. If it appears from this process that the patient can successfully live as a person of the opposite sex, he or she is considered medically eligible for sex reassignment surgery.'[50]

Second, as a matter of medical policy, a person accessing treatment or surgery must be at least 21 years of age.[51] This medical policy may be challenged on the basis that it is an arbitrary and unreasonable limitation on access on the grounds that, it is not based on the ability of a person to offer a valid consent to the surgery, and it only prejudices those who cannot afford surgery elsewhere (*i.e.* those who can afford it may have surgery overseas before the age of 21). What surgical

46 The Hong Kong Examinations and Assessment Authority Ordinance (Cap. 261).
47 <www.hkeaa.edu.hk/en/our_services/cert/sor_app/#1> accessed 28.03.2015.
48 CFA, para. 17.
49 <www.mps.gov.cn/n16/n1237/n1342/n803715/3488130.html> accessed 28.03.2015.
50 CFA, para. 11.
51 CFA, para. 15.

interventions involve, and their aims, has been explained by Dr Albert Yuen Wai Cheung, Consultant Surgeon and Chief of Surgical Service of Ruttonjee Hospital of the Hospital Authority, who gave evidence in *W*'s case. Dr Yuen Wai Cheung stated that:

> 'For male-to-female transsexual surgery, breast augmentation is done for patients whom the breast enlargement after hormone treatment is not sufficient for comfort in the social gender role. Genital surgery includes at least orchidectomy (removal of both testes), penectomy (removal of penis), creation of a new vagina. The new vagina enables penetration of penis during sexual intercourse. There is preservation of erotic sexual sensation. However, surgery cannot remove the prostate organ or provide a functional uterus or ovaries, or otherwise establish fertility or child bearing ability. Neither can it change the sex chromosomes of the person, which remains that of a male ("XY").
>
> For female-to-male transsexual surgery, the female breasts would be removed. The uterus, ovaries and vagina are removed. Construction of some form of penis is performed. There are different ways of constructing the penis, depending on the desire of person who would balance the risk of physical injuries inflicted on one's body due to the surgery with the benefits. The form of penis construction ranges from an elongation of patient's clitoris (metoidioplasty), raising an abdominal skin tube flap to mimic a penis, to the micro-vascular transfer of tissue from other parts of body to perineum to have a full construction of a penis inside which there is a passage for urine. The best outcome at present is that after surgery, the person can void urine while standing and can have a rigid penis which means it is rigid all the time, as opposed to an erected penis which is flaccid normally but becomes rigid when sexually aroused. However, the new penis, even fully constructed, cannot ejaculate or erect on stimulation, although it will not affect the person's ability to have sexual intercourse and the person can still penetrate a vagina and have sensation in the penis and achieve orgasm because the clitoris and its nerve endings are preserved. The person cannot be provided with prostate (a male sex organ which secretes prostatic fluid which when combined with sperms produced by the testes forms the semen; a female does not have such an organ) or any functioning testes and will have no ability to produce semen, to reproduce or otherwise to impregnate a female. The sex chromosomes also remain those of a female ("XX").'[52]

Apart from the 'real life experience' test and the age requirement, there is currently no legal pre-condition for obtaining GID treatment or accessing surgery. Thus, the law does not prohibit surgery being performed on a married person; nor does it prohibit surgery performed on someone under 21 years old. As mentioned earlier, the only legal obligation imposed on a post-operative transgender person is to apply for a replacement identity card (as the information stated therein has now become incorrect). However, as there is no requirement that individuals who

[52] CFA, para. 13.

seek a replacement identity card must be unmarried or have reached 21 years old. The implication of this will be discussed below.

III. CONSEQUENCES OF THE CHANGE OF LEGAL GENDER

Even prior to the Court of Final Appeal's decision, a post-operative transgender person (like Ms W) who had been issued with a replacement identity card was recognised as having their acquired gender 'for a whole range of purposes'.[53]

After the Court of Final Appeal's decision, a post-operative transgender person can now marry in his or her acquired gender to a person of the opposite gender. The Court recognised that difficult issues could arise from its watershed decision and that addressing them would involve striking a balance between 'the rights of transsexual persons and the rights of others who may be affected by recognition of the gender change'.[54] In view of this, it allowed the Government and the Legislature time to consider enacting a new law to address those issues by suspending, for 12 months, the operation of its Orders.[55] Thus, in accordance with the Court's decision, Ms W (a transgender woman) became entitled to marry her male partner from 16 July 2014, without awaiting any further action on the part of the Government.[56]

IV. LEGAL CHALLENGES OF THE EXISTING RULES

4.1. GENDER RECOGNITION – TIME AND MECHANISM

Although the Court of Final Appeal's decision in *W v Registrar of Marriages* is limited to gender recognition for the purpose of marriage, one immediate legal question arises: the time of gender recognition and whether this is linked with the gender recognition mechanism.

Prior to the Court of Final Appeal's decision, it was possible to rely upon the gender marker in a person's identity card. However, as the Court of Final Appeal held that the words 'woman' and 'female' include a post-operative male-to-female transgender person whose gender has been certified by an appropriate medical authority to have changed as a result of SRS, there appears now two separate (and alternative) points in time and mechanism for gender recognition (at least for the purpose of marriage). The first point is the time of medical certification. The second point is under the replacement identity card. To ensure uniformity, it is

[53] CFA, para. 94.
[54] CFA, para. 128.
[55] Ibid.
[56] CFA, para. 148.

argued here that obtaining a replacement identity card (currently issued based on medical certification) should be the only mechanism, as well as point in time, for recognition of an individual's acquired gender.

One argument in favour of relying on the medical certificate as the basis for recognition of an individual's acquired gender may be that an individual, such as Ms W, should have the right to decide, subsequent to surgery, whether she desires her acquired gender to appear on her identity card. However, this approach is likely to be problematic. Putting aside the point that failure to report for correction when particulars of an identity card have become incorrect is an offence, the suggestion that a transgender woman may continue to use an official document containing information inconsistent with her social gender means possible confusion to others. Although social inconveniences and confusion may not be a matter that concerns the law, to the extent that the identity card is an official document of a person's identity, the information stated therein must be treated as *prima facie* accurate, and could safely be relied upon by those dealing with the holder.[57] This is true as a principle of general application, and there is no cogent reason why a sector of the transgender people may justifiably be treated differently.

Apart from these two questions, the Court of Final Appeal mentioned two additional legal challenges which would benefit from legislative intervention: first, the question of who qualifies as a 'woman' or a 'man' for marriage, and second, who qualifies as a 'woman' or a 'man' for other purposes.[58] The Court of Final Appeal made clear that should no legislation reform be forthcoming, it could deal with cases as they arise and this would not 'pose insuperable difficulties':

> 'If such legislation does not eventuate, it would fall to the Courts, applying constitutional principles, statutory provisions and the rules of common law, to decide questions regarding the implications of recognizing an individual's acquired gender for marriage purposes as and when any disputed questions arise.'[59]

The remaining part of this chapter explores some of the legal ramifications of gender recognition beyond a transgender person's right to enter into a marriage. Some of these legal challenges, as the Court of Final Appeal's decision acknowledges, may require legislative intervention.

57 See Clause 3 of the Marriage (Amendment) Bill 2014.
58 CFA, paras. 127–146.
59 CFA, para. 147.

4.2. MARRIAGE

Hong Kong law does not permit same-sex marriage, nor does it allow civil partnerships (an example of this being the UK's Civil Partnership Act 2004). In short, marriage remains a heterosexual legal institution.[60] This is an important starting point as transgender persons raise legal issues which at some level can (and need to) be distinguished from those raised by same-sex marriage.

4.2.1. Who Qualifies for Marriage and Where to Draw the Line?

The Court of Final Appeal rejected the *Corbett* criteria on the grounds that they are incomplete as they ignore the 'psychological, post-operative and social dimensions of the transsexual person's sexual identity viewed at the time of the proposed marriage'.[61] The Court held that, in deciding whether Ms W qualifies as a 'woman' for marriage, the law ought, in principle, to consider all the circumstances – biological, psychological, medical and social – relevant to assessing that individual's sexual identity at the time of the proposed marriage.[62] As Ms W had completed a full SRS, it was held to suffice for her to be regarded as a woman in law.

The Court, however, went further and indicated that something less than full surgical intervention may suffice.[63] Thus, as the Court wrote, a person whose 'original genital organs have been removed and some form of the genital organs of the opposite sex have been constructed' ought also to qualify for marriage.[64] This is particularly relevant for female-to-male transgender men who have not

60 In the United Kingdom, the Civil Partnership Act 2004 came into force with effect from 5 December 2005. It permits two persons of the same sex to register their relationship in accordance with the Civil Partnership Act 2004. The Marriage (Same Sex Couples) Act 2013 allows same sex marriage. France, a predominately Catholic country has also recently allowed same-sex marriage, see <http://edition.cnn.com/2013/05/18/world/europe/france-same-sex-marriage> accessed 15.07.2013. New Zealand also allows for same-sex marriage, see the Marriage (Definition of Marriage) Amendment Bill which will come into effect on 19 August 2013 <www.legislation.govt.nz/act/public/2013/0020/latest/DLM4505003.html?search=qs_act%40bill%40regulation%40deemedreg_Marriage+(Definition+of+Marriage)+Amendment+Bill_resel_25_y&p=1> accessed 15.07.2013. The US Supreme Court has struck down the Defense of Marriage Act (also known as Doma) denying federal benefits to gay as it discriminated against same-sex couples, see <www.bbc.co.uk/news/world-us-canada-23068454> accessed 15.07.2013.

61 CFA, para. 90.

62 CFA, para. 103. See also CFA, para. 118 where the court said: 'the Corbett criteria are incomplete in that they are limited to a person's biological features existing at the time of birth and treated as immutable. They ignore the psychological and social elements of a person's sexual identity and ignore any sex reassignment treatment that has occurred. As such, they do not permit a full and appropriate assessment of the sexual identity of a person to be made for the purposes of determining whether he or she has the right to marry. In adopting such restrictive criteria, the provisions are inconsistent with and fail to give proper effect to the constitutional right to marry. They are therefore unconstitutional.'

63 CFA, para. 137.

64 CFA, para. 125.

had phalloplasty (surgery for the construction of a phallus (penis)), but instead, a lesser form of surgery involving the elongation of the clitoris (metoidioplasty) as mentioned in Dr Yuen's evidence above. Requiring full surgery (that is, phalloplasty in the case of female-to-male transgender persons) can be seen as inappropriate because of the medical costs involved or the risks surgery poses to the individual (in view of the current state of surgical techniques and the associated medical complications). Furthermore, some patients may not wish to have the reconstruction surgery.

However, if the requirement is that *some form* of construction of the genital organs is needed, this may exclude a person like *Re Kevin*.[65] In *Re Kevin*, a leading Australian case on the right of transgender person's to marry, the High Court of Australia placed less importance on the need for some form of reconstructive surgery and greater importance on the psychological and social dimensions of a person's sexual identity.

It might be interesting to reflect on this discussion in *W*'s case. Although the Court of Final Appeal appears to be focusing solely on genitalia as possible qualifications for entering into marriage, it is also signalling clearly that the emphasis on the biological (*Corbett* criteria) should be discarded and that the validity of a marriage for the purpose of a void marriage being unrelated to the ability of a person to consummate a marriage. In view of the emphasis of placing more weight on the psychological, medical and social, genitalia ought to have a lesser role to play in defining a person's gender in the future. Thus, it is appropriate to move away from using surgery as the sole criterion for gender recognition. Instead, other more flexible criteria similar to those employed in the Gender Recognition Act 2004 (*i.e.* a person has lived in the acquired gender for a certain period of time) should be adopted.

4.2.2. Non-Disclosure of Gender History

One potentially controversial issue is whether a prospective transgender spouse (qualify to marry) must disclose his or her gender history to a partner prior to marriage, and failing which some remedy should at least be available to an innocent party. In Hong Kong, there is no relevant legal provision offering a remedy to such an innocent spouse in the law of nullity. In the UK, section 12(h) of the English Matrimonial Causes Act 1973[66] provides that non-disclosure of gender history by a party to a marriage is a ground for voiding a marriage. This means that if at the time of a marriage a party did not know that the other had obtained gender recognition, that party may seek an annulment. This stipulation suggests that despite the relatively generous and comprehensive approach taken

65 (2001) 165 FLR 404; available at <www.wallbanks.com/PDF/Re%20Kevin_ChisholmDecision.pdf> accessed 15.07.2013.

66 Schedule 4, Part 1, paras. 4 and 5.

by the Gender Recognition Act 2004, non-disclosure of gender history amounts to a profound breach of trust, striking at the heart of a marriage.[67] This may be true. However, it raises the question as to whether remedies should equally be available for other profound breaches of trust, e.g. non-disclosure of criminal history, drug addiction and other social vices, or whether gender identity should be singled out for special attention.[68]

4.2.3. *Gender Recognition of a Married Person*

Where a married person undergoes SRS and obtains gender recognition, this results in the spouses becoming party to a same-sex marriage (*i.e.* post gender recognition, a husband has a female gender so that there are now two females within the marriage). In Hong Kong, anecdotal evidence suggests there are transgender women who are the husbands of their spouse, and transgender men who are the wives of their husbands.[69] This is one of the immediate legal challenges raised by the Court of Final Appeal's decision.

In the United Kingdom (see the England and Wales chapter in this collection for full details), the Gender Recognition Act 2004 originally avoided same-sex marriages through the requirement that a transgender person should first annul the marriage (thereby becoming single again) before obtaining gender recognition. To achieve this, the Gender Recognition Act provided that only an interim Gender Recognition Certificate could have been issued to a married transgender person. The effect of an interim Gender Recognition Certificate allowed either party to the marriage to seek an annulment of their existing marriage. After annulment, the same parties could register to be civil partners, if they so wished. This solution required transgender persons to choose between either maintaining an existing marriage or obtaining recognition of their acquired gender.[70]

67 In *ST (formerly J) v J* [1998] 1 All ER 431, the defendant was born a female, and at the age of 27, he underwent a partial sex change (consisting of hormone injections and a bilateral mastectomy). He went through a ceremony of marriage with the plaintiff (the wife), without informing her of his gender history, describing himself as a bachelor and declared that there was no lawful impediment to the marriage. The wife did not discover the defendant's female gender until his birth certificate was produced in divorce proceedings (17 years later). The wife obtained a decree of nullity on the ground that the parties were not 'respectively male and female'. Following the decree of nullity, the defendant applied for ancillary relief. The wife argued that he should be debarred from pursuing his claim on the grounds that it was contrary to public policy. The trial judge found that the defendant was guilty of perjury and that his claim for ancillary relief was barred in limine, as the court would not allow a person to profit from his own serious crime. The defendant's appeal was also dismissed.

68 Here lies the irony that while criminal activity and social vice may be issues society attaches negative connotations, there is no requirement to disclose, yet a person who obtains gender recognition, which both society and the law perceives as an individual's basic rights must disclose.

69 KTCC65661/13.

70 Today the Marriage (Same Sex Couples) Act 2013 makes same sex marriage is available. A transgender person gaining gender recognition is not required to terminate an existing marriage.

An alternative (and a more preferable) approach is to decouple gender recognition from marriage status (that is, a person ought not to be required to choose between family life and gender identity). This approach does not necessarily conflict with our current law governing nullity or impinge upon the heterosexual nature of marriage. Applying the current law on nullity, the validity of an existing marriage is not affected by SRS of one spouse.[71] This is so because a proper application of the grounds upon which a marriage is void *ab initio* suggests that the point of time for the assessment of the genders of the parties would be the time they enter into the marriage, but not any time later.[72] Thus, surgical intervention during the subsistence of a marriage, followed by gender recognition, does not render the existing marriage void.

Although a married individual's gender recognition results in the parties (in a marital relationship) being the same gender, arguably this is different from permitting same-sex marriage. This is so because the debate concerning same-sex marriage has always been about whether persons of the same-sex at the time of marriage should be permitted to enter into marriage. Further, there may not be a strong enough case for refusing gender recognition to those who are married when such a refusal may be challenged on the basis that it creates a conflict between a person's right to family life and the right to establish one's sexual identity.[73]

4.3. OTHER GENDER-SPECIFIC TERMS AND RELATIONSHIPS

Apart from the questions of who qualifies to enter into a marriage, whether there needs to be disclosure of gender history and the impact of gender recognition to an existing marriage, gender recognition also raises other legal challenges. Some are easier to tackle than others. For instance, it may be argued that following the Court of Final Appeal's decision, words such as 'woman' or 'female' and 'man' or 'male', in the context other than marriage, should also be read to include a

[71] 'Members have expressed concern over the effect on the validity of the existing marriage if one of the parties to the marriage has received an SRS subsequently. The Administration has advised that based on the legal advice it has received, a marriage celebrated in accordance with the requirements under the MO shall not automatically become void solely on the ground that one of the parties to the marriage has subsequently received an SRS. But related parties can apply for dissolving the marriage if he or she or they wish to do so.' Hong Kong Legislative Council Official Record of Proceedings, Wednesday 22 October 2014, p. 709.

[72] Contrast the current wording of section 20(1)(d) of the Matrimonial Causes Ordinance which renders a marriage void *ab initio* where the parties 'are not respectively male and female' with an alternative provision stipulating that a marriage would be *voidable* on the ground that the parties 'are not respectively male and female'. In the latter case, SRS during marriage would be a ground for the marriage to be annulled, rendering the marriage void from the time of the decree of nullity.

[73] See A. Liu, 'Gender Recognition: Two Legal Implications for Marriage' (2013) 43 *HKLJ* 407.

transgender persons who have obtained gender recognition. As the Court of Final Appeal said, at paragraph 127:

> 'it is likely that in most cases, no difficulty will be encountered in applying gender-specific statutory and other legal provisions to a person whose gender change has been legally recognized. To take a relatively trivial example, a transsexual woman who previously used the men's toilet and changing facilities will now use such facilities reserved for women without breaking any laws regulating their use.'[74]

Putting aside the issue of a transgender person marrying in his or her acquired gender, this section discusses hypothetical situations of some potential impacts of the Court of Final Appeal's decision in context other than marriage (e.g. in domestic violence protection, succession, etc.). It demonstrates that spousal or other gender-specific relationships may need to be reinterpreted to include a transgender person prior to comprehensive law reform on gender recognition.

4.3.1. Gender-Specific Relationships such as 'Wife'/'Widow' Include Transgender Persons

Following the Court of Final Appeal's decision, gender-specific relationships such as 'wife' and 'husband' should arguably be read to include transgender persons. Thus, a transgender woman who has obtained recognition of her female gender (and entered into a marriage in her acquired gender) should come within the definition of 'wife'. Likewise, a transgender man who has obtained recognition of his male gender (and entered into a marriage in his acquired gender) should come within the definition of 'husband'.

In some instances, this is unlikely to be problematic. For instance, section 3 of the Domestic and Cohabitation Relationships Violence Ordinance (DCRVO) (Cap. 189) allows an application for an injunction against 'spouses'. This can cover a person assigned a male gender at birth, who subsequently obtains recognition of her acquired female gender and marries a male person. Their marital relationship will (after the decision in *W v Registrar of Marriages*) be covered by the current legal definition of 'spouse' and 'marriage' in the DCRVO. Both parties may seek remedies against domestic violence.

However, where a person obtains gender recognition during marriage, the question arises as to whether 'spouse' can be read to include persons of the same gender. Yet this difficulty may be ameliorated if existing legislation has already cast its scope widely, reaching beyond the conventional marital relationship, and covering cohabitees and those in same-sex relationships. Thus, suppose H (who has a male gender) and W (who has a female gender) marry. During their marriage, W obtains recognition of his male gender. W now seeks an injunction

[74] CFA, para. 127.

against H on account of domestic violence. As the parties' marriage continues to be valid, are the parties 'spouses', albeit of the same gender? Fortunately, the DCRVO covers not only 'spouses', but also opposite sex and same-sex cohabitants, thus the parties are also covered as same-sex cohabitants, even if they are not spouses. Another similarly widely drawn legislation is the Fatal Accident Ordinance (FAO) (Cap. 22). The FAO makes provisions for the compensation of 'dependants' of persons killed as a result of tortious acts. As it covers those in a marital relationship as well as 'dependants', any person (irrespective of gender) who was living with the deceased in the same household immediately before the date of his or her death is covered.[75]

Another legislative provision which may potentially be affected by the Court of Final Appeal's decision is section 4 of the Intestates' Estates Ordinance (IEO) (Cap. 73). The IEO makes provision for the distribution of intestates' estates. It covers spousal as well as other familial relationships. An example of the legal uncertainties may be: suppose H (who has a male gender) and W (who was assigned a male gender at birth and has obtained recognition of her female gender) marry. When H dies intestate (leaving no issue), normally W (his wife) becomes entitled. Following the Court of Final Appeal's decision, 'wife' should be interpreted to cover W. However, suppose H (who has a male gender) and W (who has a female gender) marry, and during their marriage W obtains recognition of his male gender. When H dies intestate (leaving no issue), does 'wife' include W? The uncertainty postulated here arises because the current IEO has delineated spousal relationships (in a traditional way) without regard to transgender identities. In view of the Court of Final Appeal's decision widening the current legal boundary (of spouse) by allowing a transgender person to marry, the corresponding narrowing of the exclusionary boundary (of spouse) may need to be drawn. Although a comprehensive redrawing of the boundary is not a matter for the Court, legislative reform may be necessary. In the interim, such a case may need to be dealt with sensitively, bearing in mind the spirit of the Court of Final Appeal's decision.

The same question arises with a word like 'widow' in the context of pension entitlements.[76] 'Widow' has always been used as a gender-specific term referring

---

[75] Section 2 FAO. For other examples, see also the Employee's Compensation Ordinance (Cap 282) which provides for the payment of compensation to employees injured in the course of their employment. It covers employees' 'members of the family' such as their spouse, cohabitee, and other family relationships.

[76] See *Secretary of Department of Social Security v SRA* [1993] FCA 573 where the Full Court of the Federal Court of Australia had to consider whether the respondent (SRA) was qualified under the Social Security Act 1947 (Cth) to receive a wife's pension as being a woman who was the wife of an invalid pensioner. SRA was born a male, but lived as a woman (without undergoing SRS). SRA lived with a male person as a *de facto* couple. Under the Act, married or *de facto* couples were eligible for a joint pension. The Full Court of the Federal Court of Australia (Black CJ, Lockhart and Heerey JJ) unanimously rejected SRA's claim to a wife's pension. Black CJ stated that it would be going well beyond the ordinary meaning of the words to conclude that a pre-operative transsexual, having male external genitalia, was a 'woman'

to a female person. Following the Court of Final Appeal's decision, it should now arguably be interpreted to include a transgender woman marrying a male person who has since passed away. Take section 22 of the Widows and Orphans Pension Ordinance (WOPO) (Cap. 94) as an example. It provides that the widow of a contributor is entitled to a pension upon death of the contributor, but that the pension shall cease upon the widow's death or her remarriage. Suppose H (who has a male gender) and W (who has a female gender but who was assigned a male gender at birth) marry. H, being a contributor and upon his death, W is entitled to a pension as H's widow. Furthermore, if W marries another man, her entitlement ceases.

However, does 'widow' include a transgender man who obtains recognition of his male gender during a marriage? Suppose H (who has a male gender) and W (who has a female gender) marry, and during their marriage, W obtains recognition of his male gender. Following H's death, will W be entitled to receive a pension as H's 'widow'? Hardship would arise if SRS and gender recognition deprives W of a pension H has contributed to for the benefit of the other spouse. Again, in the absence of legislative reform, the court may need to intervene.

An extended reading of the Court of Final Appeal's decision, beyond the question of the right to marry, such that a transgender person be read to come within the definition of 'spouse', the terms 'wife' and 'husband' are likely to be inappropriate in other statutes. For instance, section 2 of the Mandatory Provident Fund Schemes Ordinance (MPFSO) (Cap. 485) defines 'spouse' to include 'a person of the opposite sex with whom the person is cohabiting in a bona fide domestic relationship as man and wife'. This juxtaposition of opposite-gender relationships is unlikely to be read to cover parties in a *de facto* same-sex marriage. Thus, suppose A (who has a male gender) marries B (who has a female gender). Where B obtains recognition of his male identity during marriage, B would not qualify as a 'spouse' because his gender is not of the 'opposite sex' as compared to A.

4.3.2. Do Familial Relationship, such as Mother and Daughter, Include Transgender Persons?

If the word 'wife' or 'widow' may sometimes be read to include transgender persons, may other familial relationships (such as mother/daughter/niece) be similarly read? Although 'parent' is a gender-neutral term, 'father' connotes a male gender and 'mother' connotes a female gender. A question may arise as to whether a person who obtains the recognition of his male gender may be registered as a father. This can be seen in the case of *X, Y and Z v United*

---

and be regarded as a 'wife'. In other words, the Court would have been prepared to hold that SRA qualified for pension had she successfully undergone the surgery recommended to her.

Kingdom[77] (a decision prior to the Gender Recognition Act 2004). In *X, Y and Z v United Kingdom,* X had been assigned a female gender at birth and subsequently underwent gender confirmation surgery. X lived with his female partner, Y. They received assisted reproductive treatment services together, and Z was born after Y received donor insemination. However, X could not be registered as Z's father on the birth certificate.[78] The applicants (X, Y and Z) all alleged that the refusal amounted to a violation of Article 8 of the European Convention on Human Rights (ECHR). The European Court of Human Rights unanimously held that although Article 8 ECHR was engaged because 'family life' covered *de facto* parent–child relationships, there was no violation of parental rights of the transgender person.[79]

Apart from registration of parent–child relationships by way of entry in a child's birth certificate, are parental rights and authority, which have always been delineated in a gender-specific manner, affected by gender recognition? This can be seen in the following example. Suppose H (who has a male gender) and W (who has a female gender) marry and C was born to the couple. W then underwent surgical treatment and obtains recognition of his male gender. Do W's parental rights and authority continue post-gender recognition? There is no reason why a person's parental rights and authority should, by reason of surgery or gender recognition, be adversely affected.[80] In the UK, section 12 of the Gender Recognition Act 2004 provides for the continuity of existing parental rights and responsibilities. That means that obtaining gender recognition does not affect the status of a person as father or mother of a child. This also means that C's birth registration need not be altered to reflect the fact that W has obtained recognition. This must be correct, as a child's need for the care of the parent (irrespective of gender) has not changed.

Other familial relationships affected as a result of W obtaining recognition of his male gender (in the scenario above) include succession, e.g. will W be entitled to inherit under the parents' testamentary disposition as a male or female person? This remains to be dealt with by the law to ensure that a transgender person is not left in legal limbo.

---

77 App. No. 21830/93, 24 EHRR 143 (1997).

78 The important point here is decision that the word 'father' under section 28(3) of the HFEA 1990 is restricted to a biological male and hence excluding someone born a female person.

79 The European Court reasoned that the Contracting States had no generally shared approach on this point: see para. 52.

80 See however the distinction between a 'parent' and a person who is not a parent but with 'parental responsibility'. A good example of the latter is a grandparent with parental responsibility. This can be seen in *T v B* [2011] 1 All ER 77, a case concerning a lesbian couple (and similar issues can arise in relation to transsexual persons). In *T v B*, T gave birth to a child (C) after donor insemination. Both parties performed the role of C's parents. Following their separation, the court made a shared residence order. T sought child support. However, under the Children Act 1989, an order for financial relief could only be made against a 'parent' and B argued that she was not a 'parent' on the grounds that she was not a biological parent, despite the fact that she had obtained a shared resident order (and acquired parental responsibility).

4.3.3. Gender-Specific Offences: Law Reform Recommended Already

Although the Court of Final Appeal suggests that no difficulty will be encountered in applying gender-specific provisions to a person arising from gender recognition, gender-specific offences, such as rape,[81] would benefit from specific legislative reform.

A case involving a post-operative transgender person committing a gender-specific offence, or being a victim of the same, has never been decided in Hong Kong. There are two potential problems with the existing law. First, should a post-operative transgender person be regarded as a person of their acquired gender? Second, to what extent does the *obiter* in *Corbett* – that a person with an artificial vagina is legally incapable of sexual intercourse – remain part of the law today?

As regards the first point, the Court of Final Appeal rejected the *Corbett* criteria only for the purpose of determining a person's gender in the context of marriage. What needs to be clarified is that the *Corbett* criteria would also be inapplicable to gender-specific crimes such as rape. The need to clarify this point can be seen in the English Court of Appeal's decision which extended the *Corbett* criteria in *R v Tan*. *R v Tan* involved Gloria (the defendant), who was assigned a male gender at birth but who had subsequently undergone hormonal and gender confirmation treatments, consisting of the removal of the external male organs and the creation of an artificial vagina.[82] As a post-operative male-to-female transsexual, she was convicted of living on the earnings of prostitution (an offence which could only be committed by a male person).[83] Brian (another defendant, a male person) was convicted of living on the earnings of Gloria's male prostitution.[84] Both defendants appealed against their convictions. It was submitted on behalf of both that Gloria was not a man, and hence, neither could be so convicted. The Court of Appeal held that, applying the *Corbett* criteria, Gloria remained a male.

In view of the Court of Final Appeal's rejection of the *Corbett* criteria, the Hong Kong courts should, if the point arises, also refuse to follow *R v Tan*. This would mean that a post-operative male-to-female transgender person would be treated as having a female gender and could be the victim of a gender-specific offence such as rape. Similarly, a post-operative female-to-male transgender person would be treated as having a male gender and could be capable of committing rape.

---

81 For example, under section 118 of the Crimes Ordinance (Cap 200), the offence of rape is committed by a man against a woman. Under sections 47 and 48, the offence of incest is committed between a man and a woman.

82 [1983] QB 1053, page 1063.

83 Section 30(1) of the Sexual Offence Act 1956 provided that it is an offence for a man knowingly to live wholly or in part on the earnings of prostitution.

84 Section 5 of the Sexual Offence Act 1967 provided that it is an offence for a man or woman who knowingly lives wholly or in part on the earnings of prostitution of another man.

On the second point, Bokhary NPJ, in the Court of Final Appeal, rejected Ormrod J's view (in *Corbett*) that a person with an artificial vagina is legally incapable of sexual intercourse. He said (*obiter*):

> 'I do not accept that what a post-operative transsexual and a person of a sex opposite to the reassigned one are capable of doing cannot amount to consummation as a matter of law. Consummation is nonetheless consummation even though only made possible by surgery and incapable of leading to procreation. Although I do not require any authority to convince me of that, I should mention that I happen to find myself in agreement with the whole of what the English Court of Appeal said in SY v SY (orse W) [1963] P 37...'[85]

Bokhary's view has been endorsed by the Hong Kong Law Reform Commission's Consultation Paper on Rape and Other Non-consensual Sexual Offences.[86] It recommended that legislative changes be made so that a person with surgically constructed sexual organ (e.g. vagina) be protected by the law.

> '[I]f modern surgical techniques could provide a surgically constructed penis, penetration by such an artificial organ should be contained within the scope of the offence of rape. It is as severe an infringement of a person's sexual autonomy if the person's vagina, anus or mouth is penetrated without consent by a surgically constructed penis as by a natural penis. We therefore consider that the definition of penis should include a surgically constructed penis. This definition should apply to all sexual offences and not just rape.'[87]

Implementing this legislative reform proposal will ensure that gender-specific offences cover transgender persons who have obtained recognition of their acquired gender.

4.4. EXCEPTION TO GENDER RECOGNITION? TSOS (祖) AND TONGS (堂) AND SMALL HOUSE (丁屋) POLICY

The discussion of Tsos and Tongs and the Small House Policy (SHP) belongs to the subject of land law. Its appearance here may be a bit curious. Local newspaper reporting suggests this may be an area of concern arising from gender recognition, thus it is mentioned only briefly here.[88] These Tsos and Tongs are sometimes called

85 CFA, para. 218.

86 <www.hkreform.gov.hk/en/docs/rape_e.pdf> accessed 19.01.2014.

87 Ibid., paras. 4.19–4.20 and recommendation 9.

88 The New Territories is a large region in the northern part of the Hong Kong SAR, which was leased to the British under the Second Convention of Peking in 1898 for a period of 99 years. Under Art. 40 of the Basic Law, '[t]he lawful traditional rights and interests of the

Chinese customary 'trusts'.[89] Both are ancestral land-holding for the worshipping of male ancestors and for the benefit of male descendants.[90] The beneficiaries of a Tso/Tong are exclusively male descendants from certain male ancestors.[91] Roger Nissim noted that there are '4000 Tsos and over 2000 Tongs which collectively control some 6000 acres of land'.[92] Another unique and relevant aspect of the New Territories land holding is the SHP.[93] The SHP is administered by the Lands Department which issues detailed definitions and eligibility criteria.[94] However, according to Sihombing and Wilkinson, there is no customary right to a small house, but it is an exercise of government policy only.[95] With the scarcity of land and land being a major asset, the Small House Policy has been the subject of much debate and has given rise to suggestions for reform.[96] Without entering into these

indigenous inhabitants of the "New Territories" shall be protected by the Hong Kong Special Administrative Region.' The 'traditional rights and interests' of the indigenous inhabitants refers to customary right affecting land and they include Tsos and Tongs. See Sihombing and Wilkinson, *A Student's Guide to Hong Kong Conveyancing*, 6th ed., LexisNexis, 2011, p. 36.

89 Ibid.

90 'Generally, the Tso is a customary land trust for the worship of a named ancestor and the upkeep of his grave. A Tong could have a similar purpose but would be more usually designed to provide funds for educational or welfare purposes of the "beneficiaries". It could also be extended to business ventures. A Tong may also build a hall to house ancestral tablets, whereas Tsos have no halls. Tongs may use a family's lucky name or other name but Tsos will always use the name of the common ancestor.' Roger Nissim, *Land Administration and Practice in Hong Kong*, 3rd ed., Hong Kong University Press, Hong Kong 2012, p. 140.

91 Mills-Owens J in *Tang Kai Chung and Another v Tang Chik Shang* [1970] HKLR 276 at 279–280: 'Speaking generally, a Tso may be shortly described as an ancient Chinese institution of ancestral land-holding whereby land derived from a common ancestor is enjoyed by his male descendants for the time being living for their lifetimes and so from generation to generation indefinitely. Thus, every male descendant of the common ancestor automatically becomes entitled at birth to an interest in the land for his lifetime; on his death his interest merges so as automatically to enlarge the interests of the surviving male descendants; thus his interest at any given moment during his lifetime depends on the number of male descendants then living and on his death it forms no part of his estate.'

92 *Land Administration and Practice in Hong Kong*, Hong Kong University Press, Hong Kong 1998, p. 111. Both the Tong and Tsos are administered by managers, and s. 15 New Territories Ordinance requires managers appointed to be reported, approved and recorded by the Secretary for Home Affairs.

93 'The Small House Policy (SHP) was introduced in 1972 with the objective of improving the then prevailing low standard of housing in the rural areas of the New Territories. Under the SHP, male indigenous villagers aged 18 or above descended through the male line from one of the recognised villages in the NT may apply for building a small house for once in their life time. They can either apply for a free building licence to build a small house on their own land at nil premium, or a private treaty grant of Government land, if available, at a concessionary premium.' Hong Kong Legislative Council paper on 'Background brief on processing of small house applications and review of small house policy', 28 February 2006 <www.legco.gov.hk/yr05-06/english/panels/plw/papers/plw0228cb1-986-1e.pdf> accessed 28.03.2015.

94 <www.landsd.gov.hk/en/legco/house.htm> accessed 28.03.2015.

95 Sihombing and Wilkinson, above n. 89, p. 52.

96 <www.scmp.com/news/hong-kong/article/1222313/civic-exchange-calls-ruling-unsustainable-small-house-policy> accessed 28.03.2015. On the problems associated with SHP, see <www.civic-exchange.org/wp/shppr_en/#more-17750> accessed 28.03.2015. The SHP has been exempted from the Sex Discrimination Ordinance (Cap 480), see schedule 5.

debates[97] the potential legal consequences which gender recognition may have on this exclusively male customary land rights and the SHP are twofold:

(i) whether a male person by birth continues (post gender recognition) to be regarded as such, and hence, remains entitled to a lifetime interest; and
(ii) whether a male descendant of a transgender woman continues to be regarded as a descendant 'from the male line'.

Take an example. A may be assigned a male gender at birth and, from birth, benefits from an interest from his Tso/Tong. Post-gender recognition, would A (as a female) continue to be so entitled? As an interest from a Tong/Tso is vested in a male descendant at birth, and it is a life interest; arguably, once vested it remains unaffected by subsequent event, such as gender recognition. Similarly, a person who obtains recognition of his male gender would not become entitled to any interest post-gender recognition. Another example might involve a person, A, who is assigned a male legal gender at birth. From birth, A benefits from an interest from the Tso/Tong. A marries W and a son (BB) is born to the couple. Arguably, BB is a male descendant from a male line despite A obtaining legal recognition of his female gender.

These postulations are based on the premise that 'male descendant' 'of the male line' denotes biological offspring, lineage and pedigree. This is consistent with the emphasis of bloodline and the patrilineal nature of traditional Chinese society which formed the basis of these customary trusts. In the Gender Recognition Act, an exemption is made such that the descent of any peerage or dignity or title of honour is unaffected by the acquired gender.[98] New Territories land rights may be such an instance.[99] If Hong Kong were to follow the approach in the Gender Recognition Act, there may be in the future a female beneficiary of

---

97 J. Chan, 'Rights of New Territories Indigenous Inhabitants' in J. Chan and C.L. Lim (eds.), *Law of the Hong Kong Constitution*, Sweet & Maxwell, Hong Kong 2011, pp. 891–895; P.H. Hase, *Custom, Land, and Livelihood in Rural South China: The Traditional Land Law of Hong Kong's New Territories, 1750–1950*, Hong Kong University Press, Hong Kong 2013.

98 Section 16 GRA.

99 The general laws of Hong Kong prevails over Chinese custom: *Wu Koon Tai v Wu Yau Loi* [1996] 2 HKLR 477; Sihombing and Wilkinson, above n. 89, p. 46. Judicial review of the New Territories Land (Exemption) Ordinance (which amended Chinese laws and custom in relation to intestate succession) on the basis that it was inconsistent with Articles 15, 19 and 23 of the Bill of Rights Ordinance (Cap 383) was unsuccessful. In *Lau Wong Fat v A-G* [1997] HKLRD 533, the plaintiff, an indigenous inhabitant, argued that since the Bill of Rights Ordinance protected rights and freedoms enjoyed by peoples of Hong Kong (Articles 15 and 19), and Article 23 protected the rights of minorities, the fact that the New Territories Land (Exemption) Ordinance abolished the well-recognised Chinese custom of succession to land in the New Territories only by the male descendants of an intestate person meant that the rights of indigenous villagers were derogated. However, the court held that there was nothing in the New Territories Land (Exemption) Ordinance that restricted the rights and freedoms of Hong Kong people. Furthermore, Article 23 of the Bill of Rights Ordinance, protecting the rights of minorities, did not apply to indigenous villagers since they were not a 'minority' under the Ordinance.

Tong and Tso, a male descendant beneficiary of a female ancestor, and to take this further, a female descendant beneficiary of a female ancestor.

V. CONCLUSION

Hong Kong currently relies on the law in the RPO to recognise a person's acquired gender. There is no reason why it should not continue to do so. It is unnecessary to impose 'being unmarried' as a precondition to obtaining a replacement identity card. A *de facto* same-sex marriage (small in number as they are) need not be a serious concern to law reform towards gender recognition. It is, however, necessary to consider whether obtaining a replacement identity card should be made a compulsory mechanism for gender recognition. Further, as the Court of Final Appeal has indicated, the qualification for marriage of a transgender person should not be rigidly focused on surgery or the lack thereof. This raises the question as to what extent a pre-operative transgender person should also be recognised in law.

In the absence of comprehensive law reform, the courts should apply generously the opinion canvassed in the Court of Final Appeal to other gender-specific terms and relationships to avoid placing transgender persons, and those with whom they have existing or new legal relationships, in limbo. Gender-specific crimes must, pending implementation of relevant law reform recommendations, be handled with sensitivity as an interim measure. New Territories customary land rights and SHP may need to be exempted from gender recognition in view of their unique characteristics.

There are other challenges to existing rules. They will require legal intervention (e.g. discrimination and the rectification of birth certificates). The Court of Final Appeal's decision represents the dawn of a paradigm shift away from entrenched gender binaries. We live in a world where sexual minority rights need to be taken seriously, and ad hoc law reform is unlikely to be the appropriate response. Hong Kong now has a valuable opportunity to review and update its law. In so doing, it will find that protecting the rights of sexual minorities liberates society and helps to realise a more tolerant and inclusive community. This opportunity for reform should not be missed.

VI. POSTSCRIPT

Nine months after *W*'s case, the Marriage (Amendment) Bill 2014 was introduced to the Legislative Council. It sought to amend the Marriage Ordinance to provide that, 'for determining the sex of the parties to a marriage, a person who has received a full sex re-assignment surgery is to be treated as being of the sex to which the person is re-assigned'.[100] A 'full sex re-assignment surgery' is a form of sterilisation. It is defined in the Bill as 'a surgical procedure that – (a) has the effect of re-assigning the sex of a person from male to female by – (i) removing the person's penis and testes; and (ii) constructing a vagina in the person; or (b) has the effect of re-assigning the sex of a person from female to male by – (i) removing the person's uterus and ovaries; and (ii) constructing a penis or some form of a penis in the person.'[101] The Secretary for Security presented the Bill stating that the government was 'duty-bound to upgrade the provisions in the Marriage Ordinance (MO) and the Matrimonial Causes Ordinance by introducing the Bill so as to align them with the CFA judgment.'[102]

At the second reading of the Bill in October 2014, it was vetoed by an overwhelming opposition (40/57 were against it, and five abstained).[103] The reasons for opposing the Bill were broadly twofold. Some conservative legislators[104] argued (erroneously) that the Bill would introduce a new meaning to the institution of marriage as it touched on sexual orientation and same-sex marriage which Hong Kong society was not ready to accept.[105] They took the view that Mr Justice Patrick Chan's dissenting judgment reflected the majority views of Hong Kong people.[106] The more liberal legislators opposed the Bill on the grounds it restricted the right to marriage only to transgender people who have received full SRS and such a restriction was inhumane and it would force a transgender person to undergo full SRS in order to get married.[107] They also opined that the government's duty was to consider gender recognition in a holistic manner, rather than to rush through the legislature the order of the Court.

The Secretary for Security indicated that the Government has formed the Inter-departmental Working Group on Gender Recognition (IWG) in January 2014. The IWG is chaired by the Secretary for Justice to follow up on the recommendations made by the Court of Final Appeal. The government has indicated that its objective is to complete an initial report in about two years' time.[108]

---

100 <www.legco.gov.hk/yr13-14/english/bills/b201402282.pdf> accessed 28.03.2015.

101 102 Clause 3 of the Marriage (Amendment) Bill 2014.

102 Hong Kong Legislative Council Official Record of Proceedings, Wednesday 22 October 2014 (hereafter 'Legco Record'), p. 772 (Secretary for Security).

103 Legco Record, p. 779.

104 Mr Ip Kwok-Him, Mr Tommy Cheung, Dr Priscilla Leung, Mr Paul Tse, Ms Starry Lee.

105 Legco Record, pp. 710–713 (Mr Ip Kwok-Him).

106 Legco Record, pp. 712, 739, 764.

107 Legco Record, p. 714 (Mr Chan Chi-Chuen), pp. 719–720 (Miss Cyd Ho), pp. 726–728 (Mr Gary Fan), pp. 746–747 (Dr Helena Wong), p. 758 (Mr Charles Peter Mok).

108 Legco Record, p. 772.

THE LEGAL STATUS OF TRANSSEXUAL AND TRANSGENDER PERSONS IN JAPAN

Yuko NISHITANI

Contents

I. LEGAL FRAMEWORK AND STATISTICS

1.1. LEGAL RULES FOR TRANSGENDER AND TRANSSEXUAL PERSONS

1.1.1. Introduction

Japan has traditionally had a unique transgender subculture, with often mystic bisexual figures in mythology and shamanism. During the period of feudalism, cross-dressing or transcending gender was not unusual, such as in *kabuki* theatres where female roles generally were played by male actors.[1] Despite modernisation since the 1868 *Meiji* Restoration, the transgender subculture has in fact endured in *kabuki*, *nô*, and even in pop culture.[2] Yet, notwithstanding this tradition, institutionalising medical and legal measures for transgender and transsexual persons has been a long process. While the legal recognition of preferred gender has been enabled by the Law Concerning Special Rules Regarding Sex Status of a Person with Gender Identity Disorder (GID Act) of 16 July 2003,[3] coming into force one year later, a series of questions remain with regard to its requirements, procedure and legal effects.

Pursuant to Article 2 GID Act, 'gender identity disorder' (*sei dôitsusei shôgai* (GID)) is defined as the state of 'a person who, against his/her defined

---

1 J. Mitsuhashi, *Josô to Nihon-jin* [Cross-Dressing and Japanese people], Kôdansha, Tokyo 2008, pp. 29–123; J. Saeki, *"Josô to Dansô" no Bunka-shi* [History of "Cross-Dressing"], Kôdansha, Tokyo 2009, pp. 12–39; M. Shirasu, *Ryôsei-Guyû no Bi* [Beauty of Bisexuality], Shinchôsha, Tokyo 2003, pp. 9–116. In the history, *kabuki* was first founded by a woman named *Okuni* from the state of *Izumo* and played by female actors from 1603 (*onna kabuki*), which was banned in 1629 to maintain public morals. After experiencing a short period of *wakashu kabuki* played by young boys, *kabuki* was established to be exclusively performed by adult male actors since mid-17th century. H. Fujita (ed.), *Kabuji Handbook* [Handbook on *Kabuki* Theaters], Sanseidô, Tokyo 2006, pp. 2–4.

2 Saeki, above n. 1, pp. 39–47.

3 *Sei Dôitsusei Shôgaisha no Seibetsu no Toriatsukai no Tokurei ni kansuru Hôritsu* [Law Concerning Special Rules Regarding Sex Status of a Person with GID: Law No. 111 of 16 July 2003]. This legislative work did not follow the usual consultation procedure of the Ministry of Justice, but was instituted and drafted by the initiative of Diet members, which was adopted by the Diet within 10 days. C. Nono, '"*Sei Dôitsusei Shôgaisha Seibetsu Toriatsukai Tokureihô*" ni kansuru torikumi to keii' [Project and Backhistory of the Law Concerning Special Rules Regarding Sex Status of a Person with GID], in: Nono (ed.), *Sei Dôitsusei Shôgai no Iryô to Hô* [Medicine and Law in relation to GID], Medica Shuppan, Osaka 2013, pp. 204–212.

biological sex, has the persistent conviction that he/she psychologically belongs to the opposite sex and has a will to make himself/herself into physical and social conformity with the opposite sex; provided that two or more physicians, who have experience and expertise required to properly make such a diagnosis, should make the same diagnosis on the subject concerned based upon generally accepted medical standards'.[4] This legal definition of GID aims to identify those transgender persons who are eligible to request the legal recognition of their preferred gender in the Family Court from a substantive and procedural perspective. The Japanese legislature consciously chose a narrow definition of GID, seeking to avoid catering to an excessively wide scope of applications and to subject the legal gender recognition to a thorough and careful examination.[5]

The nomenclature of GID has since then been established as legal and medical terminology in Japan, along the lines of F64 of the ICD-10 adopted by the World Health Organization in 1992 (last revised in 2010).[6] In the international arena, however, GID has increasingly been criticised as discriminatory and stigmatising. Hence, following suggestions by the World Professional Association for Transgender Health, the American Psychiatric Association has now substituted GID with 'gender dysphoria' in its DSM-5 (2013)[7] to ensure clinical care and clarify that gender nonconformity is not, in itself, a mental disorder. Moreover, the diagnostic name of 'gender dysphoria' was considered to be more appropriate for the symptoms and consistent with familiar clinical sexology terminology.[8] While the medical classifications and symptoms referred to in the GID Act, ICD-10 and DSM-5 differ from each other,[9] the Japanese Society of Psychiatry and Neurology (JSPN)[10] eventually proposed, in May 2014, that the terminology of GID should be replaced by 'gender dysphoria' (*seibetsu iwa*) pursuant to DSM-5. In light of these developments, the following chapter employs the terminology 'gender dysphoria'

---

4 For an English translation, *cf.* C. Nono (ed.), *Kaisetsu: Sei Dôitsusei Shôgaisha Seibetsu Toriatsukai Tokureihô* [Commentary: Law Concerning Special Rules Regarding Sex Status of a Person with GID], Nihon Kajo Shuppan, Tokyo 2004, p. 187.

5 Nono (ed.), above n. 4, pp. 83–86.

6 World Health Organization, '10th Revision of the International Classification of Diseases' (2010) <http://apps.who.int/classifications/ icd10/browse/2010/en#/F60-F69>. The 11th Revision will be completed by 2015 <http://apps.who.int/classifications/icd/en/>.

7 American Psychiatric Association, 'Fifth Edition of the Diagnostic and Statistical Manual of Mental Disorders', 2013.

8 <www.dsm5.org/Documents/Gender%20Dysphoria%20Fact%20Sheet.pdf>. For further detail, see J. Kou, 'Sei Dôitsusei Shôgai no Gainen no Hensen' [The History of the Concept of GID] [2012] 114-6 *PNJ* (*Psychiatria et Neurologia Japonica*) 673, 677–678 (with an English summary); idem, 'Sei Dôitsusei Shôgai no Gainen no Hensen' [Transition of the GID Concept] [2013] 632 *CP* (*Clinical Psychiatry*) 755, 759–761.

9 See Kou, above n. 8, pp. 675–678; idem, above n. 8, 632 *CP* 757–761; T. Yamauchi (ed.), *Sei Dôitsusei Shôgai no Kiso to Rinshô* [Basic and Clinical Principles of GID], 2nd ed., Shinkô Igaku Shuppansha, Tokyo 2004, pp. 39–53.

10 The JSPN (founded in 1902) is the most authoritative association in psychiatry in Japan consisting of 16,000 members, which includes 11,000 psychiatrists board-certified by JSPN. See <https://www.jspn.or.jp/english/index.html>.

in principle, while 'GID' is utilised to be consistent with the legal definition provided by Article 2 GID Act.

1.1.2. Past Developments

1.1.2.1. Medical Measures

The first lawsuit concerning transgenderism in Japan dates to the *Blue Boys* case in 1969, a penal case on gender identity-related surgery.[11] In that case, a gynaecologist removed the testicles of three transgender women. The doctor promptly effected the surgery upon request of the patients, without examining them cautiously during a certain period of time or keeping their records. In the judgment, the judge reasoned that gender confirmation surgery had not yet been fully established as a medical treatment. Being irreversible, such surgical interventions could only be justified on condition that (a) careful medical examinations and consultations by specialists, including a psychiatrist, had taken place, (b) the patient's records were preserved, and (c) the surgery was effected by an experienced physician on the basis of informed consent of the patient, as well as his or her spouse or parents. Since these conditions were not met in the *Blue Boys* case, the judge convicted the physician for his frivolous act that was held to violate Article 28 of the Eugenic Protection Act (EPA; amended and renamed as Maternity Protection Act (MPA) in 1996).[12]

Although the court in the *Blue Boys* case acknowledged the possibility that gender confirmation surgery could be legal and justified, its outcome was serious enough to discourage other physicians from carrying out further surgical interventions during the subsequent three decades.[13] As a consequence, a number of transgender persons either accessed illegal surgery underground in Japan or resorted to treatment abroad (e.g. in the US, Thailand, Singapore or Morocco).[14] It was not until 16 October 1998 that the first gender confirmation surgery was legally carried out as a medical treatment at a university clinic in Japan. For its preparation, the physicians had taken careful steps to obtain approval from the university ethics committee in 1996 and the JSPN in 1997. The JSPN then

11 Tokyo District Court, 15 February 1969, *Keiji Saiban Geppô* 1–2, 133 = *Hanrei Jihô* 551, 26; confirmed by Tokyo High Court, 11 November 1970, *Kôtô Saibansho Keiji Hanreishû* 23–4, 759 = *Hanrei Jihô* 639, 107 (*Blue Boys* case).

12 *Yûsei Hogo Hô* (Eugenic Protection Act [EPA]: Law No. 156 of 13 July 1947); amended and renamed as *Botai Hogo Hô* (Maternity Protection Act [MPA]) by Law No. 105 of 26 June 1996. While the violation of Art. 28 EPA only resulted in a fine, the physician was also convicted for offering narcotics in the underlying case. As a result, he was sentenced to two years' imprisonment on three years' probation and fined at 400,000 Yen (above n. 10).

13 Yamauchi (ed.), above n. 9, pp. 10–13; M. Yoshinaga, *Sei Dôitsusei Shôgai* [GID], Shûeisha, Tokyo 2000, pp. 79–81.

14 K. Harima, 'Sei Dôitsusei Shôgai no Igakuteki Gainen to Genkyô' [Medical Concept of GID and the Current State], in: Nono (ed.), above n. 4, pp. 24–25; Yoshinaga, above n. 13, pp. 37–54, 81.

issued guidelines on diagnosis and treatment of gender dysphoria on 28 May 1998 to endorse the envisaged surgical intervention and guarantee its legitimate implementation as a medical treatment.

Pursuant to the 1998 JSPN guidelines, the biological sex and gender identity of the patient was first to be verified. If gender dysphoria was diagnosed by two experienced and specialised psychiatrists, according to established international standards, such as ICD-10 and DSM-IV, psychiatric treatment was then effected through counselling and a real-life test for at least one year. If medical treatment appeared appropriate, hormone treatment was prescribed and, only if necessary, sex reassignment surgery was ultimately to be undertaken. The JSPN guidelines provided that the entire procedure be operated by a medical team consisting of psychiatrists, (plastic) surgeons, urologists, gynaecologists, endocrinologists and/or paediatrics, as well as psychotherapists, counsellors and social workers.[15] Drafted by a medical association, the guidelines were readily approved by the Ministry of Health and Welfare, giving the green light to gender confirmation surgery.[16]

The first lawful surgery was effected on 16 October 1998. It attracted considerable attention and was extensively reported within the media. This resulted in a general awareness of gender dysphoria within Japanese society,[17] and transgender persons increasingly began to present to psychiatrists, seeking a diagnosis of gender dysphoria (and subsequent counselling, hormone treatment and surgery).[18] The enactment of the GID Act in 2003 has eventually confirmed that gender confirmation surgery can lawfully be undertaken as a medical treatment without contravening Article 28 MPA.[19] Furthermore, physicians are now protected from criminal liability, insofar as they provide surgical intervention (a) for the purpose of a medical treatment, (b) in accordance with the generally accepted medical standards and (c) on the basis of informed consent of the patient.

Along with developments in medical expertise and clinical treatments, the JSPN guidelines have been renamed and continuously revised, until the latest 4th edition was adopted in 2011.[20] The current guidelines have, *inter alia,* abolished the strict order of medical treatments to reflect the broad spectrum of different symptoms and treatment needs within the transgender community. The medical team, therefore, may proceed at its discretion either to the removal of breasts or to

---

15 Yamauchi (ed.), above n. 9, pp. 227–240.

16 Yoshinaga, above n. 13, p. 140.

17 K. Harima et al., *Sei Dôitsusei Shôgai to Koseki,* 2nd ed., Ryokufû Shuppan, Tokyo 2013, pp. 23–29.

18 Yoshinaga, above n. 13, pp. 1–23, 86–155.

19 *Cf.* above n. 12.

20 Nihon Seishin Shinkei Gakkai: Sei Dôitsusei Shôgai ni kansuru Iinkai [Japanese Society of Psychiatry and Neurology: Committee on GID], 'Sei Dôitsusei Shôgai ni kansuru Shindan to Chiryô no Guidelines: Dai 4han' [4th Guidelines on Diagnosis and Treatment of GID] [2012] 114–11 *PNJ* 1250–1266; also in Nono (ed.), above n. 3, pp. 159–189.

gender confirmation surgery without first having provided hormone treatment. In addition, it was realised that a number of transgender persons already seek consultations and medical treatments when they are teenagers at school, long before they reach the threshold age of majority, set at 20 years in Japan (Art. 4 Civil Code).[21] Hence, the age restriction for hormone treatment has, under strict conditions, been lowered from 18 to 15 years, which makes it possible to prevent secondary sexual characteristics from appearing. While the removal of the breasts can be undertaken from 18 years with the consent of the custodian parents, other gender confirmation procedures are restricted to those who have reached the age of majority.[22]

1.1.2.2. Legal Measures

Prior to enactment of the 2003 GID Act, transgender persons often requested to change their first name and legal sex entered into the family register, seeking to be identified and recognised by their preferred (opposite) gender. The Japanese family register is ordered according to the unit of a couple and unmarried children. It records the detailed status of family members without due regard to privacy. In the past, a family register could be inspected by anybody. Since 1976, access has gradually been restricted,[23] though lawyers and notaries can still request access in their professional capacity, as can any other persons by proving their legitimate interests in inspection (Art. 10*bis* Family Register Act (FRA)).[24] In daily life, Japanese nationals are often requested to submit an excerpt from the family register, e.g. at school enrolment, employment, or renting an apartment.[25] It has, therefore, been a crucial issue for transgender persons to have their preferred gender reflected in the family register.[26]

Pursuant to Article 107*bis* FRA, the first name of a person can be changed by a Family Court decree, insofar as the applicant has legitimate grounds to obtain the change. Even before the GID Act was adopted in 2003, Family Courts

---

21 *Minpô* (Civil Code: Law No. 89 of 27 April 1896 and Law No. 9 of 21.06.1898 as amended). Although the Legislative Committee of the Ministry of Justice suggested in October 2009 that the majority age be lowered to 18, the proposal has remained untouched until today. For further information, see <www.moj.go.jp/shingi1/shingi2_091028-1.html>

22 Nihon Seishin Shinkei Gakkai, above n. 20, pp. 1254–1255, 1261–1263; Y. Matsumoto, '"Sei Dôitsusei Shôgai ni kansuru Shindan to Chiryô no Guidelines" no kaisetsu' [Commentary on the Guidelines on Diagnosis and Treatment of GID], in Nono (ed.), above n. 3, pp. 109–113.

23 Law No. 66 of 15 June 1976; Law No. 35 of 11 May 2007.

24 *Koseki Hô* (Family Register Act [FRA]: Law No. 224 of 22 December 1947).

25 N. Mizuno, 'Koseki seido' [1992] 1000 *Jurist* 166. Foreign nationals are not recorded in the family register, which causes particular difficulties in cross-border cases. For further detail on Japanese family register, *see* Y. Nishitani, 'Das japanische Familienregister und grenzüberschreitende Rechtsverhältnisse' (hereinafter 'Familienregister') (2002) 14 *ZJapanR/J.Japan.L.* (*Zeitschrift für japanisches Recht/Journal of Japanese Law*) 229–249; idem, 'State, Family and Child in Japan' (hereinafter 'State, Family and Child'), in: *Liber Amicorum Walter Pintens*, vol. 2, Intersentia, Cambridge 2012, pp. 987–1007.

26 Nono (ed.), above n. 4, pp. 75–76.

were generous in authorising a change of first name for transgender persons to properly reflect their preferred gender. The courts acceded to such applications in approximately 80% of cases.[27] The requirements are that the person has already been using the new name for approximately one year and is recognised by that name in society, and a diagnosis of gender dysphoria has been provided by a doctor. In the absence of such a diagnosis, the transsexual or transgender person is still entitled to change their first name on the basis of 'constant use' if he or she has been using the desired name for about five years.[28]

Nevertheless, courts would not authorise the recognition of preferred legal gender in the family register prior to the enactment of the 2003 GID Act. In 2000, the Tokyo High Court[29] dismissed a claim to amend a gender marker in the family register, although the MtF (male-to-female) transgender applicant had undergone gender confirmation surgery abroad. The judges reasoned that the legal gender of a person is determined at the point of birth registration pursuant to the biological sex prescribed by an individual's chromosomes. The requirements of Article 113 FRA for the correction of unlawful, erroneous or incomplete entries in the family register were not fulfilled, because there was no 'mistake' when indicating that the applicant should be assigned a male legal gender at birth. In *obiter dicta,* the judges further pointed out that, even though gender confirmation surgery had legally been introduced in 1998, it was not yet established or generally recognised as a valid treatment of gender dysphoria. Allowing the legal recognition of preferred gender would seriously affect the entire family register system and other legal institutions, as well as social life. The Court therefore contended that the solution could only be sought *de lege ferenda* on the basis of thorough assessments of its impact on society. This was the generally accepted standpoint of the case law.[30]

Admittedly, this reasoning differed from the cases of intersex-affected persons, who are born with a reproductive or sexual anatomy that does not fit the typical definitions of female or male.[31] In 1991, the Sapporo High Court dealt with a case where a baby was born with male chromosome and testes but with female characteristics in terms of internal and external genitals. While doctors initially identified the baby as male, the baby was subsequently held as female after undergoing thorough examinations and surgical intervention to remove the

---

27 Tokyo Family Court, 17 November 1980 [not published]; Tokyo Family Court, 10 June 1994 [not published]; for further detail, T. Ôshima, *Sei Dôitsusei Shôgai to Hô*, Nihon Hyôronsha, Tokyo 2002, pp. 41–44; T. Shoji, 'Iwayuru Sei Dôitsusei Shôgai to Na no Henkô Jiken, Koseki-teisei Jiken ni tsuite' (On Cases of the Change of Name and the Correction of Family Register in relation to GID) 52-7 *KSG* (*Katei Saiban Geppô*) 16–36, 58–69.

28 The applicant has to prove to have been receiving letters or obtaining membership of a club under the new first name, or using it at work. Harima et al., above n. 17, pp. 131–135.

29 Tokyo High Court, 9 February 2000, *Kôtô Saibansho Minji Hanreishû* 53-1, 79.

30 Also Nagoya Family Court, 27 September 1979, *KSG* 33-9, 63; Nagoya High Court, 8 November 1979, *KSG* 33-9, 61; Tokyo High Court, 27 March 2003 (below n. 35); as an only exception to grant the change of legal sex, *see* Tokyo High Court, 28 October 1980 [not published]; for further detail, Ôshima, above n. 27, pp. 57–61; Shôji, above n. 27, pp. 36–47, 70–76.

31 Sapporo High Court, 13 March 1991, *KSG* 43-8, 48.

testes. Under these circumstances, the court ordered that the legal gender in the family register ought to be changed to female, on the ground that there was a 'mistake' at the birth registration (Art. 113 FRA). The Court relied on the physical and biological self-definition of the intersex-affected person, not solely on the chromosomes.[32]

Some authors have sought to extend this argument to transgender persons with gender dysphoria, contending that the legal gender fixed at the birth registration is a 'mistake' if the person subsequently identifies with the opposite gender.[33] This academic opinion insists that recognition of preferred gender in the family register is crucial to vindicate the dignity and gender identity of the person, which are protected as fundamental rights under Article 13 (right to the pursuit of happiness) and Article 24 (dignity of individuals) of the Constitution of Japan.[34] Relying on this view, six transgender persons simultaneously filed a claim for legal recognition at Family Court in May 2001. Although the Supreme Court, in the same way as the lower courts, did not accede to the request on 28 May 2003,[35] the case attracted wide attention in society and served as the impetus for new legislation to provide sexual minorities with legal protection. The enactment of the GID Act of 16 July 2003 (entering into force on 16 July 2004) has now entitled transgender persons to alter their legal gender in the family register. Indeed, such persons are now able to freely develop their personality and to be recognised in conformity with their gender identity in society by taking an autonomous decision on their preferred legal gender.

Along with these developments, other legal protections have been introduced for the transgender community. On 20 June 2002, the Tokyo District Court rendered a decision[36] in a labour dispute, in which an employer had dismissed a transgender woman, claiming that the latter had violated his order not to be dressed as a woman. The court held that the dismissal was void and illegal due to 'abuse of right' (Art. 1(3) Civil Code). According to the court, the employer did not make sufficient efforts to respect the employee's decision to dress and present in her preferred gender, although such gender expression did not seriously disturb the order of the company or its business operations.

---

32 Similarly, Mito Family Court (Tsuchiura Branch), 22 July 1999, *KSG* 51–12, 40; for other cases, see Ôshima, above n. 27, pp. 55–57.

33 A. Ishihara, 'Seibetsu henkô no hôteki kanousei wo saguru' [Seeking legal possibilities to change the legal sex], in *Sei Dôitsusei Shôgai to Hôritsu: Ronsetsu, Shiryô, Q&A* [GID and the Law: Treatises, Materials, Questions and Answers], Kôyô Shobô, Kyoto 2001, pp. 38–40; Ôshima, above n. 27, pp. 62–65.

34 *Nihonkoku Kenpô* (Constitution of Japan, promulgated on 3 November 1946; entered into force on 3 May 1947).

35 Supreme Court, 28 May 2003 and Tokyo High Court, 27 March 2003, reprinted in: Nono (ed.), above n. 4, pp. 258–265.

36 Tokyo District Court, 20 June 2002, *Rôdô Hanrei* 830, 13.

Another case concerned a tort claim granted by the Tokyo District Court on 28 April 1999.[37] The plaintiff victim was a transgender woman, who was working at a bar where she incurred a serious facial injury when pushed down a flight of stairs by the defendant. In calculating the amount of damages, the court relied on the high standard of damages applicable to women incurring ugly scaring rather than that of men, on the ground that the victim had a female appearance, wore female clothing and used female cosmetics in her daily life.

1.2. HEALTH INSURANCE

Gender confirmation surgery often involves prohibitive costs because of the technical specificities and the required expertise. The cost is approximately US$15,000 for MtF surgery and US$45,000 for FtM surgery in Japan. Public health care is not available for such surgery or hormone treatment, although gender dysphoria is classified as a disease that requires medical treatment. In order to circumvent these restrictions, some physicians are said to declare operations, such as the removal of the womb or breasts or the cutting or constructing of a penis, as a surgery to treat polyps or wounds and apply for subsidies.[38] On the other hand, a transgender person can in any case sign an insurance contract with a private company. Depending on the premium, at least a part of the cost of gender confirmation surgery can be covered by the insurance.

1.3. STATISTICAL INFORMATION

Since the GID Act entered into force on 16 July 2004, there have been 4,353 Family Court decrees that granted legal recognition of a person's preferred gender. The number of people who obtain recognition has grown consistently year on year.[39]

Of all transgender persons who access specialised gender clinics, about 20% actually submit to gender confirmation surgery to obtain legal recognition. Judging from this ratio, there are presumably about 12,000 transgender persons in Japan who have visited a gender clinic but have not yet obtained legal gender identity recognition.[40] The most common reason for not accessing recognition of preferred gender is the strict requirements prescribed by the GID Act, particularly

---

37 Tokyo District Court, 28 April 1999, *Hanrei Times* 1018, 288; *see* Ôshima, 'Sei Dôitsusei Shôgai ni kansuru Hôteki na Shomondai' [Various Legal Questions on GID], in Nono (ed.), above n. 4, p. 66.

38 Nono (ed.), above n. 4, p. ix.

39 130 applications (97 granted) in 2004; 272 (229) in 2005; 288 (247) in 2006; 309 (268) in 2007; 468 (422) in 2008; 505 (448) in 2009; 579 (527) in 2010; 678 (609) in 2011; 802 (737) in 2012; 780 (769) in 2013. See <www.courts.go.jp/search/jtsp0010Back> (available only in Japanese).

40 Harima et al., above n. 17, pp. 98–99.

the loss of gonadal function and the acquisition of external genital features of the opposite sex (see below section 2.3). Another reason is presumably lack of information. It has been pointed out that transgender persons are not sufficiently informed of the fact that they are also eligible to obtain legal recognition of their preferred gender in Japan by submitting to gender confirmation surgery abroad.[41]

Figure 1. Family Court decrees to change the legal sex

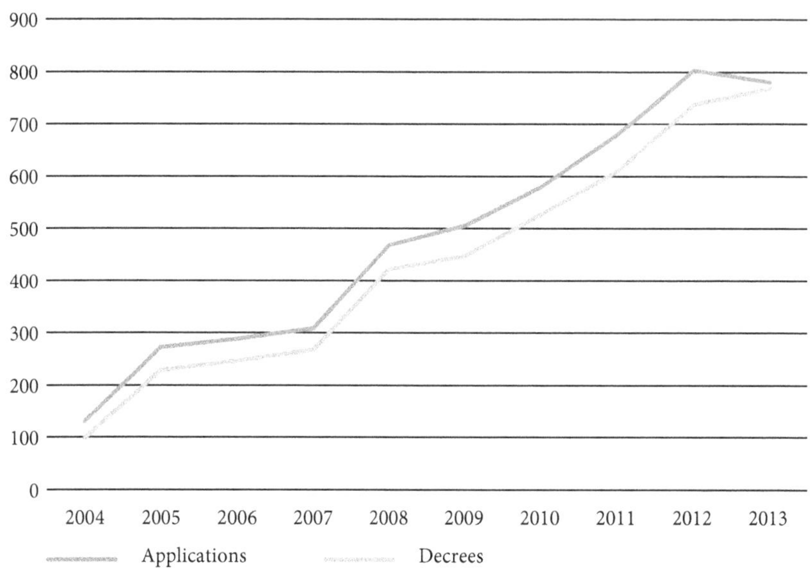

II. CHANGING LEGAL SEX AND/OR GENDER – PROCEDURE AND REQUIREMENTS

2.1. LEGAL PROCEDURE

Pursuant to Article 3 of the 2003 GID Act, the legal recognition of gender requires a Family Court decree. The proceedings at the Family Court are constituted as a non-contentious matter. They have the same characteristics as administrative measures and the state intervenes as a guarantor of general interests. The proceedings are not public (Art. 33 Family Procedure Act (FPA)). Family Courts have the authority to conduct *ex officio* examinations and to possibly order Family Court probation officers to investigate facts (Art. 56(1) and 58 FPA). The transgender person does not need to be represented by an attorney.[42] The

41 Harima et al., above n. 17, pp. 100–103.

42 Nono (ed.), above n. 4, pp. 102–103.

decision of the Family Court is subject to an immediate appeal to the High Court (Art. 232(1) FPA).[43] A special appeal to the Supreme Court is always granted in the case of a wrong interpretation or other violation of the Constitution (Art. 94(1) FPA), or subject to certiorari when there is a contradiction with the existing case law of the Supreme Court or any other important issues on the interpretation of law (Art. 97(2) FPA).

2.2. OFFICIAL DOCUMENTS

To make an application for the legal recognition of preferred gender in the family register, the transgender person is required to submit a medical certificate prepared by physicians pursuant to Article 3(2) GID Act. The medical certificate shall enter the diagnosis in the sense of Article 2 GID Act (see below section 2.3.2), along with progress of treatment, results of treatment, and other relevant information as prescribed by the Ordinances of the Ministry of Health, Labour and Welfare.

2.3. LEGAL REQUIREMENTS

The GID Act has set up strict requirements for authorising the legal recognition. Pursuant to its Article 3 (1) No. 1–5, an applicant must be (a) an adult, (b) unmarried, (c) have no (minor) children, (d) have undergone surgery to lose gonads or gonadal function, and (e) have the external genital features of the opposite sex. To guarantee the functionality of the GID Act, it was indicated in No. 2 of the Supplementary Provision that its possible revision be contemplated in light of its implementation and the development of the social environment within approximately three years after entering into force on 16 July 2004.[44] An amendment was indeed carried out in relation to requirement (c), as will be elaborated below (see below section 2.3.1.3).

2.3.1. Legal Requirements under the GID Act

2.3.1.1. Requirement of Being an Adult

Article 3(1) No. 1 GID Act requires that the transgender person be an adult, *i.e.* at least 20 years old (Art. 4 Civil Code), to obtain legal gender recognition. The legislature prescribed the reaching of majority age for a number of reasons. First, the requirement accords with the principle of civil law which provides adults with full capacity to enter transactions independently. Second, one's preferred gender

[43] *Kaji-jiken Tetsuzuki Hô* (Family Procedure Act [FPA]: Law No. 52 of 25 May 2011).
[44] *Fusoku* (Supplementary Provisions) of the GID Act; see Nono (ed.), above n. 4, p. 104.

is a crucial matter which relates to personality and causes irreversible bodily alteration, because legal gender recognition still requires surgery in Japan unlike in other progressive countries (e.g. Germany, Denmark, Argentina, the UK and the Netherlands). This is why the decision ought to be carefully taken by an adult who has attained biological maturity and mental stability, as well as being self-aware about his or her own gender. Third, this requirement is in line with the JSPN guidelines which only allowed applicants over 20 years old to access gender confirmation surgery.[45] As a result, in the recognition process, the autonomy of minors, as well as the heteronomy of their custodian parents, has been explicitly denied as a legislative policy to protect minors from a precipitate decision.

As mentioned above, however, the guidelines of the JSPN provide that transgender persons can take hormone treatment from the age of 18 years (and, under certain conditions, from as early as 15 years). Transgender persons can submit to surgery for the removal of breasts from 18 years (see above section 1.1.2.1). Furthermore, as a general principle in medical law in Japan, as well as in the UK, the US and other countries, so-called 'mature minors' who are capable of understanding the nature and consequences of their medical treatment are entitled to refuse or consent to such treatment in the same way as adults (e.g. surgery, blood transfusion and abortion). This aims to respect individual dignity and autonomous decision-making of such mature minors.[46] Even though it is not medically required, gender confirmation surgery is of crucial importance for those who mentally and physically suffer from gender dysphoria. It is, therefore, worth deliberating on lowering the threshold age for surgical intervention and legal recognition to 18 years.[47]

2.3.1.2. Requirement of Being Unwed

Pursuant to Article 3(1) No. 2 GID Act, a transgender person may not be married, insofar as he or she intends to obtain legal recognition of preferred gender. This impediment only concerns a person's current marital status. The fact that a transgender person has been married in the past is not a hindrance to altering the legal gender markers in the family register. Nor does living in a cohabitation relationship or *de facto* partnership count as 'being wed'.[48] As a result, a married

[45] Nono (ed.), above n. 4, pp. 87–88; S. Onodera, 'Sei Dôitsusei Shôgaisha no Seibetsu no Toriatsukai no Tokurei ni kansuru Hôritsu' [Law Concerning Special Rules Regarding Sex Status of a Person with GID] [2003] 1252 *Jurist* 67.

[46] See, e.g., T. Koyama, 'Kenpô-jô no Wakugumi' [The Constitutional Framework], in Koyama and Tamai (eds.), *Kodomo no Iryô to Hô* [Medical Treatment and Law for Children], 2nd ed., Shôgakusha, Tokyo 2012, pp. 72–95; T. Terasawa, 'Miseinensha he no Iryôkôi to Shôdaku: "Daidaku"-Kôsei no Saikentô' [Medical Treatment for Minors and their Consent: Reconsidering the Notion of "Consent in Representation"] [1992] *Minshôhô Zasshi*, vol. 106–5, pp. 656–677, vol. 106–6, pp. 799–823, vol. 107–1, pp. 56–69.

[47] Similarly, M. Tanamura, 'Sei Dôitsusei Shôgai wo meguru Hôteki-jôkyô to Kadai' [2008] 1364 *Jurist* 6–7.

[48] Nono (ed.), above n. 4, p. 88; Onodera, above n. 45, pp. 67–68.

transgender person has to make a difficult choice either to uphold the marriage or to divorce and seek to legal and social recognition of gender (the choice is difficult irrespective of the fact that divorce can easily be declared with the spouse's consent in Japan).[49]

The legislature has provided the requirement of being unwed because it believed that authorising the legal recognition of gender for a married person would result in same-gender marriages. It was essential in their eyes to avoid such a result so as to maintain legal order and family relations. There is a line of academic opinion that has called *de lege ferenda* for the non-marriage requirement to be abolished so as to provide greater respect for the dignity of transgender individuals in divorce (Art. 24(2) Constitution) and the right to pursue happiness (Art. 13 Constitution), as has been the case in the Netherlands and Germany.[50] The majority of commentary, however, has taken a more reserved position,[51] considering that the Japanese family law system is grounded on the heterosexual marital family unit, as is reflected in the family register. Marriage is conceived as a stable community of man and woman who give birth to and take care of children, and the status of children is clearly distinguished according to whether they are born in or out of wedlock.[52] The Japanese legislature has not yet envisaged any legal protection for same-gender couples through marriage or registered partnership.[53] Because transgender persons can subsequently enter a

---

49 H. Taniguchi, 'Sei Dôitsusei Shôgai/Seibetsu Iwa wo kakaeru Hitobito to Kazoku-seikatsu, Kazoku-keisei' [Persons of GID or Gender Dysphoria and Family Life, Family Building] [2011] 27 *Kazoku: Shakai to Hô* 52–54; for divorce in Japanese law, *see, inter alia,* N. Mizuno, 'Grounds for Divorce in Japanese Law and Mechanisms of Divorce Payment Obligation', *Japanese Reports for the XIVth International Congress of Comparative Law,* Tokyo 1995, pp. 89–102; idem, 'Die rechtliche Regelung der Ehescheidung in Japan' [1999] 7 *ZJapanR/J.Japan.L.* 120–137; Y. Nishitani, 'Privat- und Schlichtungsscheidung deutscher Staatsangehöriger in Japan und die Scheidungsanerkennung in Deutschland' [2002] *IPRax (Praxis des Internationalen Privat- und Verfahrensrechts)* 49–53.

50 S. Ninomiya, 'Koseki no Seibetsu-kisai no teisei ha kanô ka (3): Kojin no Songen to Jikokettei' [Is it possible to change the legal sex in the family register? No. 3: Dignity of Individuals and Self-Determination] [2003] 561 *Koseki Jihô* 23–37; Taniguchi, above n. 49, p. 54; idem, 'Sei Dôitsusei Shôgai Tokureihô no Saihyôka: Jinken kara no Hihanteki Kôsatsu' [Reconsidering the Law Concerning Special Rules Regarding Sex Status of a Person with GID: Critical View from a Perspective of Human Rights], in Ishida (ed.), *Sei Dôitsusei Shôgai: Gender, Iryô, Tokureihô* [GID: Gender, Medicine and the Law], Ochanomizu Shobô, Tokyo 2008, pp. 265–266; *cf.* Ôshima, above n. 37, p. 44.

51 A. Ômura, 'Sei Dôitsusei Shôgai' [GID] [2003] 278 *Hôgaku Kyôshitsu* 3; Tanamura, above n. 47, pp. 6–7.

52 At least the former Article 900 No. 4, 2nd sentence of the Civil Code, which restricted the inheritance share of children born out of wedlock to half that of children born in wedlock, has been abolished on 3 December 2013 (Law No. 94 of 11 December 2013) due to its unconstitutionality, as had been declared by the Supreme Court on 4 September 2013 (*Minshû* 67–6, 1320). Y. Nishitani, 'Kindschaftsrecht in Japan – Geschichte, Gegenwart und Zukunft –' [2014] 37 *ZJapanR/J.Japan.L.* 77–108.

53 In reality, homosexual couples are said to often carry out a simple adoption to create family relations. F. Tokotani, 'Miseinen Yôshi' [Adoption of Minors] [2014] 86–6 *Hôritsu Jihô* 26. Simple adoption between adults is regularly used for utilitarian purposes, e.g., upholding the family lineage, ensuring maintenance or falsifying the personal identity. A. Ômura,

valid marriage on the basis of their newly recognised legal gender, it would be inconsistent to uphold a previous marriage. Under current Japanese family law, it would arguably not yet be feasible to amend or repeal Article 3(1) No. 2 GID Act.

2.3.1.3. Requirement of Childlessness

The third requirement for the legal recognition of preferred gender was originally formulated in the 2003 GID Act as the 'childlessness' of the applicant (Art. 3(1) No. 3 GID Act). A transgender person was not allowed to have a child grounded on legal parentage at the time of the Family Court decree authorising recognition. Once the applicant had decided to found a family, and had produced a child, the law considered that he or she should no longer be permitted to obtain legal recognition of preferred gender, unless the child had died in the meantime.[54]

In requiring childlessness, the legislators sought to avoid disturbing the family order and contravening the best interests of the child. It was held to be inappropriate from a social and legal point of view for a child to have a legal father who would subsequently transition to her preferred female gender and become the child's 'mother', and vice versa regarding the legal mother. In addition, it was thought that having a father or mother who has obtained recognition of preferred gender may induce a psychological burden or anxiety for the child and could harm his or her relationship with the parents. In light of the still limited acceptance of gender dysphoria and the unpredictable impact of the GID Act in society, the legislators opted for a strict requirement of childlessness when first introducing legal gender recognition. During the deliberations, the legislators contemplated, but ultimately rejected, the proposition that the childlessness requirement might violate fundamental rights, such as the right to equality under the law (Art. 14 Constitution) or the right to the pursuit of happiness (Art. 13 Constitution).[55] Furthermore, the legislature also rejected as a minor consideration the idea that there was any inconsistency with the fact that paternity could be retroactively established by the father's recognition or a Family Court decree (Arts. 779 and 787 Civil Code). Finally, law makers also disregarded arguments that there was no similar provision in existing gender recognition statutes around the world. For the legislators, it sufficed that Japan was a society with unique

Kazoku-hô, 3rd ed., Yuhikaku, Tokyo 2010, pp. 203–205, 213–214. Simple adoption between adults or by stepparents/grandparents does not require any involvement of Family Court (Art. 798, 2nd sentence Civil Code). These forms of simple adoption constitute about 99% of all cases. For statistics, see Ministry of Justice, *Koseki Tôkei* <www.e-stat.go.jp/SG1/estat/List.do?lid=000001114546>; Supreme Court, *Shihô Tôkei* <www.courts.go.jp/sihotokei/nenpo/pdf/B24DKAJ03.pdf>.

54 Nono (ed.), above n. 4, pp. 91–92; Onodera, above n. 45, p. 68.

55 The legislator contended that Art. 14 Constitution does not intervene, so long as a differentiated treatment between transsexual persons with and without children has a good reason. The legislature also doubted that Art. 13 Constitution guarantees the right of autonomy to decide on his/her legal sex, since it is primarily geared to biological factors and not to the person's intent. Nono (ed.), above n. 4, pp. 89–90.

customs, traditions, family models and other specificities which could justify the imposition of childlessness in the national law.[56]

Soon after the GID Act was promulgated in 2003, the requirement of childlessness was thoroughly criticised for unnecessarily restricting the range of transgender persons eligible to access legal recognition.[57] It was argued that the legislators' rationale to require childlessness was only geared to the family order and the best interests of minor children in abstract terms. It unduly excluded the possibility for the transgender person and his or her family members to define their interests and make an appropriate decision amongst themselves. Hence, two MtF transgender persons filed a lawsuit to challenge the constitutionality of Article 3(1) No. 3 GID Act. Although the petitioners remained unsuccessful after the Supreme Court dismissed their claim in 2007,[58] on the ground that the legislature pursued a legitimate purpose and did not exceed its discretion or violate constitutional norms, their lobbying activities created the impetus to amend the childlessness requirement in 2008. Consequently, the requirement of childlessness has now been amended to the 'absence of minor children' in a revised version of Article 3(1) No. 3 GID Act.[59]

Nonetheless, the requirement of the absence of minor children is still considered as excessively strict by some transgender persons. A Tokyo High Court decree of 30 March 2009[60] concerned the revised Article 3. The applicant, X, was an MtF transgender woman, who was born in 1965 and had a daughter, Y, from a relationship with her former spouse. After undergoing gender confirmation surgery and beginning to express a female gender identity, X sought to obtain legal recognition of her preferred gender. X, her daughter and another man, Z, shared a home and lived together. In June 2008, when Y was 16 years old, she married Z,[61] who was 51 years old, and divorced eleven days later. Upon the entry into force of the amended Article 3(1) No. 3 GID Act on 18 December 2008, X applied for legal recognition at the Tokyo Family Court. The judge, however, held that X had authorised Y to marry Z (Art. 737(1) Civil Code) with a view to manipulating her daughter's legal status. In marrying Z, Y had obtained majority (Art. 753 Civil Code), thus freeing X to apply for legal gender recognition. X knew that Y did not intend to live an actual marital life with Z, who was in fact X's partner, as indicated in X's diagnosis. Consequently, the judge dismissed the application, finding that X had sought to circumvent the requirement of the absence of minor

---

56 Nono (ed.), above n. 4, pp. 90–91; Onodera, above n. 45, p. 68.

57 Harima et al., above n. 17, pp. 106–114; Ôshima, above n. 37, p. 43; K. Shimazaki, 'Kojin no Sonchô: Sei Dôitsusei Shôgaisha Mondai' [Respect of Individuals: Problems of GID] [2004] 593 *Hôgaku Seminar* 12; Taniguchi, above n. 49, pp. 267–268.

58 Supreme Court, 19 October 2007, *KSG* 60-3, 36; Supreme Court, 22 October 2007, *KSG* 60-3, 37.

59 Law No. 70 of 18 June 2008.

60 Tokyo Family Court, 30 March 2009, *KSG* 61-10, 75.

61 The threshold age for marriage is set as 18 years old for men and 16 years old for women (Art. 731 Civil Code).

children under the amended Article 3(1) No. 3 GID Act and unduly committed an 'abuse of right' (Art. 1(3) Civil Code).

Although the outcome of this case may be respectable from a legal point of view, the question remains whether the family order or the best interests of the child would have effectively been infringed in the underlying case, had X successfully obtained legal recognition of her preferred female gender. Y was already 16 years old and capable of understanding X's situation, desire and need in accessing legal recognition. Y was certainly accustomed to X's female appearance and indeed willing to support X. Article 3(1) No. 3 GID Act, which does not allow any exception, unconscionably restricts the right to self-determination and respect for individual dignity of transgender persons, where the best interests of the child would not be harmed or even enhanced by the self-realisation of the parent. Hence, as has been suggested by several authors, it would be desirable either to abolish the requirement of the absence of minor children or at least introduce an option to exempt it, depending on circumstances of the case, family relations, the age and maturity of the child.[62]

2.3.1.4. Requirement of the Loss of Gonads or Gonadal Function

As the fourth requirement, Article 3(1) No. 4 GID Act provides that the applicant is not allowed to maintain gonads or needs to have a permanent loss of gonadal function. The 'absence of gonads' implies that they have been removed through a surgical procedure or do not exist for some other reason. The 'loss of gonadal function' indicates that, although the gonads still exist, they have lost their function perpetually due to the use of anti-cancer drugs or the application of X-rays. It does not only refer to the loss of reproductive function, but that of the entire gonadal function including hormone secretion. The loss must be permanent, not temporary or reversible. As a result, depriving one of reproductive function through sterilisation pursuant to the MPA[63] does not suffice.[64] The legislators justified Article 3(1) No. 4 GID Act by contending that it is inappropriate for transgender persons who have obtained legal gender recognition to subsequently have a child on the basis of their assigned legal gender, as it could cause confusion and complications to the parentage and family order. In addition, it was opined that a transgender person should not obtain hormones typically related to their birth-assigned legal gender from gonads, as it could yield physically or mentally negative effects.[65]

This fourth requirement not only has a paternalistic ground to protect the transgender person, but also an ethical ground to permanently prevent him or her

62 M. Tanaka, [2010] 6 *Sokuhô Hanrei Kaisetsu* 115–116 (Comment on Tokyo Family Court, 30 March 2009); also Tanamura, above n. 47, p. 7; Taniguchi, above n. 49, pp. 55–57.

63 *Cf.* above n. 12.

64 Nono (ed.), above n. 4, p. 93; Onodera, above n. 45, p. 68.

65 Nono (ed.), above n. 4, p. 93.

from having a child on the basis of a previously recognised legal gender. The policy objectives pursued by this fourth requirement are closely connected with those relating to the existing of minor children addressed in the law's third requirement (Art. 3(1) No. 3 GID Act). Some authors have criticised this legislative policy, considering that transgender persons should not be deprived of or restricted in their right to reproduction and parental rights only because they seek to legally and physically transition to their preferred gender.[66]

2.3.1.5. Requirement of Having the External Genital Features of the Opposite Sex

In terms of the fifth requirement, Article 3(1) No. 5 GID Act stipulates that the applicant must have obtained a part of the body that assumes the external genital features of the opposite sex. This means that, in the case of transgender women, they must submit to the removal of their testes and penis, as well as the construction of a vagina. In the case of transgender men, they must permit to the removal of their ovaries and womb, the extension of their urethra, the narrowing of their vagina and the construction of a penis. Article 3(1) No. 5 GID Act does not require exact conformity, but an appearance similar to the external genital features typically associated with the preferred gender. The legislature considered it necessary for the sake of public policy that the transgender applicant has obtained the external genital features of the opposite gender, as otherwise there could be confusion or disturbance when, for example, a transgender person enters a public bath or toilet. This fifth requirement is qualified as both a medical and legal requirement.[67]

However, the alteration in external genital features, which cannot be observed from the outside, scarcely plays a role in everyday life. Facial and bodily features are mostly altered by taking hormone treatment, removing a beard and bodily hair for transgender women, and removing breasts for transgender men. Although Japanese people often go to a public bath that is separated between men and women, external genital features are the most intimate sphere of the individual which people would not observe. Furthermore, gender confirmation surgery is notably a complicated and severe intervention into the body and entails risk, physical burden and prohibitive costs in the absence of available public health care. Transgender persons in poor health or economic condition are not eligible from the outset. Thus the fifth requirement can hardly be justified by public policy considerations. As the examples of Germany, Denmark, the Netherlands, Sweden, the UK and Argentina show, the Japanese legislature should consider

66 Tanamura, above n. 47, p. 8; Taniguchi, above n. 49, pp. 268–269.
67 Nono (ed.), above n. 4, pp. 93–94; Onodera, above n. 45, p. 68.

abolishing the surgery requirement with a view to protecting the bodily integrity and the reproductive health of transgender persons.[68]

2.3.2. Diagnosis

Article 2 GID Act provides that two or more experienced and knowledgeable physicians, who are eligible to properly make a diagnosis of gender dysphoria, must make the same diagnosis on the necessity to obtain legal recognition pursuant to generally accepted medical standards. The diagnosis is required to indicate, in particular, the applicant's family relations, life history, social non-identification with birth-assigned ('biological') sex, persistent self-identification with the preferred ('opposite') gender, intent to transition (both physically and socially) to the preferred gender and self-identification (both social and physical) with the preferred ('opposite') gender.[69] Article 2 GID Act requires the involvement of two or more physicians to make a prudent examination on gender identity of the transgender person, viewing the serious consequences of obtaining legal gender recognition. The physicians must be licensed in Japan to deliver such a diagnosis, although the gender confirmation surgery may have taken place abroad.[70]

Pursuant to the guidelines of the JSPN, the diagnosis of gender dysphoria and the eligibility for gender confirmation surgery is decided by a specialist panel.[71] The physicians are particularly required to differentiate transgender persons from intersex affected individuals. The physicians must also separate transgender applicants from other persons who might be suffering a psychiatric illness (e.g. schizophrenics) which manifests itself in claims of uncertainty about gender identity. Physicians authorise gender confirmation surgery, having regard to the current physical and psychological burden upon the applicant. They tend to refuse to issue a medical certificate when, for example, the transgender person is vulnerable to suicide or does not have support from his or her family members.[72]

---

[68] Harima et al., above n. 17, pp. 125–127, 169–172; Tanamura, above n. 47, p. 8; Taniguchi, above n. 49, pp. 269–271.

[69] M. Kawasaki, '"*Sei Dôitsusei Shôgaisha Seibetsu Toriatsukai Tokureihô*" no kaisetsu' [Commentary on the Law Concerning Special Rules Regarding Sex Status of a Person with GID], in Nono (ed.), above n. 3, pp. 237–238.

[70] Nono (ed.), above n. 4, p. 86.

[71] See above n. 15.

[72] K. Harima, 'Sei Dôitsusei Shôgai no Gainen, Genjô, Seishinka Ryôhô' [The Notion, Current State and Psychiatric Treatment of GID], in Nono (ed.), above n. 3, pp. 50–64; Yamauchi (ed.), above n. 9. pp. 39–123.

2.3.3. *Cross-Border Cases*

2.3.3.1. General Remarks

In cross-border cases, the question arises as to when, and according to which law, the Japanese judge is entitled to grant legal recognition of a person's gender. There are no statutory rules or case law in this respect. As to the applicability of the GID Act to foreign nationals, legislators have raised the following concerns: (a) recognising a foreign national's preferred gender, where the currently recognised legal gender has been registered in a birth certificate and other documents administered by the state of origin, could violate that state's sovereignty; (b) there are no clear rules on international adjudicatory jurisdiction or conflict of laws rules regarding legal gender recognition; and (c) a 'limping legal sex' may be constituted if the foreign state of origin refuses to recognise the Japanese Family Court decree rendered for nationals of that state.[73]

2.3.3.2. Applicable Law

The rules on legal gender recognition are notably embedded in personality rights, but concern at the same time the public interests of Japanese society. Focusing on the aspect of personality rights, one could think of establishing bilateral conflict of laws rules that point to the law of nationality,[74] *i.e.* the personal law under Japanese private international law (*cf.* Art. 23 AGRAL[75]).[76] This principle would, however, presuppose the interchangeability and equivalence of domestic law and foreign law pursuant to the traditional method of private international law established by *Savigny*.[77] This could hardly be assumed in relation to substantive norms on gender recognition, because its legal and medical requirements vary considerably from country to country. While Articles 1 and 3 GID Act provide for strict requirements, including the comparatively unique condition of the absence of minor children (Art. 3(1) No. 3 GID Act), other countries, such as the Netherlands and the UK, have substantially more liberal requirements.

From a perspective of public interests, it would lead to an imbalanced and unequal law application within the forum state if Dutch or British transgender persons were allowed to obtain legal recognition of their preferred gender under the simple conditions of the law of their nationality, whereas Japanese nationals were subject to the significantly more onerous requirements of the 2003 GID

---

73 Nono (ed.), above n. 4, p. 97.

74 See K. Yamauchi, 'Kokusaishihô ni okeru "Seitenkan" ni tsuite: Europa ni okeru giron' [On "Transsexualism" in Private International Law: Discussions in Europe], in idem, *Kokusai Kôjohô no Kenkyû*, Chûô Daigaku Shuppankai, Tokyo 2001, p. 229.

75 *Hô no Tekiyô ni kansuru Tsûsokuhô* (Act on General Rules for Application of Laws [AGRAL]: Law No. 78 of 21 June 2006).

76 See Y. Nishitani, 'Global Citizen and Family Relations' (2014) 7 *Erasmus Law Review* 134–146.

77 See F.K. von Savigny, *System des heutigen römischen Rechts*, vol. 8, Berlin 1849, pp. 2–38.

Act. The possibility of referring to public policy to exclude the application of foreign law that contravenes fundamental principles and morals in Japan (Art. 42 AGRAL) would not be sufficient to uphold social order and legal certainty. Rather, bilateral conflict of law rules would become superfluous if the application of the governing foreign law is systematically excluded.

Moreover, for the sake of security in medical care, only physicians licensed in Japan should be authorised to deliver a medical certificate to Japanese courts to certify the diagnosis of gender dysphoria and the eligibility of the applicant to obtain legal recognition (*cf.* Art. 3 (2) GID Act). The physicians in Japan, however, could hardly provide a medical certificate in accordance with legal and medical requirements under the respective foreign law, particularly because the necessary degree and form of surgical intervention considerably differs depending on the jurisdiction. As a consequence, it appears to be the only reasonable and feasible solution to always subject gender recognition procedures to the requirements of the *lex fori* in Japan.[78]

Despite the fear of the legislature, even if Japanese courts order the legal recognition of gender for non-nationals, it does not infringe the sovereignty of their states of origin, because gender recognition does not affect the latters' official documents, but is only entered in official documents issued by Japan, such as the register of inhabitants, driver's licence or health care certificate.[79] Certainly, there is a risk that the foreign state will refuse to recognise the Japanese Family Court's decree, so that the applicant obtains a 'limping legal sex' (where he is male in Japan but has a legal female gender in the foreign state, or vice versa). Nevertheless, insofar as the person is closely related to Japan, the Japanese judiciary should proceed to grant recognition to guarantee respect for individual dignity and self-determination of gender identity. The objective of international harmony of decisions in private international law should not supersede the requirement to vindicate the fundamental rights of individuals.[80]

2.3.3.3. International Adjudicatory Jurisdiction

Whether and how far Japanese courts exercise international adjudicatory jurisdiction to recognise the legal gender of an individual is not yet explicitly

---

78 T. Hayashi, 'Kokusaishihô-teki Kanten kara mita Sei Dôitsusei Shôgaisha no Seibetsu no Mondai' [Problems on Legal Sex of Transsexual Persons from a Viewpoint of Private International Law] [2009] 60-7 *Dôshisha Hôgaku* 1166; Y. Tameike, *Kokusaishihô Kôgi* [Lecture on Private International Law], 3rd ed., Yuhikaku, Tokyo 2005, p. 537. When transsexual persons seek to change their first name, Japanese courts will only exercise jurisdiction over Japanese nationals by applying Japanese law, not over foreign nationals in principle. This is because the name is considered as an issue of public law in the family register practice, unlike the prevailing academic opinions that point to the law of nationality of the person as an issue of personality rights or to the *lex causae* as a status issue (e.g. the law governing the marriage). See Nishitani, Familienregister, above n. 25, pp. 234–239.

79 Hayashi, above n. 78, p. 1167; Kawasaki, above n. 69, pp. 235–236.

80 Hayashi, above n. 78, pp. 1166–1167.

provided for. This issue will be discussed within the framework of the ongoing legislative work on international adjudicatory jurisdiction in family and personal status matters.[81] Considering that gender recognition is closely related to personality rights, Japanese courts should have the authority to render a decree for Japanese nationals. Furthermore, so long as foreign nationals are domiciled or habitually reside in Japan, the judiciary should ensure their legitimate interest to obtain gender recognition. Consequently, both Japanese nationals and those who are domiciled or permanently resident in Japan should be legally recognised on jurisdictional grounds,[82] even though it is not yet clear whether the legislature will adopt a specific provision to subject foreign nationals to Japan's jurisdiction.[83]

2.3.3.4. Recognition of Foreign Court Decrees

On the other hand, when foreign courts render a decree to recognise the legal gender of an individual abroad, that recognition will be accepted as a non-contentious matter,[84] insofar as the indirect jurisdiction of the rendering state is affirmed and its recognition does not run counter to Japan's public policy (Art. 118 No. 1 and 3 Civil Procedure Code[85] *mutatis mutandis*).[86] The recognition takes place automatically without any specific court proceedings (*delibazione*) to examine whether the conditions have been fulfilled. Hence, if a foreign national obtains a court decree which legally recognises preferred gender in a country of origin and declares that gender when registering at the Municipal Office in Japan, the Municipal Office is supposed to examine the authenticity and regularity of the foreign decree to be recognised in Japan.

---

81 The Legislative Committee of the Ministry of Justice has established a Sub-Committee on International Adjudicatory Jurisdiction in Personal and Family Matters on 7 February 2014 (Consultation No. 98); see <www.moj.go.jp/shingi1/shingi03500022.html>

82 Hayashi, above n. 78, p. 1166; Tameike, above n. 78, p. 537.

83 The Sub-Committee (above n. 81) has so far taken a reserved position toward adopting a specific provision on transsexualism. See the Interim Draft of 19 March 2015 <www.moj.go.jp/shingi1/shingi04900252.html>. For preparatory work of the legislation, see Shôjihômu Kenkyûkai (ed.), *Jinji Soshô-jiken tô ni tsuite no Kokusai Saiban Kankatsu Hôsei Kenkyûkai Hôkokusho* [Report of the Working Group on Legislation of International Adjudicatory Jurisdiction in Personal Status Matters etc.], Tokyo 2014, pp. 51–53 <www.moj.go.jp/content/000122844.pdf>.

84 For recognition of foreign decrees in non-contentious matters, *see* Y. Nishitani, 'Gaikoku Hishôsaiban no Shônin Shikkô' [Recognition and Enforcement of Foreign Decrees in Non-Contentious Matters], in Shôjihômu Kenkyûkai (ed.), *Hishôjiken ni tsuite no Kokusai Saiban Kankatsu tô ni kansuru Gaikoku Hôsei tô no Chôsa Kenkyû Gyômu Hôkokusho* [Report on Foreign Legislations etc. in relation to International Adjudicatory Jurisdiction etc. in Non-Contentious Matters], Tokyo 2014, pp. 218–222 <www.moj.go.jp/content/000119005.pdf>.

85 *Minji Soshô Hô* (Civil Procedure Code: Law No. 109 of 26 June 1996).

86 Tameike, above n. 78, p. 537.

III. CONSEQUENCES OF THE CHANGE OF LEGAL SEX AND/OR LEGAL GENDER

3.1. FUTURE RIGHTS, DUTIES AND ENTITLEMENTS

3.1.1. Legal Sex and Name

Once the Family Court renders a decree to recognise the applicant's preferred gender, the applicant is immediately treated as having his or her preferred legal gender in relation to the Civil Code and other statutes and ordinances, unless otherwise provided for (Art. 4(1) GID Act). The legal recognition of gender is entered in the family register *ex officio*, unlike other status changes (e.g. divorce by judgment) that require a separate declaration by the parties. The legislature sought to alleviate the burden of transgender persons in this respect.[87] In the family register, the family status of the transgender person is modified, e.g. from the 'first daughter' to the 'first son'. For the sake of privacy, when there are other family members registered in the same family register, a new separate family register is constituted for the transgender person (Art. 20*quater* FRA). Yet the fact that the person has obtained legal recognition is indicated in the register, although this occurs in a discrete manner without using the word 'GID'.[88] The Family Court decree immediately affects other official documents and entitlements to the public health care and pension systems.[89]

In order to change one's first name to reflect the legal recognition of preferred gender, the applicant is required to make a separate application at the Family Court pursuant to Article 107*bis* FRA, pleading that he or she has legitimate grounds for the change. Once a person's legal gender has been recognised by a Family Court decree, a judge will generally assume that such legitimate grounds exist.[90] Courts have notably been generous in granting a change of first name to transgender applicants (see also above section 1.1.2.2), including those who have not fulfilled the requirements for legal recognition because of marriage or existing minor children.[91]

87 Kawasaki, above n. 69, p. 246.

88 The civil status column will indicate: 'A Family Court decree pursuant to the Law 2003 No. 113 has become effective on (the date)'. Nono (ed.), above n. 4, pp. 101, 106–108.

89 Nono (ed.), above n. 4, p. 105.

90 Nono (ed.), above n. 4, p. 101.

91 Osaka High Court, 10 November 2009, *KSG* 62–8, 75 (a married MtF); Takamatsu High Court, 12 October 2010, *KSG* 63–8, 58 (an MtF waiting for his two children to attain the age of majority in 2014).

3.1.2. Marriage and Parentage

3.1.2.1. Marriage

Pursuant to Article 4(1) GID Act, a transgender person who has obtained legal recognition is treated in law as having his or her preferred gender. Consequently, that person can thereafter enter into a valid marriage or adopt children on the basis of that recognised gender.[92] Due to the requirement that the applicant be single or divorced (Art. 3(1) No. 2 GID Act), the previous marriage of the transgender person does not persist (above section 2.3.1.2).

3.1.2.2. Parentage

With regard to parentage under Japanese law, maternity arises automatically by the fact of the child's birth.[93] Non-marital paternity is established by recognition (Arts. 779 and 787 Civil Code), whereas marital paternity is assumed so long as the child is conceived during the marriage (Art. 772(1) Civil Code). The latter paternity presumption extends to children who are born more than 200 days after the celebration of marriage or within 300 days after the dissolution or revocation of marriage (Art. 772(2) Civil Code).[94]

The marital paternity presumption has generally been applied also to children born by 'artificial insemination by donor' (AID),[95] absent clear-cut rules to legally qualify the mother's husband who consented to the AID as the father.[96] However, when a child was born through AID outside marriage to a couple consisting of a transgender man and his female partner, previous court decisions have denied the paternity presumption because there was a lack of sufficient biological relationship. Nor was the transgender man allowed to recognise the child. The individual could not be indicated as the legal father of the child on the birth registration.[97]

---

92 Nono (ed.), above n. 4, p. 99.

93 Supreme Court, 27 April 1962, *Minshû* 16–7, 1247. Art. 779 Civil Code, which subjects illegitimate maternity to the mother's recognition, has been undermined by case law.

94 Nishitani, State, Family and Child, above n. 25, pp. 987–1007.

95 Tokyo High Court, 16 September 1998, *KSG* 51–3, 165; *cf.* Osaka District Court, 18 December 1998, *KSG* 51–9, 71.

96 Even though the husband who consented to the AID is presumed to be the legal father (Art. 772 Civil Code), he could possibly reverse it pursuant to Arts. 774–778 Civil Code. There is also risk that the child claims for the recognition of paternity against the donor (Art. 787 Civil Code). A. Kubota, *Kazokuhô*, 2nd ed., Yuhikaku, Tokyo 2013, pp. 204–210; Ômura, above n. 53, pp. 224–225.

97 Tokyo Family Court, 31 October 2012, *Kin-yû Shôji Hanrei* 1437, 18; Tokyo High Court, 26 December 2012, *Hanrei Times* 1388, 284; Osaka Family Court, 13 September 2013, *TKC* No. 25501809; for its criticism, *see* S. Ninomiya, 'Seibetsu no Toriatsukai wo Henkô shita Hito no Kon-in to Chakushutsu Suitei' [Marriage and Paternity Presumption of Transsexual Persons who have changed the Legal Sex] [2012] 345/346 *Ritsumeikan Hôgaku* 576–605.

The Supreme Court reversed this position on 10 December 2013.[98] In its decision, the Court held that Article 772 of the Civil Code also applies to transgender men, even though the established case law had denied the marital paternity presumption when the husband objectively could not have cohabited with the mother at the moment of conception because of, for example, lasting factual separation.[99] Justice Terada, who has subsequently been appointed Japan's Chief Justice, contended in a supplementary opinion that the legal institution of marriage consists in forming family relations for the next generation between the couple and children born in wedlock. The paternity presumption, including its denial by the father (Art. 774 Civil Code), does not solely rely on biological connections, but rather focuses on the father's intent. In his opinion, by allowing transgender persons to celebrate marriage, after obtaining legal gender recognition, like a usual couple (Art. 4(1) GID Act), the legislature must have presupposed that a transgender man may create family relations by consent, even if he cannot be the biological father of the child. As a consequence, and by virtue of reasonable interpretation of the paternity presumption rule, the transgender male was acknowledged as the legal father and the birth registration was corrected to enter his name accordingly (Art. 113 FRA).

While this ground-breaking Supreme Court decision certainly represents major progress in acknowledging parental and custody rights of transgender persons, its scope and applicability to other questions of legal parentage is not yet clear. If a transgender woman who marries while still recognised as having a male gender divorces and obtains recognition of her preferred female gender, and her former spouse subsequently gives birth to a child within 300 days after divorce, the paternity presumption under Article 772 Civil Code should also apply to protect the child, even if there is no 'father' at the time of birth. It remains to be seen whether the ruling of the Supreme Court leads to both the restricting of the paternity presumption in such a case[100] and the enactment of rules on legal parentage based on AID in general. Insofar as transgender men are unmarried, the rationale of the Supreme Court would not include allowing such persons to recognise a child born outside of wedlock by AID, absent a biological relation and marital family unit that deserves protection under the law.

A transgender woman cannot biologically and legally constitute parentage on the basis of her recognised gender, as maternity is established by the fact of the child's birth. Such women cannot resort to surrogacy contracts because those agreements are legally null and void in Japan. Nor is surrogacy officially facilitated

---

98 Supreme Court, 10 December 2013, *Hanrei Jihô* 2210, 27 = *Saibansho Jihô* 1593, 4.

99 The paternity presumption has been denied when, e.g., the husband was living separately from his wife for a long time (Supreme Court, 29 May 1969, *Minshû* 23-6, 1064; idem., 14 March 2000, *KSG* 52-9, 85) or serving as a soldier abroad (Supreme Court, 31 August 1998, *KSG* 51-4, 75), or the marriage was fictitious (Tokyo High Court, 20 January 2010, *Hanrei Jihô* 2076, 48). In the absence of paternity presumption, a negative declaration of parentage can be claimed by the mother, the father, the child or any other persons who have legitimate interests in it.

100 Above n. 99.

by gynaecologists or other physicians,[101] even though Japanese law does not explicitly prohibit the practice. Furthermore, surrogate motherhood established in a foreign country where it is admissible (e.g. several states in the US, Greece, the UK, Ukraine, Russia and India) cannot be recognised in Japan either, as it contravenes public policy and good morals. Legal parentage, therefore, cannot be constituted between a child and the intended parent, but only with the surrogate mother.[102]

The same problem arises when transgender individuals have their sperm (in the case of MtF transgender persons) or eggs (in the case of FtM transgender persons) frozen and preserved prior to accessing gender confirmation surgery in the hope of subsequently using them to have children with the aid of a surrogate mother. Such practice would not only run counter to public policy, but also the requirement under Article 3(1) No. 4 GID Act that the transgender person needs to have lost gonads or gonadal function. In these cases, the only possible way for transgender individuals to establish legal parentage is to resort to simple or full adoption (Art. 792 ff. Civil Code).

3.1.3. *Other Consequences*

The legal recognition of preferred gender yields the following effects: (a) In labour law, rules for the protection of female workers will no longer be applicable to a FtM transgender man, but become applicable to a MtF transgender woman, except for some specific rules (e.g. menstrual leave). Transgender women generally qualify to exercise a profession that is restricted to females, such as midwifery.[103] (b) In criminal law, transgender men are capable of committing rape and transgender women may be the victim of a rape crime. Convicted persons are imprisoned as male or female captives on the basis of their recognised legal gender.[104] (c) The threshold age for the old-age employees' pension differs between men and women, so the eligibility is determined pursuant an individual's recognised legal gender. With regard to the pension rights of a wife who survives her husband (*i.e.* the widow's pension or the pension for bereaved family up to 55 years old), a transgender woman does not automatically qualify through the legal recognition of her preferred gender. If, however, an individual has been eligible to receive such

---

101 The Japan Society of Obstetrics and Gynecology (JSOG) declared with other medical associations that it would not allow implementing surrogate motherhood in Japan <www.jsog.or.jp/about_us/view/html/kaikoku/H15_4.html>.

102 Supreme Court, 23 March 2007, *Minshû* 61-2, 619; *KSG* 59-7, 72. In this case, the surrogate motherhood was constituted by a Japanese applicant couple and a US surrogate mother in Nevada, US. The Nevada court decree that declared the legal parentage between the Japanese couple and the twins was not recognised in Japan due to its contravention of public policy.

103 Nono (ed.), above n. 4, pp. 99–100.

104 Nono (ed.), above n. 4, pp. 99–100.

a pension prior to the recognition of preferred gender, the claim continues to exist afterwards.[105]

3.2. EXISTING RIGHTS, DUTIES AND ENTITLEMENTS

Pursuant to Article 4(2) GID Act, obtaining legal gender recognition does not affect the status relationship and the person's rights, duties and obligations that existed prior to the Family Court decree in principle. In other words, the rights and duties existing at the time of recognition continue to exist, unless otherwise provided.[106]

In particular, the fact that a transgender person has previously been married and obtained the status of husband or wife is not affected, even if he or she subsequently divorces for the purpose of gender recognition. Therefore, for example, provision of family allowance based on the status as wife will continue to be paid to transgender man after accessing recognition.[107] Furthermore, in the government-managed old-age pension plan, the contribution is to be paid for 15 to 19 years by men from the age of 40 years and women from the age of 35 years, depending on their year of birth. For the sake of foreseeability and effective protection, a transgender woman does not lose the entitlement to an old-age pension after obtaining recognition (No. 3 of the Supplementary Provision of the GID Act).[108]

As an exception, existing rights and duties of transgender persons will be modified, e.g. in relation to disability compensation for accidents at work or public service that happened prior to recognition.[109]

IV. LEGAL CHALLENGES OF THE EXISTING RULES

Needless to say, the GID Act has brought about significant developments and advantages for transgender persons. It has enabled them to realise their gender identity. However, the current state of legal norms and provisions entail certain drawbacks.

First, the GID Act presupposes a sharp division between the male and the female gender. The strict categorisation of transgenderism into GID or gender dysphoria does not sufficiently reflect the wide spectrum of transsexual, transgender or intersex conditions. This standpoint presupposes that they are

---

105 Nono (ed.), above n. 4, p. 100.
106 Nono (ed.), above n. 4, p. 99.
107 Nono (ed.), above n. 4, p. 101.
108 Nono (ed.), above n. 4, p. 105.
109 Nono (ed.), above n. 4, p. 101.

also medical conditions, which is itself a contentious proposition and indeed offensive to some.

Second, the requirements to obtain legal recognition of preferred gender under Articles 1 and 3 GID Act are excessively strict. In particular, the requirement to be unmarried or divorced (Art. 3(1) No. 2 GID Act) has often forced transgender persons to divorce and abandon their families. The requirement of the absence of minor children (No. 3) unduly hinders transgender persons from obtaining recognition, especially where there may not be any risk of disturbing the family order or infringing the best interests of the child. Finally, the requirement to submit to gender confirmation surgery (Nos. 4 and 5) places deep physical and financial burdens upon transgender persons. It is doubtful that the public policy arguments brought about by the legislature suffice to justify such serious intervention into bodily integrity. In view of medical as well as legal developments, and modifications of standards in other countries, the Japanese legislature should contemplate further amendments to the current GID Act.

Third, the above-mentioned Supreme Court decision of 10 December 2013 on the marital paternity presumption in favour of a transgender man (above section 3.1.2.2) certainly plays an important role in developing legal norms on transgenderism. It has, however, left uncertainties as to how far this principle can be extended to other questions of legal parentage. It would be desirable that the legislature adopt comprehensive substantive and procedural rules on medically assisted reproduction and its effects as to legal parentage and family relations.

Due to insufficient rules and legal institutions under the present Japanese law, more than a few transgender persons cannot currently afford to satisfy, or abstain from satisfying, the requirements for the legal recognition of preferred gender. Consequently, these persons continue to suffer from discrimination and the physical, as well as psychological, burden of not being able to realise their preferred gender. It remains a challenge in the future as to how Japan will achieve tolerance and true societal diversity in an effort to provide effective protection for transgender persons as a sexual minority.

THE LEGAL STATUS OF TRANSSEXUAL AND TRANSGENDER PERSONS IN SINGAPORE

Terry Sheung-Hung KAAN*

Contents

I. HISTORY

A watershed in history for transgender persons in Singapore was quietly marked with the publication of a short newspaper article in the 31 July 1971 issue of *The Straits Times*, the leading English-language newspaper in Singapore. Buried on page 17, and sandwiched between a report about a drop in water usage in water-

* The author wishes to thank the Warden and Fellows of Merton College, Oxford University for a Visiting Research Fellowship for Trinity Term 2013. A major portion of the research for this chapter was undertaken during the term of the Research Fellowship. He also wishes to thank Ms Eileena W.Y. Lee of the Pelangi Pride Centre, Singapore, for making available the resources of the library at the Centre for some of the research for this chapter.

scarce Singapore and another about the Singapore Youth Orchestra, it recorded that 'Singapore's first sex change operation was successfully carried out on a 24-year-old man' on 29 July 1971. The surgery took place at the main obstetrics and gynaecology hospital in Singapore in a three-hour operation carried out by three surgeons from the University of Singapore.[1] Although surgical procedures had previously been carried out on patients affected by an intersex condition, this appears to be the first 'complete' gender confirmation surgery procedure to be carried out specifically for the treatment of gender dysphoria in Singapore.[2,3] The lead surgeon of the team carrying out the surgery later described the operation as the 'first sex change ever done in Singapore, and for that matter in the region'.[4]

The operation went well. Within a month, the newspapers followed up with a report that the patient was on the verge of being discharged from hospital – and had 'marriage plans'.[5] The second gender confirmation surgery was carried out a few months later in November of the same year, also involving a male-to-female (MtF) transgender individual. The patient in this second case appears to have been operated upon just two weeks after being referred to the hospital. She had come to the decision about submitting to gender confirmation surgery after reading the newspaper reports about the first operation.[6] About three years later, the first surgical intervention was performed upon a female-to-male (FtM) transgender individual.[7] It, too, was successful, although the individual had to endure a series of operations as part of the considerably more complex FtM transition process (in contrast to the single-stage procedure carried out for MtF transgender persons)[8] which required among other things the construction of a neophallus through a

1 J. Yeo, 'First sex change surgery in Singapore', *The Straits Times* (Singapore), 31 July 1971, p. 17.

2 It appears that partial gender confirmation surgery procedures for the sexual reassignment of patients with both male and female physical secondary sexual characteristics had been routinely carried out in Singapore before then, but that 'these mostly involved patients who had both male and female genitalia (hermaphrodites) and the removal of one set of genitalia. The 1971 operation was regarded as a first because it involved a surgical conversion aimed at functionally changing a person's sex': M.C. Chan, 'First sex change surgery' (1971), *Singapore Infopedia*, an 'electronic encyclopaedia on Singapore's history, culture, people and events', an online service of the National Library Board, Singapore <http://infopedia.nl.sg/articles/SIP_1828_2011-08-04.html> accessed 16.12.2013.

3 See also W.L. Tan, 'Sex change patient has marriage plans', *The Straits Times*, 25 August 1971, p. 8. The article describes the patient as 'Singapore's first complete sex-change patient'.

4 S.S. Ratnam and V.H.H. Goh, 'Becoming Shonna and Becoming Sam' in S.S. Ratnam, V.H.H. Goh and W.F. Tsoi, *Cries from Within: Transsexualism, Gender Confusion and Sex Change*, Longman Singapore, Singapore 1991, p. 26.

5 Tan, above n. 3.

6 'Second sex change operation in Singapore', *The Straits Times*, p. 15.

7 M. Kwee, 'Singapore's first sex change woman', *The Straits Times*, 20 October 1974, p. 1: this time, it made the headlines, albeit a minor one.

8 A. Illancheran, 'Transsexualism and Sex Reassignment Surgery (SRS) in Singapore' in K.H. Tan and E.H. Tay (eds.), *The History of Obstetrics and Gynaecology in Singapore*, The Obstetrical and Gynaecological Society of Singapore, and the National Heritage Board, Singapore 2003, pp. 596–597.

phalloplasty procedure.[9] It was not until early 1977, some three years after the first surgical procedure, that this individual completed his medical transition.

For both 'Shonna' and 'Sam' (the pseudonyms given by the lead surgeon to these two pioneer patients), the operations opened the door to new lives and identities. Significantly, the legal obstacles in the way of their assuming and fully exercising the rights of their new-found gender status were minimal, compared to the medical and social challenges which they faced. Legal clearances had been sought, and approval had been obtained from the Ministry of Health before the operations were carried out in what were then government hospitals. The result was that within a year of submitting to surgery, Shonna, the MtF transgender individual, executed a Statutory Declaration confirming her new status before a Commissioner for Oaths at the Singapore High Court, and soon thereafter was on her way to obtaining a new and amended National Identity Card[10] and passport issued in her new name – and gender.[11] With the legal recognition of their preferred gender, both Shonna and Sam found partners and got married.[12]

II. THE SOCIAL CONTEXT

2.1. DEMOGRAPHICS

Singapore is geographically a very small country (about 716 km^2, or 276 square miles), into which is crammed a total population of 5.4 million, resulting in one of the highest population densities in the world with an average of over 7,500 persons per square kilometre (over 19,500 persons per square mile) in a 100% urban environment.[13] Founded as a British colonial trading outpost in 1819, the majority of its present population are descended from immigrants from China, the Indian subcontinent, and what is now modern Indonesia who arrived during the colonial era to trade and to find employment.

Of the current population of 5.4 million (larger than that of Norway or New Zealand), only about 3.3 million are Singapore citizens, with foreigners with permanent residency rights (about 0.5 million) and 'non-residents' (about

[9] A procedure 'fraught with difficulties', and not always successful: Ratnam, Goh and Tsoi, above n. 4, pp. 72–76.

[10] The significance of the National Identity Card is discussed further below.

[11] *The Straits Times*, 16 April 1972, p. 6.

[12] S.S. Ratnam et al., 'Sex Change Surgery' in Ratnam, Goh and Tsoi, above n. 4, pp. 25–29.

[13] Unless otherwise specified, statistical data for Singapore given here and elsewhere in this chapter are taken from those published by the Department of Statistics, Ministry of Trade and Industry, Singapore, and in particular, from *Population Trends 2012*; *Singapore in Figures 2013*, and *Monthly Digest of Statistics Singapore: November 2013*, all publications of the Department of Statistics, Ministry of Trade and Industry, Singapore. All publications are available for download from the website of the Department of Statistics at <www.singstat.gov.sg> accessed 16.12.2013.

1.5 million, with lower-skilled service workers, construction workers, domestic workers and foreign students included in this category) making up the rest, so that Singapore citizens account for less than 62% of the total population of Singapore. Only citizens have the right to vote.

Of the resident population (Singapore citizens and permanent residents, but excluding 'non-residents'), the largest ethnic group is the Chinese (2.85 million, or 74.2%), followed by the Malays (0.51 million, or 13.3%), and then Indians (0.35 million, or 9.1%) with a remaining 0.13 million (3.3%) comprising other ethnic groups and races.[14] Yet another measure of diversity in the demographic fabric of Singapore is the many religions subscribed to by its population. Buddhism has the most adherents among Singaporean non-student residents aged 15 years and older at 33.9%, Taoism (including 'Chinese Traditional Beliefs') 11.3%, Islam 14.3%, Hinduism 5.2%, and Christianity 18.2%, with other religions accounting for less than 7%. Significantly, those reporting 'no religion' accounted for 16.4%.[15] Although the census statistics do not break down religious affiliations within ethnic groups, the main diversity occurs with the majority ethnic Chinese population.

Economically, Singapore does very well. Its GDP per capita of US$51,709 is above that of the United States (US$49,965), the United Kingdom (US$38,514), Germany (US$41,514), and in East Asia, Hong Kong (US$36,796) and Japan (US$46,720).[16] Medical services are of a very high standard, as reflected in the life expectancy at birth of 79.2 for men and 84.0 for women (figures comparable to those for Australia and Canada, significantly exceeding those for the United States and the United Kingdom, but bettered by those for Hong Kong (80.1 male, and 86.0 female). The infant mortality rate is among the lowest in the world at 2.0 per 1,000 live births, but so is its total fertility rate of only 1.15 per female.[17]

In many respects, Singapore's ethnic diversity is a reflection of that of Asia in microcosm, and the responses of some of its communities may offer an insight into the likely situation in other Asian countries. This picture of diversity has been set out in detail because the ethnic and religious diversity of Singapore's present demographics have direct implications for government executive and legislative policy, particularly in areas that may impinge on community, ethnic or religious sensitivities – including many issues relating to gender identity, sexual preferences and the law relating to marriage, the family as a social and

---

14 Department of Statistics, Ministry of Trade and Industry, Singapore, *Monthly Digest of Statistics Singapore, November 2013*, at Table 2.2.

15 Department of Statistics, Ministry of Trade and industry, Singapore, *Census of Population 2010 Statistical Release 1: Demographic Characteristics, Education, Language and Religion* (data downloadable from <www.singstat.gov.sg/publications/publications_and_papers/cop2010/census10_stat_release1.html> accessed 16.12.2013).

16 The World Bank, *GDP per capita (current US$)*, dataset for 2009–2013 <http://data.worldbank.org/indicator/NY.GDP.PCAP.CD> accessed 16.12.2016.

17 Department of Statistics, Ministry of Trade and Industry, Singapore, *Singapore in Figures 2013*, p. 2.

legal construct, as well as to the law of intestacy and inheritance. In the context of this chapter, the demographic diversity of Singapore, particularly in religious affiliations and ethnic cultural and social mores, have implications for the shape of future law reform relating to gender issues and sexual preferences in Singapore. As observed by the then Chief Justice of Singapore, while 'race and religion are the traditional fault lines that have to be carefully managed' in a multicultural and diverse society that is Singapore, 'new group identities are also developing. The growth of lesbian, gay, bisexual and transgender communities the world over has not left Singapore untouched'.[18] This is the challenge for Singapore which will be discussed in greater detail below.

2.2. THE INCIDENCE OF TRANSGENDERISM IN SINGAPORE

There are no publicly available statistics for the incidence of transgenderism and gender confirmation surgeries in Singapore. Neither the Ministry of Health nor the Department of Statistics, Singapore publishes any statistics specifically on the incidence of transgenderism. One study, which used the term 'transsexual', recorded a figure of 458 transsexuals (343 male transsexuals and 115 female transsexuals – a ratio of about 3:1) for the period up to 1986.[19] The conclusion of the author (in 1988) in that study was that the prevalence of 'transsexualism' was '35.2 per 100,000 population (or 1/2,900) for male transsexualism, and 12.0 per 100,000 (or 1/8,300) for female transsexualism'.[20] Whether or not this reported prevalence can be interpolated to the current population is unknown.

A major difficulty in the way of procuring accurate statistics is of course that such statistics depend on self-reporting, which transgender persons are unlikely to do until they have decided to submit to gender confirmation surgery. Transgender individuals who have yet to make the decision to access such surgery, or who may not wish or be reluctant for personal, economic, family or social reasons to access surgery (they may, for example, already be in an existing marriage with children) are unlikely to report their transgender identity – even assuming that there was such a thing as a central registry or authority for reporting their status (there

18 S.K. Chan, 'Multiculturalism in Singapore: The Way to a Harmonious Society' (2013) 25 *Singapore Academy of Law Journal* 84, 108. The paper was delivered at the International Academy of Matrimonial Lawyers Audrey Ducroux Memorial Lecture 2012 on 8 September 2012.

19 W.F. Tsoi, 'The prevalence of transsexualism in Singapore' (1988) 78 *Acta Psychiatr Scand.* 501–504.

20 Tsoi, above n. 19, p. 501. Writing in 2003 (Illancheran, above n. 8) Professor A. Illancheran, a leading expert and pioneer surgeon in the field, mentions that 'more than a thousand patients' having been seen at the Gender Identity Clinic established by Professor S.S. Ratnam, the pioneering surgeon who led the team that carried out the first SRS operation in Singapore, with 'several hundred SRS' having been performed.

is none). Until transgender persons decide to submit to gender confirmation surgery, they tend, often because of their fear of public rejection, to live a secretive life. This is true not only before but also after accessing surgical treatments. Many individuals would move to a different vicinity or emigrate to other countries. Hence it is difficult to carry out effective follow-up treatment and comprehensive evaluations of the efficacy of the gender confirmation surgeries and to assess the extent to which individuals adapt following a process of surgical transition.[21] In a related context, it was reported in Parliament that the Government does not even have statistics on the 'number of gay teens in Singapore', with the reporting Minister noting 'the difficulty in obtaining such data' for what would presumably be a much larger group than transgender individuals.[22]

The current lack of even rough data presents difficulties not only for the public health authorities, and for the medical and social teams providing medical intervention for transgender persons, but also seriously hampers the efforts of local transgender support groups in seeking to understand the true scale and nature of the challenge. But others take the view that the incidence of transgender persons who have not opted for gender confirmation surgery and who have not made public their preferred gender may be actually lower than suggested because Singaporeans appear to be more willing than many of their peers in other Asian countries (certainly in comparison with many neighbouring countries) to seek medical advice on surgical treatments, on several arguments. These include the fact that gender confirmation surgeries are medically well-established and readily available in Singapore, and that the procedure is not only socially but, perhaps more importantly, legally acceptable in Singapore.[23] Legal acceptance operates at many levels. At the lower threshold, there is the assurance that gender-related surgical intervention is not against the law as it may be in some Asian countries. At the higher threshold, there is the assurance that transgender persons are entitled to exercise the incidental rights of their preferred gender such as official recognition of that preferred gender post-surgery, entitlement to a marriage recognised by the law, and the adoption of children.

At the lower threshold, there is indeed reasonable legal certainty. Both the courts and Parliament have made it clear that as a matter of law and of policy, transgender individuals who submit to gender confirmation surgery are entitled to the legal status of their preferred gender, and to equal protection like any other citizen by the law. As put by a psychiatrist with considerable experience with transgender persons, '[t]ranssexuals are not suppressed or harassed by the police

[21] V.H.H. Goh, 'Transsexualism: A Crisis in Gender Identity in Males and Females' in Ratnam, Goh and Tsoi, above n. 4, p. 21.

[22] Singapore Parliamentary Reports, *Hansard*, the reply of Dr Mohamad Maliki Bin Osman, the Parliamentary Secretary for Community Development, Youth and Sports, for the Minister for Community Development, Youth and Sports, Parliament No. 10, Session No. 2, Vol. 80, Sitting No. 8 (20 July 2005).

[23] Tsoi, above n. 19, p. 503.

in Singapore, and [are] therefore more willing to reveal their identity'. In speaking about 'transsexuals', the psychiatrist included transgender persons who have *not* as yet decided to access gender confirmation surgery or who are access to access such treatments.[24] For transgender persons who intend to submit to surgical interventions, this assurance is more fundamental than may be appreciated at first glance by Western readers. It is the assurance that people will not be persecuted for taking the first step towards 'outing' themselves to seek the medical treatments and advice they need. At the higher threshold, some things are clear, despite a hiccup occasioned by a decision of the Singapore High Court in 1991. Marriage, family formation and adoption all seems clear. But other incidences and rights remain uncertain. In particular, the law as it presently stands may especially disadvantage transgender persons who do not wish to embark on a process of surgical transition, and this difficulty forms the basis of an extended discussion towards the end of this chapter.

2.3. THE PROFILE OF TRANSGENDER PERSONS IN SINGAPORE

There have been few studies of transgender persons in Singapore since the early 1990s. One contributory cause may have been the closure in 2001 of the Gender Identity Clinic established by the pioneering gender confirmation surgeon in the late 1970s. But the greater impact seems to have been the result of a general trend towards transgender persons opting to go to Thailand or to other places abroad to access surgical treatments.[25] With this caution in mind, the following observations on general trends may be offered.

A significant trend noted in the earlier studies was that transgender persons in Singapore tended to be relatively young. A 1988 study found that 82% of transgender females were below 30 years old, while the corresponding figure for transgender men was 93%.[26] It has been reported that the average age at which transgender men in Singapore start contemplating gender recognition surgery was 17 years – with just an average of just 2.3 years before putting those thoughts into action.[27] The mean age of transgender females was 23.8 years at the time of surgical intervention, while that for transgender men was 24.9 years.[28] Transgender persons who accessed surgical treatments in Singapore uniformly expressed satisfaction with their gender status post-surgery, although the practical and physical difficulties and anatomical realities of constructing a 'fully functioning

---

24 Tsoi, above n. 19, p. 503.

25 'Singapore's only sex-change clinic has re-opened', *The Straits Times*, 8 June 2003, p. 32.

26 Tsoi, above n. 19, p. 503.

27 W.F. Tsoi, 'Psychological Profiles of Transsexuals' in Ratnam, Goh and Tsoi, above n. 4, p 46.

28 W.F. Tsoi, 'Follow-up study of transsexuals after sex-reassignment surgery' (1993) 34 *Singapore Med. J.* 515–517.

male neophallus' inevitably left many transgender men less than satisfied with the surgical results.[29] There is therefore a clear distinction between satisfaction with the post-surgical status, and the new sex organ functions. For transgender females, satisfaction with both outcomes was high at 91% for satisfaction with the post-surgery gender status and 82% for organ function. But for transgender men, satisfaction with organ function was much lower at 39%, although satisfaction with their post-surgery gender status remained high at 81%.[30] Significantly, no transgender person undergoing gender confirmation surgery in Singapore reported an 'adverse (regretted) outcome.'[31]

The reported social outcomes of gender confirmation surgery for transgender persons in Singapore are encouraging. Most (95%) advanced 'socially and financially'.[32] For many, surgery made possible a cherished life goal by allowing them to legally enter into marriage in their new gender. In the available Singapore studies, there appears to have been no instance of an already-married person undergoing surgical intervention post-marriage, although as previously noted, the local data is very much incomplete. In one study, transgender persons were interviewed between two to five years after their successful transition. 32% of transgender women reported that they had become legally married to men, while 39% of transgender men reported that they had become legally married to women.[33] This limited data however underscores the view that many pre-operative transgender persons in stable relationships are nonetheless prompted to consider surgery because their pre-operative status made legal marriage impossible. For many transgender persons, marriage is the one of the main driving forces in their decision to submit to gender confirmation surgery because:

> 'The married status in Singapore conferred many benefits to the couple, some of which were: (1) eligibility for low cost housing, (2) entitlement to subsidized medical treatment (for wives of married men), and (3) better chances in adopting children. Transsexuals had difficulty obtaining employment because they had to show their identity cards in which their sex status would be included. Many employers were not sympathetic towards transsexuals whose choice of occupations was therefore restricted. Many pre-operative transsexuals had to opt for entertainment jobs, e.g., working in bars, lounges and massage parlours or engaging in prostitution.'[34]

In the context of Singapore, access to subsidised housing from the government's Housing & Development Board (HDB) schemes is particularly important and even vital for all but the highest economic strata of the Singapore population,

[29] W.F. Tsoi, 'Psychological Profiles of Transsexuals' in Ratnam, Goh and Tsoi, above n. 4, p. 46.
[30] Tsoi, 'Follow-up study of transsexuals after sex-reassignment surgery', above n. 28, p. 516.
[31] Ratnam, Goh and Tsoi, above n. 4, p. 46, and Tsoi, above n. 28, p. 516.
[32] Tsoi, above n. 28, p. 516.
[33] Tsoi, above n. 28, p. 516.
[34] W.F. Tsoi, 'Psychological Profiles of Transsexuals' in Ratnam, Goh and Tsoi, above n. 4, p. 40.

given that more than 80% of Singaporeans live in subsidised housing sold by the HDB.[35] The surgical transition effected by gender confirmation procedures is therefore not only about effecting a 'new gender status', but also the entitlement to a normal family life and participation in and the exercise of social and economic rights and privileges that ordinary Singaporeans take for granted.

III. THE REGULATORY CONTEXT

Current legislative provision for transgender and transsexual people in Singapore can be very simply stated: there is no legislation governing, referring to or relating to the rights of transgender persons in Singapore apart from the 1996 amendments introducing the present section 12 provisions of the Women's Charter.[36]

It should not be imagined that the absence of legislative provisions means that there was no law governing or affecting transgender people in Singapore prior to the legislative amendment. Like many other former British colonies given their independence in the post-war era of de-colonisation in the 1950s and the 1960s, the foundation of Singapore's legal and political system is its Westminster-style constitution, which is essentially a codified version of the mostly unwritten constitutional arrangements of the United Kingdom. Founded by the British in 1819, Singapore was ruled by the British until 1963, when the British Crown Colony of Singapore was given its independence. Singapore opted upon independence for almost immediate federal union with the neighbouring new state of Malaysia. The union, however, did not work, and two years later in 1965, Singapore and Malaysia came to an agreement for peaceful secession from Malaysia, and Singapore became an independent nation on its own. From the time of its founding, English law has always been applied by the colonial authorities, at first informally, but subsequently and from 27 November 1826, when the Second Charter of Justice was issued by the Crown, the authorities in Singapore were specifically directed to apply English common law to the extent that it was not inconsonant with the customary law of the local population.[37] The result of this was that English common law effectively became the main body of applicable law in Singapore, with only minor accommodation for specific areas of private law such as the law of marriage and succession for specific ethnic and religious

35 Department of Statistics, Ministry of Trade and Industry, Singapore, *Monthly Digest of Statistics Singapore, November 2013*, above n. 14, p. v.

36 The present sections 12(1)–(4) of the Women's Charter (Cap. 353), originally introduced as a new section 11A(1)–(4) by the Women's Charter (Amendment) Act 1996 (No. 30 of 1996), which was passed by the Singapore Parliament on 27 August 1996, but only came into force on 1 May 1997.

37 For an overview of the complex development and sources of Singapore law, *cf.* Y.H. Goh and P. Tan, 'An Empirical Study on the Development of Singapore Law' (2011) 23 *Singapore Academy of Law Journal* 176–226. For a specific commentary on the Second Charter of Justice, see the monograph by A. Phang, *From Foundation to Legacy: The Second Charter of Justice*, Academy Publishing, Singapore: 2006.

communities.[38] The provisions of the Second Charter of Justice continued to apply even after independence, and the Court of Final Appeal for Singapore continued to be Her Majesty's Judicial Committee of the Privy Council.

It was only in 1993 that two separate legislative moves were made to end this dependence on English common law and on the colonial judicial system. Firstly, the Singapore Parliament enacted laws to abolish appeals to the Privy Council and to establish its own national final and permanent court of appeal in the Singapore Court of Appeal of the Supreme Court.[39] Secondly, the provisions of the Second Charter of Justice 1926 were effectively repealed and replaced by the passage of the Application of English Law Act.[40] In its place, the Application of English Law Act provided for a definitive list of English statutes which were to be 'received' as legislation in Singapore to have effect as though they were Acts of Singapore's own Parliament. More importantly, however, it rejigged the provision for the continued reception and application of English common law by specifying that 'common law of England (including the principles and rules of equity), so far as it was part of the law of Singapore immediately before 12th November 1993, shall continue to be part of the law of Singapore ... so far as it is applicable to the circumstances of Singapore and its inhabitants and subject to such modifications as those circumstances may require.'[41] The unspoken corollary of this direction was of course that the Singapore courts were freed to consider and develop its own body of common law from that date thereafter.

The combined effect of the Second Charter of Justice 1826 and its subsequent modification by the Application of English Law Act is that English common law precedents established before 12 November 1993 continue to be applied by the courts in Singapore. In the context of the law affecting transgender people, the unfortunate consequence is that the common law principles established by the English decision of *Corbett v Corbett*[42] continue to apply presumptively in Singapore, but without the benefit of the comprehensive corrective legislative regime established by the UK Gender Recognition Act 2004. It also means that, prior to 1993, the Singapore courts were directed to apply English precedents, unless there were compelling reasons to do otherwise. So it is not surprising that the Singapore High Court decided in 1991 in the controversial case of *Lim Ying v Hiok Kian Ming Eric*[43] to follow and apply the principles set out in *Corbett v Corbett*.

The decision in *Eric Hiok* overturned two decades of legal, social and governmental assumptions about the status of transgender persons, and in

38 *Regina v Willans* (1858) 3 Kyshe 16.

39 The Singapore Court of Judicature (Amendment) Act 1993. For a commentary, see Y.L. Tan, 'Legislative Comment: Supreme Court of Judicature (Amendment) Act 1993' [1993] *Singapore Journal of Legal Studies* 557–577.

40 Cap. 7A of the Revised Edition 1994, 12 November 1993.

41 Section 3, the Application of English Law Act.

42 [1971] P 83; [1970] 2 All ER 33.

43 [1991] SGHC 135.

particular their rights in relation to marriage and formation of the family. The status of transgender persons, together with marriages which had been contracted by them, as well as of the families which they had formed, and the children which they had adopted, were instantly thrown into a state of doubt and confusion as a consequence of the decision. It was not until 1996 when Parliament stepped in with the amendments to the Women's Charter that some clarity was restored – but these provisions are confined to clarifying and confirming the status and rights of transgender individuals who have submitted to gender confirmation surgeries only in relation to marriage and formation of the family. The general law relating to transgender people in Singapore remains untouched, and the some of the implications from the decision in *Eric Hiok* remain to be addressed. The decision in *Eric Hiok*, its impact and implications, and its role in the genesis of the 1996 legislative amendments will be addressed at length below.

IV. THE LEGAL STATUS OF TRANSGENDER PERSONS IN SINGAPORE

4.1. 1971–1991: THE ACCEPTED REGIME PRIOR TO *ERIC HIOK*

No regulatory procedure for the recognition of preferred gender has ever been published or mandated by either the Government, or by Parliament, and this situation obtains to this day. Given the very small number of people affected, this absence of a published formal regulatory procedure is unsurprising, but the process itself seems uncontroversial and straightforward. Under the provisions of the National Registration Act,[44] every Singapore resident attaining the age of 15[45] is required to have a national registration identity card.[46] Legally, the card is required only as a document of identity for government services, but in practice, the use of identity cards has become pervasive in every aspect of transactional life in Singapore in both the private as well the public sectors. Government departments, hospitals and medical clinics, banks, schools, telephone and internet service providers, landlords and (notably) employers among many others will all require at some time the production of a national registration identity card to confirm the identity of the holder, and to determine the holder's eligibility for services such as the provision of medical services, hospitalisation, the opening of a bank account and so forth.

For all intents and purposes, the identity card is the default document of identity in everyday life when positive identification is required or desired. This

44 Cap. 201, Revised Edition of 1992.
45 The National Registration Regulations, G.N. No. S226 of 1991, regulation 3.
46 Sections 5 and 6, National Registration Act.

practice of the universal application of the identity card has come about largely as a matter of convenience. Although Singapore residents are not strictly required by law to carry on their person their identity card, they are however required to produce it on demand by police or other statutorily authorised officers, as well as for over-the-counter government services and transactions[47] so that most Singaporeans carry their identity card with them on their person together with their bank debit cards, credit cards, bus and commuter subway cards and such, simply because it is the most convenient – and most authoritative – document of identity. The national registration identity card serves many of the functions for which Social Security numbers are used for in the United States, or drivers' licences in countries that do not have a national identity card system.

Crucially, the legal gender of the holder is shown prominently on the front of the identity card as either 'M' (Male) or 'F' (Female).[48] Under the provisions of the National Registration Act, holders of identity cards are required to inform the Commissioner for National Registration and to take steps for the correction of the relevant particulars on the identity card if the holder changes his address,[49] or '(a) changes his name; or (b) has in his possession an identity card containing any particulars, other than his address, which are to his knowledge incorrect'.[50] The most common reason for applying for corrections to be made is of course a change of address, but the change of name is sufficiently common for the Singapore Immigration and Checkpoints Authority (the government agency with responsibilities for registration under the Act) to maintain a webpage outlining the procedure for adding to a name, or changing a name altogether.[51] The prescribed procedure is straightforward, and application, like most citizen–government transactions in Singapore, may be made online. The only relevant document that the applicant has to produce in support of the change of name is a marriage certificate (for the insertion of a married name), or a baptismal certificate or other religious certificate (often for the addition of a Christian first name, or other religious name or change to a different name altogether for any religious reason whatsoever – there is no prescribed standard form for such certificates). If all else fails, a deed poll (for a name change for any reason whatsoever, which reason

47 The National Registration Regulations, regulations 7 and 8.

48 On its face, the identity card offers remarkably little information apart from a photograph and a thumbprint of the holder, the identity card number (the 'NRIC number') and its date of issue, the race, date of birth, gender, address, and country of birth of the holder. In its present form, it is not a 'smart card' in that there is no machine-readable chip embedded in the card, but it bears on the reverse a simple bar code encoding the identity card number itself (e.g. 'S1234567X'). The identity cards of Singapore citizens are immediately distinguishable by their pink colour; those of non-citizen permanent residents are blue in colour and have a field stating the nationality of the holder.

49 Section 8, National Registration Act.

50 Regulation 10(1) of the National Registration Regulations.

51 Singapore Immigration and Checkpoints Authority, *Update Change of Name in IC* <www.ica.gov.sg/page.aspx?pageid=140> accessed 20.12.2013.

need not be disclosed on the deed poll), readily executable before any solicitor or Commissioner for Oaths, may be relied upon.

It will be immediately appreciated that a change of name will be directly relevant to a person who seeks legal recognition of his or her preferred gender. But while a name change can be readily accommodated with the plain language of the Act and the Regulations, there is no specific provision for recognising a person's preferred gender, although this can be read as being implicit within the meaning of Regulation 10(1)(b) of the Regulations requiring holders to apply to the Commissioner for National Registration to make the necessary correction if he or she 'has in his possession an identity card containing any particulars, other than his address, which are to his knowledge incorrect'. If correction of a gender marker was not covered by this provision, then by implication, every person who submits to gender confirmation surgery would be in breach of the law. Fortunately, the pragmatic interpretation of the authorities has always been that when a person has submitted to gender confirmation surgery, and has altered his or her physical characteristics, then the Commissioner for National Registration will modify both the name *and* gender markers on production of a medical certificate attesting to such surgery. This procedure for change of name and gender markers for the national registration identity card was accepted as being lawful (although not with regard to the legal right to marriage and its incidents) by the Singapore High Court in *Eric Hiok*.

It is clear from the newspaper reports of the very first gender confirmation procedures in Singapore in 1971 that care had been taken by the team carrying out the operation to consult with and obtain the necessary assurances and approvals from the authorities in relation to the newly recognised gender status of their patients. The first report of such name and gender recognition was granted to the first MtF individual to submit to gender confirmation surgery on 15 April 1972. But it appears that her case was not the first such recorded official change of name and gender makers effected in Singapore. The same newspaper report records that the first case of a name change by a transgender Singapore national, who had 'undergone a gradual series of sex-operations in Hong Kong and Europe' was made consequent to a successful application to the Singapore High Court for a declaratory order some two years earlier.[52]

It is not possible to amend a birth certificate in Singapore. This reflects exactly the English common law position before the passage of the UK Gender Recognition Act 2004. The birth certificate is taken to be a record of inalterable historical fact, even though the record of gender on the identity card (or passport) can be amended to reflect the new status of the holder.[53] But for Singapore

52 'Sex change man signs statutory declaration affirming that he is now a woman', *The Straits Times*, 16 April 1972, p. 6. The declaratory order was allowed by Winslow J. The judgment is unreported.

53 The Singapore High Court in *Lim Ying v Hiok Kian Ming Eric* [1991] SGHC 135, paras. 53–56, in which the English precedents of *Rees v UK* (1987) 17 Fam Law 157, and *Cossey v UK* [1990]

residents, this is not as much an issue as it may be in many Western countries, because the production of a birth certificate is seldom required even for official purposes. The national registration identity card serves as *the* document of status, nationality and identity, not the birth certificate. For this reason, the birth certificate is largely irrelevant in the day-to-day transactions of life in Singapore. The author does not remember having been asked by any government agency or department to produce his birth certificate at any time within the last three decades. A simple illustration may suffice. Since the doctrine of *jus soli* has no application in Singapore citizenship law, a birth certificate is of little use in proving citizenship, or entitlement to any of the privileges or rights of Singapore citizenship. It may be remembered that mention was made at the beginning of this chapter to the demographics of Singapore. Singapore citizens (a fair proportion of whom were born elsewhere) account for less than 62% of the total resident population in Singapore. Therefore, the impracticability of using birth certificates (which may be from many different countries, and in languages other than English) as a standard means of identification becomes obvious. It is of note that the respondent in *Eric Hiok* did not take any steps to alter the entry made in respect of his legal gender in the Register of Births and Deaths,[54] despite changing the particulars of his identity card.[55] As far as most government agencies were concerned, the statement of gender on the identity card was conclusive. Even the Singapore military has accepted the newly recognised legal gender of transgender men in applying to them the statutory obligation of compulsory national service conscription for all male Singapore citizens.[56]

As noted above, marriage is one of the most cherished objectives for those who submit to gender confirmation surgery. Again, it is clear that this legal point was cleared in advance with the authorities by the pioneering surgical team in Singapore. The precedents established by the first cases in 1971 (for MtF transgender persons) and 1974 (for FtM transgender persons) opened the door for others in the following two decades to enter into the state of lawful matrimony.[57] Under the then-existing law for non-Muslim marriages, post-operative transgender individuals were treated as any other applicants by the Registrar of Marriages. The only relevant documents relating to their status was

TLR 664 were applied and followed.

54 The Register established under section 5 of the Registration of Births and Deaths Act (Cap. 267 of the Revised Edition of 1987). The Act allows only for 'correction of errors' (section 24). The same section makes it clear that even if a correction of an error is made, the 'register may be corrected by entry (but so that no alteration of the original entry is made)', *i.e.* the original erroneous historical record must be preserved together with the correction. Registers under the Act are not open to inspection by the public (section 7).

55 *Lim Ying v Hiok Kian Ming Eric* [1991] SGHC 135, para. 53.

56 *Cf.* the speech of Mr Mohamad Maidin B P M, the Parliamentary Secretary to the Minister for Information and the Arts, The Singapore Parliamentary Reports, *Hansard*, Parliament No. 8, Session No. 2, Vol. 66, Sitting Date 27 August 1996, at column 540.

57 Tsoi, above n. 28, p. 516.

a statutory declaration[58] essentially declaring that they met the requirements for the contracting of a lawful marriage under the Women's Charter; that 'there is no lawful impediment to the marriage.'[59]

The intent of requiring the statutory declaration seems obvious. It is a declaration to the Registrar of Marriage as to the required status, such as minimum age, residency status, and most importantly, that neither of the intending contracting parties are encumbered by a subsisting marriage, *i.e.* 'that neither of the parties to the intended marriage is married under any law, religion, custom or usage to any person other than the person with whom such marriage is proposed to be contracted.'[60] The law of marriage was in a state of transition at that point in Singapore's legal history. Polygamous marriages could be contracted according to 'customary law' during the colonial era. It was common for wealthy Chinese men to have more than one wife. The Women's Charter was enacted in 1961 with a view to ending the disadvantaged social and legal status of women under customary law marriages, and bringing about parity of rights between men and women within a marriage, and substantially boosting protection for the rights of women and children in the institution of the family.[61] To this end, a key provision of the Women's Charter was the abolition of polygamous marriages for all Singaporeans from 15 September 1961.[62] As will be explained below, Muslim Singaporeans are not affected, as they are not bound by the Women's Charter if they elect to have their marriage solemnised or registered according to the provisions for Muslim private law in Singapore.[63] So the law required that marriages contracted under the Women's Charter be monogamous marriages.

There was no mention in the Women's Charter or anywhere else in the Singapore statutes about transitioning being an impediment. But under the Interpretation Act, 'monogamous marriage' is defined as 'a marriage which is recognised by the law of the place where it is contracted as a voluntary union of one man and one woman to the exclusion of all others during the continuance of the marriage.'[64] The intent of this provision seems clear. The emphasis on 'one man and one woman' is clearly intended to underline the new policy permitting only monogamous marriage for the majority of Singaporeans. The law is not

---

58 The then section 16(2) of the Women's Charter, now section 17(2).

59 The present section 17(2)(d) of the Women's Charter.

60 The present section 17(2)(e) of the Women's Charter.

61 The Long Title of the Act reads: 'An Act to provide for monogamous marriages and for the solemnization and registration of such marriages; to amend and consolidate the law relating to divorce, the rights and duties of married persons, the protection of family, the maintenance of wives and children and the punishment of offences against women and girls; and to provide for matters incidental thereto.'

62 Part II of the Women's Charter.

63 Section 3 of the Women's Charter, and Part VI of the Administration of Muslim Law Act (Cap 3, Revised Edition of 2009) generally.

64 Section 2(1) of the Interpretation Act, Cap 1. The Act provides for general definitions of words, phrases and concepts which are to be universally applied in the statutory interpretation of all other statutes, unless there is specific provision otherwise. The Act's definition of 'monogamous marriage' accordingly applies to the Women's Charter.

interested in the history of the gender of the parties, but only in whether or not they are free and unencumbered and thus qualified to enter into a monogamous marriage. This assumption is borne out by the fact that the Registrar of Marriages, until the decision in the *Eric Hiok* case, required the intending marriage partners to produce their national registration identity cards (which would in the case of transgender persons state the gender to which they had transitioned), and not their birth certificates (which would have disclosed the parties' gender as recorded at birth).[65]

4.2. 1991–1996: THE *ERIC HIOK* DECISION

On 25 September 1991, all these comfortable, seemingly settled, legal and social assumptions in relation to the legality of marriages involving transgender persons, and indeed, in relation to the very legal status of the gender of transgender individuals, collapsed into a state of total uncertainty with the High Court decision in *Lim Ying v Hiok Kian Ming Eric*.[66] By implication, the status of children adopted by parties to such marriages was also thrown into doubt.

On 26 July 1990, the petitioner, Madam Lim Ying, had married the respondent, Mr Eric Hiok at the Singapore Marriage Registry under the provisions of the Women's Charter. She was a babysitter. He was a forklift driver. The marriage did not last long. Madam Lim filed a petition for divorce a little more than two months after the marriage. It is perhaps significant that, while Madam Lim was represented by counsel, Mr Hiok did not contest the petition and was neither present nor represented by counsel at the hearing of the petition before the High Court judge, the Judicial Commissioner Mr K.S. Rajah.

Madam Lim's case was that she had 'believed that she was marrying a man who was a bachelor and that the marriage was a monogamous marriage.' But upon starting life together, the couple had attempted to consummate their relationship without success. Madam Lim contended that it was only then that Mr Hiok revealed that he had previously submitted to gender confirmation surgery sometime in 1987. Consummation was therefore impossible. Madam Lim contended that, had she known that Mr Hiok was, in her words, 'not a man', she would not have married him 'because she wanted to have children.' She also contended that because of Mr Hiok's non-disclosure, her consent to the marriage was not obtained freely. Madam Lim therefore asked for a declaration that 'there had never been a marriage between the parties because the respondent was biologically a female.' Alternatively, she asked for an annulment on the basis of non-consummation. The response of Mr Hiok, if any, is unrecorded in the judgment.

65 *Lim Ying v Eric Hiok* [1991] SGHC 135, paras. 5 and 6.
66 Ibid.

The Judicial Commissioner granted Madam Lim the declarations that she sought. He ruled that the marriage was null and void because it was not between a man and a woman. He held that, by reason of the definition of 'monogamous marriage' in the Interpretation Act, the parties to a monogamous marriage contracted under the Women's Charter should be of the 'opposite biological sex'. If they were not, then there was a 'legal impediment' to the marriage which ought to have been made known to the Registrar of Marriages. He held that Mr Hiok was not a man for the purposes of contracting a marriage. The gender status reported on his national registration identity card (which had been 'relied upon by all parties, including the Registrar of Marriages') was not to be taken as being conclusive in law of the true gender of the holder of the identity card. He noted that Mr Hiok had not taken any steps to change the gender markers on his birth certificate (which had not been produced to the Registrar of Marriages because it was not required).

Perhaps more distressingly for transgender persons, the Judicial Commissioner held that:

> 'Reassignment surgery does not result in the acquisition of all the biological characteristics of the other sex, and where the sex of a person is in issue it must be proved to the satisfaction of the court. An identity card alone is not sufficient evidence...
>
> It is desirable in the interests of certainty and consistency for the word "man" under the Charter to be given the ordinary meaning that is in contradistinction to woman. A person biologically a female with an artificial penis, after surgery and psychologically a male, must, for purposes of contracting a monogamous marriage of one man and one woman, under the Charter be regarded as a "woman"...
>
> A person who has undergone a sex-change operation cannot be regarded as belonging to the sex for which reassignment surgery was undertaken for purposes of a monogamous marriage under the Charter.'[67]

The implications of this decision for transgender persons at that time were profound. Firstly, the decision meant that such persons could no longer contract a valid marriage in Singapore. Secondly, even if they chose to avoid this difficulty by contracting the marriage abroad, it would not be recognised as such under the laws of Singapore.[68] Thirdly, the status of the adopted children of any such marriage would be thrown into legal limbo.[69]

---

67 Ibid., paras. 56, 59 and 61.

68 On the argument that even marriages contracted outside Singapore under foreign law must still meet the requirements of 'monogamous marriage' as defined in the Interpretation Act, failing which it would be void under the present section 5(1) of the Women's Charter which provides that every 'marriage contracted in Singapore or elsewhere in contravention of section 4 shall be void'.

69 It appears that fortunately, Parliament intervened (as subsequently described) in time to prevent this question having to be brought before the courts – there are no reported judgments.

Perhaps most unfortunate of all, the legal status of *all* transsexuals (and not just Mr Hiok) who had completed a process of personal, physical transition, including gender confirmation surgery, was forthwith cast into legal uncertainty. It was clear from the *Eric Hiok* decision that transgender persons could not assert their preferred legal gender (even where they had submitted to surgery), and were therefore incapable of contracting a lawful marriage. On its own, this was bad news, as it seemed to effectively disenfranchise all transgender persons in Singapore from the exercise of what is commonly held to be a fundamental human right.[70] However, there were (possibly) worse repercussions. Did, for example, the court's decision also mean that transgender individuals who had submitted to gender confirmation surgery were now left in a state in which they would be regarded in law as having their birth-assigned gender, despite the irrevocable nature of their transition?

The Judicial Commissioner seems to have accepted that it was not inconsistent (or unlawful) for a person to hold an identity card with a gender marker which was at odds with the marker in his or her birth certificate. They were 'official documents that serve different purposes.'[71] He noted that on 'most social and official occasions, the sex shown on the identity card is accepted'. It was just that the particular rules relating to marriage under the Women's Charter *did* require (on his interpretation) the transgender party to declare his 'changed' gender as a legal impediment.[72]

Why the Judicial Commissioner should have come to such an interpretation of 'one man and one woman' has occasioned much debate.[73] On its face, there is nothing in the Interpretation Act definition that is incompatible with marriage involving a person who has had gender confirmation surgery. This concept had been recognised in law and practice without controversy for nearly two decades. But in retrospect, there was in fact legal uncertainty from the very beginning, as noted in a newspaper article about the first person to submit to gender confirmation surgery in Singapore, commenting on the fact that the individual had expressed a desire to get married. The article stated that 'chances are that if the stenographer's [the first SRS patient in Singapore] marriage to her executive fiancé goes through the marriage would be a voidable one – that is, valid until a party challenges it'. The article went on to cite a 'recent English case' as a precedent.[74] That case was

70 Articles 16 (right to marriage) and 2 (no distinction on the basis of gender) of the Universal Declaration of Human Rights, UN General Assembly, 10 December 1948.

71 *Eric Hiok*, para. 56.

72 Ibid., para. 55.

73 See C.H. Tan, 'Transsexuals and the law of marriage in Singapore: *Lim Ying v Hiok Kian Ming Eric*' [1991] *Singapore Journal of Legal Studies* 509–516.

74 W.L. Tay, 'Man-made woman may not get marriage licence', *The Straits Times*, 31 August 1971, p. 6; W.K. Leong, 'Transsexual in England still of birth sex even if this transgresses European Human Rights Convention: *Bellinger v Bellinger*' [2003] *Singapore Journal of Legal Studies* 274–284, commenting on the *Eric Hiok* decision at 279; W.K. Leong, 'Clarity in the law of valid, void and voidable non-Muslim marriages' (2009) 21 *Singapore Academy of Law Journal* 575–590, 584–587; W.K. Leong, 'Recent developments in the law of marriage and divorce',

none other than *Corbett v Corbett*.[75] So it came to be that a case decided in an English court more than two decades earlier (and more than a whole year *before*[76] the first gender confirmation surgery was conducted) came back to haunt those who had thought that the way was clear at last to an ordinary life and status in a preferred gender.

The decision in *Eric Hiok* has been much criticised but, in a sense, the decision was perhaps predictable. The regime of reception of common law at that time specifically assumed and directed the application of English common law and precedents, unless there were compelling reasons otherwise. The Application of English Law Act, which completely freed the Singapore courts to strike their own course in the development of a truly indigenous body of Singapore common law, was not passed by Parliament until more than two years after the decision in *Eric Hiok*.

The Judicial Commissioner in *Eric Hiok* chose to follow and apply Justice Ormrod's 'biological approach' to the determination of legal gender status – the argument that the gender of most people is immutably determined and therefore 'fixed at birth' by their sex chromosomes, and that it is the physical sexual attributes of a person at birth that determines legal gender.[77] The Judicial Commissioner seems to have been swayed by Justice Ormrod's argument that it would 'be nothing but bizarre' if the consequence of recognising gender confirmation surgery were to result in a transgender woman, who was already married and had already fathered a child before surgery, being regard, after treatment, as a woman 'and capable of "marrying" a man.'

The Second Charter of Justice notwithstanding, the adherence to the English approach in *Corbett v Corbett* is especially puzzling, given that a wide range of cases from various common law jurisdictions were canvassed and considered by the Judicial Commissioner in *Eric Hiok*. The Judicial Commissioner was certainly aware of the avenues open to him. He noted the very different approach in the case of *MT v JT*[78] at length, as well as the notion of 'core identity' in a New Zealand case.[79] He noted that while the Australian courts had then applied different tests for marriages and for criminal cases, 'in the name of common sense, desirability, certainty and consistency, the English matrimonial and criminal courts have followed the decision in *Corbett*'s case, both in marriage and in criminal cases'.[80]

(1993) *Singapore Academy of Law Journal* 290–308, 292–299, and S.H. Kwek and J.J. Lee, 'Transsexuals and Sex Determination' (1992) 4 *Singapore Academy of Law Journal* 86–115.

75 [1971] P 83; [1970] 2 All ER 33.

76 Mr Justice Ormrod delivered the judgment on 2 February 1970.

77 Justice Ormrod at [1971] P 83, at 100D and E, and at 104 B; and cited with approval by Judicial Commission Rajah with approval in *Eric Hiok* [1991] 2 SLR(R) 525–540, paras. 13–15.

78 355 A2d 204 (1976).

79 *Re M* (30 May 1991) (Family Court, New Zealand) FP No. 048/991/90 decided by the Family Court at Otahuhu. Unreported, facts and decision as set out in Rajah JC's judgment in *Eric Hiok* at paras. 36–43.

80 *Eric Hiok*, para. 35.

This seems to have been the overriding argument. No other reason was advanced by the Judicial Commissioner for embracing *Corbett* and rejecting *MT v JT*.

From a legal point of view, the value of *Eric Hiok* as a binding precedent is beyond challenge. Firstly, as has been already pointed out, the petition was not contested by the petitioner, nor was he represented or present in court. The court therefore had no opportunity to hear contrary arguments which might have been advanced by a contesting party. Secondly, the decision was never appealed. Arguably, these factors weaken the authority of the decision as a precedent. But there is no denying that the principle which *Eric Hiok* (and *Corbett*) established was relied upon as good law and followed by at least one reported decision also from the High Court.[81]

For Singapore's transgender community, there was little consolation so long as the decision remained unchallenged on appeal to a higher court. For that community, the end result of the *Eric Hiok* case meant that, as far as the law was concerned, no amount of surgical intervention could alter their legal gender, which was considered to have been immutably fixed by their genes at birth. There was no escape in law from the gender, assigned to an individual at birth, and with which he or she had no sense of identification.

4.3. 1996: PARLIAMENTARY INTERVENTION

The happy (for the most part, as will be explained below) denouement to this tale is that the Singapore Parliament intervened to make specific provisions for the matrimonial rights of transgender persons. It effectively reversed *Eric Hiok*, but only insofar as that decision dealt with the disqualification of transgender individuals from marriage. It should be noted that the Singapore Parliament did so well before the UK Parliament finally moved to enact the Gender Recognition Act 2004, more than three decades after the decision in *Corbett v Corbett*. On 18 January 1996, the First Reading of the Women's Charter (Amendment) Bill[82] was moved in Parliament. Among its provisions was a new section 11A.[83] This new provision provided, among other things:

- that 'a marriage solemnized in Singapore or elsewhere between two persons of the same sex shall be void';[84]
- that for the purposes of the Women's Charter's provisions relating to capacity for marriage, 'a marriage solemnized in Singapore or elsewhere between a

81 *Low Seng Siong v Lim Mei Chwen Julianna* [1995] SGHC 195.
82 Subsequently enacted as The Women's Charter (Amendment) Act 1996 (Act 30 of 1996).
83 Now section 12 of the Women's Charter.
84 The current section 12(1) of the Women's Charter.

person who has undergone a sex re-assignment procedure and any person of the opposite sex is and shall be deemed always to have been a valid marriage';[85]
- that for this purpose, 'the sex of any party to a marriage as stated at the time of the marriage in his or her identity card issued under the National Registration Act (Cap. 201) shall be *prima facie* evidence of the sex of the party';[86] and
- that 'a person who has undergone a sex re-assignment procedure shall be identified as being of the sex to which the person has been re-assigned.'[87]

In moving the Second Reading of the Bill before Parliament, the following statement was made by Mr Abdullah Tarmugi, the Minister for Community Development:[88]

> 'Mr Speaker, Sir, I am aware that this amendment has raised some concerns among some members of the public. The issue is indeed a complex one and touches on moral, cultural and religious values. Sir, permit me to explain the proposed amendments which were made after much discussion and deliberation with several parties.
>
> Sex reassignment procedure has been allowed in Singapore since 1971. A person who has successfully completed a sex reassignment procedure has to change his or her identity card to reflect the new sex and identity. A small group of individuals in Singapore have indeed undergone the procedure and have had their identity cards changed.
>
> In June 1991, things changed for this group of trans-sexuals who had married when the High Court ruled in the case of *Lim vs Hiok* that the Women's Charter did not permit marriage between two persons of the same biological sex. Until the ruling, the Registry of Marriages had all along accepted the identity card as documentary proof of the identity and sex of a person. Those who had undergone sex reassignment procedure were able to marry using their identity cards which reflected their new sex. Following the 1991 court ruling, the Registry of Marriages stopped allowing the use of identity cards and began to require applicants to bring their birth certificates as evidence of their sex instead. For those who got married before the ruling, the court's decision meant that their marriages are now void. And if they have adopted children, the status of these children is now uncertain.
>
> Sir, I must emphasise that the proposed amendments are not meant to institute a new practice. Rather they are to reinstate what was the position before 1991. The Government's stand is very clear: it is not a move to encourage or promote lesbianism, homosexuality, transvestism or sex reassignment among our people. We do not believe the amendments will result in our people reassigning their sex in droves. The Bill basically seeks a practical and humane approach to address

85 The current section 12(2).
86 The current section 12(3)(a).
87 The current section 12(3)(b).
88 Singapore Parliamentary Reports, *Hansard*, Parliament No. 8, Session 2, Vol. 66, Sitting No. 1, 2 May 1996, at column 64.

> the problems faced by this group of people and the families they have set up. It is to allow these individuals to lead a life according to their new status, as recorded in their identity cards, as we have all along used the NRIC to verify identity. It is practical. It is sensible.'

It is evident from the speech of the Minister that he was aware that this was an issue of some sensitivity among certain sectors of the population. Some ambivalence is obvious, with 'lesbianism, homosexuality, transvestism or sex reassignment' being lumped together in the category of things that are not to be encouraged. But equally clear is the government's concern for a 'practical and humane' solution, and fair treatment for a group of people and families thrown into legal limbo through no fault of their own. Following the passage of the amendment, an eminent Singapore family law expert wrote that 'we should be proud that our law does right by the small minority of people who suffer what the rest of us might never truly comprehend and who only ask that we recognize their helping themselves in the ways medical science offers'.[89] In short, the law was finally made congruent with medical science, and with physical, social, emotional and psychological reality.

The amendment brought to an end the legal inconsistency that brought about situations such as that recounted by a Member of Parliament:

> 'One of my constituents came to my Meet-the-People session. He came in full army uniform. He is currently serving national service. He came together with his fiancée and asked how come his marriage application was rejected. He said, "I serve in the Army and that means I am a man. But when I applied to register my marriage, my application was rejected (because he was born a female)". So he felt very awkward to be accepted as a man, and at the same time to be treated as a woman when it comes to marriage. …
>
> Sir, I mentioned this story because I remember the glow in his face after I explained that we are doing something about it. His fiancée was also happy that they were given a chance, despite the odd situation he was in, that he can now form a family and try his best to live happily ever after.'[90]

For Mr Hiok, however, the legislative intervention came too late. Nor did it have the retrospective effect of validating what had been declared null and void by the High Court. The Amendment Act provision makes it clear that the new provisions were not to have the effect of validating any marriage 'which had been declared by the High Court before 1st May 1997 to be null and void on the ground

---

89 W.K. Leong, 'Transsexual in England still of birth sex even if this transgresses European Human Rights Convention: *Bellinger v Bellinger*' [2003] *Singapore Journal of Legal Studies* 274–284, commenting on the *Eric Hiok* decision at 279.

90 The speech of Mr Mohamad Maidin B P M, Member of Parliament, and the Parliamentary Secretary to the Minister for Information and the Arts, The Singapore Parliamentary Reports, *Hansard*, Parliament No 8, Session No 2, Vol 66, Sitting Date 27 August 1996, at column 540.

that the parties were of the same sex'.[91] While at first sight this may seem hard on Mr Hiok, the fact is that he chose not to contest the petition, and there is no reported judgment of any other marriage declared null and void on a similar ground between the date of the decision in *Eric Hiok* and the Amendment Act. The provision makes sense in that it would be highly unlikely that any such declaration would have been made in relation to a marriage which the parties *wanted* to continue (because they would never have applied for such a declaration in the first place). Even greater legal violence would have resulted if the parties to a marriage (unwanted by at least one of the parties) declared null and void on this ground should find themselves suddenly in a state of wedlock again by legislative fiat – with further consequences for any marriage which they may have subsequently contracted after the dissolution of their first.

V. AFTERMATH: THE CONTINUING LEGACY OF THE *ERIC HIOK* DECISION POST-1996

The 1996 Amendment Act did not address all the legal problems faced by transgender persons – and especially by those persons who intend to submit to gender confirmation surgery but who have not yet accessed such treatment. For the most part, the 1996 Amendment Act appears to have been carefully drafted to put only legal gender status and marriage back onto the table for those persons who have accessed surgery – and no more. It is important to understand that what the 1996 Amendment Act did not do was to expressly overrule or declare void the entire decision in *Eric Hiok*. The result is that the correction to the law obtained under the 1996 Amendment Act is actually less than the totality of the decision in *Eric Hiok*. There remains a larger penumbra of legal implications established in the common law by *Erik Hiok* which remain unreversed or unaddressed by the 1996 Amendment Act.

The main criticism of the provisions of the 1996 Amendment Act is that it relates *only* to matrimonial rights, and to *no other* aspect of the law for transgender persons. It must be remembered that the amendment was introduced to the provisions of the Women's Charter, and not in amendment to the definition of 'monogamous marriage' in the Interpretation Act. Given that this definition in the Interpretation Act was the focus of the Judicial Commissioner in *Eric Hiok*, there was perhaps a missed opportunity to correct and establish *in the general law* (as opposed to merely status for the purposes of marriage under the Women's Charter) the principle that transgender persons who have completed a process of full medical transition should be entitled to the full legal and social incidents and privileges of their preferred gender like any other citizens, and not just in relation to marriage.

[91] The current section 12(4) of the Women's Charter.

But there is no getting around the restrictive intent of the 1996 Amendment Act provisions. The words of sections 11(2) and (3)[92] explicitly restrict the confirmation of the transgender person's right to marriage.[93] And even the privilege of using the identity card to confirm gender is restricted to the task of satisfying the requirement of gender under the Interpretation Act ('one man and one woman'). All it means is that the Registrar of Marriages may now rely on the statement in the identity card alone, and not demand also a copy of the birth certificate as appears to have happened after *Eric Hiok*.[94] And it may be further argued that even in the latter instance, an abundance of caution in the drafting of the provision means that even this use of the identity card as a document of status is not presumptively closed to legal challenge, because of the qualifying phrase '*prima facie*'.

The main problem is that the impact of the legal principles established by *Eric Hiok* go well beyond the issue of a transgender person's right to contract a marriage. In undertaking the extensive review of the cases from the common law jurisdictions then available to him, the Judicial Commissioner appears to have preferred the route taken by the English courts in *Corbett v Corbett* at least in part because of the consistent result in the law of marriage, and in criminal law, which approach the Judicial Commissioner characterised in terms of 'common sense, desirability, certainty and consistency'.[95] The implication is that the Judicial Commissioner intended (or at the least, his judgment must be construed as intending) the *Corbett v Corbett* principle of immutable gender from birth to extend to matters *beyond* the law of marriage. It must be remembered that his first concern was to establish the 'true' legal gender of the respondent, from which determination flowed the holding that the marriage was null and void.[96] If that is the correct interpretation of *Eric Hiok*, then it would mean that post-*Eric Hiok*, transgender persons must be regarded always as being immutably fixed in their birth-assigned legal gender, not only for matrimonial purposes, but for *all* other legal purposes. Thus the *Eric Hiok* decision goes to the very core of legal gender recognition for the transgender community.

And it is here that the 1996 Amendment Act complicates matters by being so restrictive in its approach. Post-1996, is the situation now that transgender persons, after surgical intervention, are considered has having their preferred legal gender for the purposes of marriage (because of the 1996 Amendment Act) but as having their birth-assigned legal gender for *all other purposes* (because of *Eric*

[92] The current sections 12(2) and (3) of the Women's Charter.

[93] Section 12(2) provides that: 'It is hereby declared that, *subject to* sections 5, 9, 10, 11 and 22' (emphasis added) marriages involving a transsexual person should be recognised.

[94] Section 12(3) of the Women's Charter explicitly provides that the use of the identity card as '*prima facie* evidence of the sex of the party' is to be restricted to 'for the purpose of this section'.

[95] [1991] 2 SLR(R) 525–540, para. 36.

[96] See the discussion of this point in S.H. Kwek and J.J. Lee, 'Transsexuals and Sex Determination' (1992) 4 *Singapore Academy of Law* Journal 86–115, 100–101.

Hiok)? It is here argued that the answer may unfortunately have to be yes, because *Eric Hiok* has not been substantively revisited by any court since it was decided. After the 1996 Amendment Act, there would have been very little in the way of grounds to mounting a challenge to *Eric Hiok*. It may be imagined that perhaps given that it was a principle of English common law (the rule in *Corbett v Corbett*) that was the source of the difficulty in the first place, the English common law might now also be employed to correct the path of the common law in Singapore. Unfortunately, this has not been the case.

For one thing, the enactment of the Application of English Law Act in 1993 by the Singapore Parliament effectively rewrote the rules of the reception of English common law cases. The regime of reception of English common law precedents that applied when *Eric Hiok* was decided no longer applies, and we can no longer automatically reach out to the current body of English common law decisions for a solution. But the current English law is not of any help, because the common law in England has now been fundamentally realigned with the passage of the Gender Recognition Act 2004. The Act forms no part of Singapore law because of the Singapore Application of English Law Act.

In a sense, Singapore is now left with an old limb of the English common law that has withered away because the UK Parliament has cut off all circulation to it. Except for the legislative clarification relating to the right to marriage introduced by the 1996 Amendment Act, the applicable principles in common law in Singapore is much as was the case in England before the passage of the Gender Recognition Act 2004. Although the Judicial Commissioner in *Eric Hiok* was aware of the arguments for the acceptance of a person's right to gender identity as determined by one's psychological, social and emotional sense of sexuality and character (particularly evident in his examination of the *MT v JT* case), it was not a path that he was prepared to take.[97] And it is equally clear that the intent of the 1996 Amendment Act is that the provisions should only apply to a transgender person 'who has successfully completed a sex reassignment procedure'.[98] In the result, there is a lack of clarity as to how gender should be interpreted for the purposes of the criminal law, in relation to transgender individuals who have completed a process of medical transition, and transgender persons who not taken steps to amend their body characteristics. As the Judicial Commissioner in *Eric Hiok* was fully aware, the law may treat these two classes of transgender individuals very differently (separated only by the fact of a surgical procedure), and this had occurred in both Australia[99] and England.[100]

Perhaps even more than in England, this distinction makes a difference. In particular, many of the offences under the heading of 'Sexual Offences'

[97] [1991] 2 SLR(R) 525–540, paras. 23–43.

[98] The speech of the Minister for Community Development, Singapore Parliamentary Reports, *Hansard*, Parliament No. 8, Session 2, Vol. 66, Sitting No. 1, 2 May 1996, at column 64.

[99] *R v Harris and McGuinness* (1988) 35 A Crim R 146, considered in *Eric Hiok* at paras. 28–33.

[100] *R v Tan* [1983] QB 1054 (Court of Appeal), considered in *Eric Hiok* at paras. 34–35.

(sections 375 to 377) in Part XVI ('Offences Affecting the Human Body') of the Singapore Penal Code are gender specific.[101] For example, the crime of rape can only be committed by a man against a woman.[102] Arguably, this might mean that a transgender woman who has submitted to gender confirmation surgery might find herself unprotected by the law against rape because she would be held to still retain a male legal gender on application of the principle in *Eric Hiok*. And unlike in England, homosexual acts *between men* remain a crime in Singapore, punishable with a term of imprisonment of up to two years. However, there is no similar prohibition on consensual sexual intercourse between two women.[103]

VI. OTHER PERSPECTIVES

6.1. MUSLIMS, GENDER IDENTITY AND THE LAW IN SINGAPORE

One fundamental qualification to all of the above information is that both the decision in *Eric Hiok* and the 1996 Amendment Act applies only to civil marriages. As has been clearly stated in Parliament, the 1996 Amendment Act applies only to civil marriages and not to Muslim marriages which are governed by a different set of laws, *i.e.* the Administration of Muslim Law Act (AMLA). Islam prohibits sex reassignment and does not recognise marriages between people who have undergone sex reassignment.[104]

The point then is that sexual reassignment through surgery is simply not recognised by Islamic law for any purposes whatsoever. While the statutory religious authority for Islamic affairs in Singapore[105] does not appear to have issued any *fatwa* or binding doctrinal ruling on the issue, the statement by the Minister for Community Development in Parliament may be taken to be authoritative on the matter. This means that if a person of the Islamic faith contracts a marriage with another Muslim, then the principle in *Corbett v Corbett* and in *Eric Hiok* applies in full force. The 1996 Amendment Act has no application. While it is legally possible for a Muslim person to contract a civil marriage with a non-Muslim under the Women's Charter, civil marriage is not an option if both

101 The Singapore Penal Code (Cap. 244, Revised Edition of 2008). The Penal Code, originally enacted in 1871, was modelled closely on the colonial Indian Penal Code.

102 Section 375, Penal Code.

103 Section 277A of the Penal Code provides as follows: 'Any male person who, in public or private, commits, or abets the commission of, or procures or attempts to procure the commission by any male person of, any act of gross indecency with another male person, shall be punished with imprisonment for a term which may extend to 2 years.'

104 Mr Abdullah Tarmugi, the Minister for Community Development, in moving the Second Reading of the 1996 Women's Charter (Amendment) Bill, Singapore Parliamentary Reports, *Hansard*, Parliament No. 8, Session 2, Vol. 66, Sitting No. 1, 2 May 1996, at column 64.

105 The Majlis Ugama Islam Singapore, or the Council of Islamic Affairs, Singapore, constituted under Part II of the Administration of Muslim Law Act (Cap 3, Revised Edition of 2009).

parties are Muslims[106] or if the parties desire that the marriage be solemnised in accordance with Muslim law.[107] Nor is cohabitation outside of lawful marriage an option for Muslims. Any person 'who cohabits and lives with a woman, whether a Muslim or not, to whom he is not lawfully married, shall be guilty of an offence.'[108]

6.2. THE PERSPECTIVE IN MALAYSIA

Singapore shares a common colonial history with Malaysia. As described above, Singapore was in federal union with and was thus a state of Malaysia between 1963 and 1965, before peacefully seceding by mutual agreement to become an independent country. Both countries have close and good relationships with one another, and both are key members of the political and economic regional bloc ASEAN.[109] It is the only country with which Singapore has land connections.[110] The ethnic and religious makeup of Malaysia, however, is markedly different from that of Singapore. Of its population of 30 million, just over 50% are Malays.[111]

Constitutionally, 'Islam is the religion of the Federation; but other religions may be practised in peace and harmony in any part of the Federation'.[112] The majority of the states forming the federal union of Malaysia have a hereditary Malay ruler – these State Malay Rulers are also constitutionally the 'Head of the religion of Islam' in their respective states.[113] 61.3% of the population were recorded as being of the Islamic faith in 2010.[114] The Conference of Rulers have made it clear that, in Muslim law, 'sex change from man to woman and vice versa through operation is prohibited in terms of Shariah'. To emphasise this point, the *fatwa* goes on to expressly state that a 'person who is born male remains a male even though he has successfully changed to female through operation', and a 'person who is born female remains a female even though she has successfully

106 Section 3(4) of the Women's Charter.

107 Section 87 of the Administration of Muslim Law Act.

108 Section 134 of the Administration of Muslim Law Act.

109 The Association of Southeast Asian Nations comprising (in alphabetical order) Brunei Darussalam, Cambodia, Indonesia, Laos (Lao PDR), Malaysia, Myanmar, the Philippines, Singapore, Thailand, and Vietnam.

110 Via a causeway, and a bridge, both over the narrow Straits of Johor separating the main island of Singapore from Malaysia, which is the most southerly point of the continent of Asia.

111 The Department of Statistics, Malaysia, Population Quick Check Info search by ethnic groups, 2013 estimates <http://pqi.stats.gov.my/result.php?token=1abc311db311727fab12f5d0249bcd1d> accessed 24.12.2013.

112 Article 3(1) of the Federal Constitution of Malaysia.

113 Article 3(2) of the Federal Constitution of Malaysia. In states not having a hereditary ruler, the position of 'Head of religion of Islam' is assumed by the Yang Di-Pertuan Agong, the federal Ruler who is elected for a term of five years by the Conference of State rulers (Article 3(3)). Under the Westminster-style constitution, the Yang Di-Pertuan Agong exercises much the same functions as Her Majesty the Queen does in the UK.

114 The Department of Statistics, Malaysia, 'Population distribution and basic demographic characteristics report 2010' <www.statistics.gov.my> accessed 24.12.2013.

changed to male through operation'. Only persons who are born '*khunsa musykil*' ('who has two private parts of male and female') are 'allowed to undergo surgery to retain the most functional private part so it can be used properly'.[115]

Until the recent landmark decision handed down by the Malaysian Federal Court of Appeal in the case of *Muhamad Juzaili bin Mohd Khamis & Ors v The State Government of Negeri Sembilan & Ors*[116] (the 'Negeri Sembilan decision'), this ruling by the Conference of Rulers effectively made it unlawful for Muslims to access gender confirmation surgery. Worse, legislation was enacted at the state level in all 13 states that make up the Federation of Malaysia to explicitly criminalise 'male person posing as woman', while 'female person posing as man' was outlawed in three states.[117]

The Negeri Sembilan decision completely overturned this hostile landscape for transgender persons, and affirmed their constitutional rights to equal protection before the law. The case originated in an action brought on behalf of three Muslim men (the appellants), who are described in the grounds of judgment in the following terms:

> 'Medically, however, they are not normal males. This is because they have a medical condition called Gender Identity Disorder (GID). Because of this medical condition, since a young age the appellants have been expressing themselves as women and showing the mannerisms of the feminine gender such as wearing women's clothes and using makeups. Indeed, they feel natural being such.'[118]

Unfortunately for the appellants, the state legislature of the state (the state of Negeri Sembilan) in which they lived had in 1992 enacted legislation in the form of section 66 of the Syariah Criminal Enactment 1992 (Negeri Sembilan) which provided as follows:

> 'Any male person who, in any public place wears a woman's attire or poses as a woman shall be guilty of an offence and shall be liable on conviction to a fine not

115 The 25th *Muzakarah* (Conference) of the Fatwa Committee National Council of Islamic Religious Affairs Malaysia (13 December 1989), referring to the decision of the Council of Malay Rulers in the Council's 126th Meeting held on 24 February 1983, as published by the Jabatan Kemajuan Islam Malaysia (JAKIM, the Department of Islamic Development Malaysia) <www.e-fatwa.gov.my/fatwa-kebangsaan/muzakarah?page=29> accessed 24.12.2013.

116 *Muhamad Juzaili bin Mohd Khamis and Others v State Government of Negeri Sembilan and Others* [2015] 3 MLJ 513.

117 The Knowledge and Rights with Young People through Safer Spaces (KRYSS), Seksualiti Merdeka, Justice for Sisters and PT Foundation, *Malaysia: Human Rights Violations against Lesbian, Gay, Bisexual, Transgender, Intersex and Queer Persons* (March 2013), submission by the author groups 'to the Human Rights Council for Malaysia's United Nations Universal Periodic Review 2013', available on the website of the Pertubahan Pertolongan Wanita (Women's Aid Organization (WAO), Malaysia) at <http://wao.org.my/file/file/Coalition%20of%20Sexual%20Orientation%20and%20Gender%20Identity%20SOGI%20Malaysia%20UPR%202013%20Submission.pdf> accessed 26.02.2015.

118 At p. 4 of the transcript of the full grounds of judgment.

exceeding one thousand ringgit or to imprisonment for a term not exceeding six months or to both'.[119]

The sad and inevitable consequence for the appellants, for whom their chosen way of dressing and presentation was an inalienable and intrinsic part of their core identity, was that they were 'repeatedly detained, arrested, and prosecuted by the religious authority of Negeri Sembilan' suffering such 'injustice and humiliation',[120] as a result of which they were eventually moved to apply to the courts for a declaration that section 66 was void as being contrary to the protection afforded to them by the Federal Constitution of Malaysia.

Their application was initially rebuffed at the first level by the High Court of Seremban.[121] The appellants appealed to the Federal Court of Appeal. The full list of the respondents arrayed against the appellants in the appeal is instructive: the State Government of Negeri Sembilan, as well as the Department of Islamic Religious Affairs, the Director of Islamic Religious Affairs, the Chief Enforcement Officer of the Islamic Religious Affairs, and the Chief Syarie Prosecutor, all of the State of Negeri Sembilan.

The appellants' case was that section 66 was void as it was inconsistent with the protection guaranteed to them by the Federal Constitution of Malaysia by virtue of Articles 5(1) (liberty of the person), 8(1) (equal protection and equality before the law), 8(2) (prohibition of discrimination on grounds of gender), 9(2) (freedom of movement), and 10(1)(a) (freedom of speech and expression).

In a stunning affirmation of the rights of transgender people, the Federal Court of Appeal in the Negeri Sembilan decision upheld the appellants' appeal on every single one of these grounds.

The Mufti of the State of Negeri Sembilan had submitted in evidence his opinion that 'the prohibition of a male Muslim dressing or posing as a woman is a precept of Islam'.[122] The Court of Appeal's response was to observe that 'whether or not section 66 is consistent with the precepts of Islam [was] not in issue in the present case': what was in issue was what was 'the position in Islam as to the appropriate dress code for male Muslims who are sufferers of GID, like the appellants?'[123] In other words, it was not asserted that section 66 was constitutional when applied to Muslim men who identified themselves as being of the male gender: what was being asserted by the appellants was that, as worded, it was unconstitutional because its application to a specific group of people (in their specific case, people with gender identity disorder) would infringe on the liberty and protection afforded to them by the Constitution.[124]

---

119 One thousand ringgit was worth about US$275 in February 2015.
120 Ibid., p. 5.
121 The city of Seremban is the capital of the State of Negeri Sembilan.
122 At p. 17 of the transcript of the full grounds of judgment.
123 Ibid., pp. 17–18.
124 Ibid., pp. 17–18.

On the point of the protection of the liberty of the person,[125] the Court of Appeal accepted the argument that the constitutional guarantee of liberty included 'the right to live with common human dignity'.[126] The Court observed that:

> 'A more disturbing effect of section 66 is that it builds insecurity and vulnerability into the lives of the appellants and other Muslim male persons with GID. The existence of a law that punishes the gender expression of transsexuals, degrades and devalues persons with GID in our society. … As long as section 66 is in force the appellants will continue to live in uncertainty, misery and indignity. They now come before this Court in the hope that they may be able to live with dignity and be treated as equal citizens of this nation.'[127]

The Court of Appeal accordingly held that section 66 was 'unconstitutional and void' on the ground of infringement against Article 5(1) of the Constitution alone. Worse yet for the respondents, the Court of Appeal also further held that the guarantee of liberty in Article 5(1) was to be interpreted broadly, so that '"life" means more than mere animal existence and includes such rights as livelihood and the quality of life',[128] and held that section 66 was doubly in contravention of Article 5(1) because the appellants would 'never be able to leave their homes, cross-dressed, to go to their respective places of work without being exposed to being arrested and punished under section 66'.[129]

On the point of equal protection under Article 8(1), the Court had strong words for the discriminatory consequences of section 66:

> '[S]ection 66 places the GID sufferers in an untenable and horrible position. They could not dress in public in the way that is natural to them. They will commit the crime of offending section 66 the very moment they leave their homes to attend to the basic needs of life, to earn a living, or to socialize; and be liable to arrest, detention and prosecution. This is degrading, oppressive and inhuman.'[130]

The Court of Appeal also noted (and affirmed) that section 66 also clearly violated the constitutional protection against discrimination on the grounds of gender under Article 8(2) because although it prohibited 'male Muslims from cross-dressing or from posing as a woman', the converse (if done by a Muslim woman) was not an offence.[131] One remarkable assertion (swiftly demolished by

125 Article 5(1) of the Federal Constitution.
126 Ibid., p. 19.
127 Ibid., pp. 20–21.
128 Ibid., p. 22, affirming the observation of Gopal Sri Ram FCJ in *Lee Kwan Woh v PP* [2009] 5 CLJ 631, 643.
129 Ibid, p. 23.
130 Ibid., pp. 24–25.
131 Ibid., pp. 26–27.

the Court of Appeal) was made by the State Legal Advisor of the state of Negeri Sembilan: that section 66 was 'not prejudicial to the appellants as they are persons of unsound mind' and hence entitled to the defence of the 'act of a person of unsound mind'![132] The net result of the Negeri Sembilan decision is that similar state legislation are now open to being challenged on similar grounds.[133]

Some difficulties remain. The scope of the ruling in the Negeri Sembilan decision is narrowly constructed, depending as it does on the acceptance by the court of gender identity disorder as a recognised medical condition 'from birth'. From this perspective, people like the appellants have to labour under the stigma of suffering from a 'disorder'. There is also the question of whether state legislative provisions such as section 66 are void entirely (*i.e.* having no effect even against Muslim men who are not identified as having GID), or whether they are void only against people who have been certified by a medical professional to be 'suffering' from GID. But the probable correct conclusion, given the unqualified wording of the declaration of the Court of Appeal in the Negeri Sembilan case ('We hold that section 66 is invalid as being unconstitutional'),[134] is that section 66 must fall entirely, even as against Muslim men without GID.

On its face, the Negeri Sembilan decision does nothing to change the position that Muslim marriages involving a transgender person are void in Malaysia under the *shariah* law compulsorily applied to private law matters for Muslims in

---

[132] Ibid., p. 43.

[133] At the time of going to press, news was received that decision in *Muhamad Juzaili bin Mohd Khamis and Others v State Government of Negeri Sembilan and Others* [2015] 3 MLJ 513 had been set aside by the Federal Court of Malaysia (Appellate Jurisdiction) on 8 October 2015 in the case of *State Government of Negeri Sembilan and Others v Muhammad Jusaili bin Mohd Khamis and Others* (as yet unreported). The Federal Court arrived at its decision on a purely technical ground: that under Article 4(4) of the Federal Constitution of Malaysia, an action by an individual challenging the validity of any law made by the Federal Parliament or by a State Legislature could not be commenced with leave of a judge of the Federal Court (paragraph 17 of the official transcript of the judgment). In this, the Federal Court chose to follow the the precedents established in *Ah Thian v Government of Malaysia* [1976] 2 MLJ 112, and *Titular Roman Catholic Archbishop of Kuala Lumpur v Menteri Dalam Negeri & Ors* [2014] 4 MLJ 765 (paras. 17 and 22): the Federal Court in these two cases held that leave was necessary in order to allow the federal or state government to be joined as a party to the proceedings. The Federal Court held, as in these two cases, that individuals had no right to challenge the constitutionality of laws 'by way of collateral attack in a judicial review proceeding' (paras. 22, and 27–29) and that the application of the Respondents ought have been dismissed by the High Court at first instance because their application for 'judicial review was in fact, a challenge to the legislative powers of the State Legislature of Negeri Sembilan' (para. 26). Significantly, this latest Federal Court decision does not touch on the substantive arguments considered by the Court of Appeal, nor on the grounds of its decision. The effect of this latest decision is that the applicants will (if they wish to continue to press their claims) have to restart the entire process anew by making an application for leave from a judge of the Federal Court under Article 4(4) of the Federal Constitution of Malaysia.

[134] Ibid., p. 44.

Malaysia.[135, 136, 137] The Court of Appeal also did not consider the issue of whether the Islamic ban against gender confirmation surgery for Muslim persons was unconstitutional. While non-Muslim citizens of Malaysia are not subject to the ban on gender confirmation surgery, there is for them still the lingering issue of whether governmental authorities are obliged to correct gender entries in official documents of identity following gender confirmation surgery.

Unlike in Singapore, it appears that the Malaysian authorities still do not allow preferred gender to be recognised on identity cards, even where a person submits to gender confirmation surgery. In *Wong Chiou Yong v Jabatan Pendaftaran Negara*,[138] Singham J rejected an application by a transgender man, who had accessed surgical treatments, for an order requiring the Registrar-General of Births and Deaths to alter his birth certificate *and* his national registration identity card (issued on a system nearly identical to that in Singapore) to reflect the recognition of his preferred male gender.[139]

The judge had considered and reviewed a wide range of decisions from common law jurisdictions (including *Corbett v Corbett*, and *Eric Hiok*). It appears that he ultimately decided against granting the order mostly on the grounds that the birth certificate could not be altered as it was a record of historical fact (the reported birth gender),[140] and that the court had no power to make the order sought as to do so 'would usurp the function of Parliament and it is trite [law] that that is something that the courts must not do as it is not the function of the court to substitute its own views to fill gaps'.[141] He declined to follow an apparent precedent on the grounds that it was granted on an *ex parte* application and was thus not fully argued before the court.[142]

But interestingly, in *Re JG, JG v Pengarah Jabatan Pendaftaran Negara*, another court of concurrent jurisdiction in Malaysia granted a transgender woman her application for recognition of her preferred gender on her MyKad (the new electronic identity card) a few short months after the *Wong Chiou Yong* case.[143]

---

135 2007 unreported case, but see 'Transsexualism in Malaysia: Syariah Court annuls same sex marriage', *Tilted World: A Malaysian LGBT Project* <http://tiltedworld.org/2008/05/31/transsexualism-in-malaysia-syariah-court-annuls-same-sex-marriage/> accessed 24.12.2013.

136 F.F. Loh, 'Zaid: Give leeway on sex change', *The Star* (Malaysian newspaper), 1 August 2011, published online at <www.thestar.com.my/story.aspx?file=%2f2011%2f8%2f1%2fnation%2f9212794&sec=nation> accessed 24.12.2013.

137 The issue of the validity of marriage in which one or both of the parties are transgender persons was not decided upon in *Muhamad Juzaili and Others v State Government of Negeri Sembilan and Others* (ibid.).

138 The National Registration Office, Malaysia.

139 [2005] 1 MLJ 551.

140 Ibid., para. 39.

141 Ibid., paras. 38, 41 and 42.

142 *Re Teh Hon Kam alias Teh Ywai Chong* (Ipoh High Court, originating summons No. 24–595 of 2002, granted 2 July 2002, before Abdull Hamid Bin Embung, J), an unreported *ex parte* application referred to in *Wong Chiou Yong* at para. 52.

143 [2006] 1 MLJ 90. *Wong Chiou Yong* was decided in the High Court, Ipoh, and the decision handed down on 4 November 2004. *Re JG, JG* was decided in the High Court, Kuala Lumpur,

The exploration of the applicable common law in *Re JG, JG* is, however, much less extensive than that in *Wong Chiou Yong*, and the ultimate basis of the decision in *Re JG, JG* is that refusing the order would otherwise be a breach of Article 5 of the Federal Constitution, which states that no person shall be deprived of his life or *personal liberty* save in accordance with law (the emphasis is that added by the judge).[144]

From the perspective of the development of a body of reasoned jurisprudence, there is much to prefer the reasoning in *Wong Chiou Yong* and, notwithstanding the later decision in *Re JG, JG*, the decision in *Wong Chiou Yong* appears to have prevailed, as far as governmental practice is concerned. One difficulty with the decision in *Wong Chiou Yong* is that perhaps the two documents of the birth certificate and the identity card ought not have been conflated. Be that as it may, the position in Malaysia is presently that transgender persons, even those who have submitted to gender confirmation surgery, will probably not succeed having their identity documents amended so as to reflect their preferred legal gender. This would prevent the transgender individual concerned from entering into a valid legal marriage. For Muslims in Malaysia, any form of recognition of their preferred gender is out of the question.

So despite the robust defence of the constitutional rights of transgender persons by the Court of Appeal, the Negeri Sembilan case leaves unanswered several critical questions of great import to the transgender community in Malaysia. There are the issues of the constitutionality of the ban on gender confirmation surgery for Muslims. There is also nothing in the judgment which would oblige or compel governmental authorities in Malaysia to recognise in their official identity documents a Muslim transgender person's preferred gender, with or without gender confirmation surgery. The Court is silent on the issue of whether Muslim men who do not qualify for a 'medical' diagnosis of GID, or who as a matter of principle do not wish to seek such a diagnosis, is entitled to the same protection as the appellants in the case. Nor does the Court say anything about the right of a transgender person (whether Muslim or non-Muslim, and with or without gender confirmation surgery) to contract a valid marriage – a case like *Eric Hiok* has yet to present itself before the Malaysian federal courts. Without these questions being answered, the constitutional protection for the rights of transgender persons in Malaysia remains incomplete. But it is a good and principled start, on which future challenges against discrimination may be brought by transgender persons in Malaysia on the same constitutional grounds.

---

and the decision handed down on 25 May 2005.

144 Ibid., para. 23.

THE LEGAL STATUS OF TRANSSEXUAL AND TRANSGENDER PERSONS IN TAIWAN

Chih-hsing Ho

Contents

I. INTRODUCTION

On Christmas Day 2014, Taiwan's Ministry of Interior announced a breakthrough change on the criteria for transgender people to obtain the recognition of their preferred legal gender. This decision reverses a previous administrative order issued in 2008 that requires psychiatric evaluation and the surgical removal of reproductive organs before transgender citizens can amend their legal gender markers on their identification cards. The decision, like a belated Christmas gift, is not only a triumph for human rights development in Taiwan, but also represents a momentous step forward for transgender rights in Asia. The government has agreed to come up with alternative criteria in a month by setting up a committee to review the application for obtaining legal gender recognition but separating this procedure from medical treatment. In the near future, those who are aged 18 or above and would like to apply for the recognition of their preferred legal gender will only need to file applications to the committee and will be given a six- month consideration period before their preferred genders are legally recognised.

This chapter discusses the legal status of transsexual and transgender persons in the Taiwanese reality and illustrates how the current situation was reached after a long struggle and human rights law development. It first introduces the general legal framework, statistics, and health insurance issues related to transgender persons. It then analyses the legal procedure and requirements for obtaining legal gender recognition. Finally, the chapter discusses the consequences of gender recognition in Taiwan, including the impact on existing and future legal relationships such as marriage and adoption, rights, duties, and entitlements.

II. THE LEGAL FRAMEWORK AND STATISTICS

The term 'transgender' mainly describes people whose gender identities are incongruent with the biological sex assigned to them at birth. Gender, according to the World Health Organisation (WHO), refers to the 'socially constructed roles, behaviours, activities, and attributes that a given society considers appropriate for men and women'.[1] Compared to the social characteristics of gender, the notion of sex is largely associated with a person's biological characteristics. For the WHO, the term 'sex' refers to 'the biological and physiological characteristics that define men and women'.[2] So, while a person's biological sex can be categorised as 'male' or 'female', her or his gender identity may not fit in this traditional biological binary. For a long period of time, incongruence between a person's gender identity and birth-assigned sex had been deemed by psychiatrists and health professionals to be a disorder, requiring to be 'healed' through hormone replacement therapy and/or sex affirmation surgery. In May, 2013, the American Psychiatric Association (APA) published the fifth edition of its Diagnostic and Statistical Manual of Mental Disorders (DSM-5). In this latest edition of the manual, APA has adopted a new diagnostic class of 'gender dysphoria' to replace 'gender identity disorder' (GID), which had previously been included in the DSM-IV, where an individual's birth-assigned gender and self-identified gender are incongruent. The 2013 revision of the diagnostic class reflects, on the one hand, a desire among health professionals to adopt terminology which both captures the lived experience of transgender persons and reduces stigma around non-binary gender identities, and, on the other hand, to ensure transgender persons can access insurance coverage for necessary medical treatment and clinical care.[3]

1 The statement is given by WHO when it tries to make a distinction between sex and gender. For more information, see: <www.who.int/gender/whatisgender/en/> accessed 25.05.2015.

2 Ibid.

3 In DSM-5, Gender Dysphoria has its own chapter which is separated from Sexual Dysfunctions and Paraphilic Disorders. In the discussions carried out by the Sexual and Gender Identity

Persons whose gender identity does not conform to their birth-assigned gender may want to establish a new gender status that accords with their preferred gender identity. With regard to the legal regulation of gender, whether and how jurisdictions recognise a person's preferred gender, which is beyond the typical categories of 'man' and 'woman', influences the rights and responsibilities of transgender persons. In some jurisdictions, a specific statute may be enacted to regulate requests for legal gender recognition.[4] In other jurisdictions, administrative rules or court practices are part of the recognition process.

In Taiwan, there is no specific statute that deals with the rights and responsibilities of transsexual and transgender persons. The Constitution does not expressly mention gender identity and sexual orientation as grounds for non-discrimination. In 1988, Taiwan allowed its first legal sex affirmation surgery.[5] Since that time, the government has created an administrative process to enable transgender persons to apply for an amendment to the gender marker on their Household Registration Certificates (HRC) and National Identification Cards (NIC). Before 2008, applicants for amendments to the HRC and NIC were required to complete an extensive process that includes a mental health assessment by two psychiatrists, the removal of reproductive organs, and sex affirmation surgery. In 2008, however, the Ministry of Interior (MOI) issued an administrative order – documented No. 0970066240 – which softened the requirements for obtaining legal gender recognition (on the HRC and NIC). According to this executive rule, the completion of sex affirmation surgery is no longer necessary for those who would like to apply for the amendment. However, both medical evaluation and removal of reproductive organs are still preconditions.

As the 2008 administrative order leads to the sterilisation of those who applied for amendment of the HRC and NIC, many human rights groups and NGOs in Taiwan have criticised this administrative rule as a violation of human

Disorders Work Group, it is noted that replacing 'disorder' with 'dysphoria' helps remove the connotation that the patient is considered to be 'disorder' but not remove the condition as a psychiatric diagnosis so without jeopardising access to care for those who need. For more information, see: Gender Dysphoria, DSM-5, American Psychiatric Association 2013 <www.dsm5.org/documents/gender%20dysphoria%20fact%20sheet.pdf> accessed 25.05.2015.

4 For example, the Gender Recognition Act 2004 in the UK illustrates the enactment of a specific legislation that provides a mechanism for transgender persons to apply for gender recognition certificate without going through surgical and hormonal treatment. The Act was enacted as a response to *Goodwin v UK* in which the European Court of Human Rights (ECHR) found that the previous UK case law in relation to transsexuals was in violation of Article 8 of the European Convention on the right to respect for private and family life. The Court further ruled that the states have positive obligations to grant legal recognition of transsexual persons and transsexuals are entitled to marry in their acquired gender.

5 The first sex reassignment surgery was performed by the Taipei Veterans General Hospital (TVGH) in 1988. For more information, see: J. Lee, 'More Men Than Women Seek Sex Change: Study', *The China Post,* 8 October 2013. However, the first case requesting transsexual change was reported a few years earlier in 1976. See: W. Chen, 'Shadow Report on Governmental CEDAW: Human Rights of Transgender People in Taiwan', Transgender Punk Activist, Taipei, February 2014.

dignity and the reproductive rights of transgender persons. It is worth noting that the Constitution in Taiwan does not refer specially to the notion of human dignity. However, in the Interpretation No. 603 of the Constitutional Court, the Grand Justices interpreted the preservation of human dignity as the core value of the constitutional structure of free democracy. In addition, the 2008 administrative order has been challenged as a violation of the principle of legal reservation, pursuant to which the administration is entitled to set up rules to restrict people's rights and obligations if, and only if, that is permitted by law. Even though the right to health is not among those rights specifically enumerated in the Constitution, such a right can be considered as a fundamental right for human dignity that is protected by the General Clause under Article 22 of the Constitution in Taiwan. According to Article 22, all other rights that are not enumerated in the Constitution shall be guaranteed and be protected so long as they are not detrimental to social order and public welfare.

Unlike some other jurisdictions that rely on specific legal statutes or courts practices to address inequality and the protection of the rights of transgender individuals, in Taiwan, the empowerment of transgender persons is more like a bottom-up process. NGOs in Taiwan play an active and important role in making international human rights law a vehicle for local transgender empowerment. In recent years, in order to ease diplomatic isolation and improve domestic human rights developments, even though Taiwan is not a member of the United Nations, the Taiwanese government has ratified several international human rights treaties with the aim of incorporating them into the domestic laws regime. These international agreements include the Convention on the Elimination of all forms of Discrimination against Women (CEDAW), the International Covenant on Civil and Political Rights (ICCPR) and the International Covenant on Economic, Social and Cultural Rights (ICESCR).

These recently ratified international human rights conventions provide useful criteria against which local NGOs and human rights groups can measure existing administrative rules in Taiwan. For example, Article 2 of the ICCPR prohibits discrimination on grounds such as 'race, colour, sex, language, religion, political or other opinion, national or social origin, property, birth or other status'.[6] For transgender rights advocates and NGOs, the term 'other status' implies that the protected grounds enumerated in Article 2 are not exhaustive. As a result, they claim that gender identity and sexual orientation should also be considered as grounds against which discrimination by law and administrative rules should be prohibited.[7]

6 Article 2 of the International Covenant on Civil and Political Rights (ICCPR)

7 For example, in the 2014 CEDAW shadow report published by the Intersex, Transgender and Transsexual People Care Association (ISTScare) in Taiwan, the international conventions of ICCPR and ICESCR were introduced as important criteria against which existing administrative rules in Taiwan can be examined.

In addition, in terms of specific rights guaranteed by the newly ratified international agreements, Article 7 of the ICCPR also states that, without free consent, no one shall be subjected to cruel, inhuman and degrading treatment. This is particularly relevant to the requirement that transgender persons submit to sex affirmation surgery as they would not normally give their full consent. For transgender rights activists, gender identity relates to one's personal conception of self and, as a result, recognition of that conception should be respected rather than decided by government authorities. That further echoes Article 5 of CEDAW which requires state parties to take appropriate measures to eliminate prejudice and address cultural and social patterns that reinforce sex role stereotyping in society.

In December 2013, following a suggestion by the Presidential Office Human Rights Consultative Committee, the Ministry of Health and Welfare organised a forum meeting, together with local NGOs, experts, and medical professionals, to discuss the possibility of allowing transgender individuals to obtain legal recognition without requiring surgery or other medical intervention, including a psychiatric diagnosis.[8] There was a general consensus reached at the meeting that it would be preferable to revise the current administrative rules, which, as noted, mandate two affidavits from certified psychiatrists and surgery to remove reproductive organs. Even though such consensus has been reached, how it is implemented remains a practical issue. On 17 January 2014, the Taiwanese Society of Psychiatry further announced its statement with regards to the medical requirements such as mental diagnosis for legal gender recognition. The Society suggested that the government should not continue to consider gender identity as something needing to be treated. Rather, it was said to be worth considering annulling the psychiatric diagnosis as one of the criteria for transgender people to obtain their preferred legal gender. Several months later, in June 2014, the Review Committee for the Taiwan CEDAW 2nd Report made a list of issues and questions for the Taiwanese government and required it to provide updated information on how the better protection of the rights of transgender individuals it once promised had been carried out. The Committee clearly indicated that the 2008 administrative order was discriminatory and a violation of the CEDAW. It further suggested that the government should take action based on the consensus reached in the meeting of the Ministry of Health and Welfare in order to respect the gender identities of transgender persons.

In October 2014, the government made a list of responses to the CEDAW Review Committee's suggestions. The Ministry of Health and Welfare was requested to propose to the Ministry of Interior its own criteria for the recognition of transsexual and transgender people. The Ministry of Interior was expected to

8 Taiwan to allow legal gender changes without transitioning – see more info at: <www.gaystarnews.com/article/taiwan-allows-legal-gender-changes-without-transitioning_091213#sthash.Eqnvmk7t.dpuf> accessed 25.05.2015.

set up implementing rules based on the suggestion and to re-evaluate what would be suitable legal procedures for the recognition of legal gender.

2.1. NATIONAL HEALTH INSURANCE

In Taiwan, under Article 51 III of the National Health Insurance Law, health care related to medical treatment for transgender persons is not covered by the national health insurance (NHI) scheme. The cost of sex affirmation surgery can be very expensive in Taiwan. According to a shadow report prepared for the CEDAW Committee by the group Transgender Punk Activist, medical expenses for male-to-female (MtF) sex affirmation surgery can reach as high as NTD 400,000 (USD 13,000). That is equivalent to approximately three years' savings for a person who earns above-average income in Taiwan.[9] In medical practices, the cost of female-to-male (FtM) sex affirmation surgery may be even higher, reaching as much as NTD 700,000 (USD 23,000). The increase in costs for FtM individuals is due to the complexity of the surgery. Before 2008, genital surgery was a precondition for obtaining legal gender recognition. This was despite the fact that many transgender persons do not want or are unable to submit to such surgery.

Taiwan started its compulsory national health insurance service in 1995. Prior to that, the health service in Taiwan was implemented by various public and private insurance groups and there was no universal and compulsory health insurance service. The NHI is a single-payer social insurance scheme that is mainly financed through the insurers' premiums, obtained from the payroll tax with a partial supplement from government funding. This scheme combines the population of Taiwan into a single client and centralises public and private health care funds into a single payer. In 2014, the National Health Insurance reached a population coverage of 99%.[10] This is out of a total population of 23.4 million Taiwanese people. However, even though the NHI's coverage rate is high, and the benefit package of NHI is comprehensive, including traditional Chinese medicine and some drug treatments for rare diseases and target therapy, the health service does not cover genital and breast surgery for transgender persons. Such surgery has been deemed to be a cosmetic surgery that is a resolution of a personal predicament.[11] For transgender groups and NGOs, if surgery was necessary to obtain recognition, then there arguably would be no case for excluding it from the NHI. To hold otherwise would create a situation where only those individuals with sufficient resources would have their preferred gender recognised in law.

---

9 See CHEN, above n. 5.

10 It was compared to the insurance coverage rate of 59% in 1995, before the health insurance plan started.

11 CHEN, above n. 5.

2.2. STATISTICAL INFORMATION

There is no official statistical information provided by the government about transgender persons in Taiwan. As far back as 1989, a psychiatrist at the National Taiwan University Hospital estimated that the percentage of transgender people in Taiwan was 0.0097%.[12] The statistics further calculated the prevalence of male-to-female 'transsexualism' in Taiwan at 1 in 37,000 and female-to-male at 1 in 107,000.[13] According to another medical journal published in 2006, the percentage for transgender people in urban cities, towns and countries in Taiwan was 0.06%, 0.20%, and 0.03% respectively.[14] Similar statistics in 2008 demonstrated that there were 30–200 transgender persons among each 100,000 people within the total population.[15] According to this percentage, the prevalence of transgender people in Taiwan was estimated in the range of 6,900–46,000 people.

III. CHANGING LEGAL SEX AND/OR GENDER – PROCEDURE AND REQUIREMENTS

3.1. LEGAL PROCEDURE AND REQUIREMENTS

Before 2008, people who wished to obtain legal gender recognition in Taiwan needed to satisfy the following conditions:

(1) they are diagnosed as 'primary transsexuals';[16]
(2) they are at least 20 years old;
(3) they have lived at least two full years in their acquired gender and they intend to live permanently in their acquired gender for the rest of their lives;
(4) they have undergone gender affirmation surgery; and
(5) they have support from their parents and families.

The requirements for obtaining legal gender recognition vary immensely across jurisdictions (as is illustrated by the various chapters in this volume). During the 1980s, Taiwan had developed its own criteria for psychiatric diagnosis about

12 S.-N. Tsai, 'Medical Legal and Ethical Analysis of Transgender Persons' (2008) *Taiwan Law Journal* 74.
13 Ibid.
14 S.-S. Chang, H.G. Hwu and E.-K. Yeh, 'Community Epidemiology of Psychosexual Dysfunctions and Transsexualism' (2006) *Medicine Today* 49–61.
15 Ibid.
16 According to Harry Benjamin's Standards of Care for Gender Identity Disorders, primary transsexuals are diagnosed as who recalled the feelings about their gender incongruence at their earliest ages that can be distinguished from secondary transsexuals who became aware of their gender incongruence at their later ages. However, such distinction has been criticised as not a proper diagnostic classification for the suitability for gender affirmation surgery.

transgender persons. The criteria for the diagnosis of gender identity disorder combined the Harry Benjamin's International Gender Dysphoria Association's (now the World Professional Association for Transgender Health (WPATH)) Standards of Care for Gender Identity Disorders (SOC, sixth version) and the Third Edition of the Diagnostic and Statistical Manual of Mental Disorders (DSM-III) published by APA. Under the criteria, it would take at least two years for a transgender individual to complete the required psychological counselling and living period (in the preferred gender), the so-called real life experience (RLE) test before the person could access hormone replacement therapy (HRT) and/ or sex affirmation surgery (SAS). In addition, parents and spouses' consent was usually considered in medical practice as one of the conditions for carrying out surgery, even though there were no further restrictions with regard to marital status, nationality and habitual residence.

After 2008, sex affirmation surgery no longer was a requirement for legal gender recognition. As stated earlier, in November 2008, the Ministry of Interior issued an administrative order No. 0970066240 according to which legal gender recognition is required to be registered with household registration offices under the following conditions:

(a) For FtM individuals, they are required to submit to the authority affidavits of a mental assessment from two psychiatrists and medical certification proving the completion of the surgical removal of female reproductive organs, including breasts, uterus and ovaries, by an accredited medical hospital or clinic.
(b) For MtF individuals, they are required to submit affidavits of a mental assessment from two psychiatrists and medical certification of the completion of the surgical removal of the male reproductive organs, including penis and testicles, by an accredited medical hospital or clinic.

The authority mentioned in the administrative order refers to the Household Registration Bureau which is in charge of the procedures for registration of legal gender recognition. It is worth noting that, unlike some other jurisdictions, changing registered information on Household Registration Certificates and National Identification Cards in Taiwan need not involve a court. The household registration agencies are required to register legal gender recognition so long as applicants have submitted the required affidavits and medical certification. Applicants can appeal against administrative a decision made by the Household Registration Bureau to refuse registration.

3.2. OFFICIAL DOCUMENTS

In Taiwan, household registration is required by law. Household Registration Certificates and National Identification Cards are foundational documents for proof of identity. These two documents are often requested for official purposes, such as voting and opening bank accounts, and can be considered as the main identity documents in Taiwan. Additional official documents, such as driving licences and educational certificates, are issued on the basis of Household Registration Certificates and National Identification Cards. Obtaining a National Identification Card in Taiwan requires proper household registration. However, unlike the *hukou* system in China, household registration in Taiwan does not function as a tool by which the government controls and manages population movement. Under the Household Registration Act, any birth in Taiwan must be registered within 60 days.[17] As the Ministry of Interior's household registration system is digitally linked with all other legal documents, the gender assigned and registered at birth will first need to be amended at the household registration agency, where the applicant's place of domicile is registered, before the applicant can change the gender marker on any other official document or paper.

In administrative practice, for an applicant who applies for legal gender recognition, the first step at the Household Registration Bureau is to amend the National Identification Number on his or her ID card. An ID card is mandatory for nationals who have household registration in Taiwan and who are aged 14 years or older. Every ID card holder has a unique ID number which consists of one English letter followed by nine Arabic numerals. The English letter refers to the ID holder's birth place, usually the first location of the card holder's household registration, and the first Arabic number denotes the gender of the ID card holder – 1 for male, and 2 for female. After the original ID number has been annulled, a new National Identification Number will be issued to the applicant and the items recorded on the household registration record, such as legal gender and the titles for the sibling relations, can be altered after the new ID number is issued. However, the photo shown on the ID card is required to be consistent with 'biological sex' rather than legal gender. This requirement can cause inconvenience for transgender persons.

A household registration record includes a person's name, gender, date of birth, parents, spouse and residency. Under the Household Registration Act, an individual is required to make a registration at a household registration office upon the following events: birth, death, marriage, adoption, guardianship, change of residency and name, and obtaining legal gender recognition. The system of household registration (*hukou*) in Taiwan can be traced back to the Japanese colonial period (1895–1945). The system was established in 1906 by categorising residents into two broad groups – local residents and temporary

[17] Article 48 of the Household Registration Act.

residents.[18] Even though the household survey was the responsibility of the police during that time, household registration was mainly carried out by clerks of the local *Baojia* authorities.[19] Invented in the Song Dynasty (960–1279) in Imperial China, *Baojia* was a community-based system designed for law enforcement and civil control. The system gave '*bao*', which was composed of several families, the authority to maintain local order and organise civil projects in order to reduce the central government's financial burden of reliance on mercenaries. It transferred responsibility for law enforcement from the central government to civil societies.[20]

The *Baojia* system was in operation in Taiwan even during the period of Japanese colonisation. Later, the Household Registration Act was enacted by the ROC government in 1931, but it was not implemented in Taiwan until 1946, after Taiwan was restored to the ROC government after World War II. According to the Act, household registration was governed by the civil administration authority. But in reality, between 1973 and 1992, household registration was under the supervision of the police authority in Taiwan.[21] In 1985, the computerisation of the household registration was initiated under a trial scheme. After a decade, household registration data was fully digitised. It has been online nationwide since 1997.[22] Digitisation ensures that the household registration data can be archived in an electronic database that makes data sharing and linkage possible, even though it also causes anxieties about the infringement of privacy.

In order to protect the privacy of individuals who apply for legal gender recognition, the Ministry of Interior issued an administrative order, documented No. 547743, that allows applicants to request a new Household Registration Transcript to be issued. Legal gender recognition can be recorded only on the notes of the de-registered Household Registration Transcript for reference, though the original data will be retained. However, by so doing, the registered records of the change of legal gender on the transcript still cannot be covered completely. In addition, under the Personal Data Protection Act in Taiwan, the records of sex and/or gender on the official documents are not regarded as personal data to be protected, even though National Identification Numbers and other identifiable personal data on medical records are protected by the Act.

---

18 The system was introduced by Wang Anshi in his implementation of the seven-year New Policies reform.

19 See F.W. Mote, *Imperial China 900–1800,* Harvard University Press 2003, pp. 918–920.

20 Ibid. In the Song Dynasty, the basic unit of a '*bao*' consisted of ten families. In the Ming Dynasty (1368–1644), the family was relabelled as a '*Jia*' and a '*bao*' usually consisted of ten *Jia* or one hundred families. Even though the structure of the system changed overtime, the *Baojia* had been an important way of governance in Imperial China to hold the Chinese society altogether.

21 For more information about the history of the household registration in Taiwan, see <www.ris.gov.tw/18;jsessionid=404867C80733D790AE07D6E6CC122FAD> accessed 25.05.2015.

22 Ibid.

IV. CONSEQUENCES OF THE CHANGE OF LEGAL SEX AND/OR LEGAL GENDER

4.1. MARRIAGE

Under the Taiwan Civil Code, an agreement to marry shall be made between a man and a woman.[23] Even though same-sex marriages have been publically discussed within Taiwanese society, they have not yet been legally recognised (nor have registered (civil) partnerships). In Taiwan, transgender persons have the right to enter into a marriage so long as the marriage satisfies the statutory conditions set out in the Civil Code. Before 2008, a marriage had to be celebrated by open ceremonies in the presence of at least two witnesses.[24] For persons who had only registered for marriages with the Household Registration Bureau, but not celebrated their marriages by open ceremonies with two witnesses, they were assumed to have married.[25] Effective from May 2008, Taiwan amended the Civil Code and changed the requirements for the validity of marriage, adopting a registration system. Since then, a marriage must be registered with the Household Registration Bureau in order to be considered as a valid union.

In summer 2013, a marriage between two transgender women attracted significant attention. Abbygail Wu and Jiyi Wu both had transitioned from male to female (MtF) and submitted to sex affirmation surgery. They married in 2012 but Jiyi Wu had not registered the legal recognition of her preferred gender with the Household Registration Bureau until a year later in 2013. According to the Taiwan Civil Code, a marriage may exist only between one man and one woman. As Jiyi Wu still retained her male status at the time of her marriage, when her spouse Abbygail Wu had a female legal gender, the Wus' marriage was recognised as a legal union because they satisfied the Civil Code. Later, Jiyi Wu applied for legal gender recognition. This application caused a dispute with regard to the validity of the existing marriage.

In June 2013, the Ministry of Interior demanded annulment of the Wus' marriage, based on the fact that, although Jiyi Wu had not yet completed registration, she had undergone sex affirmation surgery prior to her marriage. As both individuals were said to be 'physically female' at the time of their marriage, the Ministry demanded the revocation of the marriage registration and gave the couple a period of time to annul their marriage. The Ministry argued that the union violated the requirement that there be one man and one woman for a valid legal marriage. The decision to revoke the marriage licence was met with much criticism and public disapproval. On 7 August 2013, the Ministry of Interior held a conference investigating the Wus' case, and following a marathon meeting

23 Article 972 of the Taiwan Civil Code.
24 Article 982 of the Taiwan Civil Code.
25 Ibid.

with governmental officials and NGOs from the transgender rights movement, the authority finally decided to change its original decision. The Ministry thus accepted the validity of the couple's existing marriage. This decision indicates that, for the interpretation of heterosexual couples for a marriage to be recognised as a legal union in Taiwan, it refers to legal genders recorded in the Household Registration Transcripts rather than biological sex. However, even though the Wus' marriage was recognised by the Ministry of Interior as a legal union, the 'one man and one woman' rule set out in Article 972 of the Civil Code has further demonstrated a conservative mindset among the judicial and governmental administration towards marriage formation in Taiwan.

In recent years, there have been increasing calls to revise Article 972 of the Taiwan Civil Code. At the end of 2013, a campaign for 'diverse families',[26] organised by the Taiwan Alliance to Promote Civil Partnership Rights (TAPCPR), attracted nearly 30,000 signatures in support of a proposed revision. The revision would make same-sex marriages and civil partnerships possible in Taiwan.[27] The campaign aims to promote a new system that is more flexible than the traditional institution of marriage recognised by the current Civil Code. It may further open up possibilities to form a legal union for people of all kinds of gender and sexual orientation, including transgender persons. In October 2013, a draft bill for marriage equality was referred to the Judicial Affairs Committee of Legislative Yuan for review. The draft involves phrases and semantic changes, such as changing the wording 'husband and wife' to 'spouse'. Nevertheless, opposition from religious groups towards the draft remains strong. With concerns that the bill would destroy moral values and the foundation of family ethics, the Taiwan Family Alliance called for another petition for the public to support the traditional institution of marriage of one man and one woman. The bill is still in the process of review in the Legislative Yuan at the point of writing. It has not yet been approved by legislators in Taiwan.

4.2. PARENTHOOD AND ADOPTION

Under the Taiwan Civil Code, several statutory conditions are listed for prospective adoptive parents. For example, adoptive parents must have legitimate work, a stable residence and must be at least 20 years older than the child to be adopted.[28] In addition, only a married couple can adopt a child or an adult jointly.[29] On the other hand, no child adopted may be directly related by blood

---

26 In Chinese, it is called '多元成家' (Pinyin: Duo Yuan Cheng Jia); other translations for this term include 'diverse family' and 'multi-person household'.

27 A. Leach, 'Monogamy Is an Illusion: Taiwanese Lawyer Campaigns for Multiple Person Marriage Law', *LGBTI Global News 24-7*, 2 November 2012.

28 Article 1073 of the Taiwan Civil Code.

29 Article 1075 of the Taiwan Civil Code.

to the adoptive parents, nor can the adoption be related by marriage, with one exception that the adoption is for the other spouse's child as a stepchild.[30] Like many other jurisdictions, an agreement for adoption in Taiwan needs to be filed with the courts for approval before it can be executed. In practice, same-gender marriages are generally unsuccessful in Taiwan because same-gender marriage has not yet been introduced. However, a court may grant a favourable decision for adoption by a partner in a same-sex relationship given that the child to be adopted is the biological offspring of one member of the couple.[31]

In Taiwan, the first case on legal adoption by a transgender person was approved by the District Court in Chiayi in 2002. Chung Ling, 49, was a male-to-female (MtF) transgender individual who had submitted to sex affirmation surgery in Thailand at the age of 26.[32] After the surgery in Thailand, Chung went back to Taiwan to work and had been employed at several bars. The baby boy Chung adopted was not from Chung's relatives but from a neighbour of Chung's mother. The baby, who suffered from a glucose deficiency, had been abandoned by his biological mother at birth. The adoption process took about five months to complete, including going through a formal assessment from social workers and the completion of registration with the Household Registration Bureau. Under the Taiwan Civil Code, social workers are required to interview families involved in adoption and to provide home visit reports to the court. The social workers assigned to Chung's case made a favourable assessment of Chung's application after interviewing both families and they found that it would be better for the baby boy to live with Chung than with his biological mother, who had alcohol problems. The adoption was completed after Chung registered the case with the household registration office in Chiayi.

Even though Chung's case opens the possibility for transgender persons to adopt, whether an adoptive parent's sexual orientation or gender identity is a factor for consideration ultimately falls within the court's discretion. An earlier 2007 case from a court in Taoyuan, relating to lesbian parenting, demonstrated that a prospective adoptive parent's homosexuality may be viewed by courts as an unfavourable factor. Therefore their petition for adoption could be denied due to gender stereotyping.[33] In the 2007 case, even though the Court appeared to recognise that homosexual relationships are an expression of personal freedom, the Court nevertheless turned down the petition for adoption based on the application of the so-called 'best interests' doctrine, which has been incorporated

---

30 Article 1077 of Taiwan Civil Code.

31 Under Article 1074 of Taiwan Civil Code, adoption from a single person is allowed and therefore even though it is not possible for same-sex couples to jointly adopts a child or an adult in Taiwan, it is still feasible to create a single-parent family for a member of same-sex couples.

32 Tsai Wen-ting, '"Her" Story – the Transsexual Chung Ling', *Taiwan Panorama,* November 2002.

33 Yun-Hsien Diana Lin, 'Lesbian Parenting in Taiwan: Legal Issues and the Latest Developments', (2013) 14(2) *Asian-Pacific Law & Policy Journal.*

into Taiwan's family law. Under Article 1055-1 of the Taiwan Civil Code, a judge must take account of certain criteria when considering the best interests doctrine. These criteria include, but are not limited to: a prospective adoptive parent's intent and age, gender, occupation, health, character, financial conditions, lifestyle, etc. However, it has been argued that, in this case, the reason for not granting the adoptive petition was not because of any legitimate consideration of the child's best interests. Rather, the Court refused the petition because of a concern that existing homophobic attitudes in society might negatively affect a child who was being reared by two female parents.

4.3. ARTIFICIAL REPRODUCTION

Administrative order No. 0970066240 requires the removal of reproductive organs as a precondition for obtaining legal gender recognition. As surgery leads to infertility, the question is whether the gametes of a person stored before legal gender recognition can be used afterwards to create a child through artificial reproductive technology. On 10 March 2014, the Ministry of Health and Wealth issued an administrative explanation, documented No. 103301001, with regard to the application of the Artificial Reproductive Act to transgender persons. The Act limits the use of assisted human reproduction only to married couples as a medical treatment for infertility. Under the Act, a medical care institution may perform assisted human reproduction for a married couple if, and only if, certain requirements are met. These requirements include that there be 'a husband or wife of the married couple who has been diagnosed as suffering from infertility',[34] or who has been diagnosed as 'suffering from a major hereditary disease and it is suspected that natural conception and birth will cause abnormal children'.[35] In addition, at least one party of the married couple must possess healthy reproductive cells, so that there is no need for donated sperm or oocytes.

As the Artificial Reproduction Act excludes single women from accessing assisted human reproduction, and uses terminology, such as 'a husband and wife', there is an exclusion of the possibility of recognising diverse family formations. This situation has been criticised as discrimination against unmarried and single people. Under the administrative explanation, documented No. 103301001, the Ministry of Health and Welfare states that, so long as the requirements set by the Act for a married couple are met, even though transgender persons have not yet completed legal gender recognition, a medical care institution can still perform assisted human reproduction for transgender individuals according to the Act.

Article 21 II of the Artificial Reproduction Act enumerates the conditions under which stored reproductive cells have to be destroyed by an artificial

[34] Article 11 of the Artificial Reproduction Act.
[35] Ibid.

reproduction institution. The conditions include situations where the providers of the reproductive cells have died or have requested destruction. There may be circumstances where the reproductive cells have been preserved for more than ten years but such preservation period can be extended with the written consent of the providers.[36] Importantly, the Act does not require that legal gender recognition should automatically trigger the destruction of stored cells.

4.4. MILITARY SERVICE

In Taiwan, men aged 19–37 years are required to complete military service with only few exceptions, such as psychological or physical unfitness. In some jurisdictions, like Australia, Canada and the United Kingdom, voluntary military service by transgender individuals is allowed and serving in the armed forces is viewed as a right for transgender persons. Laws that prevent lesbian, gay, and bisexual individuals from enlisting in the armed forces are deemed to be discriminatory in these jurisdictions. For transgender rights advocates in those countries, there is no compelling medical reason that can justify banning transgender participation. In Taiwan, however, transgender citizens are exempted from military service based on the concern that it could cause inconvenience for both transgender and cisgender individuals in their daily military practice.

Some concerns about obtaining the recognition of preferred legal gender have been raised, in particular that it may be used as a way for individuals to avoid compulsory military service in Taiwan. Some voices in Taiwanese society are against the separation of legal gender recognition from gender confirmation surgery. These concerns have been criticised by transgender groups as that would constitute a hindrance for transgender citizens obtaining gender recognition without undergoing unwanted medical treatment. In fact, according to the current practice within the Ministry of Defense, a person who has been diagnosed by psychiatrists as identifying with a gender which does not match their birth-assigned gender will, on the basis of that diagnosis alone, be exempted from military service directly. Therefore, in Taiwan, there is no need to obtain legal gender recognition (from male to female) in order to be exempted from compulsory military service.

V. CONCLUSION

The legal status of transgender persons varies across jurisdictions. In Taiwan, there is no specific statute that deals with a transgender person's rights and responsibilities. Administrative practices constitute the major framework under

---

[36] Article 21 of the Artificial Reproduction Act.

which legal status is recognised. This chapter has introduced the historical development of the law relating to transgender identities in Taiwan. It has discussed the legal procedure and requirements for obtaining gender recognition. Faced with criticism from local NGOs and human rights groups, the Taiwanese government has gradually relaxed its administrative practices in the years since 2008. Most importantly, at the end of 2014 the administrative order that requires psychological evaluation and the removal of reproductive organs has been repealed. Even though Taiwan still has a long way to go in order to achieve full equity and respect for the rights of transgender persons, this recent decision to separate medical treatments from the recognition of preferred gender has been a triumph for human rights development in Taiwan, and represents a momentous step forward for transgender rights in Asia.

AUSTRALIA AND NEW ZEALAND

REFLECTIONS ON DECIDING *RE KEVIN*

Richard CHISHOLM*

Contents

I. INTRODUCTION

Re Kevin[1] was an application for a declaration of the validity of a marriage between a woman ('Jennifer') and Kevin, who was born with female characteristics but whose affirmed sex was male. It was common ground that a marriage required a man and a woman – the question whether a same-sex relationship could be a 'marriage' did not arise in the case.[2]

The case was conducted, magnificently, by Rachael Wallbank, who also appeared on the appeal. The Attorney-General of Australia opposed the application, saying that it was not a valid marriage, since Kevin was a woman, not a man. According to the Attorney-General (represented by a distinguished QC,

* I am grateful to Rachael Wallbank for comments on a draft of this chapter – but I should point out that she did not suggest the complimentary comments about her!

1 *Re Kevin: Validity of Marriage of Transsexual* (2001) 28 Fam LR 158 ('*Re Kevin*'). The decision and the reasoning were upheld unanimously on appeal: *Attorney-General for the Commonwealth v Kevin and Others* (2003) 30 Fam LR 1.

2 On 12 December 2013 the High Court of Australia held that the word 'marriage' in 51(xxi) of the Constitution extends to laws about same-sex relationships: *The Commonwealth v Australian Capital Territory* [2013] HCA 55. This ruling enables the federal parliament, if it chooses, to provide for marriage between same-sex couples.

Henry Burmester, as well as junior counsel), the law had been settled in *Corbett*,[3] a famous English decision of 1971. *Corbett* said that a person's sex was determined exclusively by certain physical features at the time of birth: gonads, chromosomes and genitals. If those features were congruent (as they were in Kevin's case) they would determine the person's sex, which was thus fixed at birth and could not be changed by any later development, whether the person's self-image, family life, social acceptance, or natural physical development, hormone treatment or surgery. Anything 'psychological' was irrelevant. If *Corbett* was to be followed, Kevin was a woman and the application for validity of the marriage would have to be dismissed.

Wallbank argued that *Corbett* was wrong, and that determining whether a person was a man or a woman required attention to other facts as well, especially the person's experiences since birth. Consistently with that, the case she presented was rich in detail, with much evidence about Kevin and his experiences, expert medical evidence about the nature of his condition, and evidence about his acceptance as a man into the community. Consistently with the *Corbett* decision, the Attorney-General took the view that most or all of this material was legally irrelevant, but otherwise challenged virtually none of it. So after the preliminaries, the hearing consisted of two days' legal argument, with a daunting pile of unchallenged evidence.

I have already complimented Rachael Wallbank on her presentation of the case. I should also acknowledge two features of the Attorney-General's handling of the case. First, I understand that Kevin's case was supported by Commonwealth legal aid funds. Second, the Attorney-General acted generously in formally conceding that Kevin was post-operative, thereby sparing him from any need to document the details of his surgical treatment. It also spared me the task of considering the legal position of pre-operative people in Kevin's position, as will be explained later.

Why did Kevin and Jennifer and their families care so much about the validity of Kevin's marriage? The evidence did not say. Perhaps it had something to do with social acceptance. Perhaps it had to do with promoting the human rights of others who have similar predicaments to Kevin's. Perhaps it had to do with the best interests of their two children. I suspect that they have achieved something they can be proud of in all these areas. Rachael Wallbank can also be proud of her achievement.

II. EVIDENCE ABOUT KEVIN

Part 2 of the judgment sets out the extensive evidence of Kevin's life history, including medical and psychiatric evidence, and evidence from family and work

3 *Corbett v Corbett (otherwise Ashley)* [1971] P 83 ('*Corbett*').

colleagues, showing that Kevin saw himself as a man and was treated as such by his family and community. This evidence need not be repeated here, but it was remarkably complete and impressive. Kevin passed every possible test with flying colours. For example, Kevin's mother-in-law wrote, movingly, 'There is no other man anywhere who I would prefer to have as my daughter's husband'.

It would have been possible to leave out much of this evidence, because legal acceptance of Kevin's affirmed sex might well not have required all of it. But the evidence was before me, and it was not argued that the result would have been the same had some of the evidence been missing. I thought it appropriate to set out the evidence in a systematic way, partly out of respect for Kevin and his representatives, and partly because I thought it might be in the public interest to put on record this unusually detailed picture that might personalise the plight of transsexual persons, and also to put on record the remarkably complete expert evidence that Rachel Wallbank had assembled for the court.

III. THE *CORBETT* CASE

In seeking to overturn *Corbett*, Wallbank had a formidable target. It was a 'landmark decision', that had in England 'defined the common law', informed the subsequent statutory codification of the law of nullity, and been followed in allied fields.[4] In Australia, although the reasoning had been much criticised and some courts had held that it did not determine the meaning of the words 'man' and 'woman' for other areas of law,[5] the courts had previously held[6] or assumed that *Corbett* represented the Australian law relating to marriage. It was suggested on behalf of the Attorney-General that not following *Corbett* and upholding the marriage would be a 'radical' step, an indefensible exercise of judicial activism.[7]

3.1. THE MEDICAL EVIDENCE UNDERMINED *CORBETT*

The first basis for the criticism of *Corbett* was that the decision was undermined by current medical knowledge.[8] This was the basis on which Thorpe LJ had declined to follow *Corbett* when *Bellinger* came before the UK Court of Appeal:

4 *Bellinger v Bellinger* [2002] 1 All ER 311, per Thorpe LJ (dissenting) at para. 118. For an excellent account of the case, see S. Gilmore, '*Corbett v Corbett*: Once a Man, Always a Man?' in S. Gilmore, J. Herring and R. Probert (eds.), *Landmark Cases in Family Law*, Hart Publishing, Oxford 2011, pp. 47–72.

5 *R v Harris and McGuiness* (1988) 17 NSW LR 158, *Secretary, Department of Social Security v SRA* (1993) 118 ALR 467.

6 For example *In the Marriage of C and D (falsely called C)* (1979) FLC 90–636.

7 See para. [293].

8 I know there is room for criticism of the *Corbett* treatment of the medical evidence that was then before the court, but I have not pursued this aspect.

his Lordship said that although *Corbett* was 'undoubtedly right' when given on 2 February 1970, it was rendered wrong in 2001 by subsequent developments, both medical and social.[9] Rachael Wallbank had assembled a great deal of expert medical evidence, featuring some of the world's leading authorities: its accuracy was unchallenged, and it was accepted. It occupies a substantial part of the judgment. I discussed the medical evidence in detail in *Re Kevin*, and considered that it did indeed undermine the reasoning in *Corbett*, in particular the sharp distinction drawn in *Corbett* between 'biological' and 'psychological' factors. However I will not dwell on the medical evidence here, because I have no expertise in this area and, no doubt, the science has moved on since the *Re Kevin* decision.

3.2. UNPERSUASIVE REASONING IN *CORBETT*

In this chapter I will focus more on a second reason for concluding that *Corbett* was wrong, namely that the reasoning contained logical flaws and was unpersuasive. Thus in *Re Kevin* I held that even apart from the medical evidence, *Corbett* should not be accepted in Australian law: it had always been wrong.[10]

Judicial and academic commentators had commonly criticised the consequences of the decision,[11] and there had been sustained criticism of certain passages, especially the one referring to the 'essential role' of a woman in marriage, quoted below.[12] But what also struck me was a logical flaw in the reasoning.[13] *Corbett* was a complex case with many factual and legal issues, and the reasoning is scattered throughout the judgment. But on a careful analysis, picking out the key terms used, the Court's conclusion that April Ashley was a man took this form:

(1) The biological sexual constitution of all individuals is fixed at birth and cannot be changed.
(2) Ms Ashley's biological sexual constitution at birth was male.
(3) Therefore Ms Ashley's biological sexual constitution remains male.
(4) Therefore, Ms Ashley's true sex is male.

---

9 *Bellinger v Bellinger* [2002] 1 All ER 311, per Thorpe LJ (dissenting) at para. 155.

10 Recently in Australia *Corbett* was described as of historical interest only: *Norrie v NSW Registrar of Births, Deaths and Marriages* [2013] NSWCA 145 Beazley ACJ at [134]. (The High Court appeal decision is *NSW Registrar of Births, Deaths and Marriages v Norrie* [2014] HCA 11.)

11 D. Green, 'Transsexualism and Marriage' (1970) 120 *New Law Journal* 210; J. Dewar, 'Transsexualism and Marriage' (1985) 15 *Kingston Law Rev.* 58; M. Otlowski, 'The Legal Status of a Sexually Reassigned Transsexual: R v. Harris and McGuiness and Beyond' (1990) 64 *Australian L.J.* 67. See also the quotations in *Harris* at 190, per Mathews J.

12 *Harris*, per Mathews J, 189. See in particular the fascinating account S. Gilmore, '*Corbett v Corbett*: Once a Man, Always a Man?' in S. Gilmore, J. Herring and R. Probert (eds.), *Landmark Cases in Family Law*, Hart Publishing, Oxford 2011, pp. 47–72.

13 This is set out in more detail in *Re Kevin* at paras. [76]–[84].

(5) The validity of the marriage depends on Ms Ashley's 'true sex'.
(6) Therefore, the other party being a man, the marriage is invalid.

The first two propositions were said to be based on the medical evidence before the court in *Corbett*, and the third is a logical consequence. The problem lies in steps 4 and 5. The only basis for step 4 appears to be that Ms Ashley's 'biological sexual constitution' was treated as equivalent to her 'true sex' (a term that was not explained). But this begged the question, which was whether social and psychological matters were relevant in determining whether April Ashley was a man or a woman. That was a question of law. The reasoning to this point provided no authority or argument supporting this conclusion; but this lack was obscured, I think, by a definitional sleight of hand, creating the false impression that social and psychological matters had somehow been *shown* to be irrelevant, when in truth they had simply been *assumed* to be irrelevant.

The main passage that can really count as a reason for the conclusion is this:

> '[T]he criteria must, in my judgment, be biological, for even the most extreme degree of transsexualism in a male or the most severe hormonal imbalance which can exist in a person with male chromosomes, male gonads and male genitalia cannot reproduce a person who is naturally capable of performing the essential role of a woman in marriage.'

This passage, with its notion of the 'essential role of a woman in marriage' has been subjected to severe criticism, many critics pointing out, as the late Gordon Samuels did, that 'the female spouse's ability or willingness to produce children is not a necessary incident of a valid marriage'.[14] In *Re Kevin* I agreed, saying that because marriage is a social and legal institution which includes people who are infertile or by reason of illness or otherwise are unable to engage in genital penetrative intercourse, it would be odd, rather than self-evident, to treat capacity for genital intercourse as 'the essential' role of a woman (or a man) in marriage.[15]

Finally, Ormrod J offered a *reductio ad absurdum* argument: if April Ashley were treated as a woman

> 'it would follow [from the argument] that if a 50 year old male transsexual, married and the father of children, underwent the operation, he would then have to be regarded in law as a female and capable of "marrying" a man. The results would be nothing if not bizarre...'

14 See *Re Kevin* at paras. [92]–[95].
15 Quoted in *Re Kevin* at para. [97].

In my view this is unpersuasive, for two reasons.[16] First, seeing the results as bizarre depends on adopting exclusively the point of view of *others*. From the point of view of the individual involved, *failing* to recognise the reassignment would probably seem bizarre.

Second, Ormrod J's argument is unimpressive if one actually spells out the consequences of the competing views. Suppose Jane marries Bill, and they adopt a child. Jane goes through a gender reassignment process at age 50, and, now called John, wishes to separate and marry a woman. If contrary to *Corbett* the law recognises John as a man, what will be the consequences, and are they really 'bizarre'?

The legal effect of a gender reassignment procedure on an existing marriage has not been tested. *Re Kevin* indicates that 'Jane' would have been a man when aged 50 at separation, but does not deal with the question whether in law Jane should be considered always to have been a man (in which case the marriage with Bill would have been invalid). If the marriage between Jane/John and Bill is treated as valid, as seems likely, the granting of divorce, and any issues about property division, child care or child support would be dealt with in the usual way. Consistently with virtually all other aspects of his life, except chromosomes, John would now be treated as a man for marriage as well as other legal purposes, and could remarry, to a woman. No obvious difficulties would appear to flow from this, and none seem to have arisen in other jurisdictions, such as New Zealand or many European countries, where the re-assignment is recognised for the purpose of marriage law. (If Jane/John were regarded as a person who had always been a man, the marriage with Bill would be invalid and Jane/John would be free to marry a woman.)

What if *Corbett* were correct, and the marriage law continued to regard Jane/John as a woman? The marriage with Bill would of course be valid. The law would not prevent Jane/John from going through the gender reassignment process, separating, and then obtaining a divorce. He would be free to live his life as a man. If he was like Kevin, he would now perceive himself to be a man, look like a man, and be accepted as a man by family, friends and work colleagues, and for a variety of legal and social purposes: his birth certificate, passport and other documents would all show him to be a man. He would have no female physical characteristics other than chromosomes. Under the law of marriage, if *Corbett* were right, John would be entitled to marry a man. Ironically, to the outside world such an event would appear to involve a legal marriage of a same-sex couple. If a word such as 'bizarre' is to be used, it would seem more apt to describe the consequences of the *Corbett* approach – treating John as still a woman – than the consequences of recognising the reassignment.

But calling some outcomes 'bizarre' is ultimately unhelpful (not to mention insensitive), whatever its rhetorical force might be. The fact is that the assignment

---

16 See *Re Kevin* at paras. [98]–[104].

of individuals to one category or the other will inevitably mean that some of the person's characteristics will be those of the 'other' sex. The law's task – through the definition it gives to the everyday words 'man' and 'woman' – is to reach a conclusion that is just, compassionate and sensible. And this leads to the next point.

3.3. SWAN ESSENCE – REFLECTIONS ON DECISION-MAKING

Underlying the problems that I have mentioned was, I think, a more fundamental problem with the approach in *Corbett*.

I'll start with black swans. Before Australia was discovered, I believe, the only known swans were white. When creatures that resembled swans turned up in Australia, the question arose what to call them: were they swans that happened to be black? Or were they something else, swans necessarily being white? It is a question of taxonomy, or classification. Those undertaking this task would have worked out which categorisation would be most suitable, knowing they had a choice to make. They would not have tried to solve the problem by asking whether the black creatures had some distinctive property, some 'swan essence'.

The reasoning in *Corbett* seems to be the legal equivalent of looking for 'swan essence' to find the right category for black swans. It seems to be based on the view or assumption that individuals have some basic essential quality that makes them male or female – their 'true sex' – which it is the law's task to identify.

I believe this approach is unsound. Most people, I take it, are unambiguously male or female. It does not follow that there is some single entity underlying these matters that constitutes the person's 'true sex'. In a minority of people, various incongruities arise: sometimes within the chromosomes, gonads or genitals, sometimes among them; sometimes between the self-perception and some or more of these factors. Where there are incongruities, by definition the person has some characteristics normally associated with each sex. The situation presents a question for the individual, and for legal and social systems, namely how that person's identity should be defined and managed. The law's task is not to search for some mysterious entity, the person's 'true sex', but to answer a practical human problem; as one of the witnesses in *Corbett* nicely put it, 'to determine the sex in which it is best for the individual to live'.[17]

Some decisions do this. My favourite is a rarely-quoted case, a decision of a Swiss cantonal court, *In Re Leber*, decided in 1945, a quarter of a century before *Corbett*.[18] The applicant applied to change her sex as recorded on the birth register

---

17 *Corbett* at 100, quoting Professor Dewhurst.

18 The most accessible account of this case is the summary in D.K. Smith, 'Transsexualism, Sex Reassignment Surgery and the Law' (1971) 56 *Cornell LR* 963, 971–972, quoted by Lockhart J in *Secretary, Department of Social Security* v *SRA* (1993) 118 ALR 467. The whole case is however

from male to female. Some of the language is outdated, but we can see how the court appreciated what was involved in the decision, and grasped the nettle. In a decision of conspicuous humanity, the Court granted the application. It wrote:

> 'This inclines us to attribute to the psychic element, in the determination of sex, an importance at least equal to that of the physical element … It is not only the body which determines the sex of the individual, it is also the mind. When there is a discord between body and mind, one must see which of these two elements predominates. Leber, being neither a perfect man nor a perfect woman, must be placed in the category of human beings which he most resembles. In the unanimous opinion of doctors and experts he is nearest, as a whole, to a woman …
>
> In granting him the civil status of a woman we are satisfying the most profound desire of his being while consolidating his psychic and moral equilibrium; at the same time we are facilitating his social adaptation by permitting him to lead a more normal type of life than heretofore. The personal interest which urges him to ask for a change of civic status is thus not opposed to the interests of public order and morality – quite the contrary.'

The Swiss court understood its task, namely to formulate legal criteria for assigning a person to one sex or the other. In doing so it had regard to the medical evidence, and the interests of the individual and society, rather than seeking to discover some entity that is the person's 'true sex'. Many of the more recent decisions take a similar approach.

What led to the 'essentialist' approach in *Corbett*? The legal context may have played a part. The factual issues in *Corbett*, and the presentation of the case, involved much detail about sexual matters, and this may have focused attention on this area. Another possibility is that the judge's own background played a part. As it happens, Ormrod J was, perhaps uniquely, qualified in medicine as well as in law: indeed he was remarkably distinguished in both fields.[19] This may have reinforced the focus evident in the decision. If so, his medical qualifications, which would on the face of it be a great help in a case like this, may have been a *disqualification*, distracting him from the task facing the court, the task that had been so well grasped in the *Leber* decision (which was not cited in *Corbett*).

These days, there is considerable interest in decision-making and heuristics, and *Corbett* may be an instructive case from this point of view. Our legal traditions are perhaps better at detecting some kinds of bias and preconceptions than others. No doubt all judges try to prevent their own views and experiences from distorting their judgments. For example in family law a judge will attempt to set aside any preconceptions he or she might have about, say, the respective

reproduced in E. De Savitsch, *Homosexuality, Transvestism and Change of Sex*, Heinemann, London 1958, Appendix A (pp. 96–107), from which the quoted extract is taken.

19 See generally S. Gilmore, '*Corbett v Corbett*: Once a Man, Always a Man?' in S. Gilmore, J. Herring and R. Probert (eds.), *Landmark Cases in Family Law*, Hart Publishing, Oxford 2011, pp. 47–72.

merits of private or public schools, or of different parenting styles, recognising that there are different views about such things and attempting as far as possible to ensure that the outcome does not depend on which views or life experiences the judge happens to have. In a pluralistic society, this is often no easy task, but it is a familiar challenge. A comparison between *Corbett* and *Re Leber* indicates, I think, that outcomes can also be affected by something deeper, a judge's frame of reference, or an underlying idea about the court's role – for example whether it is to discover the essence that distinguishes all men from all women (*Corbett*), or to make a policy decision about the most sensible and compassionate category for a person whose characteristics are not entirely congruent with either category. It might be arguable that judges should try to be attentive not only to the more familiar and obvious sources of bias, but also to such underlying and typically unstated beliefs or assumptions.[20]

IV. STATUTORY CONSTRUCTION AND THE MEANING OF 'MAN' AND 'WOMAN'

It's hard to get excited about statutory construction. It seems impossible not to speak of the legislature's 'intention', yet nobody takes this literally; and those old maxims, even in Latin, generally fail to give an answer. Ultimately, we all tend to end up saying it all depends on the context.

In *Re Kevin*, the submission of the Attorney-General was that the word 'man' should be given the meaning it had at the time of the relevant statute, the Marriage Act 1961, rather than its contemporary meaning (as Wallbank had submitted). I did not think the authorities established that as a general rule words should be taken to have the meaning they had at the time of the relevant enactment.[21]

There were other problems with the argument, too. *Corbett* was decided later than 1961, and there was no obvious reason to say that the Australian parliament in 1961 intended – there's that word again – that 'man' would have the meaning that Ormrod J was to give it ten years later, in 1971. Indeed, on the historical approach it might be said that the legislature might have intended the word 'man' to have the meaning it had earlier, for example in the famous statement of Lord Penzance in *Hyde v Hyde* (1866) that marriage was the 'voluntary union for life of one man and one woman, to the exclusion of all others'.[22] This would not have given us the *Corbett* meaning. The biological principles governing the development of male and female gonads became elucidated only from the middle

20 I explored this topic in a paper 'Values and Assumptions in Judicial Decisions', National Judicial College of Australia, Judicial Reasoning: Art or Science Conference, Canberra, February 2009.

21 *Re Kevin* at paras. [122]–[129].

22 *Hyde v Hyde and Woodmansee* (1866) LR 1 P&D 130, 133.

of the nineteenth century,[23] and it would be surprising if Lord Penzance was at the cutting edge of this medical research. And chromosomes, which featured largely in the *Corbett* test, seem to have become known and discoverable by tests much later, in the 1950s.[24]

Thus even if it were accepted that that the word 'man' should be given its meaning when the Marriage Act was passed in 1961, or when *Hyde v Hyde* was decided, that meaning would probably not have been the meaning given to the word in *Corbett*. Put bluntly, it would be wrong to pretend that in 1961 the legislature had thought about the meaning of 'man' and had intended to incorporate the complex definition formulated in England ten years later in *Corbett*. As Professor Gooren and a colleague put it:[25]

> 'There should be no escape for medical and legal authorities that these definitions ought to be corrected and updated when new information becomes available, particularly when our outdated definitions bring suffering to some of our fellow human beings.'

Thus the task was to determine the ordinary contemporary meaning of the word 'man'. A detailed examination of the Australian case law[26] and other aspects of the legal and social system showed that generally speaking Kevin would be a 'man' in ordinary language and would be treated as such under a wide range of laws. As a result, the Attorney-General needed to argue that there was something special about the law of marriage, so that for the purpose of marriage law, the words 'man' and 'woman' had a different meaning to the meaning they had in other legal contexts. The attempt to demonstrate this led to policy arguments about the consequences of the *Corbett* and other approaches in the context of the law of marriage.

Having reviewed these arguments, and the extensive literature, I could not accept that the word 'man' had a special meaning, namely the *Corbett* meaning, in the Australian law of marriage. In brief:

- Firstly, acknowledging sex-reassignment (to use a convenient if inaccurate term) respects the rights of the individual concerned. Sometimes, this is expressed in terms of human rights. Sometimes, it is expressed in terms of avoiding further suffering. Sometimes it is expressed in terms of compassion, or a desire to mark acceptance of people who are different.

---

23 L. Gooren and C. Doorn, 'Who determines manhood or womanhood? The biomedical and legal definitions of man and woman in relation to transsexualism' in F. Fleerackers et al. (ed.), *Law, Life and the Images of Man: modes of thought in modern legal theory*, Duncker and Humboldt, Berlin 1996, pp. 267–282, 269.

24 Ibid., p. 269.

25 Ibid., p. 281.

26 Notably *R v Harris and McGuinness* (1988) 17 NSWLR 158 (NSW Court of Criminal Appeal); *Secretary of Department of Social Security v SRA* (1993) 118 ALR 467.

- Secondly, acknowledging sex-reassignment assists individuals to integrate into society. In their re-assigned sex, these persons are more likely to live comfortably in society and to contribute to it.
- Both of these apply equally, or indeed with particular force, to the context of marriage. An examination of the submissions and the literature does not identify any reasons why the law of marriage should diverge from the general law. Indeed, there are good reasons specific to marriage for recognising the re-assignment. Doing so would be likely to promote the interests of others, in particular the spouses and children involved. Failing to do so would lead to the odd result that a person who appears to be a man, who functions in society as a man, and whose body can never function as a woman's body and has most of the characteristics of a man, would be entitled to marry a man.
- Finally, to recognise sex-reassignment would bring marriage law into conformity with other areas of law. Refusing to recognise it would mean that the words 'man' and 'woman' have a special technical meaning in marriage law, different to their general meaning. That result, while logically possible, is highly undesirable.

I concluded that there was no basis in legal principle or policy why Australian law should follow the decision in *Corbett*. To do so would create indefensible inconsistencies between Australian marriage law and other Australian laws. It would take the law in a direction that is generally contrary to developments in other countries. It would perpetuate a view that flies in the face of current medical understanding and practice. Most of all, it would impose indefensible suffering on people who have already had more than their share of difficulty, with no benefit to society.

V. EXPRESSING THE CONCLUSION

For these reasons, I rejected the *Corbett* approach, enabling a finding that Kevin was a man. As mentioned above, Kevin ticked all the boxes. One of these boxes was surgery, and as already mentioned the Attorney-General did not seek to argue that the surgery Kevin had had was in any way insufficient. So, to use terminology that was used without objection at the time, Kevin was a post-operative transsexual.[27]

Having rejected the *Corbett* definition, and holding that the word 'man' has its ordinary contemporary meaning, I had to consider what to say about that ordinary meaning, and in particular whether to formulate some other definition. Some of the Australian cases had decided that the line should be drawn at surgery, so that individuals would not have their affirmed sex legally recognised unless

[27] I have since become uncomfortable with this term: like such terms as 'the blind', it might focus unduly on the person's condition rather than their essential humanity.

they had undergone surgery. But since Kevin passed even the most rigorous test, it was not necessary for me to rule on the controversial question whether surgery was a necessary requirement for recognition of a person's affirmed sex, and the parties rightly did not argue the point, or invite me to address it. How should I express the conclusion?

There was more than one way to formulate the conclusion. I could have formulated a definition of 'man' in which surgery is not a requirement for the legal recognition of the affirmed sex; or I could have based the decision entirely on the medical evidence, and find that Kevin's brain made him a man, and so it was not necessary to rely on surgery or many of the other matters put into evidence. Deciding the case in such ways might have been rightly characterised as 'radical'. But my conclusion was, in brief, that for the law of marriage the word 'man' has its ordinary meaning; whether a person is a man is a question of fact; and a range of matters may be relevant. Since in Kevin's case all those matters indicated that he was a man, I left it open to other courts, when the question arose, to decide whether something short of that might be enough. I took the view that in accordance with the common law tradition as I understood it, I should decide what needed to be decided to resolve the particular case, and no more. Thus although the reasoning was necessarily wide-ranging, in this respect it is conventional rather than 'radical'.

Whether this approach was desirable is of course a matter of opinion, and I don't want to engage in the important and continuing debate about what the law should be, or what wider inferences might be drawn from *Re Kevin*.[28] The judgment is a public document and people can decide for themselves what it says and means. But I believe that one commentator, Professor Alex Sharpe, has misread the decision, and the mistake should be corrected.[29]

First, Sharpe has written that the *Re Kevin* decision 'provides support for the view that sex is determined at birth'. This is quite wrong.[30] *Re Kevin* held that various later life experiences were relevant in determining whether a person was a man. Indeed, the judgment states explicitly:[31]

> 'there is no rule or presumption that the question whether a person is a man or a woman for the purpose of marriage law is to be determined by reference to

---

28 See e.g. T. Bennett, 'Transsexualism and the Consideration of Social Factors within Sex Identification Law' (2014) 34 *Adelaide Law Review* 379–402.

29 A.N. Sharpe, 'Endless Sex: the Gender Recognition Act 2004 and the Persistence of Legal Category' (2007) 15 *Feminist Legal Studies* 57–84. Stephen Gilmore appears to accept Sharpe's critique in his otherwise illuminating account: 'Corbett v Corbett: Once a Man, Always a Man?' in S. Gilmore, J. Herring and R. Probert (eds.), *Landmark Cases in Family Law*, Hart Publishing, Oxford 2011, pp. 47–72.

30 Even the evidence about 'brain sex' indicated that the brain continues to develop after birth: see *Re Kevin* at paras. [222], [271].

31 *Re Kevin* at para. [330].

circumstances at the time of birth. Anything to the contrary in *Corbett* does not represent Australian law.'

Sharpe also says that the fact that Kevin had undertaken a variety of surgical procedures 'proved crucial to his legal recognition as a man'. This seems inconsistent with Sharpe's previous objection, that *Re Kevin* supported the view that sex is determined at birth. More important, the judgment makes it clear the fact that Kevin's experience of surgery was *not* crucial to his legal recognition as a man: the situation of 'pre-operative transsexuals' was expressly left open:[32]

> 'I do not need to consider the situation of a pre-operative transsexual in the context of marriage, and I do not intend to make any ruling on such cases. I will refer later to Australian authorities in areas other than marriage, recognising post-operative but not pre-operative transsexualism, but I do not intend to engage in the discussion of whether it is appropriate to draw the line in this way, in the context of marriage or any other area of law.'

Upholding the *Re Kevin* judgment on appeal, the Full Court took the same approach,[33] although hinting that surgery should not be a legal requirement.[34]

VI. REFLECTIONS – TRIAL JUDGMENTS AND LEGAL DEVELOPMENT

As in all cases, the judge must make the necessary findings of fact based on the evidence, and determine the case according to law, having regard to the submissions of the parties. Only occasionally, as in *Re Kevin*, is it the task of the judge to determine a controversy about what the law is. In *Re Kevin*, it happened to be an issue of great importance.

It seems to me that in those unusual situations, it is particularly important that the judge should not decide more than the case requires. Trial judges base their decisions on the evidence and arguments presented by the parties. It is true that the judgment in *Re Kevin* canvassed a wide range of literature, but broadly speaking it dealt only with material that was in evidence or, at least, had been canvassed in submissions. Although of course the parties would not have known the outcome in advance, I believe that none of the reasons in the judgment would

[32] Para. [19]. See also paras. [321] ('whatever might be the position with pre-operative transsexuals') and [329]. On the appeal, the Full Court also recognised that it was not necessary to determine the position of pre-operative transsexuals: *Attorney-General for the Commonwealth v Kevin and Others* (2003) 30 Fam LR 1, para. 387.

[33] *Attorney-General for the Commonwealth v Kevin and Others* (2003) 30 Fam LR 1, paras. [376]–[379], [387].

[34] Ibid., at paras. [382]–[388].

have come as a surprise to them: they were issues that had been thoroughly discussed during the hearing. (When trial judges rely on material that the parties have not had a chance to discuss, the losing party can argue on appeal that there was a lack of fairness.)

Thus in deciding *Re Kevin*, I limited the scope of the judgment by reference to the way the case had been argued. For example, the parties agreed that Australian law marriage involved a relationship between a man and a woman. It would have been wrong for me to decide the case on the basis that the marriage was valid *whether or not* Kevin was a man, or, I believe, to have expressed a view on that matter. Similarly, as I have emphasised, I did not determine whether the outcome would have been the same if Kevin had not had surgery, or had not been accepted as a man in society. Unlike a law reform commission, it was not my job to undertake original research and express my views about same-sex marriage, or where the line should be drawn in determining who is and who is not a man. And ruling on such issues would have been unfair to the parties, because if they had known I was going to do so they would no doubt have wanted to address the issues in their submissions. Further, it would have been inappropriate, since my task as a trial judge was to deal with issues that needed to be resolved in order to decide the particular case, not to make public statements on related issues.

I was aware, of course, how important the issue was, and that my decision, for better or worse, might influence the way the law was to develop. In the Family Court it is normally judges' dismal fate to deliver judgments that cause distress to one party, and sometimes both. So it was nice in this case to find a concordance between identifying the law and achieving a sensible and humane outcome. And it was professionally satisfying to have an opportunity to expose what I saw as the logical flaws in the *Corbett* judgment, and thereby help to clear the way for the development of more sensible and compassionate laws, based on careful research rather than legal dogmatism.

The task of developing such laws will have been much assisted by the conference from which this book arose. It was a privilege to participate, and see the task of law reform being assisted by the many wise, skilled and dedicated people I met there. People like Kevin deserve no less, and we will all benefit from living in a society in which the law does not tolerate discrimination against them, but instead helps them to lead what the Full Court called 'a more normal and fulfilling life'.[35]

35 Ibid., para. [388].

THE LEGAL STATUS OF PEOPLE WHO EXPERIENCE DIFFERENCE IN SEXUAL FORMATION AND GENDER EXPRESSION IN AUSTRALIA

Rachael WALLBANK*

Contents

* The author represented and appeared on behalf of 'Kevin' and 'Jennifer' at trial in *Re Kevin: Validity of Marriage of Transsexual* (2001) 28 Fam LR 158 and on appeal in *The Attorney-General for the Commonwealth & "Kevin and Jennifer" & Human Rights and Equal Opportunity Commission* [2003] FamCA 94. Wallbank is a member of the Legal Issues Committee of the World Professional Association for Transgender Health (WPATH) <www.wpath.org> and a founding member of the Australian and New Zealand Professional Association for Transgender Health (ANZPATH) <www.anzpath.org>.

I. INTRODUCTION

In this chapter I have been generously given the freedom to take a somewhat different approach to providing the Australian response to the questionnaire issued by Dr Jens M. Scherpe for this book (the 'Questionnaire').

In the course of my work as a lawyer, social advocate and writer I have been privileged to be introduced to the best of Australian and international expertise concerning the nature and medical treatment of human beings who experience Difference or diversity in sexual formation. In the course of seeking legal and social reform, I have been obliged to confront the challenges of effectively thinking about and communicating, to courts, government and community, an appreciation of the experience of Difference or diversity in gender expression.

While in sections II, III and IV of this chapter I have sought to provide the information requested in the Questionnaire, I have also sought to deconstruct and critique Australian government policy documents, legislation and case law based upon the factors I identify in section I as being the causes for what I argue is the current chaos of perception and discourse in relation to people who experience Difference or diversity in either the sexual differentiation and development of their bodies or the way they need to express gender in the world. This description includes the groups of people labelled 'Transsexual', 'Transgender' and 'Intersex'. In section V, I include my own model legislation for the reassignment of Legal Sex for your discussion and critique.

I acknowledge the considerable assistance offered to me by the wide range of ideas and perspectives shared at the conference supporting this ambitious project held at the University of Hong Kong on 6 and 7 September 2013.[1] I am

[1] Generously sponsored and conducted by the University of Hong Kong Centre for Medical Ethics and Law and St John's College (Hong Kong).

also indebted to Craig Andrews and my former client 'Kevin' for their mature and subtle insight into the distinct predicament of Affirmed Males, to the Honourable Richard Chisholm for his review of an early draft of this chapter and to the continuing benefit of the wisdom and insight of my legal colleague, mentor and friend, Teresa Anderson.[2]

As soon as the Questionnaire invites us to think about 'Transsexual', 'Transgender', 'Legal Sex' and 'Legal Gender', we are obliged to start thinking about meaning and language.

1.1. LANGUAGE AND PERCEPTION

I wrote about this issue concerning Transsexualism in 2004:[3]

> 'Language and terminology represent a major obstacle for anyone seeking to understand and meaningfully discuss this subject because the language that has developed with regard to transsexualism has been affected by the impact of long-standing diverse cultural prejudice, ignorance and mystification; whether or not that language has been the creation of medicine, law or community.'

Inaccurate and misleading language concerning people who experience Difference in sexual formation and gender expression, especially those who live with Transsexualism, reflects a continuing confusion and mystification concerning the distinct nature and needs of the diverse groups who experience these distinct phenomena and retards the evolution of cultural understanding and acceptance of these phenomena and the consequent evolution of their legal and human rights.

It is my observation that such confusion and mystification has increased in Australia in recent times as a result of the increased influence of GLBTI,[4] 'Intersex', 'Trans' or 'Trans*' interest groups on the thinking and work of academia, human rights and law reform agencies, government, the medical profession and the law.

Here the recent use of the distinctive term 'Trans*' is indicative of this conceptual and linguistic problem. As explained at *It's Pronounced Metrosexual:*[5]

> 'Trans* is an umbrella term that refers to all of the identities within the gender identity spectrum. There's a ton of diversity there, but we often group them all together (e.g., when we say "trans*" issues). Trans (without the asterisk) is best

2 Teresa Anderson of counsel, as she then was, provided extensive advice throughout the *Re Kevin* trial and appeal.

3 R. Wallbank, 'Re Kevin In Perspective' [2004] *Deakin LRev* 22; (2004) 9(2) *Deakin Law Review* 461 at 8.

4 An acronym for 'Gay, Lesbian, Bisexual, Transgender and Intersex' – which in itself either forgets people living with Transsexualism altogether or subsumes them within either 'Transgender' or 'Intersex'; in either case robbing them of their distinct representation.

5 <www.itspronouncedmetrosexual.com/2012/05/what-does-the-asterisk-in-trans-stand-for/>

> applied to trans men and trans women, while the asterisk makes special note in an effort to include all non-cisgender gender identities, including transgender, transsexual, transvestite, genderqueer, genderfluid, non-binary, genderfuck, genderless, agender, non-gendered, third gender, two-spirit, bigender, and trans man and trans woman.'

While it is becoming more popular for government and courts to support 'Intersex' and, to a lesser degree, 'Trans*' rights, such support is often being offered in the absence of any precise understanding of what these terms mean and the distinct interests and needs of the various types of people to whom such terms actually refer.

For example, it is vastly different to advocate for a right to the reassignment of Legal Sex on behalf of people who experience Transsexualism and some other intersex conditions, for whom Sex Affirmation Treatment (including Genital Reassignment Surgery) is therapeutic, needed and desired, than it is to do so on behalf of people who experience Transgenderism and other gender expression issues for whom that same medical treatment is neither wanted or needed and would be a cruel imposition.

While it is, of course, legitimate to undertake advocacy for all people who experience Difference in sexual formation and gender expression, I suggest it is misleading to use conflating and generalising terms such as 'Trans/Trans*', 'Transgender', 'Gender Identity' and 'Sex and Gender Diverse' in such advocacy or globalising and misleading 'gender'-based diagnostic terms, such as 'Gender Identity Disorder', 'Gender Dysphoria' and 'Gender Incongruence' as such terms can refer to a wide range of these distinct phenomena.

Any Australian statutory authority and government seeking to know and access the needs and opinion of people who live with the condition of Transsexualism faces a difficult challenge as the vast majority of these Australians live in a determined anonymity within the larger Australian community and not within or on the margins of Gay and Lesbian communities. Australians who live with the condition of Transsexualism, by their nature and preference, do not normally associate with, and are extremely unlikely to attend public meetings and events associated with, Trans*/Gender Queer and GLBTI communities.[6] And unlike the political 'Intersex' lobby, the advocacy of Australians living with Transsexualism has to compete with and is usually completely overwhelmed

---

6 This was the approach adopted by the Australian Human Rights Commission (AURC) for its regrettably named *Sex Files: the legal recognition: Concluding paper of the sex and gender (2009)* accessable at <https://www.humanrights.gov.au/sex-files-legal-recognition-concluding-paper-sex-and-gender-2009>. The report, responding to predominantly Transgender participants and interest groups, was ultimately primarily concerned with documentary identity issues rather than access to treatment issues and habitually referred to people who were 'sex and gender diverse' as referring to one group of people who shared the same characteristics, interests and needs.

by the advocacy from the far more numerous and visible Trans*/Gender Queer advocacy groups.

Evidence of the dominance of Trans*/Gender Queer concerns is that Australian human rights and government legislative reform concerning Australians who experience diversity in sexual formation and gender expression has become almost solely focused on legal identity rights rather than the affordable provision of Sex Affirmation Treatment; including genital reassignment surgery. While the timely receipt of such essential therapeutic medical treatment is of critical importance to the life-long health, welfare and wellbeing of a person who experiences Transsexualism (and some other intersex conditions), but is unnecessary or optional for a person living with any variety of Transgenderism, such medical treatment is increasingly being erroneously understood by statutory authorities, government and others as being chosen or optional for people living with the condition of Transsexualism.

As discussed below, the parliaments of Victoria and the Australian Capital Territory have laws concerning the reassignment of Legal Sex that legislatively privilege the rights of people who meet their legislative definition of 'intersex'.[7]

As I will argue below, even the High Court of Australia has not been immune from this growing confusion. I contend that courts determining the law on a case-by-case basis fundamentally depend upon a basic shared common sense or understanding of the world amongst the judicial officers, lawyers and expert witnesses who take part in each case in order to achieve reasonably fair, sensible and culturally intelligible outcomes and that the good functioning of the Common Law is critically challenged when dealing with aspects of human Difference concerning which these participants unconsciously lack such a shared common sense and where the subject matter has been affected by cultural taboo or mystification. I have used the term 'Cultural Prejudice' to describe this unconscious absence of a shared common sense or understanding.[8]

While the cultural understanding of diversity or Difference in sexual formation and gender expression remains mystified and contested, journalists, medical and legal authors as well as judicial officers should go to some trouble to make clear the particular meaning/s they attribute to the terms they use when dealing with these distinct and diverse phenomena if their writing and reasoning is to be really understandable and understood and capable of facilitating a general maturation of both cultural understanding and discourse.

The use of vague globalising terms such as 'Transgender' and its derivatives 'Transman', 'Transwoman', 'Trans' or 'Trans*' as well as the use of 'gender' as a euphemism for 'sex', both singularly and as a root term as in 'Gender Identity', are all likely to result in imprecision, confusion and misunderstanding.

---

7 See discussion at section 3.3 concerning the Victorian and Australian Capital Territory legislation providing for a change of Legal Sex.

8 Wallbank, above n. 3, pp. 30 and 33.

Vague and misleading 'Trans/Gender' terms may also be critiqued as reinforcing the Difference of the people to whom they are applied in the cultural psych. Such a result defeats the primary purpose of most people who experience Transsexualism and other similar intersex conditions, which is to live as other boys/men and girls/women within their community and culture and who do not primarily identify with, or seek to be identified by, their Difference.

In order to try to practice what I preach, I include the following 'Mini Dictionary' to try to clarify the language and terms I use in this chapter and elsewhere:[9]

Mini Dictionary

'*Sex*' – the medical assessment of the biological sexual differentiation of a person as either predominantly male or female. While usually based upon genital formation (only), in a more thorough assessment can include hormonal, chromosomal, genetic, neurological and behavioural/brain-based assessment.

'*Gender*' or '*gender expression*' – the cultural expression of sex through appearance and behaviour – not necessarily consistent with or limited to a person's sex.

'*Transsexual*' – describes a person who experiences the condition of *Transsexualism* – being one who experiences a critical biologically derived intersexual conflict between the individual's sexually differentiated brain or mind ('brain sex'), dictating the experience of self as either male or female, and the individual's sexually differentiated body accompanied by a critical social conflict while obliged to live as the sex they are not. Transsexualism is an intersex condition and a disorder of sexual development therapeutically medically treated by hormonal therapy and Genital Reassignment Surgery in order to mitigate the personal brain/body conflict and socially by enabling the individual sufferer to live with cultural equality and full human and legal rights in their Affirmed Sex. *Transsexualism* is not a mental illness or mental disorder. For a person with the condition of Transsexualism, Genital Reassignment Surgery or Sex Affirmation Procedures, as described below, are not optional or chosen, but therapeutic.

A person who experiences Transsexualism experiences him or herself as having always been the sex he or she affirms; being opposite to that sex to which he or she was first legally assigned based upon their infant genital formation. For such a person there is nothing about the personal experience of an innate male or female sex that has an element of choice, change, decision or the assumption of

[9] I developed what I called 'Affirmative Language' concerning Transsexualism as a result of my experience of the power of language as it affects Difference in the *Re Kevin* proceedings. I published my first references to my Affirmative Language terms in my paper entitled *The Legal Environment Following Re Kevin: New Perceptions and Strategies For Effective Law Reform* presented at the New South Wales Anti-Discrimination Board's event, Neglected Community Forum, in January 2003.

an identity they are not. A person who experiences Transsexualism experiences critical distress whilst ever there exists a conflict between the person's (brain) sex and their body's primary sexually differentiated features. Such a person also experiences critical social distress if obliged to live a life as a member of a sex that he or she does not experience him or herself to be.

Those who experience Transsexualism, including minors, will self-harm and even take their own lives as a result of the experience of this ever-present personal brain/body and social conflict. For such a person, the undergoing of Sex Affirmation Treatment, including hormonal therapy and Genital Reassignment Surgery, is the meeting of a crucial therapeutic need and not chosen, optional or cosmetic. Unlike the experience of Transgenderism, medical interventions for persons living with Transsexualism vary only minutely from person to person within each Affirmed Sex.

While there are differences in life experience and individual capacity to live with such personal conflict and distress for varying lengths of time, no person who experiences Transsexualism is able to live a content, personally comfortable and mentally healthy life without undergoing Sex Affirmation Treatment; including hormonal therapy and Genital Reassignment Surgery. Transsexualism is accurately described as a disorder of sexual development. Given the current far from fully functional and/or imperfect results of Sex Affirmation Treatment generally, and Genital Reassignment Surgery in particular, I believe that Transsexualism should also be understood as a disability with significant life-long personal and social manifestations.

For Affirmed Females, such essential medical treatment includes the suspension of puberty, the feminisation of secondary sexual characteristics by way of the administration of the 'female' hormone, Oestrogen, and Genital Reassignment Surgery for the removal of the testis and penis (to achieve the absence of the most powerful personal and social male insignia) and the creation of a functioning vagina and clitoris (Vaginoplasty & Clitoroplasty). For an Affirmed Female to not be able to undertake Genital Reassignment Surgery is to live with a deep and life-enduring sense of personal conflict, discomfort and incompleteness.

For Affirmed Males, such essential medical treatment includes the suspension of puberty, chest reconstruction surgery to provide for the removal of breasts and the creation of a male chest in the absence of pubertal suspension and the administration of the 'male' hormone, Testosterone, to stop the menses and atrophy internal genitalia (for most individuals) while also achieving the very effective masculinisation of secondary sexual characteristics such as voice, body shape, hair pattern and penis-like clitoral enlargement. The use of Testosterone for Affirmed Males is of a profoundly greater personal and physical affect than the impact of Oestrogen for Affirmed Females.

The common effect of the sustained ingestion of Testosterone on female anatomy is to cease both female genital function and menses. Those Affirmed

Males for whom the administration of Testosterone does not cease menses will usually undergo a hysterectomy in order to achieve that result. For Affirmed Males, Genital Reassignment Surgery is the surgical creation of a penis (Phalloplasty) and scrotum. Although at the time of writing Genital Reassignment Surgery for Affirmed Males is not readily available to Australians, is extremely expensive and has variable results, it is still true that for an Affirmed Male to not be able to undertake Genital Reassignment Surgery is to live with a deep and life-enduring sense of personal conflict, discomfort and incompleteness.

Variation in personal capacity to endure a life oppressed by the personal and public conflict of Transsexualism and the varying individual capacity to endure familial and cultural rejection and discrimination as well as financial circumstances, not choice or preference, determine the timing of an individual's public affirmation of their innate sex and the undertaking of Sex Affirmation Treatment.

It is now commonly understood that people who live with Transsexualism can be classified in terms of their sexual attraction as gay, lesbian or bisexual in the same way as others. Once one is able to distinguish between Transsexualism and Transgenderism, one is also able to understand that people who live with Transsexualism can also be categorised in terms of their gender expression as conforming or being different in the same way as others. In this way it becomes possible to observe and describe individuals who experience both Transsexualism and Transgenderism.

Persons living with Transsexualism usually clearly identify as being either male or female, desire to live within the general community as a member of either one of these two traditional sexes and usually do not seek to display or be socially recognised for their act of sex affirmation, their gender expression or their Difference. This desire for social acceptance, anonymous inclusion and a normal life means that people living with Transsexualism are often fearful of their difference being made known within the community in which they live, are mostly not members of interest groups associated with GLBTI communities, Trans* subcultures and associated online forums and therefore do not generally know of and/or respond to interest group, government or institutional invitations to publicly meet and discuss their needs.

'*Transgender*', 'Trans' or 'Trans*'– describes a person who experiences the condition of *Transgenderism* – being one who has a need to expresses gender, either variably, occasionally or constantly, opposite to the gender expression culturally expected of a person of their sex – who does not experience a critical personal brain/body conflict requiring Genital Reassignment Surgery or other similar medical treatment. *Transgenderism* is not a mental illness or mental disorder.

People who live with Transgenderism express the gender of a sex they are not or otherwise defy cultural norms of expected sex-aligned gender expression. People who live with Transgenderism do not affirm an innate sex different from that to which they were first assigned, but change their appearance. Unlike the experience of Transsexualism, a person who experiences Transgenderism does not have a critical need to alter the primary sexually differentiated characteristics of his or her body, and in particular the genitalia, in order to alleviate inner personal conflict and suffering. Forms of difference or diversity in gender expression that defy cultural norms or expected forms of sex-aligned gender expression may be referred to as Pangenderism or Nongenderism but are often also described as 'Transgender' or 'Trans*'. A broad definition of people who experience Transgenderism might include anyone who expresses gender differently; from a tomboy to a person who lives permanently 'cross-dressed' and uses hormonal treatment to enhance their trans-gendered appearance or simply as a form of body-art.

Almost everyone will creatively express gender in Transgender, Pangender or Nongender ways according to personal preference and cultural norms at some time in their lives. Gender and gender expression, and hence Trans/Pan-gender expression, are functions of cultural norms and differ from culture to culture.

In its most extreme manifestation, however, Transgenderism can mean the condition experienced by a person who would live with a deep sense of personal discomfort unless they are able to live exclusively undertaking the expression of their preferred gender – but without any therapeutic or other need to undergo Genital Reassignment Surgery. In its most extreme manifestation people who experience Transgenderism may make a range of cosmetic changes to their physical appearance to enhance their gender expression. In this context, however, any permanent physical bodily change is a chosen aspect of the Transgender person's overall desire to express gender differently and is not carried out to remedy or resolve a critical inner personal sexual conflict.

Transgenderism, even in its most extreme form, is not a manifestation of difference in sexual formation or a medical condition or illness requiring any diagnosis or medical treatment, but is a form of the culturally based gender expression undertaken by all human beings.

'*Pangender*' or '*Nongender*' – one who expresses gender variably, occasionally or constantly, contrary to the gender expression culturally expected of a person of either sex.

'*Intersex*' – a person possessing the physiological characteristics of both the male and female sexes.

'*Genital Reassignment Surgery*' or '*Sex Affirmation Procedure*' – all that surgery available from time to time for the therapeutic rehabilitation of the primary sexually differentiated characteristics of the body of a person experiencing Transsexualism to that resembling the appearance and function appropriate to that person's Affirmed Sex. Chest reconstruction surgery for Affirmed Males is properly included within this term.

A person is said to have *affirmed (their) sex* – rather than '*changed (their) sex*' – when a person with Transsexualism seeks to live a private and/or public life consistent with their innate or neurological sex rather than their first assigned Legal Sex.

'*Sex Affirmation Treatment*' – all that medical treatment, including hormonal therapy and Genital Reassignment Surgery as well as cosmetic and psychological support therapy required to therapeutically treat the condition of Transsexualism and facilitate a person with that condition to affirm their innate sex and live in their world with the experience of difference in a healthy way.

'*Legal Sex*' – the legal categorisation of a person's sex, usually assigned at or near the birth event, being a part of the legal identity of a person. In Australia the record of a person's legal identity is determined and maintained by States and Territories in Registers recording citizen's legal identity particulars.

'*Common Law Sex*' – the sex of a person as determined by a court for the purpose of the application of legislation where the sex of a person is significant.

'*Legal Gender*' – a legal identity distinct from an individual's Legal Sex associated with a culturally recognised appearance, behaviour or lifestyle primarily determined by gender expression or self-identification which may or may not be recorded as a part of the legal identity of a person.

'*Difference*' – the human cultural experience of diversity or variance sufficient to generate mystification or misunderstanding and attract ostracism or adverse discrimination.

Phase[10] *1 Treatment* – the administration by an endocrinologist of a GnRH agonist, such as Zoladex, to suspend or supress standard pubertal bodily development begun at about Tanner Stage 2 puberty.[11]

Phase 2 Treatment – commencing at about 15+ years of age, comprises the continuation of Phase 1 Treatment with the addition of the administration of oestrogen (Affirmed Females) or testosterone (Affirmed Males) to facilitate the adolescent's age appropriate bone development and the development of secondary sexual characteristics appropriate to his or her Affirmed Sex. While the amount of Phase 2 hormonal treatment administered is substantially reduced once the individual undergoes Genital Reassignment Surgery, it is usually continued over a similar period as standard hormone replacement therapy for women who have undergone a total hysterectomy.[12]

Phase 3 Treatment – see 'Genital Reassignment Surgery'.

I will refer to a person living with the condition of Transsexualism who has affirmed the female sex after having been first assigned to the male Legal Sex as a *female with Transsexualism* or an *affirmed female* rather than the genitocentric 'male-to-female transsexual' or 'MtF' and a person living with the condition of Transsexualism who has affirmed the male sex after having been first assigned

[10] I prefer to use the Dutch Protocol term 'Phase' instead of 'Stage' so as not to risk confusion with the numbered Tanner 'Stages' of pubertal development.

[11] See a more detailed description in section 2.2.2 below.

[12] Ibid.

to the female Legal Sex as a *male with Transsexualism* or an *affirmed male* rather than the genitocentric 'female-to-male transsexual' or 'FtM'.

While I make no claim to perfection, contrast the clarity I have sought in the language I use and the inherent respect such clarity seeks to show to the various types of people who experience difference in sexual formation and gender expression with the confusion and misrepresentation contained in this excerpt from the section dealing with 'Sex Reassignment Surgery' in the current WPATH Standards of Care:

> 'While many transsexual, transgender, and gender-nonconforming individuals find comfort with their gender identity, role, and expression without surgery, for many others surgery is essential and medically necessary to alleviate their gender dysphoria (Hage & Karim, 2000). For the latter group, relief from gender dysphoria cannot be achieved without modification of their primary and/or secondary sex characteristics to establish greater congruence with their gender identity.'[13]

Here and throughout their Standards of Care WPATH repeatedly conflate 'Transsexual', 'Transgender', and 'Gender-nonconforming individuals'. I presume that here 'Gender-nonconforming individuals' are those who express gender in a way that does not look like that expected of their assigned Legal Sex or either sex and I am left to presume that here 'Transgender' is given its 'narrow' meaning of expressing gender in a way opposite to that culturally expected of one's assigned Legal Sex on a continuous basis.

While it is apparently important enough to WPATH to distinguish 'Transsexual', 'Transgender' and 'Gender-nonconforming' individuals, it is equally apparent that WPATH do not consider it important to distinguish the quite different needs of these different groups in relation to Genital Reassignment Surgery or to make clear that for solely 'Transgender' and 'Gender-nonconforming' individuals such surgery is unnecessary and irrelevant, while for 'Transsexual' individuals such surgery is 'essential and medically necessary'.

Further, rather than this simple statement of medical necessity being in clear terms that state that for people living with the condition of Transsexualism, undergoing Genital Reassignment Surgery is necessary for their mental health, physical wellbeing and social welfare, WPATH choose to give the matter a further confusing mental disorder 'spin' by stating that Genital Reassignment Surgery is undertaken because 'relief from gender dysphoria cannot be achieved without modification of their primary and/or secondary sex characteristics to establish greater congruence with their gender identity'.

---

[13] World Professional Association for Transgender Health Standards of Care, 7th edition, pp. 54–55.

1.1.1. 'Transsexual' and 'Transgender'

While the Questionnaire refers to and asks questions about 'Transsexual' and 'Transgender' persons, I will generally prefer the somewhat more clumsy terms 'Transsexualism' and 'Transgenderism' in this chapter in order to make the point that these phenomena are examples of natural human diversity and that I consider it demeans people to be described solely in terms of their condition or their difference – as in 'She's a transsexual.'

1.1.2. 'Sex' and 'Gender'

In the English language 'sex' and 'gender' are different.[14]

As Keith Windschuttle observed in 2004,

> 'If gender is arbitrary and customary, it can be altered by changing the language. The activists saw that if sex was redefined as gender, it too became arbitrary and changeable … from the realm of biological necessity to that of custom.'[15]

I suggest that Transsexualism became entangled in this process because the 'brain-sex/Nature' explanation offered for and witnessed by the experience of Transsexualism evidenced sex as fixed and dichotomous and directly challenged the flexible Nurture explanation for sex differences favoured by Feminist and later Transgender advocacy. I hypothesise too that many politically prominent and effective Affirmed Male advocates carried over a gender-based flexible/nurture explanation of sex differences embodied in such Feminist thinking from their Lesbian community backgrounds. The commentary on the nature and veracity of Affirmed Females by leading Feminists such as Germaine Greer and Janice Raymond, if not the viciousness of that commentary, is also understandable in this context.[16]

The phenomenon of Cross-dressing, formerly also commonly called 'Transvestism', was and continues to be the basis of the all-encompassing 'Transgender'. This process of conflating difference in sexual formation as evidenced by Transsexualism with difference in gender expression as evidenced by Transgenderism appears to have first arose in the United States of America and

---

14 For a different perspective on the same issue see Diamond, *Sex and Gender are Different: Sexual Identity and Gender Identity are Different*, Clinical Child Psychology & Psychiatry, July 2002, Vol. 7(3), pp. 320–334 and <www.hawaii.edu/PCSS/biblio/articles/2000to2004/2002-sex-and-gender.html>

15 K. Windschuttle, 'Language Wars', Quadrant May 2004 © 2005 Keith Windschuttle <www.sydneyline.com/Language%20Wars.htm>

16 See, for example, J.G. Raymond, *The Transsexual Empire: the making of the she-male*, Boston, Beacon Press 1979, and G. Greer, *The Whole Woman*, Transworld Publishers Ltd, 1999. Notably, affirmed males didn't attract the same attention from these authors.

then manifested itself in the United Kingdom with the creation of the globalising terms 'Transman', 'Transwoman' and 'Trans'.

Perceiving difference or diversity in both sexual formation and gender expression as one simplified and homogenised 'gender' phenomenon, placed the focus on gender expression rather than sexual formation issues and had the advantage of providing a politically visible and palatable minority population for political activism and lobbying purposes as well as the opportunity for a more natural alliance with Gay and Lesbian interest groups. It was also a good fit with other popular movements for human rights and legal reform seeking to overcome cultural and legal discrimination based on sex.

In a further development of the same conflating process, advocates for the abandonment of the Male/Female sexual dichotomy and legal sex categories generally could then posit that Transsexualism existed as a part of a 'Trans/Gender Continuum' in the same way that they saw Male and Female as not distinct biological phenomena, but variable states on a 'Gender Continuum.'

The nurture-based and psychologically variable Trans/Gender Continuum concept saw the postulation of such misleading concepts as the 'Non-op Transsexual', while Genital Reassignment Surgery began being described as 'optional' or 'chosen' for 'a minority of Transgender/Sex and Gender Diverse/Trans* people'.

The success of the 'pro-nurture/anti-sexual dichotomy' philosophy can also be observed in the way that the imprecise 'gender' not only became popularly used as a euphemism for 'sex' in daily discourse, but in judgments and legislation as well.

Perhaps the culmination of this process has been the creation of categories of Legal Sex other than or in addition to 'Male' and 'Female': as a 'Third Sex' by the Supreme Court of India[17] or as an elective 'non-specific' or a neither Male or Female Non-sex Legal Sex by the High Court of Australia.[18]

Freedom of gender expression, the freedom to express gender in any way a person might be inspired to do from time to time, including in a Transgender form, can be seen as a natural human right to be kept free from restriction, suppression and harm by appropriate anti-discrimination legalisation. Laws that would be effective in promoting a general right of free gender expression may be seen to be fundamentally incompatible with laws that would seek to give gender expression, in whatever form, the same fixed legal status and implications as that provided for in respect of sex as part of an individual's legal identity.

'Biological Sex' is notable as a term which has survived these movements, both in terms of colloquial and expert use, to be used to distinguish a physically measurable/clinically testable claim to be biologically male, female or intersex,

---

17 *National Legal Services Authority v Union of India*, Writ Petition No. 400 of 2012 with Writ Petition No. 604 of 2013, Supreme Court of India (15 April 2014).

18 *NSW Registrar of Births, Deaths and Marriages v Norrie* [2014] HCA 11 ('*Norrie*').

such as offered by a chromosomal test, from a self-asserted sex identity which is unable as yet to be so evidenced by contemporary medical science. In this way, the individual experience of the male or female self of a person with Transsexualism, is described as 'belief', 'feeling', 'desire' or 'wish' to be a certain sex and is strictly contrasted with medically evidenced mix of male or female 'biologically characteristics' of intersex conditions. This is the dynamic and message at work with the use of terms such as 'Gender Dysphoria', 'Gender Incongruence', 'Gender Identity', 'biologically female', 'Cisgendered' and 'Natal Sex'. All these terms postulate the existence of a person's 'gender', 'Gender Identity' and innate sexual identity as a distinct psychological phenomenon and something different and distinct from a person's (true) biological sex or birth sex.

As it is a fundamental part of the legal and human rights claims of people living with the condition of Transsexualism that these experiences are not mental disorders or illnesses, but the affirmation of an innate biologically derived sex identity or 'Brain Sex', the use of such language is directly against their interests and discriminatory. As I will proceed to show below, in Australia people who experience Transsexualism continue to be medically and legally distinguished in this discriminatory way from individuals considered to have a biological entitlement to be a particular sex or to be Intersex.

1.1.3. Transsexualism and Intersex

'Intersex', another contested term, has been adopted and politically deployed by some minority lobby groups in Australia as an exclusive 'biological' and political identity. This has been achieved by subverting and restrictively redefining the ordinary meaning of 'intersex' so as to exclude the human brain as a part of the human body and by attempting to restrict its application to a limited number of readily evidenced variations in the sexually differentiated body associated with hormonal balance, chromosomal patterns and genital formation at birth.

Some Intersex advocacy maintains that until medical science makes it possible to subject the human brain to an objective 'sex test' and until references to the condition of Transsexualism are removed from diagnostic classifications associated with psychiatry, Transsexualism cannot be accepted as a biologically derived intersex condition.

Scientific observation across the natural world as well as the very existence of common traits and experience amongst people with Transsexualism and some other intersex conditions support the existence of the sexual differentiation of the human brain.

There are really only two possible and totally inconsistent explanations for Transsexualism: either an example of human intersexual diversity in sexual formation involving the sexual differentiation of the brain or a mental disorder.

As the Applicants contended in *Re Kevin: Validity of Marriage of Transsexual* (2001) 28 Fam LR 158 ('*Re Kevin*'), there is actually no accepted expert evidence or even a reasonably recognised psychological theory to support an explanation for the existence of Transsexualism as a mental disorder or illness. In his judgment in *Re Kevin* Chisholm J undertook a detailed review of the extensive expert scientific and medical evidence before him.

As a result, Chisholm J was able to make a number of significant findings concerning the nature of Transsexualism:

> 'In my view the expert evidence in this case affirms that brain development is (at least) an important determinant of a person's sense of being a man or a woman. No contrary opinion is expressed. All the experts are very well qualified. None was required for cross-examination, nor was any contrary evidence called'.[19]

> 'In my view the evidence is, in essence, that the experts believe that the brain development view is likely to be true, and they explain the basis for their beliefs. In the circumstances, I see no reason why I should not accept the proposition, on the balance of probabilities, for the purpose of this case.'[20]

> 'The traditional analysis that they are "psychologically" transsexual does not explain how this state came about. For example, there seems to be no suggestion in the evidence that their psychological state can be explained by reference to circumstances of their upbringing. In that sense, the brain sex theory does not seem to be competing with other explanations, but rather is providing a possible explanation of what is otherwise inexplicable'.[21]

> 'But I am satisfied that the evidence now is inconsistent with the distinction formerly drawn between biological factors, meaning genitals, chromosomes and gonads, and merely "psychological factors", and on this basis distinguishing between cases of inter-sex (incongruities among biological factors) and Transsexualism (incongruities between biology and psychology)',[22] and

> 'In my view the evidence demonstrates (at least on the balance of probabilities) that the characteristics of transsexuals are as much "biological" as those of people thought of as inter-sex.'[23]

Some more recent public examples of expert opinion to the same effect are:

> 'Recent advances in the field of the genetics of sexual development have shown the extreme complexity of defining males and females from a biological standpoint.

---

19 *Re Kevin*, para. 247.
20 Ibid., para. 248.
21 Ibid., para. 252.
22 Ibid., para. 270.
23 Ibid., para. 272.

There is no one biological parameter that clearly defines sex. The second point is that there are differences between male and female brains very early in development. This suggests that the sexualization of the brain happens very early during embryonic life. The last point is that significant minorities of individuals are left out of simple civil rights because they don't fit established categories of sex',[24] and

'Traditionally an individual's primary sex characteristic is the person's gonads. It is now understood that an individual's gonads or other characteristics frequently do not correspond with other features of self and variations are common. And this is the case in conditions of transsexuality and intersex (and transsexuality can be considered a form of intersexuality).'[25]

In my view, all of the evidence about the nature of Transsexualism, including that for the sexual differentiation of the brain, its consistent standard pan-cultural manifestation and experience throughout human history, the minute record of regret in respect of its medical treatment and the terrible consequences of non-treatment, compel its recognition as a disorder resulting from a natural form of intersexual variation in human sexual formation.

1.1.4. Transsexualism and Mental Disorder

It follows that in my view neither Transsexualism nor Transgenderism should be diagnostically referenced in the United States of America Psychiatrist's Diagnostic and Statistical Manual of Mental Disorders (DSM)[26] or in the International Classification of Diseases and Related Health Problems (ICD)[27] as mental disorders.

It is argued that the inclusion of Transsexualism in the DSM has facilitated access to medical treatment in such places as the United States of America where such treatment is dependent on the recognition by health insurance companies of a recognised medical condition. In such countries it is also argued that legal rights have also been dependent on such recognition. In my view, the inclusion of Transsexualism in the DSM and in the ICD as mental disorder has only

---

[24] Dr Eric Vilain, paediatrician, Chief of Medical Genetics at the University of California, USA, in an interview on Australian ABC Radio National programme 'The Health Report', 14 March 2005.

[25] H. Beh and M. Diamond, 'Ethical Concerns Related to Treating Gender Nonconformity in Childhood and Adolescence: Lessons from the Family Court of Australia', *Health Matrix: Journal of Law-Medicine*, Case Western Reserve University School of Law, Volume 15, Summer 2005, No. 2, and at the University of Hawaii <www.hawaii.edu/PCSS/biblio/articles/2005to2009/2005-ethical-concerns.html>.

[26] Diagnostic and Statistical Manual of Mental Disorders of the American Psychiatric Association.

[27] International Classification of Diseases and Related Health Problems (ICD) issued by the World Health Organization in Geneva.

delayed the creation of a non-discriminatory non-mental health based diagnostic criteria and treatment regime such as exists concerning other intersex conditions requiring the same or similar hormonal and surgical medical treatment as does Transsexualism.

People who experience Transsexualism have long been faced with the confronting irony that although their condition has to be diagnosed by psychiatry pursuant to mental health criteria in order to receive hormonal and surgical medical treatment, that diagnosis consists of a finding that their experience of their sex is not caused by any delusion, confusion or mental disorder. In other words, under the current medical model for Transsexualism, the core relevance of psychiatry/psychology is to professionally confirm its irrelevancy.

Endocrinologists and surgeons are as capable as psychiatrists in having potential patients demonstrate and evidence the distinctive history and experience of Transsexualism. As they do now when necessary in respect of other conditions, in cases of doubt such medical professionals can refer such patients to psychiatry for a ruling out of any contra-indicating mental ill health. I am aware of instances where adolescents have unnecessarily suffered through non-treatment simply because the psychiatrist 'treating' them was unaware of or confused about the time critical adolescent Phase 1 and Phase 2 hormonal Sex Affirmation Treatment available. Regrettably, these issues tend cloud the wonderful and crucial work dedicated professionals in these disciplines do in assisting people who experience diversity in both sexual formation and gender expression, and their families, to live full and fulfilling lives notwithstanding their Difference.

Transsexualism was included in the DSM-III in 1980 as a specific category of mental illness ('gender dysphoria syndrome'). Transsexualism was assimilated or subsumed into the more general category of 'sexual and gender identity disorders' in the DSM-IV in 1994. This significant change in the way psychiatry perceived Transsexualism coincided with the removal from the DSM of homosexuality as a mental disorder.[28] The DSM-IV changed the professional psychoanalytic view that there was a difference between Transsexualism and Gender Identity Disorder, while at the same time providing radically new differential diagnostic criteria for both children and adults with Transsexualism.[29]

In the DSM-IV, American psychiatry diagnostically conflated all people who experienced or exhibited any type of non-normal behaviour in respect of sexual and/or gender expression and legitimised their psychiatric 'treatment'.[30] The criteria for the diagnosis of Gender Identity Disorder in the DSM-IV included children with severe mental disorders as well as those who merely transgressed accepted norms of gender expression such as those who exhibited transgender/

---

[28] A. Michel, C. Mormont and J.J. Legros, 'A Psycho-Endocrinological Overview of Transsexualism' (2001) 145 *European Journal of Endocrinology* 365.

[29] Ibid.

[30] Ibid.

cross-dressing/effeminate/tomboyish behaviour and those who were homosexual as well as those who experienced Transsexualism.[31]

This vagueness of diagnostic criteria continues in the DSM-5 and permits psychiatrists to give the contradictory and confusing evidence of significant unreliability in the diagnosis of *Gender Dysphoria* in childhood, expressing doubt as to whether such a child will develop adult Transsexualism, homosexuality or Transgenderism, while simultaneously confirming with longitudinal evidence the extremely reliable diagnosis and successful treatment of Transsexualism in adolescence.

It is as well to remember that, while these diagnostic publications are properly given a great deal of respect, especially by lawyers and the law, their published diagnoses are derived through very human lobbying and 'political' manoeuvring by interest groups and self-interested professionals through a process of sometimes deeply divided and unresolved debate and are therefore not immune to discrimination, bias and error. Lawyers and courts should not accept the diagnostic criteria contained in these publications as medical or scientific 'gospel'.

While there are a number of disorders referred to in the DSM that are not mental health disorders, such as Insomnia Disorder and Restless Legs Syndrome, and although the new DSM-5 'Gender Dysphoria' diagnosis refers to the presence of clinically significant distress associated with Gender Dysphoria and not the condition itself, nevertheless to have a medical condition situated in a diagnostic manual for mental disorders is to invariably share the cultural prejudice and loss of human and legal rights borne by people with mental disorders.

In order to access medical treatment and legal recognition, people who experience Transsexualism have been unreasonably required to submit to inappropriate and often harmful psychiatric and psychological treatment and a diagnosis under a mental health regime – incurring all the personal and cultural discrimination associated with mental disorder.

I contend that the 2013 decision of the Full Court of the Family Court of Australia in *Re Jamie* [2013] FamCAFC 110 ('*Re Jamie*'), discussed in section 2.2, demonstrates that Australian adolescents with Transsexualism have had their timely access to therapeutic medical treatment adversely affected by the inclusion of Transsexualism in the DSM.

It is unwise to base legal rights and laws on controversial and changeable diagnostic terms and classifications, as was done in the United Kingdom in the Gender Recognition Act 2004.[32] Such legislation set up a legal right that required a person to formally concede they experienced mental ill health when they did

---

31 Ibid.

32 The UK Gender Recognition Act 2004 is also interesting in that, although the requirements of this legislation mean that it only applies to people living with the condition of Transsexualism, as the successful outcome of an application under this act does not change the record of a person's Legal Sex, but creates a 'stand-alone' 'Gender Recognition Certificate' which provides

not. Such contested diagnostic classifications are subject to regular and random change and disappear altogether.

Gender Identity Disorder has now disappeared. I trust that the same fate soon awaits Gender Dysphoria and Gender Incongruence.

II. AUSTRALIAN LEGAL FRAMEWORK AND STATISTICS

2.1. STATISTICS

There are no official or reliable statistics as to the number of people living with either Transsexualism or Transgenderism in Australia. The Australian Bureau of Statistics does not contain information about either phenomenon.

Medical treatment records, particularly those associated with Genital Reassignment Surgery, are about the only means by which the number of people living with Transsexualism in a population may be assessed, but many people with Transsexualism in Australia are obliged to obtain such treatment overseas.

Members of the Australian and New Zealand Professional Association for Transgender Health (ANZPATH) report that the number of children and adolescents presenting with Transsexualism has been steadily increasing across Australia.[33] It seems to be the common opinion amongst members of ANZPATH that this increase in presentation is primarily to be attributed to a steady cultural reduction in stigma concerning the phenomenon accompanied by an increase in parental and family support.[34]

Nevertheless, an individual publicly known to experience either Transsexualism or Transgenderism in Australia would still expect to suffer a significant degree of stigma and discrimination, particularly concerning employment and personal relationships. As such, one would not expect individual Australians to readily publicly identify themselves as experiencing either phenomena; except for those living substantially within GLB minority communities.

Because Transsexualism is a global human phenomenon, however, it is possible to estimate numbers in any given population based upon cross-cultural prevalence. National and regional variations in prevalence statistics for both Transsexualism and Transgenderism are more likely to be the result of varying degrees of cultural acceptance of Difference and the availability of social support mechanisms and medical treatment, rather than actual prevalence.

---

a limited number of specific legislative rights, I argue that it does not reassign Legal Sex (as Australian legislation does) but only creates a Legal Gender status.

33 Australian and New Zealand Professional Association for Transgender Health (ANZPATH), online forum and presentations at its international conference in Adelaide in October 2014.

34 Ibid.

The Australian Bureau of Statistics (ABS) calculates that there were 23,481,643 resident Australians as of 8 May 2014. If one adopted the typically cited prevalence numbers for Transsexualism based on Genital Reassignment Surgery per head of population averaged internationally, one would assess prevalence for Transsexualism as 1 in 11,900 for Affirmed Females and 1 in 30,400 for Affirmed Males; resulting in figures for Transsexualism in the current Australian resident population of about 1,973 Australian Affirmed Females and about 772 Australian resident Affirmed Males. This does not accord with experience.

Lyn Conway and Femke Olyslager challenged this conservative statistical approach in their 6 September 2007 paper *On the Calculation of the Prevalence of Transsexualism*[35] where they undertook a detailed and complex discussion of the prevalence of Transsexualism and how it may been assessed. Conway and Olyslager argue that the fact that the generally accepted conservative statistical methods have resulted in an increasing rate of prevalence for the same population groups year by year has to be explained. They point out that many people living with Transsexualism are unable for legal, religious, social, familial or financial reasons to either publically affirm their innate sex or to undertake Genital Reassignment Surgery, and are thus not reflected in such conservative models – which only measure the number of Genital Reassignment Surgeries actually undertaken in a given population.

Using the terms 'mf' for Affirmed Females, 'fm' for Affirmed Males and 'SRS' for 'Genital Reassignment Surgery', Conway and Olyslager conclude:[36]

> 'Our analyses of the data in key earlier reports lead to values of P(SRSImf) in the range of 1:2,000 to 1:4,500 and P(SRSIfm) in the range of 1:5,500 to 1:8,000 in a number of countries, even way back during the 1980s.
>
> Recalling Eqn. 9: P(TS) > P(SH) > P(HT) > P(ST) > P(SRS), we know that the inherent prevalence of transsexualism must be a moderate multiple of the inherent prevalence of SRS, because only a fraction of transsexual people come out to themselves and others, seek treatments to resolve their conditions, and migrate fully from the inherent TS condition to undergoing SRS.
>
> Therefore, even when using data from early reports, these factors already suggest a lower bound on the prevalence of inherent mf transsexualism on the order of 1:1,000 to 1:2,000.'

If one applies Conway and Olyslager's conservative prevalence rate for Transsexualism for Affirmed Females (1:1,200) to the Australian population for both affirmed sexes, the result is that there are likely to be about 20,000 Australians of all ages who experience Transsexualism.

---

35 Presented at the WPATH 20th International Symposium, Chicago, Illinois, 5–8 September 2007.

36 F. Olyslager and L. Conway, 'On the Calculation of the Prevalence of Transsexualism', paper presented at the WPATH 20th International Symposium, Chicago, Illinois, 5–8 September 2007, p. 23.

Conway and Olyslager postulate that in any population group about double the number of people who experience Transsexualism are likely to experience a severe degree of Transgenderism; namely 1:600 or, as of 8 May 2014, about 40,000 Australians of all ages.

Statistical issues are important, not only as the numbers involved can be decisive in determining government attention and funding, but as increasing prevalence demands explanation and study. Moreover, for every Australian who experiences Transsexualism or extreme Transgenderism, there are many more family and loved ones affected by their Difference. Nevertheless, clarity of understanding and recognition of Difference in reform agendas should not be sacrificed merely for the sake of numbers.

2.2. ACCESS TO SEX AFFIRMATION TREATMENT AND GENITAL REASSIGNMENT SURGERY

2.2.1. Availability and Health Insurance

The Australian health system is funded by a combination of government 'Medicare' payments supplemented by the individual through private health insurance and direct payments. Medicare subsidises out-of-hospital medical treatment and presently funds free universal access to public hospital treatment. Before Medicare will fund a medical procedure, however, that procedure has to have an 'Item Number'. No specific Medicare Item Numbers have been awarded for Sex Affirmation Treatment generally and Genital Reassignment Surgery in particular.

In order to facilitate access to treatment for Transsexualism, Australian medical practitioners are obliged to be 'creative' in their assignment of Medicare item numbers and seek to find and apply the item numbers that most closely relate to a particular treatment. Even with the creative use of item numbers, the minimum 'gap' cost of Genital Reassignment Surgery alone for an Affirmed Female patient is about $10,000.00 to $15,000.00 AUD.

As the total cost of other standard treatments for an Affirmed Female, such as for diagnosis for surgical approval and psychological support, voice, electrolysis and breast augmentation surgery can amount to a further $10,000.00 to $20,000.00 AUD, the total cost of Sex Affirmation Treatment for an Australian Affirmed Female, including Genital Reassignment Surgery, can amount to approximately $35,000.00 AUD. The costs facing an Affirmed Male person for the equivalent therapeutic medical treatment, involving multiple procedures, can be approximately double that amount.

While the medical expense of Phase 1 and 2 hormonal medical treatment for adolescents can be substantially covered under Medicare through the several isolated clinical programmes that are coming into existence in Australia, the legal costs of gaining access to Phase 2 Treatment, which requires the authorisation of the Family Court of Australia, and Phase 1 Treatment, which may require such authorisation, can exceed $15,000.00 AUD unless funded by legal aid. But access to legal aid is severely restricted by income and assets tests and only available in New South Wales for legal practitioners who agree to regularly carry out other legal aid work who are unlikely to have special expertise in such cases.

Many survivors of Transsexualism suffer ongoing 'post-traumatic-stress' type mental health issues; especially those who grew up subject to general familial and cultural shame and ridicule. The special needs of the growing numbers of aging Australians living with Transsexualism have been largely ignored or, if not ignored, presumed to be adequately met by measures providing specialist institutional aged assistance, support and accommodation for the Gay and Lesbian community.

While many people who experience Transgenderism may find appropriate care and accommodation within specialised Gay and Lesbian community aged care facilities, most people living with Transsexualism and some people living with extreme Transgenderism, who have lived their lives as members of the general Australian community and who do not identify as Gay or Lesbian, will not.

Most Australians living with Transsexualism will wish to continue in their later years as part of the communities in which they have lived where they have family or have carefully established a special network of friends who 'know', accept and support. These Australians, though needing specialist medical and/or psychological support in their later years, would feel their lives destroyed if their Difference was made public or if they were removed from their special network of personal and private support. For such Australians, being supported in their later years with the specialist psychological and medical care they need in their homes or in private accommodation within their communities is a need and not a preference.

In my opinion, the lack of timely and reasonably affordable access to specialist medical treatment and psychological support for Australians living with Transsexualism and Transgenderism, from childhood through to old age, is the single most important human rights issue concerning such people in contemporary Australia.

2.2.2. *Legal Restrictions on Access to Medical Treatment by Adolescents – Re Jamie*

The 2013 judgment of the Full Court of the Family Court of Australia in *Re Jamie* [2013] FamCAFC 110 ('*Re Jamie*') confirmed the law of Australia as internationally unique in strictly limiting access to the therapeutic medical treatment of the condition of Transsexualism in adolescence.

In *Re Jamie* the Full Court of the Family Court of Australia determined that only the Family Court of Australia (and not the adolescent's parents) could safely determine whether or not an adolescent living with Transsexualism might receive Phase 2 Treatment.[37]

In *Re Jamie* the Full Court of the Family Court of Australia determined that only the Family Court of Australia (and not the adolescent's treating doctors) could safely determine whether or not an adolescent living with Transsexualism was competent to the *Gillick* standard to authorise his or her own Phase 2 Treatment and that, in any case, such competence was only effective in the complete absence of parental, parent/child and/or medical conflict.[38]

While the Full Court of the Family Court of Australia in *Re Jamie* significantly determined that parental approval for 'fully reversible' Phase 1 Treatment was sufficient and that such treatment did not require the approval of the Family Court of Australia, the Full Court determined that such normal freedom of access to the time-critical Phase 1 Treatment was conditional on the complete absence of parental, parent/child and/or medical conflict when only the Family Court of Australia could safely determine whether or not an adolescent living with Transsexualism might receive Phase 1 Treatment.[39]

Thus, even a 17-year-old adolescent already receiving Phase 1 Treatment and having lived in his Affirmed Sex for many years and who was objectively competent to the *Gillick* standard to self-authorise Phase 2 Treatment, would not have, or could perhaps forfeit, the legal right to do so in the event that conflict concerning his treatment arose between him and a parent, between his parents or between any of them and a treating doctor.

The result of *Re Jamie* is to limit access to Phase 2 Treatment, and sometimes Phase 1 Treatment, to those comparatively few Australian adolescents who have family support and whose families possess the considerable financial and emotional wherewithal necessary to undertake the legal proceedings required to obtain court authorisation.

The judgment in *Re Jamie* warrants special consideration as it evidences the efforts of an Australian superior court, interacting with Australian medicine, to try to understand Transsexualism, its diagnosis and treatment and make laws for the protection and welfare of young Australians living with the condition.

This process provides an important insight into the contemporary interaction between Australian medicine, law and Difference as manifest in Transsexualism in minors. As the Hon. Justice Steven Strickland said:[40]

---

37 *Re Jamie*, para. 140.

38 Ibid.

39 Ibid.

40 S. Strickland, *To treat or not to treat: legal responses to transgender young people*, presented at the Association of Family and Conciliation Courts 51st annual conference, *Navigating the Waters of Shared Parenting: Guidance from the Harbour*, Toronto, Canada, 28–31 May 2014, p. 39, available at <www.familycourt.gov.au/wps/wcm/resources/file/ebdbe4077183420/Speech%20-%20Strickland%20-%20Transgender%20Young%20-%202014.html>.

> '*Re Jamie* was the first case where the Full Court of the Family Court had the opportunity to undertake a comprehensive analysis of earlier authorities, including that of the High Court of Australia in *Re: Marion* and Nicholson CJ in *Re: Alex*, in the context of an application for authorisation to undertake medical treatment for gender dysphoria. It is therefore a highly significant decision in the context of the limits of the Family Court's welfare or supervisory jurisdiction.'

I recommend the article *Treating the transgendered child: The Full Court's decision in Re Jamie*[41] by Fiona Kelly[42] and the paper *To treat or not to treat: legal responses to transgender young people*[43] by the Hon. Justice Steven Strickland for those interested in detailed and insightful exploration of the *Re Jamie* decision. Justice Strickland's paper is of particular interest, not only because as he was one of the members of Full Court bench who heard and determined the case, but for the detailed review he undertakes of related Australian jurisprudence.[44]

While the three members of the Full Court bench gave three separate judgments, the three judgments were in essential agreement on the primary legal and factual issues and, for the sake of simplicity, I will treat them here as a single judgment.

The legal principle that an individual minor may have sufficient competence in certain circumstances to authorise his or her own medical treatment in the absence of parental approval or court authorisation was established in the United Kingdom by the House of Lords in *Gillick v West Norfolk and Wisbech Health Authority* [1985] 3 All ER 402 ('*Gillick*') and incorporated into Australian law by the High Court of Australia in *SMB and JWB; Secretary, Department of Health and Community Services (Re Marion)* (1992) 175 CLR 218 ('*Marion's Case*').

The primary and secondary questions of law before the Full Court in *Re Jamie* were:

A. Whether, interpreting and applying the judgment of the High Court of Australia in *Marion's Case*, were either of Phase 1 or Phase 2 hormonal medical treatments for Transsexualism in adolescence of the 'special' category of medical treatment for which normal parental authority was insufficient and which required court authorisation under the court's protective Welfare jurisdiction incorporated in section 67ZC of the Family Law Act 1975; and

41 F. Kelly, 'Treating the transgendered child: The Full Court's decision in Re Jamie', *Australian Journal of Family Law*, 28 May 2014, pp. 83–94.

42 LLB (Hons), BA, LLM and PhD, Senior Lecturer, La Trobe School of Law.

43 S. Strickland, above n. 40.

44 In particular *Re Alex* (2004) FLC 93–175 ('*Re Alex*'); decided by former Chief Justice Nicholson who had been a member of the Full Court bench in the *Re Kevin* appeal, and *Re Bernadette* [2010] FamCA 94 and *Re Bernadette* (2011) FLC 93–463; the first case in Australia to authorise Phase 1 Treatment (as an interim order in 2005) and the first case to challenge the legal regime requiring court authorisation of Phases 1 and 2 Treatments.

B. Whether an adolescent living with Transsexualism could be competent to the *Gillick* standard to authorise his or her own Phase 2 medical treatment and, if so, could that competency be determined by treating doctors in the normal way or did it also require court determination?

Section 67ZC of the Family Law Act was inserted into the Act in 1995. It states:

> 'Orders relating to welfare of children
> (1) In addition to the jurisdiction that a court has under this Part in relation to children, the court also has jurisdiction to make orders relating to the welfare of children.
> Note: Division 4 of Part XIIIAA (International protection of children) may affect the jurisdiction of a court to make an order relating to the welfare of a child.
> (2) In deciding whether to make an order under subsection (1) in relation to a child, a court must regard the best interests of the child as the paramount consideration.
> Note: Sections 60CB and 60CG deal with how a court determines a child's best interests.'

Primary question A above can itself be divided into three parts:

A.1 Whether, as a matter of law, the *Marion's Case* categorisation of medical treatments requiring court authorisation is fundamentally determined by the consideration of whether or not that medical treatment is therapeutic, being carried out to alleviate suffering for the personal benefit of the patient, or whether the High Court intended such test to have two other additional essential considerations being:
A.1.1 Whether the decision to carry out the medical treatment carried with it a significant risk of the making a wrong decision; and
A.1.2 Whether the consequences of such wrong decision are particularly grave?
A.2 Whether, as a matter of law, the High Court intended its judgment in *Marion's Case* concerning the categorisation of medical treatments requiring court authorisation to be interpreted on a strictly literal basis to only a limited range of medical treatments involving surgical intervention 'appropriately carried out to treat some malfunction or disease'[45] or to the treatment of mental illness or disorder as well; and
A.3 Whether, as a matter of fact, either of Phase 1 or Phase 2 Treatments are because of their nature to be included in the category of medical treatments

[45] *SMB and JWB; Secretary, Department of Health and Community Services (Re Marion)* (1992) 175 CLR 218 ('*Marion's Case*') at 250.

requiring court authorisation determined by legal rulings in answer to A.1 and A.2?

The Full Court appeared to consider the answer to question B above to be virtually determined by the answer to question A.

In exploring the intent and effect of the High Court's judgment in *Marion's Case*, the Full Court quoted the following, in my view decisive, passage from that judgment:[46]

> 'We shall, therefore, give our reasons. But first it is necessary to make clear that, in speaking of sterilization in this context, we are not referring to sterilization which is a by-product of surgery appropriately carried out to treat some malfunction or disease. We hesitate to use the expressions "therapeutic" and "non-therapeutic", because of their uncertainty. But it is necessary to make the distinction, however unclear the dividing line may be.
>
> As a starting point, sterilization requires invasive, irreversible and major surgery. But so do, for example, an appendectomy and some cosmetic surgery, both of which, in my opinion, come within the ordinary scope of a parent to consent to. However, other factors exist which have the combined effect of marking out the decision to authorize sterilization as a special case. Court authorization is required, first, because of the significant risk of making the wrong decision, either as to a child's present or future capacity to consent or about what are the best interests of a child who cannot consent, and secondly, because the consequences of a wrong decision are particularly grave.'

The former Chief Justice of the Family Court of Australia, Justice Nicholson, sitting as a single judge, had first classified Phase 1 and Phase 2 hormonal treatment for Transsexualism in adolescence as requiring court authorisation in the case *Re Alex* (2004) FLC 93–175 ('*Re Alex*'). The Full Court quoted and effectively approved the following formulation by Nicholson CJ of the *ratio* of *Marion's Case*:[47]

> '*Marion's* case involved an application for the sterilisation of a 14-year-old teenager with a severe intellectual disability for the purpose of "preventing pregnancy and menstruation with its psychological and behavioural consequences". The gravamen of the decision was that if a child or young person cannot consent her/himself to a medical procedure, parental consent (which for present purposes may be equated with that of a guardian) is ineffective where the proposed intervention is:
>
> - invasive, permanent and irreversible; and
> - not for the purpose of curing a malfunction or disease.'

---

46 Ibid.

47 *Re Jamie*, para. 22.

In *Re Jamie* the Full Court determined that:

(1) The *Marion's Case* categorisation of medical treatments requiring court authorisation is not only determined by a consideration of whether or not that medical treatment is therapeutic, but also whether the decision to carry out the medical treatment carries with it a significant risk of making a wrong decision and whether the consequences of a wrong decision to carry out the medical treatment are particularly grave;
(2) The *Marion's Case* categorisation of medical treatments requiring court authorisation included non-surgical medical treatments such as those for the treatment of mental disorders;
(3) Transsexualism is a medically recognised category of pathology or mental illness;[48]
(4) Applying the ratio of *Marion's Case* as so determined, Phase 1 Treatment is not a medical treatment requiring court authorisation because it is a therapeutic medical treatment and its consequences, though particularly grave, are 'fully reversible' and therefore there is no significant risk of the making of a wrong diagnosis or decision to treat – except in the event of the existence of any dispute or lack of unanimity concerning such medical treatment involving any parent/guardian, the adolescent patient or any of the treating doctors when court authorisation would be required notwithstanding the High Court's categorisation of medical treatments requiring court authorisation in *Marion's Case*;
(5) Applying the ratio of *Marion's Case* as so determined, Phase 2 Treatment is a medical treatment requiring court authorisation because, although it is a therapeutic medical treatment, its consequences are particularly grave and there is a significant risk of the making of a wrong diagnosis or decision to treat because the consequences of the medical treatment, being only reversible by surgery, are not 'fully reversible';
(6) In the absence of any parent/child/doctor dispute, a young person living with Transsexualism can be competent to the *Gillick* standard to authorise his or her own Phase 2 Treatment, but, for the same considerations resulting in the treatment itself requiring court authorisation, only a court can determine whether such competence exists in each case;
(7) The High Court's categorisation of medical treatments requiring court authorisation in *Marion's Case* did not have application concerning Phase 1 or Phase 2 medical treatments in the event of the existence of any dispute or lack of unanimity concerning either such medical treatment involving any parent/guardian, the adolescent patient or any of the treating doctors; and
(8) In the event of there being any dispute or lack of unanimity concerning the administration of either Phase 1 or Phase 2 medical treatments between any

[48] Ibid., para. 69.

parent/guardian, the adolescent patient or any of the treating doctors, then Phase 1 or Phase 2 medical treatments cannot be accessed by an adolescent living with Transsexualism without court authorisation to be obtained (only) by application under section 67ZC of the Family Law Act.

Re Jamie is not an easy judgment to analyse. Findings are sometimes not readily referable to evidence and the discussion of various factual and legal issues intermix throughout the judgment to seemingly and suddenly coalesce in a series of conservative rulings which do not sit altogether comfortably with what is otherwise an insightful and compassionate judgment.

It is difficult to reconcile some of the comments and apparent findings in the judgment that seem to indicate an acceptance that the diagnosis of Transsexualism in adolescence carries with it a minute risk of the making of a wrong decision, let alone a significant one, with the core finding of fact that it does. Given the nature of Transsexualism with which the Full Court seemed informed and the apparently accepted likelihood of significant suffering, distress and permanent harm posed by non-treatment, it is hard to identify the 'grave consequences' the Full Court found, on balance, to accompany a wrong decision to undertake Phase 2 hormonal treatment. Surely here the consequences of a wrong decision to treat cannot be properly assessed independently of the likely consequences of non-treatment.

The Full Court also appeared to understand that the temporal, monetary and personal costs imposed on an adolescent and that adolescent's family by a court authorisation process concerning the authorisation of either Phase 1 and Phase 2 medical treatments or a declaration of *Gillick* capacity are significant.[49] It is unclear whether the Full Court understood that such costs are so significant as to be a bar to treatment for many young Australians and that consequently the legal regime the court determined as essential for the welfare and protection of young Australians who experience Transsexualism would undoubtedly result in many such young Australians being denied such therapeutic medical treatments altogether and thereby being condemned to experience immediate and life-long suffering and disability. That mental and physical suffering and disability is known to occur through an adolescent experiencing permanent pubertal changes to the shape and appearance of his or her body utterly at odds with his or her affirmed sex and sense of self. It is unclear whether, or the extent to which, the Full Court understood that such suffering would be shared by parents, families, loved ones and ultimately, the Australian community.

Another aspect of the judgment in *Re Jamie* that causes me concern is the legal impact on an adolescent's timely access both Phase 1 and Phase 2 medical

[49] Ibid., paras. 137 and 138. See also the address by the Chief Justice, Dianna Bryant, 'It's My Body, Isn't It: Children, Medical Treatment and Human Rights' (2009) 35 *Monash University Law Review* 193, 202–206 and the considerable thoughtfulness, insight and concern evidenced by Justice Strickland in his paper at n. 40.

treatments of a dispute arising between parents or between parent and adolescent or with or between treating doctors. I cannot find the authority in the High Court's decision in *Marion's Case* or elsewhere to support the proposition that a young Australian's access to therapeutic medical treatment should be subject to a legal process; except where there is genuine parental/parent/child or medical conflict about diagnosis – and then the matter should be a Parenting Orders case and not a Special Medical Procedure one. Nor can I find support for the proposition that medical treatment that does not require court authorisation as a matter of law or a minor who is legally competent to authorise his or her own medical treatment as a matter of law, can, by reason of circumstances of conflict beyond their control, lose such legal and human rights so as to have their access to such medical treatment made subject to an order under section 67ZC of the Family Law Act.

Such a proposition seems to be clearly inconsistent with the adolescent child's best interests, legal principal and good public policy. Dispute between parents, in particular, can happen at any time and, sadly, I do not consider it unlikely that a parent may consciously or unconsciously involve a child's access to such medical treatment in what is really parental conflict having nothing to do with the efficacy of the medical treatment.

With the respect properly due to the Full Court of the Family Court of Australia, in my opinion the majority of the High Court in *Marion's Case* provided a ruling, as applicable to the treatment of mental disorders as to the treatment of any other medical condition, that if a medical treatment is therapeutic and therefore personally beneficial to the patient in relieving suffering, it does not require court authorisation; even if such treatment might result in irreversible and grave consequences – such as the patient's sterilisation.[50] I can find nothing in Brennan J's minority judgment in *Marion's Case* that is inconsistent with that proposition.

From a practical or common sense perspective, there are any number of critical therapeutic medical procedures and treatments, such as some treatments for cancers, that have a comparatively high risk and grave consequences in terms of diagnosis, outcome and patient regret, that are carried out in Australia every day without court authorisation. No one could reasonably suggest that an assessment of the risks of a mistake in diagnosis in respect of such life-critical medical treatments or an assessment of the gravity of the effects of these medical procedures should require such treatments to be delayed or denied to patients in the absence of the completion of successful legal proceedings for court authorisation under section 67ZC of the Family Law Act.

I cannot find a basis for the proposition that the High Court of Australia intended by its judgment in *Marion's Case*, or indeed its explanatory references as to why the intended sterilisation of a minor was not a therapeutic medical

[50] *Marion's Case* at 250.

treatment, to apply a different standard to certain therapeutic medical treatments, but not others, or in some way to restrain or restrict any Australian minor in having prompt access to therapeutic medical treatment by the intervention of a court authorisation process. The very idea seems contrary to the purposes of the Welfare jurisdiction of Australian courts that such decision established, human rights principles and the precepts of the United Nations Convention on the Rights of the Child as explained by the Full Court in its judgment.[51]

I think it is arguable that the Full Court in *Re Jamie* did not follow Nicholson CJ's interpretation of the *ratio* in *Marion's Case* even though they seemed to approve it.[52] In the approach adopted by Nicholson CJ in *Re Alex*, a consideration of the matters referred to in A.1.1 and A.1.2 above are only relevant in the event that the purpose of the medical procedure in question is found *not* to be 'for the purpose of curing a malfunction or disease'.

In other words, Nicholson CJ's interpretation of the *ratio* in *Marion's Case* in *Re Alex* created a very narrow, but primarily therapeutic, test for the determination of which medical treatments required court authorisation.[53] The primary finding in *Re Alex* on which the decision turned was that Phase 1 and Phase 2 Treatments were not therapeutic medical treatments concerning which normal parental responsibility applied because they were for the treatment of a mental disorder and therefore carried unacceptable diagnostic and treatment risk.

In *Re Jamie*, by contrast, the Full Court ruled that medical treatments for mental disorders can be conceived of as being carried out for the purpose of curing a malfunction or disease and found that Phase 1 and Phase 2 medical treatments were therapeutic and necessary for adolescents living with the condition of Transsexualism and the consequences of non-treatment grave. In the circumstances I submit that had the Full Court actually applied Nicholson CJ's interpretation of the *ratio* of *Marion's Case* found in *Re Alex* to these determinations, the Full Court would have found that neither Phase 1 nor Phase 2 medical treatments were of the type which required court authorisation.

In my view in *Re Jamie* the Full Court of the Family Court of Australia established a new and distinctive interpretation of the *ratio* of *Marion's Case* that was fundamentally different from that of *Re Alex* and resulted in the Full Court virtually disregarding the factual question of whether or not either Phase 1 and 2 medical treatments were therapeutic in favour of an assessment of the risk and gravity of diagnostic and treatment error alone, with the meaning of 'gravity' disconnected from a balanced medical context and reduced to 'reversibility'. Hence, in *Re Jamie*, the question of the extent to which Phase 1 and Phase 2 Treatments were 'reversible' assumed disproportionate and unreasonable significance.

---

51 Convention on the Rights of the Child, opened for signature 20 November 1989, 1577 UNTS 3 (entered into force 2 September 1990).

52 *Re Jamie*, para. 22.

53 Ibid.

In *Re Jamie* it is notable that the Appellant Parents had not challenged the role of the Family Court in the authorisation of either Phase 1 or Phase 2 Treatments or marshalled expert evidence for such purpose at trial. The only apparent 'expert' evidence before the Full Court, therefore, was the clinical evidence of the adolescent's treating doctors. Apparently, no party sought leave to introduce additional or expert scientific evidence concerning the nature of Transsexualism, longitudinal studies concerning the reliability and safety of its diagnosis and treatment in childhood and adolescence or evidence as to the scientific and medical reasoning behind and implications for the introduction of the new diagnostic criteria for Transsexualism in the DSM-5 termed 'Gender Dysphoria' where the only disorder referenced is the distress caused by the experience of Transsexualism and not the phenomenon itself.

I can also only speculate that it was limited litigation funding that resulted in a reliance in *Re Jamie* on limited clinical opinion rather than expert evidence and the Appellant Parents adopting as one of their core factual submissions in the appeal that the Full Court should accept the DSM diagnostic categorisation of Gender Identity Disorder/Gender Dysphoria as being conclusive evidence of Transsexualism being a mental disorder or a 'diagnosed psychiatric condition which has been medically recognised'.[54] Whatever the cause, and although the Chief Justice sought to down play its significance, I believe that this core aspect of the Appellant Parents' appeal significantly adversely influenced the result of the case.

It may have assisted the Full Court in *Re Jamie* if it had been able to access expert evidence and submissions by use of an expert *amicus curiae* or 'Friend of the Court'. WPATH has appointed individual lawyers and experts to fulfil such a role in jurisdictions such as the United States of America. The evidence brought before the court in the *Re Kevin* case would not have been possible without Commonwealth Legal Aid Test Case funding. It has now become almost impossible to obtain either Commonwealth or State Legal Aid funding in Australia for test cases of this kind requiring multi-disciplined and international expert evidence. Individual applicant parents in such cases are now often dependent on the voluntary work of publicly minded lawyers and have little or no capacity to present the evidence actually required of such cases.

The roles played by government child welfare authorities, the Independent Children's Lawyer and the Australian Human Rights Commission in cases such as *Re Alex*, *Re Bernadette* [2010] FamCA 94 ('*Re Bernadette*') and *Re Jamie* are demonstrably not that of an expert *amicus curiae* and the case record indicates that such publically funded institutional parties have not assisted the court in the way I suggest is needed in order to avoid error where mystified and prejudice-laden aspects of Difference are on trial.

---

[54] Ibid., para. 26.

But what actually explains how the Full Court of the Family Court of Australia in *Re Jamie* could find that an undoubtedly therapeutic and internationally established medical treatment administered to save adolescents from immense life-long suffering with critical non-treatment implications and a negligible record of 'regret' is potentially dangerous enough to require court authorisation?

As I have argued above, I do not consider the High Court's decision in *Marion's Case* holds the answer. Nor, with respect, does the attitude or capacity of the judicial officers involved in either *Re Alex* or *Re Jamie*. Prior to *Re Alex* Nicholson CJ had led the Full Court of the Family Court of Australia to deliver a ground-breaking decision in the appeal brought by the Commonwealth Attorney General against Chisholm J's decision in *Re Kevin*[55] and his subsequent renowned human rights work clearly demonstrates his commitment to the human rights of children, including young people who experience Transsexualism. Nicholson CJ's judgment in *Re Alex* evidences his compassionate desire to understand and act in the best interests of 'Alex'. The judgment of the Full Court in *Re Jamie* evidences a similar capacity and intent. Published presentations by both Bryant CJ and Strickland J confirm their appreciation of the human rights of young people who experience the condition of Transsexualism.[56]

In searching for an explanation for the judgment in *Re Alex* in 2004 I referred to what I termed 'Cultural Prejudice' when I concluded:

> 'It is therefore important to emphasise that my criticism of the evidence, submissions and the decision of the Family Court of Australia in Re Alex neither makes or implies a criticism of the medical experts and lawyers who participated in those proceedings. Indeed, the goodwill, earnest intent and efforts of those people to seek and obtain a result in the case that honoured Alex and was in his best interests is abundantly clear. There was no conscious or individual prejudice at work in Re Alex that could be held responsible for the error of the decision in that case. There is prejudice in Re Alex, but being cultural prejudice it is so deep-rooted, self-enforcing, almost "natural" and pervasive that its presence is camouflaged. The responsibility for that prejudice belongs to us all, is cultural, and is the product of the difficulties to be met when the law seeks to deal with an unusual aspect of ourselves that we have long sought out of fear to deny; in this case transsexualism.'[57]

In her article *Treating the transgendered child: The Full Court's decision in Re Jamie*, Fiona Kelly offers two possible explanations for the Full Court's decision in *Re Jamie*:[58]

---

55 *The Attorney-General for the Commonwealth v "Kevin and Jennifer" and Human Rights and Equal Opportunity Commission* [2003] FamCA 94.

56 See Bryant, above n. 48, and Strickland, above n. 40.

57 Wallbank, above n. 3, p. 33.

58 Kelly, above n. 41, p. 93.

> 'Given that the risk of making a wrong decision is not particularly high and treatment for a transgendered child does not raise any of the conflict of interest concerns articulated in Marion's Case, why did the Full Court believe it still had a role to play in assessing competency? A possible answer is that the conclusion is simply an extension of the failure of the court to adequately interrogate the difference between therapeutic and non-therapeutic treatment, including the unique conflict of interest risks associated with the latter. However, one might also speculate that the court, while stating otherwise, continues to believe that treating a transgendered child is a special case, warranting judicial oversight. The judgment of Bryant CJ suggests this might be the case when she states that it is "the nature of the treatment at stage two [that] requires that the court determine *Gillick* competence"'.

I respectfully agree with these observations. I also think that the judgments in both *Re Alex* and *Re Jamie* may evidence that, no matter what is formally or consciously acknowledged, the diagnosis of a condition of mental disorder is 'a special case' and that judicial sensitivity or caution may be exacerbated where a psychiatric diagnosis is clearly controversial and is presented to the court associated with a phenomenon which is inexplicable in terms of mental disorder.

The fact is that medical practitioners and lawyers are no more immune from the lingering impact of cultural taboo, prejudice and mystification concerning phenomena of Difference such as mental disorder or Transsexualism than their fellow citizens. Judges are obliged to a considerable extent to rely on a varying quality of expert opinion and legal submission on a case-by-case basis to provide a foundation in technical medical and scientific cases such as *Re Jamie*.

In my respectful opinion, *Re Jamie* represents a lost opportunity for the Family Court of Australia in 2013 to end an internationally unique legal regime restricting the access by Australian adolescents living with Transsexualism to therapeutic Phase 1 and Phase 2 medical treatments. Moreover, the judgment reinforces the harmful idea, to the young people concerned, their families and the Australian community, that these children are Different; and are so Different they are not entitled to the same access to medical treatment as other Australians. Children who should be made to feel included in their world and who suffer so much for their Difference are treated by *Re Jamie* as 'special' second-class Australians simply because of the diversity in sexual formation they experience.

The following excerpts from the transcript of evidence of an American expert paediatric endocrinologist and an Australian expert psychiatrist in *Re Bernadette* seem to me to best describe the balance of risk involved in the decision to administer Phase 1 and Phase 2 hormonal medical treatments to adolescents living with Transsexualism, the fundamental therapeutic nature of that medical treatment and why it should not be subject to court authorisation:

Endocrinologist
"But since you brought up the issue of mental illness, may I make a comment about that?"
His Honour:
"Please do."
Endocrinologist
"Because I have always been impressed at how many of the patients have come to me with literally a satchel full of psychotropic medications, particularly the adults or the teenagers who have gone a bit far into their genotypic puberty, and have been labeled with depression, with anxiety, which I am sure they feel. And all too frequently labeled bipolar because of the wide swings in their mood. What has struck me more than anything at all, than anything else, is how many of them when treated with the hormones that are consistent with their affirmed gender seem to be able to shed both the most severe diagnosis that they hold psychologically and in many cases the medications. And it is my belief that the presence of the DSM4 coding of transgenderism as a psychiatric condition is really a self-fulfilling prophecy on the part of people who were not treated medically. And that indeed, by not treating them medically we are creating a mental illness, not starting with a mental illness that we need to find some way of treating medically."

The Psychiatrist
Question
"Can you tell the Court, if she [Bernadette] was your child whether you would have – whether you would have had her commence and receive phase 1 and phase 2 treatment in adolescence, as her parents have done?"
His Honour
"Would you prefer not to answer that, doctor?"
Answer
"No, I am very happy to answer it. Look, to me it is just – it is a no brainer, if you will forgive me."
His Honour
"Of course I will."
Answer
"We are allowed to try and get the maximum amount of happiness out of life. There is no guarantee that we will get it, and in fact in the 35-odd years I have been working in psychiatry, it seems to me that the odds are a bit against it. But we are allowed to try."

2.3. LEGAL FRAMEWORK

Australia is a democratic federation of six States and two Territories. The States and Territories are governed both by their own parliaments and a Federal or Commonwealth Parliament. The legislative power of each such parliament is determined and limited by the Australian Constitution and by intergovernmental agreements supported by uniform legislation, but not an overarching Bill of Rights.

Whereas, for example, the Federal or Commonwealth Parliament has constitutional power to make laws concerning marriage to the exclusion of the States and Territories, the States and Territories have the primary power to make laws concerning the legal identity of their citizens. Laws created by the Commonwealth Parliament made within jurisdiction will govern all Australians and override State and Territory laws to the degree to which such State and Territory laws are inconsistent. There are State- and Territory-based Common Law courts as well as federal courts created by Commonwealth Government legislation.

For example, while the Family Court of Australia is a federal court created by the Commonwealth Government under its constitution-based Marriage Powers, it has now acquired additional jurisdiction by agreement with the States and Territories to determine issues associated with *de facto* relationships and the welfare of children.

A decision made within power and jurisdiction by a federal court, such as the Family Court of Australia, will govern all Australians and override State laws and decisions of State courts to the degree to which they are inconsistent.

The High Court of Australia, exercising its own original and ultimate jurisdiction, determines appeals from State and Territory as well as federal courts.

III. THE RIGHT TO FREE GENDER EXPRESSION AND CHANGING LEGAL SEX IN AUSTRALIA

3.1. AUSTRALIAN ANTI-DISCRIMINATION LAWS

Anti-discrimination law dealing with the lives of people who experience Transsexualism and Transgenderism in Australia has focused its attention on two primary attributes: that of having undergone a reassignment of Legal Sex and that of expressing gender in a transgender or other diverse way.

Every Australian State and Territory, except the Northern Territory, has anti-discrimination laws that apply directly or by implication to people who experience both Transsexualism and Transgenderism.[59] Other State and federal anti-discrimination laws, mostly untested, may well also have application by implication; such as legislation protecting people living with disability. The New

[59] Australian Capital Territory Discrimination Act 1991; New South Wales Anti-Discrimination Act 1977; Queensland Anti-Discrimination Act 1991; Northern Territory Anti-Discrimination Act 1996; South Australia Equal Opportunity Act 1984; Tasmania Anti-Discrimination Act 1998; Victoria Equal Opportunity Act 1995; and Western Australia Equal Opportunity Act 1984.

South Wales Anti-Discrimination Act uses terms such as 'transgender person'[60] rather than a readily understandable description of a human attribute such as 'gender expression'. The Western Australian Equal Opportunity Act 1984 (WA) only offers protection to those who have had their Legal Sex reassigned, rather than for the free expression of gender.[61]

On 28 June 2013 assent was given to the Commonwealth Sex Discrimination Amendment (Sexual Orientation, Gender Identity and Intersex Status) Act 2013 which now provides protection from discrimination in daily life (subject to religious exemptions) for all Australians in respect of 'gender identity' defined in subsection 4(1) of the amended Act to mean:

> 'gender related identity, appearance or mannerisms or other gender related characteristics of a person (whether by way of medical intervention or not), with or without regard to the person's designated sex at birth.'

Here, although the term used is 'gender identity', the attribute itself is a broad and accurate description of gender expression as a human behaviour and protects all Australians who experience difference in gender expression from discrimination in the following terms:

> '(1) For the purposes of this Act, a person (the *discriminator*) discriminates against another person (the *aggrieved person*) on the ground of the aggrieved person's gender identity if, by reason of:
> (a) the aggrieved person's gender identity; or
> (b) a characteristic that appertains generally to persons who have the same gender identity as the aggrieved person; or
> (c) a characteristic that is generally imputed to persons who have the same gender identity as the aggrieved person;
> the discriminator treats the aggrieved person less favourably than, in circumstances that are the same or are not materially different, the discriminator treats or would treat a person who has a different gender identity.
> (2) For the purposes of this Act, a person (the *discriminator*) discriminates against another person (the *aggrieved person*) on the ground of the aggrieved person's gender identity if the discriminator imposes, or proposes to impose, a condition, requirement or practice that has, or is likely to have, the effect of disadvantaging persons who have the same gender identity as the aggrieved person.
> (3) This section has effect subject to sections 7B and 7D.'[62]

60 New South Wales Anti-Discrimination Act 1977, s. 4 and Part 3A.
61 Equal Opportunity Act 1984 (WA) s. 3.
62 Sex Discrimination Amendment (Sexual Orientation, Gender Identity and Intersex Status) Act 2013 (Clth) ('SDAct (Clth)') amended s. 5B.

This legislation also bears witness to the effectiveness of political interest groups on government in Australia in its creation of identical protection on the ground of 'intersex status' where that term is defined as:

> 'intersex status means the status of having physical, hormonal or genetic features that are:
> (a) neither wholly female nor wholly male; or
> (b) a combination of female and male; or
> (c) neither female nor male.'[63]

Here again, people living with the condition of Transsexualism, although legislatively ignored, arguably fit the statutory definition of 'intersex status', as the brain is undoubtedly a physical feature of a human being and, even if the evidence of brain and other genetic indicators of Transsexualism are discounted, a person undergoing or having undergone Sex Affirmation Treatment and/or Genital Reassignment Surgery will undoubtedly possess 'physical, hormonal or genetic features' that meet the Act's definition of 'intersex status'.

Australian anti-discrimination legislation shows the beginnings of a welcome evolution of the law to protect the right to free gender expression for every citizen and not only minority groups.

3.2. SEX AND GENDER DESIGNATIONS ON AUSTRALIAN SECONDARY IDENTITY DOCUMENTS

Two recent government publications which provide an insight to the contemporary Australian government consideration and response to the phenomena of diversity in sexual formation and gender expression are the Australian Human Rights Commission (AHRC) March 2009 report *Sex Files: The Legal Recognition Of Sex In Documents And Government Records* ('*Sex Files*') and the *Australian Government Guidelines on the Recognition of Sex and Gender* ('*AusGovt Guidelines*').[64]

The *AusGovt Guidelines* purport to 'provide guidance to Australian Government departments and agencies on the collection, use and amendment of sex and gender information in individual personal records.'[65]

The *AusGovt Guidelines* provide a means whereby an Australian can change their 'sex and/or gender information on their personal record':[66]

---

63 SD Act (Clth) amended s. 4(1).
64 Published July 2013 by Commonwealth Attorney-General's Department at <www.ag.gov.au/genderrecognition>.
65 AusGovt Guidelines, para. 3 at 3.
66 Ibid., para. 21 at 5.

> '21. Where a person requests the sex and/or gender information on their personal record be amended, or where it is necessary to verify a person's sex and/or gender to confirm identity or determine eligibility for a service or entitlement, the Australian Government will recognise any one of the following as sufficient evidence of their sex and/or gender:
> a) a statement from a Registered Medical Practitioner or a Registered Psychologist
> b) valid Australian Government travel document, such as a Valid Passport, which specifies their preferred gender, or
> c) an amended State or Territory birth certificate, which specifies their preferred gender. A State or Territory Gender Recognition Certificate or recognised details certificate showing a State or Territory Registrar of Birth Deaths and Marriages has accepted a change in sex will also be seen as sufficient evidence.
> 21. Sex reassignment surgery and/or hormone therapy are not pre-requisites for the recognition of a change of gender in Australian Government records.'

Although the *AusGovt Guidelines* appear to be quite accommodating of diversity in their purposes and intent, it is confusing in its interchangeable references to 'sex and/or gender' and its definitions of 'sex', 'gender' and 'intersex', which are globalising as well as discriminating.

Notwithstanding the use of the terms '*preferred gender*' and '*gender transition*', the document is clearly referring to the experience of Transsexualism and its medical treatment and not Transgenderism.

By contrast, and inconsistently, *the AusGovt Guidelines* define both 'sex' and 'gender' in a more or less classic way while strongly distinguishing 'intersex' Australians, as experiencing a 'biological' phenomenon, from a 'recognised' 'community' of 'sex and gender diverse' Australians who are self-determined by their feelings, appearance and behaviour alone:

> 'Gender is part of a person's personal and social identity. It refers to the way a person feels, presents and is recognised within the community. A person's gender refers to outward social markers, including their name, outward appearance, mannerisms and dress…',[67] and

> 'The term "gender diverse" is used to recognise people who do not fall within the traditional binary notions of sex and gender (male and female). This may include people who identify as a gender different to their birth sex or as neither male or female. Other terms commonly associated with gender diverse people include trans, transgender, transsexual, gender queer, pan-gendered, androgynous and inter-gender.'[68]

---

[67] Ibid., para. 13 at 4.
[68] Ibid.

The Guidelines strictly distinguish the globalised 'transgender' and 'gender diverse' from the more favourably treated 'intersex'; defining intersex in such a way, however, as to readily accommodate a *Re Kevin* understanding of Transsexualism:

> 'An intersex person may have the biological attributes of both sexes or lack some of the biological attributes considered necessary to be defined as one or the other sex. Intersex is always congenital and can originate from genetic, chromosomal or hormonal variations. Environmental influences such as endocrine disruptors can also play a role in some intersex differences.'[69]

In order to satisfy subparagraph (a) above of the *AusGovt Guidelines* to gain the right alter the sex designation on identity documents, a '*transgender*' or '*gender diverse*' person must provide a statement by a medical practitioner that confirms that the individual concerned

> 'has had, or is receiving, appropriate clinical treatment for gender transition to the new gender of (specify new gender male or female).'[70]

This is the same certification required by a '*transgender*' or '*gender diverse*' person to change the sex designation on an Australian passport.[71]

By contrast, in order to satisfy subparagraph (a) above of the *AusGovt Guidelines* to gain the right to alter the sex designation on identity documents, an 'intersex person' need only provide a mixed sex/gender statement that the person

> 'is of indeterminate, intersex or unspecified sex and lives in the gender of male/female … indeterminate/intersex/unspecified.'[72]

By way of summary, the *AusGovt Guidelines*:

- use 'gender' to mean sex except in their definition of 'gender';
- do this while seeking to deal with the designation of sex (and not gender) in secondary identity documents;
- purport to deal with a broad swathe of different types of people referred to as 'sex and gender diverse', but only provides a means for people who actually

---

69 Ibid., at 10.

70 Ibid. Appendix A – Statement from a Registered Medical Practitioner or Registered Psychologist template 1; for transitioning genders.

71 Department of Foreign Affairs and Trade, *Change of Sex: Sex and Gender Diverse*, Australian Government: Department of Foreign Affairs and Trade <www.dfat.gov.au/ publications/passports/Policy/Identity/Sex/Changeofsexsexandgenderdiverse/index.htm>.

72 Clth Guidelines Appendix A at 12 – Statement from a Registered Medical Practitioner or Registered Psychologist template 2. For people who are intersex/indeterminate/unspecified.

experience Transsexualism to change their sex designation on secondary identity documents;
- provide different rights to people living with Transsexualism than to other people who experience difference in sexual formation described as 'intersex', defined so as to include the condition of Transsexualism;
- standardise and simplify governmental requirements for a change of the sex designation on secondary identity documents;
- reduce and clarify the evidentiary requirements for those who wish to change the sex designation on secondary identity documents who do not meet the government definition of 'intersex' to a medical certification that the applicant 'has had, or is receiving, appropriate clinical treatment for gender transition to the new gender of (specify new gender male or female).'[73]

Notwithstanding the reference to '*clinical treatment*' contained in its requirements referred to above, the definition of 'Gender Diverse' in the *AusGovt Guidelines* clearly positions Transsexualism within one globalised 'community' of 'people who do not fall within the traditional binary notions of sex and gender (male and female)' who are apparently solely concerned with non-biologically issues associated with outward appearance and behaviour and who do not exist within cultural notions of the sexual dichotomy.

The concepts of both Transsexualism and Transgenderism contained in the *AusGovt Guidelines* are inaccurate and confusing. The concept of Transsexualism contained in the *AusGovt Guidelines* is clearly at odds with the understanding of Transsexualism expressed in this article and in *Re Kevin* and the long domestic and international jurisprudential history concerning Transsexualism.[74]

The linguistic and conceptual confusion contained in the *AusGovt Guidelines* is significant as an example of how difficult it is for government to accurately represent Difference and justifies the concerns expressed in this article about the failure of language and terminology to recognise and give proper regard to diversity in sexual formation and gender expression. Such conceptual misunderstanding and confusion in such a crucial government policy document that also contains a privileging of Intersex along with a sublimation of Transsexualism might be expected to have significantly negative legal and cultural impact on the understanding and appreciation of diversity in sexual formation and gender expression in Australia.

As discussed below, I contend that the 2014 decision of the High Court of Australia in *NSW Registrar of Births, Deaths and Marriages v Norrie* [2014] HCA 11 ('*Norrie*')[75] contains a similar misunderstanding of the predicament, interests and needs of Australians living with diversity in sexual formation and

---

73 Ibid.
74 *Re Kevin*, paras. 111–120.
75 Discussed below at section 4.1.3.

gender expression as well as the interaction of these distinct phenomena with Legal Sex as an aspect of legal identity.

3.3. LEGAL SEX

A person's Birth Certificate or similar cardinal document, sometimes called a '*Recognition Certificate*' or '*Document Acknowledging Identity*'[76] for those not born in a particular State, evidences their legal identity recorded in a State or Territory registry of 'Births, Deaths and Marriages' and is their cardinal or primary identity document.[77]

As stated by the Australian Human Rights Commission:

> 'Under Australia's identification systems the most important identity documents are known as cardinal documents. For people born in Australia, cardinal documents are birth certificates or change of name certificates. For people not born in Australia, cardinal documents are citizenship certificates or the information contained in the database held by the federal Department of Immigration and Citizenship (DIAC records). Cardinal documents are the most trusted evidence of identity and citizenship.'[78]

In Australia, the first or primary assignment of a person's Legal Sex is to either Male or Female and is based upon a medical practitioner's casual inspection of the external genitalia of infants. Where an infant possesses genitalia resembling that of neither or both sexes, the assignment of Legal Sex may be postponed or a preliminary assignment made subject to later correction. Australian States and Territories record a person's Legal Sex in registers of legal identity as part of the person's fixed legal identity; evidenced by the person's Birth Certificate that is the person's primary or cardinal identity document.

Thus, the standard method for the assignment of an Australian's Legal Sex is a part of a larger process of assigning legal identity and is a policy-based socio-legal process involving the assignment of individuals across a diversity of human sexual formation to one of two legally and culturally recognised categories of Legal Sex, Male or Female, based upon their external genitalia. I hypothesise that the primary purpose of this 'traditional' method for the assignment of Legal

[76] Births, Deaths and Marriages Registration Act 1996 (Vic), Part 4A Div 2.

[77] Under Australia's identification systems the most important identity documents are known as cardinal documents. For people born in Australia, cardinal documents are birth certificates or change of name certificates. For people not born in Australia, cardinal documents are citizenship certificates or the information contained in the database held by the federal Department of Immigration and Citizenship (DIAC records). Cardinal documents are the most trusted evidence of identity and citizenship.

[78] Sex Files Report N6 para. 7.1 at 13.

Sex was to facilitate the ready identification of male physical power and sexual potential as part of a person's legal identity as evidenced by their birth certificate.

Australia States and Territory laws also provide for an individual's Legal Sex to be reassigned and for an individual, born outside a particular State or Territory to have their Legal Sex recognised as different to that first assigned elsewhere.[79] The first of such legislation was introduced in South Australia (SA) in 1988. The latest substantially different version of this type of legislation was introduced by the Australian Capital Territory (ACT) and became effective on 26 April 2014. Both the Western Australian (WA) and New South Wales (NSW) versions of such legislation have been the subject of recent review and interpretation by the High Court of Australia.[80]

The different language and requirements applied in Australian legislation concerning the determination and reassignment of Legal Sex as part of legal identity has resulted in something of a hotchpotch of legal regimes across the country.

Some States take a universal approach and provide a legal pathway for all people who have undergone a 'sex affirmation procedure' to change their Legal Sex. The definition of 'sex affirmation procedure' in section 32A of the Births, Deaths and Marriages Registration Act 1995 (NSW) makes clear in subsection (b) of that section that it is applicable to all who have undergone a procedure 'to correct or eliminate ambiguities relating to the sex of the person.' The Gender Reassignment Act 2000 (WA) only provides such a universal pathway to children.[81]

By contrast, in Victoria people who experience difference in sexual formation, except those with Transsexualism, are able to change their Legal Sex by the correction provisions of the legislation without providing evidence of having undergone any Genital Reassignment Surgery or other Sex Affirmation Treatment.[82] Like the Births, Deaths and Marriages Registration Act 1996 (Vic), the Births, Deaths and Marriages Registration Act 1997 (ACT) creates two different pathways – depending on whether or not you meet a legislative definition of an 'intersex person'.[83] This legislative discrimination between people living

---

79 Sexual Reassignment Act 1988 (SA) ('SA Act'); Births, Deaths and Marriages Registration Act 1995 (NSW) ('NSW Act'); Births, Deaths and Marriages Registration Act 1996 (NT) Part 4A ('NT Act'); Births, Deaths and Marriages Registration Act 1997 (ACT) Part 4 ('ACT Act'); Births, Deaths and Marriages Registration Act 1999 (TAS) Part 4A ('TAS Act'); Gender Reassignment Act 2000 (WA) ('WA Act'); Births, Deaths and Marriages Registration Act 2003 (Qld) Part 4 ('QLD Act') and Births, Deaths and Marriages Registration Act 1996 (Vic) Part 4A ('VIC Act').

80 See *AB v Western Australia and AH v Western Australia* [2011] HCA 42 and *NSW Registrar of Births, Deaths and Marriages v Norrie* [2014] HCA 11.

81 WA Act s. 4 'Terms used in this Act' definition of 'reassignment procedure'.

82 The title of Part 4A of the VIC Act is 'Recognition of Sex (Transsexualism)' and subsection 4(1) of the Act defines 'sex affirmation surgery' to mean a procedure carried out 'for the purpose of assisting the person to be considered to be of the opposite sex.'

83 ACT Act s. 24(1)(c).

with Transsexualism and other conditions of difference in sexual formation is the same as that contained the *AusGovt Guidelines.*

In a departure from the traditional Male/Female Legal Sex categorisation, the Births, Deaths and Marriages Registration Act 1997 (ACT) and Regulations provide for the changed Legal Sex of a person to be, based upon individual self-identification, any of the Legal Sex categories of 'male', 'female', 'unspecified/indeterminate/intersex', 'unspecified', 'indeterminate' or 'intersex'.[84]

The two bases, for both adults and children, for reassignment to one of these diverse Legal Sex categories under subsection 24(1)(c) of the ACT Act are that the person:

> '(i) has received appropriate clinical treatment for alteration of the person's sex; or
> (ii) is an intersex person.'

One has to go to section 169B of the Legislation Act 2001 (ACT) to find the relevant definition of 'intersex person':

> 'An *intersex person* is a person who has physical, hormonal or genetic features that are –
> (a) not fully female or fully male; or
> (b) a combination of male or female; or
> (c) not female or male.'

Once again, it is ironic that people who experience Transsexualism meet the ACT legislative definition of an intersex person based on the findings in cases such as *Re Kevin* and their objective post-treatment state.

Whether legislative discrimination in legal identity rights between people who experience Transsexualism and other forms of intersexual diversity in sexual formation is blatant as in the Births, Deaths and Marriages Registration Act 1997 (ACT) or is carried out more in the background as in VIC practice, it is clear that some Australian legislators perceive such significant discrimination to be justified. Based upon a reading of the legislation concerned and the definitions contained or relied upon, the only apparent justification seems to be that, unlike Transsexualism, which is characterised as being solely concerned with individual 'feeling' and 'appearance', the nature of other intersex conditions is accepted by the State and Territory parliaments concerned as 'biological'.

I hypothesise, however, that there is more to such legislative discrimination than this anachronistic view of the causation of Transsexualism. In my view this legal discrimination also reflects the concern such legislators have that persons

[84] Form 204 – ACS, 'Application To Alter Birth Register To Record Change Of Sex', Births, Deaths and Marriages Registration Act 1997 (ACT) and Births, Deaths and Marriages Registration Regulation 1998 (ACT).

having a female Legal Sex not have bodies with male strength and male sexual potential combined with a legislative expectation that people with traditional intersex conditions seeking assignment to the female Legal Sex will not possess bodies with such male capacity while untreated Affirmed Females with the condition of Transsexualism could.

Although the word 'gender' and its derivative terms are used in some of the Australian State and Territory legislation which provide a legislative pathway to reassign Legal Sex, most notably in the Gender Reassignment Act 2000 (WA), it is plain from the language and definitions contained in all Australian legislation that it is solely concerned to provide for the reassignment of Legal Sex for people who have either undergone Genital Reassignment Surgery, are receiving clinical medical treatment appropriate to the condition of Transsexualism or who are considered Intersex.

Whatever the language, no Australian legislation, including the 2014 amendments to the Births, Deaths and Marriages Registration Act 1997 (ACT), provides for the recognition of Pan/Trans-gender expression as a part of a person's legal identity.

The various Australian State and Territory legislative approaches to the reassignment of Legal Sex may be summarised as:

- a self-contained statutory requirement for the undergoing of Sex Affirmation Treatment, presumably including but not specifying a form of Genital Reassignment Surgery, carried out with the purpose of affirming the male or female sex or neither sex;[85] or
- a combination of a self-contained statutory requirement for undergoing Sex Affirmation Treatment carried out with the purpose of affirming the male or female sex and an assessment (similar to that provided for in the Gender Recognition Act 2004 (UK) (UKGRA)) by a statutory board or magistrate as to compliance with Australian cultural expectations of what it means to be either male or female;[86] or
- a self-contained statutory requirement for a form of permanent Genital Reassignment Surgery carried out with the purpose of affirming the male or female sex or neither sex;[87] and

---

85 ACT Act.

86 SA Act and WA Act.

87 All States and Territories except Western Australia, South Australia and the Australian Capital Territory. With the exception of the ACT Act, I do not consider a legislative intention existed to create a 'Non-Specific' Legal Sex category, but I have included this Legal Sex option as a result of the High Court of Australia's decision in *Norrie* as I am of the view that if the High Court could impose such an intention and interpretation on the NSW Act, then there is no reason why other State and Territory legislation, similar to the NSW Act, might not be similarly construed. As is discussed below, it is significant to note that as per the High Court of Australia's decision in *Norrie* the 'Non-Specific' Legal Sex category is only available to citizens who have undergone Genital Reassignment Surgery. The requirement for Genital Reassignment

- applicants must be unmarried (except in the ACT) and adults or, if minors, have an application made by parents or legal guardian on their behalf;[88] and
- the operation of all these legal regimes is subject to administrative and judicial review.

There is simply no justification for prohibiting married persons from having their Legal Sex reassigned. I stand by what I said about this disgraceful aspect of Australian identity law in 2004 when I said:

> 'Here married people with transsexualism fall victim to a misplaced legally expressed homophobia that fails to appreciate the workings of the marriage law of Australia, as clarified in Re Kevin, that the validity of a marriage, and hence the sex of the parties to a marriage, are to be determined as at the date of the marriage. The "sex of the parties" means their common law sex and does not require or invite some scientific investigation and or argument as to which (or which set) of the sexually differentiated aspects of a person determine their possibly multi-faceted biological sex. The withholding of the right to an accurate legal identity from a person of transsexual background because that person desires to continue to honour a marriage that has endured their transsexualism has nothing to say about the sex (or sexuality) of the couple at the time of the marriage and is clearly inhumane and against the public interest that would seek to honour an enduring marriage.'[89]

All of the State and Territories of Australia, except the ACT, have adopted what I will call the *Inclusive* approach to the assignment and reassignment of Legal Sex and require some form of significant change to the sexually differentiated characteristics of the body, including the genitalia, as a precondition for the reassignment of legal sex.

Although the Births, Deaths and Marriages Registration Act 1997 (ACT) has been referred to as an example of recent radical legislative change with the abandonment of a requirement for permanent change to the sexually differentiated body as a precondition for the reassignment of legal sex, the plain language of section 24(1)(c)(i) of that act containing the precondition 'has received appropriate clinical treatment for alteration of the person's sex' indicates that this is not so. I would not anticipate that the High Court of Australia would interpret this legislative requirement in any significantly different way than the way that court construed the requirements of the Gender Reassignment Act 2000 (WA) in *AB v Western Australia and AH v Western Australia* [2011] HCA 42 ('*AB and AH v WA*').

Surgery for affirmed males is generally popularly construed by medical practitioners to be satisfied by Chest Reconstruction Surgery and long term testosterone treatment.

88 NSW Act, Vic Act, QLD Act, TAS Act and NT Act, but not the ACT.

89 Wallbank, above n. 3, p. 6.

Of considerable concern is that the 2014 amendments to the Births, Deaths and Marriages Registration Act 1997 (ACT) establish a significantly different and advantageous set of legal rights concerning the reassignment of legal sex between those people who can claim to meet the ACT's legislative definition of 'an intersex person' and those who do not.

IV. LEGAL CHALLENGES AND JUDICIAL INTERPRETATION

4.1. THE ROLE OF THE COMMON LAW CONCERNING THE ASSIGNMENT OF LEGAL SEX

The English decision of *Corbett v Corbett (otherwise Ashley)* [1971] P 83; [1970] 2 All ER 33; [1970] 2 WLR 1306 ('*Corbett*') has often been presented as a 'benchmark' decision establishing an essentialist 'biological' approach to the assignment of Common Law Legal Sex.

As Chisholm J demonstrated in *Re Kevin*, it is possible to trace a reasonably consistent judicial understanding of Transsexualism and approach to the reassignment of Legal Sex in international jurisprudence going back to 1945 that uses an inclusive approach rather than a pseudo-biological 'essentialist'[90] approach such as used in *Corbett*.[91]

In the 1988 decision *R v Harris and McGuiness*,[92] Australian criminal law came to consider a person who 'through medical intervention … has assumed the external genital features of the opposite sex, thereby bringing those genital features into conformity with the person's psychological sex' as legally of that sex.

In her leading judgment in that case, Mathews J (with which Street CJ agreed) made the pertinent and prescient observation that 'I can see no place in the law for a "third sex". Such a concept … could cause insuperable difficulties … It would also relegate transsexuals to a legal "no man's land". This, I think, could only operate to their considerable detriment.'[93]

The Federal Court of Australia examined the same issue in relation to Social Security benefits in *Secretary, Department of Social Security v SRA* (1993) 43 FCR 299 ('*SRA*'). The Applicant had been undergoing Sex Affirmation Treatment but had not undertaken Genital Reassignment Surgery. The Court ultimately determined that in order for there to be objective certainty, Genital Reassignment Surgery was a necessary prerequisite for a reassignment of Legal Sex for the

---

90 This is the term used by Chisholm J to describe Ormrod J's approach. See *Re Kevin*, paras. 106–114.

91 *Re Kevin*, paras. 111–120.

92 (1988) 17 NSWLR 158 (by majority).

93 Ibid., the majority as per Mathews J at 193.

purposes of Australian Social Security legislation. The Federal Court expressed the view that:

> 'Sex is not merely a matter of chromosomes, although chromosomes are a very relevant consideration. Sex is also partly a psychological question (a question of self perception) and partly a social question (how society perceives the individual).'[94]

At the closely following paragraph 100 of the judgment, Lockhart J concluded:

> 'In my opinion, in Australia today, the ordinary understanding of a woman or a female does not include a transsexual who has not adopted the anatomical features of the sex which he or she seeks to achieve and thinks has been achieved'.

A consideration of three further cases, *Re Kevin*, *AB and AH v WA* and *Norrie*, provides an exploration and evaluation of the contemporary development of the law of Australia concerning the legal and human rights of people who experience Transsexualism and Transgenderism; the first case ultimately determined by the Full Court of the Family Court of Australia in 2003 concerning marriage law and the other two cases determined by the High Court of Australia in 2011 and 2014, respectively, construing State legislation concerning legal identity law and the reassignment of Legal Sex.

4.1.1. Re Kevin

The first of these cases, *Re Kevin*, confirmed on appeal by the Full Court of the Family Court of Australia in *The Attorney-General for the Commonwealth v 'Kevin and Jennifer' and Human Rights and Equal Opportunity Commission* (2003) 30 Fam LR 1, established the method for determining a person's Common Law Sex for the purposes of the marriage law of Australia.

Kevin, born with an apparently female differentiated body, had affirmed the male sex and had undergone Sex Affirmation Treatment comprising hormonal treatment and Sex Affirmation Procedures including male chest reconstruction surgery and a total hysterectomy with bilateral oophorectomy.[95] Kevin had then married Jennifer; a female-bodied person with a female Legal Sex.

While Kevin had had his Legal Sex reassigned to male pursuant to the NSW Act, there was nothing in Chisholm J's judgment that indicates that the reassignment of Kevin's Legal Sex under the NSW Act was a necessary precondition

---

94 *Secretary, Department of Social Security v SRA* (1993) 43 FCR 299 ('SRA') at 325 (para. 97). Such a view was undoubtedly insightful at the time when chromosomes were considered a decisive biological sex indicator, but is somewhat problematic today in its contrasting use of the term 'psychology'; as if psychology with its associated 'self-perception' and biology were exclusive concepts.

95 *Re Kevin*, paras. 22–34.

to his Honour's finding that Kevin was a man and entitled to enter into a legally valid marriage as a man with a female at the time he married Jennifer. Here the distinction between Common Law Sex and Legal Sex is made out.

As Kevin had not undertaken a Phalloplasty procedure as a part of his Genital Reassignment Surgery, *Re Kevin* is of significance due to the implicit recognition that Sex Affirmation Treatment, and Genital Reassignment Surgery in particular, are rehabilitative medical treatments undertaken for a personal therapeutic purpose and that, in determining whether one is a male or female person for the purposes of marriage, the law of Australia is not particularly concerned that the outcome of that medical treatment precisely mimicked a standard or normal sexually differentiated body.

Also implicit in Chisholm J's judgment in *Re Kevin* was the same appreciation contained in *SRA* – that what Australians expected as necessary for a person to be culturally considered as being male or female was to a significant extent determined by practical issues associated with cultural perception and the expectations of the different physical strength and sexual potential of male and female bodies; rather than a philosophical position concerning 'maleness', 'femaleness' or self-identification.

Having dismissed the principles applied in *Corbett* as not useful to or consistent with Australian law and having reviewed the expert and lay evidence, Chisholm J determined that the marriage between Kevin and Jennifer was a valid one because he determined that 'Kevin' was a man according to the contemporary ordinary everyday meaning of that word as contained in the Marriage Act 1961 (Cth) at the date of his marriage.[96] Describing a holistic version of the Inclusive approach to the determination of a person's Common Law Sex as espoused in *SRA*, now applied to the sensitive area of Australian marriage law, Chisholm J summarised his conclusions in *Re Kevin* as:[97]

> '(1) For the purpose of ascertaining the validity of a marriage under Australian law, the question whether a person is a man or a woman is to be determined as of the date of the marriage.
>
> (2) There is no rule or presumption that the question whether a person is a man or a woman for the purpose of marriage law is to be determined by reference to circumstances at the time of birth. Anything to the contrary in Corbett does not represent Australian law.
>
> (3) In the context of the rule that the parties to a valid marriage must be a man and a woman, the word "man" has its ordinary current meaning according to Australian usage.
>
> (4) There may be circumstances in which a person who at birth had female gonads, chromosomes and genitals, may nevertheless be a man at the date

[96] Ibid., from para. 307.
[97] Ibid., para. 330.

of his marriage. Anything to the contrary in Corbett does not represent Australian law.

(5) In the present case, the husband at birth had female chromosomes, gonads and genitals, but was a man for the purpose of the law of marriage at the time of his marriage, having regard to all the circumstances, and in particular the following:
   (a) he had always perceived himself to be a male;
   (b) he was perceived by those who knew him to have had male characteristics since he was a young child;
   (c) prior to the marriage he went through a full process of transsexual re-assignment, involving hormone treatment and irreversible surgery, conducted by appropriately qualified medical practitioners;
   (d) at the time of the marriage, in appearance, characteristics and behaviour he was perceived as a man, and accepted as a man, by his family, friends and work colleagues;
   (e) he was accepted as a man for a variety of social and legal purposes, including name, and admission to an IVF program, and in relation to such events occurring after the marriage, there was evidence that his characteristics at the relevant times were no different from his characteristics at the time of the marriage;
   (f) his marriage as a man was accepted, in full knowledge of his circumstances, by his family, friends and work colleagues.

(6) For these reasons, the application succeeds, and there will be a declaration of the validity of the applicants' marriage.'

Chisholm J described his understanding of what I have called the Inclusive approach to determining the Legal Sex of all members of a community, including those who experience Difference, as:

> 'the fundamental task of the law ..., in a legal and social context that divides all human beings into male and female, is to assign individuals to one category or the other, including individuals whose characteristics are not uniformly those of one or other sex.'[98]

This Inclusive approach to Legal Sex presumes or recognises the natural diversity that exists in human sexual formation and gender expression and then seeks to assimilate and assign that diversity into either of the culturally understood and accepted 'Male' or 'Female' categories of Legal Sex based upon considerations of functionality and practicality and the best prospects for a happy life.

[98] Ibid., para. 315.

The outstanding depth and consideration embodied in Chisholm J's judgment in *Re Kevin* has earned considerable acknowledgement, such as that given by Judge Gerard O'Brien in the Florida, United States of America case of *Kantaras:*[99]

> 'it is essential that Kevin not be given a mere "citation" but studied for what it represents in the law. It is one of the most important cases on transsexualism to come on the scene of foreign jurisprudence.'

Criticism of *Re Kevin* has almost exclusively come from two distinct perspectives that I identify as the 'Political Intersex' perspective and the 'Political Transgender' perspective.

The Political Intersex perspective objects to the *Re Kevin* finding that Transsexualism is an intersex condition. Given their success in Australia in gaining favourable cultural treatment and superior legislative rights concerning the assignment and reassignment of Legal Sex, exemplified in the ACT Act as previously discussed, one can readily appreciate why Intersex advocates would object to any assertion that might weaken or dilute the purity of the Intersex 'brand'.

The Political Transgender perspective argues that the 'test' set out in *Re Kevin* for determining a person's Common Law Sex for the purpose of marriage is unfair and/or too restrictive because the judgment relies upon a new 'biological' benchmark in its recognition of 'brain sex', requires a person to have undergone some form of 'transsexual re-assignment, involving hormone treatment and irreversible surgery'[100] and requires a person's compliance with normative cultural standards of male or female gender expression.

The Political Transgender perspective is misconceived in that while these are all factors taken into account by Chisholm J in *Re Kevin* order to find that 'Kevin' was a man within the meaning of the Australian Marriage Act in that particular case, it seems to me that Chisholm J was at pains in his judgment to maintain consistency by avoiding establishing any fixed set of criteria for determining Common Law Sex for the purposes of marriage at any particular time. In so doing, Chisholm J maintained the freedom of a future court to make its own decision about its own facts and the contemporary ordinary everyday meaning of the words 'man' and 'woman' at that time in its application of the Marriage Act and the Inclusive approach to the circumstances of people who experience Difference in sexual formation and/or gender expression.

[99] *The Marriage of Kantaras,* case number 98-5375CA 511998DR00537WS (Florida/USA-2003) at 673.

[100] *Re Kevin*, para. 330.

4.1.2. *AB v Western Australia and AH v Western Australia*

In the second more recent case to be considered, *AB v Western Australia and AH v Western Australia* [2011] HCA 42 ('*AB and AH v WA*') the High Court of Australia determined the meaning and function of the Gender Reassignment Act 2000 (WA) ('WA Act') in order to determine whether the two Affirmed Male Appellants were entitled to the issue of a WA Act Recognition Certificate confirming the reassignment of their Legal Sex from female to male.

Neither of the Appellants had undergone a Hysterectomy or a Phalloplasty and so retained both their internal and external female genitalia and the possibility of female reproductive capacity if they ceased their Sex Affirmation Treatment regime. Both Appellants considered their innate sex to be male, had lived clearly male lives for a significant period, had undergone male chest reconstruction surgery and had been receiving Testosterone treatment for a medically significant period. The difference between the medical treatments these Appellants had undergone and that undergone by 'Kevin' was that Kevin had additionally undergone a hysterectomy with bilateral oophorectomy.

As the sections quoted below make clear, although the word 'gender' is used in the title and body of the WA Act, it is clear from the context of the use of 'gender' and the definitions contained in the WA Act that those drafting the act used the word 'gender' as a euphemism for 'sex'. The High Court judgment in *AB and AH v WA* generally adopts the same linguistic practice.

The parts of the WA Act that were critically examined and interpreted in *AB and AH v WA* were sections 3, 14 and 15(1)(b)(ii).

Section 14 requires that a person making an application for a reassignment of Legal Sex is first required to have undergone a 'reassignment procedure' defined in section 3 of the WA Act as:

> 'a medical or surgical procedure (or a combination of such procedures) to alter the genitals and other gender characteristics of a person, identified by a birth certificate as male or female, so that the person will be identified as a person of the opposite sex'.

Section 3 of the WA Act defines 'gender characteristics' as:

> 'the physical characteristics by virtue of which a person is identified as male or female.'

These sections of the WA Act establish a requirement for physical bodily change that is different from that in the NSW Births, Deaths & Marriages Registration Act ('NSW Act') in that it expands the type of treatment required from 'a surgical procedure'[101] to 'a medical or surgical procedure', while at the same time expanding the focus of that medical treatment from 'a person's reproductive organs'[102] to all of the culturally significant sexually differentiated aspects of a person.

The High Court determined that sections 3 and 14 were satisfied in this case because the court found that the Sex Affirmation Treatment undergone by the Appellants, namely chest reconstruction surgery and Testosterone treatment, significantly altered the Appellants' genitalia and was a medical and surgical procedure sufficient to meet the requirements of the WA Act.

Section 15(1)(b)(ii) of the WA Act also provides that before a Recognition Certificate can issue, the WA Act Gender Reassignment Board must also be satisfied that the person to whom they issue such a certificate:

> 'has adopted the lifestyle and has the gender characteristics of a person of the gender to which the person has been reassigned'.

The High Court identified the sole reason for the WA Act Board's initial refusal to issue a Recognition Certificate to the Appellants to be their finding that:

> 'The fact of having a female reproductive system is inconsistent with being male. Because it is inconsistent with being male, it is inconsistent with being identified as male.'[103]

In determining the construction to be placed upon section 15(1)(b)(ii), the High Court found that the objects of the WA Act dealing with the reassignment of Legal Sex were remedial and beneficial and therefore required that the requirements of section 15(1)(b)(ii) 'be given a fair and liberal interpretation'[104] and so determined that the Board should have been satisfied that section 15(1)(b)(ii) required no more than that Applicants be accepted as male by members of the WA society in everyday life based upon their 'observable physical characteristics'.[105]

In so doing, however, the High Court said:[106]

> 'The construction placed upon s 15(1)(b)(ii) and the identification which is its concern, does not mean that a recognition certificate is to be provided based only upon a person's external appearance, and that person's belief about his or her gender [sic]. Section 14 must be satisfied before a person can apply for a certificate.'

---

101 Section 32A of the NSW Act.

102 Ibid.

103 *AB v Western Australia and AH v Western Australia* [2011] HCA 42 ('*AB and AH v WA*'), para. 12.

104 Ibid., para. 38.

105 Ibid., para. 40.

106 Ibid., para. 39.

Of significance to the decision were the accepted facts that:

- the effect of the Testosterone treatment undertaken by the Appellants had been profound in that it had not only caused them to undergo clitoral growth and have the voices, body shapes, musculature, hair distribution, general appearance and demeanour by virtue of which a person is identified as male', but had affected their internal genitalia such that they were no longer functional in a female way;[107]
- the Appellants had refrained from undergoing a hysterectomy because their Testosterone treatment had already ceased their menses and they wished to retain their internal organs because they believed that they might be beneficial for a future Phalloplasty procedure if advances in that procedure made that procedure a more safe and feasible one;[108] and
- the evidence of the Appellants was that they would continue their Testosterone treatment indefinitely and expert evidence confirmed not only that the effect of such treatment was that the Appellants would remain infertile, but that Affirmed Males invariably did maintain Testosterone treatment indefinitely.[109]

The High Court's judgment in *AB and AH v WA* has been generally welcomed as being a humane construction of the WA Act and understood to provide a less stringent requirement for physical bodily change than that required in States and Territories which have adopted the New South Wales model.

As discussed above, both the WA Act and the Sexual Reassignment Act 1988 (SA) ('SA Act') have a dual system for determining an application to reassign Legal Sex; namely a statutory requirement for prerequisite physical bodily change and an assessment process (by a UK-style Board in the Western Australia instance and a magistrate in South Australia) to confirm that the applicant's 'lifestyle' and 'gender characteristics' are consistent with their Affirmed Sex declared in the application.

The inclusion of the assessment process and the 'lifestyle test' in the WA Act adds a requirement of normality of gender expression that is utterly absent in the NSW Act with its sole focus on the body and the undergoing of a 'sex affirmation procedure'. I presume that the intent of both the WA and the South Australian legislation was that the introduction of an assessment of 'lifestyle' or gender expression was to provide a safeguard for the authenticity of the process of the reassignment of Legal Sex for the community in circumstances where the statutory requirement for physical bodily change had been made less restrictive by the inclusion of 'medical' as well as surgical treatment in an effort to maintain

107 Ibid., para. 17.
108 Ibid., para. 15.
109 Ibid., para. 16.

a balance between the interests of the individual ('Self') and the community ('Other').

While the requirement of normative gender expression conflicts with what I have described as a human right to free gender expression, the compromise of that right is apparently intended to balance the individual and community rights – which are often at odds. Examples of this socio/legal trade-off are laws that restrict 'freedom of speech' in the interests of community peace and order. The question posed in all such cases is whether the loss of individual rights is reasonable and justified.

In New South Wales medical professionals, whose certification is relied upon to confirm compliance with the statutory test for bodily change contained in section 32A of the NSW Act, consider breasts to be a reproductive organ and consider that the combined effect of chest reconstruction surgery and significant Testosterone treatment on the female body satisfies the New South Wales legislative requirement for a 'sex affirmation procedure' for an Affirmed Male person.

Thus, perhaps ironically, people who seek to have their Legal Sex reassigned in New South Wales who have undergone a 'sex affirmation procedure' have fewer legislative requirements to meet than in Western Australia, as they do not have to be assessed by a statutory Board and demonstrate any particular gendered lifestyle. While the requirement of normative gender expression conflicts with what I have described as a human right to free gender expression in the WA Act, it does so in the interests of balancing the individual and community rights involved where there is apparently an intention in the WA Act to impose less stringent requirements for physical change.

Given the comparatively minor impact that hormone therapy has on the appearance and function of the sexually differentiated aspects of the male body as well as the significantly greater physical, sexual power and cultural significance of male genitalia, however, it is hard to imagine the High Court's construction of the requirements of sections 14 and 15(1)(ii) of the WA Act in *AB and AH v WA* being met by anything less than Genital Reassignment Surgery for male-bodied people who seek to have their Legal Sex recognised or reassigned as female. An additional factor justifying this opinion is that standard Genital Reassignment Surgery for Affirmed Female persons is more readily accessible than the equivalent Sex Affirmation Surgery for Affirmed Male persons.

It then follows arguably that, as a result of *AB and AH v WA*, the legislative requirements concerning medical treatment and bodily rehabilitation or change required by both the WA Act and the NSW Act as prerequisites for a recognition or reassignment of Legal Sex are effectively the same, but different for each sex.

In *AB and AH v WA*, the High Court of Australia construed the WA Act as establishing a statutory method for the recognition and reassignment of an individual's Legal Sex that was somewhat similar in approach to that applied in the *Re Kevin* decision. Both approaches seek to be inclusive in the assignment of people to the two available categories of Legal Sex and are not prescriptive as to which of the sexually differentiated characteristics of the body requires alteration. Both approaches seek to balance individual and community interests by having regard to the understanding and expectations of the community concerning the meaning of male/man and female/woman. Significantly, at least by implication and perhaps axiomatically, in striking that balance of interests both the High Court's *AB and AH v WA* construction of the WA Act and Chisholm J's *Re Kevin* construction of the Marriage Act treat the circumstances of an Affirmed Male and an Affirmed Female person differently.

The High Court in *AB and AH v WA* made clear that in the case of a female-bodied person seeking to be reassigned to the male Legal Sex, sterilisation was of no relevance to the requirement for Sex Affirmation Treatment in the *WA Act*. It may well be that Chisholm J would have adopted the same approach in *Re Kevin* if he had been met with the same factual circumstances. Similarly, in seeking to balance and honour both public and individual interests in the case of a female-bodied person seeking to be reassigned to the male Legal Sex, both *AB and AH v WA* concerning the WA Act and *Re Kevin* concerning the Marriage Act give significance to the individual's external bodily appearance and gender expression and not the precise results of the physical bodily change brought about by the required Sex Affirmation Treatment in evaluating whether or not a person sufficiently conforms with the ordinary every day understanding of the community of what it means to be a man.

4.1.3. NSW Registrar of Births, Deaths and Marriages v Norrie

In *NSW Registrar of Births, Deaths and Marriages v Norrie* [2014] HCA 11 ('*Norrie*'), the High Court of Australia construed the Births, Deaths and Marriages Registration Act 1995 (NSW) (the 'NSW Act') so as to rule that under Part 5A of that Act 'it was within the Registrar's power to record in the Register that the sex of the respondent, Norrie, was, as she said in her application, "non-specific"',[110] rather than 'male' or 'female'.

The High Court referred to the following provisions of the NSW Act in order to determine its purpose, intent and operation concerning its recognition of a changed Legal Sex status as an aspect of legal identity for a person not born in New South Wales:

- Section 3(d) of the NSW Act set out its relevant objects as:

> 'the keeping of registers for recording and preserving information about births, adoptions, deaths, marriages, registered relationships, changes of name and changes of sex in perpetuity ...'

[110] *NSW Registrar of Births, Deaths and Marriages v Norrie* [2014] HCA 11 ('*Norrie*'), para. 2.

- Section 6 of the NSW Act describes the Registrar's statutory role as:

> '(a) to establish and maintain the registers necessary for the purposes of this Act
> ...
> (a1) to maintain the integrity of the Register and to seek to prevent identity fraud associated with the Register and the information extracted from the Register, and
> (b) to administer the registration system established by this Act and ensure that the system operates efficiently, effectively and economically, and
> (c) to ensure that this Act is administered in the way best calculated to achieve its objects.'

- Section 43(1) of the NSW Act that requires the Registrar to 'maintain a register or registers of registrable events.'
- Section 4(1) of the NSW Act defines a 'registrable event' as 'a birth, adoption or discharge of adoption, change of name, change of sex, death or marriage.'
- A sex affirmation procedure is defined in section 32A as:

> 'a surgical procedure involving the alteration of a person's reproductive organs carried out:
> (a) for the purpose of assisting a person to be considered to be a member of the opposite sex, or
> (b) to correct or eliminate ambiguities relating to the sex of the person.'

- Section 32DA provides that a person whose birth was not registered in New South Wales may apply to register that person's sex.
- Section 32DA(1) of the Act provides that:

> 'A person who is 18 or above:
> (a) who is an Australian citizen or permanent resident of Australia, and
> (b) who lives, and has lived for at least one year, in New South Wales, and
> (c) who has undergone a sex affirmation procedure, and
> (d) who is not married, and
> (e) whose birth is not registered under this Act or a corresponding law,
> may apply to the Registrar, in a form approved by the Registrar, for the registration of the person's sex in the Register.'

- Section 32DB of the NSW Act requires that an application under section 32DA be accompanied by a:

> 'statutory declarations by 2 doctors, or by 2 medical practitioners ... verifying that the person the subject of the application has undergone a sex affirmation procedure.'

- Section 32DC of the NSW Act set out the Registrar's role in response to an application under section 32DA:

  '(1) The Registrar is to determine an application under section 32DA by registering the person's change of sex or refusing to register the person's change of sex.
  (2) Before registering a person's change of sex, the Registrar may require the applicant to provide such particulars relating to the change of sex as may be prescribed by the regulations.'

- Section 32J of the Act provides that:

  '(1) A person the record of whose sex is registered under this Part is, for the purposes of, but subject to, any law of New South Wales, a person of the sex so registered.
  (2) A person to whom an interstate recognised details certificate relates is, for the purposes of, but subject to, any law of New South Wales, a person of the sex stated in the certificate.'

The following facts of *Norrie* are apparent from the Reasons for Judgement of the High Court of Australia as well as those of the New South Wales Court of Appeal from whence the appeal to the High Court of Australia originated:[111]

(a) The Respondent 'Norrie', who was born in Scotland, was originally male bodied and initially assigned to the male Legal Sex in Scotland;
(b) In 1989 Norrie undertook Genital Reassignment Surgery specifically appropriate for a person affirming the female sex. She subsequently relocated to Australia and resides in the State of New South Wales;
(c) Norrie made an application to the New South Wales Registrar of Births, Deaths & Marriages to have a 'Recognised Details Certificate' issue to confirm the recognition of her changed Legal Sex pursuant to section 32DA of the NSW Act as her own chosen Legal Sex category of 'not specified';[112]
(d) In support of her case Norrie explained her desire to have her Legal Sex registered as 'non-specific' because she did not feel herself to be either male or female. Norrie gave evidence that she identified the source of her feeling of 'ambiguity' to be that although she was born with male reproductive organs she identified herself as having a 'non-specific gender identity'. Norrie attested that she had undertaken female Genital Reassignment Surgery, not to affirm her innate female sex, but to eliminate the 'ambiguity' she experienced in relation to her 'gender identity'. Norrie maintained that her Genital Reassignment Surgery had not been totally functionally 'successful'

111 Ibid., para. 6.
112 Ibid., para. 20.

in terms of permitting her to fully function as a female and had, as a result, failed to resolve her feelings of 'ambiguity' in relation to her 'gender identity'.
(e) Norrie declared that, in her opinion, identifying herself as male or female would be a false statement;[113] and
(f) In support of her application as required by Part 5A of the NSW Act, Norrie supplied to the Registrar pro forma statutory declarations by two doctors that supported her application as required by section 32DB of the NSW Act by confirming that Norrie had undergone a 'sex affirmation procedure'.

The High Court summarised the submissions of the Appellant Registrar at paragraphs 28 and 29 of the judgment. There are two essential parts to those submissions:

(a) That on its plain terms the NSW Act 'does not contemplate a range of categories of sex additional to the "opposite" sexes of male and female. In particular, the definition of "sex affirmation procedure" in s32A suggests a process of seeking to become male or female, given that s32A(a) states that the sex affirmation procedure is carried out for the purpose of "assisting a person to be considered to be a member of the opposite sex"; and to speak of the opposite sex is necessarily to speak only of male or female'; and 'it is reasonable to expect that an intention to recognise another category of "sex" would have been expressly stated in the Act. In this regard, the definition of "transgender" in Pt 3A of the *Anti-Discrimination Act* does refer to a person being of an "indeterminate" sex; but, significantly, this language was not used in Pt 5A of the Act'; and
(b) 'unacceptable confusion would flow from the acceptance of more than two categories of sex given that s 32J of the Act affects the operation of other laws which assume the binary division of sex.'

The High Court summarised the various submissions of the Respondent Norrie at paragraphs 30 and 31 of the judgment:

(a) '[T]he purpose of the Register is to state the truth about matters recorded in the Register to the greatest possible extent.'
(b) 'If the Act proceeded on the assumption that every person was male or female, then s 32A(b) would be superfluous because any change of sex would fall within the scope of s 32A(a). A sex affirmation procedure described in s 32A(b) of the Act, the purpose of which is to "correct or eliminate ambiguities relating to the sex of the person", was … predicated upon legislative recognition that not everyone may be classified as male or female.'

[113] Ibid., para. 30.

(c) Norrie had undergone a sex affirmation procedure, the precondition of an application under section 32DA, 'but Norrie's sex remained ambiguous so that it would be to record misinformation in the Register to classify her as male or female.'
(d) 'Norrie might more accurately be assigned to a category of sex such as "intersex" or "transgender". On this view, the expression "change of sex" in s 32DC does not mean changing from one sex (male or female) to another (female or male): a reference to change of sex simply means an "alteration" of a person's sex so that registration of categories of sex such as "transgender" and "intersex" is within the scope of the Registrar's powers under s 32DC.'

The High Court identified four significant bases to its rulings concerning the construction of the Act:[114]

(1) Section 32A of the NSW Act determined that 'a sex affirmation procedure is defined by reference to its purpose, not its outcome' and that section 32DA(1)(c) does not refer to a 'successful' sex affirmation procedure."[115] This finding is important as it confirms the High Court's construction of the NSW Act's understanding of the undergoing of Sex Affirmation Treatment compatible with *Re Kevin* and the High Court's construction of the *WA Act* in *AB and AH v WA* to the effect that such medical treatment, including Genital Reassignment Surgery, is a personally rehabilitative process in and of itself and does not have a legally relevant measure of success.
(2) The NSW Act required the Registrar to receive information from applicants and informants of registrable events, but that section 32DC did not permit the Registrar to make 'any moral or social judgements' or to attend to 'the resolution of medical questions or the formation of a view about the outcome of a sex affirmation procedure' or to make a decision in respect of a Part 5A application other than to either register or refuse to register the change of Legal Sex sought in the application. Contrast the Registrar's role with the role of the WA Board in the High Court's construction of the *WA Act* in *AB and AH v WA*.
(3) Section 32DC incorporates a legislative assumption that the first registration or assignment of a person's Legal Sex in New South Wales may differ from that first assigned to the person elsewhere. Hence, a section 32DA application under Part 5A of the NSW Act is properly determined by the Registrar pursuant to section 32DC, but in so doing the Registrar is obliged to either register or refuse to register a person's change of Legal Sex as proposed in the application – without correction or interpretation.

[114] Ibid., para. 15.
[115] Ibid., para. 15.

(4) Part 5A of the NSW Act is to be construed and applied 'in a context of express legislative recognition of the existence of persons of "indeterminate sex"' contained in the Anti-Discrimination Act 1977 (NSW). The Anti-Discrimination Act 1977 (NSW) introduced protection from discrimination based on the attribute of 'being transgender or a transgender person ... whether or not the person is a recognised transgender person', defined in section 38A(c) to include anyone:

> 'who, being of indeterminate sex, identifies as a member of a particular sex by living as a member of that sex, and includes a reference to the person being thought of as a transgender person, whether the person is, or was, in fact a transgender person.'

The High Court considering itself entitled to look to the Anti-Discrimination Act 1977 (NSW) to determine the construction of the provisions of Part 5A of the NSW Act because both these parts of their respective acts were introduced by the same 1996 Amending Act.

The High Court's reasoning in reaching this decision can be set out as follows:

(1) Because the definition of 'sex affirmation procedure' in Part 5A of the NSW Act refers to the correction or elimination of 'ambiguities relating to the sex of the person' as a purpose of such medical treatment and because section 38A(c) of the Anti-Discrimination Act 1977 (NSW) refers to people 'of indeterminate sex' as a part of its definition of 'transgender or a transgender person', Part 5A of the NSW Act contemplates a third category of Legal Sex indicative of an absence of Legal Sex classification for those individuals who consider themselves not to be of the two available registrable Legal Sex classifications of Male and Female.[116]
(2) In the absence of clear fraud in respect of an application under Part 5A of the NSW Act, it is beyond the Registrar's power to interrogate an individual concerning their application. As there was no evidence of fraud put before the court concerning Norrie's application, the Registrar was obliged to accept it at face value and either register the new classification of Legal Sex as sought by Norrie or reject it.
(3) The Registrar was obliged to register Norrie's Legal Sex as 'non-specific', given that her application under Part 5A of the NSW Act complied with the requirements of that part of the NSW Act and the act contemplated a third Legal Sex category indicating no Legal Sex.
(4) Because section 32J of the Act provides that a person's changed Legal Sex as recognised under Part 5A of the NSW Act is subject to the operation of other New South Wales laws, any legal and social problems caused by a person

116 Ibid., paras. 32 and 37.

trying to live with a Legal Sex indicating no Legal Sex can be adequately dealt with as the need arises from time to time under other New South Wales law.

The following passages from the High Court's judgment in *Norrie* are useful in better understanding that reasoning:

> 'The Registrar's submission that the Act recognises only male or female as registrable classes of sex must be accepted. But to accept that submission does not mean that the Act requires that this classification can apply, or is to be applied, to everyone. And there is nothing in the Act which suggests that the Registrar is entitled, much less duty-bound, to register the classification of a person's sex inaccurately as male or female having regard to the information which the Act requires to be provided by the applicant.'[117]

> 'The Registrar's submission must be rejected at the point at which it insists that the Registrar is required to decide whether he or she is satisfied (let alone that it has been demonstrated objectively) that, despite an application showing persisting ambiguity in the sex of the applicant following a sex affirmation procedure, the applicant's sex should be recorded in the Register as being either male or female. The registration of a change of sex records the facts supplied by the application so long as the application is supported in accordance with s 32DB.'[118]

> 'The provision of the Act which acknowledges "ambiguities" and the context of the 1996 Amending Act, which referred to persons of "indeterminate sex", are a sufficient indication that the Act recognises that, as this Court observed in *AB v Western Australia*, the sex of a person is not … in every case unequivocally male or female.'[119]

> 'As the Registrar acknowledged, the circumstance that s 32J operates subject to other laws of New South Wales serves to ensure that where another Act does differentiate between male and female it will prevail over s 32J so that an individual is not left in a "legal no-man's land".'[120]

Their Honours unanimously concluded:

> 'The Act does not require that people who, having undergone a sex affirmation procedure, remain of indeterminate sex – that is, neither male nor female – must be registered, inaccurately, as one or the other. The Act itself recognises that a

117 Ibid., para. 32.
118 Ibid., para. 36.
119 Ibid., para. 37 (footnotes omitted).
120 Ibid., para. 43.

> person may be other than male or female and therefore may be taken to permit the registration sought, as "non-specific".'[121]

While it is clear, particularly at paragraph 37 of the judgment, that in *Norrie* the High Court of Australia was motivated by a genuine desire to legally acknowledge the existence and interests of people who experience Difference or diversity in sexual formation, *Norrie* has, in fact, construed Part 5A of the NSW Act in a way that results in the record of the Legal Sex of people like Norrie being less accurate and meaningful to the community of New South Wales than it was before the decision; a 'Non-Specific' Legal Sex having nothing to say to the community about a person's physical strength and sexual capacity or an individual person's biological sex.

Whereas before *Norrie* the New South Wales community were able to use a person's Legal Sex to discern his or her male or female physical strength and sexual capacity, after *Norrie* they are unable to understand or discern anything about such sexually differentiated physical characteristics of a person with a Birth Certificate or other cardinal identity document indicating their Legal Sex as 'Non-Specific'. Where this information is relevant, those involved will be obliged to try to work their way through what is likely to be an awkward, embarrassing and potentially offensive and litigious ad hoc process for determining the sex, male or female, into which the individual's body best legally fits for a specific purpose or activity.

In *Norrie*, the 'ghost' of an anachronistic *Corbett*-like belief in the power of a person's genitalia to determine or resolve their innate sex identity seems to haunt the High Court's judgment when at paragraph 11 the High Court uncritically reports that 'Norrie considered that the surgery did not resolve her sexual ambiguity.'

The High Court also reflected positively on Norrie's submissions concerning the construction to be placed on section 32A(b):

> 'A sex affirmation procedure described in s 32A(b) of the Act, the purpose of which is to "correct or eliminate ambiguities relating to the sex of the person", was said to be predicated upon legislative recognition that not everyone may be classified as male or female. In this case, the sex affirmation procedure, which is a precondition of an application under s 32DA, was carried out, but Norrie's sex remained ambiguous so that it would be to record misinformation in the Register to classify her as male or female. There is evident force in this submission.'

Look again at section 32A(b) of the NSW Act quoted at the beginning of this section of this chapter. With respect, I suggest that any ordinary reading of that section's definition of 'sex affirmation procedure' would suggest precisely the

[121] Ibid., para. 46.

opposite meaning to that proposed in Norrie's submission. Surely section 32A of the NSW Act, either in its legislative context or read by itself, can only represent a legislative intention that a 'sex affirmation procedure' is undergone for the precise purpose of assisting those who undergo it, including those whose sex is ambiguous, to be perceived of and legally classified for the purpose of New South Wales identity laws as having either a Male or a Female Legal Sex.

The High Court's construction of section 32A(b) of the NSW Act would also appear to proceed on the erroneous presumption that only people with the condition of Transsexualism, and not people living with other conditions of diversity in sexual formation, would seek relief under Part 5A of the NSW Act. I contend that the use the High Court made of the quite differently focused and linguistically tortured Anti-Discrimination Act 1977 (NSW) as a critical aid in the construction of the purpose and function of Part 5A of the NSW Act in *Norrie* was prone to distort the distinct meaning and purpose of the NSW Act.

With the respect properly due to the High Court of Australia, I contend that the High Court erred in not requiring that the construction they placed upon the meaning of Legal Sex and the categories of Legal Sex available under Part 5A of the NSW Act be consistent with the legal regime for the assignment of Legal Sex otherwise contained in the NSW Act so that the same concept of Legal Sex could be logically and consistently applied to all of the people of New South Wales who have their Legal Sex identity assigned by the Act, pursuant to Part 5A of the NSW Act and otherwise.

In my view, there is nothing in the NSW Act itself or in its purpose of establishing and recording legal identity that suggests that the New South Wales parliament contemplated that the fundamental Male/Female categories of Legal Sex as legal identity could be different for a particular minority of people within the New South Wales community. As a result of *Norrie*, while all other members of the New South Wales community may possess only a 'Male' or a 'Female' Legal Sex, the small minority to whom Part 5A of the NSW Act applies may possess a 'Male', 'Female' or 'Non-Specific' Legal Sex.

I believe that there is an inherent risk of both social and personal discrimination when legal identity laws do not operate uniformly or universally across all people in a community. In my view, it is not in the interests of any member of the New South Wales community, and certainly not in the interests of those who have need to have recourse to Part 5A of the NSW Act, that the legal identity laws of New South Wales permit Part 5A applicants to have a different category of Legal Sex than the rest of the New South Wales community. Anyone who possesses a 'Non-Specific' Legal Sex will be singled out and is less likely to be able to assimilated into and accepted on equal terms with others and is more likely to be treated differently in a way that Part 5A of the NSW Act was surely intended to avoid.

While the judgment by the High Court of Australia in *Norrie* may not construe the NSW Act as providing for diverse Legal Sex categories, such as the optional 'male', 'female', 'unspecified/indeterminate/intersex', 'unspecified', 'indeterminate' or 'intersex' provided for in the Births, Deaths and Marriages Registration Act 1997 (ACT) ('ACT Act'), as a result of *Norrie*, the NSW Act joins the ACT Act in being the only two instances in the law of Australia where the inclusive approach to the assignment and reassignment of Legal Sex does not apply.

In *Norrie* there is no apparent recognition of Legal Sex as a socio-legal construct with a primary cultural purpose, as spelt out in *Re Kevin*, of sorting human sex and gender diversity into the two culturally recognised functional Legal Sex categories of 'Male' and 'Female' in the interests of an equal and ordered society. By contrast, *Norrie* and the ACT Act seek to legally recognise human diversity in sexual formation in a confused and imperfect way and on the error-prone basis of self-identification. This approach is hardly sufficient to satisfy the purpose of the NSW Act that the Register of legal identity 'state the truth about matters recorded in the Register to the greatest possible extent'.

While it has been popularly claimed that *Norrie* interprets the NSW Act to establish a non-binary 'intersex' third Legal Sex, given the High Court's statement in *Norrie* that 'the Act recognises only male or female as registrable classes of sex' but that does not mean 'that the Act requires that this classification can apply, or is to be applied, to everyone',[122] I think it more accurate to describe the new category of Legal Sex constructed out of Part 5A of the NSW Act by the High Court as not a 'third' Legal Sex, but a catch-all Legal Sex indicating no Legal Sex classification or a Non-Sex Legal Sex.

Although many have received the decision in *Norrie* as a welcome recognition of the right people to have self-perceived gender expression or gender identity recognised as a legal identity, the fact is that under the NSW Act such recognition is available only to those who have undergone a sex affirmation procedure and would therefore only be applicable to those people with a Pan-gender or Non-gender gender expression who also experience Transsexualism and some other intense conditions.

Notwithstanding the High Court's dismissal of the 'inconvenience proposition', I agree with the Appellant Registrar's submission that a Legal Sex indicating no Legal Sex must, axiomatically, assign individuals to whom it applies to a 'legal no-man's land'. Except perhaps for those who might live within GLBT communities, a Legal Sex of 'Non-Specific' Sex must also consign individuals to a social no-man's land whenever the individual's Legal Sex becomes relevant in their day-to-day lives; such as in sport, employment or any instance where issues of access to single-sex spaces or activities arise. While the High Court recognised that having a third Non-Sex Legal Sex was bound to create legal anomalies, it was confident that such anomalies would be able to be legally resolved. But the question remains as to how much stress and conflict will arise for both the

[122] Ibid., para. 32.

individual concerned and the community in the course of the social and legal processes involved in such resolution.

In its construction of Part 5A of the NSW Act, the High Court of Australia appears to have given individual self-perception and sense of self a greater weight than the need of the New South Wales community for an effective, objective, understandable and reliable system for the identification of a person's physical strength and sexual potential based upon their Legal Sex then as is apparent in the balance of the NSW Act.

The judgments of both the High Court of Australia and the New South Wales Court of Appeal below in *Norrie* contain a lack of clarity concerning the meaning of core concepts of sex, gender, diversity in sexual formation, diversity in gender expression and Legal Sex. In particular, in construing the NSW Act, both judgments appear to confuse Transsexualism and Transgenderism and to equate biological sex with both gender expression/identity and Legal Sex. *Norrie* conflates concepts of sex and gender, both in terms of self-perception and the gaze of Other, and, in so doing, creates a special 'No-Sex Legal Sex' category of legal identity that is not otherwise recognised within the NSW Act or in the everyday life and laws of New South Wales.

Finally, it is both ironic and instructive that while the High Court's judgment in *Norrie* recognised Norrie as being entitled to have an assigned Legal Sex that was neither Male or Female, the High Court chose to use female pronouns to describe Norrie throughout the judgment explaining: 'The respondent uses, and these reasons use, the personal pronouns "she" and "her" to refer to the respondent.'[123] In the interests of common sense and being understood, I have done the same.

V. CONCLUSION

The Questionnaire provokes an important and practical discussion.

In Australia, especially as a result of *Norrie*, but also as a result of the need for uniform legislation across all States and Territories, new laws need to be drafted concerning the reassignment of Legal Sex and the right of free gender expression. Throughout the world, new legislation, human rights instruments and medical treatment protocols are being considered in order to recognise the legal and human rights and medical needs of people who experience Difference or diversity in human sexual formation and gender expression.

The judgment of the Full Court of the Family Court of Australia in *Re: Jamie* demonstrates how the inclusion of the condition of Transsexualism and its generalised mis-description in the DSM and other international diagnostic guides not only results in doubt about diagnosis and conflicting and confused

[123] Ibid., para. 2 and footnote 4.

medical opinion but can result in crucial cultural and legal misunderstanding resulting in the loss of critical legal and human rights; including the right of children to receive therapeutic medical treatment.

In circumstances of general ignorance, prejudice and mystification, the powerful and visible cultural philosophies I have described as 'Anti-sex/dichotomy', 'Pan/Trans-Gender Rights' and 'Political Intersex' have exerted an undue influence on medical, legal, academic, government and community perception resulting in a loss of clarity of thought and discourse concerning the experience of diversity or Difference in sexual formation and gender expression; variously encouraging the substitution of 'gender' with its variable meaning for 'sex' with its fixed meaning, the conflation of Transsexualism and Transgenderism as simply 'Trans/Trans*' or 'Transgender', and the misconceived expansion of Legal Sex classifications beyond Male and Female. At the same time, a politically refined 'Intersex' identity has become legally privileged and distinguished as 'biological' from the 'psychological' 'Trans/Trans*'.

I argue that in order to empower culturally sensible and enduring law reform, the first step is to conceptually 'clean house' or get back to basics concerning our understanding of people who experience diversity in sexual formation and gender expression by recognising the fundamental difference between sexual formation issues and gender expression issues.

And to meaningfully advocate legal rights in respect of Legal Sex reassignment requires a back-to-basics appreciation of the original socio-legal basis and purpose of the assignment of Legal Sex as an aspect of a person's legal identity.

I conclude that the concept of Legal Sex as an aspect of a fixed legal identity recognised nationally and internationally is incompatible with culturally, personally and temporally variable gender expression; whether self-identified or objectively assessed.

In these considerations I have benefited from reflecting on the somewhat different way in which the Honourable Richard Chisholm identifies the different Australian Common Law approaches to the assignment of Legal Sex:[124]

- 'Essentialism' – (*Corbett*);
- policy-based allocation to a category – (*Re Leber; Re Kevin; AB v State of WA*); and
- changing or bypassing the categories – (*Norrie v NSW Registrar of Births Deaths and Marriage*).

124 The Honourable Richard Chisholm, Adjunct Professor, ANU College of Law, Australia, '*Varieties of decision-making: Reflections on deciding Re Kevin*', slide 10, presented at the conference in support of the research project on 'The Legal Status of Transsexual and Transgender Persons' throughout the world held at the University of Hong Kong on 6 and 7 September 2013.

My own model legislation concerning Legal Sex is based upon my hypothesis that a primary concern of the traditional Australian Inclusive approach to the assignment of only a Male or a Female Legal Sex to every citizen was the practical importance to the community of being able to identify the physical sexual potential and bodily strength of a person, in particular the male-bodied person, on the basis of their legal identity.

I believe that this practical underlying reason for the existence of Legal Sex remains important to the Australian community for a limited but significant range of day-to-day activities, such as with whom they physically compete in sport and with whom they share specific single-sex spaces like female refuges intended to provide a place free of male-bodied physical strength and sexual potential. While domestic physical abuse against females and male violence remain significant cultural problems, I do not see Legal Sex losing any of its core cultural or legal significance. In this context, the way an individual feels about their sex identity or gender identity is of comparatively little practical community significance.

A third Legal Sex to indicate an absence of the assignment of a Legal Sex or multiple categories of Legal Sex offer significant opportunity for conflict and discrimination rather than any benefit, to either the community or the individual, in terms of practical living, community or international legal identification, social inclusion or rights, whereas the Inclusive approach was intended to ameliorate such problems. In any case, whatever the categories of Legal Sex chosen and however they are assigned, the same concepts should apply to the whole community and not only a minority who need to have their Legal Sex reassigned. Categories of Legal Sex also need to be able to travel well; making sense and conforming to international norms.

Laws concerning Legal Sex should ignore age and marital status; enabling minors and married people to obtain a reassignment of their Legal Sex.

Laws concerning Legal Sex should provide an unconditional full reassignment of Legal Sex without religious or other exemption.

A practical and fair system for the reassignment of Legal Sex does not create legal hierarchies and provides the same rules for all people who seek to have their Legal Sex reassigned. In such a legal system, for example, infants whose genital formation does not clearly indicate a Legal Sex category can be assigned to one of the two categories of Legal Sex without the need for non-therapeutic infant Genital Reassignment Surgery on the basis that they can have that Legal Sex reassigned later if needed (see my 'secondary pathway' below).

Legal Sex assignment should also studiously ignore changeable medical and psychological diagnostic terms and confused and confusing minority terminology.

To the extent possible, an individual seeking a reassignment of Legal Sex should not be required to conform to cultural norms of sex-appropriate gender expression in a way not required of the general community.

My suggested model Legal Sex Reassignment regime, incorporating these considerations, offers only the choice of a Male or a Female Legal Sex and otherwise has only two pathways or qualifications for all applicants:

(1) A primary pathway for those applicants who are able to provide the reports of two suitably qualified doctors certifying that they had undergone a 'sex affirmation procedure' defined as:

> 'A surgical or medical procedure involving the person's reproductive organs carried out for the purpose of assisting a person to be considered to be a member of their affirmed sex.'

(2) A secondary pathway for applicants who are unable to satisfy the requirement of the primary pathway, due to age, health or financial reasons, but who are able to satisfy an expert medico-legal board that a recognition or reassignment of their Legal Sex should nevertheless be made based upon the principle that it is the fundamental task of the board, in a legal and social context that assigns all human beings in the community into either the Male or the Female Legal Sex, to assign applicants to one Legal Sex or the other, including individuals whose characteristics are not uniformly those of one or other biological sex, based upon a *Re Kevin* style holistic objective assessment of which Legal Sex is a best fit for both the applicant and the community.

In my view this dual pathway model, based on the Inclusive approach, provides a reasonable balance between the needs of the individual and community concerning Legal Sex as an aspect of legal identity and provides the law with a compassionate discretionary capacity.

While I do not consider that gender expression should be an aspect of a person's legal identity, I do consider that freedom of gender expression is a fundamental human right and that such right should have legal protection. The right to free unlabelled gender expression should be incorporated in both State and Federal anti-discrimination legalisation and Australian human rights instruments.

For all this chapter's discussion about legal identity and the law, however, in my opinion timely, affordable and safe access to age appropriate Sex Affirmation Treatment continues to be the primary human rights issue for people living with Difference or diversity in sexual formation in Australia today.

Neither Phase 1 nor Phase 2 hormonal adolescent Sex Affirmation Treatment should require court authorisation or be delayed. The Australian government should urgently act to make this legislatively certain. Access to Genital Reassignment Surgery is incredibly difficult and expensive for most Australians. The Medicare system should be urgently updated to provide specific Item Numbers for all three phases of Sex Affirmation Treatment and their ancillary cosmetic therapies for each affirmed sex.

The most practical strategy to alleviate suffering and improve the overall health and welfare of Australians who experience Transsexualism and other similar intersex conditions is the establishment of several strategically situated publicly funded e-medicine capable Centres of Excellence skilled in the treatment of the medical and psychological needs those who experience Difference in sexual formation as well as their families and loved ones. Such Centres of Excellence should also be able to offer education and expert advice to courts, medical practitioners, educational institutions, health institutions, the workplace, government and the community. Through such Centres of Excellence the specific health and welfare needs of older Australians living with Transsexualism can be properly addressed so that these Australians need not have the later years of their lives degraded by the same experiences of shame, humiliation and ostracism as pervaded and degraded their earlier years.

People who live with Transsexualism and other similar disorders of sexual development need to be seen and re-appreciated by both community and government as survivors of considerable physical and social disability who can experience mental illness if left unsupported, untreated and punished for their Difference.

While I expect that confusion and debate will continue about the accurate recognition of the different interests, needs and rights of Australians who experience diversity in sexual formation and gender expression and the nature and purpose of Legal Sex, I am optimistic that the discourse with regard to these issues will clarify and mature in Australia and throughout the world along with the evolution of increasing cultural and legal recognition and appreciation of the Difference in each of us.

THE LEGAL STATUS OF TRANSSEXUAL AND TRANSGENDER PERSONS IN AOTEAROA NEW ZEALAND

Elisabeth McDonald* and Jack Byrne**

Contents

* Elisabeth was ably assisted by Polly Johnson in researching this piece. The law is stated as at 16 February 2015.
** Trans human rights consultant, TransAction. Formerly a Senior Human Rights Specialist at the New Zealand Human Rights Commission and Project Manager of the inquiry into discrimination experienced by transgender people.

I. TERMINOLOGY AND CULTURAL AND LEGAL CONTEXT

Aotearoa New Zealand is a common law jurisdiction, with a Parliament and legal system based on the British Westminster system of government, following colonisation in the 19th century. Māori are the indigenous people of Aotearoa and signatories to the Treaty of Waitangi, which Māori consider to allow them to retain self-governance rights and, in particular, Māori customary law.[1]

Pre-colonial Māori communities were 'inclusive of whakawāhine'[2] (a Māori term describing someone born with a male body who has a female gender identity).[3] More recently takatāpui has been reclaimed as a term to describe gay, lesbian, bisexual and trans Māori.

Today Māori whakawāhine and tangata ira tane (a Māori term describing someone born with a female body who has a male gender identity) remain

[1] Disagreements about the meaning of the English translation of the Māori concepts in the Treaty still continue. There is no doubt now, however, that the Treaty is an important constitutional document for all New Zealanders and the Crown's obligations under the Treaty, including the concept of partnership with Māori, continue to inform law and policy in Aotearoa New Zealand. See further M.S.R. Palmer, *The Treaty of Waitangi in New Zealand's Law and Constitution*, Victoria University Press, Wellington 2008; Human Rights Commission, *Human Rights in New Zealand 2010*, Wellington 2010, p. 39.

[2] Human Rights Commission, *To Be Who I Am: Report of the Inquiry into Discrimination Experienced by Transgender People*, Wellington 2008, para. 2.1. See also <www.hrc.co.nz/your-rights/social-equality/our-work/inquiry/discrimination-experienced-transgender-people> accessed 16.02.2015.

[3] Gender identity can be defined as a person's internal or deeply felt sense of being male or female, or something other. A person's gender identity may or may not correspond with their sex.

visible within takatāpui communities. A support network for Māori trans people (Tapatoru), based on the traditional concept of whānau or family, now exists. There are many predominantly Pākehā (European) or Tauiwi (non-Māori) networks.[4]

New Zealand also has a large Pacific Island population, many of whom acknowledge males who take on traditional female social roles (such as fa'afafine in Samoa and fakaleiti in Tonga).[5] It is therefore not surprising that the people who made submissions to the New Zealand Human Rights Commission's Transgender Inquiry (see further at section 2.1 below) referred to themselves using a range of terms, including transgender, male-to-female (MtF) and female-to-male (FtM) transsexuals, cross-dressers, queens, intersex, androgynous, genderqueer, takatāpui, fa'afafine, fakaleiti, whakawahine and tangata ira tane.

In this chapter, as in *To Be Who I Am: Report of the Inquiry into Discrimination Experienced by Transgender People* (the Report of the Transgender Inquiry), the term 'trans' will be used when it is necessary to use a generic term to describe all of the identities listed above.[6] That is, to describe all those 'who identify their gender in some way in opposition or outside the gender role which they are meant to fulfil as a result of their sex designation at birth.'[7]

The focus of this chapter, as elsewhere in this book, is on the issues for trans people who wish to have their 'nominated sex' (the sex they self-identify with) recognised as their legal sex (for the purposes of official identity documentation). Until the early 1990s, little recognition or accommodation was accorded in post-colonial New Zealand society to those whose legal sex did not accord with their self-identified gender. However, not all trans people wish to identify as either male or female, yet for most purposes only these two options are available and have legal and social implications. The law in New Zealand, as elsewhere, does not adequately accommodate those who wish to live outside the male/female binary.[8]

That issue is not squarely for consideration in this chapter, nor are examples of discrimination against trans people, except as part of the broader context and rationale for this work. Also outside the scope of this piece are issues of sexuality and sexual orientation. As with cisgender people (those whose sex assigned at

---

4 <www.hrc.co.nz/files/7014/2378/4851/TGI-Fact-Sheet-C.html> accessed 16.05.2015.

5 See further P.J.A. Feu'u, *Ia e Ola Malamalama I lou Fa'asinomaga: A comparative study of the fa'afafine of Samoa and the whakawahine of Aotearoa/New Zealand*, Victoria University of Wellington Master's thesis, 2013.

6 Human Rights Commission, above n. 2, para. 13. New Zealand pieces of primary legislation (statutes) do not use the terms 'trans' or 'transgender' or 'transsexual'. In secondary legislation (rules and regulations) the term 'transgender' was used but not defined in reg. 190 of the Corrections Regulations 2005 (repealed by reg. 5 of the Corrections Amendment Regulations (No. 2) 2013: see 4.1.4.3 below). There are a few references to 'gender identity' (see s. 9(1)(h) of the Sentencing Act 2002, for example).

7 S. Whittle, *Respect and Equality: transsexual and transgender rights*, Cavendish Publishing, London 2002, p. xxiii.

8 Also outside the scope of this chapter is a discussion of the consequential effects of allowing people to self-identify as being of 'indeterminate' sex: see section 3.1.4 below.

birth is congruent with their gender identity), the sexual orientation of trans people is varied: 'You can look at it like a graph with two separate axes, gender and sexual orientation ... You can be anywhere on that graph, anywhere you want. You can be as straight as they come, or completely genderless and asexual.'[9]

In a recent criminal case, the New Zealand Court of Appeal acknowledged that identifying as trans is a separate matter from issues of sexuality or sexual orientation.[10]

II. HISTORY, HEALTH CARE AND STATISTICS

2.1. TRANS HISTORY IN AOTEAROA NEW ZEALAND

The history of the legal status of trans people in Aotearoa New Zealand is largely characterised by invisibility. The historical record is almost silent with regard to the legal status of trans people in colonial New Zealand society. It was not until 1995 that Parliament passed legislation that allowed trans people to change their legal sex, with many Parliamentarians speaking of the importance to trans people of having a legal mechanism through which to have their nominated sex officially recognised.[11]

Up until 1995 legal recognition had been slow. The 1970 decision in the English case of *Corbett v Corbett*,[12] in which it was held that sex is fixed at birth, was influential throughout the common law world, including New Zealand. This decision was widely criticised and five years later, in *Re T*,[13] the notion that legal sex could not be changed was challenged in a New Zealand court. T, who was assigned male at birth but had lived as a female for at least 16 years, sought a declaratory judgment from the High Court to require the Registrar-General to change her recorded sex from male to female. She had undergone 'sex conversion' surgery some years prior and, according to medical evidence, could be regarded as female in all respects except for genetic sex and lack of female reproductive organs.[14] While the Judge expressed sympathy with T's position, he found that there was no jurisdiction to do as T requested under the Declaratory Judgments Act 1908, nor was there any statute that could be invoked in the applicant's

---

9 N. Fowler, 'A Transgender Inquiry', *Salient*, 7 September 2009 <http://salient.org.nz/columns/a-transgender-inquiry> accessed 16.02.2015.

10 *V (CA107/2008) v R* [2012] NZCA 14, para. 29.

11 (5 December 1989) 503 NZPD 14021; (20 March 1991) 513 NZPD 943; (28 March 1995) 547 NZPD 6463. Michael Cullen MP commented that it was pleasing to see a piece of legislation which enabled people 'to give full expression to who they are.'

12 [1970] 2 All ER 33.

13 [1975] 2 NZLR 449 (HC).

14 *Re T*, above n. 13, p. 450.

favour.[15] There was no legal procedure in New Zealand by which an applicant could obtain a declaration as to their sex.

Although T's application was not successful, the case did provide a starting point for public and judicial consideration of the status of trans people in New Zealand. The early 1990s saw a number of related cases before the courts. These cases reflected changing attitudes towards the place of trans people in New Zealand. *M v M*[16] and *Attorney-General v Family Court at Otahuhu*[17] concerned the position of trans people in relation to marriage. These cases established that where a person had undergone full gender affirmation surgery (although the cases use the term 'reassignment') they could enter a marriage as a person of their preferred sex, suggesting that legal recognition of sex was possible. However, emphasis was placed on the appearance of a person's genitals as a significant determinant of sex,[18] which necessarily excluded the overwhelming majority of trans people who have not had those medical interventions.

The Births, Deaths and Marriages Registration Act,[19] first introduced in 1989 and passed in 1995, made statutory provision for trans people who wished to amend their legal sex. This provision was arguably the most controversial in the Bill, and went through several iterations. Much debate in Parliament focused on its operation and effects.[20] Overwhelmingly, however, the response to the proposed provision was positive and the significance of the reform to the lives of trans people in New Zealand was widely recognised.

The debate that accompanied the Act reflected changing social attitudes towards trans people. The Act's passing also coincided with a high-profile moment in New Zealand's trans history when, also in 1995, Georgina Beyer became the first openly and self-identified transsexual in the world to be elected as a mayor of a small rural New Zealand town.[21] Her second 'first' was when she became a Member of Parliament (MP) when elected to represent the Wairarapa electorate in 1999.

Georgina Beyer served as an MP from 1999 until 2007. In 2004, her Private Members Bill, the Human Rights (Gender Identity) Amendment Bill, was pulled from the ballot. This Bill sought to amend section 21 of the Human Rights Act 1993 to include gender identity as a prohibited ground of discrimination. However, Ms Beyer withdrew the Bill after the Solicitor-General issued an opinion on 2 August 2006 which concluded that the New Zealand courts would likely

---

15 *Re T*, above n. 13, p. 453.

16 [1991] NZFLR 337. See also R. Mackenzie, 'Transsexuals' Legal Status and Same Sex Marriage in New Zealand: *M v M*' (1992) 7 *Otago Law Review* 556.

17 [1995] 1 NZLR 603, [1995] NZFLR 57 (HC). See also A. Alston, 'Transgender Rights as Legal Rights' (1999) 7 *Canterbury Law Review* 329.

18 *Attorney-General v Family Court at Otahuhu*, above n. 17, pp. 607 and 631.

19 The name of the Act was changed to the Births, Deaths, Marriages and Relationship Registration Act 1995, as from 24 January 2009. See further section 3.1.1.1 below.

20 (5 December 1989) 503 NZPD 14017–1408; (15 May 1990) 507 NZPD 1537–1540.

21 <www.teara.govt.nz/en/photograph/12060/georgina-beyer> accessed 16.02.2015.

follow the approaches of the UK, European and Canadian courts, and construe the existing sex discrimination provisions in the Human Rights Act 1993 in a way that would protect against discrimination on the grounds of gender identity.[22] This opinion has yet to be tested in the New Zealand courts.

While social attitudes towards trans people were changing, it was clear by 2006 that legislation and government policy and practice still had to catch up. That year the Human Rights Commission began an Inquiry into the experiences of trans people in New Zealand – the world's first such inquiry by a national human rights institution. It focused on the three most significant issues faced by trans people – discrimination, access to health services and legal recognition of sex.[23]

During the 18 months of the Inquiry, approximately 200 people made submissions, including farmers, business-people, tradespeople, academics, artists, sex workers, health professionals, economists, managers, parents and grandparents.[24] The Report was released in January 2008 and the information and recommendations it contained provide essential material and significant context for this chapter. In particular, it is due to the work of the Inquiry that a number of important reforms, both in law and policy, have occurred in the subsequent seven years.

The Human Rights Commission's Transgender Inquiry Report and the following national public education programme, which involved local trans communities, was a very visible response to the situation that trans people in New Zealand face. It was in stark contrast to the silence that had characterised the experience of trans people throughout much of the 20th century. While the legal status of trans people is still evolving, and their history is yet to be written, the current record demonstrates that, relatively swiftly, New Zealand has made significant progress in recognising trans people and their rights.

2.2. PROVISION OF TREATMENT FOR TRANS PEOPLE

The Report of the Transgender Inquiry summarised trans people's experience of health services, including those related to gender affirming treatment in the following words:

[22] Human Rights Commission, above n. 2, paras. 8.45 and 9.9. The ground of 'sex' may well cover discrimination against transsexuals, for example, but would not easily cover discrimination that related to a person's gender expression. See further E. McDonald, 'Discrimination and Trans People: The Abandoned Proposal to Amend the Human Rights Act 1993' (2007) 5 *New Zealand Journal of Public and International Law* 301.

[23] Human Rights Commission, above n. 2, para. 1.3.

[24] Human Rights Commission, *Transgender Inquiry: Summary of Submissions*, Wellington 2007.

> 'Trans people and health professionals consistently raised the difficulties trans people have in obtaining general health services and being treated with dignity and respect when they did use them. The Inquiry has identified major gaps in availability, accessibility, acceptability and quality of medical services required by a trans person seeking to transition. The provision of public health services is patchy and inconsistent. Trans people and health professionals need to work together to address these issues.'

The Report's health recommendations focused on providing clear information about gender affirming health services available regionally through the public health system, developing treatment pathways and agreed standards of care, and looking into the absence of health insurance coverage for trans people. In response to the concerns expressed by trans people and clinicians, in 2009, the Counties Manukau District Health Board was funded to manage a national project looking at gender affirming health services for trans people in New Zealand.[25] The project's work, *Good Practice Guide for Health Professionals* (the Guide) was available online on 2 August 2011,[26] and a slightly revised version was published in May 2012 by the Ministry of Health.[27] The Guide is now considered to be out of date as it was primarily based on Version 6 of the Standards of Care published by the World Professional Association for Transgender Health (WPATH). A much improved Version 7 of these standards was published very soon after the Guide was completed. Notwithstanding this concern, the Guide does provide a readily accessible resource for trans people and medical professionals regardless of which Health Board area they live in.

The Guide confirms that four types of hormone interventions are publicly funded, while the initial diagnosis to allow hormones to be prescribed may involve referral to a mental health practitioner, which is typically not funded.[28] This initial assessment is likely to be expensive and is therefore a significant barrier to many trans people. In New Zealand, as elsewhere, there is also concern that a mental health diagnosis is routinely required in order for hormone treatment to be made available.[29]

---

25 See further background and information about the consultation process at <www.hrc.co.nz/human-rights-environment/action-on-the-transgender-inquiry/health-of-trans-people> accessed 16.02.2015.

26 <www.health.govt.nz/publication/gender-reassignment-health-services-trans-people-within-new-zealand> accessed 16.02.2015. This publication is due for revision.

27 <www.health.govt.nz/system/files/documents/publications/gender-reassignment-health-services-for-trans-people-nz-2012-v2.pdf> accessed 16.02.2015.

28 Human Rights Commission, above n. 2, para. 5.23. Nor are other important procedures, such as hair removal, publicly funded: para. 5.28.

29 Human Rights Commission, above n. 2, para. 5.21. At the time of the inquiry, the commonly used diagnosis in New Zealnd was 'Gender Identity Disorder', from the 4th edition of the Diagnostic and Statistical Manual of Mental Disorders (DSM-IV). Subsequently, this has been replaced with the term 'gender dysphoria' in the updated DSM-5.

With regard to surgeries, only some are regularly performed in public hospitals – such as chest reconstruction, hysterectomy and orchidectomy. However, trans people often struggle to be prioritised on waiting lists. In September 2013, the only surgeon currently providing chest reconstruction to trans men through the public health system announced this procedure would no longer be available in Auckland, New Zealand's largest city.[30] On 8 October 2013 the Sexual Health Clinic announced that they could not take any more referrals (necessary for trans people to begin hormone treatment).[31] In February 2014 the only plastic surgeon performing genital surgery for trans women in New Zealand retired.[32]

There is limited state funding available for genital surgeries through the Special High-Cost Treatment Pool,[33] which is public funding for treatments not available through the public health system. Every two years it provides for up to three surgeries for trans women and one for a trans man. The historical backlog of people requiring such surgeries, and the growing size of the trans community, mean people face years on a waiting list with no guarantee their surgery will ever be funded. A large proportion of trans people who want to have genital surgery therefore choose to travel overseas, which is an expensive option.[34] Virtually no gender confirming health services required by trans people are covered by health insurers in New Zealand.[35]

2.3. STATISTICS – NUMBERS OF TRANS PEOPLE IN AOTEAROA NEW ZEALAND

There is limited information about the numbers of trans people in New Zealand. What does exist is primarily government agencies' data about people accessing their services. This excludes those parts of the trans community who are unaware of, or cannot afford to access, such services. For example, the Transgender Inquiry was told that from 1 September 1995 until 16 August 2007 114 people had applied to the Family Court to have their legal sex details amended. Subsequent data from the Department of Internal Affairs shows an increase, with 20 applications being lodged in 2014.[36]

---

30 <www.gayexpress.co.nz/2013/09/top-surgery-no-longer-offered-by-auckland-surgeon> accessed 19.12.2013.

31 'Dialogue follows suspended health clinic' <www.gaynz.com/articles/publish/2/artcile_14024.php> accessed 29.01.2015.

32 A. Dudding, 'Gender Mender', *Sunday Magazine, Sunday Star-Times*, 26 October 2014, p. 16.

33 Human Rights Commission, above n. 2, paras. 5.88–5.95; <www.health.govt.nz/our-work/hospitals-and-specialist-care/high-cost-treatment-pool> accessed 16.02.2015.

34 Human Rights Commission, above n. 2, paras. 5.44–5.45.

35 Human Rights Commission, above n. 2, para. 5.55.

36 Human Rights Commission, above n. 2, para. 2.9. The number of applications received by the Department of Internal Affairs between 1 January 2008 and 31 December 2013 was 105. 16 of these related to people born overseas who wanted a declaration in order to change their birth information in another jurisdiction. 24 of the applications were unfinished at the time

As of April 2007 almost 400 people had obtained passports with an indeterminate legal sex marker ('X' – see further below at section 3.1.2). This figure does not include those trans people who had been able to change their details from female to male or vice versa, and may reflect the high threshold to make changes from M to F or vice versa at that time. Despite some activism on the issue, neither gender identity nor sexual orientation information is gathered by Statistics New Zealand, including through the population census, which is usually conducted every four years.[37] Statistics New Zealand has however recently developed a statistical standard for gender identity, which is a necessary step towards collecting such data.[38]

The Transgender Inquiry's Report estimated that between 400 and 800 people belonged to trans organisations and networks that contributed to its Inquiry and the trans population itself would be significantly larger.[39] Heightened visibility since the Inquiry, and a growing trans youth community, mean that there is likely to be at least a few thousand trans people in New Zealand.

III. CHANGING LEGAL SEX – PROCEDURE AND REQUIREMENTS

3.1. LEGAL PROCESS OF CHANGING OFFICIAL DOCUMENTS

In New Zealand the process of changing legal sex classification on official documents varies depending on the document. Changes to passports and driver licences for example are possible through a straightforward administrative process; changes to birth certificates require an application to the Family Court. The applicable processes of making changes to sex markers or classifications, and how those changes are recorded and accessed, are discussed below in relation to each type of document.

---

of getting advice from the DIA. No applications were received under section 29 (for those under 18). Email from Eileen Kennedy, 16 January 2014, on file with the authors. A further 20 applications under section 28 were received between 1 January and 31 December 2014 (email of 10 February on file with the authors).

37 Statistics New Zealand, *Considering Sexual Orientation as a Potential Official Statistic: Discussion paper*, Wellington, Statistics New Zealand, 2008; <www.stuff.co.nz/national/8375951/Census-taking-stock-of-NZs-changing-society> accessed 16.02.2015.

38 <www.stats.govt.nz/methods/classifications-and-standards/current-classifications-and-standards-review.aspx> accessed 11.02.2015.

39 Human Rights Commission, above n. 2, para. 2.8.

3.1.1. *Birth Certificates*

3.1.1.1. Change of Name

A person's name may be changed on their birth certificate by application to the Registrar-General, although in practice this is done by presenting the declaration at the local Department of Internal Affairs office (section 21A of the Births, Deaths, Marriages and Relationships Registration Act 1995: BDMRRA). This can be done by a person who 18 years or older, or by the person's guardian. The 'eligible person' or the guardian must make a statutory declaration declaring their intention to abandon the name in their certificate, and after payment of the relevant fee, the Registrar-General must register the name change 'as soon as practicable' (section 21B of the BDMRRA).

Following amendments to the definition of 'eligible person' in section 21A, which took effect from 24 January 2009,[40] people born overseas but residing indefinitely in New Zealand may take advantage of this administrative process which has the effect of the Registrar-General including the new name 'in the person's name change information' (section 21B(2)(b)). Access to information about a person's change of name is governed by sections 74–75G and section 78–78I.[41] These sections allow public access in most cases (section 74), however when a change of name accompanies a change of sex classification different rules apply (see below section 3.1.2.2).

The Transgender Inquiry was told that many trans people over 18 years of age had changed their name and '[a]lmost without exception this proved to be a simple and straightforward exercise for them.'[42] For a very small number of people, the fee involved had meant they had not made an application. Recently the University of Auckland has begun providing financial support to trans students who wish to change their name on their birth certificate, including providing them with a new academic transcript in their chosen name and paying for a new passport.[43]

---

40 These changes were made in response to the recommendation of the Transgender Inquiry: 'allow the Family Court to make a declaration as to sex for overseas-born NZ citizens': Human Rights Commission, above n. 2, para. 9.50.

41 These provisions were due for review in 2013 as required under section 78J of the BDMRPA. On 10 February 2015, no information was available about the status of this review (email from Eileen Kennedy, on file with the authors).

42 Human Rights Commission, above n. 2, para. 6.18.

43 <www.auckland.ac.nz/en/about/eo-equity-office/eo-information-for-students/eo-information-for-students-information-for-students-and-staff-LGBTI/guidelines-for-the-university-of-auckland-support-for-trans--stu.html> accessed 29.01.15.

3.1.1.2. Change of Sex Classification

In order for a person to amend the sex classification on their birth certificate, an application must be made by an 'eligible adult' (or the guardian of an 'eligible child' – as defined in section 27A) to the Family Court (sections 28 and 29 of the BDMRRA). These definitions also now entitle persons born overseas to make an application for a declaration,[44] an amendment that responded to the recommendation of the Transgender Inquiry that the Family Court should have jurisdiction to 'make a declaration as to sex for overseas-born NZ citizens.'[45]

The effect of the declaration is that 'birth certificates issued in respect of the applicant should contain the information that the applicant is a person of the sex specified in the application' (section 28(1)). As this is an application for a court order, a filing fee is involved, and the applicant may wish to engage a lawyer, but this is not a requirement.[46] However, as the process relies on the presentation of a number of affidavits, more being required for those who have had few or no surgical interventions, it can be an overwhelming process for a layperson to undertake. The Court may appoint an *amicus curiae* (literally a friend of the court) to assist the judge when coming to his or her decision, in the absence of either party being legally represented (it is not always the case that the Registrar-General appears as a party).[47] Some Community Law Centres in New Zealand offer free assistance to trans people wishing to make an application as a result of the comments made to the Transgender Inquiry:[48]

> '[T]rans people said that it was difficult for them to obtain clear information about the process of applying to the Family Court. Lawyers with expertise in this area were difficult to find. Some trans people had successfully applied to the Court without legal representation, but this did not appear to happen very often. Some thought that the procedures were complex, while others found it intimidating to talk to lawyers and found the legal costs high.'

Although the BDMRRA does not provide for an appeal from a refusal to make a declaration, as this application is a proceeding in the Family Court a judge's decision can be appealed in the usual way to the High Court – although this

---

44 Section 15 of the Births, Deaths, Marriages, and Relationships Registration Amendment Act 2008, that took effect on 24 January 2009. See *AB* FAM Auckland, FAM 2009-004-1341, 16 November 2009, in which AB, a permanent resident, was granted a declaration that despite his UK birth certificate showing his sex classification as female, the birth certificate should contain information that he is male.

45 Human Rights Commission, above n. 2, para. 9.50. See also the discussion at para. 6.29.

46 For details on the process see also: <www.justice.govt.nz/courts/family-court/what-family-court-does/transgender-declaration-as-to-sex-on-birth-certificate-application> and <www.dia.govt.nz/diawebsite.nsf/Files/GeninfoDeclarationsofFamilyCourt/$file/GeninfoDeclarationsofFamilyCourt.pdf> accessed 16.02.2015.

47 See, for example, *Hemmings v Births, Deaths and Marriages* [2014] NZFC 85.

48 Human Rights Commission, above n. 2, para. 6.23.

would be a prohibitively expensive process for most people. Further, Family Court proceedings are usually closed to the public (but the media can be in attendance, with reporting limitations in place: section 11D(f) of the Family Courts Act 1980) whereas High Court proceedings would not necessarily be, unless a further application was made in order to protect the applicant's privacy, with regard to both the hearing and the reporting of the outcome. Decisions of the Family Court with regard to some section 28 applications are accessible on legal databases but identifying details of the person are removed.

Once the Registrar-General has received the declaration from the Family Court, a further fee is payable to update the person's birth certificate. This ensures that included in 'the information relating to the birth recorded under the Act ... that the person is a person of the nominated sex' (section 30) ('nominated sex' meaning the sex specified in the application – section 28(1)). If the declaration under section 29 (regarding a child) was conditional on certain medical treatment being undertaken which has not occurred, the Registrar-General may delete the amended sex details made on the child's birth certificate (section 31).[49]

Section 64 of the Act has the effect of ensuring that once the section 30 process is complete, the birth certificate issued contains 'the information that such a certificate would contain if the person had always been a person of that sex' and shall contain 'no other information'. Section 71 provides that any birth certificate 'shall in any proceedings be received as prima facie evidence of the truth of the information it contains'.[50]

Once the birth information details are changed pursuant to section 28 or 29, there is limited access to that information. Section 77 of the BDMRRA provides that only the Registrar-General may permit any person (other than the person to whom the information relates) 'to inspect [or print out] any document' which contains a correction to the birth information relating to the person's sex (and new names adopted by that person). The Registrar-General may allow inspection to occur after 120 years has passed since the birth of the person, or when the situations covered in section 77(8) and (9) are satisfied. Section 77(8) provides for inspections following an order from the Family, District or High Court – the order being made to allow inquiries into the making of a false statement or the validity of a marriage, for example.[51] Section 77(9) provides that notwithstanding the general presumption of non-disclosure in section 77, any government agency 'that has an interest in ensuring that people should not have more than one

---

49 The same provision does not apply in relation to applications under section 28 seemingly, even if the declaration has been made on the basis that medical treatment (particularly surgery) is yet to be undertaken. That is, there is no follow up in such cases.

50 This is really an evidential rule (a specific exception to the hearsay rule) – and would not preclude evidence of the previous birth information being offered in evidence if relevant.

51 This second ground is unlikely to now be a valid basis for a disclosure order following the amendments to the Marriage Act 1955, which allows two people to marry regardless of sex or gender identity, and the repeal of section 30(2) of the BDMRRA.

identity' can be told about the additions to the birth information (including sex classification and name changes).

3.1.2. *Passports*

In response to concerns expressed to the Transgender Inquiry and the recommendations made in the final report,[52] as of 1 December 2012 a passport may now be issued in a person's nominated sex/gender identity without the need for a change to their birth certificate. This is an administrative process undertaken after the person has made a relevant statutory declaration. Those under the age of 18 years must provide additional information, namely a declaration from a parent or legal guardian and from a registered counsellor/medical professional supporting this change. The choices for the sex/gender identity recorded are 'M', 'F' or 'X' (meaning indeterminate or unspecified). Trans people who are either in the early stages of their transition or who do not wish to identify as either male or female may prefer the latter option. It may also be a preferred option for some intersex people, although any person may apply to have their sex/gender identity details amended, not only those who identify as trans or intersex.

Prior to this policy change, trans people who had not had the details on their birth certificate changed could only request an 'X' (or a '–' prior to 2005) as the sex data on their passport, in line with the International Civil Aviation Organisation (ICAO) specifications for a symbol for unspecified sex.[53] This was also done by a statutory declaration stating how long the person had 'lived as a member of the opposite sex' and they must have changed their name to a name 'more suitable to a member of the opposite sex, or have a unisex name'.[54] In 2007 the Department of Internal Affairs (DIA) advised the HRC that approximately 400 New Zealand passport holders had an 'X' or '–' (dash) in the sex details field.[55] The DIA stated to the Inquiry that they did not have information as to how many people with an 'X' or a '–' had changed to M or F. However, subsequent research by Jaimie Veale in 2008 revealed that 11 passport holders had changed from X to M, and 65 had changed from X to F.[56] The Transgender Inquiry was told that although access to the 'X' (or dash) option was a progressive step for those transitioning or wanting to identify as androgynous or gender neutral, it was not always a safe option for travel into some countries:[57]

---

52 Human Rights Commission, above n. 2, para. 9.50: 'Simplify the requirements for changing sex details on a birth certificate, a passport or other documents to ensure consistency with the Human Rights Act'.

53 Human Rights Commission, above n. 2, para. 6.12.

54 J.F. Veale, 'Prevalence of transsexualism among New Zealand passport holders' (2008) 42 *Aust NZ L Psychiatry* 887, 888.

55 Human Rights Commission, above n. 2, para. 6.13.

56 Veale, above n 54, p. 888.

57 Human Rights Commission, above n. 2, para. 6.16. The main ongoing issue seems to be at the checking-in stage for those travelling on 'X' passports – as airlines' computer systems often

> 'I believe the dash on the passport or a gender that does not represent what you appear to be leaves you vulnerable and open to all kinds of violations at borders. I have travelled extensively since having gender reassignment with female on my passport and have not encountered the scrutiny that I experienced when I had a dash on my passport.'

If a trans person is applying for their first New Zealand passport after changing the details on their birth certificate, the Passport Office will have no previous record of their sex details. Usually there is no requirement to return a previous passport with the application, although it is DIA policy to require the return of a passport when there has been more than one change to a person's legal sex marker (although the DIA website refers to a change to a person's 'gender identity'). That passport is cancelled, defaced and returned to the applicant.[58] This process may apply, for example, to a trans man who has changed from F to X and then seeks a new passport and requests, by way of statutory declaration, for the sex details to be recorded as M. The DIA has however stated that the multiple change of sex/gender identity from M to X to F is considered to be a 'transitional change' but it also advises on its website that 'multiple changes in gender identity are likely to have implications for a person at overseas border controls or may affect a person's ability to confirm their identity in the wider community.'

In the absence of specific statutory provisions regarding the disclosure of information about the sex or gender history of a person, the information privacy principles in the Privacy Act 1993 apply. This means that information held by an agency in connection with one purpose must not be used for any other purpose, except in limited circumstances. Similar principles apply to disclosure of personal information. These principles allow trans people the ability to obtain confirmation that personal information about them is being held and to request correction where appropriate. Agencies that hold personal information must not use it unless they have taken reasonable steps to ensure that it is accurate and up to date. The Office of the Privacy Commissioner stated, in its submission to the Transgender Inquiry, that such a principle:[59]

> 'has significant implications for agencies that record and keep gender status information. Where a transgender person has for example undergone surgery and identifies with a gender other than the one recorded on their birth certificate, questions about the accuracy of the recorded information will arise ... difficulties experienced by one person who contacted this Office show that accuracy of

---

only accept an M or F option – and not all countries are members of the IACO. See however the more recent unexceptional experience of Joey Macdonald (reported in S. Collins, 'X marks the spot on passport for transgender travellers', *The New Zealand Herald*, Auckland, 5 December 2012).

58 See <www.passports.govt.nz/Transgender-applicants> accessed 16.02.2015.

59 Human Rights Commission, above n. 2, para. 6.90.

> gender status information is not simply a semantic or conceptual question. When incorrect gender status information is allowed to persist in the "official" record the result can be very real humiliation and detriment to the individual concerned.'

With regard to information about a person's application, including a statutory declaration regarding the person's nominated sex, the privacy statement on the application form is consistent with New Zealand privacy principles:[60]

> 'The information you provide helps us establish your identity and determine if you are eligible for a New Zealand passport.
>
> We may obtain information from other sources (including, but not limited to, the Citizenship Office and the Registrar-General of Births, Deaths and Marriages) using an authorised information-matching programme (under Section 78A of the Births, Deaths, Marriages and Relationships Registration Act 1995 or Section 26A of the Citizenship Act 1977).
>
> *How is your privacy protected?*
>
> All relevant information about you is collected in line with the Passports Act 1992 and is held securely by the New Zealand Passport Office, Department of Internal Affairs, 120 Victoria Street (PO Box 10–526), Wellington.
>
> Under the Privacy Act 1993 you may access and request a correction of any of that personal information.
>
> *When may information from your passport records be disclosed?*
>
> Under the Passports Act 1992 and the Privacy Act 1993, this information may be disclosed, subject to agreement in writing between the Secretary of Internal Affairs and the Chief Executive of the organisation requesting the information, to any appropriate agency, body, or person to aid border security, facilitate the processing of passengers, verify the identity of a holder of a travel document, or determine whether a person is a New Zealand citizen.
>
> Information may also be disclosed under authorised information matching programmes and information sharing agreements in accordance with the Privacy Act 1993 ...
>
> The information that may be disclosed includes the information recorded in your passport; your eye colour; your height; the status of your passport; our passport database key number; and any other information relating to your passport that may be required.'

The Department of Internal Affairs has been recording information for statistical purposes since changes to the Department's policy for recording a change in sex/ gender identity were introduced in late 2012. The Department advises that this information is stored in a secure manner and may only be accessed by a very small number of authorised personnel.

---

60 <www.passports.govt.nz/vwluResources/adult-new-form.pdf/$file/adult-new-form.pdf> accessed 29.01.2015.

3.1.3. Driver Licences

On 13 June 2013, the New Zealand Transport Agency (NZTA) announced its new policy with regard to sex or gender identity records for driver licences. Although New Zealand licences do not include sex details, this information has always been held on the national Driver Licence Register (DLR), which can be accessed by police officers when requested. This information has historically matched what is on the person's birth certificate. As a consequence, a person stopped by the police who has a male name and appearance may be recorded as female on the register (and vice versa).[61] Once the officer finds this out, it may well be that they are concerned about the validity of the licence or the identification of the person presenting it:[62]

> 'If a person is stopped and they say one name and the check shows another legal name or gender, the initial reaction is "they lied to me". Strike one and it becomes an interrogation.'

Although the requirement for sex or gender information to be collected and recorded on the DLR is authorised by legislation, there is no statutorily mandated way of gathering this information. The NZTA was aware that inconsistency of processes to changing sex or gender details might expose the Agency to challenges under the Human Rights Act 1993 (NZ). The NZTA also 'looked to the Yogyakarta Principles which show that human rights approaches internationally are now steering toward individuals self-declaring their gender identity'.[63] As a consequence, changes to the sex or gender details on the DLR are now possible without needing to provide an amended birth certificate. The options are 'male', 'female' or 'indeterminate'. This is an administrative process that can be undertaken at any NZTA agency (available in all cities and major towns in New Zealand). There is no charge for changing sex details on the DLR at any time. If this is done when a person is renewing their licence, the usual renewal fee applies.

Section 199 of the Land Transport Act 1998 governs access to the DLR. Although there is provision for access to some of the details by insurance companies and those who employ drivers (class of vehicles, endorsements, etc.: see section 199(6)), only some employees of the NZTA may access the identification history of any person (including any change of name or sex details: section 199(a)) and only in very limited circumstances. Although the statutory declaration would be kept along with the licence application for the period for which the licence is valid, this information would only be disclosed to the person themselves in the absence of exceptional reasons.

---

61 Human Rights Commission, above n. 2, para. 6.10.

62 Human Rights Commission, above n. 2, para. 6.10.

63 Email from Charmaine Berry, NZTA, 30 July 2013, on file with the authors.

3.1.4. *Citizenship and Evidentiary Certificates*

Citizenship certificates, issued when a person has been granted citizenship, may be issued with the sex classification different from the sex on the applicant's birth certificate in two situations. First, if the applicant has a Family Court declaration (under section 28 of the BDMRRA as discussed above) or second, if 'the applicant has provided a court order or other official documentation from another country recognising the gender identity they are currently maintaining, which is assessed as being suitable'.[64] This process is therefore similar to the requirements for changing sex details on a birth certificate.

Following the 2009 amendment to the BDMRRA,[65] those who are citizens or have the right to remain in New Zealand indefinitely (a permanent resident, for example) may apply for a declaration that, if granted, will allow for the citizenship certificate to reflect their nominated sex. However, if the granting of citizenship precedes the application for a declaration as to sex, a person may apply for an *evidentiary* certificate that will record their nominated sex, but their citizenship certificate cannot be changed retrospectively. Regulation 15 of the Citizenship Regulations 2002 provides that access to the details about a person held on the citizenship register is limited to the person themselves, or for public interest reasons (see regulation 15(2)).

The position is somewhat different with regard to those who wish to have no indication of sex on their citizenship certificate. In such a case, prior to the granting of citizenship, a person who is of indeterminate sex or intersex may apply to have no sex recorded on the certificate. A person who has changed their name to one suitable to a member of their nominated sex, or has a unisex name, and produces a statutory declaration that they live as a member of the nominated sex, may also have a citizenship certificate issued with no indication of sex. However, such certificates may not necessarily be accepted by the NZTA as the basis for changing details on the driver licence register – their publicised policy regarding acceptable evidence of identity notes that '[citizenship or evidentiary] certificates that do not confirm your name, date of birth, *gender* and effective date of citizenship will not be accepted' (emphasis added).

A citizenship or evidentiary certificate may also be issued showing indeterminate or intersex in the sex field if that appears on the person's birth certificate, or 'if the applicant has provided both a statutory declaration and a medical certificate or records confirming that the applicant is of indeterminate sex or intersex'.

Pursuant to regulation 15, any statutory declaration will be kept on the person's file, along with their application for citizenship, and may only be accessed

---

64 <www.passports.govt.nz/transgender-applicants#citizenship> accessed 16.02.2015.

65 Section 27A, which extended the definition of eligible adult for the purposes of section 28, was inserted, as from 24 January 2009, by section 15 of the Births, Deaths, Marriages, and Relationships Registration Amendment Act 2008.

by the person themselves or by state officials (such as border control agents) in limited circumstances.

3.2. LEGAL REQUIREMENTS FOR CHANGING DOCUMENTS

As with the procedural rules, the substantive requirements for changing the sex classification on official documents differs between the various types. The most rigorous test is that for changing birth certificates. This is understandable in the sense that most people view a birth certificate as being 'all the proof required that they are New Zealanders',[66] although the Department of Internal Affairs stresses that a birth certificate is only proof of the registration of a birth. However, it is the most significant form of identity as it cannot be revoked or altered by the State, and a birth certificate is the document used by most people to obtain other important documents such as a passport or driver licence. Amending the sex details on a birth certificate will therefore allow these other documents to be amended accordingly, but with the exception of evidentiary certificates (relating to citizenship status) most identity documents can now be changed even without first amending the sex classification on a birth certificate.

Further, since 2 July 2013 New Zealanders can sign up for RealMe – an online identity verification service backed by the New Zealand government.[67] A person completes a one-off identity verification process (involving a visit to a Post Office), after which they will be able to use their verified RealMe account online to apply for services from participating organisations online. RealMe does not allow New Zealand Post or the Department of Internal Affairs to see or access the information on individuals held by organisations that use RealMe as their verification system. It simply serves as an authentication and identity verification tool, and will not track any data or activities carried out by members once its function (of providing verified information) is completed. No personal identity information is held by New Zealand Post – all information collected for the identity verification process is handed to the Department of Internal Affairs.[68] As RealMe accepts a passport as evidence of someone's identity, trans people who have not changed their birth certificate can still share their nominated sex details with government departments and agencies that use RealMe as their verification

[66] Human Rights Commission, above n. 2, para. 6.3.

[67] <www.realme.govt.nz> accessed 18.12.2013.

[68] <www.nzpost.co.nz/about-us/media-centre/media-release/government-backed-online-identity-verification-system-realme-ready-to-go> accessed 18.12.2013. See also the Electronic Identity Verification Act 2012.

system.[69] Such a process renders birth certificates less significant as proof of identity and sex than they were historically.[70]

3.2.1. *Birth Certificates*

Changing the sex or gender details on a birth certificate of an adult (aged 18 and over) requires an application to the Family Court, pursuant to section 28 of the BDMRRA,[71] which provides:

> '(1) Subject to subsection (3) of this section, a Family Court may, on the application of [an eligible adult (the *applicant*)], declare that it is appropriate that birth certificates issued in respect of the applicant should contain the information that the applicant is a person of a sex specified in the application (in subsection (3) of this section referred to as the nominated sex).
> [(2) The Court must cause a copy of the application to be served on –
> (a) the Registrar-General, if the applicant's birth is registered or is registrable under this Act but is not yet registered; and
> (b) any other person who, in the Court's opinion, is interested in it or might be affected by the granting of the declaration.]
> (3) The Court shall issue the declaration if, and only if, –
> (a) It is satisfied [either that the applicant's birth is registrable under this Act but is not yet registered, or that there is included in the record] of the applicant's birth –
> (i) Information that the applicant is a person of the sex opposite to the nominated sex; or
> (ii) Information that the applicant is a person of indeterminate sex; or
> (iii) No information at all as to the applicant's sex; and
> (b) It is satisfied that the applicant is not a person of the nominated sex, but –
> (i) Has assumed and intends to maintain, or has always had and intends to maintain, the gender identity of a person of the nominated sex; and
> (ii) Wishes the nominated sex to appear on birth certificates issued in respect of the applicant; and

69 A person may also change their sex details for the purposes of their 'electronic identity': section 30 of the Electronic Identity Verification Act 2012.

70 Birth certificates are no longer required when people make an application for a passport, register a birth or apply for a marriage licence – although usually there will be sharing of the relevant records within the Department of Internal Affairs. A death may also be registered without reference to a person's birth certificate – usually the funeral director will advise the Department based on the information given by the family, although the Department may note the inconsistency when issuing the death certificate. Universities, however, still require a change of birth certificate in order to make changes to the sex of a person on the University record, and therefore on the official transcript: <www.ousa.org.nz/support/queer-support/transgender/> accessed 29.01.2015. As already noted at section 3.1.1.1 the University of Auckland is now providing financial assistance for a name change on a birth certificate and the consequential changes to identity documents, but not for changes to sex/gender markers.

71 The relevant provision for those under 18 is section 29 of the BDMRRA.

(c) Either –
  (i) It is satisfied, on the basis of expert medical evidence, that the applicant –
    (A) Has assumed (or has always had) the gender identity of a person of the nominated sex; and
    (B) Has undergone such medical treatment as is usually regarded by medical experts as desirable to enable persons of the genetic and physical conformation of the applicant at birth to acquire a physical conformation that accords with the gender identity of a person of the nominated sex; and
    (C) Will, as a result of the medical treatment undertaken, maintain a gender identity of a person of the nominated sex; or
  (ii) It is satisfied that the applicant's sexual assignment or reassignment as a person of the nominated sex has been recorded or recognised in accordance with the laws of a state for the time being recognised for the purposes of this section by the Minister by notice in the *Gazette*.'

The leading authority regarding the application of section 28 is *'Michael' v Registrar-General of Births, Deaths and Marriages*.[72] In this case, Judge Fitzgerald in the Auckland Family Court held that the following requirements must be satisfied in order for the applicant to be successful:[73]

'(a) that the applicant must be 18 years of age or older (s 28(1) and s 27A);
(b) that the application has been served on the Registrar-General (s 28(2);
(c) that the Court is satisfied that the applicant's birth registration includes information that the applicant is a person of the sex opposite to the nominated sex (being the gender which the applicant wishes to adopt) (s 28(3)(a));
(d) that medical evidence is necessary to establish that:
  (i) the applicant has assumed the gender identity of the nominated sex;
  (ii) the applicant has undergone medical treatment, both psychological and surgical, of a type regarded by medical experts as desirable to obtain a physical confirmation with the gender identity of the nominated sex. It is not necessary that every possible medical intervention has been undertaken but, on a case-by-case basis, sufficient treatment as in the opinion of medical experts is desirable to achieve a physical change of identity;
  (iii) that as a result of the medical treatment undertaken, the new gender identity will be maintained by the applicant (s 28(3)(c)).

[72] (2008) 27 FRNZ 58. See commentary of the case in N. Seuffert, 'Case Comment: *'Michael' v Registrar-General of Births, Deaths and Marriages*' (2009) 17 *Waikato Law Review* 115 and P.R.H. Webb, 'Case Note: Getting a new birth certificate' (2008) 6 *New Zealand Family Law Review* 110.

[73] As set out and applied in *KRM v Registrar-General of Births, Deaths and Marriages of Wellington*, FAM New Plymouth, FAM 2009-043-82, 1 April 2009, para. 4.

(e) that the applicant has assumed and intends to maintain, or has always had and intends to maintain, the gender identity of the nominated sex and wishes that to appear on their birth certificate (s 28(3)(b)).'

It is the inquiry in section 28(3)(c)(i)(B), that the applicant 'has undergone such medical treatment as is usually regarded by medical experts as desirable to enable persons of the genetic and physical conformation of the applicant at birth to acquire a physical conformation that accords with the gender identity of a person of the nominated sex', which has caused the most concern for trans people. Many of those who made submissions to the Transgender Inquiry thought this part of the test meant that they needed to have undergone 'full gender reassignment surgery'.[74] This was also the view of the Department of Internal Affairs who told the Inquiry that their understanding was that 'full gender reassignment surgery is required'.[75] If that was the case, this would be an impossible test for most trans people to meet. Most surgeries are not available in New Zealand, or are too costly, medically unnecessary or undesirable:[76]

> 'I can't change [my birth certificate] legally until I have had all surgeries deemed necessary, which for transguys is no mean feat if it includes "lower" surgery. We can't get that done in New Zealand, most of us don't have [the] $50 – $100k needed to do it overseas, it can involve as many as five risky operations with very variable outcomes, and many of us will never choose to have it. In short, I'm convinced that this criteria [sic] was set only with reference to MtFs. No one else is legally defined by surgery.'

'Michael' was decided six months after the report of the Transgender Inquiry was published. Judge Fitzgerald, after considering the legislative history of the section (which included the deletion of the original reference to 'surgical' procedures), concluded that 'Parliament did not intend an applicant should necessarily have to undergo all available surgical procedures, including full genital surgery, to satisfy the test under the section.' All that is required is 'some degree of permanent physical change as a result of the treatment ... received.'[77] The Judge also noted that during the Third Reading of the Bill, Richard Northey MP stated:[78]

> 'The select committee ... recognised that it was principally a psychological, rather than a surgical, matter of identification, and to require people to go through the full gamut of very expensive surgery in order simply to have themselves recorded on their birth certificate as being the sex with which they identify was inappropriate.'

---

74 Human Rights Commission, above n. 2, para. 6.21.
75 Human Rights Commission, above n. 2, para. 6.54.
76 Human Rights Commission, above n. 2, para. 6.22. See also *C-DT* [2012] NZFC 10036, para. 17.
77 *'Michael'*, above n. 72, para. 50.
78 (28 March 1995) 547 NZPD 6465.

Since *'Michael'* there have been a number of cases in which trans people who have not undergone surgery,[79] or have had no genital surgery,[80] have been successful in obtaining a declaration under section 28. In May 2012 Judge Hikaka noted that 'the applicant cannot afford full genital surgery but such surgery is not a mandatory requirement'.[81] He accepted, when hearing an application from a trans woman, the endocrinologist's evidence that the effects of long-term hormone treatment were irreversible and had 'brought her measurements completely into the normal female range.'[82] The Family Court has also acknowledged, regarding an application from a trans man, that the 'surgical procedure for the artificial construction of a penis, known as phalloplasty, is still quite imperfect, and is unlikely to have a suitable result'.[83] Although sometimes an applicant is due to have surgery in the future, either in New Zealand or overseas, the fact that this is yet to occur has not deterred judges from making the declaration, even though section 28 requires evidence of medical treatment that has occurred.[84]

Consistent with the previous case law, on 13 March 2013 Judge Russell made the declaration sought and held:[85]

> 'The Court needs to be satisfied that the person has lived their life in this way for a sufficient period of time that it can be confident that there is no sudden urge about making the application which may be later regretted or that an applicant is likely to change his/her mind. *Evidence of gender re-assignment surgery having been undertaken, while helpful, is not an essential pre-requisite for such an application being granted.*'

3.2.2. Passports

A New Zealand passport may be issued in a person's nominated sex or gender without the need to change these details on a birth certificate or citizenship record. A person needs to complete the usual adult application form (if 18 years of age or over) and a statutory declaration.[86] This must include which sex or gender

---

79 *C-DT*, above n. 76 (FtM); *Basinger v Registrar-General* [2013] NZFC 3562 (MtF)

80 See *KRM v Registrar-General of Births, Deaths and Marriages of Wellington*, above n. 73 (FtM); *H v Registrar-General of Births, Deaths and Marriages* FAM Waitakere, FAM 2009-090-2000, 21 September 2010 (MtF); *MMT v Registrar-General of Births, Deaths and Marriages* [2012] NZFC 3533, 15 May 2012 (MtF); *DAC v Registrar-General of Births, Death and Marriages* [2013] NZFC 1998, 13 March 2013 (MtF); *Lucas v Registrar-General of Births, Deaths and Marriages* [2013] NZFC 6612 (FtM).

81 *MMT v Registrar-General of Births, Deaths and Marriages*, above n. 80, para. 7.

82 *MMT v Registrar-General of Births, Deaths and Marriages*, above n. 80, para. 4.

83 *KRM v Registrar-General of Births, Deaths and Marriages of Wellington*, above n. 73, para. 9.

84 *H v Registrar-General of Births, Deaths and Marriages*, above n. 80, para. 28; *C-DT*, above n. 80, para. 21.

85 *DAC v Registrar-General of Births, Death and Marriages*, above n. 80, para. 12 (emphasis added).

86 <www.passports.govt.nz/Transgender-applicants> accessed 18.12.2013.

identity is preferred for inclusion in the passport (M, F or X) and how long the current sex or gender identity has been maintained. As with a driver's licence (see below section 3.2.3) there is nothing stated in the publicly available information regarding a minimum time for a person to have 'maintained' their nominated sex or gender.

Applicants under the age of 18 also need to provide a statutory declaration from a parent or legal guardian and a counsellor or health professional, which 'supports the change in sex/gender identity in their passport.'

These changes must be seen in the wider context of technological advances regarding facial recognition programmes and the use of fingerprinting at borders. In such a context, identifying people by their sex or gender is less significant. In fact, New Zealand departure and arrival information documentation no longer requires a person to fill out either their name or their sex details – only their passport number.

3.2.3. Driver Licences

In order to change the sex or gender details on the driver licence register (DLR) a person must provide confirmation of the gender they wish to have recorded by presentation of an original 'evidence of identity' document, which states that gender.[87] Evidence of identity includes a birth certificate, passport or certificate of citizenship. If the gender on the document does not match the one the person wishes to appear on the DLR then they must also provide an original statutory declaration, in the form provided on the website (Form DLR25). The declaration must state the gender the person wishes to have recorded on the DLR and the period of time they have maintained their gender – however, none of the policy documents publicly available indicate a particular period of time is required for the change in gender to be recorded.[88] The declaration also allows amendment of the sex or gender information on the motor vehicle register. The making of the declaration must be witnessed in the usual way by a Justice of the Peace, Member of Parliament, lawyer, a registered legal executive or any government officer authorised to take statutory declarations.

Applicants under the age of 18 years must also provide two further statutory declarations: one from their parent or guardian which documents their support of the applicant's change of gender identity as recorded on the DLR, and one from a registered counsellor or medical professional in support of the change to the DLR.

---

87 <www.nzta.govt.nz/licence/renewing-replacing/replacing-changing.hmtl> accessed 18.12.2013.

88 Representatives of New Zealand Transport Agency and the Department of Internal Affairs have both stated there is no minimum time period – although if this is the case, the requirement that it is specified is otiose.

3.2.4. Citizenship and Evidentiary Certificates

As discussed in section 3.1.4, citizenship and evidentiary certificates will reflect the nominated sex of a person only if they have changed their birth certificate or have received a relevant court declaration of similar effect, at the time the certificate is issued. This means the access issues, in terms of cost and legal knowledge, are the same.

If a person has changed their birth certificate or obtained a court order *after* the issuing of a certificate of citizenship, it cannot be changed retrospectively, but an evidentiary certificate can be issued with the nominated sex included. The reason for this is that a citizenship document is only of historical effect. It shows the gender of the person on the date they were granted citizenship. It is not proof of someone's current identity – it is 'only proof that the person named on it was granted New Zealand citizenship on the specified date'.[89] Citizenship certificates are issued only once and are not re-issued unless it is shown that the information on it was incorrect at the time it was first issued.[90] If details about the person have changed since the citizenship certificate was issued, these changes can only be reflected in an evidentiary certificate. The Department of Internal Affairs has stated that this is the appropriate process:

> 'We believe the ability to issue an evidentiary certificate showing a person's new sex (or showing no sex) is an appropriate balance for the need for the Department to keep the historical record accurate, and an individual's desire to have the gender as they presently are, recorded on a certificate'.[91]

However, even an evidentiary certificate can only be issued showing the person's nominated sex (male or female) when a court declaration (under section 28 of the BDMRRA) is obtained. A person who wishes to have no sex recorded on their citizenship or evidentiary certificate can succeed in this request through a statutory declaration process. However for many trans people not having sex details on the certificate is unlikely to be their first option, as it will not reflect their gender identity. As stated by a trans woman in relation to the use of 'X' on a passport: 'I don't want to be in the middle. I've been in the grey area for too long.'[92]

---

89 Human Rights Commission, above n. 2, para. 6.83.
90 Human Rights Commission, above n. 2, para. 6.84.
91 Human Rights Commission, above n. 2, para. 6.84.
92 *Submissions Analysis*, above n. 24, p. 22.

IV. CONSEQUENCES OF THE CHANGE OF LEGAL SEX

In this part, the change focused on is the change to the sex details recorded on a person's birth certificate, as this is the change with the most wide-ranging impact. Other changes, to passports or the driver licence register for example, have significance only in that specific context. The important statutory provision for this discussion is therefore section 33 of the BDMRRA which provides that '[n]otwithstanding this Part of this Act, the sex of every person shall continue to be determined by the general law of New Zealand'. The effect of this section is that 'the registration of information that the person in question is of the nominated sex does not, *per se*, determine that person's sex in the eyes of the law in all respects.'[93] On 8 January 2014, Judge Hikaka made the following statement:[94]

> 'I note, and am grateful to counsel to assist the Court, Mr McCarthy's reminder that the [section 28] application itself was on the basis of gaining legal recognition of a transition from male to female by *legally changing gender to female*. That is not possible by law, but what is possible as a result of further definition of the issues at hand, is a declaration that the applicant's birth certificate record sex as female rather than male as currently recorded.'

This limitation has had particular significance with regard to the ability to marry as a person of the nominated sex.[95] This example was discussed in *'Michael'*,[96] where Judge Fitzgerald noted the comments of Ellis J in *Attorney-General v Family Court at Otahuhu*.[97] Ellis J drew a distinction between the recognition of a change of sex on a birth certificate and whether a trans man was a male for the purposes of marriage, although holding that there would be no social advantage in the law not recognising the validity of a marriage 'of a transsexual in a reassignment case'.[98] In *'Michael'* the *amicus* submitted that 'if the test in [section 28] can be met by a lower threshold than the test for marriage, transsexuals with amended birth certificates' may not be able to marry, only enter into a civil union. She pointed out that 'a [FtM] may live as a male, be socially perceived as a male, and be legally recognised as a male in official identity documents, but only be able to marry as a

---

93 P.R.H. Webb, above n. 72, p. 114.
94 *Hemmings v Births, Deaths and Marriages* [2014] NZFC 85, para. 2 (emphasis added).
95 In fact, it has been the only meaningful example ever provided by the DIA of where section 33 might be a relevant limitation. There is no discussion concerning the scope of the section in the Parliamentary debates.
96 *'Michael'*, above n. 72, para. 104.
97 *Attorney-General v Family Court at Otahuhu*, above n. 17.
98 *Attorney-General v Family Court at Otahuhu*, above n. 17, p. 607.

female.'[99] This was the rather unpalatable effect of the combination of section 28 and section 33.[100]

4.1. FUTURE RIGHTS, DUTIES AND ENTITLEMENTS

This section outlines the impact of changing the sex details on a birth certificate to a range of situations – including intimate relationships, participation in gender-specific sporting activities and interaction with the criminal justice system.

4.1.1. Marriage and Civil Partnerships

On 19 August 2013 section 2 of the Marriage Act 1955 (NZ) came into force, which defines marriage as 'the union of 2 people, regardless of their sex, sexual orientation, or gender identity'. Although much of the public debate focused on the impact of the change on same-sex couples, the definition in the Act, unlike reforms in many other jurisdictions, also had significance for those who are not legally recognised in their affirmed sex, do not identify as male or female, or choose not to do so for the purpose of the legal recognition of their intimate relationship.[101]

This definition is important as it allows the marriage of any two people, without the need for either person to define themselves as either the same or different sex as their partner, or to be legally recognised as either male or female. The definition therefore allows, for example, a trans man to legally marry a cisgender woman without having to first establish his legal sex. The definition also allows a person who identifies as intersex and whose birth certificate records their sex as indeterminate to marry any other person. What this reform means is that a change to the sex details on a birth certificate is no longer required before a trans man may marry a cisgender woman, and even if this step is taken, section 33 of the BDMRRA can no longer prevent the marriage occurring. These couples are no longer limited to the option of a civil union as a marker of their commitment.

4.1.2. Parental Status and Responsibilities

Once a person has changed their sex details on their birth certificate there is no reason they cannot be treated as a mother or father with regard to any children born *after* that process (including their status as such on the child's birth certificate).[102] However New Zealand law (including rules of succession and

99 *'Michael'*, above n. 72, para. 106.
100 P.R.H. Webb, above n. 72, p. 115.
101 See <jurist.org/forum/2013/05/elisabeth-mcdonald-samesex-marriage.php> accessed 16.02.2015.
102 Human Rights Commission, above n. 2, para. 4.12.

testamentary rights) generally draws no material distinction between men and women (or mothers and fathers).

4.1.3. *Participation in Sport*

The sporting exception in the Human Rights Act 1993 that permits sex-segregated sports activity is limited. Section 49(1) of the Act, which permits limited discrimination, does not apply if the young person is under 12 (section 49(2)(d)) – therefore the prohibition of discrimination under section 44 applies to young children. The exception also only applies if the sport is a *competitive* sporting activity and one where 'strength, stamina or physique of competitors' is relevant.

That competitive advantage would only apply to a trans woman, fa'afafine or whakawahine who has reached puberty *and* is not taking any form of hormone blockers or hormones to counteract the effect of male sex hormones. This is because gender affirming surgeries and/or hormone treatment would reduce her strength and muscle tone.[103]

The Human Rights Commission was involved in resolving an issue that concerned a trans woman who played in a woman's cricket team:[104]

> 'After a game of women's club cricket, the losing team complained to the local cricket association that the winning team had included a trans woman. It asked that the club's winning points be taken away. The player's club supported Anne's right to play. It asked her to provide information about her gender identity and history playing for another association so it could report back to the local association. Anne contacted the Commission for information about her rights under the Human Rights Act so she could pass this on to her club …
>
> The Commission told Anne the view of the Commission and the Crown Law Office is that trans women are covered under the HRA, as outlined in the Transgender Inquiry report. A trans woman who had taken decisive steps to live as a woman should be recognised as such and should be free from discrimination under the ground of sex. However, the HRA also includes a sport exception, which allows women-only and male-only sports where strength, stamina or physique are relevant. This meant it was necessary to also consider whether other female competitors would be disadvantaged by competing against a trans woman. The Commission told Anne that overseas sporting organisations are increasingly taking into account the impact that taking female hormones for a number of years would have in reducing any competitive advantage a trans woman might have over other women …
>
> The information was passed on to the cricket association, which ruled that Anne was eligible to play and supported her right to do so.'

[103] These principles were used in the 2nd Regional Asia Pacific OutGames held in Wellington, New Zealand in March 2011 (Participation Policy, 11 June 2010, on file with the authors).
[104] Human Rights Commission, above n. 2, p. 317.

In those instances where a trans woman or girl wants to play competitive sport and has a physical competitive advantage over other girls because of male hormone levels, mixed netball may be a good option. Ideally a trans girl or woman in that situation would be able to play as a female (wearing a female uniform if the team has different uniforms for females and males) but she would be counted as one of the 'male' team members.[105] However, internationally these arguments are evolving as more is learnt about the actual effects of hormones on the performance of female athletes. Care has to be taken in order to avoid the risk of intersex athletes being required to take hormones in order to compete as the gender they identify as.[106]

4.1.4. Criminal Liability, Bodily Searches and Imprisonment

Aside from some competitive sporting contexts and schooling, interaction with the criminal justice process is one of the few areas in New Zealand where sex matters – that is, it is essential to identify as male or female and particular consequences flow from that identification. In some contexts, self-identification is sufficient, but in others it is sex details of the person's birth certificate that will dictate how they will be classified and treated.

4.1.4.1. Criminal Liability

With very few exceptions, New Zealand's criminal law is gender neutral. This is arguably the flow-on effect of the Human Rights Commission Consistency 2000 Project, which has resulted in, for example, specific reforms to the sexual offence provisions. The project was set up to discover any conflicts between the Human Rights Act 1993 (HRA) and Acts and regulations in force in New Zealand, government policies or administrative practices, as required by section 5(1)(i)–(k) of the HRA. The exemption for the government for non-compliance with the 1993 Act was originally planned to end on 1 January 2000. In May 1998 however the Government announced that rather than introducing permanent exemptions for the government, its policies would be required to comply with the HRA, unless expressly exempted.[107] Legislation and regulations would be considered for any inconsistencies as they came up for review. In 1998 the Cabinet introduced an Amendment Bill to the HRA to give effect to these changes. The Commission however, in line with its statutory obligation, did publish its report in December

---

105 See also: <www.hrc.co.nz/wp-content/uploads/2011/11/TGI-Fact-Sheet-A.html> accessed 18.12.2013.

106 <www.oii.org.au/27647/no-scientific-basis-for-current-policy-excluding-elite-intersex-women-from-sport/> accessed 29.01.15. See also K. Karkazis et al 'Out of Bounds? A Critique of the New Policies on Hyperandrogenism in Elite Female Athletes' (2012) 12 *The American Journal of Bioethics* 3.

107 Human Rights Commission, above n. 2, p. 311.

1998, commencing with the line: 'This is the report that the government did not want'.[108]

One of the notable exceptions to gender neutrality is the 'male assaults female' assault provision in section 194 of the Crimes Act 1961. This carries a higher penalty than so-called 'common' assault (two years' imprisonment as opposed to six months').[109] Periodic review and discussion of this section has not resulted in its repeal, with police indicating it is a very valuable charging option in cases of family violence.[110]

Although the specific offence of 'rape' was retained as part of the 2005 amendments, as a form of the crime of sexual violation (section 128 of the Crimes Act 1961), the *actus reus* was re-defined as being the 'penetration of person B's genitalia by person A's penis' (that is, without reference to the sex or gender of the offender or victim).[111] Section 2 of the Act defines genitalia as including 'a surgically constructed or reconstructed organ analogous to naturally occurring male or female genitalia (whether the person concerned is male, female, or of indeterminate sex)', and 'penis' as including 'a surgically constructed or reconstructed organ analogous to a naturally occurring penis (whether the person concerned is male, female, or of indeterminate sex)'. Prior to these amendments, rape could only occur between a biologically male offender and a biologically female victim.

4.1.4.2. Bodily or Strip Searches

Current police policy is that anyone can nominate their gender identity and that will govern who searches them, and will apply where practicable (e.g. if there is a police officer of that sex on duty and it is not an emergency such as when police suspect someone has a weapon). For example, if someone identifies as a trans woman, they will be searched by a female police officer. As reported in the Transgender Inquiry: 'In short, the [various governing police] instructions state that a trans person should be asked which gender they identify with and that due accord be given to their answer where practicable.'[112]

The Inquiry noted that the recently completed Law Commission report, *Search and Surveillance Powers*,[113] did not 'consider the practical issues for trans

108 Human Rights Commission, *Consistency 2000: Report to the Minister of Justice pursuant to Section 5(1)(k) of the Human Rights Act 1993*, Wellington 1998, p. 6.

109 Section 9 of the Summary Offences Act 1981 (NZ).

110 New Zealand Law Commission, *Review of Part 8 of the Crimes Act 1961: Crimes Against the Person*, Report 111, Wellington 2009. See also E. McDonald, 'Contemporary feminist thought in Aotearoa/New Zealand: Feminist legal theory in Aotearoa New Zealand: The impact of international critical work on local criminal law reform' (2014) 28(2) *Women's Studies Journal* 68, 72.

111 Cisgender women have been convicted of rape under this provision: see *L v R* [2006] 3 NZLR 291 (SC).

112 Human Rights Commission, above n. 2, para. 4.78.

113 Law Commission, *Search and Surveillance Powers*, NZLC, R97, Wellington, 2007.

people who are searched'.[114] However, progress has been made in this area since the Inquiry, as following the enactment of the Search and Surveillance Act 2012 Part 8 of the Police Manual on search and surveillance contains internal guidelines, which are applicable in such cases. The guidelines in this context relate to section 126(4) of the Search and Surveillance Act 2012 which provides that a 'strip search may be carried out only by a person of the same sex as the person to be searched, and no strip search may be carried out in view of any person who is not of the same sex as the person to be searched.' The Act does not define 'same sex', which may 'cause difficulty when the sex is unclear'.[115] However, the guidelines state:[116]

> '[T]he search should be undertaken by a person of the same sex as the preferred sex stated by the person to be searched. If a transgender person refuses to state a preference, the sex should be determined on the basis of gender presentation, such as name and clothing. If an intersex person refuses to state a preference, the search should be undertaken by two persons, one of each sex.'

4.1.4.3. Imprisonment

The Transgender Inquiry highlighted some significant areas of concern for trans prisoners, with a number of trans women reporting that they had been held in a male prison, as consistent with the information on their birth certificate.[117] They told of having to follow male dress codes, as well as being subject to physical and sexual harassment and abuse. Inmates who had not been prescribed hormones prior to sentencing were unable to obtain hormone treatment while in prison.[118] Although the Inquiry did not receive submissions from trans men inmates, trans men did raise concerns 'about their potential vulnerability within prisons particularly their physical safety within a male prison, but also the extent to which their male gender identity would be recognised if they were sent to a female prison.'[119]

The Department of Corrections advised the Inquiry that at any one time 'there might be 10 to 20 inmates who were identified as "transgender". All were

---

114 Human Rights Commission, above n. 2, para. 4.76. See also K. Stove, *Preserving Human Dignity: An Advocation for the Consideration of Trans and Intersex People in Accordance with 'Human Rights Values' when Conducting Strip Searches under the Search and Surveillance Act 2012*, Victoria University of Wellington LLB Honours Research Paper, 2013, on file with the authors.

115 W. Young, N. Trendle and R. Mahoney, *Search and Surveillance Act and Analysis*, Brookers, Wellington 2012, para. SS126.03.

116 W. Young, N. Trendle and R. Mahoney, above n. 115, para. SS126.03.

117 Human Rights Commission, above n. 2, para. 4.64.

118 One prisoner is currently exploring mediation with the Department of Corrections through the Human Rights Commission regarding this issue: see *Forrest v Chief Executive of the Department of Corrections* [2014] NZHRRT 47.

119 Human Rights Commission, above n. 2, para. 4.67.

trans women who were held in men's prisons.'[120] This number did not include trans women who had changed their sex details on their birth certificate, as they were considered by the Department to be female rather than trans.

In early 2012 the New Zealand Office of the Ombudsman also raised concerns about the treatment of trans women in male prisons.[121] This investigation noted a Health Centre Manager's comment that 'abuse [of transgender prisoners] goes unrecorded in male prisons'.[122] Risk of abuse may be managed by voluntary segregation but that can reduce the inmate's access to prison activities, including rehabilitation programmes. The Office recommended that the Department of Corrections should review 'its policy regarding the placement of transgender prisoners. For transgender prisoners who have not completed full sexual reassignment, consideration should be given to their placement in a women's prison, if it is their wish to do so.'[123] The Department initially did not accept this recommendation.[124] Despite public concern and pressure from the opposition Members of Parliament, the Minister of Corrections remained unwilling to review the policy regarding the treatment of trans prisoners and stated in Parliament on 29 February 2012 that there 'is no evidence of widespread sexual abuse.'[125] However in December 2012 a trans woman was given a reduction in sentence in recognition of the difficulties she would face in a men's prison.[126]

On 10 June 2013 the Equal Justice Project, a youth run pro bono organisation led by students from the Faculty of Law at the University of Auckland, published their report on the treatment of trans prisoners under the Department of Corrections policies, entitled *Transgender Prisoners' Rights Ignored*.[127] The report argued that the policies were in breach of both domestic and international human rights obligations, including sections 9, 19 and 23 of the New Zealand Bill of Rights Act 1990 and section 21 of the Human Rights Act 1993 (NZ).[128] The report recommended that prisoners should not need to have initiated medical treatment to 'receive protection and recognition of their gender identity.'[129] Trans prisoners should also be free from harassment and discrimination and should receive 'the same quality of care as they would expect to receive through the public health

---

120 Human Rights Commission, above n. 2, para. 8.36.

121 <www.ombudsman.parliament.nz/system/paperclip/document_files/document_files/456/original/own_motion_prisoner_health.pdf?1349735789> accessed 18.12.2013.

122 Office of the Ombudsman, above n. 121, p. 105.

123 Office of the Ombudsman, above n. 121, Recommendation 27.

124 Office of the Ombudsman, *Annual Report of the Ombudsman 2011–2012*, Wellington 2012.

125 (29 February 2012) 677 NZPD 667.

126 'Transgender woman to serve time in male jail', *New Zealand Herald*, 19 December 2012.

127 <http://equaljusticeproject.files.wordpress.com/2013/03/equal-justice-project-transgender-prisoners-rights-ignored-report.pdf> accessed 18.12.2013.

128 See also S.F. Dewing, *Women Among Men; Human Rights Jurisprudence and Pre-Operative Male-to-Female Transgender Imprisonment*, MA Thesis, University of Auckland, completed July 2013. On file with the authors.

129 Equal Justice Project, above n. 127, p. 22.

service, including counselling, pre-operative and post-operative care, and continued access to hormone treatment.'[130]

On 25 September 2013 the same Minister of Corrections, the Hon Anne Tolley, announced a more flexible system would be introduced for trans prisoners, 'in line with international practice' and in response to the report of the Office of the Ombudsman. However the only reform is that transgender prisoners whose sex on their birth certificates has not been changed may apply to the Chief Executive to be moved into a prison congruent with their 'identified gender'.[131] This process does not apply to those serving or facing charges for serious sexual offending.

Regulations now provide:[132]

> '*65 Accommodation of male and female prisoners*
> (1) Male and female prisoners must be detained–
> (a) in separate prisons; or
> (b) within the same prison in separate quarters that are secured by different locking systems.
> (2) Where there is doubt about whether a prisoner is male or female, the chief executive must determine whether the prisoner is a male or female prisoner for the purpose of subclause (1).
> (3) If a prisoner supplies a copy of the prisoner's birth certificate that records the prisoner's sex as female or male, the determination under subclause (2) must be made in accordance with that sex.
> (4) If a prisoner supplies a copy of the prisoner's birth certificate that records the prisoner's sex as indeterminate, or records no sex, the chief executive must–
> (a) undertake a review of the determination made under subclause (2); and
> (b) inform the prisoner that a review is being undertaken.
> (5) If a prisoner is not satisfied with the determination made under subclause (2), the prisoner may make an application for review under regulation 65B.
>
> *65A Interpretation*
> In regulations 65B to 65D,–
> *nominated sex* means the sex, whether male or female, nominated by a prisoner
> *sentence expiry date* has the same meaning as in section 4(1) of the Parole Act 2002
> *serious sexual offence* means a sexual offence under Part 7 of the Crimes Act 1961 that is punishable by a period of imprisonment of 7 years or more.

130 Equal Justice Project, above n. 127, p. 22.

131 <www.beehive.govt.nz/release/prison-changes-increase-rehab-and-safety> accessed 18.12.2013.

132 See also the Operating Manual update: <www.corrections.govt.nz/resources/prison-operations-manual/Movement/M.03-Specified-gender-and-age-movements/M.03-4.html> accessed 29.01.15.

65B Prisoner may apply for review of determination as to sex

(1) A prisoner may apply to the chief executive for a review of the determination made under regulation 65(2).

(2) However, a prisoner may not make an application under subclause (1) if the prisoner–

(a) is serving a sentence of imprisonment for a serious sexual offence against a person of the prisoner's nominated sex; or

(b) is remanded in custody charged with, or awaiting sentence for, a serious sexual offence against a person of the prisoner's nominated sex; or

(c) has served a sentence of imprisonment for a serious sexual offence against a person of the prisoner's nominated sex, and the sentence expiry date is 7 years or less before the date on which the application is made.

(3) An application must state the prisoner's nominated sex for the purpose of regulation 65(1).

65C Review of determination as to sex

(1) This regulation applies if–

(a) a prisoner applies under regulation 65B for a review of a determination made under regulation 65(2); or

(b) the chief executive is required by regulation 65(4) to undertake a review of the determination made under regulation 65(2).

(2) The chief executive must review the determination as soon as is reasonably practicable and–

(a) confirm the original determination that the prisoner is a male or female prisoner; or

(b) determine that the prisoner should be recognised as being of the opposite sex to that originally determined.

(3) In reviewing a determination, the chief executive must consider the following matters:

(a) the prisoner's nominated sex; and

(b) any evidence provided by the prisoner about whether, and, if so, for how long, the prisoner has lived as a person of the nominated sex; and

(c) any evidence provided by the prisoner about whether the prisoner intends to live permanently as a person of the nominated sex; and

(d) the advice of–

(i) a senior employee of the department who has responsibility for custodial services; and

(ii) a senior employee of the department who has responsibility for health services for prisoners; and

(iii) any other person that the chief executive considers has relevant expertise; and

(e) any advice from a medical practitioner who has seen the prisoner; and

(f) any evidence provided by the prisoner about whether the prisoner has undergone, or is undergoing, medical treatment to acquire a physical conformation that accords with the gender identity of a person of the nominated sex; and

(g) the safety and well-being of the prisoner; and
(h) the safety and well-being of other prisoners (of either sex) with whom the prisoner may be accommodated; and
(i) the security of the prison; and
(j) whether any determination could make it more likely that the prisoner will be segregated from other prisoners in accordance with section 57 to 60 of the Act; and
(k) the likely effect of any determination on the prisoner's rehabilitation, including the prisoner's access to special treatment programmes; and
(l) any other matters raised by the prisoner.'

These changes have been welcomed, but also criticised as not going far enough to address the health and safety issues faced by trans prisoners, including those put in a prison that corresponds to their nominated gender.[133] The Equal Justice Project team also note that cisgender prisoners (those whose gender identity matches the sex they were assigned at birth) convicted of sexual assault 'do not face secondary punishment by being housed in a prison where their chances of facing assault are disproportionately high'.

4.1.5. Ceremonial Titles and Practices and Gender-Specific Honours

The highest honour awarded to New Zealand citizens is the title of 'Sir' (for men) and 'Dame' (for women). No other honours are gender-specific. They also vary in that the wife of a Sir may choose to be known as 'Lady', whereas there is no equivalent for the husband of a Dame. There is no available information as to whether any person in New Zealand holding this honour changed their nominated sex after receiving the award. Although the title should follow the nominated sex in principle, as this is a bestowed honour it is unclear whether a change to a birth certificate would have this effect of itself.

In accordance with tikanga Māori (Māori culture or custom) there is a gender-specific role for women as part of a pōwhiri (the welcoming of visitors onto a marae, which is the meeting place of a tribe or iwi). Karanga is the first stage of the pōwhiri, which is an exchange of calls that takes place when the visiting group moves onto the marae. Carried out virtually exclusively by women and in te reo (the Māori language), karanga are initiated by the hosts, with women from the visitors' side then responding. It is usual for both kaikaranga (women who carry out the karanga) to address and greet each other and the people they are representing, as well as to pay tribute to the dead known by each other and to refer to the reason the groups are meeting. There is no restriction on how long the exchange lasts or the number of women involved. However, not all women are skilled in karanga and typically only a few women may karanga on any one

133 See Equal Justice Project, 'Policy changes on transgender prisoners: a step forward', *LawTalk: Magazine of the New Zealand Law Society*, 22 November 2013, p. 30.

occasion. The exchange usually continues until the visitors have made their way to stand outside the meetinghouse. At this point a final karanga may be given by a host kuia (female elder) to indicate the visitors should be seated.

The issue as to whether whakawāhine are able to karanga was considered by the Human Rights Commission. The following is some background information the Commission has collated on this issue after consultation with its kaiwhakarite (senior Māori staff) and with whakawāhine:[134]

- Some whakawāhine have been taught to karanga by their kuia (female elders).
- Kawa (protocol on the marae) varies. Sometimes a whakawahine is able to karanga on a marae in one tribal area but not in another (even if she is linked by whakapapa, or family relationships, to both).
- Purpose is important. A group of whakawāhine were able to karanga on a marae because they were bringing someone back from overseas to be buried at home. They were given the blessing of a kuia from that marae to karanga, and that practice continues today on that marae.
- Roles are important – a whakawahine who has learnt to karanga is not always the most appropriate person to do so in any given instance – and this may or may not be because of her gender identity.
- In some instances a whakawahine can karanga only if there is another whakawahine on the other side to balance her call.
- Tikanga evolves. Traditionally only widows were able to karanga. Similarly, the requirement to have menstruated and given birth (in order to be able to karanga) is relatively traditional, and often young women do karanga within a school environment.
- There is no 'right to karanga'. It is about role, purpose, context and competence.
- It is important to create a safe environment where people are aware of tikanga and the dignity and rights of everyone are respected.

4.2. EXISTING RIGHTS, DUTIES AND ENTITLEMENTS

4.2.1. Marriage and Civil Partnerships

Since 19 August 2013, with the repeal of section 30(2) of the BDMRRA by section 9 of the Marriage (Definition of Marriage) Amendment Act 2013, trans people who are married no longer need to have their marriages dissolved before changing the sex classification on their birth certificate. Section 30(2) had operated to prevent married people from doing so.[135] There was no similar limitation in place with

134 Provided by the Human Rights Commission, correspondence on file with the authors.

135 This provided: 'The Registrar-General shall not at any time act under subsection (1) of this section if the person concerned is then lawfully married to a person of the nominated sex'.

regard to people in civil unions (which have been permitted for same-sex couples in New Zealand since 26 April 2005).[136]

4.2.2. *Parental Status and Responsibilities*

Trans parents report difficulties enforcing their rights as parents, at all stages of their transition, including after changes to legal documents.[137] Anecdotal information suggests that trans men who had their children before transitioning seem to be judged particularly harshly when considering the rights of the child, as they are seen as having denied their child a mother. This particular judgement may well be part of a conservative concern that a child should not have two (gay) male parents. In New Zealand however there are very limited gender-specific rights or obligations attaching to parents on the basis of their status as mother or father.

One exception is provided in section 5 of the Status of Children Act 1969 which creates a rebuttable presumption of parenthood. It provides that a child born to a woman during her marriage, or within 10 months after her marriage has been dissolved, shall be presumed to be the child of her husband. If the husband now identifies as a woman, and has completed the section 28 process, she is no longer a 'husband' and therefore arguably no longer a 'father' for the purposes of section 17 of the Care of Children Act 2004. It is unlikely that guardianship responsibility could be avoided in this way; however, section 33 of the BDMRRA may have a role to play in this regard.

An unresolved issue for those who have transitioned after the birth of their child, and changed the sex details on their birth certificate, is the inability currently to change their status (from father to mother or vice versa) on their child's birth certificates.

For those who have chosen not to change their birth certificate, but live in their nominated sex, parental status on the child's birth certificate may be more problematic, although this issue has yet to arise in New Zealand. For example, if a trans man wishes to be recognised as a parent of a child born while married to the mother of the child it is not clear that he could be named as father on the child's birth certificate. In this situation he may be treated similarly to a non-biological lesbian mother and listed as another parent, not as the father (see section 14 of the Status of Children Act 1969). Guardianship rights and responsibilities would still flow from this recognition however (see Part 2 of the Care of Children Act 2004).

---

136 Human Rights Commission, above n. 2, para. 6.86.

137 Human Rights Commission, above n. 2, para. 4.8.

4.2.3. *Gender- or Sex-Specific Employment*

The Human Rights Commission have pre-employment guidelines that concern situations where sex is a genuine occupational qualification and how that applies to trans people. This includes advice as to whether a person should disclose that they are transgender in a job interview:[138]

> 'In most cases it is solely your decision whether you wish to disclose that you are transgender, as your sex or gender identity has no bearing on your ability to do the job. There are some very limited circumstances where it is legal to employ only a woman or a man for a particular position, *i.e.* being female or male is a genuine occupational qualification. In these limited situations, some transgender people may need to provide evidence about their sex.'

Section 27 of the Human Rights Act 1993 allows discrimination in employment because of the sex of a job applicant or employee:[139]

- where for reasons of authenticity, being of a particular sex is a genuine occupational qualification, or
- the position is one of domestic employment, or needs to be held by one sex to preserve reasonable standards of privacy, or
- the position is that of a counsellor on highly personal matters such as sexual matters or the prevention of violence.

The Human Rights Commission advises employers that a trans woman, who has legally changed the sex details on her birth certificate to female, is able to apply for jobs that are legally advertised for women only. Similarly, a trans man with a male birth certificate may apply for jobs where being male is a genuine occupational qualification.

In addition, the Human Rights Commission's policy is that some trans people who have not changed the sex details on their birth certificate may also be able to apply for such jobs. This is possible where the trans woman (or man) can show evidence that they have taken decisive steps to live fully and permanently as a woman (or as a man).

The language 'taken decisive steps to live fully and permanently' as a woman or as a man was based on the Human Rights Commission's interpretation of international case law in 2007 when the Report of the Transgender Inquiry was finalised. The pre-employment guidelines were due to be redrafted by the Human

---

138 Human Rights Commission, *Getting a job: An A to Z for employers and employees*, p. 32 <www.hrc.co.nz/files/3014/2360/3784/HRC_A-Z_Pre-employment_Guide.pdf> accessed 16.05.2015.

139 See further Department of Labour, *Transgender People at Work* <www.dol.govt.nz/er/minimumrights/transgender/Transgenderpeople.pdf> accessed 16.02.2015.

Rights Commission in 2014 and may yet change to reflect the new interantional context.

4.2.4. *Health and Life Insurance*

Anecdotal evidence suggests that most trans people are able to assert their affirmed sex, whether or not they have had their birth certificate changed, for the purposes of health and life insurance (and car insurance, which also varies on the basis of sex).[140] This has a tendency to raise premiums across all categories for trans men and lower them for trans women. However, insurance companies in New Zealand typically exclude any gender affirming health services from coverage under health insurance schemes.

V. CHALLENGES TO THE EXISTING RULES

5.1. CHANGES TO BIRTH CERTIFICATES

The Report of the Transgender Inquiry recommended that the 'physical conformity' threshold in section 28 of the BDMRRA be replaced with the requirement that a person has 'taken decisive steps to live fully and permanently in the gender identity of the[ir] nominated sex'.[141] This recommendation did not stipulate any specific medical interventions but would still have been dependent on the evidence of expert medical witnesses as that is the framework of the BDMRRA.

Since the Transgender Inquiry there has been considerable debate internationally by courts, governments, human rights experts, health professionals and trans people about trans people's right to define their gender identity, the medical pathologisation of gender diversity and legal gender recognition. In New Zealand this has seen trans people increasingly arguing that sex details on birth certificates should be able to be changed in the same way that passports are: that is, by self-identification and without the need for medical or surgical intervention. The Human Rights Commission facilitated the Passports Office's consultation with trans communities about this proposed policy change and welcomed this new focus on self-defined gender identity.

The Human Rights Commission has acknowledged that since *To Be Who I Am* was published there has been significant progress internationally in both of these areas and the Inquiry's recommendations are now modest compared to current international best practice – such as gender recognition laws that enable

---

140 One trans woman did report difficulties based on being a perceived higher risk due to having had gender affirming surgery: <www.hrc.co.nz/hrc_new/hrc/cms/files/9914/2353/5059/28-Nov-2008_10-45-06_TeRitoNov08web.pdf> accessed 16.02.2015.

141 Human Rights Commission, above n. 2, para. 9.50.

birth certificates to be changed through a simple process, and gender identity being explicitly stated in anti-discrimination laws.[142]

In 2013 the Aotearoa New Zealand's Sexual Orientation, Gender Identity and Intersex (SOGII) UPR Coalition 2013 made a submission to the United Nations' 2014 Universal Periodic Review (UPR) of New Zealand's human rights record.[143] Both that submission and one made by a coalition member, GenderBridge,[144] highlighted the importance of 'depathologising' gender diversity, drawing on the international context, particularly the Yogyakarta Principles.

The SOGII Coalition's concerns were included in the Office of the High Commissioner for Human Rights (OHCHR) compilation documents for New Zealand's second UPR. These are the two documents that, together with the government's report, were taken into account when the government's human rights performance was considered during the 18th Session of the UPR Working Group in Geneva in January 2014:[145]

> 'GenderBridge (GB) reported on New Zealand's health system failing to respond to the needs of gender diverse populations. *GB made recommendations to remove any requirement to undergo medical procedures to acquire legal recognition of gender identity* ... ANZSOGII/JS3 recommended prioritising improving data collection about sex, gender and sexually diverse people's use of health services and their health outcomes.'

The SOGII Coalition's comments on the New Zealand government's draft UPR report resulted in the final submitted report including the following acknowledgment: 'The Ministry of Health changed its guidelines on the availability of gender reassignment surgery in 2011 but work still remains to ensure equitable access to health services and outcomes for transgender people.'[146]

None of the SOGII Coalition's recommendations were picked up by other countries in their assessment of New Zealand's human rights record. However when formally responding at the UN Human Rights Council to recommendations it received, the New Zealand government acknowledged that further work was needed in this area:[147]

---

142 <www.gaynz.com/articles/publish/32/printer_14246.php> accessed 16.02.2015.

143 <www.hrc.co.nz/files/7014/2406/3081/SOGII-Coalition_joint-UPR-submission_New-Zealand_Jan-Feb-2014-with-appendices.doc> accessed 25.05.2015.

144 <www.hrc.co.nz/files/2814/2406/3074/Submission-on-Depathologising-Gender-Diversity-in-New-Zealand.docx> accessed 16.05.2015.

145 <www.converge.org.nz/pma/A-HRC-WG.6-18-NZL-3-PMA.pdf> accessed 16.02.2015.

146 <www.mfat.govt.nz/downloads/humanrights/New%20Zealand%20UPR%20national%20report%20-%20submitted%20version%20(3).pdf> accessed 16.02.2015, para. 65.

147 <www.hrc.co.nz/wp-content/uploads/2013/03/New-Zealand-Government-Response-to-2014-UPR-recommendations.pdf> accessed 29.01.15, para. 3.

> 'The New Zealand Government is aware that some issues raised by the Human Rights Commission and NGOs in their UPR submissions were not reflected in the interactive dialogue and Working Group recommendations, for example issues around legal abortion and the rights relating to sexual orientation, gender identity and intersex people. We intend to follow up on these issues separately as part of our commitment to ongoing engagement with civil society on the UPR.'

ITANZ (the Intersex Trust Aotearoa New Zealand) has also called on the government, in its submission on New Zealand's draft periodic report on the Convention Against Torture (CAT), to 'remove any requirement to undergo or intend to undergo medical or surgical procedures, including those that may result in sterilisation, as a prerequisite for changing sex details on a birth certificate or other official document.'[148]

ITANZ was of the view that this statement was a clear direction to the New Zealand government to review the current laws and practices which impact in these ways on members of trans and intersex communities – in particular: sections 28 and 29 of the Births, Deaths, Marriages and Relationships Recognition Act 1995; section 204A of the Crimes Act 1961; and, the current medical practice of cosmetic genital surgery on intersex infants without the free and fully informed consent of the child or the child's parents. However, no mention of these issues was made in the New Zealand government's sixth periodic report on compliance with the CAT.[149] ITANZ has therefore recently joined other community groups in voicing its concerns directly to Secretariat of the Committee against Torture.[150]

Given that the amendment to the Marriage Act 1955 has removed the requirement to either change a birth certificate in order for a trans person to marry as their nominated sex, or to seek dissolution of their existing marriage as a condition of changing their birth certificate, the way is clear for less stringency in the section 28 (or section 29) process. This point has been recently made in the Australian context:

> 'Removing the perceived obstacle of same-sex marriage may enable Parliament and courts to facilitate a more genuinely transformative approach to gender regulation whereby, for example, gender could be self-determined without any medical intervention or treatment.'[151]

There are also calls to repeal section 33 of the BDMRRA, which would ensure that a change to sex details on a birth certificate would have effect for all legal purposes.

[148] Copy on file with the authors, p. 3.
[149] <www.hrc.co.nz/index.php/downloadfile/1316> accessed 16.05.2015.
[150] Submission on file with the authors.
[151] L. Grenfell and A. Hewitt, 'Gender Regulation: Restrictive, Facilitative or Transformative Laws?' (2012) 34 *Sydney Law Review* 761, 783.

At present, however, no legislative reform has been proposed, although a number of opposition Members of Parliament are interested in considering an alternative process. Currently section 28 is flexible enough to accommodate a declaration made in the absence of any requirement to undertake treatment. The concern for the trans community is that interpretation of the section turns on judicial discretion, which may not be consistent or transparent. The Human Rights Commission's report *Human Rights in NZ 2010* stated these outstanding concerns:[152]

> 'New Zealand law does not clearly state that trans people do not need to undergo medical or surgical steps that result in sterilisation in order to change sex details on official documents. Currently, under New Zealand law, a trans person may or may not be required to undergo sterilisation in order to change the sex on their birth certificate. In the *Re Michael* decision, the applicant was able to obtain a male birth certificate without having undergone a hysterectomy. However, the Commission has been informed of other decisions where trans women have been required to show evidence of full sex-reassignment surgery.'

One possibility to ensure consistency of judicial decision-making is for a Practice Note to be issued by the Principal Family Court Judge. These and other advocacy strategies are being actively considered. It should be noted that in the SOGII Coalition's recommendations included the call that the New Zealand government be directed to:[153]

> '(e) remove any requirement to undergo or intend to undergo medical or surgical procedures, including those that may result in sterilisation, as a prerequisite for changing sex details on a birth certificate or other official document;
> (f) enable adults with intersex conditions and trans and other gender diverse adults to change the sex details on any official documentation to male, female or indeterminate based solely on the individual's self-identification, without any requirement for medical treatment and without the need to resort to a court process.'

5.2. CHANGES TO CITZENSHIP CERTIFICATES

A trans woman, born in England, who has obtained a declaration under section 28 of the BDMRRA, has been campaigning for changes to the law that would allow a citizenship certificate to be re-issued to reflect changes to a person's sex after the certificate was issued. The most recent response from the Minister of

[152] Human Rights Commission, above n. 2, p. 319.
[153] <www.hrc.co.nz/wp-content/uploads/2013/08/SOGII-Coalition_joint-UPR-submission_New-Zealand_Jan-Feb-2014-with-appendices.doc> accessed 16.02.2015.

Internal Affairs is that this will require an amendment to the Citizenship Act 1977 and that he is unable to indicate 'when a bill to amend the Act will next be on the legislative programme'.[154] However, it should be possible to allow trans people to request an evidentiary certificate to reflect their nominated sex without requiring them to obtain a court order. If this is an available procedure for those who wish to have no sex details recorded, it is unclear why it should not also be possible for those who wish to have sex details changed.

---

[154] Letter to Allyson Hamblett from the Hon Chris Tremain, 23 October 2013, on file with the authors. See also Human Rights Commission, above n. 2, p. 17.

NORTH AND SOUTH AMERICA

THE LEGAL STATUS OF TRANSSEXUAL AND TRANSGENDER PERSONS IN ARGENTINA

Laura María Giosa, María Victoria Schiro and Peter Dunne

Contents

I. LEGAL FRAMEWORK AND STATISTICS

1.1. ACT NO. 26.743 ON GENDER IDENTITY

1.1.1. Self-Identification and Perception

In Argentina, the current law on the legal recognition of preferred gender is set out in Act No. 26.743 ('Gender Identity Act' or '2012 Act'), which was enacted in May 2012. The Gender Identity Act has established a radically new regime for legal gender recognition in Argentina, moving away from the previous, court-centred system towards a process which prioritises the self-identification and self-perception of transgender individuals. This new departure is evident not only in the way persons can obtain legal recognition but also in the extended and simplified rights which transgender individuals now enjoy regarding appropriate health care. The far-reaching changes which have been enacted by the 2012 Act are evident in Article 2 of the 2012 Act, which defines 'gender identity' as 'the internal and individual way in which gender is *perceived by persons*, that can correspond or not to the gender assigned at birth, including the personal experience of the body' (emphasis added). Article 2 continues that a person's perception of their own gender 'can involve modifying bodily appearance or functions through pharmacological, surgical or other means, provided it is freely chosen.' Gender identity also includes 'other expressions of gender such as dress, ways of speaking and gestures.'[1]

1.1.2. Argentina's Constitutional Regime

The Gender Identity Act is a product of Argentina's constitutional environment, particularly the right to privacy set out in Article 19 of the National Constitution. Article 19 declares that 'private personal' acts, which offend neither public order nor morals and which do not harm third parties, fall within God's will and are not subject to review by judges. Under Article 19, a person cannot be compelled to engage in any act which is not prescribed by law nor can he be prevented from actions which are not proscribed by law. Article 75, subsection 22, incorporates a number of international treaties, conventions and charters into Argentina's constitutional regime. These international agreements, many of which have already recognised the protection of individuals on the basis of gender identity, include, *inter alia*, the International Covenant on Economic, Social and Cultural Rights, the International Covenant on Civil and Political Rights and the American Convention on Human Rights.

1 Act No. 26.743, Art. 2 (translation provided by Transgender Europe) <www.tgeu.org/Argentina_Gender_Identity_Law> accessed 07.07.2014.

1.1.3. The Recognition of Preferred Gender Pre-2012: An Evolving Jurisprudence

Prior to 2012, the system for legal gender recognition in Argentina was characterised by extensive judicial control. Before the Gender Identity Act, the legal status of transgender and transsexual persons in Argentina was, in terms of statute, governed by two laws: Act No. 17.132 on medical, dentistry and similar collaborative practice rules and Act No. 18.248, which set out procedures for changing legal name. Under Article 19 of Act No. 17.132, gender confirmation surgery was heavily restricted, except where an individual could show that he or she had obtained judicial consent. Article 15 of Act No. 18.248 provided for similarly limited procedures in relation to amending a person's name.

It is possible to identify three distinct stages in Argentina's evolving jurisprudence on preferred gender recognition.[2] The first stage was defined by a landmark ruling from the National Civil Court of Appeals, Tribunal E,[3] in 1989. In this case, which involved an application made by a post-operative transgender woman for recognition, a majority of the court held that the applicant's request could not be accepted. While the Court acknowledged that an individual's 'sex' is the product of many, complex factors, it nevertheless held that priority had to be given to biological sex characteristics, which the Court stated were 'immutable'. The case, however, is notable for a dissenting opinion issued by Judge Catalayud, in which he strongly advocated for a more liberal, understanding approach. Judge Catalayud wrote that:

> 'once a person has managed, after surgery, to adjust her anatomy with her psychological sex, she must be helped to get into society by legally acknowledging her new status, because she has freely and willingly chosen the hard and irreversible path that led her to adapt her physical appearance with her inner feeling. The contrary would take her to social marginalization.'

During the second stage in the law's development, the courts began to permit legal gender recognition, but only where the applicant could prove that he or she was affected by an intersex condition. In 1993, the First Instance Civil National Court No. 18[4] allowed an individual to amend their name and gender markers on a birth certificate where the individual produced evidence of 'Klinefelter's Syndrome'. In 1994, the San Nicolás Civil and Commercial Court of Appeals permitted another individual (a) to amend the gender markers on their identity documents[5]

---

[2] G. Medina, 'Bioética, libertad sexual y derecho (Libertad de elección sexual, libertad de contracepción, libertad de cambio de sexo. Límites y responsabilidades' (2002) *Revista de Derecho de Familia Lexis Nexis* 21, 91.

[3] Cámara Nacional de Apelaciones en lo Civil, sala E, 31/03/1989 (RDF 1990-4-133; JA 1990-III-97; MP: Juan C. G. Dupuis – Osvaldo D. Miras. Disidencia: Mario P. Catalayud).

[4] *B., J. L.*, Juzgado Nacional de 1era Instancia en lo Civil No. 18, ED 152–733.

[5] *C., L. J.*, Cámara de Apelaciones en lo Civil y Comercial de San Nicolás, 11/08/1994, JA 1995-II-380.

and (b) to submit to surgical intervention in order to treat a congenital genital dystrophy condition. In such cases, the courts noted that it was not, as had been suggested in 1989, possible to assign the individual a definitive legal gender based upon unambiguous biological sex characteristics. Therefore, the courts would permit legal recognition so as to create greater coherence between legal gender and a person's socio-psychological identification. These cases in the mid-1990s are important for an emerging consciousness among judges of the difficulties which gender-variant individuals face when there is incongruence between gender presentation and legal gender status. These difficulties are particularly pronounced when considering access to basic rights, such as employment and voting.

The third and final stage in the case law witnessed increasing judicial support for the legal recognition of preferred gender, and a movement away from the medicalisation of recognition procedures. While there remained dissenting judicial voices, particularly regarding 'when' and 'how' to recognise gender,[6] this third stage was overwhelmingly characterised by court-led efforts to remove biology, and later pathology, from gender identity rules. In 2008, the Mar del Plata Criminal and Correctional Court No. 4[7] stated that:

> 'subjecting the sex reassignment judicial judgment ... to a previous surgical intervention, which is certainly settled for a future time, would carry a serious inconsistency: it would mean to still remain in a reductionist viewpoint which identifies the sex as gender with only one of its expressions, in this case the external male genital organs disregarding the personal identity examined from an all-embracing approach and considering expert opinions and complemented by other relevant evidence'.

In October, 2010, the Autonomous City of Buenos Aires Administrative and Tax Court rejected a requirement that, before obtaining legal recognition of preferred gender, an applicant should submit to psychological analysis of his gender identity. According to the Court, it was 'not relevant to produce such tests or examinations because they are unnecessary and because they involve undue state scrutiny of private personality aspects.' Where an individual seeks legal recognition of his

---

6 The jurisprudence that preceded the norm established the birth certificate rectification trough a marginal note. For instance: Tribunal de familia No. 1 de Quilmes, 30/04/2001 (La Ley 2001-F, 217; MP: Dalla Via); Juzgado de Primera Instancia Civil y Comercial No. 3 de la provincia de Formosa, 10/09/2009 (MP: Judith E. Sosa de Lozina); Juzg. Crim. y Corr. Transición Mar del Plata, n. 1, 19/07/2001 (Lexis No. 20014211; MP: Pedro Federico Hooft); Juzgado en lo Correccional No. 4 de Mar del Plata, 16/03/2009 (AR/JUR/67615/2009; MP: Pedro Federico Hooft). Suprema Corte de Justicia de la Provincia de Buenos Aires, 21/03/2007 (AR/JUR/4098/2007; MP: Eduardo Néstor de Lázzari. – Francisco Héctor Roncoroni. – Juan Carlos Hitters. – Luis Esteban Genoud. – Daniel Fernando Soria. – Hilda Bogan).

7 *P., R. L.*, Juzgado en lo Criminal y Correccional No. 4 de Mar del Plata, 10/04/2008, La Ley Online.

or her gender identity, it should suffice that the individual can support his or her claim through evidence which does not constitute an unnecessary assault on individual decency. For the Buenos Aires judge, it was 'highly desirable' to have one general law regulating the status of transgender persons in Argentina so that such persons were not subject to ad hoc, inconsistent procedures when seeking access legal gender recognition.

1.2. STATISTICS – THE NUMBER OF INDIVIDUALS ACCESSING GENDER RECOGNITION POST-2012

The National Registry of Persons is the sole office in Argentina which records information about the legal recognition of preferred gender. According to available statistics, following enactment of the Gender Identity Law in 2012, 2,147 individuals applied for a modification of the gender markers on their National Identity Card between May 2012 and May 2013. Among those who applied for legal recognition of gender, 1,888 applicants (88%) sought recognition of their preferred female gender. Two-hundred and sixty-six applicants (12%) sought the legal recognition of their preferred male gender.[8]

The following chart illustrates the age structure of those people who applied for modification of their National Identity Card during the period May 2012 to May 2013:[9]

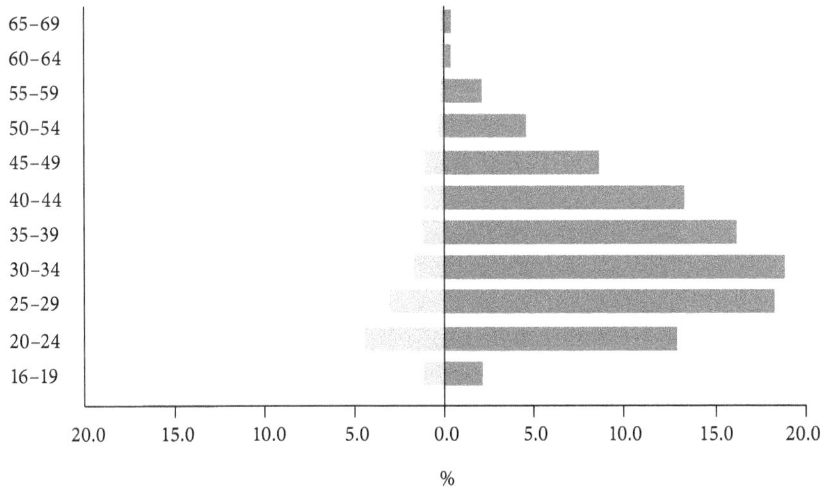

[8] 'Explorar una nueva perspectiva de la información', Conversación con Flavio Brocca, Subdirector de Gestión Informática Ministerio del Interior y Transporte de la Nación, *Población*, Publicación de la Dirección Nacional de Población, Registro Nacional de las Personas, Año 6, No. 11, p. 12.

[9] 'Explorar una nueva perspectiva de la información', above n. 8, p. 12.

In 2012, the National Institute of Statistics and Censuses (INDEC) established the first-ever survey on the lives of transgender persons in Argentina. The aim of the survey was to expose the living conditions of transgender individuals, and to investigate how Argentina's transgender community experiences discrimination, navigates the courts system and accesses justice. A pilot survey was completed in La Matanza City, in June 2012, and the subsequent report shed light on transgender experiences in areas such as self-identification, relationship status, discrimination within education, access to health care and treatment within the legal system.

II. CHANGING LEGAL GENDER: PROCEDURE AND REQUIREMENTS

2.1. ACT NO. 26.743 AND THE RIGHT TO SELF-IDENTIFICATION

2.1.1. *Requirements for Gender Recognition*

Under the Gender Identity Act, Argentina has adopted an administrative procedure for the legal recognition of preferred gender. This new departure contrasts sharply with the prior regime, which, as already noted, relied heavily upon judicial intervention. The requirements for recognition of gender, name and image are set out in Article 4 of the 2012 Act. An individual must first provide proof that he or she is 18 years old. There is, however, an exceptional procedure for minors built into Article 5 (see below). Individuals must next submit to the National Bureau of Vital Statistics (or their corresponding district offices), a request stating (a) that they fall under the protection of the current law and (b) that they wish an amendment of their birth certificate in the records and a new National Identity Card, with the same number as their current card. Finally, the individual must provide the new first name (where applicable) with which they want to be registered. Absent from Article 4 is a requirement for surgical intervention, hormone treatment or gender dysphoria diagnosis. Rather, the new law focuses on the self-identification of the applicant, placing determination of gender in his or her own hands.

2.1.2. *Minors*

The legal age of majority is reached in Argentina at 18 years (Civil Code, Article 126 – Act 26.529). In that context, Article 4 of the 2012 Act specifically requires that an applicant for gender recognition must be 18 years old before he or she can apply for gender recognition. However, under Article 5, individuals who wish to obtain legal recognition, but who have not yet reached the age of majority, may take advantage of a special procedure created for minors. Article 5 permits a minor to make an application for recognition through a legal representative. The child must be consulted and agree to any application before it is made. In considering whether to make such an application, the legal representative must have regard to the child's evolving capacities and best interests, as expressed in the United Nations Convention on the Right of the Child and in Law 26061 for the Comprehensive Protection of the Rights of Girls, Boys and Adolescents. The minor must be assisted by a children's lawyer as prescribed by Article 27 of Law 26061. Where the child's legal representative refuses his or her consent, or is unable to provide such consent, the decision as to whether to allow an application may be conferred upon a judge.[10]

In 2013, global media attention was drawn to the application of Article 5 when national authorities were asked to consider the application of a six-year-old transgender girl for legal recognition ('the *Lulu* case'). Article 5 does not place an age limit on applications. In the *Lulu* case, the applicant's mother had contacted the Argentine President, Cristina Fernández de Kirchner, complaining that, although her daughter had been diagnosed with gender dysphoria, the national registry officials were refusing to process her application for recognition because the registry authorities believed that the six-year-old was incapable of giving full, informed consent to such recognition. According to the evidence, the young girl had self-identified as female for four years and presented as female at her kindergarten. The National Secretariat of Childhood, Adolescence and Family (SENNAF) from the Social Development Ministry intervened on the applicant's behalf, noting that the decision to refuse recognition violated, *inter alia*, the right to equality based on sex and age, the right to preserve identity and the right to be heard.[11] The SENNAF report compelled the Department of Legal Affairs to file a claim at the provincial branch of the national registry which had rejected the application. The provincial branch ultimately allowed rectification of the girl's gender markers.

---

[10] Some Argentinean theorists, like Silvia Fernandez, consider that the Gender Identity Act has not ruled this matter with constitutional criteria since the legal statement referred to the fact that 'the application shall be filed through the legal guardians and with the express consent of the child' does not follow the constitutional principle of progressive autonomy in the exercise of the children's right (Art. 5 CRC). This principle embraces the different stages throughout which a child develops his existence regarding his psychophysical evolution, setting a gradation in the decision-making level. This concept fits the notion of competence regardless of the place the child takes from the viewpoint of the hard-determined civil capacity. S.E. Fernandez, 'Reconocer y restringir. Un debate latente en el acceso al ejercicio del derecho constitucional al proyecto de vida autorreferencial… ¿para tod@s?', *MJ-DOC-6046-AR/MJD6046*.

[11] In addition, it was held that the refusal violated the right to respect for the applicant's parents' rights and duties related to her guidance when exercising her rights according to her evolutionary stage, to get protection against arbitrary intrusion, to being raised by her parents, to enjoy the highest level of health, to a proper life level regarding her physical, mental, spiritual, moral and social development

2.1.3. *Non-National Applicants*

As a general rule (there is an exception in Sections 73 to 77 of the Civil Registry Law No. 26.413), Decree 1007/2012, issued by the Argentinian National Executive, prohibits national authorities from amending the foreign-issued birth certificate of a non-citizen, even if he or she has obtained permanent resident status in Argentina.

Where a non-citizen, who has obtained permanent resident status in Argentina, seeks the legal recognition of his or her preferred gender on other documentation (such as his or her residence card), the situation is governed by Decree 1007/2012 (02/07/2012) and Joint Resolution 1/2012 and 2/2012 passed by the National Bureau of Vital Statistics and the National Migration Office. These provisions draw a distinction between those applicants who have already obtained legal gender recognition in their country of origin and those who are citizens of a country which does not recognise preferred gender (as set out in Law No. 26.743)

In terms of non-citizens, who are applying for, or have already been granted, permanent resident status in Argentina and, in addition, who have also already obtained legal gender recognition in their country of citizenship, section 9 of Decree 1007/2012 provides that such persons may request the legal recognition of their preferred gender by providing appropriate evidence of that extra-territorial recognition (e.g. submitting a national identity card, birth certificate, passport, court order or any other documentation from the country of citizenship). Such documentation is sufficient for the individual to obtain an amendment to the gender marker on his or her residence card, National Identity Card for Foreign Residents and any other documentation issued by the Argentine state.

A non-citizen who has permanent residence status in Argentina (or who has the status of refugee or stateless person), but who has not obtained legal gender recognition in his or her country of origin, is subject to Joint Resolution 1/2012 and 2/2012. Where such an individual seeks legal gender recognition in Argentina, the request is forwarded to the National Migration Office, subject to Law No. 26.743. As part of his or her request, the applicant must produce:

(a) evidence of his or her permanent resident status in Argentina;
(b) the National Identity Card for Foreign Residents (or a police report explaining that the card has been lost); and
(c) notification from the Consular Office of the country of citizenship which affirms that the laws of that country do not permit the individual to obtain legal gender recognition.

Where the applicant is able to provide such evidence, the public officer will proceed with the administrative procedures required for the notification of amendments to legal gender markers. The National Migration Office must take all appropriate measures to provide the applicant with a National Identity Card for Foreign Residents which reflects the applicant's preferred legal gender, as recognised by the National Bureau of Vital Statistics. There is general parity – in terms of the obligations and entitlements owed and enjoyed as a result of legal gender recognition – between non-citizens and Argentine citizens who have obtained recognition of their preferred gender. However, one important point of difference is that the documentation issued to non-citizens is only valid for use within Argentina. The issued identity card cannot be used to enter or exit the Argentine territory. Instead, individuals must continue to rely upon their travel documentation issued by the country of citizenship, even if this documentation retains their birth-assigned legal gender.

Pursuant to section 3 of Joint Resolution 1/2012 and 2/2012, once an individual has been issued with residence documentation which reflects his or her preferred gender, the National Migration Office is required to notify the Ministry of Foreign Affairs, INTERPOL and the consulate of the country of citizenship, subject to the legal reservations specified in Law No. 25.326 for the Protection of Personal Data.

2.1.4. *Rectification of the Civil Register and Issuance of New National Identity Cards*

Once the procedures set out in Articles 4 and 5 have been satisfied, the Public Officer will issue, without any other judicial or administrative formality, an *ex officio* notification to the Civil Registry where the birth certificate had been originally registered. The person's preferred legal gender and name is recognised on the Civil Register, and the individual is entitled to be issued with an amended National Identity Card. That card, which maintains the individual's personalised identity number, now reflects the individuals preferred gender and name (if different from the originally issued identity card). Article 6 of the 2012 Act prohibits any reference to Act No. 26.743 on the applicant's amended birth certificate or on the new National Identity Card. The only people who are entitled to access the original birth certificate are those who have either been granted authorisation by the applicant or the courts. The 2012 Act prohibits publication of information regarding the legal recognition of a person's preferred gender, save where the individual or a court grants authorisation. Article 6 affirms that the procedure for obtaining gender identity recognition is personal, free and without the need for a lawyer's intervention.

2.2. ACCESS TO HEALTHCARE

In addition to its ground-breaking work to 'depathologise' gender identity, Argentina's 2012 Act differs from many other recognition regimes in that it specifically provides for a right to access appropriate healthcare treatment.

Article 11, entitled 'Right to Free Personal Development', sets out the entitlement of transgender individuals to access medical care. According to Article 11, all persons over the age of 18 have the right to access 'total and partial surgical interventions and/or comprehensive hormonal treatments to adjust their bodies, including their genitalia, to their self-perceived gender identity, without requiring any judicial or administrative authorization.' Article 11 does not make access to hormone treatment conditional on proof that an individual has submitted to total or partial gender confirmation surgery. Rather, it suffices that the individual provides his or her informed consent. A particularly interesting and welcome feature of the Gender Identity Act is the law's ability to decouple the legal recognition of preferred gender from questions of pathology, and still vindicate, in a comprehensive manner, the healthcare rights and needs of transgender individuals.

The healthcare rights of minors differ from those of applicants who have already reached the age of majority. Under Article 11, consent for medical intervention may only be achieved through the process set out in Article 5 (discussed in section 2.1.2 above). However, in the context of healthcare, even if the minor's legal representative consents to gender confirmation surgery, the judicial authorities must also provide their agreement, taking into account the evolving capacities and best interests of the child as expressed in the Convention on the Right of the Child and in Law 26061 for the Comprehensive Protection of the Rights of Girls, Boys and Adolescents. Therefore, the provisions in Article 11 regarding minors remain a notable exception to the removal of the judiciary from the gender recognition process. When the question of youth healthcare arises, judges retain a central role.

Article 11 ends with a statement as to the obligations and responsibilities of third-party actors in relation to transgender healthcare. All public health officials and employees (whether state, private or trade union) must continuously uphold and enforce the healthcare rights set out in the 2012 Act. Reflecting the significant costs of gender identity-related healthcare, and the difficulties which many transgender persons have historically experienced affording such care, Article 11 guarantees that all medical procedures contemplated within the Gender Identity Law are included within Argentina's Compulsory Medical Plan (and its possible successors). As a result, individuals who access healthcare through private or trade union-run plans cannot be required to pay additional costs for their care.

III. CONSEQUENCES OF THE CHANGE OF LEGAL GENDER

3.1. LEGISLATING RESPECT FOR THE LEGAL RECOGNITION OF PREFERRED GENDER

Article 13 of the Gender Identity Law provides that:

> 'every norm, ruling or procedure shall respect the human right to gender identity. No norm, ruling or procedure shall limit, restrict, exclude or suppress the exercise of the right to gender identity. The application and interpretation of norms must always be done in favour of this right's enjoyment.'

The law must, in principle, guarantee an individual the full exercise of his or her citizenship in accordance with that individual's preferred legal gender. Indeed, even before the 2012 Act had been introduced, the Civil and Commercial Court of Mar de Plato had ruled (in a case concerning a transgender woman) that:

> 'the judicial decision on sex reassignment should influence every concerning aspect of the benefited person … If the judicial system – as in this case – orders her registration as a female, she will be able to adopt children, enjoy maternity leave so as to establish her relationship with the child, enjoy the breast-feeding benefit in order to assist to her baby's feeding during the first stage of life; she will also be able to get married, even though she does not have the bearing possibility, and enjoy every right she is entitled to by this institution; she will be able to work under the legislation that rules women's employment; and so on because who is able to do more is consequently able to do less, and because the judicial assistance must be complete, without pitfalls, for the contrary would carry the risk of never solving the person's conflict.'[12]

Having regard to the fact that the Mar de Plato court delivered this statement while the rule on legal gender recognition was still governed by the highly restrictive previous regime, it must be assumed that the consequences of the Gender Identity Act, which is based upon the principles of dignity and equality, must be equally as advantageous for transgender individuals.

3.2. EFFECTS OF LEGAL RECOGNITION – NEW AND EXISTING RIGHTS AND DUTIES

Article 7 of the Gender Identity Law provides that, from the point of first legal recognition, an individual's preferred gender and name are enforceable as

[12] Juzgado en lo Civil y Comercial No. 11 de Mar del Plata, 12/12/2005, LLBA 2006, 85.

against third parties. The legal recognition of preferred gender does not, however, amend or terminate existing rights and duties owed to or by the individual. In particular, the mere fact that an individual has obtained recognition of his or her gender identity does not mean that the individual escapes, or can be stripped of, all the rights and duties which that individual owes as a matter of family law. According to Article 7, it is the serial number on a person's National Identity Card, rather than the specific gender and name markers, which assumes priority for the purposes of identifying the individual. This number remains constant, even where the individual makes a successful application to amend the latter data.

It is possible to identify distinctions between the consequences of gender recognition which arise for marital relationships and filial relationships. In terms of marriage, Argentina has, since Act No. 26618 of 2011, allowed same-sex marriages. Where a married individual obtains legal recognition of his or her preferred gender and, in doing so, transforms his or her marriage into a same-sex union, such recognition does not impugn the validity of the existing marriage. It is, however, necessary to amend the marriage certificate to reflect the fact that there are now two spouses of the same legal gender in the relationship. The consequences which arise where a parent obtains legal gender recognition are, however, more complex and less well defined. In a recent case from the province of Salta, two parents, each of whom had obtained legal gender recognition and amended their names on their National Identity Cards, sought to rectify their daughter's birth certificate so that the certificate carried the couple's preferred names. The Civil Registry of Salta considered that such rectification could only be achieved through a judicial process. The director of the Salta Civil Registry required the government ministry to intervene, and the state attorney office also submitted an opinion. In the end, the State Attorney, as well as the Guardian's Office for Minor and Incapacitated Persons, issued reports in favour of rectification without the need for an additional court-based process.[13] However, the case stands as a cautionary tale of the difficulties which may still exist for transgender parents, even after they have obtained general legal recognition of their preferred gender.

3.3. NOTIFICATIONS

Following the legal recognition of an individual's preferred gender and the amendment of his or her National Identity Card, the National Registry of Persons must notify the National Registry of Criminal Records, the Secretary of the Electoral Registry and the Central Bank. Further notifications to other public offices may be permitted by a regulatory measure, provided the measure complies

[13] 'La familia trans que logró su derecho', 2014 <www.pagina12.com.ar/diario/sociedad/3-249456-2014-06-26.html> accessed 27.06.2014.

with the requirements of confidentiality and ensures sufficient protection for the individual's personal data. The individual himself or herself should notify additional public or private officials, such as doctors, banks and universities, if that notification is necessary for the individual to continue (or begin) accessing important services in their preferred gender. Article 10 concludes by requiring the National Registry of Persons to provide notification to any additional body which might have information on existing precautionary measures involving the individual.

3.4. PRISONS

In the particular sphere of Argentina's prisons, a national working team has been established to promote greater visibility and understanding of the problems caused by the absence of gender considerations within the planning for, and operating of, the Federal Penitentiary Service. The team's work focuses on the experiences of non-national women and lesbian, gay, bisexual, transgender and intersex-affected persons (LGBTI) in Argentina's jails.[14]

3.5. LABOUR AND EMPLOYMENT POLICIES

The Argentine government, both before and after the 2012 Act, has taken steps to tackle workplace discrimination based upon gender identity. In September 2011, the Ministry for Work, Employment, and Social Security signed a Framework Agreement of Cooperation in Matters of Employment and Sexual Diversity ('Framework Agreement') with the National Institute against Discrimination, Xenophobia and Racism (INADI). The Framework Agreement promotes greater collaboration between the Government and INADI in various areas relating to employment and sexual diversity, including the realisation of INADI's National Programme against Discrimination and increasing labour rights for LGBTI-

[14] The Procuration, in its annual report from 2012, points out the existence of a Unit in the Federal Penitentiary Establishment created for the transgender and homosexual population. In 2012 there were an average of 28 inmates held in this place, not having equal conditions with those inmates held in Ezeiza Federal Jail. Procuración Penitenciaria de la Nación 'Informe Anual 2012', Capítulo VIII, Colectivos Sobrevulnerados <http://ppn.gov.ar/sites/default/files/Cap%C3%ADtulo%20g%C3%A9nero%20Informe%20Anual%202012.pdf>. We can also cite the Highest Court of the Province of Cordoba's judgment, *P. L. D (o) R. J.* on enforcement of a judgment involving deprivation of liberty that stated that an inmate that has been awarded the registry sex reassignment from male sex to female sex, the first name and image reassignment according to her female gender identity without undergoing surgical genitalia-reassignment interventions, is entitled to the right to be held in a penitentiary unit for women. Thus, the protection given by Act No. 26743 regarding the right to the self-perceived gender identity comprises the right to apply for penitentiary housing according to her inner and individual experience of gender.

identified persons. As a direct result of the Framework Agreement, a number of projects have been initiated with the aim of addressing the specific difficulties faced by the LGBTI community in Argentina's workplaces. One such project has created a workshop space, providing an opportunity for dialogue and proposal making. This workshop uses the employment and sexual diversity resources from MTEySS, INADI's sexual diversity area, and invites representatives and activists from LGBTI groups.[15] In addition, since the passage of both the same-sex marriage and gender identity laws, and as a means of encouraging better and more equal participation by transgender individuals within Argentina's labour market, the Employment Ministry has introduced a number of policies seeking to enhance the employment experiences of the transgender community. The Social Action Ministry and the National Institute on Associativism and Social Economy were directly involved in supporting the country's first transvestite cooperative, called 'Nadia Echazú'.[16] In 2013, the Ministry for Work, Employment and Social Security passed Resolution 331/2013. This resolution broadens the existing access to training and employment insurance coverage, established by Decree No. 336/06, extending such coverage to an individual whose preferred gender differs from the legal gender assigned to that individual at birth.

IV. CURRENT AND FUTURE CHALLENGES IN THE EFFECTIVENESS OF RIGHTS

The introduction of a radically reformed system for legal gender recognition, hailed as the most progressive in the world, as well as same-sex marriage constitute important breakthroughs for the rights of LGBTI persons in Argentina. Both measures are a reflection of Argentina's commitment to international human rights law, a law which now forms part of the country's national constitutional order. However, these progressive laws cannot and will not, in themselves, ameliorate the undoubted challenges which transgender and homosexual persons face in Argentina. The effects of legislation can only go so far. As a next step, Argentina must now seek to address not only the legal discrimination still faced by LGBTI communities, but also, and perhaps more importantly, the cultural stigma which continues to frustrate LGBTI inclusion and equality.

15 <www.trabajo.gov.ar/diversidadsexual/> accessed 09.07.2014.
16 <www.trabajo.gov.ar/diversidadsexual/inclusion.asp?subcat=2> accessed 09.07.2014.

THE LEGAL STATUS OF TRANSSEXUAL AND TRANSGENDER PERSONS IN THE UNITED STATES

Jameson Garland

Contents

I. LEGAL FRAMEWORK AND STATISTICS

1.1. OVERVIEW

The legal status of individuals with regard to gender is a complex matter in the United States (US), made even more so by the divisions of legal power within the nation.[1] The US Constitution enumerates the powers that it confers on the legislative and executive branches of the federal government, authorising them to regulate taxation, interstate commerce, and international travel.[2] As such, the federal government issues passports and establishes a national registry with identity numbers for individuals in relation to taxes, employment, and receipt of federal benefits. However, the states also have broad powers to regulate the public health and welfare within their borders, provided that they do not conflict with federal law, the US Constitution, or their own state constitutions.[3] These jurisdictions register births and provide identity cards used in daily life. Both the federal government and the states allocate responsibility for each identity document to different agencies, with separate rules for the documents and registries that they maintain. As a result, citizens and residents of the United States may have multiple legally registered identities that are independent of each other, such that changing one document often has no impact on the other.[4]

Persons wishing to correct their registered gender in much of the United States face numerous administrative barriers in doing so. This is largely due to the diversity of rules in the states, which are often inconsistent, even within individual jurisdictions. The most recent comprehensive study of transgender persons in the

---

1 This chapter covers the fifty States and the District of Columbia (DC) but excludes other US territories. Except where clarification is needed, references to the 'states' include DC, as it has similar powers to the states for purposes of this chapter. While 'the United States' generally includes these territories when dealing with foreign entities, questions remain about the extent to which the Constitution and regulatory authority of the United States extends to these territories. *Downes v Bidwell*, 182 U.S. 244, 261 (1901); *Valmonte v I.N.S.* 136 F.3d 914, 918–920 (2d. Cir. 1998). See also US Const., Amend. XXIII. This is not meant to diminish that persons born in these territories are citizens of the US by birth. See 8 U.S.C. §§ 1402 (Puerto Rico), 1406 (US Virgin Islands), 1407 (Guam), 1408 (American Samoas) and 48 U.S.C. § 1801 (Northern Mariana Islands).

2 US Const., Article I, § 8, cl. 1 (tax and spending power), cl. 3 (foreign and interstate commerce), cl. 4 (naturalisation of immigrants), cl. 10–12 (national security) and cl. 4 (powers necessary and proper for the government). The Constitution further empowers the Executive Branch and the Presidency with powers to control foreign relations. US Const. Article II, § 3, cl. 2, *Haig v Agee*, 453 U.S. 280 (1981), *United States v Curtiss-Wright Export Corp.*, 299 U.S. 304 (1936). These powers, taken together, have given the legislative and executive branches broad powers to control entry into the United States.

3 *Jacobson v Massachusetts*, 197 U.S. 11 (1905); *Village of Euclid v Amber Realty*, 272 U.S. 365 (1926).

4 This chapter cannot begin to capture fully the difficulties faced by transgender persons in controlling their legal documents and status. For comprehensive analysis, see D. Spade, 'Documenting Gender' (2008) 59 *Hastings L.J.* 731; A.W. Howell, *Transgender Persons and the Law*, American Bar Association, Chicago 2013.

United States reported that only approximately one-fifth (21%) of persons who transitioned gender had been able to correct all of their identity documents, and two-fifths (41%) had not corrected their identity cards used in daily life.[5] These administrative problems may explain why quality data is lacking to estimate the numbers of Americans who may have been diagnosed as transsexual or who have successfully corrected their registered gender. The US Census Bureau collects data on gender,[6] but does not ask respondents whether their gender identity matches their gender registered at birth. Federal law protecting the privacy of health care information also effectively prevents substantial disclosure of statistics about the transgender population.[7] As such, the full extent of the population most affected by gender registry laws remains largely unknown.

Access to medical care poses additional burdens for persons experiencing gender distress in the United States. In particular, financing of surgery is widely inaccessible, either from the government or through private insurance coverage. The lack of finance for surgery may also explain why very few specialists in sex reassignment and other gender surgeries for adults actually exist in the United States.[8] More broadly, the lack of universal, comprehensive healthcare poses significant barriers to individuals seeking treatment to support their gender identity. Approximately 65% of the US population receives healthcare through their employers or through private insurance.[9] Increasingly, some private insurers have removed restrictions for financing sex reassignment surgery and hormone therapy, though often they do not expressly cover such treatments.[10] Most private insurance plans, however, do not cover significant health care costs related to gender transition,[11] while even supportive plans may have 'medical

---

5 J. Grant, L.A. Mottet, and J. Tanis, *Injustice at Every Turn: A Report of the National Transgender Discrimination Survey*, National Center for Transgender Equality and The Task Force, D.C. 2011, p. 5 (NTDS).

6 For the latest information on gender at the US Census Bureau see <www.census.gov/population/age/> accessed 24.05.2015.

7 45 C.F.R. §§ 160 and 164 and 42 U.S.C. 1320d–1320d–8 (2013), enacted by the Health Insurance Portability and Accountability Act, Pub. L. 104–191, 110 Stat. 1936 (1996) and the Genetic Information Nondiscrimination Act, Pub. L. 110–233, 122 Stat. 881 (2008).

8 See Howell, above n. 4, pp. 181.

9 Government-funded plans, including military health care, provide coverage to 34.3% of the population, and is the only coverage for 22.5%. US Census Bureau, *Health Insurance Coverage in the United States: 2013* (2014). Most of the population (64.2%) obtains health care coverage through private sources, mainly employers, ibid., partially subsidised by the federal and state governments. See Joint Committee on Taxation, US House of Rep. Ways and Means Committee and US Senate Finance Committee, *Estimates of Federal Tax Expenditures for Fiscal Years 2012–2017* (GPO: JCS-1-13), 1 February 2013, pp. 2–8 and 40; see also 26 U.S.C. § 105 and 106 (excluding benefits from income tax) and 26 U.S.C. § 62(l)&(n) (authorising the self-employed and employers to deduct premiums as business expenses).

10 See Howell, above n. 4, pp. 94 and 259–275.

11 Only California, Connecticut, Oregon, Vermont, and Washington DC currently require all public and private insurers to provide such coverage. See Howell, above n. 4. For inclusive coverage examples, see also Human Rights Campaign, *Transgender Inclusive Health-Care Coverage and the Corporate Equality Index*, HRC, D.C., 2012.

necessity' clauses that allow restrictions on procedures deemed non-essential for treatment of gender identity disorder or distress.[12] For most of the remainder of the population – particularly those who receive public health care benefits or have no health care insurance – the costs of most gender-related treatments are borne entirely by the individual.[13] Individually financed treatments are partially tax-deductible[14] – effectively a limited subsidy – but this requires the individual to pay for such care first before claiming any such deduction.[15] Despite all of these barriers to healthcare, a majority of states generally require a person to have undergone surgery to authorise change of gender markers on birth certificates. Thus, particularly regarding registered gender status, the full impact of the lack of access to health care is difficult to estimate.

1.2. LEGAL BACKGROUND AND ORGANISATION

1.2.1. Historical Developments

Gender surgeries in the United States began before registration of personal identities became a national governmental practice. Surgeries developed in the 1800s to enhance genital function for persons with differences in sex development were increasingly offered after the 1920s to help them appear more typical for one gender.[16] These surgeries, often resulting in a change in social or legal gender,

---

12 See NTDS, above n. 5, pp. 76–79. Regarding early successful challenges to these clauses and to state health care plans for coverage, see N. Ben-Asher, 'The Necessity of Sex Change: A Struggle for Intersex and Transsex Liberties' (2006) *Harv. Jrnl. of Law & Gender* 55–60 and Howell, above n. 4, p. 94.

13 See Howell, above n. 4, pp. 91–92 (most states do not subsidise coverage or require insurance coverage for corrective surgery). The exceptions are for the elderly and disabled, as well as veterans. On 30 May 2014, the Medicare Appeals Board held that the government cannot categorically deny coverage for gender assignment surgery to the elderly and disabled, but little coverage has been affirmed at this writing. See National Center for Transgender Equality, *Fact-Sheet on Medicare-Coverage of Transition-Related Care*, 2014. Regarding veterans, see section 3.4.

14 26 U.S.C. §213(d)(9)(b). The US Tax Court has confirmed that surgery and hormonal treatments are deductible. *O'Donnabhain v Commissioner*, 134 T.C. 34, Tax Ct. Rep. (CCH) 58.122 (U.S. Tax Ct. 2010).

15 The Internal Revenue Code only permits medical expenses to be deduced in excess of 10% of adjusted gross income (AGI), 26 U.S.C. §213(d)(9)(b), with AGI generally meaning income minus all costs of earning that income or certain education expenses. 26 U.S.C. §62. Assuming a person earned $45,000 in AGI before taxes and spent $10,000 on medical care, the first $4,500 would be excluded from the deduction. Thus, the person would only be allowed to deduct $5,500. Assuming that this amount would have been taxed at 25%, the value of the deduction is the tax avoided, or $1,375. Thus, for the $10,000 spent on treatments, only $1,375 would be offset by reduced taxes as a result of the deduction.

16 A. Fausto-Sterling, *Sexing the Body*, Basic Books, New York 2000, pp. 3–5 and E. Reis, *Bodies in Doubt: An American history of intersex*, Johns Hopkins University Press, Harvard 2009, pp. 82 ff. J. Meyerowitz, *How Sex Changed: A History of Transsexuality in the United States*, Harvard, Cambridge 2002, pp. 38–44.

became more widespread by the 1950s, particularly on children.[17] For persons whose bodies were typical for their genetic sex, however, surgeons nationwide initially declined to perform such procedures out of concern that they might be covered by criminal laws prohibiting the removal of organs.[18] Surgeries on such persons did not officially begin until the late 1960s in the United States, prompting many Americans to travel abroad for care.[19] By then, several states already had laws permitting correction of gender on birth certificates, a few restricted to persons with atypical sex development.[20] And yet, while legal authorities had often harshly punished non-conforming gender behaviour as early as colonial times,[21] a national framework for using legal documents as the basis for administering legal gender was not in place until the mid-twentieth century.

Before that time, registration of birth data was not considered within federal powers and was left to the states, even though the federal government conducted a constitutionally required census, primarily to allocate representation in Congress.[22] In the early 1900s, the US Census Bureau began to encourage states to register births using standardised criteria. All states except Alaska and Hawaii had birth registries in place by 1933, with the latter two states having standardised registries once becoming states in 1959.[23] The federal government began using registered identities to track contributions to social security systems in 1936, but the government did not use this registry in connection with all federal benefits and taxes until the 1960s.[24] Though the government had issued passports as early as the eighteenth century,[25] it did not formally require registration with the government to leave or enter the United States, except in wartime, until 1942,[26] a rule that was codified for peacetime in 1978.[27] Thus, by the time US citizens began to be able to receive gender surgery at home, a complex legal scheme had developed whereby legal identity registries were fragmented into separate controls by state and federal agencies. The legal framework that emerged placed the states at the front lines for gender registration, often with conflicting standards within or among the states, as well as with those set by the national government.

---

17 Reis, above n. 16, pp. 116–152.
18 Meyerowitz, above n. 16, pp. 47, 120–121 and 212–225.
19 Ibid., pp. 42–70 and 145–150.
20 Committee on Public Health, New York Academy of Medicine, 'Change of Sex on Birth Certificates for Transsexuals' (1966) 42:8 *Bull. N.Y. Acad. Med* 721–724 (surveying laws and presumed legitimacy of surgeries on persons with atypical sex development).
21 See generally, Reis, above n. 16, pp. 1–45.
22 US Const. Art. I, §2. For more historical information, see H.L. Brumberg, D. Dozor and S.G. Golombek, 'History of the birth certificate: from inception to the future of electronic data' (2012) 32 *Journal of Perinatology* 407–411.
23 Ibid., p. 408.
24 W. Long, 'Social Security Numbers: A 20-year review' (1983) *Social Security Bulletin* 83–86.
25 For a brief history of the United States passport, see *Haig v Agee*, 453 U.S. 280 (1981).
26 See 6 Fed. Reg. 6069 (1941) (effective 1942).
27 See Foreign Relations Authorization Act, Fiscal Year 1979 §707(b), Pub.L. 95–426, 92 Stat. 993 (enacted 7 October 1978).

1.2.2. *State Law: Birth Certificates and Identity Cards*

Each birth in the United States is expected to be registered with a *birth certificate* issued in the state where the birth took place.[28] The certificate is the primary means a person first uses as identity to obtain other legal documents, even though it generally does not serve as a keystone document that must be updated in order to change other records. It is, however, an important document, particularly for young people in gaining access to multiple agencies, for example, to obtain first passports and identity cards, as well as to register in schools.[29] The birth certificate in the United States has historically not been part of a collective registry but, rather, a single record from which copies can be made from the original on file in the agency of the state that maintains those records.[30] The notable exception in this regard is New York, which gives separate authority to New York City to register births within its jurisdiction.[31] The rules for amending and correcting birth certificates vary from state to state, with some permitting the former certificate to be permanently amended, but others permitting the agency to retain the original and issue a new one.[32] Today, the documents are routinely computerised, and federal law requires states to maintain digital copies of birth certificates for access by law enforcement as a national security matter.[33]

The identity cards that most individuals use to prove identity in daily transactions is the *driver's licence* or the *non-driver's identity card.*[34] These cards serve as daily identification because they contain the address and photograph of the cardholder, as well as the holder's name and gender. The Department of Motor Vehicles (DMV) in each state controls the registries for these cards, even for those who do not drive, so that a person who does not drive or pass a driver's test can obtain a card for identification purposes. The card is not permanent and must be renewed in every jurisdiction, such that persons who live in a different gender from the one registered on the card will have an expired licence if it is not renewed, placing those who have undergone a physical gender transformation at a significant disadvantage if they are not prepared to disclose their personal history to the DMV.

---

28 Office of Inspector General, US Department of Health and Human Services, Birth Certificate Fraud (1988), pp. 8–10 (explaining how the states collectively delegate this authority to thousands of local offices).

29 Spade, above n. 4, p. 766.

30 Ibid.

31 See <www.health.ny.gov/vital_records>.

32 See Howell, above n. 4, pp. 203–239; Spade, above n. 4, pp. 832–841.

33 6 C.F.R. Part 37. For analysis of the impact of national security policy on transgender persons, see Spade, above n. 4, pp. 791–821.

34 For extensive analysis, see Spade, above n. 4, pp. 770–775.

1.2.3. Federal Law – National Identity Numbers and Travel Documents

The *Social Security Number* (SSN) is a nine-digit number administered by the Social Security Administration (SSA). The SSN is now the primary means by which individuals identify themselves in major public and private transactions.[35] Its original purpose was to identify persons for all federal benefits enumerated in the Social Security Act, a function it continues to serve.[36] The number is also used for the payment of taxes,[37] as well as to identify any child for whom parents claim a tax credit or deduction.[38] As a result, most children receive their SSNs at the latest in the year after they were born. Because employers must withhold taxes from income,[39] they must collect the SSN in reporting withheld taxes to the federal government. The SSN does not have a gender marker in the number itself, but the SSA's database contains identifying information, including gender.[40] As such, if the gender marker in an employment record does not match the SSA's records, the first report of an employee's withheld tax to the Internal Revenue Service might trigger an alert for the employer to verify that the SSN is not being used fraudulently.[41] The same match problem has occurred when the Department of Homeland Security, checking for identity fraud, has asked states to revoke drivers' licences when the SSN and the licence did not match through vital data.[42] Today, because of the ease of use, most private financial services and many other businesses use SSNs as a means to identify customers in their transactions, if only because the SSN is a unique, coded identity monitored by the government.[43]

Passports are administered by the Department of State (DoS).[44] The DoS also issues consular reports for citizens born abroad and certain nationals.[45] *Resident permits* are issued by the Department of Homeland Security's US Citizenship and Immigration Services.[46] Federal law requires US citizens and nationals to use the US passport to enter or leave the country, even if they have dual citizenship.[47] As such, a citizen of another country who has changed registered gender in that country may not use a foreign passport to pass through US borders if he or she is also a US citizen or national. The DoS provides passport cards that may be used

35 K.S. Swendiman, *The Social Security Number: Legal Developments Affecting Its Collection, Disclosure, and Confidentiality* Congressional Research Service, Washington, D.C. 2008; Spade, above n. 4, p. 762.

36 42 U.S.C. § 405(c)(2).

37 26 U.S.C. § 6109 and 42 U.S.C. § 405(c)(2)(A).

38 See 26 U.S.C. § 32 (c)(3)(D)(i) *and* 26 U.S.C. § 151(e).

39 26 U.S.C. § 6051 and 42 U.S.C. § 405(c)(2)(A).

40 Spade, above n. 4, pp. 737 and 761.

41 See ibid., pp. 800–801.

42 Ibid., p. 737.

43 Spade, above n. 4, pp. 761–764.

44 22 U.S.C. § 211a.

45 22 C.F.R. 50.7

46 USCIS, *I Am a Permanent Resident: How Do I... Renew or Replace My Permanent Resident Card?*, USCIS, District of Columbia 2010, p. 1.

47 8 U.S.C. sec. 1185(b).

as ID for travel within the US,[48] though they do not provide the details that may be needed for some transactions, and, therefore, are not complete substitutes for a state ID. Without a birth certificate, individuals bear the burden of proof to locate witnesses or compile other evidence to prove their identity to obtain their first passport, but not to change it.[49]

II. CHANGING LEGAL GENDER – PROCEDURES AND REQUIREMENTS

2.1. LEGAL PROCEDURES AND REQUIREMENTS – GENERALLY

Because each legal document or record with a gender marker is controlled by a separate agency within the federal, state, or local government, there is no single procedure for changing gender markers in these documents or records. Moreover, because each document or record does not have an automatic effect on other documents or records, changing one document will not change the other. As explained below, a state court order is often required for a change of certain registered information, which then must be presented to the requisite agencies in order to receive new identity documents. Some individuals may choose to go to such a court first, as it can order state agencies to correct registered gender and change a name. State court orders will not bind the federal government but may be used as evidence in applications to federal agencies. Across all jurisdictions, the procedure for changing all documents is extensively administrative and in all but a few instances is expressly governed by statute or regulation. These actions are judicially reviewable under federal and state law, though the procedures across the states and the federal government are too intricate to summarise here. Discrimination and violations of procedural requirements may also trigger constitutional violations as independent grounds to access judicial review. All decisions where court orders are required automatically have judicial review and are, therefore, subject to appeal.

The requirements summarised below are divided by jurisdiction and the record to be changed. As the structure of the text indicates, the streamlining of the rules for changing gender markers on SSNs, passports, and other federal documents suggests that the national process for changing gender markers is relatively easier, apart from the time-consuming process of appearing before multiple federal agencies. State law, however, provides documents that may be used to facilitate further legal changes and are essential to identification in daily

48 22 C.F.R. § 51.3(d).
49 22 C.F.R. § 51.40 and 41.

life. Thus, the complexity and diversity of state practices provide the primary encumbrances to securing a correct juridical identity for transgender persons.

2.2. CHANGES ON BIRTH CERTIFICATES AND IDENTITY CARDS

2.2.1. Overview: Changing Gender Markers and Names

For birth certificates and basic identity cards – documents under state control – the first layer of complexity in correcting documents is determining *which state* controls the document to be changed. Regardless of where a person resides in the United States, that person's birth records are controlled by the state in which the person was born.[50] In sharp contrast, a person's driver's licence or state identification card is issued by the jurisdiction in which the person resides, through that state's DMV.[51] For individuals who move from one state to another, states generally require that drivers register with the DMV in the state of residence, even if a driver has an active licence from another jurisdiction, which must be exchanged for a licence within the new jurisdiction.[52] Because the right to travel within the United States is considered a fundamental right,[53] a person may move without penalty to a state where it is easier to obtain a driver's licence or identity card for daily life. It is not possible, however, to fully escape the reach of the state that has control over birth records. Thus, a person who is born in a state that is not transgender-supportive, like Alabama, but later seeks gender identity correction in a state that is more supportive, like California, must still correct the birth certificate in the birth state and the drivers' licence in the state of residence.

It would be an extreme understatement to say that the requirements for gender change imposed by the individual states vary substantially. All states and the District of Columbia (DC) permit changes of gender markers on drivers' licences and identity cards,[54] whereas all but five states permit alterations of gender markers on birth certificates.[55] From these general starting points, however, the divergences among the states' approaches multiply considerably. Though forty-five states and DC permit changes of birth certificates, only nine of these jurisdictions set forth the medical requirements for changes on all documents in the same manner *within* their own jurisdictions.[56] Moreover, while these jurisdictions can be categorised according to degrees of medical treatment

---

50 Howell, above n. 4, p. 18.
51 Spade, above n. 4, pp. 770–775.
52 Howell, above n. 4, p. 23.
53 *Sáenz v Roe*, 526 U.S. 489 (1999).
54 See Tables 1, 2 and 3.
55 See Table 4.
56 See columns 2 and 3 in Tables 1, 2 and 3.

required for gender marker changes, the language in their laws is often vague and differs radically from state to state. This does not mean that an individual will need to do the impossible – undergo separate gender treatments – to satisfy two different agencies within one or more states to change documents. In most states, the identity card requirements are less stringent than those for changing birth certificates, driven by concerns that the need for an identity document is a pressing one, as well to meet medical requirements to live openly in a particular gender before undergoing further medical or legal corrective procedures. Nevertheless, for a person without legal experience attempting to understand the legal process, the inconsistencies may be extremely daunting to decipher, particularly for those who must work with two jurisdictions, not just one.

Finally, all jurisdictions require a state court order for a name change.[57] For most US citizens and residents, this is a much simpler process than it seems. Most states provide simple forms that can be filed with the court to request such a change, and courts frequently approve the change without a hearing. Perhaps of most importance, no state has any requirement whatsoever that a name change must be gender appropriate or that any medical procedure must be required for that change. The process, however, may be much more complicated depending on the timing of the change and its connection to other legal document corrections. On the one hand, applicants in all states can consolidate a request for change of both registered name and gender in a single court petition, which can then be sent to agencies for processing of birth certificate and driver's licence changes. On the other hand, consolidation converts what is a simple petition for a name change to a process with more complicated pleadings, requiring extensive documentation and, perhaps, attorney assistance. Depending on the needs of the applicant, the timing of these choices may be awkward – for example, if the applicant feels a change of a gender marker is more urgent than a name change. Nevertheless, individuals seeking a name change should expect that the request, in most circumstances, will face little judicial resistance.[58]

2.2.2. Requirements for Psychiatric Diagnosis and Care

No jurisdiction in the United States formally requires a psychiatric diagnosis of gender identity disorder or dysphoria to change gender markers on drivers'

---

[57] See HOWELL, above n. 4, p. 309 (listing all state statutes and federal policies).

[58] This is not to say that applicants for name change may not face bias from judges. Heterosexual men and gay couples have faced problems of this kind as well. M. ROSENSAFT, 'The Right of Men to Change Their Names upon Marriage' (2002) 5 *University of Pennsylvania Journal of Constitutional Law* 186, 193–196. The reported cases where judges have refused to change names for transgender persons indicate that appellate courts have overturned such judgments because of an abuse of discretion to deny such a change. See e.g. *In the Matter of Jhirard Tahiem Powell*, 945 N.Y.S.2d 789 (N.Y. App. Div. 2012), *In the Matter of the Application of Leah Uri Winn-Ritzenberg for Leave to Change His/Her Name To Olin Yuri Winn-Ritzenberg*, 891 N.Y.S.2d 220 (N.Y. App. Div. 2009) *In re Eck*, 584 A.2d 859, 861 (N.J. Super. Ct. App. Div. 1991).

licences or identity cards or to change names. Of the jurisdictions that permit gender marker changes on birth certificates[59] only Virginia currently requires a doctor to certify that the applicant has been diagnosed with gender dysphoria, but even this requirement is retrospective, after other procedures are complete. The rarity of this requirement is not particularly surprising, given that specific medical practices are rarely regulated in the United States. Indeed, no law in the United States requires psychiatric diagnosis before receiving further treatment for gender identity matters, and no law requires such treatments to proceed in any stages.

This does not mean, however, that the law does not have the effect of requiring medical assessment, as most states require medical confirmation that a requested gender marker on an ID card is likely to be the applicant's gender for the foreseeable future. The standard of medical care in the United States also requires some psychiatric evaluation and waiting period before recommending surgery or other treatment.[60] Of course, some psychiatrists will provide recommendations for further treatment without a diagnosis of illness, instead assessing only mental fitness to proceed with significant treatment.[61] So, too, a smaller but substantial percentage of transgender patients surveyed in the United States oppose counselling altogether and may find ways to obtain gender conforming care without it.[62] Limited research, however, suggests that many transsexual and transgender persons have sought such care if only to obtain further additional treatments that they need or desire.[63] Because all jurisdictions that change drivers' licences or birth certificates require, at a minimum, some medical documentation of the appropriateness of change of registered gender, an unspecified medical diagnosis may be effectively necessary to obtain both additional medical care and changes of registered gender markers in most states.

2.2.3. Requirements for Hormonal Treatments or Surgery

While no jurisdiction requires surgery or other medical treatment for a name change, forty-five states, DC, and New York City permit changes of gender markers on birth certificates only after some medical treatment. The requirements for changes of gender markers on these and other legal documents differ from state to state. Of the jurisdictions that change birth certificates, six states, DC, and New York City only require clinically appropriate treatment,[64] while five other states have no surgery requirements or clearly stated policy.[65] None of these jurisdictions

59 See listing Virginia in Table 3, column 2.
60 See W. Byne et al. 'Report of the American Psychiatric Association Task Force on Treatment of Gender Identity Disorder' (2012) 41 *Archives of Sexual Behavior* 759–796.
61 Ibid.
62 See NDTS, above n. 5, p. 78.
63 Ibid.
64 See Table 1.
65 See Table 2.

require surgery for state identity cards, such as a driver's licence, although four indicate that 'gender' must be medically 'changed' or 'altered'. In stark contrast, of the remaining states, thirty-four require gender reassignment surgery for birth certificate changes, but only nine of these states clearly require surgery to correct identity cards – with the remainder of these jurisdictions requiring as little as entry into a gender identity program, confirmation of intent to live in the requested gender or, more broadly, clinically appropriate treatment.[66] Finally, of the five jurisdictions that do not change gender markers on birth certificates, all allow changes of gender markers on drivers' licences and identity cards – two requiring sex reassignment surgery, two requiring appropriate clinical treatment, and one requiring treatment according to WPATH standards of care.[67]

Of the jurisdictions requiring surgery to correct registered gender, none statutorily specify precisely what surgery is required, though a survey of the statutory language in these jurisdictions broadly suggests that the surgery must be substantial. Perhaps the most remarkable of all jurisdictions is New York, where, until recently, both state and city agencies – without support of any statutory language – graphically detailed surgical requirements for gender marker changes on birth certificates. New York State required total hysterectomy and mastectomy for persons seeking to change legal gender from female to male, and penectomy and orchiectomy for persons seeking to change legal gender from male to female.[68] New York City considered vaginoplasty or phalloplasty as prerequisites to such changes.[69] As of 2014, however, New York State requires only 'appropriate clinical treatment'[70] whereas New York City requires affirmation of gender identity to a health professional or social worker 'in keeping with contemporary medical standards'.[71] Other states have administratively varied surgical requirements along gender lines – requiring mastectomy for persons changing a gender marker from female to male and substantial genital surgery for persons changing the marker from male to female – while still other states grant exemptions from surgery judicially.[72] Among the states that require a court order for birth certificate or identity card changes, it is unclear what these courts require as proof, or to what degree practitioners' medical assessments receive deference. Indeed, in one famous early case, the court affirmed the female gender

66 See Table 3.

67 See Table 4.

68 See Spade, above n. 4, pp. 735–736.

69 Ibid.

70 N.Y. Comp. Codes R. & Regs. Tit 10, § 35.2 (2014).

71 24 RCNY Hlth. Code § 207.05(a)(5) (2014).

72 See e.g. Correspondence between author and CT Trans Advocacy Coalition, 18 Oct 2013 (explaining that Connecticut requires breast surgery for female to males, and genital surgery for males to females); Spade, above n. 4, p. 768 (explaining Virginia's negotiated administrative action requiring only breast surgery).

of a person on the grounds that she could post-operatively 'function as a female' in sexual intercourse.[73]

While the US Constitution prohibits class-based sterilisation and requires due process before such procedures are compelled,[74] no constitutional challenges of surgery requirements have been officially reported for persons correcting registered gender. In part, this may be because courts may grant variances to surgery requirements,[75] or because the vagueness of statutory language makes challenges to the statutes difficult, as no state expressly requires *de jure* sterilisation and most may not require *de facto* sterilisation. Without strong judicial precedent supporting a right to change gender without surgery, it is, perhaps, not surprising that some surgery remains a requirement for gender reclassification in many states.

2.3. SSNs, PASSPORTS AND OTHER FEDERAL DOCUMENTS

The current federal process for gender reclassification seems remarkably simple when compared with procedures in most states. For adults seeking a change of the gender marker on a passport and Social Security Administration records, the applicant must (1) appear in person at the nearest office for the agency in question, (2) apply for the reclassification of gender on former documents, (3) submit proof of clinically appropriate treatment, and (4) submit a copy of a court order for any change of name.[76] This last requirement means that a person wishing to change a federal record in a single application will need to obtain a state court order for a name change first before proceeding to change federal documents, if a name change is desired. Surgery is *not* required for any change of SSN records or passports. The same is true for records controlled by other federal agencies, such as US Citizenship and Immigration Services and the Department of Veteran Affairs.[77] The Department of State issues a new passport and returns

[73] *M.T. v J.T.*, 355 A.2d 204 (N.J. Sup. Ct. App. Div. 1976) *cert. den.* 364 A.2d 1076 (N.J. 1976).

[74] See *Skinner v Oklahoma*, 316 U.S. 535 (1942) (sterilisation based on a characteristic of a class violates equal protection and due process); *Stump v. Sparkman*, 435 U.S. 349 (1978) (courts may violate due process when ordering sterilisation without cause). For extensive discussion of the history of sterilisation and how it has become disfavoured in the United States, see P. Reilly, *The Surgical Solution: A History of Involuntary Sterilization in the United States*, Johns Hopkins Univ. Press, Baltimore 1991.

[75] See e.g. *In re the Petition of Jamie Miranda Glistenberg*, Case No. 13AR-CV00240 (Mo. Cir. Ct., 20 May 2013) (holding that a Missouri court may grant a variance from the statute where surgery is not medically advisable).

[76] See US Department of State, *Foreign Affairs Manual Volume 7: Consular Affairs*, 7 FAM 1300 Appendix M: Gender Change (CT:CON-464) (2013) and Social Security Administration, *Program Operations Manual System (POMS), RM 10212.200 Changing Numident Data for Reasons other than Name Change* (2013).

[77] See USCIS, *0.22 Document Issuance Involving Status and Identity for Transgender Individuals* (Amended 8/10/2012; PM-602-0061.1. Added 4/10/2012; PM-602-0061. AD12–02) and VHA

the nullified passport to the applicant, as in all applications for renewed passports. The SSN does not contain gender markers, so the Social Security Administration merely changes the information in its database associated with the number, which is generally unavailable to the public. These changes have all been made by the Obama Administration, by each agency's civil administrative orders, not legislation.

III. CONSEQUENCES OF THE CHANGE OF LEGAL GENDER

3.1. OVERVIEW

Because changes of legal documents are primarily confined to those documents, changes of registered gender generally do not confer any formal legal gender status. One exception to this rule formerly arose in states that restricted marriage to male–female couples – a practice today considered unconstitutional – as changes of birth certificates were theoretically needed for transgender persons in most jurisdictions to obtain marriage licences according to their corrected gender. Today, however, transgender persons still face significant consequences simply for being transgender, regardless of their legal documentation or whether they undergo medical treatment. Consequently, legal protection depends on other laws and regulations, particularly those prohibiting discrimination on the basis of gender identity. The United States has few national laws prohibiting such discrimination expressly. Currently, only federal hate crimes law does so, but the federal government currently considers 'gender identity' included within the meanings of other civil rights legislation, as set forth below. Several states also have laws prohibiting gender identity discrimination, though they represent less than half of the country.

3.2. CIVIL RIGHTS

Civil rights protections for transgender persons have recently become national in the United States. Federal law has, for many years, prohibited discrimination on the basis of sex in employment[78] and housing,[79] and also prohibits such discrimination by any health care[80] or educational[81] institution or program

---

DIRECTIVE 2013-003, *Providing Health Care For Transgender And Intersex Veterans*, 2013, pp. A-6 and A-7.

[78] 42 U.S.C. § 2000e et seq.; see also 42 U.S.C. § 1983 (state employers).

[79] 42 U.S.C. § 3601 et seq.

[80] 42 U.S.C. § 18116 (2010).

[81] 20 U.S.C. §§ 1681–1688.

that receives any federal funds, reaching most such institutions and programs in the United States. A growing number of federal courts have demonstrated a willingness to hold that discrimination against a person for gender non-conformity is discrimination on the basis of sex and gender.[82] As a result, the federal government also now considers gender identity discrimination to be covered under the Civil Rights Act,[83] as well as under the Fair Housing Act for federally financed housing assistance.[84] The Patient Protection and Affordable Care Act extends these protections to any health care institution or program receiving federal funds.[85] At the state level, these laws are limited in number. Only eighteen states and DC prohibit gender identity discrimination in private employment, housing, public benefits, education, and public accommodations.[86] Approximately 100 towns and municipalities also have similar laws.[87]

The extension of federal civil rights protection to persons on the basis of gender identity means that federal authorities now join several state and local governments in the ability to receive complaints and take independent law enforcement actions against discrimination on the basis of gender identity in some areas. There are, however, two significant gaps in all of these laws. First, none of the laws require educational facilities to provide updated school records with the correct name and gender identity to persons who have had those records under a prior name or gender.[88] Second, very few, to date, guarantee access either to changing rooms in sports facilities or public restrooms, which are largely gender segregated throughout the United States, often by law.[89] Several hundred state and private universities have adopted non-discrimination policies and have made

---

[82] This interpretation of the Civil Rights Act began with *Price Waterhouse v Hopkins*, 490 U.S. 228 (1989), when the US Supreme Court held that gender stereotyping, such as failing to hire or promote a woman for not being feminine or wearing sufficient jewellery, constituted sex discrimination. Courts are currently split on whether this fully extends protection to all transgender persons. Compare *Schoer v Billington*, 577 F.Supp.2d 293 (D.D.C. 2008) and *Barnes v City of Cincinnati*, 401 F.3d 729 (6th Cir. 2005) with *Etsitty v Utah Transit Auth.*, 502 F.3d 1215 (10th Cir. 2007) and *Ulane v Eastern Airlines, Inc.*, 742 F.2d 1081 (7th Cir. 1984); see also *Glenn v Brumby*, 663 F.3d 1312 (11th Cir. 2011) (holding transgender discrimination to be unconstitutional). For other cases assessing gender stereotyping as unlawful bases for adverse employment conditions, Howell, above n. 4, p. 141–153.

[83] This is recognised by the Department of Justice, the Equal Employment Opportunity Commission, as well as the Department of Education. See Office of the Attorney General, *Treatment of Transgender Employment Discrimination Claims Under Title VII of the Civil Rights Act of 1964* (15 December 2014), *Macy v Holder*, E.E.O.C. Dec. 0210120821, 2012 WL 1435995, pp. 1 and 11 (2012), United States Department of Education, Office for Civil Rights, *Letter to Educators*, 26 October 2010, pp. 3–8. Successful litigation on these grounds was rare before these recognitions. For a notable successful case, see e.g. *Nabozny v Podlesney*, 92 F.3d 446 (7th Cir. 1996); *Henkle v Gregory*, 150 F.Supp.2d 1067 (D.Nev. 2001).

[84] See e.g. 24 C.F.R. § 5.105 200.300 and 570.3 (2013) (FHA regulation on housing funding).

[85] 42 U.S.C. § 18116 (2010).

[86] National Gay and Lesbian Task Force (NGLTF), *State Nondiscrimination Laws in the U.S.*, NGLTF, D.C. (2014).

[87] See Howell, above n. 4, pp. 253–261 and 277–293. See e.g. NYC Admin. Code § 8-107(4)(a).

[88] Ibid., p. 78.

[89] Ibid., pp. 273–291 (comparing city ordinances).

efforts to accommodate students.[90] Nevertheless, because transgender persons are not considered disabled under the Americans with Disabilities Act, most facilities offering restrooms for their own employees or public restrooms are not required to provide reasonable accommodations in most of the nation.[91] Notably, in 2013, California passed the first state-wide law of its kind when it authorised student access to restrooms and sports programs on the basis of gender identity, regardless of how gender is registered in school records or other legal documents.[92]

3.3. RELATIONSHIP RECOGNITION

Marriage is considered a 'fundamental right' in the United States, one of the 'basic civil rights' so 'fundamental to our very existence and survival' that it is protected by the US Constitution, even though it is not enumerated therein.[93] The Constitution does not grant the federal government any power to licence and regulate marriage. Rather, that power belongs to the states, pursuant to their general powers to regulate public health and welfare. Nevertheless, the US Supreme Court has held that the Constitution places limits on the ability of the states to penalise or restrict access to marriage licences as a matter of right,[94] as well as that state regulation is subject to the Constitution's equal protection guarantees.[95] The Court has, for example, held that states cannot restrict 'the freedom of choice to marry … by invidious racial discriminations'.[96] However, as 'marriage' is not mentioned in the Constitution; rather, the Court has considered marriage to be a right drawn from pre-Constitutional 'tradition'.[97] Because the Court had, until recently, declined to reverse lower court decisions upholding gender requirements for marriage,[98] the right to marry without regard to gender was left in doubt for most of US history. In June 2015, however, the Court in

[90] See HOWELL, above n. 4, p. 79. For further analysis, see T.B. WOLFF, 'Civil Rights Reform and the Body' (2012) 6 *Harvard Law & Policy Review* 201.

[91] See HOWELL, above n. 4, p. 140.

[92] CAL. EDUC. CODE, § 221.5(e) ('A pupil shall be permitted to participate in sex-segregated school programs and activities, including athletic teams and competitions, and use facilities consistent with his or her gender identity, irrespective of the gender listed on the pupil's records').

[93] See *Loving v Virginia*, 388 U.S. 1, 12 (1967).

[94] See *Zablocki v Redhail*, 434 U.S. 374, 381–391 (1978).

[95] *Loving*, 388 U.S. at 11–12.

[96] Ibid., at 10–12.

[97] The US Supreme Court has frequently used tradition to reject claims of fundamental rights when the tradition is not 'deeply rooted'. See *Troxel v Granville*, 120 S.Ct. 2054 (2000). The question of the degree of how specifically to read the tradition, however, has split the Court, see e.g. *Michael H. v Gerald D.*, 491 U.S. 110, 127 n. 6 and 132 (1989). Indeed, regarding a fundamental right to sexual privacy, the Court first held that tradition permitted prohibitions on 'homosexuality', *Bowers v Hardwick*, 478 U.S. 186, 196 (1986) but reversed that decision in part on this point in *Lawrence v Texas*, 539 U.S. 558, 576–578 (2003).

[98] See *Baker v Nelson* 409 U.S. 810 (1972); *Littleton v Prange*, 531 U.S. 872 (2000).

Obergefell v Hodges held that the right to marry – read through the lens of equal protection – could not exclude same-gender couples.[99]

The decision in *Obergefell* is the culmination of the rapid evolution of marriage law in the US. As of June 2013, only thirteen states and the District of Columbia authorised the issuance of gender-neutral marriage licences, which the federal government did not recognise.[100] In *Windsor v the United States*, however, the Supreme Court held that federal refusal to recognise these marriages violated the Fifth Amendment's promise of equal protection, as such 'differentiation demeans the couples, whose moral and sexual choices the Constitution protects' and 'humiliates tens of thousands of children now being raised by same-sex couples'.[101] Shortly thereafter, two more states legalised same-gender marriage,[102] while courts nationwide in rapid succession struck down other states' denials of marriage licences to same-gender couples.[103] By February 2015, thirty-seven states and the District of Columbia issued marriage licences without regard to the couples' gender, with most federal Courts of Appeals – except the Sixth Circuit Court of Appeals – holding gendered marriage restrictions unconstitutional. Resolving that disagreement, the Supreme Court in *Obergefell* held that exclusion of 'same-sex couples' from marriage resulted in substantive inequality that left those couples 'consigned to an instability many opposite-sex couples would deem intolerable in their own lives', such that it 'demeans gays and lesbians for the State to lock them out of a central institution of the Nation's society', with

---

99 135 S.Ct. 2584, 2605 (2015).

100 Of these jurisdictions, ten did so legislatively or by referendum: D.C. (D.C. Code § 46–401), Delaware (Del. Code tit. 13 §101 et seq. and 129 (2013)), Maine (Me. Rev. Stat. Ann. tit 19-A § 701 (2012)), Maryland (Md. Code Ann. Fam. Law §§ 2–201 and 2–202 (2013)), Minnesota (Minn. Stat. § 517.01), New Hampshire (N.H. Rev. Stat. Ann. § 37:1–1 et seq. (2010)) New York, N.Y. Dom. Rel. Law §§ 10a and 10b (2011), Rhode Island, R.I. Gen. Laws (2013), §15-1-1 and 15-1-7, Vermont (Vt. Stat. Ann. tit. 15 § 8 (2009)), and Washington (Wash. Rev. Code § 26.04.010(1) and (3) (2012)). The rest did so after litigation: California, *In Re Marriage Cases* 183 P.3d 384 (2008), Connecticut, *Kerrigan v Commissioner of Public Health*, 957 A.2d 407 (Conn. 2008), Iowa, *Varnum v Brien*, 763 N.W.2d 862, (Iowa 2009), and Massachusetts, *Goodridge v Dept. of Public Health*, 798 N.E.2d 941 (Mass. 2003). In California, the state supreme court's decision was nullified by referendum, which was then struck down in federal court under the US Constitution, with appeals by opposed citizens dismissed by the US Supreme Court for lack of standing, see *Perry v Schwarzenegger*, 704 F.Supp.2d 921 (N.D. Cal., 2010) *aff'd* 671 F.3d 1052 (9th Cir. 2012) *vacated and dismissed sub. nom. Hollingsworth v Perry*, 133 S.Ct. 2652 (2013). Delaware, Minnesota, and Rhode Island passed their laws in May 2013 but became effective shortly after *Windsor*.

101 *United States v Windsor*, 133 S.Ct. 2675 (2013).

102 These states are Hawaii (Hawaii Rev. Stat. §572–1 (2013)) and Illinois (750 Ill. Comp. Stat. 5/201 (2013)).

103 Federal appellate court decisions bound most of these states. *See Bostic v Schaeffer*, 760 F.3d 352 (4th Cir. 2014); *Baskin v Bogan*, 766 F.3d 352 (7th Cir. 2014). *Kitchen v Herbert*, 755 F.3d 1193 (10th Cir. 2014); *Latta v Otter*, 771 F.3d 456 (9th Cir. 2014). The exceptions are New Jersey, *Garden State Equality v Dow*, 82 A.3d 336 (N.J. Super. Ct. 2013) *stay denied* 79 A.3d 1036 (N.J. 2013); New Mexico, *Griego v Oliver*, 316 P.3d 865 (N.M. 2013); Oregon, *Geiger v Kitzhaber*, 994 F.Supp.2d 1128 (D.Or. 2014), Pennsylvania, *Whitehood v Woolf*, 992 F.Supp.2d 410 (M.D.Pa. 2014), Florida, *Brenner v Scott*, 999 F. Supp. 2d 1278 (D. Fla. 2014) and Alabama, *Searcy v Strange*, --- F.Supp.3d ----, 2015 WL 328728 (S.D. Ala. 2015).

'the effect of teaching that gays and lesbians are unequal'.[104] Thus, the Court held that the Fourteenth Amendment required all states to respect the 'right to marry' in a gender-neutral manner, as a right that protects 'personal choices, central to individual dignity and autonomy, including intimate choices that define personal identity'.[105]

While *Obergefell* did not address the importance of gender-neutral marriage to transgender persons, it has dramatically eliminated legal barriers that such persons once faced in marriage. Before *Obergefell*, transgender persons only had the complete freedom to marry if they lived in or moved to a state that issued gender-neutral marriage licences.

That freedom of movement, therefore, provided limited access to equality, especially for individuals who could not leave states restricting marriage along gender lines. In four states in particular, courts expressly refused to recognise the gender identity of persons who changed registered gender, ruling that their marriages were effectively 'same-sex marriages' and, therefore, not recognised as legal. In the leading case, the Texas Court of Appeals, Seventh Circuit held:

> 'The evidence fully supports that Christie Littleton, born male, wants and believes herself to be a woman. She has made every conceivable effort to make herself a female, including a surgery that would make most males pale and perspire to contemplate … Her female anatomy, however, is all man-made. The body that Christie inhabits is a male body in all aspects other than what the physicians have supplied.
>
> Christie was created and born a male. Her original birth certificate, an official document of Texas, clearly so states … Christie amended the original birth certificate to change the sex and name … At the time of birth, Christie was a male, both anatomically and genetically. The facts contained in the original birth certificate were true and accurate, and the words contained in the amended certificate are not binding on this court … We hold, as a matter of law, that Christie Littleton is a male. As a male, Christie cannot be married to another male.'[106]

Thereafter, courts in Kansas, Florida, and Ohio followed suit restricting marriage recognition based on the parties' gender as registered at birth.[107] Even after the Texas legislature amended its laws to enable proof of sex for a marriage licence through legal 'sex change', the Texas Court of Appeals' Thirteenth Circuit affirmed the change to be law,[108] leaving Texas courts divided on the issue. As a result, state

---

[104] 135 S.Ct. at 2601–2604.

[105] Ibid., at 2597.

[106] *Littleton v Prange*, 9 S.W.3d 223, 230–31 (Tex. App. 1999) *rev. den.* (Tex. 2000) *cert. den.* 531 U.S. 872 (2000).

[107] *In re Estate of Gardiner*, 42 P.3d 120, 124–135 (2002) *cert. den.* 537 U.S. 825 (2002), *Kantaras. Kantaras*, 884 So.2d 155, 158–61 (Fla. App. 2d. Dist. 2004) *rev. den.* 898 So.2d 80 (Fla. 2005), and *In re Marriage License for Nash*, 2003 WL 23097095 at 8–9 (Ohio App. 2003).

[108] *In re Estate of Araguz*, 443 S.W.3d 233 (Tex Ct. App. 2014).

law doctrine in the field remained muddled through 2015, particularly because of hostility to 'same-sex marriage'.[109]

State court decisions opposing marriage recognition for transgender persons had always been difficult to reconcile with the freedom to marry as protected by the US Constitution, but they also conflicted with state law permitting changes of legal gender. No court had denied that persons who have corrected their legal gender have a right to marry someone. Even if that right under the US Constitution encompassed only the right to marry someone of the so-called other gender, restriction of legal gender to the one on the original birth certificate meant that a person who had changed registered gender – and perhaps had undergone gender correction surgery – could only marry a cisgender person with the same registered gender or another transgender person who had also undergone a change of registered gender, perhaps without any noticeable physical change. In many of these cases, a marriage would appear to the public to be a *de jure* same-gender marriage, as well as a *de facto* one – in essence, perceptible only as a 'male–female' marriage by agencies with access to birth certificate records. Today, in the wake of *Obergefell*, prior court decisions in the US interfering with marriages of transgender persons remain an historic record of how such discrimination manifested in uniquely denigrating and intrusive ways – intrusions that in marriage, at least, have been eliminated by gender neutrality.

3.4. PARENTHOOD AND FAMILY

As in other areas of US law, changing individual legal documents may not have any measurable impact on parenthood for transgender persons, including those who have undergone medical treatment to support their gender identity. Transgender persons remain vulnerable to discrimination in parenthood simply because they are transgender. In large part, that vulnerability has extended to all sexual minorities wherever privileges have been closely associated with traditional heterosexual marriage – for example, where presumptions about legal parenthood and gendered parental status applied only to certain married couples.[110] In other matters, however, particularly relating to custody of children in relationship disputes, a troubling number of courts have awarded custody to a cisgender parent out of concerns of how the transgender parent might

---

109 See A.C. Stirnitzke, 'Transsexuality, Marriage, and the Myth of True Sex' (2011) 53 *Ariz. L. Rev.* 285.

110 For an overview of the patterns in the states, see J. Shapiro, 'The Law Governing LGBT-Parent Families' in A. Goldberg and K.R. Allen (eds.), *LGBT-Parent Families: Innovations in Research and Implications for Practice*, Springer, New York 2013, pp. 291–304 (surveying the US, explaining 'there is so much variation in the law as well as near constant change in law' in this field in the United States, 'it is practically impossible to accurately summarize the current state of the law at any given moment').

affect the child.[111] In adoption matters, being transgender – or even refusal to disclose transgender history – may also have an impact on state approval for adoption.[112] These decisions have been difficult to challenge on appeal because the judicial or administrative authorities in question typically claim to make highly individualised, fact-based decisions for each child in each particular case. In the absence of categorical statements by authorities that transgender persons should not be parents or have custody, judicial challenges claiming status-based discrimination in these cases may be difficult to mount.

Nevertheless, actual governmental interference with parenting is rare in the US, as the US Constitution generally protects the rights of individuals to decide to have a child.[113] As such, it is extremely common that transgender persons in the United States are parents.[114] This is true even for persons who have had children after some gender-correction surgery, even though many states require sex assignment surgery to change registered gender in ways that might be presumed to interfere with reproductive capacity. Without detailed private information and further study, it is impossible to draw general conclusions about such parents' circumstances, namely whether they have not sought a change of registered gender or whether any corrective procedures that they may have had spared reproductive capacity. Assisted reproduction and surrogacy are also relatively accessible in the United States, with many clinics nationwide assisting non-traditional families in reproduction.[115] Many states have extended gender-neutral protections in adoption and legal parental status to gay and lesbian parents, even in some cases making it possible for such parents to be listed as legal parents at birth without adoption or other government intervention.[116] These latter advances may assist and shelter transgender parents. Nevertheless, barring legal reform, the security of transgender parents may depend on the strength of their relationships with co-parents and children, as well as hope for progressive support from public

111 See Howell, above n. 4, pp. 67–74; see also S. Perez, 'Is It a Boy or a Girl? Not The Baby, The Parent: Transgender Parties In Custody Battles And The Benefit Of Promoting A Truer Understanding Of Gender' (2011) 9 *Whittier Journal of Child & Family Advocacy* 367

112 See Shapiro, above n. 110, p. 294.

113 See. e.g. *Planned Parenthood of Southeastern Pennsylvania v Casey*, 505 U.S. 833, 851 (1992), *Eisenstadt v Baird*, 405 U.S. 438, 453 (1972).

114 See J.B. Downing, 'Transgender-Parent Families' in A. Goldberg and K.R. Allen (eds.), *LGBT-Parent Families: Innovations in Research and Implications for Practice*, Springer, New York 2013, pp. 105–115.

115 For an overview, see A. Goldberg and K.R. Allen (eds.), *LGBT-Parent Families: Innovations in Research and Implications for Practice*, Springer, New York 2013, pp. 21–85. Regarding surrogacy, D. Hinson, *State-by-State Surrogacy Laws: Actual Practices, Family Advocate* (American Bar Association), 34:2 (2011) see <www.creativefamilyconnections.com/state-map-surrogacy-law-practices>. See also C.G. Joslin and S.P. Minter, *Lesbian, Gay, Bisexual and Transgender Family Law*, West, Egan, MN 2011.

116 For a summary of state laws on second-parent adoption where couples are same gender pairings, see Human Rights Campaign, *Parenting Laws: Joint Adoption*, 2013, and Human Rights Campaign, *Parenting Laws: Second Parent Or Stepparent Adoption*, 2013.

officials in individual cases when government involvement is necessary to settle custody disputes or legally affirm parenthood.

3.5. SPECIALISED AREAS OF CONCERN

In three specialised areas, persons perceived as non-conforming in their gender are at particular risk of legal harm. In all branches of the US Armed Forces, any discovery or disclosure of transgender or transsexual identity, difference in sex development, or impairment of genital function from genital surgery is a ground for discharge from service.[117] In jails and prisons, transgender inmates are also placed in precarious positions – often housed according to their legal gender but left susceptible to prisoner violence, or formally isolated to protect them from other prisoners but placed in harsh prison conditions that may fall below constitutional standards.[118] No state or federal correctional service provides for sex reassignment surgery, and many restrict access to treatments associated with gender identity care.[119] Finally, despite being statistically at greater risk of murder and assault,[120] transgender persons receive only limited legal protection from bias-motivated violence. The states are primarily responsible for police powers, but gender-identity violence is specifically covered by law in only fifteen of them and the District of Columbia.[121]

In each of these areas, federal efforts have made some steps toward improved conditions for gender minorities. In 2009, Congress amended federal hate crime law to cover bias-motivated violence against persons on the basis of gender identity.[122] Enforcement is, however, limited to interstate crimes or instances of a showing of unequal law enforcement against such crimes in the states. In 2012, the Department of Justice promulgated regulations under the Prison

---

117 Dep't Of Defense Instruction 6130.03, Medical Standards for Appointment, Enlistment, or Induction in the Military Services, ¶¶ E4.14(e) E4.15(l), and ¶ E4.28(r) (2010). As one scholar has noted, the repeal of discharge provisions for gay and lesbian service members leaves uncertain whether discharge will be honourable for one of these conditions. See Howell, above n. 4, pp. 42–43.

118 See *Farmer v Brennan*, 511 U.S. 825 (1994) (surveying the constitutional standards and how difficult it may be to prove violations). The scope of this problem in the US is reflected in the considerable volume of scholarship on this subject, see e.g. G. Arkles, 'Safety and solidarity across gender lines: Rethinking segregation of transgendered people in detention' (2009) 18 *Temp. Pol. & Civil Rts. L. Rev.* 515; S. Tarzwell, 'The gender lines are marked with razor wire: Addressing state prison policies and practices for the management of transgender prisoners' (2006) 38 *Colum. Hum. Rts. L. Rev.* 167.

119 NDTS, above n. 5, p. 160; Howell, above n. 4, pp. 173–190. See also *Kosilek v Spencer*, 774 F.3d 63 (1st Cir. 2014) (holding that refusal to provide surgery is not a constitutional violation).

120 See National Coalition of Anti-violence Programs, *Lesbian, Gay, Bisexual, Transgender, Queer and HIV-Affected Hate Violence in 2012*, 2013, pp. 32–33.

121 See National Gay and Lesbian Task Force, *Hate Crime Laws in the United States*, NGLTF, D.C. 2013.

122 8 U.S.C. §249(a) as amended by Pub. L. No. 111–84 (2009).

Rape Elimination Act[123] requiring all prisons in the US receiving federal funds to regularly review placement of transgender and intersex prisoners, as well as prison security – for example, ensuring prisoners' rights to shower separately to protect their safety.[124] Finally in 2013, the Department of Veteran Affairs extended its directive requiring equal treatment for all transgender and intersex patients, guaranteeing all treatment related to their gender conditions except for gender surgery,[125] including post-surgical treatment, if necessary.[126] Apart from the obvious limitations in these reforms, it should be noted that these latter two regulations are the only two federal regulations that expressly provide protection for persons with atypical sex development as 'intersexed' individuals, illustrating how much more work in this area remains.

3.6. IN PRACTICE

Because of the complexity of the law in this field, it may be helpful to view potential scenarios of how a change of legal gender works in concert with civil rights laws and other regulations in the United States, as presented in this chapter.

Example 1 – Living in a Progressive State

Persons born in one of eight jurisdictions – California, the District of Columbia, Iowa, New York, Rhode Island, Oregon, Washington, and Vermont – can be assured of the ability to change both their birth certificates and state identification cards administratively without any surgery. These individuals will face no greater burdens applying for such a change on a passport or SSN records from the federal government. In all of these states but New York, they will be protected under state law from discrimination in employment, housing, and other areas in their gender identity. They will also be protected by local hate crime laws in all of these jurisdictions but Iowa and New York.

Example 2 – Risks of Moving from One State to Another

A person born in any state permitting change of gender on birth certificates might move to Kansas, Ohio, Oklahoma, Idaho, Tennessee, or Texas – for example, for a new job or to be with family. In each of those new states of residence, the person will not be protected by a state-specific anti-discrimination law or hate crime law and will also have to turn to federal law enforcement for help in housing or employment. Until 2015, if that person fell in love with someone in the new state of residence, the couple would only receive a marriage licence if their birth

---

123 42 U.S.C. § 15601 et seq.

124 28 C.F.R. §§ 115.5, 115.41, 115.42 and 115.231(a)(9).

125 38 C.F.R. § 17.38 and 32 C.F.R. § 199.4(e)(7).

126 Department of Veterans Affairs, VHA Directive 2011–024, Providing Health Care for Transgender and Intersex Veterans (2011).

certificates did not reflect the same gender, often based on their uncorrected certificates, with uncertainty of what the state's position was regarding the right to marry anyone at all.

Example 3 – Increased Liberty after Moving from One State to Another
A person born in Ohio, Idaho, or Tennessee categorically cannot change a gender marker on a birth certificate but may decide to leave the state. Even before same-sex marriage was recognised nationwide, that person could move to one of eighteen states that had (and still have) gender-neutral marriage laws and also prohibit discrimination on the basis of gender identity, only three of which do not have laws with specific penalties for gender-identity violence. In all of these states, no permanent physical changes are required to obtain a new state ID card. Even without a new birth certificate, the person can apply for a passport with the old certificate and change the registered gender following clinically appropriate treatment, equally changing the SSN registration with relative ease.

Example 4 – Territorial Border Perplexities
Until recently, a person born in New York City who needed to change gender markers on a birth certificate was required by law to have reconstructive surgery, but if born elsewhere in New York State was required to have certain organs removed. Today, both the city and state have abandoned these requirements, but only New York City prohibits gender identity discrimination. Neither the city nor the state punishes crime motivated by gender identity bias. Neighbouring state Connecticut has both such laws, but still requires surgery for gender marker changes on birth certificates. As such, a person from Connecticut might be better off for gender registry purposes if born in New York, but a New York native might be better protected from discrimination and violence by moving to Connecticut.

IV. CONCLUSIONS

The United States has often been called a 'laboratory' of democracy, where 'a single courageous state may, if its citizens choose … try novel social and economic experiments without risk to the rest of the country'.[127] As such, from an academic standpoint, the United States offers a rich variety of legal approaches of tying legal status to gender. This has been even more true over time as these laws frequently change, offering a collective experience that has demonstrated that a single approach is not necessary for a state or the federal government to function but, rather, reflects attitudes about gender particular to that jurisdiction that may not stand the test of time. Unfortunately, from a human perspective, these 'legal experiments' in the United States have also imposed significant

---

[127] *New State Ice Co. v Liebmann*, 285 U.S. 262, 311 (1924).

hardships on individuals most directly affected by rules and regulations, in ways that are difficult to reconcile, even within their own jurisdiction's gender norms. If nothing else, the US experience with legal status based on gender identity emphasises the need for progressive national regulation so that all citizens and residents can be treated with dignity.[128]

From a more positive point of view, the United States offers examples of just how progressive jurisdictions can rapidly become. For example, ILGA Europe and Transgender Europe have recently cited California as a model jurisdiction for European nations to follow in ensuring equality for transgender persons through anti-discrimination law.[129] Recent reforms made by the federal government also demonstrate that even a nation like the US – with controversial policies on national security – can function quite well without strict legal control of gender status. If the trend in the US continues toward relaxing restrictions on correcting gender registries, it may permit more probing and profound questions about the degree to which gender classifications are necessary in law at all. As one scholar has explained:

> 'Overall, a detailed examination of the gender classification rules of the United States exposes the internal contradictions and assumptions that are for the most part ignored or unrecognized in the numerous administrative contexts where these rules operate day-to-day ... the under-discussed policy matrix that messily and incoherently defines gender categories in the United States ... Further, it allows us to see at work the production of insecurity and vulnerability for certain populations in the creation of systems of classification that administer caretaking programs ... It offers a chance to re-imagine political responses to surveillance and to question whether caretaking functions of the state, such as the redistribution of wealth through taxes and public benefits, national security, disease control, and even the remediation of long histories of oppression and exploitation, require the kinds of data collection that are increasing at a rapid pace in the United States, or whether they could be better accomplished through other means.'[130]

---

[128] The federal government has authority to take action against state government for class-based discrimination under US Const., Amendment XIV, §5. See *United States v Morrison*, 529 U.S. 598 (2000); *United States v Harris*, 106 U.S. 629 (1883); *Civil Rights Cases*, 109 U.S. 3 (1883).

[129] S. Agius, R. Köhler, S. Aujean and J. Ehrt, *Human Rights and Gender Identity: Best Practice Catalogue*, ILGA/TGEU, Brussels 2011, p. 37.

[130] Spade, above n. 4, pp. 817–821.

TABLES: COMPARISONS OF MEDICAL REQUIREMENTS FOR CHANGE OF GENDER MARKERS IN THE UNITED STATES[131]

Table 1. Jurisdictions that have no requirement for surgery to change gender markers on birth certificates

Jurisdiction	Prerequisites for birth certificate correction	Prerequisites for state ID correction	Court order required for gender change
California	Clinically appropriate treatment	Currently living in the requested gender	Birth certificate only
District of Columbia	Clinically appropriate treatment	Physician statement that applicant is expected to live in the gender requested for the foreseeable future	Neither document
Iowa	Surgery or 'other treatment'	'Corrected birth certificate'	Neither document
New York State	Clinically appropriate treatment only	'Proof of sex change' from physician stating that the requested gender is the 'one' and 'main' gender.	Neither document
New York City	Confirmation according to 'contemporary medical standards'	Controlled by state agency	Neither document
Oregon	Clinically appropriate treatment	Medical opinion of gender for foreseeable future	Birth certificate only
Rhode Island	Clinically appropriate treatment	Medical opinion of gender for foreseeable future	Neither document
Vermont	Surgery, hormonal or other treatment	Medical opinion of gender 'for foreseeable future'	Birth certificate only

131 The information in these tables is based on 2015 data. For up-to-date information on birth certificates, *see* the National Center for Transgender Equality's website at <http://transequality.org/documents> accessed 26.03.2015.

Table 2. Jurisdictions with no express medical requirements to change gender markers on birth certificates

Jurisdiction	Prerequisites for birth certificate correction	Prerequisites for state ID correction	Court order required for gender change
Indiana	No requirements specified	Court order or proof of 'all medical treatment necessary' for gender change	Birth certificate only
Mississippi	No requirements specified	Documentation of 'gender change' (no official rules)	Birth certificate only
Minnesota	No requirements specified	Clinically appropriate treatment	Birth certificate only (formally)
South Dakota	No requirements specified	Gender has been 'medically altered'	Both birth certificate and driver's licence
Washington	Clinically appropriate treatment (official policy)	Appropriate gender transition clinical treatment	Neither document

Table 3. Jurisdictions requiring surgery for changing gender markers on birth certificates

Jurisdiction	Prerequisites for birth certificate correction	Prerequisites for state ID correction	Court order required
Alabama	'Changed by surgical procedure'	Sex reassignment surgery	Birth certificate only
Alaska	'Change of sex' (surgery)	Appropriate clinical treatment	Birth certificate only
Arizona	'Sex change operation'	Committed to gender change process	Neither document
Arkansas	'Changed by surgical procedure'	Uncertain – documents showing gender change	Both documents
Colorado	'Changed by surgical procedure'	Medical confirmation of gender identity or completion of surgery	Birth certificate only
Connecticut	Surgical procedure (admin. practice)	Medical opinion of gender for foreseeable future	Birth certificate only
Delaware	'Changed by surgical procedure'	Medical opinion of gender for foreseeable future	Birth certificate only
Florida	'Sex reassignment surgery'	Appropriate clinical treatment	Neither document
Georgia	'Changed by surgical procedure'	'Gender reassignment operation'	Both documents
Hawaii	'Sex change operation'	Medical opinion of gender for foreseeable future	Neither document

Jurisdiction	Prerequisites for birth certificate correction	Prerequisites for state ID correction	Court order required
Illinois	'An operation' that warrants that sex 'should be changed'	Gender change has taken place or is in the process of change	Neither document
Kentucky	'Changed by surgical procedure'	Changed passport or birth certificate	Neither document
Louisiana	Surgery changing the 'anatomical structure of the individual' to a sex 'other than on the birth certificate'	'Undergone a gender change/reassignment procedure and desires to change the gender'	Birth certificate only
Maine	'Change by surgical procedure'	Medical opinion of gender for foreseeable future	Birth certificate only
Maryland	'Permanent' and 'irreversible' surgery	Medical documentation of hormone therapy and living in the requested gender	Birth certificate only
Massachusetts	'Sex reassignment surgery, so-called'	Medical opinion of gender for foreseeable future	Neither document
Michigan	'Sex reassignment surgery'	Changed birth certificate	Neither document
Missouri	'Changed by surgical procedure'	Undergone gender surgery (policy)	Birth certificate only
Montana	'Changed by surgical procedure'	Changed birth certificate	Birth certificate only
Nebraska	'Sex reassignment surgery'	Necessary sex reassignment procedures for social gender recognition	Neither document
Nevada	'Sex transformation'	Lives in the identity and is undergoing treatment	Neither document
New Hampshire	'Sex change'	Medical opinion of gender for foreseeable future	Birth certificate only
New Jersey	'Changed by surgical procedure'	Medical opinion of gender for foreseeable future	Neither document
New Mexico	'Changed by surgical procedure'	Medical opinion of gender for foreseeable future	Neither document
North Carolina	'Sex reassignment surgery'	No clear rule – policy seems to require surgery	Neither document
North Dakota	'Sex conversion operation'	'Medical documentation'	Neither document
Pennsylvania	Sex reassignment surgery	Medical opinion of gender for foreseeable future	Neither document
South Carolina	Sex reassignment surgery (admin. practice)	Medical documentation of gender change	Both documents

Jurisdiction	Prerequisites for birth certificate correction	Prerequisites for state ID correction	Court order required
Texas	Called into doubt by courts in some parts of the state, officially permitted by department with court order	Court order of change of gender; anticipates surgery.	Both documents
Utah	'Sex changed' / surgical procedure (admin. practice)	Change of gender on birth certificate or passport	Birth certificate only
Virginia	'Surgical gender reassignment procedure' and 'pre-operative and post-operative diagnosis'	Certification of gender identity by physician with practice including treatment or counselling of persons with gender identity issues	Birth certificate only
West Virginia	Sex reassignment surgery (admin. practice)	Gender change is complete	Both documents
Wisconsin	Surgical procedure	Physician certification of the gender change	Birth certificate only
Wyoming	Sex changed / surgical procedure (admin. practice)	'All operations necessary to effect a change of sex'	Birth certificate only

Table 4. Jurisdictions that currently do not permit changes of gender markers on birth certificates

Jurisdiction	Legal ground for denying change of birth certificate	Prerequisites for state ID correction (sex)	Court order required
Idaho	Statute does not permit change	Documentation of change of gender (appropriate treatment without surgery)	For driver's licence
Kansas	Administratively halted on grounds of unclear statute	Appropriate clinical treatment or proof of physical change	Neither document
Ohio	Court confirmed statute does not permit change	Documentation of clinically appropriate treatment according to WPATH standards of care	Neither document
Oklahoma	Administratively halted on grounds of unclear statute	Documentation of a 'complete physical sex change' that is 'irreversible and permanent'	Neither document
Tennessee	Expressly barred by statute	Documentation of sex reassignment surgery	Neither document

PART IV
CONCLUSION

THE LEGAL STATUS OF TRANSSEXUAL AND TRANSGENDER PERSONS – COMPARATIVE ANALYSIS AND RECOMMENDATIONS

Jens M. Scherpe and Peter Dunne

Contents

I. PURPOSE OF THE COMPARATIVE ANALYSIS AND RECOMMENDATIONS

When comparing and analysing the development of the legal status of transsexual and transgender persons,[1] what is striking is how fraught with – at best – misapprehensions and misunderstandings[2] and – at worst – social rejection and even hatred the debates have been and, in many jurisdictions, still are. Looking back, the history of recognition of the preferred gender of transsexual and transgender persons has been, and remains, a battle against discrimination, stigmatisation, social exclusion, anxiety, pain and suffering, violation of dignity and physical integrity, and sometimes even prosecution and persecution.

While the legal and social situation of transsexual and transgender persons has improved greatly in many jurisdictions, that certainly is not the case globally. As already said in the introduction, this book therefore aims to make a contribution to the ongoing scholarly and political debates concerning the legal status of transsexual and transgender persons, both inside and outside of potential legislative reform processes.[3] It is also meant to function as a resource for judicial and administrative decisions. One purpose of this final chapter is to compare, categorise and, where possible, explain the legal developments in the jurisdictions covered in this book. This hopefully will enable readers to see where their home jurisdictions stand, and whether the positions taken there are tenable in the light of social developments, current medical and psychological research, and international human rights standards. The other purpose of this final chapter

1 See below for an explanation of the terminology used.

2 Perhaps best captured be the infamous statement by the German Bundesrat (Upper House) who criticised the Bill which would later become the 1980 *Gesetz über die Änderung der Vornamen und die Feststellung der Geschlechtszugehörigkeit in besonderen Fällen (Transsexuellengesetz – TSG)* (on which see the chapter by A. Dutta in this volume) with the following words: it was too early to legislate because 'transsexualism could not sufficiently be distinguished from other phenomena such as homosexuality and transvestitism' (Stellungnahme des Bundesrates, Bundestags-Drucksache 8/2947, p. 18).

3 This chapter, as indeed does the book, mainly focuses on the legal status of transsexual and transgender persons, and therefore many fundamentally important areas including discrimination laws and access to health care unfortunately cannot be explored in greater depth.

is to identify what the developing trends are. This should allow readers to not only see the stages of development and surrounding discussions – which are surprisingly similar in many, socially diverse jurisdictions – but perhaps also see why some of the points and concerns raised in the discussions are considered to lack sufficient basis in other jurisdictions. This, it is hoped, ideally (and perhaps somewhat over-optimistically) might lead to legislatures and courts avoiding what can be referred to as 'repeating other people's mistakes' – in the sense that certain development stages could be 'leap-frogged' and a better legal standard of recognition and protection for the persons concerned achieved at the outset. In order to achieve this, the chapter will make recommendations on the criteria for legal recognition of preferred gender which are based on the comparative analysis, as well as general policy and human rights considerations.

Finally, it is important to state that the views expressed in this chapter are the views of the authors of this chapter alone. This chapter was not discussed with the contributors to this book, and while many of them might agree with the views expressed here, others will not. The same is true for the terminology used in this chapter.

II. TERMINOLOGY

The issue of terminology was already addressed in the introduction.[4] However, as terminology is both an important and an extremely sensitive concern, what was said there said will be repeated here.

The precise wording and terms used in debates surrounding gender identity often reflect the intensely personal views and feelings of the persons concerned. They are often an area of strong debate or disagreement. The authors realise that any terminology used, even with the best of intentions, may be imprecise or even hurtful and insulting. Given the inherent difficulties in terminology, the language used in this chapter will not, and cannot, reflect the many different ways in which persons experience and express their preferred gender. In some cases, despite the best efforts of the authors, the terminology used may offend. With this in mind, it is important to repeat that no offence or disrespect is intended.

This chapter uses the terminology coined by Professor Stephen Whittle OBE. Professor Whittle has made an immense contribution – both in terms of his scholarship and his activism – in advancing transgender rights in the United Kingdom and elsewhere. He previously served as President of the World Professional Association of Transgender Health (WPATH), and his definitions have the benefit not only of the authority of someone immensely knowledgeable in the field but also, and perhaps crucially, of being accessible to the lay reader. In *Respect and Equality: Transsexual and Transgender Rights*, Professor Whittle

[4] Above pp. 2 f.

defines 'transgender person' to indicate all persons who live, or desire to live, in the role of a gender which is not the one designated to that person at birth, while 'transsexual person' is meant to refer to those transgender persons who desire or have undergone gender reassignment treatment/surgery.[5] In writing this chapter, the authors have also had regard for the definition of 'gender identity' set out in the Introduction to the Yogyakarta Principles.[6]

Furthermore, many terms have been used to describe the change of legal gender status of a person, some offensive like 'sex change', some suggestive and – at least in the view of the authors of this chapter – inappropriate, such as 'acquired gender',[7] some neutral such as 'registered gender' or 'nominated gender'. For this chapter – and indeed many of the chapters in this book – we have chosen the term 'legal recognition of preferred gender', as this in our view places the emphasis where it belongs – on the individual concerned. The use of the term 'preferred' or 'affirmed' change also highlights the fact that individuals do not 'change' gender through a process of legal transition. Rather, legal recognition provides a mechanism through which the law can acknowledge a person's true identity. In terms of medical interventions, we have rejected terms such as 'sex change operation' and 'gender reassignment surgery' and opted for 'gender confirmation surgery' and 'gender confirmation treatment'.

III. THE HISTORICAL LEGAL DEVELOPMENT

Mapping the historical legal development of the legal status of transsexual and transgender persons is not an easy task, as at first the developments seem somewhat disparate and the legislation enacted and court decisions rendered deeply embedded in the respective national legal culture. However, closer analysis reveals similarities, undoubtedly based on the fact that legislatures and judges were essentially always asked to answer the same questions. The main question (in those jurisdictions which permit legal recognition) has been what the prerequisites for recognising the preferred gender of a person should be. Often this question arose implicitly in a different context, namely whether a person who has undergone gender confirmation surgery (or some other medical treatment) can get married in their preferred gender (e.g. Australia, England and Wales, Singapore, Hong Kong, etc.). As can be seen from the contributions in this book, where the issue of the legal status of transsexual and transgender persons was first addressed in

---

5 S. Whittle, *Respect and Equality: Transsexual and Transgender Rights*, Routledge-Cavendish 2002, pp. xxii f.

6 The Yogyakarta Principles define gender identity as 'each person's deeply felt internal and individual experience of gender, which may or may not correspond with the sex assigned at birth, including the personal sense of the body (which may involve, if freely chosen, modification of bodily appearance or function by medical, surgical or other means) and other expressions of gender, including dress, speech and mannerisms.' See Yogyakarta Principles <http://www.yogyakartaprinciples.org/principles_en.pdf> accessed 15.10.2015.

7 See the UK's Gender Recognition Act 2004.

the latter context, this led to an unfortunate and unhelpful conflation of a what a marriage is/should be about (and often, somewhat misguidedly, a discussion of same-sex marriages)[8] with the actual core question about the right to a gender identity/recognition of preferred gender.

Unhelpful conflations are somewhat of a theme for the history of the legal status of transsexual and transgender persons.[9] As can be seen from many of the preceding chapters, a further and often very harmful one for the individuals concerned is the conflation of the medical and the legal issues in many jurisdictions; only in more modern legislation/procedures have the two finally been detached. While this will be looked at in more detail later, it is important to state at the outset that one of the key recommendations is to separate legal and medical transitions.

The details of the approaches in the various jurisdictions, and particularly the changes to these approaches, are detailed in the contributions in this book preceding this chapter and therefore need not be repeated here. But what might be helpful for the understanding of the development is a classification into different stages of development.

3.1. STAGE 1 OF LEGAL RECOGNITION: FIRST STEPS: THE 'MEDICAL PHASE'

If one leaves aside the period of non-recognition (best illustrated by the infamous, yet influential, *Corbett* decision),[10] the first stage, which begins in 1972 with Sweden's *Lag (1972:119) om fastställande av könstillhörighet i vissa fall* is characterised by a restrictive, medicine-centred approach. Knowledge of the medical and psychological foundations of transsexualism and transgenderism was limited at the time, and the political discussion exhibited an attitude that the law must 'help these poor people in their dreadful condition'. Gender confirmation surgery was (and unfortunately in many jurisdictions still is) seen as 'the cure' for the 'medical problem'.

---

8 On which see section 4.4.3 below.

9 See for example the quote given in n. 2.

10 *Corbett v Corbett (otherwise Ashley)* [1971] P83. For comment on the decision see the chapter by S. Gilmore in this volume as well as S. Gilmore, '*Corbett v Corbett (Otherwise Ashley)* – Once a man, always a man?' in S. Gilmore, J. Herring and R. Probert (eds.), *Landmark Cases in Family Law*, Hart Publishing, Oxford 2011, pp. 47–72; K.K.S. Tso, 'Accident of birth or matter of choice: legal recognition of transsexual people in the common law' (2014–15) 21 *Cardozo Journal of Law & Gender* 683–727. For a pertinent and convincing critique of the *Corbett* decision see the chapter by R. Chisholm in this volume and of course *Re Kevin: Validity of Marriage of Transsexual* (2001) 28 Fam LR 158 and *Attorney-General for the Commonwealth v Kevin and Others* (2003) 30 Fam LR 1 (on this see also Tso (this n.)). Despite this criticism and particularly the *Re Kevin* decision, *Corbett* was nevertheless followed in Singapore (*Lim Ying v Eric Hiok* [1991] SGHC 135, on which see the chapter by T. Kaan in this volume and the references in n. 15 below).

Often prompted by court decisions, jurisdictions increasingly began to take action. Germany legislated in 1980,[11] Italy in 1982,[12] the Netherlands in 1985,[13] Turkey in 1988,[14] Singapore in 1996,[15] Finland in 2002,[16] and Japan in 2003.[17] Other jurisdictions, which included Belgium,[18] Austria,[19] Denmark[20] and Spain,[21]

---

11 See the chapter by A. Dutta in this volume; see also F. Pfäfflin, 'Fünf Jahre Transsexuellengesetz – Eine Zwischenbilanz, *StAZ* 1986, 199 ff. and generally J. Basedow and J.M. Scherpe (eds.), *Transsexualität, Staatsangehörigkeit und internationales Privatrecht*, Mohr Siebeck, Tübingen 2004.

12 See M.G. Cubeddu Wiedemann in this volume, and S. Patti and M. Will, 'La "Rettificazione di attributione di sesso": Prime considerazioni', *Rivista di diritto civile* 1982, II, 729–762; S. Patti and M. Will, *Mutamento di sesso e tutela della persona – Saggi di diritto civile e comparato*, CEDAM, Padua 1986, esp. pp. 17–39; P.M. Vecchi, *Der Transsexualismus im deutschen und italienischen Recht – Eine rechtsvergleichende Untersuchung des deutschen und italienischen Gesetzes*, Verlag für Standesamtswesen, Frankfurt am Main 1991; S. Wagner, 'Italien', in Basedow and Scherpe, above n. 11, pp. 42 ff.

13 See the chapter by W. Pintens in this volume; see also W. Breemhaar, 'Das niederländische Transsexuellengesetz', *StAZ* 1986, 204 ff.; J. d'Oliveira, 'Transsexualität im internationalen Personenrecht', *IPRax* 1987, 189 ff.; A. Metzger, 'Niederlande' in Basedow and Scherpe, above n. 11, pp. 48 f.

14 See the chapter by Y. Atamer in this volume; see also M. Will, 'Die Sängerin im Zivilgesetzbuch – Zum neuen türkischen Transsexuellengesetz', in B. Pfister and M. Will (eds.), *Festschrift für Werner Lorenz zum 70. Geburtstag*, Mohr Siebeck, Tübingen 1991, pp. 825 ff.; M. Will, 'Allah Kimseyi Hekime, Hakime Muhtaç Etmesin! Das Menschenrecht auf Geschlechtsidentität im Normenwirrwarr: Türkei und Finnland – Pioniere im Europäischen Familienrecht' in *Festschrift Kalpsüz (Prof. Dr. Turgut Kapsüz'e Armağan)*, Ankara, pp. 741–776; M. Will, 'Das Gespenst im Zivilgesetzbuch – Zum neuesten türkischen Transsexuellengesetz' in H.P. Mansel et al. (eds.), *Festschrift für Erik Jayme*, Sellier European Law Publishers, Munich 2004, pp. 1625 ff.; Y. Atamer, 'Türkei' in Basedow and Scherpe, above n. 11, pp. 74 ff.

15 See the chapter by T. Kaan in this volume. See also H. Tan, 'Transsexuals and the law of marriage in Singapore: *Lim Ying v Hiok Kian Ming Eric*' [1991] *Singapore Journal of Legal Studies* 509–516; W.K. Leong, 'Clarity in the law of valid, void and voidable non-Muslim marriages' (2009) 21 *Singapore Academy of Law Journal* 575–590; W.K. Leong, 'Recent developments in the law of marriage and divorce' (1993) *Singapore Academy of Law Journal* 290–308; S.H. Kwek and J.J. Lee, 'Transsexuals and Sex Determination' (1992) 4 *Singapore Academy of Law Journal* 86–115; Tso, above n. 10, pp. 706 ff.; P. Jiang, 'Legislating for Transgender People: A Comparative Study of Legal Gender in Hong Kong, Singapore, Japan and the United Kingdom' (2013) 7 *Hong Kong Journal of Legal Studies* 31–74.

16 *Laki transseksuaalin sukupuolen vahvistamiseta/Lag om fastställande av transsexuella personers könstillhörighet*, 28 June 2002/563. On this see V. Pimenoff and M. Will, 'Zum finnischen Transsexuellengesetz', *StAZ* 2003, 71 ff. (with a German translation of the act on p. 90 f.); M. Will, 'Allah Kimseyi Hekime, Hakime Muhtaç Etmesin! Das Menschenrecht auf Geschlechtsidentität im Normenwirrwarr: Türkei und Finnland – Pioniere im Europäischen Familienrecht' in *Festschrift Kalpsüz (Prof. Dr. Turgut Kapsüz'e Armağan)*, Ankara, pp. 741–776; J.M. Scherpe, 'Finnland' in Basedow and Scherpe, above n. 11, pp. 36 ff.

17 See the chapter by Y. Nishitani in this volume.

18 See the chapter by W. Pintens in this volume. See also W. Pintens, 'Belgien' in Basedow and Scherpe, above n. 11, pp. 20 ff.; W. Pintens, 'Belgisches Familien- und Erbrecht 2006–2007', *FamRZ* 2007, 1491 ff.; and generally P. Senaeve and K. Uytterhoeven (eds.), *De rechtspositie van de transseksueel*, Intersentia, Antwerp 2008.

19 See M. Roth, 'Österreich' in Basedow and Scherpe, above n. 11, pp. 50 ff.

20 See the chapter by N. Videbæk Munkholm in this volume; see also J.M. Scherpe, 'Dänemark' in Basedow and Scherpe, above n. 11, pp. 31 f.

21 See the chapter by J. Ferrer Riba and A. Lamarca Marqués in this volume; see also C. Eckl, 'Spanien' in Basedow and Scherpe, above n. 11, pp. 69 ff.; by J. Ferrer Riba, 'Neueste

at the time relied on administrative or judicial procedures to amend legal gender – and hence recognise the preferred gender – of a person.

Discussions on what the requirements for legal gender recognition should be usually focused on similar issues: the age of the person concerned, their nationality, their marital status and – often most importantly – certain medical requirements. This latter consideration usually included (and in some of the jurisdictions still includes) invasive surgery, including sterilisation, hormonal treatment, the so-called 'real life test', and requirements regarding specific medical and/or psychological diagnoses. The discussions surrounding the individual requirements will be addressed below (section IV).

Medical requirements generally formed the core of any legal recognition regime. In most scenarios, they were the most onerous requirements for legal recognition and, in a number of cases, became insurmountable obstacles. In hindsight it is apparent that many of these 'well-meaning' statutes or administrative/court procedures inflicted (and continue to inflict) unnecessary suffering on the persons concerned. As will also be described later, many of the original stipulations were later found to be human rights violations by national constitutional courts. In any event, many of the requirements of this stage today are outdated and lagging behind social and legal (and particularly human rights) developments and medical/psychological research.

3.2. STAGE 2 OF LEGAL RECOGNITION: RIGHTS NOT REMEDIES

In the second stage, the question of legal recognition – slowly – began to detach itself from the medical sphere. We see a 'legalisation' of the issue, particularly through the human rights lens. Increasingly the issues came to be phrased in terms of rights (rather than mere remedies), and we saw a number of legal challenges in national and international fora.

In the national sphere, the most striking examples for what might be termed as 'transadvocacy' on the national level can be seen in Germany.[22] Here almost every single one of the recognition criteria originally contained in the German Act has been found to violate the German Constitution. One individual here deserves special mention – Maria Sabine Augstein, who as a *Rechtsanwältin* was the main driving force behind these decisions and in 2015 was awarded the highest German honour, the *Bundesverdienstkreuz*, by the German President.[23] In Australia one of

Entwicklungen im spanischen Personen- und Familienrecht in den Jahren 2006–2007', *FamRZ* 2007, 1513 ff.

22 On which see the chapter by A. Dutta in this volume. See also Basedow and Scherpe, n. 11 above, pp. 3–11.

23 On Maria Sabine Augstein see I. Gukema-Augstein, *Der intime Blick. Maria Sabine Augstein*, Perfect Paperback 2008.

the authors of this volume, Rachael Wallbank, played a similarly leading role in transforming Australian law as the advocate in two landmark cases, *Re Kevin*[24] and *Norrie*.[25]

In the international sphere the decisions of the European Court of Human Rights (ECtHR) in *Goodwin v United Kingdom* and *I v United Kingdom*[26] clearly stand out as decisive landmark decisions. They are the result of a long line of legal challenges in the ECtHR[27] and an example of how relentless legal activism can be successful.

In this stage gender identity and the recognition of preferred gender became part of the rights discourse, and were recognised as such. *Goodwin* makes absolutely clear that for Contracting States of the European Convention on Human Rights there is a duty to allow for the recognition of preferred gender. However, the modalities – i.e. the requirements – for such recognition were left to the Contracting States. Nevertheless, the requirements by the national laws themselves now increasingly come under scrutiny, both on the national level[28] and also in the ECtHR.[29] Further developments can be expected, at least in the European jurisdictions. However, the human rights discourse certainly was not, and is not, limited to the European jurisdictions, as the contributions in this volume show.[30] Indeed, the authors recognise that, while litigation has played a key role in advancing the recognition structures discussed in this chapter, these legal advancements merely reflect a broader movement – at local, regional and international level – for transgender equality, without which any legal development would not have been possible. The crucial progress in the second

---

24 *Re Kevin: Validity of Marriage of Transsexual* (2001) 28 Fam LR 158 and *Attorney-General for the Commonwealth v Kevin and Others* (2003) 30 Fam LR 1. On *Re Kevin* see in particular the chapter by R. Chisholm in this volume, and of course the chapter by R. Wallbank.

25 *Norrie v NSW Registrar of Births, Deaths and Marriages* [2013] NSWCA 145 Beazley ACJ at [134] and the High Court appeal decision *NSW Registrar of Births, Deaths and Marriages v Norrie* [2014] HCA 11. On these see the chapter by R. Wallbank in this volume.

26 *Goodwin v United Kingdom* (application no. 28957/95) [2002] ECHR 588 (11.07.2002); *I v United Kingdom* (application no. 25680/94) [2002] ECHR 592 (11.07.2002). For ease of exposition only the *Goodwin* decision will be referred to in the following.

27 Space precludes a discussion of the preceding decisions/developments/cases such as *van Oosterwijck v Belgium* (application no. 7654/76); *Rees v United Kingdom* (application no. 9532/81); *Cossey v United Kingdom* (application no. 10843/84); *B. v France* (application no. 13343/87); *X, Y and Z v United Kingdom* (application no. 21830/93); *Sheffield and Horsham v United Kingdom* (application nos. 22985/93 and 23390/94). But see e.g. J.M. Scherpe, *The Present and Future of European Family Law*, Edward Elgar Publishing, Cheltenham 2016, pp. 11 ff. and 119 ff.

28 See the chapters in this volume, particularly the last sections on 'Legal Challenges of Existing Rules' on this, particularly the chapters on Germany and Italy.

29 See e.g. *Hämäläinen v Finland* (application no. 37359/09) [2014] ECHR 787 (16.07.2014) (on this case see below section 4.4.3 and the case note by P. Dunne, 'Marriage dissolution as a pre-requisite for legal gender recognition' (2014) 73 *Cambridge Law Journal* 506–510) and *YY v Turkey* (application no. 14793/08) [2015] ECHR 257 (10.03.2015) (on this case see below section 4.4.5 and by Y. Atamer, in this volume, p. 321).

30 See especially the chapters on Taiwan, Hong Kong Special Administrative Zone, Australia, New Zealand and the United States.

stage was to amend the popular discourse so that legal recognition was no longer simply viewed through the lens of medicine, but began to be conceived through the language of human rights.

3.3. STAGE 3 OF LEGAL RECOGNITION: MOVING AWAY FROM PATHOLOGISATION

In this third stage human rights discourse – developing through the 1990s and early 2000s – became the core concern and medicine was side-lined as a related, but more directly applicable, matter. The 'pathology approach' therefore was no longer present in this stage.

One existing controversy is whether the UK's Gender Recognition Act 2004 should be seen as part of the second or the third stage (as described here). Without doubt, the 2004 Act was something of a minor revolution in legal gender recognition.[31] The absence of an express surgical requirement (or indeed any medical treatment beyond diagnosis) placed the UK in the vanguard of international practice. The legislation has rightly been heralded as a great leap forward for transgender equality. Yet the fact remains that section 2(1) of the 2004 Act (even in its current form) continues to require a diagnosis of 'gender dysphoria'. The UK has not (yet) depathologised gender recognition because, in order to come within the terms of the law, an applicant must still present as 'ill'. Although there is no requirement for treatment, the 2004 Act therefore reproduces the idea that legal gender recognition is a 'cure', not a right.

Yet internationally the discourse increasingly is focusing on human rights. Professor Stephen Whittle OBE, along with a group of distinguished human rights experts including Professor Philip Alston (current UN Special Rapporteur on Extreme Poverty and Human Rights), Mary Robinson (former President of Ireland and UN High Commissioner of Human Rights), Professor Manfred Nowak (former UN Special Rapporteur on Torture and Other Cruel, Inhuman or Degrading Treatment or Punishment and Professor of Law, Vienna University) and Professor Michael O'Flaherty (former member of the UN Human Rights Committee and Chief Commissioner of the Northern Ireland Human Rights Commission), was a signatory to Yogyakarta Principles on the Application of International Human Rights Law in relation to Sexual Orientation and Gender Identity.[32] One of the core provisions with regard to gender identity is Article 3 of the Yogyakarta Principles, which states:

> 'Everyone has the right to recognition everywhere as a person before the law. Persons of diverse sexual orientations and gender identities shall enjoy legal

31 On the act see S. Gilmore, in this volume, pp. 192 ff.
32 Available at <http://www.yogyakartaprinciples.org/principles_en.htm>.

> capacity in all aspects of life. Each person's self-defined sexual orientation and gender identity is integral to their personality and is one of the most basic aspects of self-determination, dignity and freedom. No one shall be forced to undergo medical procedures, including sex reassignment surgery, sterilisation or hormonal therapy, as a requirement for legal recognition of their gender identity. No status, such as marriage or parenthood, may be invoked as such to prevent the legal recognition of a person's gender identity. No one shall be subjected to pressure to conceal, suppress or deny their sexual orientation or gender identity.'

The Principles thus 'set the tone' for what is quickly becoming the norm in legislation in the third stage, namely self-definition and the absence of restrictive (or indeed any, in some cases) medical requirements such as gender confirmation surgery, sterility or hormonal therapy (on which see section 4.4.5 below), as well as legal requirements regarding a person's vertical or horizontal family relationships (on which see sections 4.4.3 and 4.4.4 below).

While not internationally binding on any jurisdiction, the Yogyakarta Principles have rapidly become an international point of reference and accepted human rights standard. In the reform discussions in many jurisdictions they were expressly referred to, and it is fair to say that, in many ways, they have become the yardstick for laws in relation to gender identity (and sexual orientation). In April 2015, the Parliamentary Assembly of the Council of Europe (another important regional actor in this area) then called upon State Parties to 'develop quick, transparent and accessible procedures, based on self-determination, for changing the name and registered sex of transgender people on birth certificates, identity cards, passports, educational certificates and other similar documents.'[33]

The standards set by these international statements are (very) far from being universally applied, but it is interesting and encouraging to see that modern law and practice – in jurisdictions such as Argentina,[34] the Netherlands,[35] Taiwan,[36] Ireland[37] and Denmark[38] – is increasingly adhering to these standards.

IV. LEGAL CRITERIA FOR RECOGNITION OF PREFERRED GENDER

As already mentioned above, certain issues feature in most reform discussions at various stages as to which criteria should be required for recognition of the

33 Parliamentary Assembly of the Council of Europe, *Discrimination against Transgender People in Europe,* Resolution 2048 (2015) at para. 6.2.1 <http://assembly.coe.int/ASP/Doc/XrefViewPDF.asp?FileID=21630&Language=EN> accessed 15.10.2015.

34 See L.M. Giosa, M.V. Schiro and P. Dunne, in this volume.

35 See W. Pintens, in this volume.

36 See C. Ho, in this volume.

37 See B. Sloan, in this volume.

38 See N. Videbæk Munkholm, in this volume.

preferred gender. These will now be looked at in turn. As will become apparent, some of the criteria are actually considered to be unnecessary and redundant by the authors of this chapter, others to be harmful and counter-productive, and several to be violations of international human rights standards. However, as they are likely to be raised in reform discussions, it is important to discuss them here and in particular explain why these should not be criteria for legal recognition. One of the key issues, as will become apparent, is that in many jurisdictions the medical and the legal procedure are inextricably linked. In many jurisdictions certain medical procedures are required in order to obtain recognition of the preferred gender, while in others a court authorisation for certain medical procedures is required. While this chapter argues very strongly that the medical and the legal procedures should be independent of each other, the existing links between the two need to be borne in mind when approaching the comparison below, as this will have repercussions for other requirements, for example the age at which the person becomes eligible for recognition of preferred gender.

4.1. AGE REQUIREMENTS

In all jurisdictions studied for this volume, minors (or at least some minors) are subject to different recognition criteria than those who have already achieved the age of majority.[39] Around the world, the age limit for gender recognition is typically set at legal majority,[40] which is often 18 years (but for example is 20 years in Japan).[41] In the Netherlands and Ireland, the age limit is set at 16 years (although in Ireland, 16- and 17-year-old persons are subject to an amended application procedure).[42] In Germany the original age limit of 25 years was struck down by the German Constitutional Court. It has not been replaced, so that, in terms of legal right, no specific age limit exists.[43] The same is apparently true in Belgium, where minors can apply for legal recognition of their preferred gender if assisted by their parents or legal representative.[44] In addition, in several jurisdictions, exceptions are made for commencing certain forms of medical treatment.[45] In other jurisdictions, such as Hong Kong, access to gender confirmation surgery is restricted to persons over 21 years of age, thereby effectively banning any person

39 Except in Germany, where the Constitutional Court struck down the age limit of 25 years, see A. Dutta, in this volume, p. 212, and below.
40 See (all in this volume) for the Czech Republic, pp. 367 f.; Denmark, p. 167; England and Wales, pp. 193 f.; Ireland, p. 235; Italy, p. 252; Spain, p. 268 f.; Sweden, pp. 299 f.; Turkey, pp. 317 f.; Singapore, pp. 410 f.; Taiwan, pp. 425 f.; New Zealand, pp. 545 f.; Argentina, p. 576.
41 See Y. Nishitani, in this volume, p. 368.
42 See W. Pintens, in this volume, p. 117 and B. Sloan, in this volume, p. 235.
43 See A. Dutta in this volume, p. 212, and below.
44 See W. Pintens, in this volume, p. 117.
45 See for Japan Y. Nishitani, in this volume, p. 368.

below that age from obtaining recognition of their preferred gender.[46] Hong Kong is thus the jurisdiction with the highest age threshold of the jurisdictions canvassed in this volume.

The 'link' with medical treatment also seems to be the reason most commonly given for the existence of an age limit. There seems to be a belief that young people are incapable of expressing a stable gender identity, and many judges and policy makers have argued that, before the age of majority, it would be inappropriate for the law to validate a child's expression of preferred gender. Given that many jurisdictions still require invasive surgery and sterility for recognition of the preferred gender, aligning the ability to consent to medical treatment with the ability to apply for gender recognition appears to make sense, at least superficially. In essence, the underlying assumption is that minors need to be protected from decisions with far-reaching and life-long consequences they may later come to regret. As with all age limits, the age of legal majority of course is a legal fiction (although in many other contexts arguably a necessary one). Nobody seriously believes that a person 17 years and 364 days old is intrinsically less competent than the same person three days later. The maturity of a person cannot in reality be pinned to a specific date or age. But in the context discussed here, the effective bar from legal recognition (and indeed in many jurisdictions desired medical treatment) can have very serious consequences for the persons concerned and inflicts unnecessary suffering (see below).

Even in jurisdictions such as the Netherlands, Denmark, Taiwan and Argentina – where policy makers have removed many of the most onerous preconditions for legal recognition (and particularly the need for invasive medical treatment) – there are still certain restrictions for minor applicants.[47] Perhaps law makers fear that that a more liberal regime is more susceptible to misuse, and therefore there is an increased need to protect young individuals. In wider public (and frequently tabloid media) discussions, there is also a fear of 'pushy' parents, who encourage or project a transgender identity onto their children. Age restrictions are considered as a proportionate 'gatekeeper' to ensure that, where a person decides to obtain legal recognition, that decision is made with full, informed and free consent. It is further interesting to note that in Belgium, where invasive surgery still *is* required, minors can apply for legal recognition of their preferred gender if assisted by their parents or legal representative.[48] A similar system has now been established in Argentina and Malta.[49]

---

[46] See A.N. Liu, in this volume, p. 345.

[47] See for the Netherlands W. Pintens, in this volume, p. 117 (age limit 16); for Denmark N. Videbæk Munkholm, in this volume, p. 167 (age limit 18); for Taiwan C. Ho, in this volume, p. 425 (age limit 18); and for Argentina L.M. Giosa, M.V. Schiro and P. Dunne, in this volume, p. 576 (age limit 18, but with generously interpreted exceptions, on which see the '*Lulu*' case, p. 577 and below).

[48] See W. Pintens, in this volume, p. 117.

[49] See for Argentina L.M. Giosa, M.V. Schiro and P. Dunne, in this volume, p. 576. For Malta see the Gender Identity, Gender Expression and Sex Characteristics Act 2015.

The question of minors is an intensely sensitive area of legal gender recognition. Without doubt, the paramount consideration must always be the 'best interests of the child'. If jurisdictions are to extend legal gender recognition to minors, this must be done in a manner which creates sufficient legal safeguards, and which reflects the changing maturities and capacities of individual applicants. It is reasonable and, perhaps, unsurprising that in all the jurisdictions reviewed for this volume, more stringent requirements and conditions are established where children and adolescents seek legal gender recognition.

Accepting those caveats, however, the current legal position – where most countries refuse to acknowledge any recognition of transgender youth, particularly those under the age of 16 years – raises a number of concerns and, in specific situations, may be highly problematic. The reality is that, irrespective of whether the law recognises the existence of transgender young people, such children and adolescents are present in society.[50] A significant minority of transgender young people now self-identity as gender non-conforming. While many of these young people are satisfied with their current identity documentation, others struggle on a daily basis with the inability to access services according to their true gender. Frequently, these children have already commenced a process of social transition – where they live and are accepted in their preferred gender.[51] In most jurisdictions there are no legal or regulatory prohibitions on social transitions and, indeed, young people may even be encouraged and facilitated (e.g. through the provision of state services and benefits) in expressing their preferred gender. However, this situation creates circumstances of potential danger for young transgender individuals. Where a child or adolescent lives and presents in their preferred gender, but must bear the burden of incongruent identity documents, that individual will be subjected to continuous 'outings', where their transgender history is involuntarily revealed to others and where they may be exposed to peer bullying, social discrimination and, in extreme cases, transphobic violence.[52] If the primary concern of legal gender recognition is truly the 'best interests of the child', it makes little sense to force a person who has, from an early age, expressed a clear and consistent gender identity to live in a way which does not reflect his or her lived experience of gender, and which may create significant emotional harm.

Recent studies suggest that young transgender individuals are just as capable of expressing a consistent identity as other children.[53] It is also important to emphasise that where transgender persons (irrespective of age) are not required to undergo medical treatment in order to obtain recognition, there would be no threat of involuntarily medicalising children. Much of the public concern in this

[50] P. Dunne, 'Ten Years of Gender Recognition in the United Kingdom: Still a "Model for Reform?"' (2015) *Public Law* 530.
[51] Ibid.
[52] Ibid.
[53] K.R. Olson, A.C. Key and N.R. Eaton, 'Gender Cognition in Transgender Children' (2015) 26(4) *Psychological Science* 467.

area relates to a fear that, if the law were to recognise the preferred gender of minors, it would involve carrying out highly invasive and irreversible surgeries on young children. (However, as will be discussed later in this chapter, legal gender recognition should not be contingent on medical intervention.) Medical transitions are conceptually distinct from legal recognition. Children and adolescents should be able to access legal recognition without the need to amend best practice medical standards for treating young persons who exhibit gender dysphoria. However, if one is to consider the questions of medicine, it may be asked why, in countries such as Ireland, young people are capable of consenting to medical treatments, such as hormone therapy, from 16 years but will not be allowed to access legal recognition on the same terms as adults.[54] Similarly, certain medical procedures are permitted for minors in Japan (including some forms of surgery) but legal recognition only possible at the age of 20.[55] Indeed, this very subject was addressed by the 1982 Germany Constitutional Court in striking down that jurisdiction's 25-year age limit – there simply was no medical justification for that age limit if medical treatment could be obtained before.[56]

As both medical and legal understandings of gender identity increase, there have been recent movements towards a more nuanced policy for transgender children and adolescents. In the Netherlands, recent reforms to the gender identity laws mean that any person over the age of 16 years can access recognition of their preferred gender.[57] Even so, the Dutch law can be criticised for failing to deal with the plight of transgender children who, given the extent to which identity documents are required during childhood, should be considered as particularly in need of recognition. However, at the very least, the reforms are welcome from the point of view of creating parity of application procedure between, on the one hand, 16- and 17-year-olds and, on the other, adult applicants. Similarly, by way of exception, 16- and 17-year-olds in Ireland will also be entitled to access recognition, although the onerous application requirements for these adolescents mean that, in reality, few, if any, persons may be able to access gender recognition before reaching 18 years of age.[58]

In terms of respecting children's rights, as well as their lived experience of gender, there is ample evidence that strict age limits can be counterproductive and harmful. Germany effectively does not have an age limit and no major problems have been reported; on the contrary, the previous strict age limit was deemed to be a human rights violation.[59] Likewise Malta does not have an age limit, and section 7(1) of the Gender Identity, Gender Expression and Sex Characteristics

[54] B. Sloan, in this volume, p. 236.
[55] See Y. Nishitani, in this volume, pp. 368, 373.
[56] Bundesverfassungsgericht (16.03.1982), BVerfGE 60, 123. On this see A. Dutta, in this volume, p. 212.
[57] See W. Pintens, in this volume, p. 117.
[58] See B. Sloan, in this volume, p. 236
[59] See above n. 56.

Act 2015 allows 'persons exercising parental authority over the minor' to apply to a Civil Court seeking legal gender recognition on the minor's behalf. In any proceedings to determine such an application, the Court must 'ensure that the best interests of the child [...] be the paramount consideration' and 'give due weight to the views of the minor having regard to the minor's age and maturity.' Belgian law, despite currently still requiring invasive surgery, also appears to take a similar approach.[60] In Argentina, an age limit of 18 exists in principle, but there is also a special procedure for minors and the minor can make an administrative application for recognition through a legal representative.[61] Once again, the voice and best interests of the child are the primary concern. Where the child's legal representative refuses his or her consent, or is unable to provide such consent, the decision as to whether to allow an application may be conferred upon a judge. While recognising the preferred gender of minors is unlikely to be a frequent occurrence, the high profile *'Lulu'* case in Argentina illustrates how important legal acknowledgement may be for a child's mental and physical wellbeing. It may be instructive that, in 2015, both Sweden and Norway announced plans to relax their rules for minor applicants.[62]

Recommendation 1: Age limit
There should be no absolute age limit for obtaining legal recognition of preferred gender. Where legislatures restrict access for minors, exceptions must be available and should not be excessively onerous to achieve. Decisions regarding the legal recognition of preferred gender of children should solely be based on the best interest of the child and should take account of the opinion of the minor concerned.

4.2. NATIONALITY OR RESIDENCY REQUIREMENTS

Early statutes (such as the 1980 law in Germany)[63] often stipulated nationality requirements. Only the nationals of the state in which the decision was to be taken could have their preferred gender recognised. This limitation was deemed necessary for both practical reasons and for reasons of comity. No state can issue identity papers for citizens of other states, such as passport and ID cards. The underlying assumption was that each state should be responsible for the legal status of its own citizens, including a person's registered gender. Another consideration probably also played a role: the fear of 'trans tourism' or 'transmigration' (i.e. the fear that if a jurisdiction offered favourable legislation, it would find itself the target of mass immigration by transsexual and transgender persons). In reality, such fears

60 See W. Pintens, in this volume, p. 117.
61 See L.M. Giosa, M.V. Schiro and P. Dunne, in this volume, p. 576.
62 J. Garland, in this volume, p. 300.
63 See A. Dutta, in this volume, pp. 215 f.

never materialised. A final concern was that recognising the preferred gender of a person when their home jurisdiction did not also extend recognition might result in a 'limping' (i.e. split) legal gender: a person might have different legal genders depending on the jurisdiction.

But the restriction to one's own nationals came under increasing political and social pressure. The decision by the German *Bundesverfassungsgericht* (German Constitutional Court) on the matter may be deemed to be exemplary. The Court held unanimously that the existing restriction to German nationals constituted a violation of basic human rights, as enshrined in the German Constitution.[64] There was not sufficient justification for treating German and foreign citizens differently. While German authorities might not be able to provide new personal identification documents etc., they could recognise the preferred gender of foreign nationals for all intents and purposes on the German territory and for German law. The issue of 'limping' legal gender was accepted, but the recognition of preferred gender was considered more important.

Given that the right to be recognised in one's preferred gender is a human right, it must be a violation of human right standards to restrict such recognition to a limited class of people based on nationality. The reasons for such a conclusion are clearly spelled out in the German Constitutional Court decision. Jurisdictions, such as Spain, which deviate from the German position appear to be open to legal challenge.[65] The question arises how the issue of foreign nationals applying for recognition of preferred gender should be processed, and which law should be applicable.[66]

In many cases, there actually are no specific rules. This means that civil status matters are generally subject to the law of the nationality of the person concerned. If, however, the law/jurisdiction so designated does not allow for a recognition of the preferred gender, then this has to be deemed a violation of public policy (*ordre public*) by any state that adheres to the human rights standards just outlined above. In consequence, the courts/authorities of the 'application jurisdiction' then apply their own law. This is currently what happens in Germany, Italy, France and Austria.[67] This approach can also be taken when the legislation specifically stipulates the law of the nationality as the connecting factor, as happens in

---

64 Bundesverfassungsgericht (18.06.2006), BVerfGE 116, 243. On this see the case notes by A. Röthel, 'Inländerprivilegien und Grundrechtsschutz der Transsexualität: Gleichwertigkeit von Staatsangehörigkeits- und Aufenthaltsanknüpfung', *IPrax* 2007, 204 ff.; M. Roth, *StAZ* 2007, 17 and J.M. Scherpe, *FamRZ* 2007, 271 and also A. Dutta, in this volume, pp. 215 f. and the amicus brief in the proceedings, published as Basedow and Scherpe, above n. 11.

65 See J. Ferrer Riba and A. Lamarca Marqués, in this volume, pp. 267 f.

66 On this generally see J.M. Scherpe, 'Transsexual and Transgender Persons' in J. Basedow et al., *European Encyclopedia of Private International Law*, Edward Elgar, forthcoming in 2016.

67 For Germany see A. Dutta, in this volume, pp. 215 f.; for Italy see M.G. Cubeddu Wiedemann, in this volume, pp. 251 f. and esp. Court of Milan, 17.08.2000 [2000] *Famiglia e diritto* 6 and 14.07.1997, [1998] *Riv.Dir. Int'le Priv. & Proc.* 508; for France see Cour d'appel Paris, 14.06.1994, [1995] 84 *Rev.crit.DIP* 308; for Austria see VwGH, 30.09.1997, [1999] *ZfRV* 185 and the national reports in Basedow and Scherpe, above n. 11.

Belgium.[68] Other jurisdictions, such as Japan and Argentina apparently will merely apply the *lex fori* if they have jurisdiction.[69]

The modern, and certainly less cumbersome approach, is to apply the law of the country in which the person concerned is habitually resident (e.g. Denmark, Sweden and Finland),[70] often combined with a minimum residency requirement of one year (e.g. Ireland and the Netherlands).[71]

Recommendation 2: Nationality and residency requirements
It is preferable to regulate expressly that the courts/competent authorities have jurisdiction to decide on the recognition of preferred gender irrespective of the applicant's nationality.

The applicable law should also be regulated expressly. This may be done either

- by using residence (with or without a modest minimum residency period) as the connecting factor for the applicable law and thus apply the *lex fori*, or
- by using nationality, provided it is made clear that the public policy exception applies if the law so designated does not permit recognition of the preferred gender.

4.3. REQUIREMENTS REGARDING HORIZONTAL FAMILY RELATIONSHIPS (ESPECIALLY MARRIAGE AND REGISTERED PARTNERSHIPS)

Requirements for legal gender recognition often touch upon the marital status or registered partnership[72] status of an applicant (i.e. pre-conditions relating to existing formalised horizontal relationships – intimate partnership relationships with another adult). Indeed, historically, it has often been the question of the

---

68 See W. Pintens, in this volume, p. 117.

69 For Argentina see L.M. Giosa, M.V. Schiro and P. Dunne, in this volume, p. 578; for Japan see Y. Nishitani, in this volume, pp. 381 f.

70 For Denmark see N. Videbæk Munkholm, in this volume, p. 167; for Sweden J. Garland, in this volume, pp. 290 ff.; for Finland see V. Pimenoff and M. Will, 'Zum finnischen Transsexuellengesetz', *StAZ* 2003, 71 ff. (with a German translation of the act on p. 90 f.)

71 For the Netherlands see W. Pintens, in this volume, p. 117 f.; for Ireland B. Sloan, in this volume, p. 235.

72 The term registered partnership is used for all legal relationships which come into existence through a formal act such a registration or contract, and this includes registered partnerships which are exclusively open to same-sex couples only (such as the German *eingetragene Lebenspartnerschaft* or the English civil partnership) or those that are open to two persons irrespective of their legal gender/sex (such as the French *Pacte civil de solidarité*, the Dutch *geregistreerd partnerschap* or New Zealand civil unions). On registered partnerships more generally see J.M. Scherpe and A. Hayward, *The Future of Registered Partnerships*, Intersentia, Cambridge/Antwerp, forthcoming in 2016.

validity of a marriage of a person in their preferred gender that has brought the legal issues of gender recognition to the fore.[73]

Many jurisdictions require that an applicant be either single or divorced (or have their registered partnership dissolved) before seeking gender recognition. No similar rules apply to informal cohabitation/*de facto* relationships. If the person in question is living in a formalised relationship, such as marriage or registered partnership, they may have to either terminate their legal relationship (e.g. Czech Republic[74] and Japan)[75] before recognition, or have their relationship automatically terminated upon recognition (e.g. Turkey).[76] In these jurisdictions, the law essentially forces the couple to divorce even if both spouses/partners want to remain in the existing marriage/registered partnership. This was also the legal position in jurisdictions such as England and Wales,[77] Spain,[78] Sweden[79] and New Zealand,[80] before they extended marriage to same-sex couples.

The justification for the divorce/partnership dissolution requirement is generally the gendered nature of these relationships. There is a belief that such a gendered structure should be maintained. So when, in 1972, Sweden first enacted its landmark gender recognition statute, national law did not allow persons of the same legal gender to marry. There was a fear that, if a spouse in a heterosexual union obtains recognition, that would create a situation whereby there were two persons of the same gender in the marriage; hence a requirement to dissolve the marriage was introduced.[81] This is still the position in many countries today. There are notable exceptions in Germany and Italy, which will be discussed further below. Similarly, below, and under section 3(2)(a) of Malta's recent Gender Identity, Gender Expression and Sex Characteristics Act 2015, legal gender recognition is 'without prejudice' to a person's 'relationship', even though Malta does not recognise same-sex marriages conducted on its territory.

But the advent of same-sex marriage in many jurisdictions has meant that requirements to dissolve marriages have become obsolete.[82] Where legislation concerning recognition of preferred gender was introduced after marriage

73 For example in Singapore, Hong Kong, England, Australia and NZ (on which see the chapters on these jurisdictions in this volume).
74 See B. Havelková, in this volume, pp. 126, 129.
75 See Y. Nishitani, in this volume, pp. 373, 375.
76 See Y. Atamer, in this volume, p. 316 for the 1988 law.
77 See S. Gilmore, in this volume, p. 196.
78 In Spain, contrary to the *Goodwin* decision, a person could actually not even marry in her recognised preferred gender before the introduction of same-sex marriage/the 2007 legislation, see J. Ferrer Riba and A. Lamarca Marqués, in this volume, pp. 262, 269.
79 See J. Garland, in this volume, pp. 286 f. Indeed, it took several years after the introduction of same-sex marriage before the requirement to dissolve a marriage was removed from the 1972 Act.
80 See E. McDonald and J. Byrne, in this volume, pp. 552, 561.
81 See J. Garland, in this volume, pp. 286 f.
82 e.g. in the Netherlands, Belgium and Denmark, see W. Pintens and N. Videbæk Munkholm, in this volume, pp. 119 and 168 ff.

equality (e.g. Ireland and Argentina), dissolution requirements never formed part of the law.[83]

England in this context remains a curiosity. There is a continuing requirement to dissolve a civil partnership for full legal gender recognition. It is also the only jurisdictions of those canvassed where, even though same-sex marriage was introduced, the spouse retains a 'veto right' with regard to the full gender recognition of the other spouse, as only with consent will there be a full gender recognition and the marriage continues. Should the spouse not consent, only an interim gender recognition certificate can be issued and a dissolution of the marriage is required before a full certificate can be issued.[84] The legislature apparently felt that spouses needed to be protected from the 'stigma' of suddenly finding themselves in a same-sex marriage. This is problematic for number of reasons, not least because it implies that there are two kinds of marriage (same-sex and opposite-sex) and not just one institution of marriage. Given that the whole point about opening up marriage to same-sex couples was to end discrimination of same-sex relationships and ensure that all couples are treated the same, the current legal situation seems somewhat counter-intuitive (as indeed is the current legal situation regarding civil partnerships).[85] A preferable approach would have been to provide a spouse with notification of recognition (with the possibility for exceptions where to notify would give rise to a threat of harm) but not allow that spouse to dictate the terms of the recognition process (i.e. by requiring that an applicant seek spousal consent). A spouse should be permitted to apply for divorce should he or she be uncomfortable remaining in the marriage. While unwilling individuals should not be required to remain in a marriage which is no longer mutually committed and consensual, the law must equally be capable of conceptually separating gender recognition from the distinct matter of relationship status. It may be instructive that, in Scotland, legislative measures enacting marriage equality in that jurisdiction have removed forced divorce without introducing a spousal consent provision.[86]

In jurisdictions which do not accept same-sex marriage, courts and law makers continue to require that an applicant dissolve horizontal legal relationships before obtaining recognition (Malta, as mentioned above, being an exception). From one perspective, this 'forced divorce' is unsurprising. Given the absence, or even express rejection, of same-sex marriages in many jurisdictions (such as Germany, Italy, the Czech Republic, Japan, Turkey, Australia, Hong Kong SAR and Singapore)[87] it is perhaps understandable that those who oppose 'gay

[83] On Argentina see L.M. Giosa, M.V. Schiro and P. Dunne, in this volume, pp. 580 f.; on Ireland see Gender Recognition Act 2015 (as commenced), conjunction with the Marriage Act 2015; see also B. Sloan, in this volume, pp. 241 ff.

[84] See S. Gilmore, in this volume, p. 196.

[85] On this see e.g. J.M. Scherpe, 'Quo vadis, civil partnership?' (2015) 46 *Victoria University of Wellington Law Review* 755–768.

[86] See Marriage and Civil Partnership (Scotland) Act 2014, s. 29 and Schedule 2.

[87] See the respective chapters in this volume.

marriage' would seek to close off any avenue which suggests state acceptance for such unions. The legal reality indeed is that, post-recognition, if a married applicant is able to validate his or her preferred gender without divorcing, there will be two individuals in the marriage who have, as a matter of law, the same legal gender. In recent years, however, 'forced divorce' both in Europe and beyond has been subject to increasing scrutiny. Within human rights discourse, there is a growing sentiment that individuals' relationship status should not determine their access to legal recognition.

In 2008 the German *Bundesverfassungsgericht* (Constitutional Court) held that a requirement to dissolve an existing marriage to obtain full legal gender recognition violated the German Constitution.[88] Marriage was protected as an institution by the German *Grundgesetz* (Basic Law, the German Constitution) in Article 6(1). Forcing a person to choose between a constitutionally protected legal position (marriage) and the constitutional right to recognition (as part of the *Allgemeine Persönlichkeitsrecht* – general personality right) under Article 2(1) was held to unconstitutional. Not only was it not an actual free choice, but the applicants would also have had to lie about the requirements for divorce. They would have had to feign an irretrievable breakdown of the marriage. In addition, the constitutionally protected position achieved through marriage needed continued protection. As a result, the legal situation in Germany now is that, although same-sex marriages are not permitted, a person in a marriage can nevertheless apply for recognition of preferred gender without marriage dissolution. The same applies, in the reverse, for existing *eingetragene Lebenspartnerschaften* (registered partnerships). The 'side-effect' of this of course is that for this situation, namely where a married person has their preferred gender recognised, it is now possible to have same-sex marriages in Germany. But it was deemed that, compared with the infringement of the rights of the persons immediately concerned, this very limited exception was acceptable. The Court's judgment does not introduce same-sex marriage generally. Thus, the only way for a same-sex couple to formalise their relationship in Germany remains the *eingetragene Lebenspartnerschaft*.[89]

In Italy, the *Corte costituzionale* (Constitutional Court) has similarly held that, while a post-recognition transgender individual and their same gender spouse are no longer entitled to marriage protection under Article 29 of the Italian Constitution, stripping the couple of all their legal rights would violate the spouses 'inviolable rights of man' as set out in Article 2 of that Constitution.[90] In April 2015, the Italian Court of Cassation held that, pending the introduction

---

88 Bundesverfassungsgericht 27.05.2008, BVerfGE 121, 175; on this see A. Dutta, in this volume, p. 212 f.

89 On this see J.M. Scherpe, 'The Legal Status of Same-sex Relationships in Germany' in J. Basedow, U. Kischel and U. Sieber (eds.), *German National Reports to the 18th International Congress of Comparative Law*, Mohr Siebeck, Tübingen 2010, pp. 75–107.

90 Constitutional Court of Italy, 11.06.2014, no. 170; *cf.* M.G. Cubeddu Wiedemann, in this volume, p. 257.

by Parliament of registered partnerships or civil unions with 'substantially equivalent' value to marriage, transgender persons should not be required to divorce before the law recognises their preferred gender.[91]

Another way of looking at this is to solely judge the validity of a marriage at the point of entry. Where two persons contract a valid heterosexual marriage, the subsequent conduct of the spouses then is irrelevant. In Ireland advocates and legislators opposed a proposed divorce requirement (not commenced after the passage of same-sex marriage in a May 2015 referendum) precisely because, where two people have entered into a valid opposite-sex marriage, their relationship remains valid even if one of the spouses later has a different legal gender recognised.[92] Taiwan also offers an illustration of this approach. Abbygail Wu and Jiyi Wu retained different legal genders at the point of marriage. Their union thus satisfied the marriage requirements of Taiwan's Civil Code. It was subsequently deemed not appropriate for the Ministry of Interior to require an annulment when Jiyi later applied for recognition of her preferred gender.[93] Admittedly, this line of reasoning creates issues of legal consistency. A spouse will have one legal gender for marriage and another legal gender for all other purposes. This may not be satisfactory to a transitioning individual who might prefer full recognition of their gender in all circumstances. However, where, in order to maintain his or her marriage, an individual is willing to retain their birth-assigned gender for limited purposes, there does not appear to be any compelling legal reason why that person's marriage should have to be dissolved.

Although there are movements away from 'forced divorce', particularly in Europe, this trend was somewhat stunted by the recent judgment of the European Court of Human Rights (ECtHR) in *Hämäläinen v Finland*[94] (despite compelling dissenting opinions by the Judges Sajó, Keller and Lemmens).[95] Finnish law requires that all married applicants for recognition must either divorce their spouse or automatically convert their marriage into a registered partnership (the law is currently under review and there is a proposal to amend at the time of

[91] Cassazione Civile, sez. I, sentenza 21/04/2015 n° 8097. It also needs to be noted, though, that the European Court of Human rights in *Oliari and Others v Italy* (application no. 18766/11 and 26030/11) [2015] ECHR 716 (21.07.2015) held that the legal protection currently afforded to same-sex couples fell short of the requirements of the ECHR, and that a civil union or registered partnership would be the most appropriate way for same-sex couples to have their relationship legally recognised. Legal reform in this area therefore seems likely.

[92] B. Sloan, in this volume, p. 243.

[93] See C. Ho, in this volume, pp. 435 ff.

[94] *Hämäläinen v Finland* (application no. 37359/09) [2014] ECHR 787 (16.07.2014); noted by P. Dunne, 'Marriage dissolution as a pre-requisite for legal gender recognition' (2014) 73 *Cambridge Law Journal* 506–510; D. González Salzberg, 'Confirming (the Illusion of) Heterosexual Marriage: Hämäläinen v Finland' (2015) 2 *Journal of International and Comparative Law* 173–186.

[95] As the development up to *Goodwin* has shown, these dissenting opinions often become important and even decisive in later decisions, *cf.* Scherpe, above n. 27.

writing).[96] In *Hämäläinen*, the ECtHR found that there was no disproportionate interference with the applicant's Convention rights. The vast majority of rights enjoyed by married couples were also afforded to registered partners. The Court concluded that Finland's 'forced divorce' requirement was within a Contracting State's margin of appreciation.

Of course, it needs to be borne in mind that the European Convention on Human Rights is an international instrument. It provides a floor of rights but not a ceiling.[97] The ECtHR as a supranational body therefore treads particularly carefully in sensitive areas of law like family law.[98] Its judges are unlikely to impose obligations on a Contracting State unless the State in question has fallen below the minimum standard required by the European Convention. *Hämäläinen v Finland* cannot necessarily be regarded as determining the matter conclusively – it merely says that currently the Finnish law is within the margin of appreciation afforded to Contracting States. But as the development leading up the *Goodwin* decision has shown,[99] this may change over time. In addition, in Finland there are (almost) equivalent rights available for registered partners, so the decision may well have been different had that not been the case. Indeed, a number of the European jurisdictions canvassed for this volume would not satisfy the *Hämäläinen* test.

Still, a number of criticisms can be raised against the Grand Chamber's reasoning in *Hämäläinen*. The Court adopts a rather reductive interpretation of the right to marry under Article 12 ECHR. In effect, the Grand Chamber's decision means that, while two individuals of opposite legal gender may be protected in their right to enter a marriage, those persons can subsequently be stripped of their marital status simply because one spouse invokes another Convention right by wanting to have their preferred gender recognised. As outlined above, for that reason both the German and the Italian highest courts found that this violated their national constitutions. This critique of the majority opinion was adopted by the dissenting Judges Sajó, Keller and Lemmens. They argued that the applicant had not only been denied effective enjoyment of her marital rights under Article 12 ECHR but also, on the basis of her gender identity alone, was now being

---

96 It is worth noting that Finland will introduce same-sex marriage on 1 May 2017 and that the matter therefore will become obsolete, at least for Finland.

97 *Cf.* N. Wikeley, 'Same sex couples, family life and child support' (2006) 122 *LQR* 542; see also J.M. Scherpe, 'Family and private life, ambits and pieces' [2007] *Child and Family Law Quarterly* 390–403.

98 On this particular issue see W. Pintens and J.M. Scherpe, 'The Marckx Case: A "Whole Code of Family Law"?' in S. Gilmore, J. Herring and R. Probert (eds.), above n. 10, pp. 155–174; and W. Pintens and J.M. Scherpe, 'Die Marckx-Entscheidung des Europäischen Menschengerichtshofs als Keimzelle eines europäischen Familien- und Erbrechts. Ein Rück- und Ausblick nach fünfunddreißig Jahren' in N. Witzleb, R. Ellger, P. Mankowski, H. Merkt and O. Remien (eds.), *Festschrift für Dieter Martiny zum 70. Geburtstag*, Mohr Siebeck, Tübingen 2014, pp. 127–146; J.M. Scherpe, 'The Gametes of a European Family Law' [2008] *International Family Law Journal* 98–101.

99 See the references in n. 27 above.

treated unequally with all other couples who had contracted a valid heterosexual marriage. Judges Sajó, Keller and Lemmens raised an additional point, also referring to the German Constitutional Court's reasoning. The reality is that requiring transgender individuals to divorce before obtaining recognition is not going to prevent the actual 'phenomenon' of same-sex marriage. Even before the couple seek official acknowledgement in *law*, many married transgender persons have already undertaken a process of *social* transition. They are accepted in their preferred gender for all personal and professional matters. They remain in a committed relationship where there are *de facto* two persons of the same gender. To the outside world, these relationships will generally already be perceived as same-sex marriages by members of the public. If a jurisdiction is really concerned about the consequences of post-recognition same-sex marriage, they would also have to take measures to prevent married transgender persons from socially transitioning. The fact that law makers have not affected such prohibitions in the jurisdictions canvassed in this volume,[100] and that *de facto* same-sex marriages have not yet caused any appreciable social disintegration in the jurisdictions concerned, seriously undermines arguments in favour of 'forced divorce'.

The reasoning of the German Constitutional Court outlined above is equally convincing in a different constitutional context. To impose on a person the loss of an important legal status such as marriage (or registered partnership) in order to be recognised in their preferred gender is an infringement of their rights. This infringement cannot be justified through a desire to maintain the gendered structure of adult relationships without any (and very limited) exceptions. In addition, as the examples from Germany and Italy show, it does not necessarily mean that this is a step on the road to the introduction of same-sex marriage. Opponents of the recognition of same-sex relationships should also find consolation in the fact that for the very limited number of marriages in question the union was an opposite-sex one when entered into/solemnised.

Recommendation 3: Requirements relating to existing adult relationships
Legal recognition of preferred gender should not require the dissolution of an existing formalised adult relationship (such as marriage or registered partnership).

4.4. REQUIREMENTS REGARDING VERTICAL FAMILY RELATIONSHIPS (PARENT–CHILD RELATIONSHIPS)

Of the jurisdictions examined in this volume, only one jurisdiction has legal requirements regarding vertical family relationships (i.e. legal parent–child relationships existing at the time of recognition of preferred gender). That

100 For an interesting development in Malaysia see T. Kaan, in this volume, pp. 419 ff.

jurisdiction is Japan.[101] The original statutory provisions required the applicant for recognition of preferred gender to be childless – which effectively meant that any person who had children was barred from gender recognition.[102] The legislature explained this internationally unique requirement with the need to prevent 'disturbance of the family order' and potential 'harm for children' as well as Japan's unique customs, traditions and family structures, and found that such a requirement therefore would not violate fundamental rights such as the right to equality under the law (Article 14 of the Japanese Constitution) or the right to pursuit of happiness (Article 13 of the Japanese Constitution).[103] The constitutionality of this rather extreme requirement was even confirmed by a Supreme Court decision in 2007.[104] But the continuing criticism led to reforms in 2008, and now only the absence of any minor children is required.[105] While this reformed requirement at least allows persons whose children have reached the age of majority (which in Japan is 20), it still creates extreme hardship for the persons concerned who might have to wait a very long time to have their preferred gender recognised.

The requirement not to have any minor children is incompatible with human rights law. The arguments in support of the requirement are unconvincing. It is unclear how barring the recognition of the preferred gender for an extended period could possibly maintain the 'family order' or prevent any 'harm for children' (described as 'psychological burden' and causing 'anxiety')[106] if the persons concerned can and indeed will transition socially even without legal recognition. Surely the 'disturbance of the family order' and the potential 'harm for children' do not arise from the *legal* recognition as such but, if at all (and there are more than serious doubts about this in any event), rather from the *social* transition of the parent. Moreover, the inability to achieve the legal recognition of the preferred gender will in all likelihood have a profound negative impact on the person concerned, which in turn will have an impact on any existing family relationships, including parent–child relationships. Thus nothing is really gained by such a requirement, except unnecessary suffering of the persons concerned. It appears that the requirement is rooted in an overly medicalised and outdated view (see also section 4.5.1 below). It should be abolished.[107]

---

101 For parent–child relationships after recognition of preferred gender see section 5.5.2 below.
102 See Y. NISHITANI, in this volume, pp. 376 ff.
103 Ibid., pp. 376 f. and there esp. n. 55.
104 Supreme Court, 19.10.2007, *KSG* 60–3, 36 and Supreme Court, 22.10.2007, *KSG* 60–3, 37. On this see Y. NISHITANI, in this volume, p. 377.
105 Ibid., p. 377. For an interesting (but ultimately unsuccessful) attempt to circumvent this requirement see ibid., pp. 377 f.
106 *Cf.* ibid., p. 376.
107 This is supported also by academic authors in Japan, see ibid., p. 378 and there esp. n. 62.

Recommendation 4: Requirements relating to existing parent–child relationships
Legal recognition of preferred gender must not require the absence of any existing legal parent–child relationships.

4.5. MEDICAL AND DIAGNOSTIC REQUIREMENTS

4.5.1. Gender Confirmation Surgery and Sterility

In the wider public debates there often is the misguided perception (a) that *all* transgender persons wish to physically alter their bodies, and (b) that *every* transition will inevitably result in surgery. Indeed, the contributions in this volume have a described a judicial and policy landscape in which surgery and genitalia, rather than self-identity and lived experience, become the primary determinants of a transgender individual's legal status – while at the same time revealing national perceptions/stereotypes about 'proper' male and female identities.

For many of the jurisdictions canvassed for this volume, medical intervention conditions – and particularly the requirements for gender confirmation surgery and sterilisation – remain *the* central consideration in their gender recognition schemes. Ever since northern European countries began recognising preferred gender in the mid- and late 20th century, legal acknowledgement for gender identity has been intimately bound up with considerations of medicine[108] – so much so that it often appears that the decisions on recognition of preferred gender ultimately remain within the sphere of the medical profession. Furthermore, in many jurisdictions, medical and legal procedures are utterly intertwined. One often sets pre-conditions for the other. This is not only unhelpful but, in many cases, extremely harmful for the individuals concerned.

But it is important to make clear at the outset that both of the perceptions mentioned at the beginning of this section simply are wrong – and easily disproved by the fact that a significant number of transgender persons do not desire any, or only some, medical intervention. While transgender and transsexual individuals who just wish to medically transition should of course have access to quality medical treatment, any requirements that exceed what the individual concerned wishes to receive in way of medical or other treatment therefore becomes an imposition – and a infringement of personal autonomy and bodily integrity, as is discussed in the following.

---

[108] See section III above.

4.5.1.1. Jurisdictions with Medical Intervention Requirements

Some of the jurisdictions canvassed for this volume require more extreme and invasive medical procedures than others as part of the legal transition process. Full gender reconstructive surgery is, for example, required in Turkey according to Article 40 of the Civil Code.[109] Similarly, in Japan transgender persons who seek legal recognition must obtain the 'external genital features' associated with their preferred gender.[110] Comparable rules apply in the Czech Republic.[111] In Hong Kong, the Court of Final Appeal's decision in *W v Registrar of Marriages*[112] established that recognition of preferred gender must be available for transgender individuals who have submitted to gender confirmation surgery (which was the case at hand) but also strongly hinted that gender recognition requirements similar to those of the United Kingdom's Gender Recognition Act 2004[113] might be appropriate. Given the failure of the Legislative Committee to pass an Act on the matter, however, surgery and sterility currently remain prerequisites.[114] In Singapore legislation following the decision in *Hiok,*[115] requires a 'sex re-assignment procedure'.[116] In Belgium, a transgender person will not obtain gender recognition unless he or she has 'undergone gender reassignment'. However, this procedure must be 'possible and justifiable from a medical perspective'. The individual must also be incapable of 'producing children in accordance with his or her previous sex'.[117] While the latter requirement is absolute, there is some scope for a more generous interpretation of the surgery requirements, and there is a debate whether psychological reasons would be sufficient to justify dispensing with gender confirmation surgery.[118]

In other jurisdictions, surgical requirements fall below full genital reconstruction (and sterility) but nevertheless mandate significant internal and external alterations to body. For example, in the United States, a majority of states continue to require gender confirmation surgery in order to access amended birth certificates.[119] While none of these states specifically mention the exact

---

[109] Y. Atamer, in this volume, pp. 317 ff.; this requirements was expressly confirmed by the Turkish Court of Cassation in 2006, *cf.* ibid., pp. 324 f.

[110] Y. Nishitani, in this volume, pp. 378 ff.

[111] With detailed regulation what surgery is required for a 'sex change', including the 'disabling of the reproductive function', see B. Havelková, in this volume, p. 131.

[112] [2013] HKEC 716.

[113] On which see S. Gilmore, in this volume, and below.

[114] A. Liu, in this volume, pp. 361 f.

[115] *Lim Ying v Eric Hiok* [1991] SGHC 135.

[116] At least for the purpose of being able to marry someone of the opposite sex: now section 12 of the Women's Charter (originally s. 11A); see T Kaan, in this volume, p. 411.

[117] Art. 62*bis*, § 2 Belgian Civil Code; see W. Pintens, in this volume, p. 118. But Belgium now has committed to amending its laws, *cf.* 'Malta and Belgium sign Transgender Agreement', *Malta Star,* 16 May 2015 <http://www.maltastar.com/dart/20150516-malta-and-belgium-sign-transgender-agreement> accessed 15.10.2015.

[118] Ibid., p. 118.

[119] J. Garland, in this volume, pp. 609 ff.

procedures to which applicants must submit, 'a survey of the statutory language in these jurisdictions broadly suggests that the surgery must be substantial.'[120] In Italy (until the decision of the Italian Supreme Court)[121] case law on the Sex Reassignment Act 1982 required that applicants for gender recognition had to undergo surgery.[122] However, it was not clear whether such interventions related to internal or external sex characteristics, and whether it was necessary to have full reconstructive procedures. In Spain the 2007 Act does not expressly require surgery or sterility but rather evidence that applicants have transitioned their physical characteristics to those associated with the preferred gender. Under pressure to show how they have amended their bodies, many applicants may feel that they have little choice but to submit to hormone and other treatments.[123] However, there is an exception from this requirement where compliance cannot be expected for health and age reasons,[124] so there again is scope for a generous interpretation in order to avoid medical intervention requirements.

The contributions in this volume offer an interesting insight into how medical intervention requirements often have been challenged before national and regional court systems. One of the most successful litigation strategies has been to argue that particular surgical or sterilisation procedures are not specifically required by the existing laws or regulation. In many of the jurisdictions canvassed for this volume, legal gender recognition rules, particularly the provisions relating to medical intervention, are drafted in broad, sometimes vague, language and rely upon the relevant implementing body – either the courts or an administrative agency – to establish specific policies and practice. In order to permit legal gender recognition, an implementing body may interpret the foundational statute or regulation as requiring specified medical procedures, even though those procedures are not expressly referred to in the primary rules. Where an applicant for recognition objects to the implementing body's practices, it has fallen to the superior courts to determine whether enforcing the impugned medical intervention is compatible with, or at least can be justified by, the original statute or regulations. For example section 28(3)(i)(B) of New Zealand's Births, Deaths, Marriages and Relationship Registration Act 1995 requires that, in order to obtain an amended birth certificate, individuals should provide proof that they have submitted to 'such medical treatment as is usually regarded by the medical experts as desirable to enable persons of the genetic and physical conformation of the applicant at birth to acquire a physical conformation that accords with the gender identity of a person of the nominated sex'. In the case of *'Michael' v*

---

120 Ibid., p. 596.

121 Decision no. 15138 of 20.07.2015, on which see M.G. Cubeddu Wiedemann, in this volume, pp. 252 ff. and further discussion below. The decision was confirmed by the Italian Constitutional Court on 21.10.2015 (Sentenza 221/2015).

122 M.G. Cubeddu Wiedemann, in this volume, pp. 252 f.

123 Art. 4.1; see J. Ferrer Riba and A. Lamarca Marqués, in this volume, p. 271.

124 Art. 4.2. of the 2007 Act, see ibid., p. 271.

Registrar of Births, Deaths and Marriages[125] it was argued by the Registrar that this required proof of full gender confirmation surgery. However, the presiding judge rejected that expansive interpretation, concluding instead that 'Parliament did not intend that an applicant should necessarily have to undergo all available surgical procedures'; rather, it sufficed that there was 'some degree of permanent physical change as a result of the treatment'.[126]

A similar result was reached by the High Court of Australia in the case of *AB v Western Australia* and *AH v Western Australia*.[127] In that instance, Western Australia's Gender Reassignment Act 2000 in sections 14 and 15 required that applicants submit to a 'reassignment procedure' (defined in section 3 as a 'medical or surgical procedure ... to alter the genitals and other gender characteristics of a person ... so that the person would be identified as a person of the opposite sex') and 'has the gender characteristics of a person of the gender to which the person has been reassigned' (section 15(1)(b)(ii)). Neither AB nor AH had undergone a hysterectomy or a phalloplasty operation, and both retained their internal and external female genitalia, as well as their capacity to reproduce. Both appellants had, however, accessed chest surgery and were following a course of hormone therapy. Australia's High Court held that, on a proper interpretation of the 2000 Act, AB and AH had satisfied the specific statutory requirements and were therefore entitled to legal gender recognition.[128]

In jurisdictions where it would be politically unfeasible for policy makers to adopt a non-medicalised regime for gender recognition, the experience in New Zealand and Australia may serve as a blueprint for positive (and incremental) reform. The New Zealand and Western Australian statutes obviously still conceive of gender recognition as a medicalised concern as both the 1995 and 2000 Acts presuppose that at least some medical treatment will be appropriate for individuals who want to legally transition (for a criticism of this see below). But by omitting to establish specific medical requirements, and by placing the ultimate analysis in the hands of medical practitioners, policy makers at least increase the likelihood that applicants will only be required to access such procedures as are both necessary and desired. It is not possible to spare transgender persons the burden of full genital reconstruction surgery where a statute expressly requires this. However, where transgender persons need only access, for example, 'medically appropriate' interventions, judges and other implementing bodies have a much wider discretion. Indeed, where applicants for recognition can access a sympathetic physician, who understands both medical and socio-political dimensions of gender identity, flexible statutory language, based on the idea of 'appropriate' medical care, may create the possibility of obtaining legal recognition without any formal medical interventions. In the United States an

125 (2008) 27 FRNZ 58; on this case see E. McDonald and J. Byrne, in this volume, pp. 546 ff.
126 Ibid.
127 [2011] HCA 42; on this case see R. Wallbank, in this volume, pp. 506 ff.
128 Ibid.

increasing number of jurisdictions (including e.g. New York City in 2014) have moved away from explicitly surgery-based recognition models in favour of a requirement for 'clinically appropriate treatment'.[129] The result is that transgender persons in such jurisdictions are increasingly capable of accessing appropriate documentation without compromising their physical and emotional autonomy.

The potential value of flexible or open-ended statutes should not be overstated, however, and they certainly are not, in any way, a generally acceptable solution for the problems posed by medical requirements. At a practical level, it is clear that many national laws leave no room for interpretation and that some of the existing legal rules are interpreted strictly. For example, in the Czech Republic, transgender persons apparently have no real chance of successfully arguing that the requirement to 'transform' an applicant's internal organs does not require submitting to a hysterectomy operation or the removal of testes.[130] Flexible statutory language also only works when it can be interpreted by sympathetic and informed medical officers and judges. In New York City, it is not unreasonable to assume that, where individuals can access the services of specialised transgender health professionals, such as officers at the Callen-Lorde Community Center, who have a nuanced appreciation of gender identity, there may be experts who will support their application for gender recognition without requiring medical treatments. However, in other jurisdictions canvassed for this volume, it is evident that health professionals continue to view gender recognition through a solely medicine-orientated (and even surgery-orientated) lens. Even if a margin of appreciation did exist for doctors in these jurisdictions, it is unlikely that they would support a person's application without proof of significant medical interventions. The same reasoning applies to judges. In both Turkey and France the highest courts have recently affirmed that the statutory and regulatory language should be interpreted as requiring full reconstructive surgery (Turkey)[131] and medical sterilisation (France).[132]

4.5.1.2. Jurisdictions without Medical Intervention Requirements

By contrast, several jurisdictions have moved away from/abolished surgery and sterility requirements – or never had such requirements in the first place.

While the courts and targeted litigation have proved a useful vehicle through which to challenge the legality of medical intervention requirements (on which see below the passages on Germany and Italy), the contributions included in this volume illustrate that, in recent years, many of the most radical movements away

[129] *Cf.* J. Garland, in this volume, pp. 609 ff.
[130] See B. Havelková, in this volume, pp. 127 ff.
[131] Y. Atamer, in this volume, pp. 318 ff.
[132] Court of Cassation (French Supreme Court), Civil Chamber, 11–14.515 (13 February 2013).

from medicine have actually been introduced through statute.[133] This may seem both counter-intuitive and ironic, considering the historical reluctance of many policy makers to acknowledge and engage with transgender identities.

In 2004, the United Kingdom enacted the Gender Recognition Act 2004. As noted already, this landmark statute, introduced in direct response to *Goodwin v United Kingdom*,[134] was considered revolutionary at the time of its enactment. The 2004 Act specifically omits requirements for surgery, sterilisation and hormone therapy. A key feature of the UK legislation is the extent to which the draft law generated scrutiny and debate in Parliament.[135] One of the main concerns raised, quite rightly, by the House of Lords and House of Commons Joint Committee on Human Rights, was whether a medicalised gender recognition model would be practically accessible to all applicants. The reality is that, for many people, considerations of age, health and indeed resources may prevent submission to surgery or sterilisation. In addition, as Terry Sheung-Hung Kaan states in his contribution for Singapore and Malaysia, religious restrictions may also affect a person's willingness to undergo body modifications.[136] Therefore, if medical procedures are a mandatory gateway to legal gender recognition, many transgender persons will be denied official recognition of their preferred gender. In recognising and addressing these limitations, the UK's Members of Parliament exhibited a capacity to engage with the lived experience of gender recognition in a way that previous English and Welsh case law, particularly *Corbett v Corbett* and *Bellinger v Bellinger*, had failed to do. Indeed, while strategic litigation focuses, often with great success, on specific issues, such as bodily integrity, the contributions in this volume prove that statutory measures have frequently been more successful in impacting transgender lives specifically because parliamentarians have be able to consider the wider social consequences of reform. In Ireland, the Joint Oireacthas Committee on Education and Social Protection was instrumental in encouraging the Irish Parliament to adopt human rights focused gender recognition rules.[137] With regard to Denmark and Sweden, the recent reforms are largely the product of government-sponsored reports which engaged with the lived realities of transgender lives in both jurisdictions.[138] Recent changes to the gender recognition rules in Taiwan,[139] Argentina,[140] the Netherlands[141] and Malta[142] mean that no form of medical intervention is required.

---

133 Notable exceptions being the Czech Republic and Singapore where the statues introduced actually were a regression with regard to the rights of transgender persons, see B. Havelková and T. Kaan, both in this volume, pp. 127 ff. and 401 ff.

134 ECtHR (application no. 28957/95) [1996] ECHR 16 (27.03.1996).

135 S. Gilmore, in this volume, pp. 188 ff.

136 T. Kaan, in this volume, pp. 416 ff.

137 *Cf.* B. Sloan, in this volume, pp. 231–235.

138 See N. Videbæk Munkholm and J. Garland, in this volume.

139 See C. Ho, in this volume.

140 See L.M. Giosa, M.V. Schiro and P. Dunne, in this volume.

141 See W. Pintens in this volume.

142 Gender Identity, Gender Expression and Sex Characteristics Act 2015.

In all these jurisdictions fundamental human rights considerations – and indeed in many cases the Yogyakarta Principles – played a pivotal role in shaping the 'non-medicalised' approach.[143]

Considerations of physical integrity and human rights were central concerns for the German Constitutional Court when it addressed physical intervention requirements in 2011.[144] The original German Act from 1980 required infertility as well as sterility, having modified 'secondary sex characteristics through surgery to the other sex'.[145] Building on previous decisions regarding the (non-)marriage requirement,[146] the Court held that a surgery and sterility requirement was in violation of the German Constitution. The German statute essentially put the applicant in a position of choosing between two constitutionally protected rights, namely the right to recognition of one's gender identity and the right to one's physical integrity. In order to exercise the fundamental right to recognition of one's gender identity a violation of physical integrity (in the form of surgery) had to be accepted; without physical intervention, recognition would be withheld. While this technically left the person in question with a 'choice', in reality that was not a choice at all. First, no matter what the person in question chose, he or she was forced to forfeit one of his or her constitutionally protected rights. Second, the assumption of the law seemed to be that every transgender person would want to submit to these requirements, which of course is disproven the very moment somebody does not. Third, for the people concerned, recognition of preferred gender is not a 'choice' in any sense of the word. It involves aligning the law with their self-identity. This is not optional; it is a necessity, both from a legal and a social point of view.[147] Fourth, and perhaps most importantly, this legal rule essentially forced the violation of physical integrity on the person, with the state requiring surgery and sterility which the person in question does not desire. The only justification offered for this, the desire to protect the existing 'gender structures' of the law, was utterly insufficient to warrant such an intensive and invasive act. In a civilised jurisdiction, it is unthinkable that the state forces its citizens to undergo involuntary sterilisation and surgery.

The Court of Appeals in Stockholm in 2012[148] came to very similar conclusions regarding the 'choice' individuals are given in Sweden (where sterilisation was a requirement for recognition of preferred gender). In considering the compatibility

[143] e.g. in the Netherlands (see W. Pintens, in this volume, pp. 113 and 119) Denmark (see N. Videbæk Munkholm, in this volume, pp. 157 ff.), Sweden (see J. Garland, in this volume, p. 290) and New Zealand (see E. McDonald and J. Byrne, in this volume, pp. 542 and 565).

[144] BVerfG 11.01.2011, BVerfGE 128, 109 = NJW 2011, 909. See also BVerfG 27.08.2011, NJW 2012, 600.

[145] Original version of §8(1) nos. 3 and 4 Transsexuellengesetz; *cf.* A. Dutta, in this volume, p. 212.

[146] On which see above section 4.4.3.

[147] *Cf.* also R. Wallbank, in this volume, p. 470.

[148] Kammarrätten, *Socialstyrelsen v NN*, Mål nr 1968–12; on this see J. Garland, in this volume, p. 289.

of Sweden's sterilisation requirement with both the national Constitution and Article 8 ECHR, the Court suggested that, where sterilisation is a pre-condition for obtaining basic recognition from the state, an individual's decision to undertake that procedure cannot be considered 'voluntary'. The Stockholm Court of Appeal's judgment has been referred to by Judges Keller and Spano in their concurring opinion for *YY v Turkey*.[149] The judgment is an important, and overdue, recognition of the stark choices facing many transgender persons. While sterilisation requirements do not force transgender persons to compromise their reproductive capacities – in the sense that they do not physically compel compliance – they do nevertheless leave applicants for recognition in an untenable situation where they either accept sterilisation or forfeit their right to meaningful participation in the social and economic life of the state.

For essentially the same reasons as the German and Swedish courts, the Italian Supreme Court, confirming a decision by the Court of Trento,[150] held that 'medical treatment' required by the Law no. 164/82 for recognition of preferred gender does not necessarily include invasive medical procedures and sterilisation.[151]

As far as Germany is concerned, the decision by the Constitutional Court means that, since the relevant provisions which were held to be unconstitutional have not been replaced with any other medical intervention requirements, German law now no longer requires any form of medical intervention for recognition of preferred gender.

4.5.1.3. Access to Gender Confirmation Healthcare

Before discussing the justification for medical intervention requirements for recognition of preferred gender, it is necessary to dispel any suggestion that gender confirmation healthcare – whether surgical, hormone-based or psychological – is always a bad thing. On the contrary, in many cases, appropriate medical treatment is vital for transgender persons' physical and mental well-being, and can be an important vehicle through which individuals obtain a true sense of self. In recent times, much of the global transgender community's advocacy efforts have focused on increasing access to necessary, consensual healthcare procedures. For example, in the *YY v Turkey* case,[152] the applicant was actually seeking to ease access requirements for gender confirmation surgery in that jurisdiction. However, there is a difference between medical transitions and applications for legal gender

[149] ECtHR, *YY v Turkey* (application no. 14793/08) [2015] ECHR 257 (10.03.2015); on this case see Y. Atamer, in this volume, p. 321.

[150] Court of Trento, 19.08.2014, n. 228. On this case see M.G. Cubeddu Wiedemann, in this volume, p. 253.

[151] Decision no. 15138 of 20.07.2015. The decision of the Supreme Court was confirmed by the Italian Constitutional Court on 21.10.2015 (Sentenza 221/2015).

[152] ECtHR, *YY v Turkey* (application no. 14793/08) [2015] ECHR 257 (10.03.2015); on this case see Y. Atamer, in this volume, p. 321.

recognition. Where a person wishes to medically transition, it is essential that he or she should have recourse to healthcare treatments, the exact details of which will be decided by the individual and his or her physician. Ensuring the health and well-being of its citizens are fundamental aims for any state irrespective of whether that person also seeks legal recognition of their preferred gender. In other words: health is health, and medical decisions need to be medical decisions alone. These decisions should not be tied up with legal rules and considerations. It must be possible to provide healthcare where healthcare is needed. Therefore there must not be any specific legal requirements or procedures necessary for access to gender confirmation healthcare. This should not be interpreted to mean that state actors cannot legally require that all applicants for legal gender recognition have full capacity to consent. It does mean, however, that transgender persons should be able to access appropriate gender confirming treatments without having to satisfy unnecessary, onerous legal tests.

Recommendation 5: No specific legal requirements for access to gender confirmation healthcare
No special procedures or specific legal requirements should be required for access to gender confirmation healthcare.

4.5.1.4. Justifications for Medical Intervention Requirements

Numerous justifications have been offered for the medicalisation of legal gender recognition, many of which have been referenced and discussed by the contributions in this volume. At their core, surgical requirements reflect what Friedemann Pfäfflin describes as the rigid 'binary' approach to sex and gender.[153] Within the jurisdictions canvassed for this volume, there is significant evidence that many policy makers and judges continue to view gender through an 'either/or' lens. According to this view, *all* human beings are born with either unambiguously male or unambiguously female sex characteristics.[154] Further, according to this view these physical attributes – both internal and external – are considered determinative of a person's legal gender. Therefore, in order to be legally recognised in their preferred gender, transgender persons must bring their bodies, by surgical means if necessary, into line with the binary model. Any other approach would give rise to 'unnatural' bodily diversity, which might create a fear of social 'confusion or disturbance'.[155] Concern about social 'normalities' also underlie the requirement for sterilisation, particularly when considered in the context of 'unnatural' human reproduction. The requirement for sterilisation often reflects wider fears about men 'mothering' and women 'fathering' future

---

153 F. Pfäfflin, in this volume. See also D. Dormor, in this volume, p. 37 and esp. n. 22.
154 Which of course, as is well known, is factually incorrect.
155 Reasons given by the Japanese legislature, see Y. Nishitani, in this volume, p. 379.

offspring. The vista of the 'pregnant man' is thought to be so unpalatable, both as a matter of science and policy, that laws and regulations must prevent its realisation.[156] There is, of course, the possibility that the children of transgender persons may experience peer bullying or institutional discrimination because of their parents' legal status. However, the way to address such discrimination cannot be to restrict the family and parental rights of transgender persons.[157] Any such restriction would only validate the unproven notion that transgender persons should not be parents, and would encourage a belief that families headed by transgender individuals are less important. It also is a chicken-and-egg problem: by preventing the existence of such parent–child relationships because they are 'unusual', one automatically ensures that they remain so and thus no legal change will ever be possible. In any event, as many individuals who transition already have children and thus there inevitably are transgender parents with children, this problem needs to be dealt with by providing sufficient protections to young people who are targeted because of their parents' gender identity and enact meaningful equality provisions to counteract transphobic youth bullying – in the same way that children need to be protected from bullying for other reasons.

Many of the justifications for medical requirements can be challenged at both a conceptual and practical level, and indeed a number of contributors in this volume have openly questioned the reasoning employed by judges and policy makers in their jurisdictions. As a matter of pure biology, the existence of two rigid and absolute binary genders appears, at best, highly questionable. As research from other disciplines shows, the human experience of sex and gender is characterised by bodily diversity. Intersex persons in particular undermine any notion that all persons have unambiguously male or female sex characteristics.[158] Why then must transgender persons alter their bodies to uphold a binary standard that in fact does not exist in reality? And even if one accepted that such a binary

---

156 See e.g. the reasoning reported for the Turkish legislation in Y. Atamer, in this volume, p. 320.

157 Similar arguments and discussions can be seen regarding same-sex parenting; on this see the conclusive study conducted by M. Rupp (ed.), *Die Lebenssituation von Kindern in gleichgeschlechtlichen Lebenspartnerschaften*, Bundesanzeiger Verlag, 2009.

158 It needs to be repeated here that the term 'intersex person' and the understanding of the term is controversial (see e.g. the contribution by R. Wallbank, in this volume, pp. 470 ff.). This is not the place to discuss these issues, and for the purposes of this volume and the statement made here it is sufficient to note that rigid legal binary of gender based on the notion that every person physically is unambiguously male or female simply is wrong. It is noteworthy that several jurisdictions now have legal rules that allow a person not to have a legal gender of male or female, e.g. Germany (new § 22(3) Personenstandsgesetz; on this see W. Sieberichs, 'Das unbestimmte Geschlecht', *FamRZ* 2013, 1180–1184 and T. Helms, 'Personenstandsrechtliche und familienrechtliche Aspekte der Intersexualität vor dem Hintergrund des neuen § 22 Abs. 3 PStG' in I. Götz, I. Schwenzer, K. Seelmann and J. Taupitz (eds.), *Familie – Recht – Ethik, Festschrift für Gerd Brudermüller*, Beck 2014, pp. 301 ff.), Australia (following *NSW Registrar of Births, Deaths and Marriages v Norrie* [2014] HCA 11) and India (following Supreme Court of India, *National Legal Services Authority v Union of India and others*, Writ petition (civil) no. 604 of 2013 <http://supremecourtofindia.nic.in/outtoday/wc40012.pdf> accessed 15.10.2015).

exists, why does it follow from that that every human being must be forced to 'fit' into that binary?

In the landmark case of *Goodwin v United Kingdom*, the European Court of Human Rights noted the increasing importance of social and psychological factors in determining the make-up of gender.[159] This line of reasoning has been adopted by superior courts in many of the jurisdictions canvassed for this volume, including New Zealand, England and Wales and Germany. Defining a person's legal gender solely by reference to external sex characteristics is now considered an overly reductive approach.[160] To take a simple example, one need only think of how we access gender segregated restroom facilities. What is more important where transgender persons seek to enter their preferred service: genitalia or social acceptance in their expressed gender? If a restroom operator perceives a person to be male, does he or she verify that the individual actually has male genitalia? It is doubtful that sex characteristics truly determine a person's gender in any meaningful way for practical social interaction.

The sole argument in favour of sterilisation appears to be that the 'normal' categories of gender need to preserved, or in other words the 'normal' gendered order of family should not be disturbed. That things need to stay as they have always been is in itself not a particularly strong argument, and particularly in a day and age where there are more and more single-parent families, more and more children born outside of marriage, where same-sex couples in an increasing number of jurisdictions can formalise their relationship (either as marriage or some other legal regime such as register/civil partnerships/unions) and can adopt children and have access to artificial reproductive techniques, this presumed 'normal', traditional order of families often does not exist anymore and has been replaced by a new and much more gender-flexible family order.

But even if one accepted that preserving the traditional gendered approach to families might be an acceptable aim, it simply cannot justify the severity of the interference that the mandatory medical treatment, surgery and sterilisation rules impose on the individuals concerned. The clearest and most convincing exposition of this can be seen in the decision by the German Constitutional Court

---

159 *Goodwin v United Kingdom* (application no. 28957/95) [2002] ECHR 588 (11.07.2002), esp. paras. 53, 82

160 Again this is not the place to discuss this issue, but in *Re Kevin*, Justice Chisholm (as he then was) referred to increasing evidence within medical science of a biological basis for gender identity. At trial in *Re Kevin*, some of the world's leading transgender healthcare experts, including Louis Gooren and Milton Diamond, offered opinions on the origins and causes of transgender identities. Drawing upon their testimony, Chisholm J concluded that 'on the balance of probabilities ... [the applicant's] sense of being a man is based on some biological characteristics of his brain' (*Re Kevin: Validity of Marriage of Transsexual* (2001) 28 Fam LR 158, [312]; see also R. Chisholm's contribution in this volume, esp. pp. 449 ff., as well as R. Wallbank, in this volume, pp. 471 ff.). From this perspective, one could argue that a non-medicine based gender recognition system would not challenge the biological sex binary because a person's gender identity is a factor which must be considered in determining whether the individual is biologically male or female.

discussed above[161] which therefore need not be repeated here. Requiring unwanted medical intervention and particularly surgery and sterilisation in order to obtain recognition of preferred gender simply is a violation of the fundamental human rights of the persons concerned. The desire to maintain a (perceived) normality of gender and family is utterly insufficient to justify the violation of the physical integrity of a person through mandatory medical treatment, surgery and sterility requirements.

The German (and indeed the Italian) highest courts are not alone in this view – far from it.[162] When law reform was discussed in Denmark, human rights obligations, such as the Yogyakarta Principles, heavily influenced the Danish Parliamentary Working Group's 2014 conclusion that 'any framework involving medical or surgical treatment procedures would render Denmark in breach of international regulation.'[163] In his contribution, Walter Pintens has also noted the impact of evolving human rights norms and the Yogyakarta Principles in the Netherlands,[164] and these considerations also played a prominent role in the shaping of the new gender recognition rules in Ireland[165] and Taiwan.[166] In Malta, where Parliament has recently enacted a fully de-medicalised gender recognition scheme,[167] Article 3(1)(d) of the Gender Identity, Gender Expression and Sex Characteristics Act 2015 expressly affirms that each citizen of Malta has a right to 'bodily integrity and physical autonomy'. In Hong Kong, pro-transgender rights representatives in the Legislative Council in 2014 vetoed legislation which limited marriage rights to post-operative transgender individuals. Legislators, as well as the region's Equal Opportunities Commission, argued that such legislation would encourage people to undergo unnecessary treatment, particularly sterilisation, and was thus 'inhuman and degrading.'[168]

Medical treatment and especially surgery and sterility requirements for recognition of preferred gender are an unjustifiable infringement of the fundamental human rights of the persons concerned, particularly their right to physical integrity and private autonomy. The 'choice' between submitting to such procedures or not having one's preferred gender recognised is simply not a choice. Even considering that this might be a choice is based on a misconception of the gender identity issues this volume is concerned with.

---

161 See esp. section 4.4.5.1.2 above and A. Dutta, in this volume, pp. 213 ff.

162 Indeed the German jurisprudence recently was cited with approval by the ECtHR in *YY v Turkey* (application no. 14793/08) [2015] ECHR 257 (10.03.2015); on this case see Y. Atamer, in this volume, p. 321.

163 N. Videbæk Munkholm, in this volume, pp. 156 ff.

164 W. Pintens, in this volume, p. 119.

165 B. Sloan, in this volume, pp. 224 ff.

166 C. Ho, in this volume, pp. 427 ff.

167 Gender Identity, Gender Expression and Sex Characteristics Act 2015.

168 *Cf.* A. Liu, in this volume, pp. 361 ff.

Recommendation 6: No specific medical treatment or sterility for access to recognition of preferred gender
Recognition of preferred gender must not require any specific medical treatment or sterility.

4.5.2. *Diagnosis Requirements versus Self-Identification*

Many jurisdictions require a medical diagnosis for recognition of preferred gender. Diagnoses are explained as ensuring that applicants are 'true transsexuals'. In jurisdictions in which invasive surgery still is a requirement, such as the Czech Republic,[169] Turkey,[170] Hong Kong,[171] Singapore,[172] Japan[173] and Belgium,[174] this is hardly surprising. But even in jurisdictions which have moved away from surgical intervention requirements (or indeed any mandatory treatment), medical diagnoses are still used. Examples include Germany (two separate diagnoses required)[175] and Spain.[176] In England and Wales, two medical experts must confirm that an individual has, or has had, gender dysphoria.[177] In New Zealand, medical evidence is required that the applicant 'has assumed gender identity of the nominated sex'.[178] This appears to be less restrictive than an explicitly clinical diagnosis.

At the other end of the spectrum, there are jurisdictions like Argentina, Malta, and Ireland (for individuals above 18 years) where there are no medical requirements whatsoever. In these countries, a simple self-declaration suffices.[179] The same is true for Denmark[180] and Taiwan;[181] however, in both these latter jurisdictions a waiting period and affirmation of the application after six months is required (to prevent spontaneous and/or spurious applications leading to immediate legal consequences.)

A 'middle ground' position is taken by the Netherlands. Under the current Dutch rules, applicants must present a report from an expert (or expert team) to confirm that they hold the conviction that they are their preferred gender. The expert must also confirm that the application is not due to mental disorder or

169 B. Havelková, in this volume, p. 135.
170 Y. Atamer, in this volume, pp. 317 f.
171 A. Liu, in this volume, pp 345 ff.
172 T. Kaan, in this volume, pp. 410 ff.
173 Y. Nishitani, in this volume, p. 380.
174 W. Pintens, in this volume, p. 118.
175 A. Dutta, in this volume, pp. 215 f. Japan also requires two diagnoses, see Y. Nishitani, in this volume, p. 380.
176 J. Ferrer Riba and A. Lamarca Marqués, in this volume, p. 270.
177 S. Gilmore, in this volume, pp. 193 ff.
178 E. McDonald and J. Byrne, in this volume, pp. 545 f.
179 For Argentina see L.M. Giosa, M.V. Schiro and P. Dunne, in this volume, p. 576; for Ireland see Gender Recognition Act 2015, section 10 and B. Sloan, in this volume, p. 241.; for Malta see Gender Identity, Gender Expression and Sex Characteristics Act 2015, section 3.
180 N. Videbæk Munkholm, in this volume, pp. 165 ff.
181 C. Ho, in this volume, pp. 425 ff.

'caprice'.[182] In principle, the gender team do not have to provide a diagnosis and there is no requirement for treatment. However, in practice, the extent to which the Dutch model has actually de-medicalised the legal recognition remains unclear. It is apparent that, unlike the Maltese and Argentine regimes, the Netherlands' current laws (due for review next year) have not fully broken the link between legal gender recognition and medicine.

The question of diagnosis represents a key frontier in the struggle for transgender rights. Despite the heated debate which diagnosis requirements have generated, and continue to create, within gender identity activism, linking recognition to mental illness has, until recently, not been challenged as frequently as one would expect within legal and political discourse. It is perhaps instructive that the most high profile case on the topic in this volume, the 2014 judgment of the Administrative Court of Stockholm (*NN v Socialstyrelsen*),[183] did not specifically consider whether linking gender recognition to mental health violates an applicant's rights or whether transgender identity is symptomatic of illness. Rather, in that case, the Swedish court struck down the practice of requiring a mental health examination because, on a proper construction of the relevant legal and administrative rules, there was no basis for imposing such a requirement. *NN v Socialstyrelsen* is an important affirmation of the rights of transgender persons in Sweden but unfortunately it offers little substantive guidance for courts and policy makers who may face similar considerations in other jurisdictions.

The question of medical diagnosis is complicated by the fact that such requirements often appear to enjoy at least tacit support within parts of the transgender community. Historically, individuals have for a long time been denied effective access to safe, publically funded healthcare; transgender persons may grudgingly accept diagnosis requirements as a necessary price for obtaining gender confirming treatments, and regrettably that still is the case in many jurisdictions. There is a fear that, if gender identity is not considered a medical concern, public authorities may cease providing and funding appropriate healthcare. This line of reasoning is encouraged by cases such as *YY v Turkey*, where the ECtHR emphasised the fact that 'transsexualism is a medical condition which justifies treatment for the purpose of helping the persons concerned.'[184] The message which transgender persons receive from such statements is that gender identity rights are contingent upon the existence of a mental health concern. The message therefore appears to be that the transgender community should embrace diagnosis as the only sure way of protecting their rights.

Such sentiments, even if perhaps unintended by courts and policy makers, are extremely unfortunate. As already outlined above, medical and legal transitions are conceptually distinct and need to be treated separately. Decoupling *legal*

---

182 W. Pintens, in this volume, p. 119.

183 Mål nr. 24931-13 (23.05.2014), *cf.* J. Garland, in this volume, pp. 293 ff.

184 ECtHR, *YY v Turkey* (application no. 14793/08) [2015] ECHR 257 (10.03.2015); on this case see Y. Atamer, in this volume, p. 321.

recognition from a diagnosis requirement does not necessarily mean that transgender identities cannot be treated as a healthcare concern in other contexts. It is perfectly consistent for medical professionals to require a diagnosis for medical treatments even though the legal gender recognition has been 'depathologised', i.e. that legal recognition no longer requires medical diagnoses. In 2014, WPATH urged 'the avoidance of pathologizing gender variance', noting that 'scientific and medical evidence indicates that gender variance should not be regarded as something wrong or something to be corrected.'[185] Rachael Wallbank has put the issue like this:

> 'People who experience Transsexualism have long been faced with the confronting irony that although their condition has to be diagnosed by psychiatry pursuant to mental health criteria in order to receive hormonal and surgical medical treatment, that diagnosis consists of a finding that their experience of their sex is not caused by any delusion, confusion or mental disorder. In other words, under the current medical model for Transsexualism, the core relevance of psychiatry/psychology is to professionally confirm its irrelevancy.'[186]

Wallbank also argues that, contrary to the perception that a classification as 'disorder' facilitates treatment, it actually merely delayed the creation of non-discriminatory, non-mental-health based diagnostic criteria and treatment regimes.[187]

Gender confirming healthcare should be provided on an 'informed consent' basis, so that failing or refusing to obtain a medical diagnosis would not deprive individuals of necessary treatments. As the contributors for Argentina note, such an 'informed consent' model has now been pioneered under that jurisdiction's 2012 Gender Identity Act.[188] There cannot be any doubt that transgender persons who experience no distress or discomfort because of their gender identity should not be required to feign mental illness to access appropriate healthcare treatments.

Diagnosis requirements have a heavily stigmatising effect on the transgender community. It reinforces stereotypes of transgender individuals as confused and unstable, as 'mentally ill'. In a number of jurisdictions canvassed for this volume, linking transgender identity to mental illness has subsequently been

---

185 World Professional Organisation for Transgender Health (WPATH), *WPATH Statement Concerning Cross-dressing, Gender-Nonconformity, and Gender Dysphoria*, 15.07.2014 <http://www.wpath.org/uploaded_files/140/files/WPATH%20Statement%20Concerning%20Cross-dressing_15%20July%202014.pdf> accessed 15.10.2015.

186 R. Wallbank, in this volume, p. 473.

187 Ibid., p. 472.

188 Article 11 of the 2012 Act provides that all persons over the age of 18 have the right to access 'total and partial surgical interventions and/or comprehensive hormonal treatments to adjust their bodies, including their genitalia, to their self-perceived gender identity, without requiring any judicial or administrative authorization.' On this see L.M. Giosa, M.V. Schiro and P. Dunne, in this volume, pp. 572 ff.

used to validate institutional discrimination in areas such as employment and parental rights. Quoting Judith Butler, Barbara Havelková notes that 'diagnosis singles transgender persons out as "ill, sick, wrong, out of order, abnormal", leaves them open to stigmatisation and can legitimise their discrimination.'[189] The requirement to obtain a diagnosis has a direct and extremely negative impact on the social and political status of transgender persons.

Conscious of the strong objections raised against the diagnosis requirement, a number of jurisdictions (as outlined above) have recently acted to remove mental health considerations from the legal gender recognition regimes or introduced new schemes without such requirements. If policy makers are serious about depathologising legal gender recognition, they should look to the reforms outlined in the Argentine and Danish contributions.[190] Joined by Malta and Ireland in 2015,[191] Argentina and Denmark have established the 'gold standard' in terms of separating legal gender recognition from medicine.

Of course, objections can be, and are, raised in opposition to self-determination. Some observers complain that an unsupervised system is open to abuse. A typical objection is that a person may misuse gender recognition in order to obtain legal or social benefits (such as pension rights, etc.). While there is no reported evidence of such abuse, it might be thought that insufficient data has been analysed to determine the true risk of self-declaration. For example, the fact that there is no abuse of legal gender recognition in France and Germany – where individuals have to either undergo sterilisation or obtain a medical diagnosis – cannot be proof that misuse would not arise where such safeguards are removed. Even in jurisdictions such as Denmark and Taiwan, which have embraced a model of self-determination, lingering fears have led policy makers to implement a six-month waiting period. Such a 'waiting time' does not infringe on the principle that individuals can self-define their own gender, but it may reduce the likelihood of improper applications.

For the purposes of this chapter, the authors have reflected hard on all the legal and policy arguments surrounding the 'medical supervision versus self-determination debate'. The authors acknowledge that concerns about possible fraud are legitimate. While they are unlikely to arise with great frequency, the risk of abuse should give lawmakers reason to pause. However, balancing the existing rights and policy arguments, this chapter does recommend self-declaration as the most appropriate, desirable and human rights conscious regime. The – abstract – risk of abuse is insufficient to justify the interference with the right to legal gender recognition. All legal processes in principle are at risk of being abused

[189] B. Havelková, in this volume, p. 132.

[190] See the contributions by L.M. Giosa, M.V. Schiro and P. Dunne (Argentina) and N. Videbæk Munkholm (Denmark) in this volume. At the time of writing, Sweden and Norway have indicated that will implement similar legislation.

[191] Gender Recognition Act 2015, section 10 (Ireland) (on which see B. Sloan, in this volume) and the Gender Identity, Gender Expression and Sex Characteristics Act 2015 (Malta).

(one only needs to think of sham marriages for immigration purposes) but this has not led to calls for abolishing or restricting these processes. Potential abuse of legal gender recognition simply needs to be monitored like all other potential abuses. Medical supervision of the legal transition can, and does, cause individuals significant harm and/or distress. The authors believe that a properly maintained and administered self-determination system is capable of avoiding widespread fraud. It is therefore the most appropriate system for acknowledging an individual's preferred legal gender.

Recommendation 7: No medical diagnosis requirement
The legal recognition of preferred gender must not require a specific diagnosis but should be effected on the basis of self-determination.

4.6. LIVED EXPERIENCE REQUIREMENT – 'REAL LIFE EXPERIENCE'

Several of the jurisdictions examined in this volume require that an applicant for recognition observe a period of what has been called a 'real life experience' (RLE), often a minimum of two years, before the preferred legal gender is formally acknowledged.[192] In others RLE is a requirement for access to gender confirmation surgery (which then in turn is a requirement for gender recognition).[193] RLE conditions are considered a trial-run for gender recognition, allowing transgender persons to 'prove' their capacity and desire to live in their preferred gender, and creating an opportunity to understand the consequences of transitioning without crossing a legal threshold.

---

192 e.g. England and Wales: 'lived in acquire gender for two years' (see S. Gilmore, in this volume, pp. 193 f.); Germany: 'compulsion' to live 'according to the other gender' for at least three years (see A. Dutta, in this volume, p. 215); Spain: evidence of medical treatment for two years is required, see J. Ferrer Riba and A. Lamarca Marqués, in this volume, p. 271; Sweden: requirement to have lived according to requested gender identity for 'some time' before applying for legal change (see J. Garland, in this volume, p. 293).

193 For example in Turkey: two years before access to medical procedure (see Y. Atamer, pp. 318 f.); Czech Republic: 'real life test' lasting at least 12 months before access to gender confirmation surgery (see B. Havelková, in this volume, p. 137). That there internationally often seems to be a two-year RLE requirement was also noted by the Hong Kong Court of Final Appeal in its seminal *W v Registrar of Marriages* decision: 'If the diagnosis of gender identity disorder is confirmed, the patient is usually required to go through a "real life experience", living in the preferred gender for about two years while having hormones of the opposite sex administered to produce reversible physical changes in the body and to ease the patient's psychological discomfort' (*W v Registrar of Marriages* [2013] HKEC 716, [11]). According to A. Liu, in this volume, p. 345, in Hong Kong such a real life experience is required by medical practitioners before they consider gender confirmation surgery, which in turn currently still is requirement for gender recognition.

In one sense, it is not surprising that transgender individuals should have to observe a waiting period before accessing legal gender recognition.[194] In the seventh edition of its Standards of Care, the World Professional Association for Transgender Health (WPATH) recommends that persons seeking access to specific surgical procedures, including a hysterectomy or orchiectomy, should complete at least '12 continuous months of hormone therapy as appropriate to the patient's gender goals.' Where legal gender recognition is contingent upon medical treatment, it is correct that applicants should access healthcare procedures in accordance with international best practice. However, this line of reason presupposes the validity and necessity of medical intervention requirements. In reality, the main objection to RLEs is not that transgender persons must observe a waiting period before surgery. Rather, the problem lies in the fact that medical intervention is a prerequisite for gender recognition. But, for the reasons discussed above, medical preconditions for legal transition are to be rejected as a violation of the fundamental rights of the persons concerned. Therefore, whether or not RLE conditions can be medically justified as a basis for surgery and other medical treatment decisions, they cannot on that basis form a legitimate pre-condition for legal gender recognition.

In jurisdictions such as the United Kingdom, which have already repealed medical requirements for gender recognition,[195] RLEs appear to have even less justification. The idea of a trial-run living as a man or woman is highly problematic in a number of key respects. It suggests that there is only one, identifiable way of living in a particular gender. What exactly does it mean for a transgender woman to prove that she can function socially and professionally as a female? How do 'normal men' live their lives? There is a real fear that, in requiring applicants for recognition to prove their capacity to live a 'real life', policy makers will merely reinforce biased and stereotyped presumptions about male and female conduct which do not conform with the lived reality of the vast majority of the population. RLE requirements hold transgender persons to a false standard of maleness and femaleness which is not expected of any other person. Nowhere in the law are men and women denied recognition of their gender simply because they do not conform to gendered assumptions. RLE conditions may result in a bizarre situation where, prior to obtaining official recognition, applicants will feel obliged to express an accentuated version of their preferred gender which they have no intention of subsequently maintaining.

RLE conditions also misunderstand the complex ways in which people experience their gender. Transgender individuals do not begin to self-identify and express their preferred gender on the day they first apply for recognition or think about making such an application. As the recent litigation in *YY v Turkey*

194 Indeed, in Denmark and Taiwan where no RLE exists a six-month waiting period is required for legal recognition of preferred gender, see N. Videbæk Munkholm, in this volume, p. 165 and C. Ho, in this volume, p. 426.

195 See S. Gilmore, in this volume, pp. 183 ff.

illustrates, personal reflection on gender identity is often a lifelong process.[196] In many instances, a transgender person will have self-identified with his or her preferred gender for numerous years before applying for recognition. Transgender individuals do not need a trial period to know what it is like to live their preferred gender, because they experience that gender on a daily basis.

That the jurisdictions which have recently reformed or implemented their gender recognition laws have omitted and thus actively rejected RLE conditions illustrates that such requirements are not a necessary (and probably not even an effective)[197] safeguard against potential abuse and should not be imposed to obstruct gender recognition for transgender persons.[198]

Recommendation 8: No 'real life experience' conditions
Recognition of preferred gender must not require a 'real life experience'.

V. LEGAL CONSEQUENCES OF RECOGNITION OF PREFERRED GENDER

The final consideration is the consequences of legal gender recognition. Here, the law must have regard to what institutions, rights and benefits a person will enjoy/have access to, or will continue to enjoy/have access to, once their preferred gender has been acknowledged by the state. As a general rule, a transgender person who has obtained recognition in the jurisdictions examined in this volume is legally acknowledged in their preferred gender.[199] However, some exceptions to this approach can be identified. First and foremost these can be found with regard to family relationships, particularly the horizontal relationships (relationships between adults; see section 5.1 below) and vertical relationships (parent–child relationships; see section 5.2 below), but other areas of law are concerned as well (see section 5.3 below).

---

196 ECtHR, *YY v Turkey* (application no. 14793/08) [2015] ECHR 257 (10.03.2015); on this case see Y. Atamer, in this volume, p. 321.

197 Anecdotal evidence suggests that there is sufficient information available on internet websites and other media so that a RLE can be faked; apparently, that information even is 'tailored' towards specific jurisdictions, panels and even individuals who judge the RLE.

198 See e.g. the Irish Gender Recognition Act 2015 and on this B. Sloan, in this volume, pp. 241 and 244; in Denmark the application needs to include a statement that the application for legal gender recognition is based 'on an experience of belonging to the other gender', but nothing further (and particularly no proof) is required, *cf.* N. Videbæk Munkholm, in this volume, p. 166.

199 See generally the relevant sections the contributions in this volume.

5.1. HORIZONTAL RELATIONSHIPS

As already noted, questions of legal gender recognition have often arisen in the context of marriage (e.g. Texas, Kansas, Florida and Ohio in the United States,[200] England,[201] and Singapore).[202] In those cases, common law courts were typically unwilling to allow transgender persons to marry in their preferred gender because the law itself did not acknowledge that self-actualised identity. However, courts in, *inter alia*, New Jersey,[203] Hong Kong,[204] Australia[205] and New Zealand[206] have taken a different view and permitted the marriage of persons in their preferred gender.

The landmark case of *Goodwin v United Kingdom*[207] decided this issue for all Contracting States of the ECHR. The Court not only found a conflict with Article 8 ECHR, but also held that the United Kingdom had violated Article 12 ECHR because Christine Goodwin had no right to marry her male partner. As the case makes abundantly clear, where the law recognises transgender and transsexuals in their true gender, there is no reason to prevent access to marriage. Transgender and transsexual persons should be entitled to enter a legal relationship on the same terms as all other persons who share their legal gender. Denying the right to enter into a legally recognised adult relationship, which otherwise is afforded to all other persons, is, as held in *Goodwin*, a human rights violation.

Furthermore, in the light of the position taken by the authors – that there should not be any change to the legal nature of *existing* horizontal relationships (such as marriage, civil/registered partnership and cohabitation/*de facto* relationships) in the event of recognition of preferred gender[208] – allowing marriage according to the legally recognised preferred gender is merely consistent.

5.2. VERTICAL RELATIONSHIPS

Legal gender recognition also raises complex questions in terms of vertical family relationships (i.e. parent–child). A common approach in the jurisdictions looked at in this volume is that the existing legal parent–child relationships of

---

[200] J. Garland, in this volume, pp. 602 ff.
[201] S. Gilmore, in this volume, pp. 185 ff.
[202] T. Kaan, in this volume, pp. 406 ff. and the references in n. 15.
[203] *MT v JT* (1976) 335 A 2d 204 (Appellate Division of the Superior Court of New Jersey).
[204] *W v Registrar of Marriages* [2013] HKEC 716, on which see A. Liu, in this volume, pp. 335 ff.
[205] *Re Kevin: Validity of Marriage of Transsexual* (2001) 28 Fam LR 158 ('*Re Kevin*') and *Attorney-General for the Commonwealth v Kevin and Others* (2003) 30 Fam LR 1. On this see especially the chapter by R. Chisholm, in this volume, pp. 443 ff.
[206] *M v M* [1991] NZFLR 337 (Family Court at Otahuhu), and *Attorney-General v Family Court at Otahuhu* [1995] 1 NZLR 603.
[207] *Goodwin v United Kingdom* (application no. 28957/95) [2002] ECHR 588 (11.07.2002). See also S. Gilmore, in this volume, pp. 189 ff.
[208] See above section 4.4.3.

transgender or transsexual persons do not change where he or she transitions legally.[209] This is the result of an important development for the law. Many of the contributions in this volume have recounted stories of parents being denied access to their children (e.g. Spain).[210] Specifically acknowledging the rights of transgender parents in a legal recognition statute, as for example Argentina and Ireland have done,[211] expressly states that transgender and transsexual persons are equally capable of raising children.

With regard to children being born after the legal transition, the approaches in the jurisdictions looked at are less clearly aligned. In some jurisdictions, only the 'new' legal gender determines the parent–child relationship.[212] Hence a person can technically be the father of one child and the mother of another. In other jurisdictions, it is the genetic/biological gender or rather the actual reproductive capacity that determines legal relationship to the child.[213] As a result, a legal male can become the mother of a child in these jurisdictions.[214] That said, recently a court in Sweden has held that a legal male giving birth to a child should be regarded as the legal father of the child in the particular circumstances of the case.[215]

No specific recommendation is made here on the potential impact a legal transition should have (or should not have) on existing and future parent–child relationships. The preferences of the individuals concerned will inevitably differ, and the law should be able to accommodate these individual preferences. The easiest way forward for this would be to simply abolish the legal categories of 'mother' and 'father' and simply determine who is the 'parent' of a child, as one of the authors of this chapter has advocated elsewhere.[216] Where more and more jurisdictions allow same-sex couples access to adoption and artificial reproductive technologies (including surrogacy) this path may even be inevitable.

209 For Belgium and the Netherlands see W. Pintens, p. 121; for Denmark see N. Videbæk Munkholm, pp. 168 f.; for Argentina see L.M. Giosa, M.V. Schiro and P. Dunne, pp. 581 f.; for England and Wales see S. Gilmore, pp. 200 f.; for Germany see A. Dutta, p. 218; for Italy see M.G. Cubeddu Wiedemann, p. 258; for Spain see J. Ferrer Riba and A. Lamarca Marqués, p. 275; for Sweden see J. Garland, pp. 302 ff.; for Turkey see Y. Atamer, p. 328; for Japan see Y. Nishitani, p. 385; for Taiwan see C. Ho, p. 425 (all in this volume).

210 J. Ferrer Riba and A. Lamarca Marqués, in this volume, pp. 275 f.

211 See L.M. Giosa, M.V. Schiro and P. Dunne, in this volume, p. 582; Gender Recognition Act 2015, s. 19, on which see B. Sloan, in this volume, p. 247

212 For Belgium see W. Pintens, p. 121; for England and Wales see S. Gilmore, pp. 200 f.; for Japan and particularly the Supreme Court decision on the matter see Y. Nishitani, p. 385; for Taiwan see C. Ho, p. 425 (all in this volume).

213 For the Netherlands see W. Pintens, p. 121; for Denmark see N. Videbæk Munkholm, pp. 168 f.; for Germany see A. Dutta, p. 218; for Sweden see J. Garland, pp. 302 ff. (all in this volume).

214 In Denmark, even co-motherhood is possible for legal male as again the actual reproductive *capacity* determines the parent–child relationship and the fact of giving birth, *cf.* N. Videbæk Munkholm, p. 169.

215 *NN v Socialstyrelsen*, Mål nr. 24685–13 (14 May 2014) (non-public decision), but an appeal is pending at the time of writing, *cf.* J. Garland, pp. 309 f.

216 See Scherpe, above n. 27, pp. 130 ff. If need be, one of the parents could be designated as the 'birth parent' or 'gestational parent', which might for example be relevant for parental leave.

It is important to note that merely abolishing the legal categories of mother and father does not change the social categories, and the vast majority of children will of course continue to refer to their individual parents as 'mum' and 'dad'. In the case of transgender parents (and indeed parents of the same legal sex) this approach would accommodate individual preferences without any difficulties.[217]

5.3. OTHER AREAS OF LAW

5.3.1. Criminal Law

Criminal law may require exceptions from the general rule that the recognised preferred gender will be regarded as the person's gender for all intents and purposes. For example, under the United Kingdom's Gender Recognition Act 2004, gender-specific crimes fall outside the scope of legal recognition.[218] Similar legal provisions exist in numerous other jurisdictions canvassed for this volume.[219] A person who commits a gender-specific crime must not be able to escape criminal liability because the victim has obtained a gender recognition certificate. Even if, as a matter of law, the victim has a recognised gender against which the specific crime cannot be committed, the perpetrator must still be held accountable. Similarly, where a person who has obtained gender recognition commits a crime that, as a matter of law, can only be committed by somebody who has the perpetrator's birth-assigned gender, the law may convict the perpetrator as though the birth-assigned gender still applies. In short, individuals who commit identifiable crimes should not be able to circumvent the criminal process by relying on legal gender recognition. Legal gender recognition must not be an instrument of abuse.

However, whenever these crimes are prosecuted this must be done with the utmost sensitivity. Every effort should be made throughout the criminal process to ensure that the prosecution, and the surrounding legal procedures, affirm and respect, to the greatest possible extent, the victim's gender identity and thus avoid compounding a situation of trauma and distress. The same also applies if a transgender or transsexual person is prosecuted and/or sentenced to imprisonment; here every effort must be made to respect the preferred gender of the individual in question.[220]

---

217 It would also allow for multiple parenting, on which see e.g. ibid., pp. 112 ff.

218 See S. Gilmore, in this volume, p. 201.

219 Gender Recognition Act 2015, s. 23 (Gender Specific Offences).

220 See e.g. the recent case of Tara Hudson <http://www.bbc.co.uk/news/uk-england-34675778> accessed 15.10.2015.

5.3.2. *Sport*

Numerous jurisdictions have adopted sporting policies which exclude transgender individuals from their preferred sporting teams, even where they have obtained legal gender recognition. The justification for such exclusions is 'fair competition' and 'safety'. There is a belief that transgender women who legally transition pose a physical and competitive threat to women's competitions. It is not possible to identify any one, consistent policy across the jurisdictions when it comes to sport. Indeed, in some countries, different formal and informal policies apply, depending upon the gender, age and skill level of the participants. While no specific recommendation on transgender participation in sport is made here, the importance of participation in sporting competitions for many transgender individuals, particularly transgender youth, needs to be emphasised. The systematic exclusion of transgender individuals, and especially transgender youth, from sport can result in further marginalisation for an already side-lined social group. Furthermore, any policy which would limit transgender participation in sport needs to be based on actual scientific evidence, rather than mere intuitive beliefs about human biology. The recent Court of Arbitration for Sport decision in the *Dutee Chand Case*[221] illustrates the complexity of human biology in this area, and the need to avoid misinformed assumptions about female–male capabilities.

5.3.3. *Access to Healthcare, Medical Services and Insurance*

There cannot be any doubt that with regard to healthcare and medical services the legal gender of a person should not prevent adequate treatment in line with best practice medical care. For example, a legal male must, if the circumstances require it, have access to breast cancer or cervical cancer screening and treatment; similarly, a legal female must of course have access to prostate cancer screening and treatment. The legal gender must not prevent medically necessary treatments and healthcare services.[222]

However, an exception from attaching legal consequences solely to the recognised preferred gender under certain circumstances might be required for insurances and pensions. Both of these rely on mathematically complex calculations, some of which include considerations of the genetic gender/physical characteristics. For example, private health insurance policies for women tend to require payment of higher premiums if the 'risk' of pregnancy and birth is covered. As this 'risk' can exist without regard to the legal gender of a person, insurance calculations might need to be based on the actual reproductive capacity. The same may be true for other physical characteristics (e.g. risk of prostate cancer) and

---

221 *Dutee Chand v AFI and IAAF* (CAS 2014/A/3759) <http://www.tas-cas.org/fileadmin/user_upload/award_internet.pdf> accessed 15.10.2015.

222 In Denmark this matter is addressed specifically, *cf.* N. Videbæk Munkholm, in this volume, p. 168.

calculation of life and pension insurance premiums (because of different life expectancies based on genetic characteristics). Another difficult issue is raised by the existence of different retirement ages/state pension entitlements for men and women in some jurisdictions, which under certain circumstances may require reference to the genetic/biological characteristics of a person rather than their legal gender.[223] Exploring these highly complex issues conclusively is beyond the scope of this contribution.

Recommendation 9: Legal consequences of recognition of preferred gender
Individuals who have obtained legal gender recognition in principle must be acknowledged in their preferred gender for all legal purposes, particularly marriage (and adult relationships in general). Where exceptions to this rule are introduced (such as in the law regarding parents and children, criminal law, healthcare, sport, etc.), they must be necessary and proportionate for achieving an important social goal.

VI. RECOMMENDATIONS

Recommendation 1: Age limit
There should be no absolute age limit for obtaining legal recognition of preferred gender. Where legislatures restrict access for minors, exceptions must be available and should not be excessively onerous to achieve. Decisions regarding the legal recognition of preferred gender of children should solely be based on the best interest of the child and should take account of the opinion of the minor concerned.

Recommendation 2: Nationality and residency requirements
It is preferable to regulate expressly that the courts/competent authorities have jurisdiction to decide on the recognition of preferred gender irrespective of the applicant's nationality.

The applicable law should also be regulated expressly. This may be done either

- by using residence (with or without a modest minimum residency period) as the connecting factor for the applicable law and thus apply the *lex fori*, or
- by using nationality, provided it is made clear that the public policy exception applies if the law so designated does not permit recognition of the preferred gender.

[223] See e.g. England and Wales where the pension age is determined by the 'acquired' gender (*cf.* S. Gilmore, in his volume, p. 204), and Germany where existing pension rights are unaffected by legal transition (*cf.* A. Dutta, in this volume, p. 218).

Recommendation 3: Requirements relating to existing adult relationships
Legal recognition of preferred gender should not require the dissolution of an existing formalised adult relationship (such as marriage or registered partnership).

Recommendation 4: Requirements relating to existing parent–child relationships
Legal recognition of preferred gender must not require the absence of any existing legal parent–child relationships.

Recommendation 5: No specific legal requirements for access to gender confirmation healthcare
No special procedures or specific legal requirements should be required for access to gender confirmation healthcare.

Recommendation 6: No specific medical treatment or sterility for access recognition of preferred gender
Recognition of preferred gender must not require any specific medical treatment or sterility.

Recommendation 7: No medical diagnosis requirement
The legal recognition of preferred gender must not require a medical diagnosis but should be effected on the basis of self-determination

Recommendation 8: No 'real life experience' conditions
Recognition of preferred gender must not require a 'real life experience'.

Recommendation 9: Legal consequences of recognition of preferred gender
Individuals who have obtained legal gender recognition in principle must be acknowledged in their preferred gender for all legal purposes, particularly marriage (and adult relationships in general). Where exceptions to this rule are introduced (such as in the law regarding parents and children, criminal law, healthcare, sport, etc.), they must be necessary and proportionate for achieving an important social goal.

www.ingramcontent.com/pod-product-compliance
Ingram Content Group UK Ltd.
Pitfield, Milton Keynes, MK11 3LW, UK
UKHW051917100926
8556IPUK00021B/1230

9 781780 681962